# THE BRITISH AND THE TURKS

**Edinburgh Studies on Modern Turkey**

Series Editors: Alpaslan Özerdem and Ahmet Erdi Öztürk

**International Advisory Board**

- Sinem Akgül Açıkmeşe
- Samim Akgönül
- Rebecca Bryant
- Mehmet Gurses
- Gareth Jenkins
- Ayşe Kadıoğlu
- Stephen Karam
- Paul Kubicek
- Peter Mandaville
- Nukhet Ahu Sandal
- M. Hakan Yavuz

**Books in the series (published and forthcoming)**

*Islamic Theology in the Turkish Republic*
Philip Dorroll

*Turkish–Greek Relations: Foreign Policy in a Securitisation Framework*
Cihan Dizdaroglu

*Policing Slums in Turkey: Crime, Resistance and the Republic on the Margin*
Çağlar Dölek

*The Kurds in Erdoğan's Turkey: Balancing Identity, Resistance and Citizenship*
William Gourlay

*The Politics of Culture in Contemporary Turkey*
Edited by Pierre Hecker, Ivo Furman and Kaya Akyıldız

*Peace Processes in Northern Ireland and Turkey: Rethinking Conflict Resolution*
İ. Aytaç Kadioğlu

*The British and the Turks: A History of Animosity, 1893–1923*
Justin McCarthy

*The Alevis in Modern Turkey and the Diaspora: Recognition, Mobilisation and Transformation*
Edited by Derya Ozkul and Hege Markussen

*Religion, Identity and Power: Turkey and the Balkans in the Twenty-First Century*
Ahmet Erdi Öztürk

*A Companion to Modern Turkey*
Edited by Alpaslan Özerdem and Ahmet Erdi Öztürk

*The Decline of the Ottoman Empire and the Rise of the Turkish Republic: Observations of an American Diplomat, 1919–1927*
Hakan Özoğlu

*Turkish-German Belonging: Ethnonational and Transnational Homelands, 2000–2020*
Özgür Özvatan

*Contesting Gender and Sexuality through Performance: Sacrifice, Modernity and Islam in Contemporary Turkey*
Eser Selen

*Turkish Politics and 'The People': Mass Mobilisation and Populism*
Spyros A. Sofos

*Electoral Integrity in Turkey*
Emre Toros

*Erdoğan: The Making of an Autocrat*
M. Hakan Yavuz

edinburghuniversitypress.com/series/esmt

# THE BRITISH AND THE TURKS

*A History of Animosity, 1893–1923*

## Justin McCarthy

EDINBURGH
University Press

*For*
*Mira Julian and Tara Margaret*

Edinburgh University Press is one of the leading university presses in the UK. We publish academic books and journals in our selected subject areas across the humanities and social sciences, combining cutting-edge scholarship with high editorial and production values to produce academic works of lasting importance. For more information visit our website: edinburghuniversitypress.com

© Justin McCarthy, 2022, 2019

Edinburgh University Press Ltd
The Tun – Holyrood Road
12 (2f) Jackson's Entry
Edinburgh EH8 8PJ

First published in hardback by Edinburgh University Press 2022

Typeset in 11/15 Adobe Garamond by
IDSUK (DataConnection) Ltd, and
printed and bound by CPI Group (UK) Ltd
Croydon, CR0 4YY

A CIP record for this book is available from the British Library

ISBN 978 1 3995 0004 3 (hardback)
ISBN 978 1 3995 0005 0 (paperback)
ISBN 978 1 3995 0006 7 (webready PDF)
ISBN 978 1 3995 0007 4 (epub)

The right of Justin McCarthy to be identified as author of this work has been asserted in accordance with the Copyright, Designs and Patents Act 1988 and the Copyright and Related Rights Regulations 2003 (SI No. 2498).

# CONTENTS

| | |
|---|---|
| Maps | vii |
| Tables | ix |
| Abbreviations | x |
| Acknowledgements | xii |

| | | |
|---|---|---|
| **Part I** | **Broken Promises** | **1** |
| 1 | The British and the Ottoman Armenians | 7 |
| 2 | The British Plan for the Armenians | 46 |
| 3 | Crete and the 1897 War | 73 |
| 4 | Macedonia | 117 |
| 5 | British Politicians and Macedonia | 169 |
| 6 | Ottoman Revolution, Italian War | 209 |
| 7 | The Balkan Wars | 239 |
| 8 | The Inspectorates | 292 |
| 9 | World War | 325 |
| **Part II** | **The Final Confrontation** | **343** |
| 10 | The Paris Peace Conference | 353 |
| 11 | The Smyrna Commission | 397 |
| 12 | Britain, France, and Italy | 410 |
| 13 | Creating Resistance – Mustafa Kemal | 427 |

| 14 | The Treaty of Sèvres | 450 |
| 15 | At War with the Turks | 471 |
| 16 | Kurds and Armenians | 511 |
| 17 | The Fall of Venizelos – Neutrality | 532 |
| 18 | Sakarya | 560 |
| 19 | Chanak | 588 |
| 20 | Lausanne | 617 |

| | |
|---|---|
| Appendix: Government Officials | 633 |
| Bibliography | 636 |
| Index | 649 |

# MAPS

| | | |
|---|---|---|
| 1.1 | The Six Provinces, called 'Turkish Armenia' | 8 |
| 3.1 | Crete | 73 |
| 3.2 | Greece, 1876–81 | 90 |
| 4.1 | Bulgarian borders. San Stephano and Berlin Treaties | 119 |
| 4.2 | Macedonia | 120 |
| 6.1 | Bulgaria and Eastern Rumelia | 219 |
| 7.1 | Balkan War conquests | 243 |
| 7.2 | Eastern Thrace and the Enez–Midye Line | 251 |
| 7.3 | The Aegean Islands | 258 |
| 7.4 | Muslim refugees from the Balkan Wars | 272 |
| 8.1 | The inspectorates | 313 |
| II.1 | Anatolia, Eastern Thrace, Northern Syria and Iraq | 344 |
| II.2 | The Sykes–Picot Agreement | 345 |
| 10.1 | Foreign Office recommended boundaries | 363 |
| 10.2 | 'Greek Patriarchate Statistics' | 365 |
| 10.3 | Eastern Thrace and the Straits Zone | 368 |
| 10.4 | Greek Territorial Committee award to Greece | 371 |
| 12.1 | Ottoman Syria, Iraq and Palestine | 413 |
| 14.1 | Aydın Province. Greek boundaries in the Treaty of Sèvres | 453 |
| 14.2 | The Tripartite Agreement | 459 |
| 15.1 | The İzmit–Yalova region | 488 |

| | |
|---|---:|
| 16.1 Northeast Anatolia and the Caucasus, 1919–20 | 512 |
| 16.2 The Armenian Commission proposal | 514 |
| 16.3 Woodrow Wilson's Armenia | 517 |
| 16.4 Southeastern Anatolia and Northern Iraq, 1919 | 521 |
| 17.1 Cilicia: Treaty boundaries | 546 |
| 18.1 The Greek army advance and retreat | 561 |
| 18.2 Paris proposals, British plans for Greek evacuation | 573 |
| 19.1 Chanak and the Dardanelles | 589 |
| 20.1 Lausanne Treaty and demilitarised zones | 626 |

# TABLES

| | | |
|---|---|---|
| 1.1 | Population of Eastern Anatolia and Cilicia, 1912 | 10 |
| 2.1 | Ottoman administrative units | 47 |
| 4.1 | Population of Ottoman Macedonia and Edirne Province, 1911, by province and religion | 120 |
| 8.1 | Population of the 'Six Vilâyets' by religion | 293 |
| 10.1 | İzmir Kaza (district): Population in Cuinet and the 'Patriarchate Statistics' | 364 |
| 10.2 | Population by religion in Western Anatolia and Eastern Thrace, 1911–12 | 366 |
| 20.1 | British plans for Turkey | 628 |

# ABBREVIATIONS

Affaires      France, Ministère des Affaires Étrangères, *Documents Diplomatiques*, cited by sub-heading, for example, *Affaires De Macédoine, 1903–1905*.

BDOW          Gooch, G. P., and Harold Temperley, eds, *British Documents on the Origins of the War, 1898–1914*, vols 1–18, London: 1926–38. Cited by volume.

DBFP          E. L. Woodward and Rohan Butler, eds, *Documents on British Foreign Policy 1919–1939*, First Series, vols 1–18, London: HMSO, 1947–72. Cited by volume.

DD (number)   Ministère des Affaires Etrangères. Commission de publication des documents relatifs aux origines de la guerre de 1914, *Documents diplomatiques français, 1871–1914*, Série 3, Paris: Impr. Nationale, 1929–59. Cited by volume, for example, DD 2, no. 141.

DD (year)     Ministère des Affaires Etrangères. Commission des archives diplomatiques, *Documents diplomatiques français*, Bruxelles, etc.: Peter Lang, 1997–2010. Cited by year and volume, for example, DD 1920, T 1, no. 36.

Dugdale       Dugdale, E. T. S., ed., *German Diplomatic Documents 1871–1914*, vol. 2, New York and London: Harper, 1929.

| | |
|---|---|
| GP | Lepsius, Johannes, Albrecht Mendelssohn Bartholdy, Friedrich Thimme, eds, *Die Grosse Politik der Europäischen Kabinette 1871–1914: Sammlung der diplomatischen akten des Auswärtigen amtes, im auftrage des Auswärtigen amtes*, Berlin: Deutsche Verlagsqesellschaft für Politik und Geschichte, 40 vols in 54, 1922–7. Cited by volume. |
| Papers Relating | United States, Department of State, *Papers Relating to the Foreign Relations of the United States, the Paris Peace Conference, 1919*, vols 1–12, Washington: Government Printing Office, 1942–7. Cited by volume. |
| US | United States National Archives. Cited by digital file and number (Film Series M and T). |

Great Britain, The National Archives

| | |
|---|---|
| ADM | Admiralty |
| CAB | Cabinet |
| FO | Foreign Office |
| T | Treasury |
| WO | War Office |

British Parliamentary Command Papers, *Blue Books*, are cited by title and year.

# ACKNOWLEDGEMENTS

*The British and the Turks* depends on nearly fifty years of archival research. The large majority of documents that form the basis of the book came from the vast collections of the British National Archives. I especially praise the National Archives' liberal policies on reproductions, personal copying by researchers and online documents. Without these policies, it would have been impossible for anyone who did not live in London to do this type of research. The United States National Archives also provided valuable documents.

For books and articles, I particularly depended on the collection and online resources of the University of Louisville Library, especially its efficient Interlibrary Loan Department. Over the years, other major sources for my research have been the British Library, the Library of Congress, the library of the School of African and Asian Studies, the Türk Tarih Kurumu, the Başbakanlık Arşivi, the ATASE SAREM Başkanlığı and many university libraries.

While the writing of this book was funded purely from my own bank account, many of the documents and books that formed the basis of this study were collected during previous projects. These were funded by the University of Louisville, the United States National Endowment for the Humanities and Department of Education, the Social Science Research Council, the Istanbul Chambers of Commerce, the Institute of Turkish Studies, the American Research Institute in Turkey, the Baykan Foundation and the İmre Foundation.

Those who assisted my research are too many to list. Prominent among them were Stanford J. Shaw, Şükrü Elekdağ, Heath Lowry, Kâmuran Gürün, Melih Berk, Hakan Yavuz and Andrew Mango. Librarians and archivists, most of whose names I never knew, aided me always.

As always, my greatest debt is to my wife, Carolyn Beth, and my family – Justin Nicholas, Caitlin Elizabeth, Anne Maureen and John Patrick. They have always been my support, and they contributed greatly to this work with valuable advice and suggestions, editing, proofreading and by copying thousands of documents in the British National Archives. *The British and the Turks* particularly benefitted from John Patrick's manuscript editing and Elizabeth Welsh's copy-editing.

I thank them all.

*Justin McCarthy,*
*Louisville, Kentucky,*
*April 2021*

# Part I

## BROKEN PROMISES

In 1914, as the Ottoman Government contemplated allying with the Germans in World War I, British Foreign Secretary (Foreign Minister) Sir Edward Grey admonished the Ottomans for turning their back on Britain – 'Turkey's oldest friend'. Britain had in fact long since ceased to be a friend to the Ottoman Empire.[1]

**Promises**

The Crimean War was ostensibly fought to defend the possessions of the Ottoman Empire. The 1856 Treaty of Paris confirmed the commitment to Ottoman territorial integrity by Britain, Austria, France, Russia, Sardinia and Prussia:

> Their Majesties engage, each on his part, to respect the Independence and the Territorial Integrity of the Ottoman Empire; guarantee in common the strict observance of that engagement; and will, in consequence, consider any act tending to its violation as a question of general interest.

The provision was short of a commitment to defend the Ottoman Empire, but Britain, Austria and France committed themselves to the Empire in a separate treaty:

> The High Contracting Parties Guarantee, jointly and severally, the Independence and the Integrity of the Ottoman Empire, recorded in the Treaty concluded at Paris on the 30th of March, 1856.
>
> Any infraction of the stipulations of the said Treaty will be considered by the Powers signing the present Treaty as a *casus belli*. They will come to an understanding with the Sublime Porte as to the measures which have become necessary, and will without delay determine among themselves as to the employment of their Military and Naval Forces.

The signatories of the Paris Treaty specifically stated that they did not have 'the right to interfere, either collectively or separately, in the relations of His Majesty the Sultan with his subjects, nor in the Internal Administration of his Empire'.[2]

The Powers had committed themselves to the integrity of the Ottoman Empire and to non-interference in Ottoman domestic affairs. In an 1871 treaty they reaffirmed their commitment to the Treaty of Paris.[3]

For the Ottoman Empire the promises in the treaties were worthless. When the Russians invaded the Ottoman Empire in 1877, Britain, France, Italy and Germany remained neutral. Austria colluded with the Russian invasion in exchange for Austrian occupation of Bosnia. Despite past promises, the Ottomans stood alone against the Russians. In the Treaty of San Stephano (3 March 1878), the Russians forced the Ottomans to cede large areas of Eastern Anatolia and to create a Great Bulgaria out of Ottoman Europe. Only the fear of Russian aggrandizement caused the other Powers, in the Treaty of Berlin (13 July 1878), to allow the Ottomans to retain some of their European possessions.[4]

The Treaty of Berlin renewed some of the previous treaties' provisions: 'The Treaty of Paris of March 30, 1856, as well as the Treaty of London of March 13, 1871, are maintained in all such of their provisions as are not abrogated or modified by the preceding stipulations.' The 'previous stipulations' in the treaty, of course, were acceptance of the occupation and dismemberment of Ottoman Europe. The worthless promise of Ottoman integrity in theory remained, as did the equally worthless promise not to interfere in Ottoman domestic affairs.

## Balkan Muslims and the Treaty of Berlin

For the people of what had been Ottoman Europe the most important provisions of the Berlin Treaty dealt with the rights of Muslims in the new states that were carved out of Ottoman Europe. The treaty stipulated for each country that civil and religious rights and Muslim real property in the new states, including the property of refugees who had fled the states, would be guaranteed. Muslims would be able to retain their property or, if they were no longer in the country, to lease out or sell their property at a fair price: if a country expropriated property 'by legal process for the public welfare', an indemnity would have to be paid.[5]

These treaty provisions proved to be as valueless as the guarantees in the Treaty of Paris. Virtually all the property of Muslims who had been forced out of the new states was expropriated without compensation. Montenegro and Serbia were the worst offenders. By ten years after war's end, virtually all the property of Muslims in the new Montenegrin and Serbian territory had been either taken illegally or destroyed. The process of expropriation was echoed to an equal or somewhat lesser extent in the other conquered regions. Mosques, medreses and other Muslim institutional buildings were destroyed or converted to other uses, but this made little difference to many of those who had depended on them, because the Muslims were so often dead or gone. Worse than the confiscation of property was the murder and forced exile of the Muslim population of the conquered territories. By 1879, 55 per cent of the Muslims of the occupied territories had been forced out as refugees; 19 per cent were dead.[6]

The British were well aware of events in the conquered territories. British consuls reported in great detail attacks on, and murders of, Muslims, illegal expropriations of Muslim property, as well as Muslims forced to flee from Bulgaria, the Dobruja, Montenegro and Serbia. The British and the other Europeans did nothing. Their status as guarantors of the Berlin Treaty was forgotten. While the British were later to concern themselves extensively with Christian suffering in Macedonia and Eastern Anatolia, they did nothing to defend Muslims from much greater suffering from 1878 to 1922.

## Dismembering the Ottoman Empire

Fearful of Russian aggrandizement, Britain had belatedly assisted the Ottomans at the Congress of Berlin, but only in exchange for the island of Cyprus. After that, in every crisis that beset the Ottoman Empire, the British were to act to dismember the Ottoman domains. Promises to guarantee Ottoman territorial integrity and not to interfere with Ottoman domestic affairs were disregarded in Crete, the Balkans and Anatolia. British leaders from the 1890s to the 1920s – Rosebery, Kimberley, Lansdowne, Salisbury, Grey, Curzon and Lloyd George – were driven by anti-Turkish public opinion. But they themselves simply did not like the Turks. They felt no wish to protect them. The Ottoman Christians, on the other hand, were to be protected, their interests fostered. The interests of Ottoman Muslims, the majority population, were ignored.

## Notes

1. Grey to Beaumont, Foreign Office, 4 August 1914, in BDOW 11, p. 313.
2. 'Convention between Great Britain and France, relative to Military Aid to be given to Turkey. Signed at London, 10th April, 1854' and 'Protocol of Conference between Great Britain, Austria, France, Russia and Prussia, relative to the Maintenance of the Integrity of the Ottoman Empire. Vienna, 23rd May, 1854'. 'General Treaty of Peace between Great Britain, Austria, France, Prussia, Russia, Sardinia and Turkey. Signed at Paris, 30th March, 1856'. 'Treaty between Great Britain, Austria, and France, guaranteeing the Independence and Integrity of the Ottoman Empire. Signed at Paris, 15th April, 1856'. Edward Hertslet, *The Map of Europe by Treaty*, vol. II, London: Butterworths, 1875, pp. 1254–5 and 1280–1.
3. 'Treaty between Great Britain, Austria, France, Germany (Prussia), Italy, Russia, and Turkey, for the Revision of certain Stipulations of the Treaties of 30th March, 1856, relative to the Black Sea and Danube. Signed at London, 13th March, 1871'. Hertslet, p. 1922. The changes, which were all on treaty provisions on the Danube and Black Sea, did not affect the other treaty provisions, which were specifically reaffirmed. See Barbara Jelavich, *The Ottoman Empire, the Great Powers, and the Straits Question*, Bloomington: Indiana University Press, 1973.
4. Thomas Erskine Holland, *The European Concert in the Eastern Question*, Oxford: Clarendon Press, 1885: Treaty of San Stephano, pp. 335–48. Treaty of Berlin, pp. 277–307.

5. The same wording was put in articles for each state – Montenegro, Serbia, Romania and Bulgaria. The same provisions were applied to Greece when its borders were set in 1881.
6. In Bulgaria in 1876, nationalist revolutionaries had attacked and killed Turkish villagers and Ottoman officials. The Ottoman Government, already fighting Serb rebels in Bosnia, had set free local Turks, who killed both rebels and innocent civilians. Russian had intervened in the Russo-Turkish War of 1877–8. 288,000 Bulgarian Muslims, mainly Turks, had died and a further 515,000 had been forced out of Bulgaria as refugees, a total loss of 54 per cent. The Muslim population of the Dobruja, taken by Romania, decreased by 83 per cent. Nearly all the Muslims in regions taken by Serbia and Montenegro were dead or refugees (Justin McCarthy, 'The Demography of the 1877–78 Russo-Turkish War', in Ömer Turan, ed., *The Ottoman-Russian War of 1877–78*, Ankara: Middle East Technical University and Meiji University Institute of Humanities, 2007, pp. 51–76). Alexandre Popovic, *L'Islam Balkanique: les musulmans du sud-est européen dans la période post-ottomane*, Berlin: Osteuropa-Institut an der Freien Universität Berlin, 1986; Justin McCarthy, *Death and Exile: The Ethnic Cleansing of Ottoman Muslims, 1821–1922*, Princeton: Darwin, 1995, pp. 59–108; 'The Population of Ottoman Europe before and after the Fall of the Empire', in *Proceedings of the Third Conference on the Social and Economic History of Turkey*, Heath W. Lowry and Ralph Haddox, eds, Istanbul: Isis, 1990, pp. 275–98 and Justin McCarthy, 'Muslims in Ottoman Europe: Population from 1800 to 1912', *Nationalities Papers*, vol. 28, no. 1, 2000, pp. 29–43. McCarthy, 'The Demography of the 1877–78 Russo-Turkish War', p. 72. Derya Derin Paşaoğlu, 'Muhacir Komisyonu Maruzatı'na Göre (1877–78) 93 Harbi Sonrası Muhacir İskânı', *History Studies*, vol. 5, Issue 2 (March 2013), pp. 347–86.

# 1

# THE BRITISH AND THE OTTOMAN ARMENIANS

The creation of the Balkan States by Russia during and after the 1877–8 War was a manual of rebellion for Armenian nationalists. That war had cemented the demographic predominance of Christian groups in the Balkans by killing or expelling Muslim minorities. However, in Bulgaria the Christian Bulgarians had always been a majority; the war only increased their relative proportions. The situation in the Eastern Anatolian region claimed by Armenian nationalists was quite different. For them, the difficulty was demographic. In the Erivan Province of Russia, they made up slightly more than 50 per cent of the population, but in the provinces that they claimed in Ottoman Eastern Anatolia, they were a minority in every province. Militarily, Armenians could not have stood even against the local Muslims, much less the Ottoman army. Their only hope was to elicit the help of the European Powers – to follow the example of Bulgaria.[1]

The strategy of the Armenian nationalist revolutionaries in the 1890s was cold-hearted. Russian military attack had created Bulgaria. Armenian nationalists knew that similar European intervention was the only path to the creation of an Armenia. There would have to be massacres of Armenians, followed by European intervention. As in Bulgaria, the Muslim population would have to be dispensed with, either by death or forced exile. It was a callous plan, sacrificing both Muslims and Armenians to nationalist goals.

The revolutionaries who devised the plan were not native to the Ottoman Empire. Some small and unsuccessful Armenian rebel groups had existed in

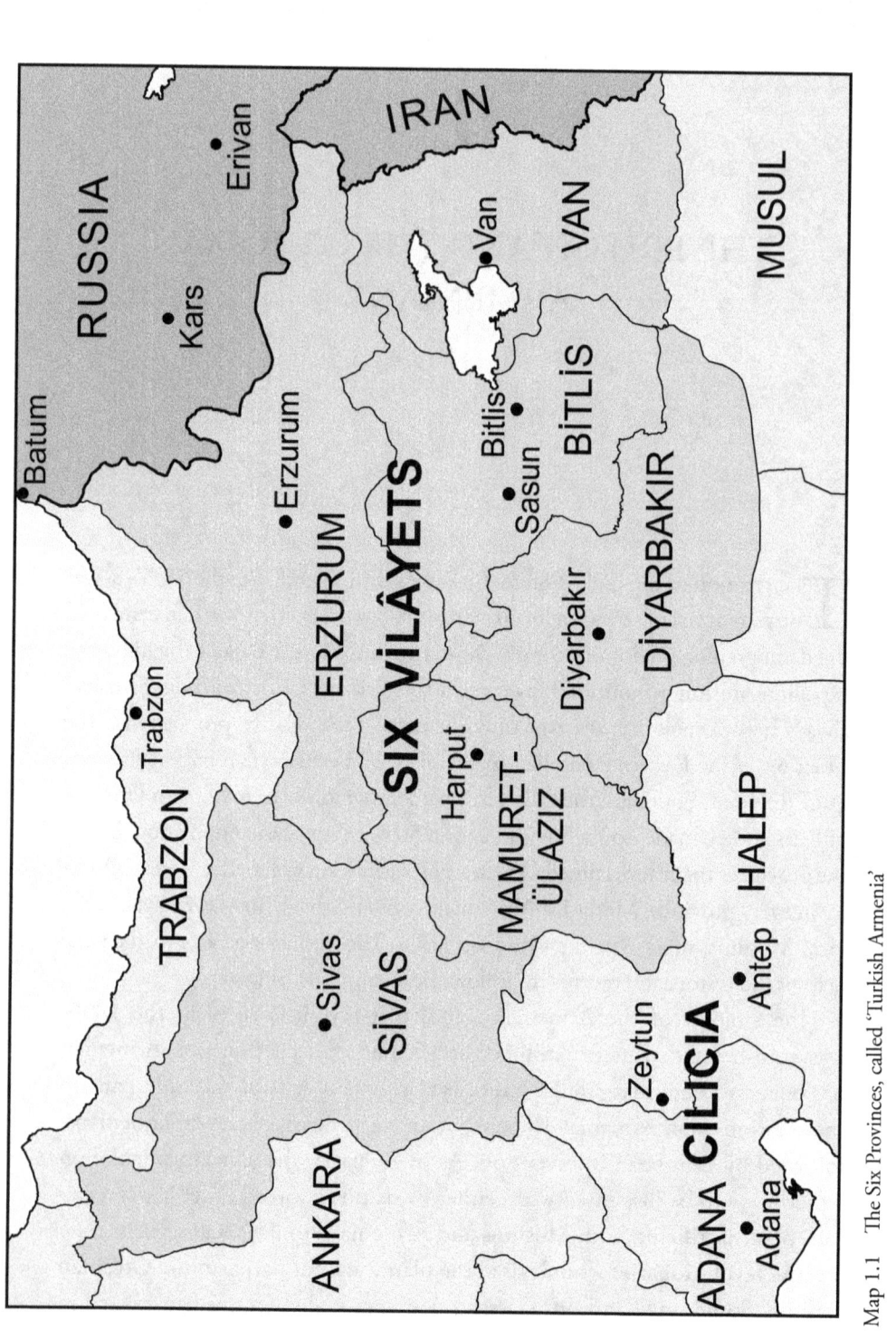

Map 1.1 The Six Provinces, called 'Turkish Armenia'

Southeastern Anatolia, but significant Armenian rebellion only began at the end of the nineteenth century with two new organisations founded in Europe and the Russian Empire – the Hunchaks and Dashnaks.[2]

## Hunchak Rebellion

The Hunchaks (the Hunchakian Revolutionary Party), who were to take the lead in revolt in the Ottoman Empire, were founded in Geneva, Switzerland, in 1887 by students from the Russian Empire. Theirs was avowedly a terrorist organisation, as declared in their party platform. Attacks on Muslims, followed by revenge massacres of Armenians by Muslims, and European intervention was always their plan. Conditions in Eastern Anatolia were ripe for rebellion: poverty, poor government administration, and control of Armenians by Kurdish landowners provided a number of dedicated followers, never close to a majority of the Armenians, but enough to further the Hunchak plan.

At first the Hunchaks engaged in small actions, killing government couriers and officials. By 1890 they had advanced to more significant actions. In July 1890, they kidnapped the Armenian Patriarch in Istanbul, who had to be rescued by Ottoman soldiers. Small-scale offences continued, attracting a number of Armenians to the Hunchak cause. For the new adherents, the Hunchaks represented the chance for Armenian rule or, more likely, a protest against poor conditions.

From 1894 to 1896 the Hunchak plan was implemented in earnest – prominent attacks that would draw reprisals. In Bitlis in 1895 Armenians fired on Muslim worshippers at the Friday Prayer and shot Muslims in the streets. Muslims then attacked Armenians. One hundred and twenty Armenians and thirty Muslims were killed. Similar attacks came in Diyarbakır, and then at Merzifon, where European consuls reported a great number of both Turks and Armenians killed. In Erzurum, Armenian rebels fired on Muslims in a crowded marketplace, sparking a riot in which eleven Muslims and 111 Armenians died. Similar events took place all over Eastern Anatolia – Muş, Akdağmadeni, Arapgir, Bayburt, Mamahatun, Eğin and many others. The Hunchak strategy progressed as planned; after the Hunchak attacks, many more Armenians died than Muslims. Some Kurdish tribes took advantage of the fact that Ottoman soldiers were occupied by the riots to steal from Armenian villages and fight the Armenians when they resisted. Unquestionably,

Armenians suffered a substantially higher mortality rate than did the Kurds and Turks, as was the plan.

Table 1.1   Population of Eastern Anatolia and Cilicia, 1912

|  | Muslim | Greek | Armenian | Other | Total |
|---|---|---|---|---|---|
| The 'Six Vilâyets' | | | | | |
| Sivas | 1,196,300 | 90,419 | 182,912 | 3,207 | 1,472,838 |
| Bitlis | 408,703 | 0 | 191,156 | 11,532 | 611,391 |
| Mamuretülaziz | 564,164 | 1,227 | 111,043 | 3,807 | 680,241 |
| Diyarbakır | 598,985 | 2,355 | 89,131 | 63,980 | 754,451 |
| Van | 313,322 | 1 | 130,500 | 65,974 | 509,797 |
| Erzurum | 804,388 | 5,811 | 163,218 | 779 | 974,196 |
| Total | 3,885,862 | 99,813 | 867,960 | 149,279 | 5,002,914 |
| Cilicia | | | | | |
| Adana | 573,256 | 14,825 | 74,930 | 3,567 | 666,578 |
| North Haleb | 1,017,539 | 25,474 | 123,129 | 23,536 | 1,189,678 |
| Total | 1,590,795 | 40,299 | 198,059 | 27,103 | 1,856,256 |

Source: McCarthy, *Muslims and Minorities*.[3]

These figures are the most accurate available, but populations in the 1890s were somewhat smaller.

The most important Hunchak rebellions took place in Sasun, Zeytun and Van.

In 1893, long-standing conflicts between Armenians and Kurdish tribes erupted in Sasun in Southeastern Anatolia. The deaths were part of a war in which Armenians and Kurds took part as combatants.

The Sasun district (*kaza*) had a small Kurdish Muslim majority, 53 per cent; the larger region, which included Kulp and Muş kazas, was slightly more Armenian in population, 55 per cent. Armenians in Sasun largely were independent, sometimes allied with, or clients of, Kurdish tribes. They sided with 'their Kurds' in conflicts with other tribes. The Ottoman Government applied what little power it had in the region on the side of the Armenians and their Kurdish allies. The Ottomans sent a battalion of troops to the Sasun region because they wanted to control the Kurds and out of fear of European repercussions if Armenians were harmed. The system was fairly stable until the Hunchak Revolutionary Committee sent organisers to Sasun. These went into alliance with Armenian bandit groups, who now espoused revolutionary ideals in their own interest. Armenian peasants and religious leaders sided with either the traditional system or with the rebels.

Battles between the Kurds allied with the Armenians and other Kurds erupted in 1893, with the Kurdish/Armenian side victorious. Led by the Hunchaks, Armenian rebels and bandits then began to attack Ottoman officials, tax collectors and gendarmes. Open warfare broke out in Sasun, with Armenians attacking Kurds during their tribal migrations and Kurds retaliating. Armenian and settled Kurdish civilians fled and suffered the plights of the now homeless.

The Ottomans intervened. Deciding that the small force of soldiers already in the region was insufficient, more troops were sent. As they moved into the region, they were attacked by Armenian rebels, but fought them off. The Hunchaks in Sasun had been promised aid from the Hunchak Central Command. Aid and reinforcements never appeared, because the Hunchaks had no forces to send them. The local rebels had been betrayed. The real intention of the Hunchak leaders had been to spark massacre of Armenians that would be reported in Europe and bring European intervention. Insofar as the British were concerned, the Hunchak policy was a success. Sasun was reported in the British press only as the scene of massacres of Armenians.[4]

Zeytun (today Süleymanlı), in a mountainous region in South Central Anatolia, was a town with a solely Armenian population, except for an Ottoman garrison. The surrounding region was populated by both Armenians and Muslims. The Armenian revolt there was led by a Hunchak organiser known as Aghassi. His first revolt, in Suedia near Antakya, had been a failure, and Aghassi and his band of supporters concentrated on Zeytun, where the local Armenians had previously revolted a number of times to preserve independence and oppose taxation. Aghassi was received enthusiastically by the Zeytun population. Armenians from around the region flocked to his cause. In October 1895, they began to attack gendarmes and burn Muslim villages, killing the inhabitants. On 25 October, they attacked a greatly outnumbered company of 200 Ottoman soldiers, who were only saved by Muslim villagers who joined the fight. The Ottoman Government called out the reserves and prepared, very slowly, to oppose the rebels.

In Zeytun City itself, an Ottoman force was besieged in an army barracks. The rebels surrounded them, and after two days of fighting the garrison surrendered. Some of the soldiers' families were allowed to leave, but the soldiers were killed. The rebels extended their attacks to Muslim villages throughout the region, plundering and burning houses and torturing and killing those who could not escape.

The Ottomans at first attempted to negotiate with the rebels. A Commission of Armenian Notables was sent to Zeytun to negotiate with the rebels. The rebels imprisoned them as government spies.

In December, the Ottoman army advanced. They were not gentle. In response to attacks on the Muslim villages in Yenice Kale, the soldiers burned Armenian villages in the same district. Cannon were used to dislodge rebels resisting in the town of Fırnıs, setting fire to the town. Some 800 Armenian women and children were sent to Maraş by the soldiers, where they were cared for by American missionaries. The other Armenians from Fırnıs and all around the region fled to Zeytun, swelling the numbers in the town. Typhus, dysentery and smallpox killed an estimated eighty a day in Zeytun. The army surrounded Zeytun. When the rebels refused to surrender, the troops opened fire with cannon.

The Ottoman forces at Zeytun under Edhem Paşa were orderly. A large force of Circassians who had arrived at the city were disarmed and sent away. Local Muslims seeking revenge were not allowed to take part in the battles, surely saving Armenian lives. Armenians who had not been able to flee their villages were not so lucky. Muslim villagers took their revenge.

Sultan Abdülhamid II, faced with European pressure and routinely uninformed and prejudiced European press, requested European intervention. European consuls, led by the British Consul Henry Barnham, negotiated with the rebels. They negotiated a general amnesty for all the rebels; the Hunchak leaders were to be freed but expelled from Ottoman territory. Muslims and Armenians were to be disarmed. A Christian was to be named *kaymakam* (district governor) of the Zeytun Kaza. On 13 February, the Hunchak leaders went to the port of Mersin. They boarded a ship for Marseilles on 12 March.[5]

The astonishing thing about the assault on Zeytun City is that the Ottoman soldiers kept such good order and so seldom engaged in reprisals, despite what they saw the Armenian rebels had done to their comrades. As British Consul Barnham recounted:

> This afternoon I visited the Zeitoun river and saw the bodies of the Turkish soldiers who were killed by the Zeitounlis. One of them admitted yesterday that 230 had been massacre. In many cases they are tied hand and foot, their heads split open by axes, or they are killed by sword cuts or shots, and in some cases their hands and feet cut off. One of the Turkish authorities told me that a zaptieh (rural gendarme) had his eyes cut out, filled with gunpowder, and his head blown to pieces. I have no reason to doubt this story.[6]

It is instructive that in both Sasun and Zeytun the Hunchaks had promised rebels they would receive British support. It was assumed that the British would take the side of Armenian rebels. The support they expected was military; however, the support that they received was diplomatic – the Europeans forced the Ottomans to set the rebel murderers free.

Rebel preparations for revolt in Van began in spring of 1896. The revolt began on 3 June. Fighters from the Dashnak (see below) and Hunchak Committees barricaded the Armenian Quarter of the city and began to fire on Ottoman soldiers and Kurdish civilians who approached, killing many. British Consul Williams estimated 600 Armenian fighters armed with Russian rifles. Requested by the government to intervene, European consuls attempted to negotiate with the rebels, to no avail. Sporadic fighting continued until the rebels fled the city on 9–10 June. Ottoman forces retook the Armenian Quarter. British Consul Williams estimated that 300 Muslims and 200 Armenians had died in the city; Ottoman General Sadettin Paşa listed 349 Muslim and 219 Armenian dead.

The Armenian revolt spread to other towns in Van Province, with attacks on Muslim properties and murders of Muslims, but was put down by Ottoman forces. Armenians fared worse in the countryside. When firing began from the Armenians in Van City, Kurdish tribes asked if they should come into the city to fight the Armenians. Fearing a bloodbath, the Ottoman commander, Sadettin Paşa, ordered them to stay back. However, Ottoman forces were insufficient to control the countryside. When the Armenian rebels fleeing Van City attacked Kurdish villages, Kurdish tribes attacked Armenians, by no means all of them rebels. Sadettin Paşa listed 1,715 Armenians and 363 Muslims dead in the countryside and the city. Fighting between tribes and Armenian rebels from Iran continued into 1897.

The rebellion in Van Province never had a chance of success. The Ottoman army, undermanned as it was, was still much more powerful than the rebels. Moreover, even if the army had somehow been defeated, there were the forces of the Kurdish tribes to consider. Why did the rebels revolt? Part of the reason, as elsewhere in Anatolia, was to spark massacre and draw European intervention. The other reason could be labelled absurd over-confidence. The Van rebels considered themselves to be an advance guard, holding the city until they could be relieved by an Armenian army that would arrive from an Armenian base in Iran. An Armenian force, much smaller than an army, did indeed leave Iran, heading for Van. However, it was cut down by Kurds when it attacked Kurdish towns on its line of march. Survivors fled back to Iran.

Sadettin Paşa's force in Van acted correctly throughout the events. Neither the British consul nor the American missionaries in Van faulted the troops' discipline, but there were never enough of them to properly constrain the Kurdish tribes. Armenians in the countryside suffered.[7]

One factor in the rebellions should be emphasised: in both Sasun and Zeytun, local organisers were promised aid and reinforcements from the Hunchak Committee. No such reinforcements existed; those who revolted were sacrificed so that Armenian deaths in war could be portrayed in Europe as massacres. That was the Hunchak plan. It was very successful. Newspapers all over Europe portrayed the Armenian deaths as massacres of innocents, not including any other reasons for the troubles or the fact that Muslims had died or that Muslims had been the first victims. The propaganda surrounding the Armenian troubles was particularly well received by British politicians and by Christian and humanitarian interests that were always willing to believe the worst of Muslims.

**The Dashnaks**

The other main Armenian rebel group, the Dashnaks, proved to be more successful than the Hunchaks, slowly organising Armenian nationalist rebellion until it flowered in World War I. The Dashnak Party was founded in Tiflis, in the Russian Empire. Its aim, as inscribed in its manifesto, was to implement a 'people's war against the Turkish government'. Like the Hunchaks, they were willing to accept Armenian losses to achieve their goals. On 26 August 1896, an armed band of twenty-six Dashnaks invaded the Ottoman Bank in Istanbul, taking the bank's employees hostage. They shot at police and passersby from the bank windows. Dashnak supporters throughout the city occupied schools, warehouses and houses, shooting and throwing bombs at civilians. As expected, this drew Muslim reprisals. Hundreds died, the majority of them Armenians. Their actions drew no European intervention, although Europeans did arrange safe passage for those who had occupied the bank.

The Dashnaks adopted a programme of assassination, extortion and the slow organisation of rebel cadres. The majority of those extorted and murdered were Armenian who refused to support the rebel cause or to pay 'revolutionary taxes'. Ottoman officials were also attacked; the Dashnaks killed chiefs of police, local gendarmes and policemen, one governor and other officials. Dashnak bands, mainly from Russia and Iran, attacked Muslim villages, Kurdish tribes and government outposts; the Dashnaks themselves recorded more than 100 incursions. The main Dashnak purpose was to establish their control over the Armenians of the Ottoman East and to organise the Armenians in preparation for ultimate battle against the Ottoman Government and the Turks and Kurds that was to come.[8]

## British Public Opinion and the Armenians: The Anglo-Armenian Association

The Anglo-Armenian Association was founded in 1893 by James Bryce (later Viscount Bryce of Dechmont). It was the intellectual and emotional child of Gladstone's anti-Turkish agitation on the 'Bulgarian Horrors' of 1876. It held a symbiotic relationship with Gladstone's Liberal Party, and Gladstone remained a supporter of the association after his retirement from politics. Headed by Francis S. Stevenson, a Liberal member of parliament, the association included many members of parliament and others from Liberal political circles, including Sir Edward Grey, later the foreign secretary. Thirteen of the association's committee and officers were members of parliament in 1893. It thus had influence in parliament and the government. The association's MPs deluged parliament with its version of Armenian events. From 1893 to 1896, Francis Stevenson, the president, entered fifty-one questions or speeches on the Armenians in the House of Commons; its treasurer, C. E.

Schwann, entered twenty-two. Deputations from the association, including MPs, influential citizens and church leaders, visited Prime Minister Rosebery and other officials to plead their case.[9]

The association's most pronounced effect was on British public opinion and, through public opinion, on politicians. British newspapers reported in great detail the claims the Anglo-Armenian Association made against the Turks in press releases and public meetings. Reporters from the English press and press agencies used the Anglo-Armenian Association as a primary source of information.[10]

The Anglo-Armenian Association held 'mass meetings' in the largest venues in Britain. Audiences included 'members of parliament, irrespective of party, ministers of all denominations, and others who sympathize with the Armenian people' and, of course, the public and reporters. At the public meetings, descriptions were not temperate: at one public meeting organised by the Anglo-Armenian Association, the audience was told the Turks were 'a disgrace to humanity and civilization'. At another, the Turks were 'a constant and chronic evil'. Audiences were told that Ottoman law forced Christian women to be 'at the disposal' of Turks sexually. At a meeting on 3 April 1895, President Stevenson of the association evaluated Turkish rule: 'The Turk had never done anything good, or had made the slightest improvement, except under the compulsion of one or more Powers. (Cheers.)' The Rev. Dr J. Clifford stated: 'Turkish Government had been a blight wherever it had ruled, and it was a blight and a curse still.' Canon Gore added: 'Every kind of outrage to life, liberty, religion, and the honour of women had been perpetrated with a cold-blooded fanaticism which it was impossible to exaggerate. (Cheers.)' 'A mass meeting of several thousand persons' in Manchester was told, 'the suffering people have been exposed to outrage, slaughter and hideous barbarities, until it is in peril of extermination, to the disgrace of Europe, especially England.' Ex-Prime Minister Gladstone, in retirement, delivered a speech to the Anglo-Armenian Association in which he called Turkey 'the scourge of the world', 'a disgrace to civilization at large' and 'a curse to mankind'. The speech appeared in newspapers across Britain. The multitude of public meetings held across Britain described the Turks using similar language.[11]

It is impossible to attempt to describe here the many 'mass meetings' organised by the Anglo-Armenian Association. One example was the great meeting held at the 2,000 seat St James's Hall in London on 19 October 1896. Members of all parties in both houses of parliament attended, as did bishops, 'leading Nonconformists' and professors. More than 100 provincial mayors attended, wearing their insignias of office. The Duke of Westminster originally planned to take the chair, but he was indisposed, so the Bishop of Rochester chaired the meeting. Those on the platform included members of parliament, various lords and ladies, bishops, mayors, the chairman of the London County Council and many other worthies. Organisers said they had been forced to turn away two-thirds of those who had applied for tickets. The meeting opened with a prayer, followed by a long list of dukes, marquesses and bishops who sadly could not attend, but sent their best wishes for the cause. A letter from ex-Prime Minister Gladstone was read in which he demanded action against the 'Great Assassin (the sultan)'. Reading of other letters deploring the Turks followed. All demanded action by the British Government. The bishop chairman then spoke of the necessity of action by Christendom. A resolution of 'indignation and abhorrence at the outrage, torture, and murder of defenceless subjects of the Sultan' was brought forward. The mayors of Belfast and Worcester seconded the motion, stating that the Ottomans would never reform unless forced. Wholly spurious accounts of Turkish atrocities were offered (for example, 10,000 Armenians were murdered at Urfa). Other speakers kept up the theme, describing the sultan as 'an evil genius', whose actions were 'abominations'. One speaker stated that Britain must not stand in the way of Russia's taking Armenia, Constantinople and the Straits. Speakers said that the honour of England demanded that the Turkish Government be ended. Speakers were often interrupted by loud cheers. After numerous orators had castigated the Turks and further calls were made 'not to allow the Armenian people to perish helplessly', the meeting ended with the singing of 'God Save the Queen'.[12]

The above was but one of a multitude of large-scale meetings, including others with packed audiences also held at St James's Hall. The tenor of the speeches was nearly identical across all; only descriptions of specific atrocities changed.[13]

The impacts of the Anglo-Armenian public meetings went far beyond their effect on attendees. Newspapers across Britain reported the meetings, often quoting verbatim from the speakers. They listed the names of prominent speakers, audience members and those whose letters of support were read at the meetings. Readers would have been impressed, all the more so because newspapers printed almost nothing that disagreed with the Anglo-Armenian Association's assertions. In computerised searches for years 1893 to 1914: *The Times* printed 404 articles including the phrase 'Anglo-Armenian Association' (although for *The Times* these included letters to the editor and a small number of indexes). The British Library's British Newspaper Archive – mainly a collection of provincial newspapers – listed a staggering 1,196 entries for 'Anglo-Armenian Association', almost all of them actual articles.[14]

The association asserted that Armenian massacres had been carried out by order of the Ottoman Government and the sultan personally. The sultan could not be allowed to continue to rule over Christians. The association stated that the reforms that had been suggested by the European Powers fell far short of what was needed. It brought forward a solution to the 'Turkish problem' that was to become a staple of British policy in upcoming years – the British Government was to intervene to create an 'Armenia' ruled by a high commissioner/governor-general approved by the Great Powers. In a meeting at Oxford, Francis Stevenson, president of the association, stated that: 'A European High Commissioner should be appointed, who should not be a subject of the Sultan, but should be appointed by the Powers, and be responsible only to them.'[15]

The British Government did not officially admit how many of its plans and proposals were influenced or directed by the association, but the evidence supports that the British Government's plan for the Ottoman Empire was to be essentially the same as that of the Anglo-Armenian Association.

The association made requests that the British Government secure the release of named rebels who had been imprisoned and even the replacement of an Armenian Patriarch, whom the association felt had been too cooperative with the Ottoman Government. They assured that they knew that those convicted of treason had been innocent victims of a government plot. The Foreign Office made assurances that their views were being acted on in Istanbul, as they were.[16]

London forwarded to the Istanbul embassy Armenian Association publications, memoranda and resolutions, along with requests for diplomatic action. The diplomatic record is full of Anglo-Armenian Association requests for actions against individual Ottoman officials and in favour of individual Armenians. Members of parliament that were officials of the association brought the association's requests for intervention to parliament and were promised action. Ambassador Philip Currie in Istanbul and Her Majesty's consuls acted on these requests, with varying results. For example, responding to the association's concerns over Armenians condemned to death for treason in Yozgat, Foreign Secretary Kimberley asked the sultan to grant them clemency, which 'cannot fail to produce a favourable impression in this country'. It was granted. Prime Minister Salisbury instructed the British embassy in Istanbul to intervene in court cases against Armenians to gain acquittals or to obtain reduced sentences.[17]

**The Churches**

British churches took up the campaign against the Turks. Methodist, Congregationalist, Universalist and Anglican churches all held meetings blaming Turks for massacres of Armenians. The meetings were sometimes held in conjunction with the Anglo-Armenian Association, sometimes organised by the churches themselves. Ministers made 'the Turkish Evil' the subject of sermons. Bishops and ministers were also prominent speakers at the public meetings held by the Anglo-Armenian Association and later the Balkan Committee, which was to use the same tactics to advocate for Balkan Christians.[18]

Both the Anglo-Armenian Association and the Balkan Committee made extensive reference to 'common Christianity' and the need to rescue brother Christians from Muslim rule. The churches, both independently and in concert with the committees, preached against the Turks. The Bishop of Hereford, prominent among supporters of the Anglo-Armenian Association and later member of the Balkan Committee, called on his churches to support the Armenian cause. Petitions from 209 parishes, containing 10,000 signatures, in the diocese of Hereford were sent to the queen.[19] Sermons were preached, and special meetings were held on Armenians and Bulgarians. In one such meeting, at St Andrew's Church in London, congregants were told Britain had to repent of its sin in supporting the Turks at the Congress of Berlin.[20]

The Archbishop of Canterbury gave his support to the intentions of the Anglo-Armenian Association, as did many bishops. Bishops, other Anglican clergy and Nonconformist leaders and ministers often spoke at the mass meetings. Churchmen united in asking their followers to join in great rallies against the Turks called by the association. Such meetings were held across Britain, often presided over by bishops and nearly always featuring bishops and members of the clergy as speakers.[21]

When the Anglo-Armenian Association spoke with politicians and presented 'memorials' (petitions), the deputations uniformly contained members of the clergy, mainly bishops and leaders of Nonconformist churches. For example, a deputation from the Anglo-Armenian Association met with the Earl of Kimberley, foreign secretary, on 30 March 1895. Sir Edward Grey, later foreign secretary and a member of the Anglo-Armenian Association, was in attendance. In addition to thirty-five members of parliament, the delegation included Anglican clergymen and representatives of the Baptist churches, the Free Church Congress, Dissenting churches and the Salvation Army.[22]

Protestant church organisations outside the Anglican Communion were prominent in the Armenian cause. These often supported the Anglo-Armenian Association, but sometimes lobbied the British Government alone. The General Presbyterian Alliance sent memorials to Kimberley. Many memorials were sent to Kimberley and Salisbury by the Evangelical Alliance. The Evangelical Alliance was mainly concerned with problems of the Protestant Armenians in the Ottoman Empire. It portrayed Ottoman actions as 'a war on the Christian Religion'. The alliance stated that all over Anatolia Armenians were starving and would only be allowed to eat if they became Muslims. Many Christians were supposedly threatened with death if they did not convert. The Foreign Office forwarded their complaints to Ambassador Currie and promised they would be investigated. (One assumes that they were simply placating the alliance, since the Foreign Office could not have believed that all the Armenians were starving.)[23]

Complaints of ill-treatment and of Ottoman governance from the Anglo-Armenian Association, British religious organisations and individual Armenians were forwarded to the Istanbul embassy for investigation. Ambassador Currie was very receptive to the complaints. He himself solicited what amounted to anti-Turkish religious propaganda from the Evangelical Alliance, asking the alliance to produce a paper against the Turks. The British Government reported back to the association that it was taking action on its complaints.[24]

The British ambassador at St Petersburgh, Frank Lascelles, had a frank discussion on the Armenian issue with the Russian Foreign Minister, Prince Lobanov (Aleksey Lobanov-Rostovsky). Lobanov blamed excessive British zealousness on the Armenian issue on pressure from the Anglo-Armenian Association, which he described as 'so-called public opinion'. He said he knew the association aimed to create an autonomous district for Armenians, which they intended to eventually become an Armenian state, which the Russians would not allow.[25]

**Newspapers**

It is obviously impossible to cite here the thousands of articles on the Armenian Question that appeared in the British press, only a sample of the almost universal condemnation of Turks and misrepresentation of both Turks and Armenians. Some features were common in British newspaper reporting on the Armenians: numbers of Armenian dead were grossly inflated; Muslim deaths were seldom listed and, if occasionally mentioned, were minimised; the actual causes for troubles were not given, the actions of Armenian rebels unmentioned. According to the newspapers, Muslims had simply decided to massacre Armenians or were ordered to do so. The sultan was declared to be responsible for everything. It was often claimed that he had ordered massacres. Many of the events described were pure invention and never took place; others were so distorted as to be demonstrably false.[26]

Analyses of the informants of the British articles on Armenians are hindered by their lack of verifiable sources. Sources were seldom identified: 'private reports received', 'private advices from Armenia', 'an Armenian Correspondent', 'A Special Correspondent', 'a letter received from Smyrna (İzmir)', 'from private reports received', 'A report from Moosh', etc. Where sources were occasionally given, they were questionable. In an article sent to its subscribing newspapers the Central News Bureau even interviewed Avetis Nazarbek (Nazarbekian), who alleged that the Ottoman Government had sent 10,000 Kurds to kill the Sasun Armenians, a complete falsehood. The article did not mention that Nazarbekian was the leader of the Hunchak Party, whose members were instrumental in causing the Sasun troubles. *The Times*, the *Daily News* and many other newspapers reported a harrowing scene of massacre in Sasun, Van and elsewhere, told by a group of Armenian refugees who had somehow made it to the Black Sea and taken a ship to Athens. The story had originated with an Armenian organisation and *The Times* correspondent in Athens. The problem was that the British ambassador in Athens, Edwin Egerton, reported that he had investigated, and the refugees did not exist; the whole story was a fabrication.[27]

Articles purporting to describe massacres were bylined Athens, Vienna, Tiflis, Paris and even Washington. Reports of massacres were sent to Vienna 'from Armenian sources in Constantinople' and were printed as fact. In a typical article, 'Our Correspondent' in Istanbul reported that '[n]othing is known of the massacre at Hesra', then proceeded to describe the alleged massacre.[28]

The most egregious articles on the Armenian troubles appeared in the Liberal press, especially the London *Daily News*. The *Daily News* reports and what were in fact editorials posing as news were reprinted in full or summarised throughout Great Britain, the colonies and the United States. The *Daily News* summarised its stance in an editorial: 'Every spot on the earth's surface redeemed from the Turkish Government has been a subtraction from the sum of evil which afflicts mankind.'[29]

Much of the reporting on the Ottoman Empire in the *Daily News* and the rest of the Liberal press was either invented by reporters or from sources that invented tales to advance their cause. There are many demonstrable examples of false reporting, particularly in the *Daily News*: for example, it was reported that Turks had burned down the city of Harput, an event that never occurred. Most of the Armenian priests in and around Harput (the city and fifty-three villages) supposedly had been tortured and killed because they would not accept Islam, which also never happened. The paper wrote that the British consul at Van had reported that in that city, '[t]housands of women and girls are wandering through the snow piled streets without shelter or food, and barefooted, their ravishers having only left them a chemise and some of them only a cloth to cover their nakedness'. In fact, the British consul in Van never made such an observation, because it was untrue, as can be seen in his reports to the Foreign Office. 'A secret Armenian committee at Bitlis' was supposedly organising a mass uprising of 200,000 Armenians in spring 1896, a ridiculous assertion of a revolt that, of course, never occurred. The *Daily News* reported that Armenians had been massacred in Merzifon in February 1896, but the

French consul who investigated the claims on the scene and the American ambassador both reported that there had been no such massacre. A Turkish force of soldiers and irregulars supposedly sacked villages near Erzincan and captured 5,000 Armenians. 'According to the invariable Turkish practice, the men were cruelly tortured, and women and young children ravished.' The author of this information was 'the Kars correspondent of the *Daily News*'. Kars, in the Russian Empire, was 300 miles from Erzincan by bad roads.[30]

A common assertion, such as one from an 'an occasional correspondent of *The Times*', was that the Ottoman Government had decided to engage in a massive massacre of Armenians as a response to reforms demanded by the Powers. 'The object has been to destroy everything so effectually that the Armenians would have no means of living, and would have to choose between death and Islam.' Spurious 'Turkish Statistics' were produced, showing that 425,000 Armenians were starving, and 79 per cent of the Armenian villages had been destroyed. *Reynolds's Newspaper* published a report taken from an Armenian newspaper stating that the British consul had reported 6,000 Armenians had been massacred at Van in 1894, and that the British consul had asked for Great Britain's intervention. Neither had happened. There were troubles and an attempted Armenian revolt in Van, not one-sided massacre, but they occurred in 1896, two years after the report, not in 1894.[31]

While newspapers such as *The Times* or the *Daily News* are well known today, others were significant only in their day. For example, *Reynolds's Newspaper*, a Radical, working-class publication that appeared on Sundays only, but had a circulation of more than 350,000, was as vociferous as the *Daily News* in its condemnations of the Turks: in an article headlined 'The Unspeakable Turk Again', it described the Turks as 'a handful of lying, thieving cutthroats who are still permitted to pollute European soil'. It printed articles with sub-heads such as 'Women Hacked to Pieces' and 'Mothers and Babes Slaughtered'.[32]

The provincial Liberal press often outdid the London papers. They took articles from the London dailies or news services and added embellishments of their own. The *Bristol Mercury* wrote of 'Turkey – a festering sore upon the body politic of Europe', which must be excised for the health of Europe. The *Hampshire Telegraph* headlined 'Unspeakable Turk: Atrocities in Armenia', and went on to describe rapes and massacres, based on the testimony of the non-existent Athens refugees. The *Belfast News-Letter*, after claiming the Turks had massacred 10,000 in Sasun alone, declared that the sultan planned to exterminate all the Christians in his Empire. Where the provincial press articles sources were identified, they often originated with the Anglo-Armenian Association.[33]

Even those who did not read beyond the headlines could not escape the anti-Turkish news. Common headlines were 'Armenian Outrages', 'The Massacres in Armenia', 'The Atrocities in Armenia', 'Turkish Atrocities. Horrible Outrages. Massacre and Pillage', 'The Armenian Atrocities: Ten Thousand Reported Massacred', 'The Armenian Atrocities: Sickening Barbarities' and 'The Armenian Atrocities: Fiendish Tortures'. Had they read on, the readers would have most often found press releases from the Anglo-Armenian Association or extended quotes from Gladstone's condemnation of the Turks.

Editorials demanded British action against the Ottomans. *The Times* wanted all Armenian reforms to be 'placed under the continuous power of the Great Powers'. *The Times*, however, did not agree with Gladstone's call for an autonomous Armenia, which would lead to conflict in which the Armenians would suffer most. What was needed was European control. The *Daily News* editorials, as might be expected, described horrors committed by Turkish soldiers and Kurds, calling for British action. Armenia, the *Daily News* declared, must be ruled by a Christian governor and have a constitution written by Europe – in effect, a separate state, created by force. The newspaper held nothing back in its editorial condemnations of the Kurds ('as savage as Red Indians') and the 'ignorant Turks'.[34]

The events in Sasun and Zeytun were particularly plagued by false reporting. The *Daily News* reported that in Sasun, 3,000 Armenians had been killed by Kurds and Ottoman troops and twenty-five Armenian villages destroyed. Other reports alleged that 6,000 or 10,000 Armenians had been killed. The *Daily Telegraph* printed completely invented stories of men and women in Sasun hacked to pieces, little children cut in half, priests flayed alive, 100 women sent off to Van for soldiers' pleasure and all the Armenian villages plundered by Hamidiye Kurds. (The Hamidiye Kurds were irregular cavalry in the Ottoman forces. They had a bad reputation in Europe, and thus were convenient scapegoats, but they had, in fact, never been in Sasun.)[35]

*The Times* never had the same effect on the British populace as the *Daily News* or the *Telegraph*, both of which had many times its circulation. *The Times*, however, had its effect on the Establishment. *The Times*, which stated that its information came from Istanbul, Vienna and İzmir – all far from Sasun – gave an almost completely incorrect picture of events in Sasun in long articles: one article wrote that the Ottoman Government had mistakenly believed that the Armenians were in revolt, so it sent in Hamidiye troops under Zeki Paşa, their leader, 'to annihilate all those who had resisted the authority of local officials'. It related that Turkish soldiers had not wanted to kill defenceless women and children, but followed orders and did so. In another article it reported that the Ottomans had ordered the massacre of the Sasun Armenians by Kurds because the Armenians were too independent. Torture, murder and rape were described in gruesome detail. Sometimes 6,000 Armenians were reported killed, sometimes 10,000. The stories were mainly without attribution, but *The Times* was not above accepting the sort of sources seen elsewhere. In one article, it quoted 'an Armenian in a humble position in life, who is temporarily resident here (Bucharest), has received a letter from his wife'.[36]

The Hamidiye Kurds were never at Sasun during the troubles. Zeki Paşa only arrived at the end of the fighting, when he brought order, not massacre. As reported in the press, the estimates of the number of Armenians who died and the number of Kurds who fought were ridiculous, because there were only 13,000 Armenians in Sasun (the districts of Sasun and Kulp). The actual numbers of deaths among combatants were ninety-seven Armenians, 117 Kurds and fourteen soldiers. An unknown number of noncombatants also died of exposure.[37]

The British public was particularly interested in a Commission of Investigation sent to investigate the events at Sasun. British, French and Russian consuls served as delegates to the commission and wrote a report. In Britain it was confidently expected that the commission would return evidence of massacre of Armenians by Turks and Kurds. The *Daily News* and the *Daily Telegraph* sent leading correspondents to report on the Sasun Investigation Commission, Emile J. Dillon and Frank Scudamore. Their reports were printed in many newspapers.

The correspondents had a major difficulty – they were not allowed to go near the sittings of the commission. The Ottoman Government, fearing the sort of reports that were seen in the press, had forbidden all journalists at the meetings; the reports of the consuls, they felt, would suffice. (In terms of public relations, this was probably a mistake, because reporting could not be worse than what was reported.) The answer for Dillon and Scudamore was simply to invent the news. What they reported as the commission's deliberations was the opposite of the truth: tens of thousands of Kurds ordered by the Government to attack the Armenians. Many thousands of Armenians were killed, '(Armenians were) butchered, often with refined contumely and cruelty, and always with a savage delight'. According to Dillon and Scudamore, no soldiers died at Sasun. This was the opposite of what was found by the commission.[38]

Dillon's reports included extensive spurious reports of testimony before the commission, testimony that advanced his thesis that soldiers, acting on Orders from the Ottoman Government, had tortured and massacred Armenians. His reports were filled with the sort of gory detail already featuring in, and reinforcing, the stories already seen in the British press. He said he had interviewed the members of the commission, who had agreed with Dillon that 'the Armenians were butchered wherever they were found'. But Dillon had never actually interviewed commission members. Dillon simply lied. The actual minutes and report of the commission, which included the statements of witnesses before the commission, were completely different to Dillon's reports and gruesome tales. Dillon said he had received commission reports while he was in Muş, close to the commission's sittings, and when he visited Sasun itself. In fact, he had never been to either place. He was in Erzurum and Kars, hundreds of miles away.[39]

Scudamore also reported on commission matters that he could not have known. He reported 5,000 to 8,000 Armenians dead at Sasun, killed with appalling cruelty, based on what he said were commission findings. He stated that eighty Armenian villages were destroyed. This was many more Armenians and Armenian villages than ever existed in Sasun. He wrote that 28,000 to 30,000 Kurds and Turks attacked the Armenians; again, many times the actual numbers of Turks and Kurds. Scudamore supposedly received reports from inside Ottoman prisons and from Ottoman soldiers that had escaped to join him in Kars, across the border in Russia. As with Dillon, Scudamore's reports were never borne out by the actual commission testimony.

The sort of article sent in by Scudamore is exemplified by a report he supposedly sent from Muş to Kars. It was stated to be testimony before the Sasun Commission, although the commission never heard it, and it was a complete invention:

The savagery of the Kurds was tame compared with the diabolical cruelties perpetrated by the soldiers of the regular army, who flayed people alive; gouged out the eyes of priests, and then made them dance; and seized children by the hair of the head, afterwards amusing themselves with cutting their little necks asunder at one stroke.[40]

These were the 'first-hand' reports on Sasun that reached the British public. While Dillon's and Scudamore's false reports of the Sasun Commission's deliberations were printed across Britain, stories quoting the actual commission report, when it was published, were few. They identified the reporting on Sasun as false. That was not what the public or the politicians wanted to hear.[41]

The only major publication to never join the anti-Turkish crusade was the relatively low circulation *Pall Mall Gazette*, which repeatedly wrote that the evidence was too untrustworthy for any conclusions to be made. Other newspapers, tied to Conservative politics, occasionally questioned the Liberal journals. In addition to the standard claims against the Turks, *The Morning Post* printed some articles questioning the standard stories of massacres. A very few newspapers printed remonstrances of the Turkish ambassador against false reports, usually along with statements that the ambassador could not be trusted. Even the papers that printed a few hesitant articles questioning some massacre reports, however, still printed spurious massacre reports as news.[42]

Although the British newspapers embellished and exaggerated stories of Armenian suffering and often simply lied, not all the stories printed in the press were completely false. There were massacres of Armenians. But by not printing either the actual events in the Ottoman East or news of the corresponding deaths of Muslims, the newspapers told less than half the story of the Armenian troubles. Added to the manifest lies printed almost universally in the newspapers, these omissions left the British public with a false picture of events. The fabrications and omissions fed on themselves: having been fed a diet of massacres, the public expected more. Editors obliged. Public indignation rose, and with it the real or feigned indignation of politicians.

## Public Opinion and the Politicians: Rosebery and Kimberley

Prime Minister Archibald Philip Primrose, fifth Earl of Rosebery, had long been an enemy of the Ottoman Empire. During and after the 1877–8 Russo-Turkish War he had been an ardent apostle of Gladstone's anti-Turkish policy. In 1877 he suggested that the British negate the guarantee of Ottoman borders that Britain, France and Austria had made in 1856. Rosebery delivered a long speech at Aberdeen on 18 October 1878, in which he praised the Russian division of the Ottoman Empire in the Treaty of San Stephano. ('As to the partitioning of the Turkish Empire, that is a result which some of us may not be particularly inclined to regret.') The British Government, he said, had left the Christians of Macedonia under a 'debasing yoke'. The Disraeli Government's treatment of the Ottoman Empire like other European Powers was a grave mistake. ('Turkey is not a great Power; she is an impotence.')[43]

While in office as foreign secretary from 1892 to 1894 and prime minister from 1894 to 1895, Rosebery seldom explained publicly his opinions on the Armenian Question or, indeed, most other issues. Only when his party had been defeated in the 1895 election did Rosebery express what one assumes were his true feelings: out of power in 1896, in his speech on the opening of parliament, Rosebery lamented the loss of the spirit in Christendom that had once opposed Islam: 'The inspiration and perhaps the faith which impelled embattled Christendom to rescue the Cross from the dominion of the Crescent are not present in these days.' In a speech at Edinburgh Empire Theatre on 9 October 1895, he accepted as true the press reports on Armenian massacres ('the horrors that have transformed an earthly paradise into an organized hell'). He accused the sultan, whom he obviously hated, of organising them. In taking action against the Ottomans, he felt, Britain should not bound by its previous commitments to the Ottomans, although for reasons of European politics he did not feel Britain could act alone, despite the moral justification to do so. Expressing his feelings, Rosebery described the Ottoman capital as: 'Constantinople, in what was once the capital of Eastern Christianity, and which, I pray, may yet be the capital of Eastern Christianity.'[44]

The Foreign Office under Foreign Secretary John Wodehouse, 1st Earl of Kimberley, was beset by notes and petitions from the Anglo-Armenian Association and church groups. These demanded action for the Armenians and asked that deputations be received by the foreign secretary to plead the Armenian case. Kimberley rejected meetings with the Anglo-Armenian delegations, as he did with meeting other pressure groups, but the Foreign Office corresponded with the groups, explaining how much the British were doing for the Armenians.[45]

While he did not meet with the British pressure groups, Kimberley was willing to express his opinions on the source of the Armenian troubles to the Ottomans. He told them that he doubted that Armenian rebels were an important source of the problems in Eastern Anatolia. He declared to the Ottoman ambassador, Rustem Paşa, that the Armenian troubles stemmed not from the Armenian 'agitators', but from 'corrupt and vicious administrators'. When the Ottoman Government complained over a vehemently anti-Turkish speech by Gladstone, Kimberley authorised Ambassador Currie to tell the sultan that Gladstone was representing the general feeling in Britain.[46]

In addition to his personal feelings against the Ottomans and Islam, Kimberley admitted that his motives were greatly affected by British public opinion. During negotiations on Armenian reforms, he demanded onerous requirements for the Ottomans because the British public demanded it. When he thought they were too lenient toward the Ottomans, he told the Russians that 'measures of restraint' would have to be used against the sultan, because of 'the excited state of feeling in this country on the subject of the Armenians'.[47]

**Salisbury**

Robert Arthur Talbot Gascoyne-Cecil, 3rd Marquess of Salisbury, served simultaneously as both prime minister and foreign secretary during the height of the Armenian agitation in Britain. His views and actions on the Armenian Question were framed by his religious beliefs. He shared the opinions of the clergy, who were so vocal in support of the Armenians. A firm believer in the superiority of Christianity, he had a quite intolerant view of non-Christian faiths and their believers. Lord Salisbury was in varying degrees intolerant of every religion except the Church of England, and that only in its High Church version. Methodist and Presbyterian beliefs and those of Roman Catholics in Ireland shared in his disdain. In Britain, he worked against inclusion of even non-Anglican Protestant values in universities and public life. But Salisbury reserved his greatest dislike for Islam. He once stated that Islam was 'capable of the most atrocious perversion and corruption of any religion on the face of the globe'. (Peter Marsh, in his analysis of the motives behind Salisbury's Ottoman policies, made a convincing case that Salisbury's antipathy to the Turks and sympathy for the Armenians arose from moral and religious conviction, not reasons of state.)[48]

Immediately on taking office in 1895, the Conservative Salisbury indicated that on the one subject of the Armenian Question his views were the same as those of Rosebery's Liberals. He proposed a plan that mirrored the plan of the Anglo-Armenian Association: Armenians were to be put in government positions throughout Eastern Anatolia, with overall control in the hands of a European governor-general or, at the least, the approval of European ambassadors for government actions. Lord Salisbury's efforts were supported. At the Anglo-Armenian Association St James's Hall meeting, described above, Bryce and Stevenson spoke of the need to support Salisbury 'to put an end to the root of the evil – the Government of the Porte'. It was declared that mass meetings would strengthen the prime minister's hand in bringing the other Powers to agree to intervene in the Ottoman Empire.[49]

When Salisbury took office, he was as concerned with British public opinion as had been Kimberley. He told the Turkish ambassador that 'it was absolutely necessary that the Turkish Government should make concessions to public opinion, particularly in Britain'. When the Ottomans rejected the one European proposal, Salisbury complained that the problem with the Ottomans' response was that it would not satisfy British public opinion.[50]

Salisbury's approach to the Ottomans can only be called radical. When he met with Tsar Nicholas at Balmoral in 1896, Salisbury suggested that the solution to the Armenian Problem was that the sultan should be deposed:

> When he (the next sultan) took the Sultanate he would know that his predecessor had been deprived of it by the voice of the Powers, and would know that if he shocked the feeling of Europe, or disregarded the advice of the Powers, a similar fate might await himself.

Salisbury did not hesitate to suggest gunboat diplomacy. If the Ottomans did not comply with his wishes, he proposed various measures to force their cooperation: sending the British fleet to the Bosporus, seizing Ottoman ports, even seizing Jeddah and blockading the Muslim Holy Land. Although never able to put the plan into effect, because the river was too shallow for British ships, he proposed sending gunboats up the Tigris, a proposition that gained cabinet approval. He moved the British fleet to Salonica to impress on the Ottomans the possible effect of British might.[51]

German Ambassador Count Paul von Hatzfeldt met with Salisbury on 10 and 31 July 1895. He reported to Berlin that Salisbury felt that Britain had made a great mistake in the Crimean War by not accepting Russia's plan to divide the Ottoman Empire. Salisbury told him that public opinion in Britain was forcing him to action. Salisbury felt the Ottoman Empire was doomed; the question was what to do with its remains, or perhaps how to speed its demise. Hatzfeldt felt that Salisbury was contemplating a division of the Ottoman Empire. (It should be kept in mind that Salisbury was only considering the possibility, not making a formal decision, but his conversation does illuminate his mindset.) Salisbury's wish was to take Syria and Iraq for Britain; Austria would take Macedonia and the port of Salonica, Russia Anatolia, Italy Albania, and France Libya.[52]

Salisbury's radical proposals were frustrated by the other European Powers. When he met with Kaiser Wilhelm II in August of 1895, Salisbury brought up the impending 'dissolution' of the Ottoman Empire. Wilhelm told Salisbury that things in the Ottoman Empire had improved, and there was no need to consider any dissolution. Salisbury's own naval advisors said that his proposals were wholly impractical. Frustrated in his plans, Salisbury was forced to accept a plan that would have put Eastern Anatolia in the hands of an Ottoman subject as governor-general and an Ottoman Commission, and even this plan never came to fruition.[53]

Salisbury's mind was closed on any subject relating to the Turks. One can search in vain in Salisbury's assertions for any consideration of the human losses of Muslims in the 1877–8 War, the actions of Armenian and Bulgarian revolutionaries against Muslims in Eastern Anatolia and Macedonia or any other knowledge that might lead to, if not sympathy for the Turks, at least understanding of their situation. He showed so little understanding that his knowledge of the Ottoman Empire might have come mainly from the popular press, which may have been the case. His beliefs on crises in Eastern Anatolia and Macedonia surely do not reflect the correspondence of consuls in those regions. It must be admitted, however, that Salisbury depended on his ambassador to the Ottoman Empire, Philip Currie, whose prejudices reflected his own.

Among the many British politicians with an anti-Turkish bias, Salisbury stands out as the most hostile. Although frustrated by the Europeans, he never abandoned his hope of dissolving the Ottoman Empire. Even had there been no such evidence of his antipathy toward Islam from his own words, Salisbury's actions would have demonstrated it. Throughout his time as prime minister and foreign secretary, Salisbury showed great concern for the Christians of the Ottoman Empire, but certainly showed no concern for the Ottoman Muslims.[54]

**Ambassador Currie**

Philip Henry Wodehouse Currie, the wealthy son of a banking family, entered the Foreign Office in 1854 and rose rapidly through its ranks. He had a close connection with Lord Salisbury, who was a personal friend and mentor. Currie served as private secretary to Salisbury when Salisbury became foreign secretary in 1878. He served as permanent under-secretary of state, the head of the Foreign Office, in 1888, working closely with Salisbury. He was then appointed by Lord Rosebery in December 1893 as British ambassador at Istanbul, where he remained until he was sent as ambassador to Rome in 1898.

Lord Kimberley usually had been content to follow Currie's lead in dealing with the Ottomans, but Currie's influence increased when his personal friend, Lord Salisbury, became both prime minister and foreign secretary. Salisbury's daughter and biographer, Lady Gwendolen Cecil, described Currie as Salisbury's first friend in the Foreign Office, 'the most intimately trusted of those who worked with him'. Salisbury praised Currie in both public speeches and in parliament. Salisbury and Currie were so much to share opinions and policies that it was difficult to know which of them had originated them. Currie contended that it was at his initiative that the British Government invited the French and Russians to join them in joint protests at Istanbul, which was probably correct.[55]

With Salisbury's approval, Currie repeatedly used threats to force the sultan to bow to British demands. The use of force was Currie's own predilection, not only a reflection of Whitehall policy. Currie told his cousin and confidant, Wilfrid Blunt, that he was in favour of using the fleet to enforce British demands. Like Salisbury, Currie considered blockading Jeddah and detaching the Muslim Holy Land from the sultan's rule, and he may have been the source of Salisbury's ideas. Currie further believed that British occupation of İzmir would bring the Ottomans to heel. He told Blunt that it was absolutely necessary to be rid of Abdülhamid: '"We have come to the conclusion," he said today, "that it will be necessary to kill him (the sultan). To depose him would be very difficult, perhaps impossible".'[56]

Ambassador Currie was not what one would expect in a diplomat. He did not hesitate to broadcast his opinions of the Turks. Prince Hugo Fürst von Radolin, German ambassador to Russia who had also served in Istanbul, wrote of Currie:

> A rumor has recently spread in Petersburg that Sir Philip Currie does not feel safe either and that an assassination attempt against him is feared. With Sir Philip Currie's passionate demeanor and his careless utterances, which I remember very well from Constantinople, I should not be surprised if the passion of the Muslims also turns against him. He said to me a few days after his arrival in Constantinople, when he hardly knew me, in the most brutal way that he did not understand why some of the stable generals of the empire did not thrust a dagger into this 'weak wretched man', so he will probably have used similar utterances in other ways with the same carelessness, which some could perhaps use against himself, and which could others to act on his provocations.[57]

Currie treated Ottoman officials and even the sultan as recalcitrant servants who would be forced to accept British authority. Sultan Abdülhamid described a meeting with Currie:

> The British Ambassador was a very nasty man. He had an audience with me once, at the time of the Armenian crisis. He crossed his legs and began to yell at the top of his voice, saying you do such and such things to the Christians. I was so angry that I said to myself, now I shall get at your throat and kill you, but what can I do, I am in a responsible, official position (*memurum*). My Ottoman nerves were so infuriated that I was barely able to control myself. Tears came to my eyes after the Ambassador left; I cried . . .[58]

Whether or not Abdülhamid actually cried, the British ambassador had certainly left him with an understanding of British feelings toward the Ottoman Empire and its sovereign.

## Notes

1. A list of the books on the Armenian troubles would take up a chapter on its own. See, for example, the very differing viewpoints in: Justin McCarthy, *Turks and Armenians: Nationalism and Conflict in the Ottoman Empire*, Madison, WI:

Turco-Tatar Press, 2015. Esat Uras, *The Armenians in History and the Armenian Question*, Istanbul: Documentary Publications, 1988. Türkkaya, Ataöv, ed., *The Armenians in the Late Ottoman Period*, Ankara: Turkish Historical Society/Grand National Assembly of Turkey. Ankara: 2001. Kamuran Gürün, *The Armenian File*, London: Rustem and Weidenfeld and Nicolson, 1985. Jeremy Salt, *The Last Ottoman Wars: The Human Cost, 1877–1923*, Salt Lake City: University of Utah Press, 2019, pp. 38–70. Anahide Ter Minassian, *Nationalism and Socialism in the Armenian Revolutionary Movement*, trans. A. M. Berrett, Cambridge, MA: Zoryan, 1984. Louise Nalbandian, *The Armenian Revolutionary Movement*, Berkeley: University of California, 1963. George A. Bournoutian, *A Concise History of the Armenian People: (From Ancient Times to the Present)*, Costa Mesa, CA: Mazda Publishers, 2002. Richard G. Hovannisian, ed., *The Armenian People*, vol. II, New York: St. Martin's, 1997. Other sources are also listed in the notes below.

2. On the Hunchaks and Dashnaks, see: Altan Deliorman, *Türklere Karşı Ermeni Komitecileri*, Istanbul: Boğaziçi Üniversitesi, 1975. Mehmed Hocaoğlu, *Arşiv Vesikalarıyla Tarihte Ermeni Mezâlimi ve Ermeniler*, Ankara: Anda, 1976. Hüseyin Nâzım Paşa, *Ermeni Olayları Tarihi*, 2 vols, Ankara: Osmanlı Arşivi Daire Başkanlığı, 1994. Jeremy Salt, *Imperialism, Evangelism and the Ottoman Armenians 1878–1896*, London: Frank Cass, 1993, pp. 61–4, 71–80 and 92–4.

   In the British National Archives: FO 195/1863, 1887, FO 424/183, 184, 186, 196, 197, FO 881/6957, 6959. Alternative view: Richard G. Hovannisian, ed. *Armenian Van/Vaspurakan*. Costa Mesa, CA: Mazda, 2000. Hratch Dasnabedian, *History of the Armenian Revolution Federation, Dashnaktsutiun*. Bryan Fleming and Vaha Habeshian, trans., Milan: GEMME Edizione, 1989, and Hratch Dasnabedian, 'The Hnchakian Party'. Mariné A. Arakelians, trans., *Armenian Review* 41, no. 4 (Winter 1988), pp. 17–39.

3. Justin McCarthy, *Muslims and Minorities: The Population of Ottoman Anatolia and the End of the Empire*, New York: New York University Press, 1983, pp. 109–12.

4. On the conflicts in Sasun, see Justin McCarthy, Cemalettin Taşkıran and Ömer Turan, *Sasun*, Salt Lake City: University of Utah Press, 2014, which contains an extensive bibliography. Başbakanlık Devlet Arşivleri Genel Müdürlüğü, Osmanlı Arşivi Daire Bşk., *Ermeni Komiteleri (1891–1895)*, Ankara: T. C. Başbakanlık Devlet Arşivleri Genel Müdürlüğü Osmanlı Arşivi Daire Başkanlığı, 2001. Great Britain, Foreign Office, *Correspondence Relating to the Asiatic Provinces of Turkey: Turkey, No. 1 (1895), part 1: Events at Sassoon, and Commission of Inquiry at Moush*, London: HMSO, 1895, and *Correspondence Relating to the Asiatic Provinces of Turkey: Turkey, No. 1 (1895), part 2. Commission of Inquiry at Moush: procès-verbaux and separate depositions*, London: H. M. Stationery Office, 1895.

Hüseyin Nazım Paşa, *Ermeni Olayları Tarihi*, 2 vols, Ankara: T. C. Başbakanlık Devlet Arşivleri Genel Müdürlüğü, 1994. Nurşen Mazıcı, *Belgelerle Uluslar arası Rekabette Ermeni Sorunu'nun Kökeni (1878–1918)*, İstanbul, 1987.

Sasun in the British National Archives: FO 78/4006, 4562. FO 195/1728, 1766, 1821, 1860, 1863, 1891, 1892. FO 424/169, 175, 178, 181, 182, 183, 184. FO 881/6555X, 656X.

Alternative view: Antranig Chalabian, *Revolutionary Figures*, trans. Arra S. Avakian, USA (sic): no publ. data, 1994. Poghosyan, H. M. (Haykaz Manuki), *Sasuni patmut'yun (1750–1918)*, Erevan: 'Hayastan' Hratarakch'ut'yun, 1985. Louise Nalbandian, *The Armenian Revolutionary Movement*, Berkeley: University of California Press, 1963.

5. On the Zeytun Rebellion, see Latif Dinçaslan, *Zeytun ve Çevresindeki Ermeni İsyanları*, Kahramanmaraş: Ukde Kitaplığı, 2008. Mehmed Hocaoğlu, *Arşiv vesikalarıyla tarihte Ermeni mezâlimi ve Ermeniler*, İstanbul: ANDA Dağıtım, 1976. Hüseyin Nâzım Paşa, *Ermeni Olayları Tarihi*, 2 vols, Ankara: Osmanlı Arşivi Daire Başkanlığı, 1994. Erdal İlter, *Ermeni Meselesinin Perspektifi ve Zeytun İsyanları*, Ankara: Türk Kültürünü Araştırma Enstitüsü, 1988.

National Archives: FO 195/1883, FO 424/181, 184, 186, 189, FO 881/6739, FO 78/ 4614, 4617, 4621, 4702, 4735, especially FO 78/4735, 'Memorandum by Consul Barnham Respecting the Zeitoun Insurrection, 1895–96', London, 18 June 1896.

Alternative view: Aghassi, *Zeitoun: Depuis les Origines Jusqu'a l'Insurrection de 1895*, Paris: Mercure, 1897. Dasnabedian, 'The Hnchakian Party', pp. 17–39.

6. FO 424/186, Currie to Salisbury, Aleppo, 3 February 1896. All place names, which sometimes differed, are as in the diplomatic correspondence.

7. On the 1896 Van rebellion, see: Justin McCarthy, Esat Arslan, Cemalettin Taşkiran and Ömer Turan, *The Armenian Rebellion at Van*, Salt Lake City: University of Utah Press, 2006 (hereafter McCarthy et al., *Van*), which contains an extensive bibliography. Ergünöz Akçora, *Van ve Çevresinde Ermeni İsyanları (1896–1916)*, Istanbul: Türk Dünyası Araştırmaları Vakfı, 1994. Sami Önal, *Sadettin Paşa'nın Anıları*, Istanbul: Remzi Kitapevi, 2003.

8. On the Dashnaks, see the sources in Notes 1 and 2, above, and: Hagop Manjikian, ed., *Houshamatyan of the Armenian Revolutionary Federation: Album-Atlas*, vol. 1, Los Angeles: Western United States Central Committee of the Armenian Revolutionary Federation, 2006. Dikran Mesrob Kaligian, 'The Armenian Revolutionary Federation under Ottoman Constitutional Rule, 1908–1914', unpublished PhD dissertation, Boston College, 2003. Salt, *Imperialism, Evangelism*, pp. 106–10.

9. An earlier society with the same name had been founded by Bryce in 1878 or 1879 (sources differ). The officials and members of the committee were listed in Francis S. Stevenson, *The Case for the Armenians*, London: Harrison and Sons, 1893, p. 27. All the members of parliament who were officials or members of the committee were Liberals except two. Speeches and questions were prominent in *Hansard* for 1893–6. After then, much more parliamentary attention was addressed to Crete and Macedonia. On the deputations, see, for example, FO 800/35, Meeting with Anglo-Armenian Association, 9 May 1893. FO 424/178, 'Anglo-Armenian Association to the Earl of Rosebery', London, 17, 23 January, 17, 20 November 1894 and FO 424/181, 19 March 1895, as well as numerous mentions in FO 800/39. Rosebery seldom wished to receive deputations, preferring to communicate with the association by letter. Kimberley did not comply with some of the more radical requests of the association; the association asked the Foreign Office for copies of all recent consular documents on the Armenians. Kimberley understandably refused. (FO 424/178, 'Anglo-Armenian Association to the Foreign Office', London, 20 November 1894; 'Foreign Office to Anglo-Armenian Association', Foreign Office, 21 November 1894.)

   The National Moslem Association sent a note to Kimberley complaining of the unjust treatment of the sultan and his government in the agitation being carried out in Britain. The Foreign Office responded, briefly, that they could do nothing about the anti-Muslim actions of individuals, and that the pro-Armenian organisations were simply investigating the truth about actions in the Ottoman Empire. (FO 424/181, 'The National Moslem Association to the Earl of Kimberley', London, 14 January 1895; 17 January 1895.)

10. See, for example, articles in which the connection with the Anglo-Armenian Association is acknowledged: 'Reported Rising in Armenia', *Birmingham Daily News*, 26 November 1894; 'The Massacres in Armenia', *Birmingham Daily Post*, 5 December 1894. It is impossible to quote here from the hundreds of press articles originating from, or reporting on, the Anglo-Armenian Association. (Note that it has sometimes not been possible to give page numbers for all articles, because they are not given online and in sources.)

    Another main source of propaganda against the Turks on the Armenian Question was the Armenian Patriotic Association, which has not been considered here, because it was primarily made up of ethnic Armenians, and this study concentrates on native Britons. Although none were as important as the Anglo-Armenian Committee, organisations such as the Armenian Relief Fund and the International Arbitration and Peace Association also called for British coercion of the Ottomans. (See, for example, FO 424/178, Foreign Office to International Arbitration and Peace Association, Foreign Office, 30 April 1894. FO 424/183. Duke of Westminster to Salisbury, London, 14 September 1895.) The Friends of Armenia, founded in 1897, with Lady Frederick (Lucy J.) Cavendish as president, forwarded numerous letters on Armenia suffering to the Foreign Office, but does not seem to have been taken very seriously. The International Friends of Armenia, founded by the Bishop of Rochester (president) and the Bishop of Hereford (Chairman of the Committee) in 1896, seems to have disappeared quickly.

The most complete listing and description of the Armenophile secular and religious organisations is in Yahya Bağçeci, *İngiltere'de Ermeni propagandası (1878–1898)*, İstanbul: Yalın Yayıncılık, 2013. The work also contains extensive descriptions of the British press. Most of its contents came from the Ottoman embassy in London, which kept a scrupulously complete record of anti-Ottoman activities, analysing them from the Ottoman perspective. The development of British opinions on Ottoman Muslims, not only Kurds, is thoroughly considered in Adnan Amin Mohammed, 'British Representations of the Kurds and the Armenian Question 1878–1908', unpublished PhD dissertation, University of Leicester, 2018.

11. Letter to *The Times* from Francis Seymour and other committee members, *The Times*, 10 December 1894, p. 10. 'The Armenian Commission', *Daily News*, 22 May 1895, p. 5. 'The Armenian Commission', *Daily News*, 5 May 1895. 'Meeting at Ripon', *Leeds Mercury*, 29 December 1894. 'The Turkish Atrocities in Armenia', *Daily News*, 4 April 1895. 'The Armenian Massacres', *The Times*, 13 January 1996, p. 6. See, for example, in addition to the London newspapers, 'Mr. Gladstone and the Armenians', *Freemans Journal Dublin*, 31 December 1894; 'Mr. Gladstone and the Armenian Outrages', *Liverpool Mercury*, 31 December 1894; 'The Armenian Atrocities', *Glasgow Herald*, 21 December 1894; 'Armenia and the Powers', *Leeds Mercury*, 31 December 1894; 'The Armenian Atrocities', *Northern Echo*, 31 December 1894.

12. 'The Armenian Question: Great Meeting at St. James Hall', *The Times*, 20 October 1896. *The Times* reported this meeting and others like it in great detail.

13. See, for example, 'The Atrocities in Armenia', *The Times*, 8 May 1895, p. 10; 'The Armenian Question', *The Times*, 24 May 1895, p. 7.

14. For examples of reporting on these public meetings, see 'The Baptist Union', *Glasgow Herald*, 27 April 1894; 'The Armenian Commission', *Daily News*, 26 February 1895; 'The Persecution of the Armenian Christians: A Protest from Leeds',

*Leeds Mercury*, 18 September 1894. There was an audience of 'nearly 1,000 men' in Huddersfield ('Armenia', *Daily News*, 13 December 1894. The article also listed other meetings.) See also, 'The Armenian Christians and their Suffering', *Leeds Mercury*, 5 December 1894; 'Atrocities in the East', *Bristol Mercury*, 4 December 1894; 'The Armenian Massacre', *Leeds Mercury*, 4 December 1894.

15. 'The Armenian Association', *The Times*, 26 October 1895, p. 9. 'The Armenian Atrocities: Protest Meeting at Oxford', *Jackson's Oxford Journal*, 22 June 1895. Letter to *The Times* from Francis Seymour and other committee members, *The Times*, 25 January 1895, p. 10. FO 424/182, 'Anglo-Armenian Association to the Earl of Kimberley', 6 June 1895. A letter from the Duke of Argyll was read at one Anglo-Armenian Association meeting. The duke advocated an end to Turkish rule in Eastern Anatolia and demanded that prisons be immediately put under the control of European consuls. ((Untitled), *Daily News*, 14 December 1894.)

    Stevenson believed that there was no hope for Ottoman administration: 'The whole country is under a reign of terror, to which judicial administration affords no redress and no mitigation.' There was no need, he felt, to pay any attention to the Sasun Commission – the commission that included European delegates and was investigating reported massacres in Sasun – because the facts were already known. The only solution was, in effect, European rule over Eastern Anatolia, with a governor approved by the Powers and a gendarmerie under European commanders. Europeans would head all the higher courts. Stevenson made no concession to the wishes of Muslims, only stating that they would also benefit from European rule. (Francis Seymour Stevenson, 'Armenia', *The Contemporary Review*, vol. 67 (January–June 1895), pp. 201–9.)

16. FO 424/178, 'Foreign Office to Anglo-Armenian Association', Foreign Office, 1 February, 4, 17, 19, 20 April, 3 September 1894; 'Anglo-Armenian Association to the Foreign Office', London, 5, 13 April 1894.

17. FO 424/178, Kimberley to Currie, Foreign Office, 7 September 1894. FO 195/1911, Salisbury to Currie, 15 May 1896. Musa Şaşmaz, *British Policy and the Application of Reforms for the Armenians in Eastern Anatolia 1877–1897*, Ankara: Türk Tarih Kurumu, 2000, pp. 134–5. FO 195/1911, Salisbury to Herbert, Foreign Office, 1 July 1896. Further examples are too numerous to cite. See also, for example, 'The Armenian Prisoners', *Daily News*, 2 October 1894. 'Armenia', House of Commons Debate, 21 March 1895, *Hansard*, vol. 31, cc. 1562–3. 'Armenia', House of Commons Debate, 16 May 1895, *Hansard*, vol. 33, cc. 1325–6. Even high officials were removed at British insistence, such as the governor of Diyarbakır. (FO 195/1911, Salisbury to Currie, Foreign Office, 3 July 1896.)

18. For examples of the many sermons and memorials against the Turks on the Armenian Question, see the articles in the *Daily News* that listed many meetings in one two-week period: Untitled, 13 May 1895. 'The Armenian Commission', 21 May 1895. 'The Armenian Reforms', 28 May 1895.
19. 'The Armenian Question', *The Times*, 11 May 1895, p. 16.
20. For example, 'The Armenian Question', *The Times*, 27 October 1896, p. 10.
21. See 'The Armenian Question', *The Times*, 3 October 1896, p. 6 for an extensive list of clergy and their opinions. It would be impossible to list all the hundreds of meetings reported in the provincial press. Some examples: a meeting led by the Bishop of Aukland (sic), Aukland, 11 September 1896 ('The Armenians', *Northern Echo*, 22 September, p. 4); an Oxford Diocese Conference, led by the Bishop of Oxford, 24 September 1896 ('The Armenians', *Exeter Flying Post*, 26 September 1896, p. 6); a Norwich meeting presided over by the Bishop of Norwich, 18 February 1896 ('The Bishop of Norwich on Armenian Atrocities', *Tamworth Herald*, 22 February 1896, p. 6); the Bishop of Llandaff presided at a meeting in Cardiff on 22 September 1896 ('The Armenian Agitation', *York Herald*, 23 September 1896, p. 6); the Bishop of Salisbury presided at a meeting in Salisbury, 31 December 1895 ('The Armenian Massacres', *Western Gazette*, 3 January 1896, p. 7).

    The Archbishop of Canterbury was more temperate than many of the others, and more willing to support the efforts of the British Government. He seldom wrote on Armenian issues to the Foreign Ministry, but he did forward complaints of the treatment of Assyrian Christians, who were served by Anglican missionaries. See FO 424/182, 'The Archbishop of Canterbury to the Earl of Kimberley', London, 27 May 1895. FO 424/183, 'The Archbishop of Canterbury to the Marquess of Salisbury', London, 10 July 1895.
22. Virtually all the meetings with politicians cited here contained members of the clergy; almost all contained bishops and Nonconformist leaders. 'The Government and Armenia', *The Times*, 30 March 1895, p. 15.
23. FO 424/181, 'General Presbyterian Alliance to the Earl of Kimberley', London, 18 February 1895. FO 424/178, 'Evangelical Alliance to Foreign Office', London, 3, 12 July, 22 October 1894. FO 424/181, 'Evangelical Alliance to the Earl of Kimberley', London, 23 January 1895; Evangelical Alliance, 'Brief Epitome', London, 29 March 1895. FO 424/182, 19 April 1895. FO 424/182, Foreign Office to Evangelical Alliance, 10 April 1895. FO 424/184, Evangelical Alliance to the Marquess of Salisbury, London, 9 December 1895.
24. For examples of these, see FO 195/1911, Salisbury to Currie, Foreign Office, 5 May 1896. FO 195/1912, Salisbury to Herbert, Foreign Office, 3, 30 June,

19 August, 6 September 1896. FO 195/1913, Salisbury to Currie, 24 October 1896; Salisbury to Currie, 1 December 1896. Evangelical Alliance, *Violations of the Hatti Humayoun: A Paper Prepared at the Request of Sir Philip Currie, British Ambassador to the Sublime Porte, by the Evangelical Alliance of Constantinople*, London: Evangelical Alliance Office, 1895.

25. FO 424/182, Lascelles to Kimberley, St Petersburgh, 4, 5 June 1895. Lobanov called the Anglo-Armenian Association 'the Armenian Committee'. He said they were in touch with, and supported, Armenian revolutionaries in Russia.
26. Jeremy Salt has written a valuable summary on the differences of reporting and reality in the Armenian Question. Jeremy Salt, 'The Narrative Gap in Ottoman Armenian History', *Middle Eastern Studies*, January 2003, vol. 39, no. 1 (January 2003), pp. 19–36.
27. Nazarbekian article: 'Turkey and Armenia: Thousands Killed and Imprisoned', *Leeds Mercury*, 22 November 1894 and other papers. The lengthy article on the refugees appeared in many newspapers. See, for example, 'Armenian Atrocities', *Leeds Mercury*, 5 December 1894; 'Armenian Outrages', *The Standard*, 5 December 1894, p. 6. See also 'The Porte and the Armenians', *The Times*, 5 December 1894, p. 5 and 'The Armenian Question', *The Times*, 17 December 1894, p. 6. A more complete list is in McCarthy et al., *Sasun*, pp. 44–6 and 287–8. FO 424/178, Egerton to Kimberley, Athens, 12 December 1894.
28. 'The Armenian Inquiry', *London Standard*, 23 February 1895. 'The Armenian Question', *London Standard*, 19 February 1895. I have not been able to find any town named Hesra in gazetteers or on maps.
29. Unsigned editorial, *Daily News*, 18 December 1894, p. 2.
30. 'Outrages in Armenia', *Birmingham Daily Post*, 9 November 1895. See the extensive list on these fabrications and reports in McCarthy et al., *Sasun*, pp. 38–71. See also the description of the deceptions in the press reports by British Consul George Pollard Devey in Van. (FO 424/169, Devey to White, Van, 12 January 1891.) Much of the information and sources for Sasun are in McCarthy et al., *Sasun*.
31. 'A Summary Review of the Armenian Massacre', *Birmingham Daily Post*, 31 December 1895. 'The Alleged Armenian Atrocities', *Reynolds's Newspaper*, 6 December 1894. McCarthy, *Van*, pp. 54–77.
32. *Reynolds's Newspaper*, 9 December 1894, 25 November 1894.
33. *Bristol Mercury*, 17 December 1894. *Hampshire Telegraph and Sussex Chronicle*, 8 December 1894. *Belfast News-Letter* editorial, 8 August 1895. Some other examples are above. See and compare, for example, 'The Attacks on Armenians', *Daily News*, 17 November 1894, and 'Atrocities in Armenia', *Bristol Mercury*, 19 November 1894.

34. *The Times* editorial, 7 August 1895, p. 7. See also, *The Times* Editorial, 29 March 1895, p. 9. 'The Armenian Atrocities', *Daily News*, 19 December 1894. 'The Sultan and the Powers', *Daily News*, 24 December 1894.
35. 'London, Monday, November 12', *Daily News*, 12 November 1894. 'The Armenian Question: A Reign of Terror', *Daily Telegraph*, 9 January 1895, p. 3 (a Reuters story from Vienna). 'The Troubles in Armenia', *Daily Telegraph*, 7 January 1895, p. 5. 'The Armenian Question', *Daily Telegraph*, 13 February 1895, p. 3. While it is usual to cite page numbers for newspaper articles, this often has not been possible here, because the computerised files of newspapers from the British Library and some others do not give the page numbers.

    On the Hamidiye, see: Janet Klein, 'Power in the Periphery: The Hamidiye Light Cavalry and the Struggle over Ottoman Kurdistan, 1890–1914', unpublished doctoral dissertation. Princeton University, 2002. Bayram Kodaman, 'Hamidiye Hafif Süvari Alayları; II. Abdülhamid ve Dogu-Anadolu Aşiretler', *Tarih Dergisi*, vol. 32 (1979), pp. 427–80. On the British views of the Hamidiye, see Mohammed, 'British Representations', pp. 105–17.
36. 'The Reported Atrocities in Armenia', *The Times*, 19 November 1894, p. 5. 'Disturbed Armenia: The Massacres Confirmed', *The Times*, 4 December 1894, p. 6. 'The Armenian Atrocities', *The Times*, 29 March 1896, p. 10. 'The Armenian Atrocities', *The Times*, 30 March 1895, p. 7. 'The Armenian Question', *The Times*, 28 January 1895, p. 5. *The Times* had at first summarised a fairly accurate report from the Ottoman Government, along with an Armenian denial. ('Trouble in Armenia', *The Times*, 17 November 1894, p. 5.) Two days later, it had completely adopted the Armenian line.
37. McCarthy et al., *Sasun*, pp. 7 and 186–8.
38. 'The Truth about Armenia: Inquiry at the Scene of Massacre, Evidences of Witnesses, a Pit of Death, Important Special Despatch', *Daily Telegraph*, 27 February 1895, bylined Moush, 23 February.

    Dillon's name was not revealed by the *Daily News* until his last articles. He was identified only as 'Our Own Correspondent' or 'Our Special Correspondent'. 'Armenia: Moush Commission of Inquiry', *Daily News*, 23 August 1895. See also 'Armenia: Moush Commission of Inquiry', *Daily News*, 21 August 1895.
39. Most of Dillon's reports were published in the *Daily Telegraph* under the title 'The Truth about Armenia'. These are cited extensively in McCarthy et al., *Sasun*, pp. 288–9.

    On the problems with Dillon's claim that he received news from the commission in Muş and Kars, see McCarthy et al., *Sasun*, pp. 50–6. Members of parliament and rival newspapers rightly questioned how Dillon could have received the information he claimed.

40. Seen in quote from the *Daily Telegraph* in the *Leeds Mercury*, 3 March 1895.
41. There seems to be no need to describe the accounts of the Reuters Agency, often as bad as those in the *Daily News* and *Telegraph*, or in the many newspapers that quoted, with or without attribution, from the three sources. They are considered in McCarthy et al., *Sasun*, pp. 38–75. One example: *The Times* printed a Reuters report that the Sasun Commission had fully confirmed newspaper past reports on Sasun massacres, which was completely untrue. ('The Armenian Inquiry', *The Times*, 10 April 1895, p. 5.)
42. On questioning the standard version on massacres, see, for example, 'Armenian Rising in Sasun: Official Story of the Turkish Reprisals', *Pall Mall Gazette*, 29 January 1896. 'Any Porte in a Storm', *Pall Mall Gazette*, 4 May 1895. The *Pall Mall Gazette* delighted in exposing British hypocrisy, and even had the effrontery to remind its readers of the horrors the British had inflicted in subduing India. ('The Shadow of God and the "P.M.C."', *Pall Mall Gazette*, 16 May 1895.) 'The Armenian Stories', *The Morning Post*, 18 April 1895, p. 5. 'The Situation in Armenia', *The Morning Post*, 5 January 1895, p. 5.
43. 'Question. Observations', House of Lords Debate, 14 May 1877, *Hansard*, vol. 234, cc. 829–49. 'Question. Observations', House of Lords Debate, 26 July 1878, *Hansard*, vol. 242, cc. 344–85. Thomas F. G. Coates, *Lord Rosebery: His Life and Speeches*, vol. 1, London: Hutchinson, 1900, pp. 311, 315–22, 336.
44. 'Address in Answers to Her Majesty's Most Gracious Speech', House of Lords Debate, 11 February 1896, *Hansard*, vol. 37, cc. 9–61. Coates, vol. 2, pp. 842–86.
45. See the various communications in FO 424/178 and 181.
46. FO 424/178, Kimberley to Currie, Foreign Office, 7 November 1894. Kimberley reiterated this to Rustem on 27 March 1895. (FO 424/181, Kimberley to Currie, Foreign Office, 28 March 1895.) FO 424/181, Kimberley to Currie, Foreign Office, 8 January 1895.
47. FO 424/182, Kimberley to Currie, Foreign Office, 28, 29 April, 3, 6, 9, 27 May 1895; FO 424/182, Kimberley to Lascelles, Foreign Office, 30 May 1895; Lascelles to Kimberley, St Petersburgh, 4 June 1895.

It is beyond the scope of this study to consider the religious, nationalist and racialist British views of the Ottoman peoples. These are well considered in H. J. R. Odoms, 'British Perceptions of the Ottoman Empire 1876–1908', unpublished DPhil dissertation, Oxford, 1995. See also Justin McCarthy, *The Turk in America: Creation of an Enduring Prejudice*, Salt Lake City: University of Utah Press, 2010.

48. Speech to the Nonconformist Unionist Association, 31 January 1896 (*The Times*, 1 February 1896), quoted on p. 75 of Peter Marsh, 'Lord Salisbury and the Ottoman Massacres', *The Journal of British Studies*, vol. 11, no. 2 (May 1972), pp. 63–83. Often an informative analysis of Salisbury's attempted actions against the Ottoman Empire. Marsh considers Salisbury's religiosity and sense of morality, which is often neglected in such studies. The difficulty with this article, like many others on the British response to the 'Bulgarian Massacres' and 'Armenian Massacres', is that no consideration is given to the actual history of events in the Ottoman Empire. Marsh assumes that Salisbury's understanding of the massacres was correct, which it demonstrably was not.

On Salisbury's religious development and beliefs, see Gwendolen Cecil (Salisbury's daughter), *Life of Robert, Marquis of Salisbury*, vol. 1, London, Hodder and Stoughton, 1921, pp. 24–30, 99–122 and 310–35, and Frederick Douglas Howe, *The Marquis of Salisbury*, London: Isbister and Company, 1902, pp. 197–214. For a prime minister with many concerns, Salisbury spent an incredible amount of time on religious matters. Bismarck called Salisbury, 'Çe clergyman laïque'.

49. FO 78/4006, Salisbury to Curry, 10 July 1895 and *Hansard*, 4th series, XXXVI, 49 (15 August 1895), cited in Marsh, p. 75.
50. FO 424/183, Salisbury to Currie, Foreign Office, 4 July 1895; Currie to Salisbury, Constantinople, 2 and 12 August 1895.
51. Cabinet Memorandum by Lord Salisbury, 27 and 29 September 1896. Salisbury Private Papers, F. O. (Private Correspondence), vol. 89, Cabinet Memoranda, no. 20, very secret, 'Balmoral Castle, Sunday, 27 September 1896', in Margaret M. Jefferson, 'Lord Salisbury's Conversations with the Tsar at Balmoral, 27 and 29 September, 1896', *The Slavonic and Eastern European Review*, vol. 39, no. 92 (December 1960), pp. 216–18. See also, G. S. Papadopoulos, *England and the Near East: 1896–1898*, Thessaloniki: Institute of Balkan Studies, 1969, pp. 91–4. J. A. S. Grenville, *Lord Salisbury and Foreign Policy*, London: Athlone Press, 1964, p. 29, Papadopoulos, pp. 164–6. Marsh, pp. 76–9.
52. Hatzfeldt to Holstein, 31 July 1895, in GP 10, pp. 10–13, and Hatzfeldt to Foreign Office, 3 August 1895, in GP 10, pp. 16–18. Grenville, p. 31. Grenville questioned whether this was a serious proposal, implying that Salisbury was joking with the ambassador! Hatzfeldt reported to Berlin that it was serious. Gregor Schöllgen (*Imperialismus und Gleichgewicht: Deutschland, England und die orientalische Frage 1871–1914*, München: R. Oldenbourg Verlag, 1984, pp. 64–6) believed that Salisbury's plan was a 'trial balloon' to gain reactions, which was categorically rejected by the German Foreign Office. See also Margaret M.

Jefferson, 'Lord Salisbury and the Eastern Question, 1890–1898', *The Slavonic and East European Review*, vol. 39, no. 92 (December 1960), pp. 44–60. Jefferson advanced a thesis that Salisbury's main concern, often his only concern, was to keep the Russians from occupying the Straits, and that Salisbury had progressively become more and more detached from the Ottoman Empire proper, instead concentrating on Egypt. I believe that the evidence, particularly concerning Crete and the 1897 War, does not support this. Jefferson also gave no consideration to Salisbury's own convictions, and little to the effect of British public opinion and political pressure groups on him.

The plan for division also appeared in a letter to Philip Currie, a plan later shared with ambassadors. (Gwendolen Cecil, *Life of Robert, Marquess of Salisbury*, 4 vols, London: Hodder and Stoughton, 1929–32, in David Steele, *Lord Salisbury: A Political Biography*, London: UCL Press, 1999, p. 321, quoting from an unpublished volume 5.)

53. Hatzfeldt to Foreign Office, London, 7 August 1895, in GP 10, pp. 25–7. The political secretary in the Foreign Office, Friedrich von Holstein, noted: 'Lord Salisbury is probably annoyed because the emperor did not allow himself to be converted to the idea of division.' (Holstein to Hatzfeldt, Berlin, 14 August 1895, in GP 10, p. 29.) Marsh, pp. 78–81. For the final version of the reforms, see FO 424/184, Enclosure 1 in Currie to Salisbury, Therapia, 17 October 1895 and FO 424/184, Enclosure 1 in Currie to Salisbury, Therapia, 22 October 1895. Salisbury later told Hatzfeldt that he would prefer to preserve the Ottoman Empire rather than see Istanbul and the Dardanelles fall to Russia. (Hatzfeldt to Foreign Office, London, 14 August 1895, in GP 10, p. 28.) Still later, Salisbury said that he expected the Dardanelles to fall to Russia, and that Britain was only interested in Iraq, not Egypt. (Hatzfeldt to Hohenlohe, London, 31 August 1895, in GP 10, p. 28.) I can only assume that Salisbury was thoroughly confused in his own intentions or, more likely, was sounding out the German ambassador as to German views or passing false information to Berlin. By October, Salisbury was telling Hatzfeldt he was 'particularly pleased with the settlement of the Armenian question'. (Hatzfeldt to Foreign Office, London, 25 October 1895, in GP 10, pp. 35–6.)

W. N. Medlicott advanced the theory that Salisbury abandoned his desire to partition Ottoman regions out of fear that Russia would take Istanbul and the Straits. I find Medlicott's reasoning questionable. ('Historical Revisions: XLIII.—Lord Salisbury and Turkey', *History*, new series, vol. 12, no. 47 (October 1927), pp. 244–7.) Salisbury's opinions on Russia and the Straits vacillated. See Lillian M. Penson, 'The New Course in British Foreign Policy, 1892–1902', *Transactions of the Royal Historical Society*, vol. 25 (1943), pp. 121–38, especially pp. 134–5.

54. See the analyses of David Steele (Steele, especially pp. 244–5, 320–3). Salisbury intervened to save the Greeks when they were defeated in the 1897 War, forcing the Ottomans to advance no farther and to accept an armistice. He stated that no territory that had ever been under Christian rule should ever be returned to the Turks. (Grenville, pp. 92–4; 'Foreign Office Vote: Turkey and the European Powers', House of Commons, 19 July 1897, *Hansard*, vol. 51, cc. 418–79. Note that this included territory that had only been taken from the Ottomans in 1881.) See Chapter 4.
55. Gwendolen Cecil, *Life of Robert, Marquis of Salisbury*, London, Hodder and Stoughton, 4 vols, 1921–32: vol. 2, p. 94 and vol. 3, p. 205. Blunt, p. 234. 'Lord Mayor's Day', *The Times*, 11 November 1895, p. 6. In the Commons, Edward Grey stated that Currie had 'received the warm approval of his chief, Lord Salisbury'. ('Armenian Christians', House of Commons Debate, 3 March 1896, *Hansard*, vol. 38, cc. 37–125.)
56. Wilfrid Scawen Blunt, *My Diaries*, part one, London: Martin Secker, 1919, pp. 228, 229 and 231. Blunt (pp. 235–6) believed that Currie knew of, and encouraged, the Istanbul Armenian revolt of 1895. Currie to Salisbury (private), 27 June 1895, Salisbury Mss, 3M/A/135/1; Currie to Kimberley (private), 11 March 1894, Kimberley Mss, Ms.Eng.c.4397. Sanderson to Rosebery, 25 May 1894, Rosebery Mss, MS 10135, cited in T. G. Otte, *The Foreign Office Mind: The Making of British Foreign Policy, 1865–1914*, Cambridge: Cambridge University Press, 2011, p. 211.
57. Radolin to Hohenlohe, St Petersburg, 24 October 1895, in GP 10, pp. 83–4. Radolin was not the only German diplomat to think poorly of Currie. The ambassador to the Ottoman Empire Adolf Marschall von Bieberstein thought Currie opinionated and afraid of taking decisive action, even when following orders from London. He thought Currie a hothead (whenever Currie heard the name of the sultan, he developed a *roten Kopf*) who could not control his temper. (Marschall to Hohenlohe, Pera, 25 December 1897, in GP 12/2, pp. 441–6.) Unless otherwise indicated, all translations of quotations are my own.
58. Atıf Hüseyin, TTK Lib., Y-255, defter 11, pp. 98–9, quoted in Engin Deniz Akarlı, 'The Problems of External Pressures, Power Struggles, and Budgetary Deficits in Ottoman Politics under Abdulhamid II (1876–1909): Origins and Solutions', unpublished PhD dissertation, Princeton University, 1976, p. 52.

# 2

# THE BRITISH PLAN FOR THE ARMENIANS

Driven by public opinion and imperial hubris, the British decided to solve the Armenian Problem. Their plan was to be imposed on the Ottomans by Europeans. It took little account of realities such as the make-up of the population of Eastern Anatolia or the difficulties of governing there. The assumption was that if the Ottoman Government followed the advice (or orders) of Europeans, all would be well. The essence of the plan, like all the plans to come, was the removal of Ottoman control over parts of the Ottoman Empire.

**The British Plan**

British Ambassador Currie in Istanbul was in close touch with the Armenian Patriarch, Matthew II (Simeon Martirosi Izmirlian). He shared with the Patriarch his plan for reforms, which drew on the Patriarch's own suggestions: provincial governors were to be approved by the Powers and were to serve for five years. A provincial council elected from members of each religious community according to the ratio in the population was to be in charge of finances. Each district was to have an administrative council made up of members of each community. A mixed gendarmerie would be made up of Christians and Muslims in proportion to their communities' sizes. Justice would be in the hands of a court of assize made up of two Muslim and two Christian judges. The court would have control over judgments, appeals and the prisons. Unspecified 'special measures' would be created to protect Armenians.

Table 2.1   Ottoman administrative units

| Unit | | Official |
|---|---|---|
| *Vilâyet* | Province | *Vali* |
| *Sancak* | Sub-Province | *Mutasarrıf* |
| *Kaza* | District | *Kaymakam* |
| *Nahiye* | Sub-District | *Müdür* |

Currie's plan envisaged Armenian representation in government down to the district level. Patriarch Izmirlian approved of Currie's plan, but wanted one inclusion – in addition to the governors, all provincial officials should be named by the governors approved by the Powers. Foreign Secretary Kimberley told Currie to make sure the other ambassadors knew of the views of the Patriarch as they drew up plans for reforms.[1]

Currie's plan was totally unworkable and would not have achieved the Armenian control Currie and the Patriarch desired. Not only were Armenians in a minority in every province (Table 1.1), but there were extremely few Armenians in so many places. For example, if the proportionate representation on councils were as planned, the councils of Genç Sancak would need fifteen Muslim delegates for every Armenian. Cizre Sancak's would need forty-seven Muslims and one Christian. Kebanmadeni Sancak's sixty-three to one; Narman Sancak's fifty-two to one; Ovacık Sancak's 417 to one; Alucra Sancak's 1,025 to 1. The Court of Assize would be particularly unrepresentative. In Diyarbakır Province, there were seven Muslims for every Christian; in Sivas Province, six Muslims for every Christian. Yet there would be two of each community deciding all judicial matters. Ignoring the unfairness, such a court would often be unable to render judgments, the four judges deadlocked two to two.[2]

Currie may have been unaware of the demographic problems with his plan. Ignoring the reports on population sent in by his consuls, he included with his proposal a population table (drawn up by the Armenian Patriarchate) that showed one million Christians and 780,000 Muslims in 'Armenia'. (There were supposedly only 330,000 Kurds.) The real population was more than three-fourths Muslim.

## The Plan of Britain, France and Russia

In April of 1895, at the behest of their governments, the ambassadors of Britain, France and Russia composed a set of reforms to be accepted by the Ottoman Government in the 'Six Vilayets'. This region, which the Europeans called 'Armenia', was composed of the provinces (*vilâyet*s) of Van, Bitlis, Erzurum, Sivas, Diyarbakır and Mamuretülaziz. The plan, like all subsequent Great Power projects, was described as 'reforms'. In the strictest sense of the word, it was indeed a plan to reform – that is, to reorganise – the Ottoman Empire. However, it was also described by the Europeans in the connation of 'reform' – that is, to greatly improve.

- The number and boundaries of provinces would be changed to better conform to ethnographic lines.
- The nomination of provincial governors would be supervised by the Powers, although the sultan retained the right to name them.
- All Armenians convicted of 'political crimes' would be amnestied.
- All Armenian emigrants and exiles would be allowed to return.
- Kurdish 'brigands et autres malfaiteurs' would be kept in check and prosecuted by special courts.
- A judicial commission of a president and two assessors, one Muslim and one Christian, would sit in each province and sancak (sub-province) to decide matters of law. Investigating judges and prosecutors (one a Muslim and one a Christian) would be attached to the judicial commission. Provincial courts would be similarly divided.
- Inspectors and adjutants, one Christian and one Muslim, would examine prisons.
- Sancaks and kazas with the greatest number of Christians ('le plus grande nombre de Chrétiens') would have Christian governors. If the governor was a Muslim, he would be assisted by a Christian associate.
- A high commissioner would supervise the implementation of reforms. He would be assisted by an adjutant – a Muslim if the commissioner were Christian or a Christian if the commissioner were Muslim. He would have authority over the provincial governors.
- A permanent Commission of Control would sit at Istanbul to supervise the enactment of administrative, financial and judicial reforms. It would

be composed of three Christian and three Muslim delegates. Provincial governors and the high commissioner would describe their actions to the commission. The commission would in turn be supervised by the embassies of the Powers.
- Claims for damages submitted by Armenians would be paid after investigation by the high commissioner.
- Religious conversions were to be 'regularised'. After a declaration of intent to convert was made, a person might only do so after a week under surveillance by the leader of the religion (in practice, officials of the Armenian Apostolic, Catholic or Protestant churches, since almost no Muslim ever converted).
- Kurdish nomad migrations and encampments were to be regulated, and tribes' arms to be restricted. The Ottoman Kurdish Cavalry (Hamidiye) was only to be used in conjunction with the regular army and was to otherwise be unarmed.
- There would be strict application of the rights and privileges granted to Armenians (unspecified).
- Special officers would be appointed for the provinces outside the Six Vilayets to represent the interests of Armenians there.

The plan went into great detail on some matters; detail that showed an arrogant belief that all things administrative and political could be best ordered by Europeans. For example: for village groups, the plan decided election procedures and the number of representatives on the council ('a maximum of eight, a minimum of four'). Village finance rules were set, as were the age and salaries of town council members. For some reason, teachers were excluded from membership on the councils. The duties of town police and rural gendarmes were set. The proposal decided precise fines to be exacted by criminal courts – 500 kuruş and three months in prison for lesser offenses, etc.[3]

There was an almost complete lack of understanding of the actual situation in Eastern Anatolia. Kurdish tribes were to be disarmed and regulated in their migrations, although understandably no statement was given on how this was to be done. (The Ottomans had been trying to control the Kurdish tribes for fifty years, with some limited success, but without sufficient finance or manpower to carry out the programme completely.) Armenian villages were to be grouped together into separate administrative sub-districts (*nahiye*), as were Muslim villages. This neglected the problem that the populations were usually thoroughly mixed, both between villages and within villages and towns. The demographic problems were the same ones described in Currie's plan above. No sensible plan would have ignored the real nature of the Eastern Anatolian population.

The ambassadors conveniently demanded Christian governors for sancaks and kazas with 'large Christian populations', not majorities, because only one kaza of the 106 in the Six Vilayets (Muş) had an Armenian majority. Three others (Ahlat, Bulanık and Sasun) were close. In any case, what constituted a 'large Christian population'? Only eleven kazas were more than a third Armenian. Seventy-five (71 per cent) were less than 20 per cent Armenian. Six kazas had no resident Armenian population at all. Except for Muş, Muslims (Turks and Kurds) were a majority in every sancak. Of course, there was no guarantee that the ambassadors ever planned to consider demographic facts. They expected Armenians to be named to official positions, no matter demographic realities.

The Ottoman Government could never have accepted such an unworkable plan unless forced. If accepted, it would never have worked. And the Ottomans knew that they would be blamed for the inevitable failures.

The plan was entirely the work of the British, French and Russian ambassadors. Germany, Austria and Italy were kept in the dark on the plan until it was presented to them in a complete form.

## The British are Not Satisfied

Bad as the ambassadors' plan was, Ambassador Currie attempted to make it more stringent: Currie wanted one governor who ruled over all the provinces, not a high commissioner who only supervised. If he had his wish, all provincial governors and members of the Commission of Control would have to be approved by the Powers – in effect, a veto on government appointments. Currie stated that he wanted 'the Powers to exercise an efficient control', but the French and Russian ambassadors would not agree. They would only propose more moderate measures. Currie was sorry that the Armenians would not be receiving what they wanted, but he was confident that the Armenians' 'superior culture and intelligence' would eventually triumph.[4]

Foreign Secretary Kimberley was worried that the ambassadors' plan 'will be subjected to severe criticism in this country on the ground that unless the appointment of the Valis (provincial governors) is made subject to the consent of the Powers, no reform can be effective'. Like Currie, he preferred a powerful governor-general, not a weaker high commissioner, but he was willing to yield to French and Russian pressure on the issue of the governors and high commissioner. The one thing Kimberley demanded was that the high commissioner would have to be approved by the Powers; that was necessary to satisfy public opinion in Britain. The French and Russian Governments finally agreed to Kimberley's demand that the Powers must approve the high commissioner.[5]

After some debate, the ambassadors presented their demands to the Ottoman Government on 11 May 1895. Sultan Abdülhamid II, who had already known roughly what the proposals might be, attempted to preempt the Powers' proposals with a plan of his own: Abdülhamid did not reject all the reforms. He accepted that some would be beneficial. He proposed the assignment of Christian assistants to all governors and the naming of Christians as some sancak governors. Christians would be admitted to the gendarmerie. A permanent commission would be appointed in the Ottoman Government to supervise reforms. These reforms would be applied throughout the Empire, not only in the Six Vilayets. The three ambassadors and their governments found these proposals unacceptable.[6]

The sultan met his adversaries with delaying tactics. Presented with an unworkable reform scheme, he hoped for time to convince the Powers to accept less stringent and more workable reforms. The Ottoman Government told the Powers' ambassadors that state ministers had developed a counter-proposal, but the sultan had rejected it. A new consideration would take time. The ambassadors were told to wait for a response until the government had time to consider everything after the upcoming Kurban Bayramı (*'īd al-'aḍḥā*) holiday celebration, because no work could be done until the festivities ended. Two weeks elapsed without a response. Kimberley told the Ottomans that an answer would have to be delivered by 1 June. Ambassador Currie used veiled threats that an unspecified action would result if no response was received.[7]

On 3 June the Ottoman Government finally sent its reply to the ambassadors' plan. The reply refused all parts of the plan, except those that were already in Ottoman law or in the sultan's earlier reform proposal. The sultan stated that reforms were needed, but should be applied to the entire Empire, not only to the Six Vilayets. Ambassador Currie told them that all the demands must be met. The French and Russian ambassadors were more open to compromise, but the British refused.[8]

Kimberley decided that the Ottomans must be forced to submit; what he called 'measures of restraint' – a euphemism for some sort of limited military, perhaps naval, or financial pressure. He proposed that the ambassadors demand a reply from the Ottomans in forty-eight hours, 'in order that the Governments may be in a position to decide what course they shall pursue'. His plan for coercion was thwarted by the Russians, who would agree to no coercion. Pressed repeatedly by the British, the Russians still refused.[9]

The Liberal Party of Prime Minister Rosebery and Foreign Secretary Kimberley lost the election of June 1895. Kimberley declared that he left the Armenian Problem to his successor, Lord Salisbury. Salisbury proved to be even more anxious than Kimberley to force the Ottomans to accept the reforms. Like a true politician, Salisbury blamed the previous Liberal government for the bad situation. It had threatened, he said, but did not have the power to enforce its demands, because it did not have the other Powers behind it. 'Frightful events' had followed from the Liberals' policies. Salisbury said he had been left with an impossible situation. He then proceeded to enact what was essentially the same policy – threats without the support of the other Powers.[10]

The sultan's government named a commission to study the ambassadors' proposal. On 1 August it returned a report that once again denied most of the proposal. The Ottomans did agree to a Commission of Control to oversee reforms and to name a high commissioner, Şakir Paşa, to supervise reforms. France, Russia and Britain approved the appointment, the British reluctantly, but the Ottomans refused the suggested judicial and administrative changes set forth in the ambassadors' proposal. The Ottoman Government promised reforms, but not under European auspices. Salisbury objected, but the Russians still refused to coerce the Ottomans.[11]

Of the three Powers who attempted to impose their will on the Ottomans, Russia was the least vociferous. In the 1890s, the Russians supported the territorial status quo in the Ottoman Empire, which the British obviously wanted to upset. Russia shared none of Britain's emotional support of the Armenian Cause. Instead, the Russians feared Armenian separatism as a threat to their Empire in its Caucasian possessions. The Armenians in Russia had always been a restive population, and the Russians wanted no Armenian state, or even an autonomous region, in Eastern Anatolia that would attract Russia's own Armenians. (As will be seen in Chapter 8, Russian was to begin its own suppression of Armenian separatists in 1903.) In addition, after Japanese victory in the First Sino-Japanese War of 1894–5, Russia was concentrating on threats to its own plans for expansion in the Far East. A decade later, all that was to change, but in 1896 the Russians were opponents to Britain's more radical plans.[12]

On 15 August 1895, Salisbury told parliament that the sultan was deluded if he thought he could stand against the wishes of Britain, France and Russia. The Ottomans, he said, had hidden too long behind the treaty guarantees granted by the Powers. Those treaties would not be allowed to stand in the way of the Powers' demands. If the sultan refused to accept the 'assistance and advice of the European Powers', the effect on the Ottoman Empire would be fatal. It was an unvarnished threat, but one Salisbury, despite great effort, could not carry out.[13]

Frustrated by the Russians, Salisbury presented a new plan: an investigation commission composed of four Ottoman members and three delegates named by Britain, France and Russia would reside in Eastern Anatolia. They would have the right to investigate all matters and report back to the three Powers. It was obviously a face-saving measure, since the British consuls were already fulfilling that function. The French agreed to it. The Russians were willing to agree to propose Salisbury's plan to the sultan, providing that it was understood that it was to be a temporary measure, not permanent, and that no force was to be used to coerce the Ottomans to accept. The Russians stated that they only accepted the plan 'in order to avoid raising difficulties and to show a conciliatory spirit', but they did not think it could work. The Germans advised the Ottomans to accept, because British public opinion was forcing Salisbury to act against them, and Salisbury could not moderate his plan. The Ottomans still refused to accept it. The impasse continued.[14]

The sultan once again tried compromise: he would accept the Commission of Control as long as his minister of foreign affairs was its president. If this were agreed, he would approve the naming of Christians to administrative positions, except province and sancak governors, in proportion to their population numbers. Christian officers would be appointed to the gendarmerie. Leaders of the nahiyes would be chosen, as stipulated by the three ambassadors' plan. The British once again found this unacceptable, although the Russians approved of it and hoped Salisbury would do so also. Currie instead presented a new plan that was, in almost all particulars, the old plan. It demanded that the Ottomans lose much effective control. Salisbury was only willing to accept a plan in which the Ottomans agreed to European delegates sitting on the Commission of Control, Christian assistants to each governor and perhaps a fixed number of Christian officials. Salisbury felt that the prohibition of Christian governors was unacceptable. Salisbury maintained the British policy of demanding the Ottomans accept the substance of all the original plan of reforms in its entirety.[15]

The British finally relaxed their demands somewhat and convinced the Russians and French to tell the Ottomans that they wished the high commissioner and the governors to employ Christian assistants. Ambassador Currie tried to convince his colleagues to ask for more concessions. The three ambassadors agreed to a new programme on 7 October 1895: a Christian assistant would be assigned to the high commissioner, 'whose name should be unofficially submitted to the Powers'. (What these assistants were to do was never defined.) The ambassadors and their agents reserved the right to 'remonstrate' against the appointment of governors they did not accept and to address other matters, such as the Kurdish cavalry, amnesties, the return of Armenian emigrants, etc. Province and sancak governors could be Christians. The Commission of Control would set the number of Christian administrators in proportion to the communities' population. The proposal extended the reforms to apply to 'all the sandjaks and cazas of Asia Minor where the Christians form a notable part (unspecified) of the population'. Half of the judicial inspectors in each province would be Christian. Kurdish tribes would be regulated and disarmed.

For the British, the important matters became appointing a Christian assistant to the high commissioner, naming Christians as half the judicial inspectors and the fixing of the number of Christian administrators by the Commission of Control, not the government. Disarming Kurdish tribes was too impossible to be anything but lip service. On many points, the proposal was in direct contradiction to the reform plan of the Ottoman Government, which reserved all appointments to the government and asserted that all governors must be Muslims. Some of the proposed reforms were only superficial: the embassies were already intervening in many areas of Ottoman governance. The proposal only requested that the sultan listen to them, which he was already doing. The idea of applying the reforms all over Anatolia, which had been the sultan's suggestion, was dropped.[16]

The sultan complained of the pressure brought on him to deny his rights, but he nonetheless bowed to the Powers' demands. He probably believed he had no choice: Currie had threatened to bring in the British fleet if the proposal were not accepted. On 20 October, the sultan formally accepted.[17]

On 29 October the three ambassadors submitted to the government a list of persons 'suitable to serve on the Commission of Control or as *muavins* (governor's assistant) in the six vilayets'. The British Chargé d'Affaires (Currie was on leave) protested the Ottoman plan to appoint the foreign minister as head of the commission, and the Ottomans agreed not to do so. The Commission of Control was constituted and held its first meeting on 26 November. Within two weeks Currie was complaining that the commission was not acting expeditiously. He told the sultan that the commission was useless.[18]

The sultan received Ambassador Currie in an audience on 29 November. He complained of the presence of naval warships in Ottoman waters, sent by the Powers, that planned to pass through the Dardanelles to Istanbul. These were ostensibly there to protect the lives of foreign nationals, but the sultan stated, correctly, that foreign nationals were already being protected by Ottoman forces. There had been no instance of attacks on foreigners: 'Has even one foreigner's nose bled either in the capital or in the provinces?' Currie admitted this was true, but the ships were necessary to prevent trouble. The sultan replied that they were more likely to provoke it. Currie threatened that, 'if the permission was refused the Powers were united, and resolved to carry the matter through'. Abdülhamid believed that the presence of the ships was at the instigation of Britain.[19]

Abandoning any diplomatic niceties, Currie denied the sultan's statements that Armenian rebels had instigated recent troubles; he said Abdülhamid had been 'hoodwinked' by lying officials. Currie openly threatened the sultan with the 'danger to himself and his Empire' if he did not listen to Currie's admonishments.[20]

## Salisbury and Enforcing the Reforms

Salisbury, feeling political pressure at home and personally convinced that reforms would never succeed, planned for what he believed would be the dissolution of the Ottoman Empire. He began to attempt to convince the other Powers that drastic action was needed. Salisbury wanted the other Powers to follow his suggestion that the ambassadors at Istanbul should 'concert together on the general state of the Ottoman Empire'. At first, he told the other Powers only that they must concert to take unspecified action, although it was obvious that the only action open to them was military. Taking advantage of blame attached to the Ottoman Government in the Ottoman Bank troubles, Salisbury once again proposed strong action in Istanbul. He told other Powers that the ambassadors should meet and devise new, more stringent reforms and present them to the sultan. 'If, on their being placed before the Sultan, His Majesty should refuse to accept them, measures should be taken by the Six Powers to enforce their acceptance.' Salisbury declared that if any of the Powers should refuse to take action (as they surely would), they should not object to others (that is, Britain) doing so.[21]

The Russians felt that conditions in the Ottoman Empire were improving. They were not sure that such drastic action was needed. Instead, they proposed that the sultan be assisted by the Powers in carrying out reforms. Russian Foreign Minister Aleksey Lobanov-Rostovsky believed the sultan had shown a conciliatory spirit and was ready to apply reforms. He should be given time. (The sultan had agreed to the reforms less than three months before.) On the other hand, Salisbury's proposal would be perceived 'as evidence of the imposition of a kind of guardianship on the Sultan'. This perception would lead to disorder. Moreover, Lobanov-Rostovsky objected that Salisbury's proposal was in direct contradiction to the Treaty of Berlin. The Austrians gave the British qualified support, but believed that Russia would never agree to the coercion proposed by Salisbury.[22]

The Russians had a point. How could the British have believed that a ponderous state system could be completely changed in a few months? The answer, one suspects, is that Salisbury and Currie did not ever expect the reforms would succeed. What Britain actually wanted was the progressive end of the power of the Ottoman Empire over its provinces. Later British policies in Crete, the Balkans and Eastern Anatolia were to prove this to be true.

Salisbury's cabinet indicated that it did not expect much for the Ottoman Empire. In parliament, the Lord Chancellor, Hardinge Giffard, speaking for the government, stated: 'I look upon the condition of the whole of those countries as hopeless under Turkish rule. It has been, it is, and it will be a curse and a blight upon every country in which it exists.' Giffard stated that he and Salisbury had no hope that the sultan would undertake reform unless forced, but that other Powers stood in Britain's way. In the same session, Salisbury said that the Ottoman Empire was doomed unless it followed Britain's plans, but that the doom might be delayed – only delayed – by the actions of the Powers. Military action against the Ottomans was desirable. Salisbury had little hope of success for the Armenians without it. Britain, however, did not have sufficient force to attack the Ottoman Empire alone, and would risk European war if it tried. Britain was, he declared, unfortunately forced to continue to act through diplomacy, which would probably fail.[23]

On 20 October 1896, the same day Abdülhamid accepted the reforms, Salisbury sent a long letter to his ambassadors in the major European countries, instructing them to transmit the letter to the respective foreign ministers. In it, Salisbury gave a long list of what he considered Turkish crimes, magnifying all the troubles suffered by Armenians and denying that Armenian rebels had paid any significant part in those troubles. He cited the Istanbul riots without mentioning any Armenian bomb-throwers, stating instead that the Istanbul riots 'had every appearance of being organized by authority'. He cited the conflict in Sasun as if the Armenians there had never attacked the Kurds. He blamed all on the sultan and his government, who, he claimed, had either fomented or guided massacres. Salisbury admitted that the Ottoman finances were in a perilous state, but, amazingly, he held that Ottomans' poverty was due to their treatment of Christians. Salisbury's solution to Ottoman ills was force. A new set of orders to the Ottomans should be written. The Ottomans would be forced to accept them:

> I trust that the Powers will, in the first instance, come to a definite understanding that their unanimous decisions in these matters is to be final, and will be executed up to the measure of such force as the Powers have at their command.

The letter was an astonishing statement of pugnacious ill will.[24]

In response to Salisbury, other Powers expressed their qualified and theoretical support of his demands for new reforms, carefully not committing themselves to Salisbury's desire for military intervention. The only encouragement expressed for military coercion was valueless: the Austrian Foreign Minister, Count Agenor Goluchowski, said Austria was willing to cooperate in coercion, but only if all the Powers agreed. It was an easy commitment, since Goluchowski himself had often stated that Russia would never agree to coercion.[25]

Throughout the month of November 1896, the British Government laboured diplomatically to bring about a Russian change of mind. The results were never satisfactory for the British, but the Tsar did finally agree that '[t]he Russian Government would consent to discuss the methods of pressure to be chosen'. The Russians agreed that the ambassadors should tell the Ottoman Government that the Powers were committed to a new unspecified pressure on reforms. This was far from a Russian commitment on coercion, which the Russians never accepted.[26]

While the Powers were considering new demands on the Ottomans, the sultan was attempting to bring about the reforms already agreed upon. Those guilty of disorders would be prosecuted, presumably Muslims, since Armenians were to be set free. Of 1,900 persons in prison for political crimes and rebellion, mainly Armenians, 1,800 had been released. The sultan named an Armenian Reform Commission to suggest and oversee new laws and enforcement of old laws. By 30 September 1896, the commission reported on laws passed for the provinces that conformed to the Powers' reform plan. Laws implementing much of the ambassadors' plan had been initiated, although, due to the administrative difficulty of matters such as redrawing nahiye boundaries, some parts were not yet implemented. Christian assistants were to be named to the provincial governors. Judicial inspectors were to be named. Christians were named to the gendarmerie and police. Kurdish tribes were to be accompanied by soldiers on their migrations to protect the settled populace.

Some of the new laws had already been put into effect. Some had been less than successful: numbers of innocent Armenians had been released from prison, but so had been rebels who continued to take part in actions against the government and local Muslims. Armenians had been enrolled in the police and the gendarmerie, but their numbers were limited because of poor or nonexistent salaries and threats to those enrolled by Armenian rebel groups. Although efforts were made, patrolling all the Kurdish tribes could never be achieved with the manpower available. Although judicial commissions and commissions to decide property titles had been named in the provinces, there were great difficulties in finding Christians willing to serve as administrators. Nevertheless, by November of 1896, in the six provinces of Eastern Anatolia, six Christians had been chosen as governor's assistants, six as judicial inspectors, four as assistants in sancaks and two named kaymakams.[27]

In December of 1896, less than three months had passed since the sultan accepted the scheme of reforms. Strides had been made, although the administration was always hampered by the lack of funds. Currie, however, stated that none of the reforms had worked properly. Neither Prime Minister Salisbury nor Ambassador Currie were willing to make any allowances for Ottoman difficulties in carrying out reforms. Despite reports of limited improvements in the Empire, Currie felt that the reforms had been a complete failure, because the Ottomans had never meant to carry them out.

> In a word, we are confronted by an organized official conspiracy to thwart all attempts at improving the state of the Empire. The history of the introduction of reforms in the past year is one long record of pretense, evasion, counterfeit, and sham.[28]

Undaunted by their failure to find real support from other Powers, the British brought forth an even more drastic plan at the beginning of December 1896: Salisbury wanted the Powers to force a change in the Ottoman Cabinet, creating an Ottoman Government 'which would be truly responsible', a policy that had long been advanced by Currie. The Ottoman Government was described as 'almost universally corrupt and incapable'. This new proposal was even less acceptable to the other Powers than had been Salisbury's plan for coercion. The French believed the British plan was impossible and would in itself lead to disruption among 'the fanatical Moslem population'. Neglecting the imputation of fanaticism, the French were correct. Exerting drastic European control over the Ottoman Government could only have caused a great adverse reaction.[29]

Salisbury's vehemence against the Ottomans was counterproductive. By the middle of December, the opinion of even those who had at least half-heartedly supported the British plans for coercion, never shared by the Russians, began to turn. The French Minister of Foreign Affairs stated, somewhat duplicitously, that he had always opposed coercion on principle. France would only accept it if intervention by the Powers was necessary to quell violence, which did not appear likely to occur. The French ambassador in Istanbul was authorised to 'examine' coercion if the sultan refused to cooperate with the ambassadors, but only if 'isolated action' was avoided, an impossibility. The Germans and Austrians concurred. This was a definite change in French and Austrian attitudes. The Russian ambassador in Istanbul was instructed by his government not to discuss coercion at all.[30]

The ambassadors in Istanbul continued to discuss the implementation of reforms. They disagreed on what was to be done. Lists of 'critical evils' and remedies were written. The sultan was threatened with unnamed consequences for inaction, which the Ottoman Government must have known were empty threats.[31]

## The Financial Problem

The poverty of the Ottoman Empire is too well documented to need much consideration here. The picture is of an empire forced to spend more and more to defend itself and attempt to develop economically. By the 1890s the economic picture was dismal, yet the British expected the Ottomans to somehow find the funds to rapidly improve the state of the Armenians. The British knew the perilous economic state of the Empire. It is hard to believe that they ever truly believed that their plans could be achieved. It is easier to believe that they never truly expected them to succeed, leaving open the path to destruction of the Ottoman Empire.

The Ottoman Empire unquestionably suffered from a lack of financial expertise and from corruption. The financial problems inherited by Abdülhamid derived from the mistakes of his predecessors. They had borrowed heavily from European banks in the mistaken belief that they could use the money to finance economic development, not an uncommon problem in developing nations. The result was bankruptcy and the passage of a significant portion of state revenue to European control under a Public Debt Administration.

Much of the Ottoman economic difficulty was beyond the government's control. Like all other countries that did not undergo the Industrial Revolution, the manufacturers of Ottoman industry often (although not always) could not compete with those of their European rivals. The protective tariffs used by other countries were denied to the Ottomans. In order to gain British support against Muhammad Ali of Egypt, the Ottomans were forced to sign the Treaty of Balta Limanı in 1838. The treaty allowed the British to trade freely in the Ottoman Empire. France and, later, other nations, including the United States of America, were included under the same terms. The Europeans paid a 5 per cent import duty, raised to 8 per cent in the 1860s. Ottoman produce and manufacturing, on the other hand, paid an Ottoman tax and a further 3 per cent export duty, 12 per cent in total, later reduced to 9 per cent (in sum, 8 per cent local tax plus 1 per cent export tax). For comparison, the independent nations of the Balkans, which were able to set their own tariffs, exacted duties on imports much higher than was allowed to the Ottomans: Greece: 20–7 per cent, Bulgaria: 14–21 per cent, Serbia: 42–57 per cent. Unlike the Ottomans, they were able to set different tariffs on different goods, which was important to protect domestic manufacturing. The Ottomans had tried to institute this, but the Europeans refused to allow it. In addition, the British and other Europeans levied protectionist duties on imports from the Ottoman Empire. It is doubtful if the Ottoman Government at the time realised what would be the economic outcome of the treaty.

Economists have argued, and probably will always argue, over the value of protectionism. To the Ottomans, it was a simple matter – they needed the money from customs duties. The Ottoman Empire was forbidden the protectionist policies that were used to advance other economies. Worse, Ottoman domestic industry, particularly in textiles, was destroyed. The Empire was traditionally an exporter of cereals, but the price of wheat declined by more than 60 per cent from 1873 to 1894 as American produce increasingly entered the world market. The result was a chronic balance of payments problem. From 1892 to 1897, the value of imports was 13,914,021,000 kuruş, of exports 8,892,230,000 kuruş.[32]

The government became permanently unable to collect enough in taxes to cover state expenditures and debt payments. Tax collection from 1892 to 1897 averaged 6 per cent less than expenditures. Troubles in Anatolia and

Crete caused this deficit to jump to 9 per cent in 1896–7. The deficit had to be made up by short-term loans from institutions such as the European-owned Ottoman Bank and other 'local' banks controlled by Europeans.

The Ottoman Empire was in a rough neighbourhood, and the primary duty of the government was defence. In the years from 1892 to 1897, the Ottoman Empire spent 40 per cent of its revenues on the army and navy, and another 7 per cent on the police and gendarmerie. This was nearly three times the amount spent on servicing the national debt, in itself an average of 17 per cent of expenditures in the period.

Provincial governors attempted to carry out many of the reforms, particularly the ones that did not cost money, which they did not have. Amnesties were granted. Prisons were improved. Lax officials were sacked. Battalions of troops were even sent to watch over the Kurdish nomads. But few Christians were enrolled in the gendarmerie in the East, because they could not be paid. The best men could not be hired as local officials, for the same reason.[33]

Şakir Paşa, the new high commissioner, set about his task with great energy, touring Eastern Anatolia and creating extensive lists of reforms. For Erzurum Province, for example, he detailed steps to be taken for each of the points in the reforms: lists of the numbers of Armenians to be enrolled in the security forces and the administration were drawn up. Christian *muavins* (deputies) for each province were named. Troops were sent in limited numbers; all that could be afforded were sent to watch over Kurdish tribes. Reforms in government administration, transportation and other matters were put on paper and sometimes implemented, but it was never possible to properly pay for them all. British Consul Williams in Van evaluating the slow progress of reforms: 'The Vali is sincere in his wish to carry them (reforms) out, both in the letter and the spirit, but most of them cost money and none is available.' Williams felt that pressure from the Istanbul Government and the Powers was useless unless funding could be found. The best men had all left the gendarmerie and police because of lack of pay, and Armenians would not serve unless paid regularly.[34]

Money problems fed on themselves. In the Eastern provinces, taxes were usually in arrears; often only a quarter of them were collected. Yet to collect them officials would have to have both gendarmes and officials who could collect them, and lack of money meant that good gendarmes and officials were not available. The situation was not helped by the Powers' insistence that only unarmed tax collectors be used, not gendarmes. Without some force, peasants and merchants would not pay. Moreover, the lack of good men meant that corruption flourished in the system. The Central Government, beset by its financial problems, continually demanded taxes from the provinces, but this was in itself an intractable difficulty. The governor (*mutasarrıf*) of the sancak of Muş described to the British consul a situation in which the villagers simply could not pay their taxes:

> A terrible difficulty is the absolute bankruptcy of the govt., the pay of officials, soldiers and police being many months in arrear, and the central govt. continually demanding money. And, as the mutessarif justly says, to press the villagers for taxes now is only to complete the ruin.[35]

**Informing Parliament and the Public**

British prime ministers and foreign secretaries seldom felt the need to inform parliament of their actions or even to tell parliament the truth. The picture Salisbury presented to parliament late in 1895 was one of complete agreement among the Powers with British plans. Salisbury promised that if the sultan did not act on the reforms presented to him, it would lead to his doom and that of his empire. He stated that the Powers would all stand together, and that no Power should ever act on its own. 'I believe the Powers are thoroughly resolved to act together upon everything that concerns the Ottoman Empire.' It was all untrue; the Powers were in disagreement on many issues, especially on Salisbury's proposal for coercion of the sultan. Moreover, rather than believing the Powers should act in unanimity, Salisbury was later to suggest to the others that Britain wanted to act alone if the others would not support him.[36]

The Under-Secretary of State for Foreign Affairs, George Curzon (later foreign secretary), spoke for the Salisbury Government in the House of Commons. On 3 March 1896 Curzon described in parliament the government's justifications for its actions in the Ottoman Empire. Although he had access to all the consular reports, Curzon's descriptions of events in Anatolia were duplicitous and uniformly wrong. He described for the MPs what the government declared had occurred there (Curzon's statement is in italics below, with accompanying evaluations):

*'They (the troubles) all occurred posterior to the granting of the reforms in Constantinople, which in itself suggests some connection with that step.'*

The sultan granted the reforms on 20 October 1895. Armenian rebel actions actually began in 1890, accelerating significantly in 1893. The Sasun troubles started in 1893, the Suedia/Zeytun Revolt in 1893, both long before the decree of reforms. Major attacks on Muslims and Muslim retaliation did indeed occur after October 1895, but the timing was set by the Hunchak rebels, not the government or local Muslims.

*'They occurred almost simultaneously in widely-scattered parts of Asia Minor.'*

Curzon had an odd definition of 'simultaneous'. Although they had begun before, rebel attacks on Muslims and subsequent Armenian and Muslim deaths began in earnest in 1893 and extended at various times and places to 1897. Of course, Curzon did not consider the actual timetable, because he falsely declared all had begun as a government-directed opposition to the granting of reforms.

*'They were begun in most cases by the Turks.'*

This was very seldom the case. The troubles began with attacks on Turks and Kurds, not by them. Later attacks were begun by Muslims in retaliation, but these never began the troubles.

*'The massacres were openly participated in by Turkish soldiers and gendarmes.'*

On the contrary, Ottoman soldiers were hard put, but often effective, in stopping Muslim attacks on Armenians. Despite major provocations, such as the slaughter of their fellows in Zeytun, they generally acted professionally. Undoubtedly the soldiers did kill Armenians in battle with rebels, and there were instances of inhumanity by soldiers, but their 'open participation' in massacres was another invention.

*'The proceedings were conducted with an organisation that was perfect and almost mathematical.'*

There is no evidence from British consular reports or other diplomatic sources of any such organisation, which Curzon implied must have been governmental. As to the 'perfect and almost mathematical', a major complaint of British representatives in the Empire was the disorganisation of Ottoman actions in Eastern Anatolia. Although it was far from mathematically precise, there was an organisation at work – the Hunchak Committee.

'*These massacres were followed by the forcible conversion of the survivors to Mahommedanism, accompanied by the greatest cruelty.*'

There were forced conversions of Armenians, particularly in the Birecik region. These were limited, not the general conversion following massacre Curzon described. The Ottoman Government refused to accept the conversions and negated them, partly affected by European pressure, although it had always declared the inadmissibility of forced conversions.

'*The massacres in some cases began and ended by sound of trumpet.*'

This is a complete invention, unsupported by any consular evidence. It appears to have originated with tales told by pro-Armenian organisations in Britain.

'*The number of Turks killed was quite insignificant.*'

It is true that in the troubles more Armenians were killed than Muslims, as was the rebels' plan. Muslim death was not insignificant, however: in Bitlis, 120 Armenians and thirty Muslims were killed; in Erzincan, eleven Muslims and 111 Armenians; in Erzurum, ten Muslims and ten Armenians; in Hisnimansur, forty Muslims and 150 Armenians; in Sasun, 131 Muslims and ninety-seven Armenians, etc. The question, not considered by the British Government, was if these were massacres of inoffensive Armenians, why did so many Muslims die at all, and why were Muslims the first to die?

The intention of the British Government is obvious. Blame was placed on the Ottomans, and the Ottomans alone, for the debacle in Anatolia. By claiming a central organisation and coordination, Curzon was in effect claiming that massacres of Armenians had been organised by the Ottoman Government in reaction to European plans for reform. This was a step beyond claiming that the Ottomans should not govern because of incompetence. It was an allegation that they should not rule because of their evil actions.[37]

Curzon, significantly, did not admit the actions of the Armenian rebels – attacks that began the troubles and led to so many Armenian and Muslim deaths. Ignoring any wrongdoing by Armenians was the general policy of the British Government. The British blamed all on the Ottomans and local Turks and Kurds. Some of their criticisms were valid. Most were the result of describing only one side of an intercommunal conflict.[38]

In 1902 Sultan Abdülhamid II described what he believed had been the cause of the calamities that beset his empire:

> May God grant peace to us! No other country needs it more than ours! I am fully aware that the defects of our administration and the laxity of our officials are among the reasons that create the endless and intolerable confusion which our state is in. The principle (sic) factor which pushes our state into a catastrophe, however, is the intriguing of the great powers. The powers instigate the nations under our rule to rebellion one after another and impoverish us more year by year. So many useful deeds could have been accomplished with the millions we have spent on quelling rebellions every year. Alas! the powers never allow us either the time or the peace to build our wide-flanked empire! We cannot advance our people, again because of the powers . . . We could have repeated the much-praised progress of the Japanese, if we, too, were allowed peace for only ten years, at least. They are fortunate people compared to us, for they are at a distance from the claws of the Europeans and live in security. Unfortunately, our tent is pitched at the crossroads of the European hyenas.[39]

There were surely more reasons for the disasters that beset the Ottoman Empire, including mistakes made by the sultan himself, but there is more than a little truth in his criticism of the Europeans.

## Notes

1. FO 424/181, Currie to Kimberley, Constantinople, 19 and 22 January 1895, and Kimberley to Currie, Foreign Office, 7 February 1895. Kimberley approved Carrie sharing his plan with the French and Russian ambassadors (FO 424/181, Kimberley to Currie, Foreign Office, 7 February 1895). Musa Şaşmaz, *British Policy and the Application of Reforms for the Armenians in Eastern Anatolia 1877–1897*, Ankara: Türk Tarih Kurumu, 2000, pp. 131–9. Currie's plan built on a British plan immediately after the Congress of Berlin. (Şaşmaz, pp. 24–230.)

    On Salisbury's earlier attempts to intervene earlier in Ottoman domestic affairs, see W. N. Medlicott, *The Congress of Berlin and After*, London: Cass, 1963, pp. 311–48, an account very unsympathetic to the Ottomans, and F. A. K. Yasamee, *Ottoman Diplomacy: Abdülhamid II and the Great Powers, 1878–1888*, Istanbul: Isis Press, 1996, p. 71. Yasamee considers in detail Ottoman–British diplomatic relations in an earlier period than is covered here. The Russians believed that the Armenian population was not as great as alleged. (FO 424/183, Lascelles to Salisbury, St Petersburgh, 3 July 1895).

2. Ottoman Empire, Dahiliye Nezareti, Sicil-i Nüfus İdare-yi Umumiyesi Müdüriyeti, *Memalik-i Osmaniye'nin 1330 Senesine Nüfus İstatisitği*. Istanbul: 1336M.
3. FO 424/182, 'Memorandum Mars-Avril 1895', and other enclosures in Currie to Kimberley, Constantinople, 18 April 1895. The plan actually only implied the Powers' control over the naming of governors:

> Les Puissances, attachant la plus grande importance au choix des Valis, dont dépendra essentiellement l'efficacité des réformes prévues par le Traité de Berlin, sont résolues à faire à la Sublime Porte des représentations chaque fois que le choix se porterait sur des personnes dont la nomination pourrait présenter des inconvénients; c'est pourquoi elles trouveraient nécessaire que le Gouvernement Impérial Ottoman, afin d'éviter sur ce point des malentendus fâcheux, voulût bien tenir officieusement les Représentants des Puissances nu courant des choix qu'il aurait l'intention de faire.

The ambassadors included deceptively chosen and incomplete references to existing Ottoman laws and government statements to justify some of their proposals.
4. FO 424/182, Currie to Kimberley, Pera, 18 April 1895.
5. FO 424/182, Kimberley to Currie, Foreign Office, 28, 29 April, 3, 6, 9 May 1895; Kimberley to Howard, Foreign Office, 3, 4 May 1895.
6. FO 424/182, Currie to Kimberley, Constantinople, 18 April 1895. On the general position of Abdülhamid II vis-à-vis the European Powers, see F. A. K. Yasamee, 'Ottoman Diplomacy in the Era of Abdülhamid II (1878–1908)', İsmail Soysal, ed., *Çağdaş Türk Diplomasisi Sempozyumu*, Ankara: Türk Tarih Kurumu, 1999, pp. 223–32.
7. FO 424/182, Currie to Kimberley, Constantinople, 25, 30 May 1895; Kimberley to Currie, Foreign Office, 27 May 1895.
8. FO 424/182, Currie to Kimberley, Constantinople, 3, 4, 11, 13 and 18 June 1895.
9. FO 424/182, Kimberley to Lascelles, Foreign Office, 30 May 1895; Lascelles to Kimberley, St Petersburgh, 4 June 1895; Kimberley to Dufferin, Foreign Office, 19 June 1895; Lascelles to Kimberley, St Petersburgh, 21 June 1895. The Russians and French did plan to apply their ultimate weapon to force the sultan to comply. If he did not do so, they would withdraw and tell the sultan that he would have to deal with Britain alone. (FO 424/182, Currie to Kimberley, Constantinople, 28 May 1895.)
10. FO 424/182, Kimberley to Currie, Foreign Office, 24 June 1895. 'Lord Salisbury on Political Affairs', *The Times*, 30 April 1896, p. 8. Before he took power, Salisbury had stressed the need for unanimous support from the other Powers. Britain by herself could do nothing, but must depend on the agreement of others,

particularly Russia and France. 'Impotent threats' would be useless; they would only make things worse for the Armenians. He was also less critical than he was to become of the sultan and his government: 'I doubt myself if the (Ottoman) Government of the country is responsible for those things. I believe the Sultan to be a humane man.' ('Lord Salisbury at Bradford', *The Times*, 24 May 1895, p. 8.)

11. FO 424/183, Currie to Salisbury, Constantinople, 2 and 12 August 1895; 'Observations on the Draft of Reforms Presented by the Ambassadors of the Three Powers for Certain Vilayets in Anatolia', enclosure in Currie to Salisbury, Therapia, 3 August 1895; Salisbury to Currie, Foreign Office, 7 August 1895; Salisbury to Lascelles, Foreign Office, 7 August 1895. Saurma to Hohenlohe, Therapia, 14 July 1895, in GP 10, pp. 42–4. GP 10 has extensive documentation on the Armenian Crisis, little of which is cited here, because it duplicates other sources. German diplomatic efforts were not aided by the idiocy of Wilhelm II, who at the time believed in a worldwide Muslim conspiracy that had to be stopped. (Message from the Kaiser, Hohenlohe to Foreign Office, Munich, 21 October 1895, in GP 10, pp. 76–8.)

   A further statement on reforms planned by the Ottoman Government tightened Ottoman rule and laws in the East, but still refused to acquiesce to the three Powers' plan. (FO 424/183, enclosure in Currie to Salisbury, Therapia, 21 August 1895.)

12. The French believed the Russian intransigence on the Armenian Question derived from their desire to have a change in the position of the other Powers on the Straits Question. They would barter acceptance of British plans for an opening of the Straits to the Russian fleet. FO 424/189, 'Memorandum by Mr. Block', enclosure in Currie to Salisbury, Pera, 25 November 1896.

13. 'Address in Answer to Her Majesty's Most Gracious Speech', House of Lords Debate, 15 August 1895, *Hansard*, vol. 36, cc. 19–58.

14. FO 424/183, Salisbury to Howard, Foreign Office, 13 August 1895; Salisbury to Lascelles, Foreign Office, 16 August 1895; Lascelles to Salisbury, St Petersburgh, 9 and 28 August 1895; Salisbury to Currie, Foreign Office, 21 August 1895. Rotenham to Hehenlohe, Berlin, 3 August 1895, in GP 10, pp. 45–6.

15. FO 424/183, Currie to Salisbury, Constantinople, 28 August, 4, 7, 8 September 1895; 'Turkish Government to Rustem Pasha (ambassador in London), Communicated by Rustem Pasha', 6 September 1895; Lascelles to Salisbury, St Petersburgh, 11 September 1895; Salisbury to Currie, Foreign Office, 11 September 1895; Salisbury to Lascelles, Foreign Office, 27 September 1895. Salisbury not only demanded that the sultan agree to his plans, but that the sultan do so in writing, because

his verbal assurances could not be trusted. (FO 424/183, Salisbury to Dufferin, Foreign Office, 24 and 27 September 1895.)

16. FO 424/184, Currie to Salisbury, Therapia, 4, 10, 17 and 22 October 1895. 'Note Verbale' from the Ottoman Government, enclosure in FO 424/184, Currie to Salisbury, Therapia, 7 October 1895. The Austrians offered support for the plan. (FO 424/184, Salisbury to Currie, Foreign Office, 10 October 1895.) The Armenian Patriarch notified Currie that he wanted all the reforms to be under the control of the Powers. (FO 424/184, enclosure in Currie to Salisbury, Constantinople, 9 October 1895.)

17. FO 424/184, Currie to Salisbury, Constantinople, 16, 20 October 1895. The deliberations on the reform proposals and their execution can only be summarised here. For a more complete rendering, see Şaşmaz, pp. 110–252.

18. FO 424/184, Herbert to Salisbury, Constantinople, 29 and 30 October, and 3 December 1895; Currie to Salisbury, Constantinople, 16 December 1895; Salisbury to Currie, 3 January and 20 March 1896.

19. FO 424/184, Currie to Salisbury, Constantinople, 29 November 1895.

20. FO 424/184, Currie to Salisbury, Constantinople, 16 January 1896.

21. FO 424/186, Goschen to Salisbury, St Petersburgh, 16 and 30 January 1896. FO 424/188, Salisbury to Monson, Foreign Office, 23 September 1896.

    According to the Germans, in January of 1896, the British began to canvas the European governments with Salisbury's plan to effectively end the Ottomans' control of their government. They said the Ottoman Empire was about to collapse. They therefore proposed that the Powers' ambassadors in Istanbul should confer to do draw up plan for the Empire's demise. The Germans and Russians refused to consider a conference under those terms. Salisbury recanted and said he had not intended such 'far reaching proposals'. (Marschall to Saurma, Berlin, 19 January 1896 in GP 12/1, p. 4. Radolin to Hohenlehe, St Petersburgh, 23 January and 6 February 1896, in GP 12/1, pp. 7–8 and 11. Hatzfeldt to Hohenlohe, London, 29 January 1896, in GP 12/1, pp. 8–9.)

22. FO 424/186, Goschen to Salisbury, St Petersburgh, 16 January 1896; 'Memorandum of the Contents of a Despatch from Prince Lobanow, dated St Petersburgh, January 10 (33), 1896.' FO 424/188, Monson to Salisbury, Vienna, 24 September 1896. FO 424/189, Monson to Salisbury, Vienna, 24 September 1896.

23. 'Address in Answers to Her Majesty's Most Gracious Speech', House of Lords Debate, 11 February 1896, *Hansard*, vol. 37, cc. 9–61.

24. FO 424/189, Salisbury to O'Conor, Foreign Office, 20 October 1896. Salisbury stated the Powers had forced a satisfactory solution to the Cretan problem

(although not very satisfactory to the Ottomans), and they could do something similar in Eastern Anatolia.

25. FO 424/189, Monson to Salisbury, Vienna, 23 October 1896; Lascelles to Salisbury, Berlin, 26 October 1896; Ford to Salisbury, Rome, 26 October 1896; Gosselin to Salisbury, Paris, 4 November 1896; Milbanks to Salisbury, Vienna, 7 November 1896; O'Conor to Salisbury, St Petersburgh, 12, 18 November 1896. Radolin to Foreign Office, St Petersburg, 20 November 1896, in GP 12/1, p. 222.

26. FO 424/189, Salisbury to O'Conor, Foreign Office, 25 November 1896; O'Conor to Salisbury, St Petersburgh, 25 November 1896; Currie to Salisbury, Constantinople, 5 December 1896. The Austrians believed the Russians would still never agree to coercion. (FO 424/189, Milbanks to Salisbury, Vienna, 24 November 1896.)

27. FO 424/189, enclosure in Currie to Salisbury, Therapia, 30 September 1896; Salisbury to Gosselin, Foreign Office, 14 November 1896; Anthopoulu Pasha (Ottoman ambassador, a Christian) to Salisbury, London, 30 November 1896. Anthopoulu included reports on reforms in individual provinces. See also FO 424/189, Anthopoulu Pasha to Salisbury, London, 9, 22 and 28 December 1986. In October 1896, the sultan sent telegrams to his officials in the Six Vilayets ordering compliance with the reforms. Currie believed nothing would come of it. (FO 78/4717, Currie to Salisbury, 28 October 1896.)

28. FO 424/189, Currie to Salisbury, Constantinople, 17 December 1896. See also FO 424/189, Currie to Salisbury, Constantinople, 16 and 25 November 1896. Despite all, on 25 November Currie wrote: 'We are entering on a calmer period in the Armenian question'.

29. FO 424/189, Monson to Salisbury, Paris, 3 and 4 December 1896.

30. FO 424/189, Monson to Salisbury, Paris, 17 and 18 December 1896 (a number of communications); the Austrians continued to prevaricate, but stated they were willing to discuss enforcement measures if all the others agreed, once again duplicitous. (FO 424/189, Salisbury to Milbanks, Foreign Office, 21 December 1896.) FO 424/189, Currie to Salisbury, Constantinople, 17 December 1896; Currie to Salisbury, Constantinople, 23 December 1896. The Germans' response to the Armenian troubles was confused and contradictory, primarily due to the Kaiser's changes of mind, but the Germans opposed military coercion. (Schöllgen, pp. 70–2.)

31. See especially FO 424/189, Currie to Salisbury, Constantinople, 25, 27 December 1896. There are many examples of these fruitless discussions in FO 424/189. Rosebery, out of office, accused Salisbury of making threats that

he could not back up, because Russia would never support him. 'And what is the result? The Porte has triumphed all along the line.' ('Lord Rosebery on the Situation', *The Times*, 4 March 1896, p. 10.)
32. See Şevket Pamuk, *The Ottoman Empire and European Capitalism, 1820–1913*, Cambridge: Cambridge University Press, 1987, especially pp. 18–21, 46–52 and 108–26.
33. FO 78/4706, Cumberbatch to Currie, Erzurum, 31 March 1896. A certain distrust of the Gregorian Armenian establishment was evident in the naming of the muavins. For the Six Vilayets, five of the muavins were Catholic Armenians, one a Greek Orthodox.
34. FO 424/188, Williams to Herbert, Van, 7 June 1896. See also, FO 424/188, Williams to Herbert, Van, 15 August and 9 December 1896, Currie to Salisbury, Constantinople, 30 October 1896, and Williams to Currie, Van, 27 October 1896. It should be added that Williams felt that nothing could be done unless the Powers completely took over Ottoman finances. He gave no indication of how this would solve the money problems.

   By no means were the financial problems restricted to Eastern Anatolia. See, for example, FO 424/189, Gilbertson to Currie, Broussa, 17 December 1896. FO 424/184, Eyres to Currie, Damascus, 8 December 1895. FO 424/186, Eyres to Currie, Damascus, 31 December 1895. Other examples: lack of government money in Muş: 'The Government chests are empty.' Salaries had not been paid: 'Even the families of many of the police are starving, the Government being without the means to pay salaries.' (FO 424/186, Hampson to Cumberbatch, Mush, 10 December 1895 and 5 February 1896.) Even the salaries of high officials were not paid. At one point the governor of Sivas Province had not been paid for four months. (FO 424/189, Graves to Currie, Erzurum, 17 September 1896.)
35. FO 424/189, Monahan to Currie, Bitlis, 26 October 1896. FO 78/4704, Hampson to Currie, Moush, 27 January 1876.
36. 'Lord Mayor's Day', *The Times*, 11 November 1895, p. 6. On the relation of officials and the parliament, a relationship with much duplicity and outright deception, see Zara S. Steiner, *Foreign Office and Foreign Policy, 1898–1914*, Cambridge: Cambridge: University Press, 1969, pp. 192–200.
37. 'Armenian Christians', House of Commons Debate, 3 March 1896, *Hansard*, vol. 38, cc. 37–125.
38. On the few occasions where Armenian attacks on Muslims were mentioned in reports from Istanbul, Currie described them as 'alleged', whereas attacks on

Armenians, no matter how exaggerated and embellished, were described as fact. See, for example, FO 78/4706, Currie to Salisbury, Pera, 21 April 1896. FO 78 4717, Currie to Salisbury, 16 October 1896.

39. Ali Vehbi, *Siyasi Hatıratım*, İstanbul: Hareket, 1974, p. 99, translated and quoted in Engin Deniz Akarlı, 'The Problems of External Pressures, Power Struggles, and Budgetary Deficits in Ottoman Politics Under Abdulhamid II (1876–1909): Origins and Solutions', unpublished PhD dissertation, Princeton University, 1976, p. 75. Akarlı's dissertation is an excellent source on the sultan and his administration, drawing on Ottoman documents.

# 3

# CRETE AND THE 1897 WAR

The Greek Orthodox of Crete, who made up two-thirds of the island's population, had revolted many times against their Ottoman rulers, most recently in 1866 and 1878. In response to the 1878 revolt and pressure from the Powers at the Congress of Berlin, the Ottomans had instituted the Halepa (Chalepa) Pact, granting Crete a limited amount of self-government: a Christian was to be governor, an assembly (forty-nine Christians and thirty-one Muslims) was elected, a local gendarmerie created, Greek, as well as Turkish, was made an official language of the courts and the assembly, Greek officials were selected by the Greeks for provincial administration, taxes were reduced and half of the

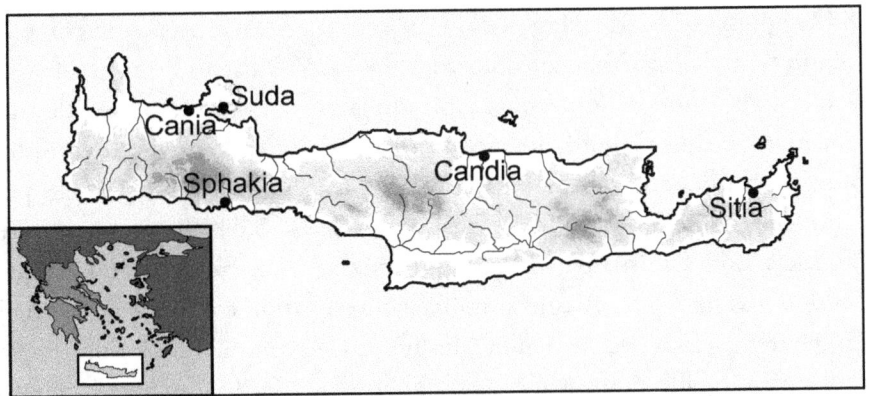

Map 3.1   Crete

island's customs were allocated to the provincial government. In effect, Crete was granted a certain degree of autonomy, more than other Ottoman provinces.[1]

The Halepa system was less than successful. It did not greatly reduce tensions on Crete or opposition to Ottoman rule. Finances became a shambles. Conflicts arose in the Assembly among political parties and between politicians and the governor. A new revolt broke out in 1889. It quickly dissolved into inter-communal warfare between Christians and Muslims. In 1889, Sultan Abdülhamid II restricted the Halepa Pact. Most of the prerogatives of the Assembly were abrogated. Martial law was declared, and the rebellion was put down. All customs receipts were sent to Istanbul, leaving all finances under Central Government control and ending any financial autonomy. From that point, the Ottoman governor alone ruled Crete.[2]

Beginning slowly in 1895, increasing in 1896 and dissolving into a total civil war in 1897, Greeks in Crete revolted against the Ottoman Government. Their stated intention was union (*enosis*) with Greece. It became a two-fold war – Greek rebels against Ottoman troops and intercommunal war between Christians and Muslims, in which each side engaged in massacres of the other. The Greeks, in greater numbers and well supplied with weapons from Greece, had the upper hand. Ottoman troops, scattered across the island, were too few to effectively intervene. The troops concentrated in coastal fortifications. Muslims in the interior, unprotected, fled to the coasts; Greeks from the coasts fled to the interior.[3]

Alfred Biliotti, the British consul-general in Canea (Chania), Crete, was an exemplar among diplomats. By no means always correct in his assessments, he did scrupulously avoid taking sides in the conflict. He did his best to compile statistics on the sufferings of both Muslims and Christians. The result was at odds with those who portrayed the situation only as the persecution of Christians. Neither Biliotti, nor anyone else, had data on mortality, but he did provide statistics on homelessness: of 18,129 Muslim families, 5,180 (29 per cent) were homeless. Of 49,961 Christian families, 3,099 (6 per cent) were homeless. Both Christians and Muslims had been driven from their homes, the Muslim loss far worse. A British military investigation commission reported on the tremendous destruction of Muslim property in the interior of Candia Province. Virtually all the Muslim houses in villages in this province had been either destroyed or occupied by Greeks.[4]

The Ottomans were in fact in an undeclared war with Greece from 1896. It was a guerilla and partisan war in which Cretan Greeks and soldiers and officers of the Greek army attacked Ottoman forces and local Muslims. The Greeks were armed with shipments of weapons and ammunition from Greece. Foreign consuls reported the arrival of thousands of weapons and of 'volunteers' from Greece, many of whom were actually Greek army officers and men. Given the long and ragged coastlines of both Crete and Greece, many of the deliveries of weapons and men must have passed unnoticed by diplomats. Nevertheless, British Consul-General Biliotti reported a great number arriving in Crete, and Ambassador Egerton in Athens reported a great number as leaving Greece.[5]

The driving force behind the support in Greece for revolution in Crete was the Ethniki Etaireia ('National Society') – a Greek nationalistic organisation created in November 1894. The group and others like it advocated an irredentist policy of uniting Greeks of the Ottoman Empire with Greece – the *Megali Idea*. The Ethniki Etaireia grew quickly and, although theoretically a secret organisation, became a force in Greek politics, primarily because it represented an ideal of the populace and many Greek leaders. Rampant nationalism drove reluctant Greek leaders to intervene in the Cretan rebellion. As Thomas Gallant described:

> Romantic nationalism was reaching a fever pitch and, as a consequence, for (Prime Minister Theodore) Deliyiannis and King George I, it was increasingly clear that external conflict in the name of the Megali Idea was the only way to avoid internal unrest. And developments in Macedonia and Crete provided them with the *casus belli*.[6]

Greeks in Greece and abroad took up collections for arms and supplies. A Cretan Committee in Greece provided surplus weapons purchased inexpensively from government stores. Cretan Greeks who had gone to Athens were well-armed by the committee and returned by steamer to Crete; one was noted by the British ambassador in Athens as leaving from near Piraeus, the port of the Greek capital, with 400 men, arms and ammunition. The Greek Government stated that it was trying to stop the exodus of arms and ammunitions to Crete, but it was a ridiculous assertion. Ships leaving from near, or at, Piraeus could not have escaped government attention. Even cannon were sent to Crete, and these could not have come from anything but government arsenals. The Greeks actually made little effort to disguise their actions: Greek soldiers sent to Crete were led by officers in uniform. Consul-General Biliotti stated that Greek soldiers and their officers had landed in every district of the island.[7]

A mixture of military power and European diplomacy had put down previous Cretan revolts. The Ottomans planned the same policy. The Grand Vezir told the British Chargé d'Affaires, Michael Henry Herbert, that the Ottomans planned to use the army to restore order. He said sixteen battalions had been ordered to Crete, in addition to the fifteen already there. Others were held in readiness. The Ottomans were following a basic principle of halting intervention – stopping it before it spread to adherents who would join only if it seemed successful. The Powers were not to allow the Ottomans to act. They were convinced that it was the European Powers, not the Ottomans, who should pacify Crete.[8]

## The 'August Agreement'

The Russians and British, seconded by the other Powers, told the Ottoman Government that they would only allow Crete to be pacified if reforms were instituted. On 4 July 1896, therefore, the sultan agreed to name a Christian governor-general, convene the General Assembly, and restore the Halepa Constitution. He declared a general amnesty on Crete. He also ordered the Turkish military on Crete not to take the offensive against the insurgents. Two weeks later, Abdülhamid sent a message that the announcement of reforms had achieved nothing. The insurgents were still in revolt, and men and supplies were still arriving from Greece. The Ottoman Government asked that the Powers take strong action against the insurgents, since they had kept the Ottomans from doing so themselves. The Powers' response, instead of intervention, was to codify rules for their suggested reforms. Ignoring the nationalist dedication of Greeks on Crete and in the Greek kingdom, the Europeans assumed that reforms of the Ottoman administration would pacify the rebels.[9]

The proposal drafted by the Powers' Istanbul ambassadors returned provisions of the Halepa Constitution that had been abrogated by the sultan. Measures of Cretan autonomy and Christian power were increased: domestic matters would be in the hands of the Assembly, where a majority (that is, the Greek deputies) would approve the budget, although the governor retained veto power. Two thirds of the administrative appointments were reserved for Christians. Half the customs revenues and all the tax on tobacco imports would remain on the island. Significantly, the Powers were to be expressly given rights on the island ('The Powers shall satisfy themselves of the execution of all these measures.'): the governor-general would be a Christian, named by the sultan, but approved by the Powers. A commission of European officers would reorganise the gendarmerie. Foreign jurists would supervise reforms of the judicial system.[10]

The Powers presented the plan to the Christian deputies elected to the old Assembly for approval. The deputies were notified that their approval included the promise that the Greeks would stop fighting. If the insurgency continued, the plan would be null and void. The Greek delegates agreed, but the insurgency continued.[11]

In keeping with the spirit of the August Agreement, the seventeen battalions of Ottoman reservists that had been sent to Crete were returned home, cutting the Ottoman force on the island in half, to seventeen battalions of regulars. The governor adopted a policy of stationing troops only in centres of Muslim population. The rest of the island was to be patrolled by small contingents, accompanied by Christian gendarmes (paramilitary rural police). But the Christian gendarmes themselves began to revolt, and, despite elaborate regulations drawn up for the gendarmerie, the plan was ineffective, because gendarmes were often not paid. Money to apply the reforms was scarce. Biliotti felt that one month after the reforms had been promulgated, the situation had become worse. Neither the Muslims nor the Christians believed that the reforms would work, nor did they believe that the Powers would enforce them – a very accurate belief. The Muslims were afraid to return to their villages. Insurgents told British officers that their only aim was the union of Crete with Greece, not a reformed Crete remaining in the Ottoman Empire.[12]

The intervention of the powers had two basic flaws that showed a misunderstanding of the situation on Crete. One was what can be styled as imperialist hubris. The Powers had planned that Crete would be pacified simply because they had drawn up a plan. The sultan had been coerced to agree with the plan. In any case, the Ottoman Government could do nothing in the face of Great Power opposition. The other was the belief that all the insurgents wanted was reformed government and a measure of Christian local control. In fact, the insurgents were well beyond that, if it had ever been their intention. What they wanted was union with Greece. The August Agreements never worked.

The Powers decided to take the pacification of Crete into their own hands.

**Naval Intervention**

The British battleship *Hood* and a French gunboat arrived at Crete in May of 1896. By the beginning of March 1897, there were on station in Cretan waters ships from Italy (ten, including five older battleships), Austria (seven), France (six), Russia (nine, including three battleships), Germany (one) and Britain (fourteen, including five British battleships). Even though many of the ships were older than more modern ones, it was a formidable fleet, especially because it had no naval opposition. The major drawback of the fleet was that its power only extended to the range of its naval guns. The interior of Crete was beyond its control. This meant that control of the interior remained with the rebels.[13]

The naval commanders agreed:

> [T]o use force if needed to prevent 1. Towns being bombarded. 2. Troops, arms, or ammunitions of war being disembarked from Greek war-ships. 3. Greek regular forces being disembarked from merchant-vessels. 4. Greek ships of war attacking Turkish ships of war or merchant vessels.

On 15 February 1897, the Allied fleet landed 450 men, mainly marines, at Canea, taking effect control of the Cretan capital. Occupation of other coastal cities followed. The admirals organised themselves into an Admirals Council on 16 February. It was to function as a *de facto* government over the area the fleets controlled.[14]

The admirals' flotilla did effectively protect the Ottoman coastal garrisons with naval gunfire and occasional limited forays of troops. The European forces were effective in halting rebel advances on the main cities of Canea (Chania) and Candia (Heraklion) and in defending smaller Ottoman outposts, usually with naval gunfire. However, when the Powers created an international force to police the island, it was instructed not to base troops beyond the range of naval gunfire. The effect was to leave the centre of the island, now mainly denuded of its Muslim population, in the hands of the insurgents. Despite diplomatic efforts, Greek army officers remained. The admirals failed in their attempts to broker agreement between the insurgents and the Muslim population and Ottoman troops to end the revolt. The admirals, the consuls in Crete and the ambassadors in Istanbul developed elaborate proposals for reforming important matters, such as the judiciary and the gendarmerie, with little effect.[15]

**Greek Incursion**

In February 1897, the Greek Government began an open war with the Ottomans. A Greek naval squadron was sent to Crete on 8 February 1897 with the intention of aiding the revolution. It was followed by a Greek torpedo flotilla under the command of Prince George, the second son of King George. Two boatloads of arms were landed at the diplomatically protected consulate-general of Greece in Canae. George was ordered by the Powers' admirals to leave, which he did, but on 15 February the Greeks landed more than 1,000 soldiers, with cannon and military supplies, on the island. The Greek minister of war announced that he had dispatched a force under Colonel Timoleon Vassos to Crete. Vassos was instructed to claim the island for Greece:

> Landing with the troops under your command on Crete and in a proper locality, you will, in the name of the King of the Hellenes, George I, occupy the island, driving away the Turks from the forts, and taking possession of them. Every action that you will take you will base upon the established Greek laws in the name of the King and under the responsibility of the Greek Government.

Greek Government actions were no secret. The orders to Vassos were published in the official gazette. Once in Crete, Vassos announced that he had come under orders from the king. Six days before Vassos's arrival the insurgents had passed 'a Decree of Annexation', which declared union with Greece.[16]

All the Great Powers, except Britain, agreed that 'coercion' should be applied to the Greeks to compel Greek forces to leave Crete. The principle that revolutionaries should succeed against an established government was too dangerous to accept. German Emperor Wilhelm II wanted 'vigorous measures' taken against the Greeks, including naval blockade of Greece if the Greeks did not leave Crete. Gabriel Hanotaux, the French Foreign Minister, desired the Powers 'marcher au Pirée'. He reiterated that in various meetings with other Powers. When the Greek Government threatened to incite rebellion in Macedonia and even in Istanbul if the Powers acted against them, Hanotaux responded:

> These threats are regarded by Mr. Hanatoux as evidence that Greece, finding herself bankrupt alike in honour, in credit, and in domestic and foreign policy, is ready, in the hope of extricating herself from her disgraceful position, to ruin her own existence.[17]

The German Emperor announced: 'A formal proposal to blockade the Greek Coast would now be made to the Powers by the Imperial Government.' The Austrians and French agreed with the German proposal, and the French had hopes that the Russians and Italians would join them. The Germans wished the British to join in their plan. It was not to be.[18]

All changed when the British broke with the others and took an independent stand. Under Lord Salisbury, the British began to offer support for Greek aspirations that would extend until 1923. The British were thenceforward to do what they could to turn Crete over to the Greeks. The British position on Crete effectively reversed the Powers' plan of forcing the Greeks, who were responsible for the troubles in Crete, to abandon their rebellion to one of advocacy of forcing the Ottomans to abandon Crete. The British refused to support a blockade of Greece, and proposed a measure that would in effect remove Crete from Ottoman rule:

> Her Majesty's Government have received from the German Government proposals in the direction of a policy for blockading Greece. In the view of Her Majesty's Government, it is not possible usefully to consider a proposal of this kind until the Powers have resolved upon a course of action as regards the island of Crete, which is now occupied by them.
>
> A strong feeling is entertained by Her Majesty's Government that though Crete may continue to form a part of the Ottoman Empire, it cannot continue subject to the administration of Turkey, but must be converted into a privileged province of the Empire.[19]

What the British proposed was autonomy for Crete, in effect removing it from the Ottoman Empire in all but name.[20]

At first the British proposal met strong resistance from other Powers. The Russian Government stated that the ultimate governance of Crete could not be considered until coercive measures had forced the Greeks to abandon Crete. The Germans were particularly incensed by the British proposal. They held to their blockade proposal, declaring that the Greeks had 'violated the law of nations and defied the orders and advice of the Great Powers', a precedent that could not be allowed to stand.[21]

The British Government nevertheless made a public declaration of policy on 24 February 1897:

1. That the establishment of administrative autonomy in Crete is, in their (the Powers) judgment, a necessary condition to the termination of the international occupation.
2. That, subject to the above provision, Crete ought, in their judgment, to remain a portion of the Turkish Empire.
3. That Turkey and Greece ought to be informed by the Powers of this resolution.
4. That if either Turkey or Greece persistently refuse when required to withdraw their naval and military forces from the island, the Powers should impose their decision by force upon the State so refusing.[22]

The Powers, other than Great Britain, had opposed Greece on the basis of the perceived need to preserve the status quo in Europe. All feared that taking sides in such disputes might lead to a greater conflict, as Powers backed their own surrogates in local conflicts. Britain's actions in favour of the Greeks over Crete drew this policy into question. One Power had taken a side. The others could either placate Britain or risk conflict. None were concerned with the theoretical rights of the Ottoman Empire, nor with past promises to retain the territorial integrity of the Empire. Their concern was for the unity of Europe, the so-called 'Concert of Europe', and avoiding European war. Lord Salisbury was willing to take the chance that the other Powers would acquiesce to his wishes rather than risk the alternative. He was right. The Powers, even the Germans, agreed to implement the British proposals. The Italians made no objections. The Russians, Germans and Austrians agreed with all of the proposal except point four. They wanted the Greeks to leave the islands before the Ottoman garrisons, some of which should remain 'in accordance with the maintenance of the suzerainty of the Sultan'. Salisbury was forced reluctantly to agreed that there need not be simultaneous withdrawal of the Greeks and Turks.[23]

The Russians proposed a collective representation by the Powers: the Ottomans were to be told that Crete would become autonomous. The Greeks were told to leave Crete in three or four days or face forcible measures 'either by blockading the island, or by entering on active measures on the mainland'. But the British still opposed any specific threats to the Greeks. In addition, the British demanded that the Ottomans be formally blamed for their own losses; they should be told that Crete was becoming autonomous because the Turks had failed to execute reforms. The Ottomans, in other words, were gratuitously to be told that it was all their fault. The British refused to send the ultimatum without that accusation. The British form of the plan was adopted and sent to Athens and Istanbul.[24]

Two communiques notified the Ottomans that, while Crete would not become part of Greece, it would be autonomous, under a face-saving 'sovereignty of the sultan'. All blame was put on the Ottomans, because they had not properly instituted reforms. The Greeks were also told that the need for Cretan autonomy was due to failures of the Ottoman Government; no Greek fault was mentioned. Nevertheless, Greek forces had to leave Crete. The Powers announced their intention 'not to shrink from any measure of compulsion' if the Greeks had not decided in six days on the evacuation of their forces from the island.[25]

The Ottoman response accepted Cretan autonomy and asked to discuss the form of autonomy with the Powers' ambassadors. The Greek Government, however, rejected autonomy. They asked the Powers to make Crete part of the Greek kingdom. They accepted the withdrawal of Greek ships, but not the Greek army, which would remain.

> It is, above all, our duty not to leave the Cretan people at the mercy of Mussulman fanaticism, and of the Turkish army, which has always intentionally and by connivance, been a party to the acts of aggression of the populace against the Christians.

They intended the Greek army to be 'entrusted with the mandate of pacifying the country'.[26]

Salisbury wanted consideration of the Greek proposal to use the Greek army to police Crete, which he thought reasonable. If the other powers would not accept an army under Greek command, perhaps the Greeks could be put under officers from the Powers. The Greeks refused to accept that, however, and the other Powers would not consider anything but complete evacuation of all Greek and Ottoman troops. France and Germany declared that any Greek soldiers that remained would only aid and encourage the insurgents. Salisbury then proposed what was originally a Russian plan that 10,000 to 12,000 European troops would occupy the island. The other Powers also disagreed with that. They felt it would be enough for each power to send 600 men to defend the Powers' areas of occupation on the coasts, which was the plan adopted.[27]

On 17 March 1897, the Powers' admirals announced to the people of Crete

> that the Great Powers have formed an irrevocable decision to secure for Crete complete autonomy under the suzerainty of His Imperial Majesty the Sultan, and that it is well understood that, as regards the internal affairs of the island, the Cretans will be free from all control of the Porte.

The admirals' declaration of autonomy was unanimously accepted and praised by the Christian Assembly, which wrote that all the problems of Crete had been caused by the Muslims, but, they expected, all would now be well. Cretan Muslims and Ottoman officials, on the other hand, felt betrayed.[28]

## Blockade

The situation in Crete had become more serious by February of 1897. The admirals reported that villages all across Crete in which Muslims still remained were besieged by the insurgents. For example, the international force was needed to rescue the Ottoman troops and 2,500 Muslim civilians of the Selinos district. Of these, 1,570 Muslims of Candanos went to the shore to be rescued 'with literally nothing more than the clothes on their backs'. Others were able to take a bit more, but all their flocks were left to the Greeks.[29]

The question for the Powers was what to do about the refusal of the Greeks. The six-day deadline came and went with no change in Greek resolve. The Powers, again excepting Britain, felt it necessary to enforce their wishes, because it was intolerable that a small state would disobey the orders of the Great Powers. The Powers, however, were unwilling to force the Greeks militarily to comply with their wishes. The only weapon at their disposal was a naval blockade of Crete and Greek ports on the mainland. It was the blockade of Greek ports, especially Piraeus, the port of Athens, that would be most effective in forcing a withdrawal from Crete. The damage to the Greek economy, it was felt, would be the deciding factor.

As they had throughout the Crete situation, the British wanted no effective coercion of the Greeks. Salisbury was completely against any blockade of Greek ports. He stated that he was not sure that any coercive measures against Greece were necessary. In the face of determination from the other Powers, however, he was willing to accept a blockade of Crete only. The admirals who were in charge of the Powers' fleets at Crete, including British Rear-Admiral Harris, disagreed with Salisbury. They considered blockading Piraeus as 'an integral part of the operations to be undertaken for the coercion of Greece'. The Germans also disagreed. They wanted blockades of the Greek mainland ports. German Foreign Minister (State Secretary) Adolf Marschall von Bieberstein stated: 'Indeed, there would be no necessity for blockading Crete if the Greek ships were blockaded in their own ports.' The Austrian Government told Salisbury that it was 'greatly concerned by your Lordship's communication (opposing the Greek ports blockade)'. They wanted unison of the Powers and feared the break-up of the European Concert and of European prestige, with unforeseen effects, if the British did not cooperate. The Italians threatened that, if Britain did not cooperate, the European Concert would be imperiled and 'the peace of Europe would be in great danger'. The British were unmoved. British commitment to the Greeks was more important to them than the Concert of Europe.[30]

The British were in command of the situation. They knew that the others were unwilling to break up the unison of the Concert of Europe. Moreover, the British fleet was needed to enforce any effective blockade. Salisbury proved willing to gamble that obstinacy would be rewarded.[31]

The admirals announced a blockade of Crete to begin on 21 March. They notified the commander of the Greek forces that they would intervene militarily if the Greeks bombarded villages, landed troops or military supplies or attacked Turkish buildings and commerce. This would help pacify the island

and would keep Greece from reinforcing its soldiers and the insurgents on the island, but would do little to force out the Greek soldiers already there. (The Greeks estimated well over 12,000 Greek soldiers and insurgents on the island, only a slight exaggeration.) Something still had to be done to force the Greeks to leave Crete.[32]

The Russians attempted to break the deadlock with a compromise for Britain. Only the port of Volo in the North (Map 3.2) would be blockaded, with some later consideration of other blockades. All the Powers except Britain accepted a blockade of Volo. It was viewed as a measure to keep the Greeks from extending the conflict to Ottoman Europe, because Volo was the closest port to the Ottoman Macedonian border. It seems to have been a measure to do something, though only symbolic, in light of British refusal to admit a more effective blockade, even if it would have little effect on Crete. But the British had no wish to cooperate even in the limited Volo blockade, not because it would be ineffective, which was true, but because they wanted no coercion, even a symbolic one, of the Greeks. Great pressure was put on Britain to participate in the blockade of Volo. Britain's refusal to apply any coercive measures on the Greeks to leave Crete led to great consternation among the other Powers. The Russians felt that Britain's rejection would lead to the end of the European Concert. Britain vacillated, and her delay allowed the Greeks to bring troops and supplies through Volo. The Germans were particularly incensed. Finally, the British agreed to diplomatically 'support' a blockade of Volo and some other parts of the Greek coast by the other Powers, but Britain would send no ships of her own.[33]

At the end of March 1897, the Germans and Austrians were still committed to a blockade of Piraeus, but the war between the Ottoman Empire and Greece intervened and made all the plans for blockades irrelevant.[34]

## British Public Opinion

Others were not unmindful of the cause for British reticence to coerce the Greeks. The Kaiser blamed the British position on British public opinion, which would not allow Salisbury to act against the Greeks, but supported any actions against the Ottomans. The Italian foreign minister noted the same, saying the public opinion would keep the British from doing anything that seemed to support the Turks. British diplomats explained to foreign leaders that British actions 'were mainly based on the state of opinion which had shown itself in parliament on the subject of Crete'. Salisbury himself acknowledged that he had made his 24 February declaration on Cretan autonomy in order to placate public opinion and the voices against the Turks in parliament.[35]

> (British ambassador in Berlin Frank Lascelles) The Emperor expressed doubts as to whether Great Britain would take part in coercive action against Greece. Upon my reminding him that Her Majesty's Government had so far acted in complete accord with the other Powers, he replied that that it appeared from the utterances in the English press that English public opinion would not allow Her Majesty's Government to coerce Greece.

The Kaiser thought the best solution would be to support a Turkish attack in Thessaly, something which the British would never approve.[36]

As judged by British newspapers, Salisbury was indeed correct in interpreting public opinion against the Turks, although how much newspapers reflected actual public opinion is unknown. Nevertheless, newspaper readers would have found anti-Turkish and pro-Greek opinions and highly selective news. Muslim attacks on Greeks in Crete were reported, but seldom Greek attacks on Muslims. When a few Greek raids on Muslim villages were admitted, they were styled as reprisals for Muslim ill-doings; Greeks supposedly fought only after Muslims had attacked them. Actions against Greeks by Turkish refugees, real or imagined, were described with no mention of the Greek attacks that had forced the Turks to become refugees.[37]

*The Times* featured emotive descriptions of the evils of the Ottoman Empire: 'suffering and crime'; 'a system of government that has produced untold suffering in the past and threatens to engender fresh calamities in the future'; 'horrible barbarity'. Spurious statistics of population and mortality emphasised Greek numbers and suffering, without considering Muslim deaths or privations. The *Daily Telegraph* wrote of 'Muslim atrocities' and 'the rottenness of the Turkish System'. *Daily News* editorials described 'the Sultan in his diabolical work', and noted: 'The Turkish dominion in Crete means not only oppression, but anarchy.'[38]

The standard of evidence was what might be expected: most writers offered no sources for their reporting. Those that did cited 'an informant', 'authentic information' or 'trustworthy information'. As was the journalistic custom of the time, articles were unsigned, attributed to 'Our Own Correspondent' or 'Special Correspondent'. These unidentified authors presented often contradictory information from unnamed sources. Their undisclosed identities gave great scope to invention for which they would never be called to account. Supposed news articles were often in fact editorials.[39]

Newspapers instructed the British Government, and Salisbury in particular, to support Greek annexation of Crete, or at least Cretan autonomy. For example, the *Evening Standard* was concerned with forcing the British Government to take action against the Ottomans in Crete and, it implied, everywhere. The *Standard* called for an end to Ottoman rule in Crete, 'because Turkish rule is bad everywhere'. It was not because the Greeks were worthy: 'As far as fanaticism and cruelty are concerned, there is, in all probability, nothing to choose between the Mussulmans and the Christians of Crete . . . Scratch any of them and you will find a savage.' Nevertheless, it was the Turks that should be punished.[40]

The byline most cited in articles was Athens.

The public opinion that concerned Salisbury was led by pressure from the anti-Turkish political groups, described in the previous chapter, and their supporters in parliament. Liberal politicians and members of the partisan committees, prominently including Herbert Asquith and David Lloyd George, publicly pressured the government to deal more harshly with the Cretan Muslims and the Ottomans. The members of the Anglo-Armenian Association supported the public agitation over Crete. Stalwarts of the association such as Francis Stevenson, its president and members of the association's governing committee – F. A. Channing, J. Arthur Price and Canon MacColl – lent support to the Greek cause and spoke at mass meetings on Crete. In addition, a Greek Committee published pamphlets and lobbied the government for the Greek cause in Crete. The committee had been formed in 1879 'for the purpose of promoting the interests of Greece in the East'. Its first presidents were the Marquis of Lansdowne and the Earl of Rosebery, sometime prime minister and foreign secretary. 'The method of the Committee was to evoke public opinion in favour of the Greek claims.'[41]

Like the Armenian and later Macedonian Questions, the Cretan Question inspired great public meetings to protest against the Ottomans and demand

British action against them. Audiences were often in the thousands. One prominent public meeting was held in Hyde Park on 6 March 1897, with an estimated attendance of 100,000 (probably a gross overestimation, but a sizeable number.) Members of parliament and clergymen regaled the crowd with stories of murderous Turks and innocent Greeks. The calls for Britain to eject the Turks from the island were universal. Salisbury was condemned as being too pusillanimous in supporting the Greeks. The reason for Salisbury's policy, according to the speaker Havelock Wilson, MP, was that 'the present policy of the Government was to support Jew financiers and bondholders'. Another speaker characterised the Cretan uprising as 'a crusade of the Cross against the black crescent'. Common Christianity was the universal theme. It was not a temperate meeting. Similar meetings, with somewhat smaller attendance, were held all over Britain – at various venues in London, Eastbourne, Glamorgan, Lancaster, Bedford, Birmingham, Liverpool, Norwich, etc.[42]

Is an attribution of Salisbury's actions solely to the force of public opinion and parliamentary politics a completely accurate assessment? Neither Salisbury nor later researchers had the benefit of opinion polls in 1896. Any politician might have been affected against the Turks by the sentiment in the press. It would be a mistake, however, to assume that Salisbury's actions were solely a calculated concession to popular opinion. As seen in previous chapters, Salisbury himself was deeply committed to detaching Christians from Ottoman rule. He also held an overwhelming majority of 153 seats in the House of Commons that would have allowed him great leeway in policy decisions. In parliament it was only Liberals who attacked the government policy, and they wanted it to be even more forceful. When Crete was debated in the Commons in 1897, the British Government actually defended the Muslims of Crete and blamed the Greeks for the troubles. Anyone hearing the government statement in the debate of 7 May 1897 would have expected Salisbury to be doing all he could for the Muslims of Crete. In fact, rather than fearing the parliament, Salisbury was advocating one position in the House and pursuing another policy in Europe and the Ottoman Empire. Nothing in the limited debates on Crete in 1896 and 1897 indicated that parliament was forcing Salisbury into anything. The force of public opinion in favour of the Greeks was real, but it was also a convenient excuse to be offered to the other Powers for Salisbury's consistent personal advocacy for the Greeks.[43]

## 1897 War

War fever, stoked by the Megali Idea and reports – often false reports of attacks on Cretan Greeks – spread in Greece. As it had in Greek intervention on Crete, popular sentiment in Greece drove the actions of politicians in Macedonia. The Ethniki Etaireia sent volunteer guerillas across the border into Ottoman Macedonia, where they assured themselves that local Greeks would welcome them and join their cause. That did not happen, but the incursions did cause the Ottomans to send troops to the border. The Greeks sent their own army to face them.[44]

The British were deeply concerned that Greece would be the loser in a war with the Ottoman Empire. They joined with the Russians in the demand that Greek and Ottoman forces each withdraw from the border, which was ignored by both. From the first, the British and Russians took a stance against the Ottoman forces. The British announced that 'a passage of the frontier by Turkish forces would be regarded by Her Majesty's Government as a hostile act to Great Britain'. Baron von Marschall, the German Foreign Minister, concluded that the British threat to the Ottomans was intended to satisfy public opinion in England. He was convinced that the Turks had no intention to cross the border, but would only defend themselves against hostile Greek actions.[45]

It was the Greeks that attacked over the border. The attack was folly. The Ottomans could field more than twice as many men as the Greeks, and they were better equipped. Unlike their warning to the Turks, the British made no assertion that the Greek attack was 'a hostile act to Great Britain'. Announcements in Athens on 9 April 1897 stated that 2,000 armed men had crossed the border into Macedonia. This was announced on the same date as the incursion, indicating previous planning. The Ottomans communicated news of the Greek attack on 10 April. Further attacks, with Turkish dead and wounded, continued through the week. While the first Greeks to attack were described by Athens as irregular forces not attached formally to the Greek army, by 17 April the Ottomans reported, and the Greeks admitted, that their regular army was attacking Turkish positions. The Ottoman Government notified the foreign embassies that it would take measures to defend its territory, but would suspend military action if the Greeks withdrew.[46]

Map 3.2   Greece, 1876–81

The Greeks refused to retreat. The Ottomans went to war, quickly defeating the Greeks. By the middle of May, Northern Greece was in Ottoman hands. Athens was threatened, with no effective Greek force between it and the Ottoman army. Greece had allowed its grandiose plans for a Greater Greece to interfere with sound military judgement.[47]

On 17 May, the Tsar wrote to the sultan congratulating him on Ottoman successes on the battlefield, and stated that it was time for the acceptance of Great Power mediation for peace. The danger of Russian intervention was obvious. The sultan responded on 18 May, suspending hostilities and accepting mediation. The Greeks requested mediation on 19 May. Hostilities officially ceased, although Greek bands continued to attack Ottoman occupation forces.[48]

The Greek army began to leave Crete at the beginning of May 1897. In all, 1,885 officers and men, fourteen guns and ammunition left the island by 26 May. The Powers' blockade was raised on 10 September. After the departure of the Greek soldiers, conflict in Crete diminished, but did not end. Muslims seem to have been the principal sufferers. Admiral Harris noted: 'Robbery and murder continue on both sides both between Moslems and Christians. I regret to say principally by Christians who kill all Moslems they can find outside the outposts.'[49]

On 25 July 1898, the European admirals turned over control of all Crete outside the cities occupied by the Europeans to an assembly made up entirely of Christian politicians and leaders of the insurrection. It became obvious to the Muslims that they had been excluded from any part in rule over the island. In addition, the Muslims, on the coasts and under European control, were required to pay taxes, whereas the Christians in the interior did not do so, and proceeds from the agricultural tax (*aşar*) were to be paid to the Christian authorities, by order of the admirals. The admirals had begun disarming the Muslims, under their control on the coasts, in April 1897, leaving the Greeks in the interior armed, so the Muslims had no means to resist.[50]

## An Enforced Peace

The Ottoman Government presented the Powers with its proposals for peace with Greece: the pre-1881 border would return, leaving Thessaly to the Ottomans. The Greeks would pay an indemnity of £T 10,000,000. Treaties that gave Greece special status and extraterritoriality in the Ottoman Empire – the Capitulations – would be renegotiated. As soon as Greece agreed to these conditions, hostilities would formally cease.[51]

By the standards of past wars, in which the Ottoman Empire had lost much, the Ottomans would seem to have been able to retain most, perhaps all, of what they had conquered. The region of Thessaly had only been taken from them in 1881, sixteen years earlier, by a decision of the Congress of Berlin, but Britain refused to countenance any reversion of Thessaly to the Ottomans. It was Salisbury's fixed principle that no land which had been taken from Muslim rule should ever be returned to Muslim rule. Salisbury would only admit that the Greeks pay an indemnity, because the Ottomans had not been guilty of starting the war and had a right to some compensation. Salisbury stated that he would accept no plan that included Muslim administration over any Christian community.[52]

The ambassadors of the Powers at Istanbul drew up a notice to the Ottomans stating that the Ottoman desires were unwanted and unacceptable. All matters would be decided by the Powers. The note was not initially sent; the Germans and Austrians refused to agree to it, because the Greeks were continuing to attack the Ottoman forces that had ceased their advance. German opposition continued until the Greeks finally signed an armistice (at Arta, 19 May 1987). The Germans then agreed to the note being sent, but they continued to work to lessen the blow on the Ottomans. The ambassadors presented the Powers' memorandum on peace to the Ottoman Government on 28 May. It responded to the Ottoman proposals for peace by presenting a set of proposals from Salisbury: he Ottomans could only expect a slight modification of the Thessaly borders for strategic reasons. An indemnity would have to fit the ability of the Greeks to pay, which was less than the sum suggested by the Ottomans. The Greek Capitulations would not change.[53]

On 5 June 1897, the ambassadors at Istanbul submitted a joint memorandum to the Ottoman Government on their proposals for a peace treaty: they stated that they did not wish to upset the settlement in the Treaty of Berlin, and therefore Thessaly would not be retained by the Ottomans. There would only be small border rectifications. The ambassadors assured the Ottomans that the Greeks would protect Muslim rights in Greece. The Greek Capitulations were to be unchanged, but further negotiations between the Ottoman Empire and Greece were suggested. An indemnity would be set by the Powers. The Ottomans were to get none of their requirements.[54]

Nothing is as instructive of the British attitude toward the Ottoman Empire as Salisbury's desires for military coercion. He had wanted the Europeans to use their navies to force the Ottomans to conform to Britain's wishes in Anatolia. Salisbury intended to militarily coerce the Ottomans in Crete and on the Mesopotamian border. Yet he was unwilling to coerce the Greeks, even when his refusal threatened the Concert with the other Powers. Now he wanted to once again send in the navies to compel Ottoman acceptance of his plans. He fully intended to use force if the Ottomans did not agree with his plan. He wrote to the Russians, stating that he knew they would agree with him that the Ottoman demand to retain Thessaly was unacceptable. He suggested that Russia and Britain send ships to Istanbul to threaten the sultan. The Russians agreed with the British, stipulating only that the Straits not be closed. But the Ottomans bowed to military reality. They could not stand against the Russians and the British. On 15 July 1897, the Germans told them that they could not help. With no other option, on the same day the German refusal arrived, the Ottoman Government formally accepted the loss of Thessaly.[55]

The Ottomans had accepted the loss of Thessaly. The sticking point in negotiating the treaty was a guarantee that the indemnity would be paid. The Germans accepted that the Ottomans would have to abandon most of Thessaly, but they wished the evacuation to be gradual, the Ottomans only progressively leaving as the Greeks continued to pay portions of the indemnity. The French agreed with the German solution. The Ottomans proposed that there were only two possibilities: they would be allowed to garrison points in Thessaly until the indemnity had been paid, gradually leaving when partial payments had been received. They preferred the second choice – a guarantee from the Powers that the indemnity would be paid.[56]

The British opposed any gradual payment plan, because it would still leave Christian populations under Muslim rule, even for a time. Salisbury was completely against any plan that would allow the Ottomans to remain in any part of the conquered territory for any period. The ostensible justification for his position was that Greece would not be able to pay, leaving the Turks in control of the territory, but he admitted that it was British public opinion that was behind his position. He wanted a definite date for withdrawal. The Powers, he stated, should guarantee nothing; the Ottomans would have to be satisfied with a promise from the Greek Government to pay.[57]

Salisbury was advancing his unending support of the Greeks. He must have known that, once Thessaly was theirs, the Greeks would never pay. Even the Russians disagreed with the British, and tried to dissuade Salisbury from his stance on the indemnities. They felt that Greece could afford to pay if the Powers supervised their finances, their payments to European bond holders and their indemnity payments. The Russians also believed that Greece could not be trusted to make the annual payments that Salisbury suggested. The French, Germans and Austrians also urged Salisbury to change his position. The Russians and Austrians noted that 'the abstention of Great Britain would increase the mistrust felt in certain countries'. They felt that once again Britain was threatening the unity of the Concert of Europe.[58]

The solution advanced by the other Powers was to arrange indemnity payments in one lump sum or a few payments over a short period. They recognised that the Greeks could not pay, so they proposed European control ('supervision') of Greek finances, guaranteeing that European lenders would receive Greek payments and interest. Salisbury did not believe that a European loan to pay the indemnities in a lump sum could be arranged; he still wanted the Ottomans to be forced to accept illusory annual payments. But Salisbury was proven wrong. European bankers agreed to the loan. The one force Salisbury could not stand against was the bankers. On 24 August, Salisbury was forced to abandon his plan and accept a European loan guaranteed by the Powers. The British regretfully told the Greeks that they had no choice but to accept financial control by the Powers.[59]

There was never a question of any of the Powers accepting alteration of the Capitulations enjoyed by Greeks in the Ottoman Empire. All the Powers benefitted from the Capitulations. Any change in them would be a dangerous precedent.[60]

The ostensible reason to deny the Ottomans their conquests in Thessaly was the preservation of European peace. The Powers agreed that Thessaly must remain Greek because it had been awarded to Greece in the Treaty of Berlin, and the Treaty of Berlin must not be upset. Although even the Germans, the Power most friendly to the Ottomans, believed that the Berlin Treaty could not be violated, this position was ridiculous. The Treaty of Berlin had been violated by all the Balkan States. More major violations were to come in 1908, when Austria took Bosnia and Bulgaria took Eastern Rumelia. And, of course, the treaty had guaranteed Ottoman borders, a stipulation that the Powers were about to violate in Crete. There was indeed potential danger to European peace, but it had little to do with the Berlin Treaty: Russia and Britain wanted to defend Greece and make sure that Greece lost as little as possible. The Germans and Austrians had somewhat defended Ottoman rights. A collision was possible. In fact, however, there was no threat to European diplomatic cohesion, because the Germans and Austrians abandoned their defence of the Ottomans rather than risk European war.[61]

Behind the denial of Thessaly to the Ottomans was the British desire, shared by others, that no land that had come under Christian rule, even for a short time, should ever be returned to Muslim rule. Salisbury made this an essential requirement of any peace treaty. He told Ambassador Currie, who was negotiating the treaty: 'Her Majesty's Government will not be able to take part in any Treaty or Arrangement under which any Christian community is placed under the Sultan's Government.'[62]

A peace treaty was signed on 4 December 1897. Greece ratified it on 16 December.

**Family Connections**

George I of Greece had been named King of Greece through the intercession of Great Britain, France and Russia. In 1863, when the Greek National Assembly deposed King Otto, the three Powers had interceded to arrange the nomination of Prince Philip of Denmark as King George I. The new king enjoyed close family connections to both Russia and Britain. His sister, Maria Feodorovna (born Dagmar), was the mother of Nicholas II of Russia. Another sister, Alexandra, was the wife of the Prince of Wales (later Edward VII), and thus was the daughter-in-law of Queen Victoria. George himself had married Olga Constaninovna, niece of Nicholas II's grandfather. King George was thus closely related to the royal family of Russia through both his wife and his sister. Prince George of Greece, later governor-general of Crete, was a close personal friend of Nicholas II. George I's daughter Marie also married into the Romanov family. Throughout the Cretan Crisis Britain and Russia were concerned that actions might damage the place of the Greek King. There was the precedent of his predecessor's deposition.[63]

The Russians, at first willing to coerce the Greeks over Crete, began to adopt a conciliatory position in 1897. The longstanding Russian desire to weaken the Ottoman Empire or opposition to the Germans, who had taken a strong position against the Greeks, does not seem to satisfactorily explain this. European officials contended that the Tsar had changed his views because of the influence of his mother, the Tsarina dowager Maria Feodorovna, the sister of King George I of Greece. She undoubtedly had great influence as Tsar Nicholas's advisor, but her actual effect on the Crete issue is undetermined. Her attempts to bring about Nicholas's intervention in Greece's war with the Ottomans, on the other hand, is well documented: Maria Feodorovna's intercession with her son, aided by Nicholas's cousin (once removed), the wife of George of Greece, was a major factor in Russia's intervention in the 1897 War, and in advocacy for lenient terms for the Greeks. Queen Victoria, another relative, became involved, asking the Tsar to support Salisbury's lenient terms for the Greeks. In any case, it is certain that Russia began to join Britain in a pro-Greek policy by late February of 1897. Both Russians and British often emphasised the close connection between the British and the Russians and the unison of their plans for Crete, Greece and the Ottoman Empire.[64]

## Choosing a Governor for Crete

The one Ottoman condition for the governor of autonomous Crete was that he be an Ottoman subject. This was not to be. The British opposed the selection of any Ottoman subject. Two Christian Ottoman officials were proposed, Karatheodori Paşa and Mavroyeni Bey; Salisbury rejected both. He wanted no one with a close connection to the Ottoman Government. Any Ottoman candidate was rejected. None of the other powers was concerned enough with the wishes of the sultan to oppose the British demands.[65]

The Powers agreed that a European should become governor of Crete. That was as far as their unity prevailed. Hanotaux of France wanted Numa Droz, ex-president of Switzerland. Hanotaux blamed Germany when Droz was not accepted. Germany suggested Colonel Charles Schaefer, who had served the British in Egypt and knew both Greek and Turkish. To many Europeans he appeared to be an excellent choice. Only the Ottomans seemed to object to him, because they had not been consulted, and Schaefer had been involved in anti-Ottoman 'agitations'. Somewhat affected by the Ottoman stance, and perhaps more by their view that Schaefer would be too pro-British, the Powers abandoned his candidacy. Bojedar Petrovitch of Montenegro was considered, but the Prince of Montenegro would not allow him to serve.[66]

When other possibilities had been exhausted, the Russians suggested Prince George, the second son of the King of Greece. Whether they coordinated the nomination with the British is unknown. In any case, Salisbury immediately and forcibly supported the Greek prince. British ambassadors were instructed to advance George's case. The British plan was plain: Ambassador Horace Rumbold in Vienna told both Austrian Foreign Minister Agenor Maria Goluchowski and German Ambassador Philipp Friedrich Alexander zu Eulenburg that the appointment of Prince George would be a very good thing, because it would ultimately lead to the annexation of Crete by Greece. For the British, this was the desired end.[67]

The Ottomans would never accept Prince George. They saw it as the equivalent of annexation of Crete by Greece. Indeed, it was difficult to see it in any other way. For Sultan Abdülhamid II this was a step too far. Germany and Austria joined the Ottomans in opposition. Austrian Foreign Minister Goluchowski noted, with prescience, that rewarding Greece in this way would upset the tenuous peace in the Balkans; others would want to follow the Greek example.[68]

The Russians and British put great pressure on the Ottoman Government to accept Prince George. The Russians threatened the sultan with direct annexation of Crete by Greece if the Ottomans did not agree to Prince George, because Russia would accept no other candidate and great problems would ensue. Salisbury notified the Ottoman Government that Prince George was the only possibility if troubles in Crete were to be quieted. The appointment of any Ottoman subject, he said, would lead to a further rebellion that could only be quelled with 'overwhelming military force'.[69]

The sultan pleaded personally with the British to change their minds on the appointment, calling on what he called the traditional friendship of Britain. His government, he pleaded, had cooperated in every way with the demands for Cretan autonomy, but he had to retain at least this one mark of sovereignty – naming his own officials. If Britain showed friendship in this matter, the sultan promised that he would reciprocate with a friendly policy toward England. But Salisbury had no wish for friendship with the Ottoman Empire.[70]

Despite the pressure from Britain and Russia, the Ottoman Government continued to reject Prince George. It declared that naming a foreigner as governor infringed on the rights of any sovereign to name his own officials.

The Ottomans continued to insist that the governor be an Ottoman Greek Orthodox subject.[71]

## The Withdrawal of Ottoman Troops

The Ottomans had little leverage left in the Crete crisis. Only the Germans seemed to have any sympathy for them, and the Germans felt they could do nothing about the situation. The sultan, they felt, could not win. Although the Germans claimed that their interest in the Cretan Question continued, they in fact withdrew diplomatically and militarily from Crete. The one German ship in the Crete blockade was withdrawn. Austria also washed its hands of Crete. Count Goluchowski said it had been a mistake to ever join in the international efforts there: 'Crete was an object of indifference to Austria-Hungary. The only Powers really interested in it were England and Russia.' The question was whether it was worthwhile to antagonise both Russia and Britain. Furthermore, the insistence of Russia and Britain to force their own way on Crete and in the Balkans had brought the Germans and Austrians closer together, something applauded by the German Foreign Ministry. Both Austria and Germany were willing to show their support for the Ottomans diplomatically by opposing naming Prince George as governor of Crete, but only that. The Germans nevertheless continued to declare their support to the sultan.[72]

For the Ottomans, the only bargaining point, although admittedly a weak one, was the presence of Ottoman soldiers and officials stationed at various points on Crete. Salisbury and Count Mouravieff, the Russian Foreign Minister, agreed that the sultan would have to somehow be forced to take Ottoman forces from Crete, because nothing could be done to enforce their wishes as long as the Ottomans had an armed force on the island. They agreed that all the sultan's objections would be set aside. Once the Ottoman troops and officials had been removed from the island, the British and Russians would be able to do what they wished.[73]

The British suggestion for the removal of Ottoman troops had an ominous tenor:

> With regard to the method of coercion to be applied, if necessary, Her Majesty's Government would prefer that each of the Four Powers (Russia, Britain, Italy, and France) should proceed to remove the Turkish troops from the district under its control.[74]

Any Ottoman chance to oppose the British was greatly damaged by a Muslim riot against the British, sole occupiers of the city, in Candia on 6 September 1898. Although the attacks were put down the same day by Ottoman troops, seventeen of the British occupiers were killed and approximately thirty-nine injured. Approximately 150 Muslims and 200 Christians died in intercommunal fighting and the British naval bombardment of the city, but only the Christian deaths were reported in Europe. In response, the British destroyed thirty-nine Muslim houses of those they considered to have taken part in the rioting. Seven Muslims were hanged. All the Muslims of the Canea region were disarmed, but not the Christians. The incident was used in the press and by British diplomats as evidence that the Ottomans were unable to control public safety, although Ottoman forces had been specifically excluded from doing so by the Powers, until they were needed to put down the riots.[75]

The Italians, who had previously done little concerning Crete, prepared a plan for the acceptance of the other Powers: the Ottoman forces must begin to leave Crete on 5 October 1898. All military power would be in the hands of the admirals. A collective note to that effect would be sent to the Ottomans. The French, British and Russians agreed with the Italian proposal. The Germans and Austrians did not, but were forced by the usual fears of conflict to agree not to oppose action by the other four Powers. They could only have opposed the four others militarily, an impossible option. Coercing the Ottomans was to be the work of four Powers alone.[76]

The British were insistent that Ottoman forces withdraw, which the Ottomans initially refused to do. The British told the Russians that, if the Powers did not take joint actions, the British would consider acting alone. There was, however, no need for the British to act alone. The Russians suggested the four Powers concentrate enough force to compel the Turkish soldiers into collection points, from which they would be evacuated by sea. The admirals notified Salisbury that they could expel the Ottoman soldiers by force if they were given enough resources.[77]

The British suggested on 28 April that if the Ottomans did not reduce their forces on the island and concentrate the remainder in specific places, 'they must bear the whole responsibility for any consequences which may result from their refusal'. By September the British had escalated their demands; they would now only accept the complete removal of Ottoman forces, except perhaps for a token force, not only their concentration. Then a concrete threat to the lives of the Cretan Muslims was made: the British and Russians suggested that the sultan be told that unless the Ottoman force left, '[i]t is impossible for us to guarantee the protection of the Muslims'.[78]

It was this threat to the Muslim population that finally convinced the Ottomans to remove their troops and officials. The Ottoman military governor on Crete advised the government to yield because of what the Muslims would suffer if the Ottomans did not yield. On 10 October, the Ottoman Government agreed to withdraw the troops on Crete, asking only that a small contingent remain 'for the purpose of safeguarding its sovereign rights and its flag'. The Istanbul ambassadors of Britain, Russia, Italy and France notified the Ottomans that even the retention of a small contingent was unacceptable. Ottoman troops on Crete had left by the beginning of November. The admirals complained that they took too long to do so. Not all the Ottoman troops left willingly. A number were disarmed by soldiers of the Powers and marched to ships in the harbour at gun-point.[79]

On 18 October, the admirals announced that they would become a provisional government of Crete once the Ottoman officials and soldiers had left. All administration, law and taxes would be in their hands, although domestic matters outside the occupied cities would be left to the Christian Assembly. The British Government concurred in the decision. On 4 November the admirals took over governance. Most of the small number of Ottoman officials who remained relinquished their posts. The admirals resolved to use force against any who did not comply. All Ottoman administration was removed.[80]

## Prince George, the Governor-General of Crete

Departure of Ottoman troops from Crete left the Ottomans with no power to negotiate. The Ottoman Government still continued to oppose Prince George, asking if the fact that Prince George was an enemy of the Ottomans had been forgotten. How could they accept someone who had led a fleet to Crete and disembarked Greek soldiers there, adding to the disaster on the island? The Ottomans continued to demand the right of the sultan, in consultation with the Powers, to name the governor of Crete. Ottoman protests were useless. The British, Italians and French stated that the departure of the Ottomans from Crete cleared the way for Prince George to become the governor. The Russians naturally agreed, calling for Prince George to be named immediately after the Ottomans had left. Britain and Russia had already agreed that the sultan's agreement on a governor was not necessary.[81]

On 8 November 1898, the Russians formally proposed the appointment of Prince George to be governor-general to administer Crete. Prince George was in fact to rule until 1906, when he was removed by the Cretan Assembly.[82]

Prince George notified the four Powers of his acceptance on 26 November. The embassies of the four Powers officially notified the Ottoman Minister of Foreign Affairs of the selection of Prince George on 1 December 1898. Queen Victoria conveyed to Prince George her satisfaction on his appointment. The Ottoman Government could only lodge ineffectual complaints that the rights of the sultan had been unjustly abrogated.[83]

Prince George sailed to the island of Milos on the Greek royal yacht, where he was taken aboard an honour flotilla of ships from Britain, France, Russia and Italy, which transported him to Crete. The military and naval officers of the four Powers and a military band greeted him there, along with the 21-gun salute usually reserved for heads of state. The admirals officially transferred control of Crete over to him. A parade followed.

An astute observer, the German ambassador in Istanbul Marschall, described the naming of Prince George as 'an acute, indeed immeasurable, injustice'. Because of his past activities in Crete, Prince George was known to be 'the image of disorder bordering on anarchy'. Marschall presciently predicted that the actions of the Powers in Crete would inevitably encourage rebels elsewhere and lead to bloodshed. He felt that England had achieved what it desired in Crete:

> Lord Salisbury will not be concerned that the treatment of the Cretan question will inevitably strengthen the revolutionary elements in Macedonia and encourage them to emulate them; a conflagration on the Balkan Peninsula is unlikely to be regarded as an undesirable event in London today.[84]

Britain had created Greek rule in Crete. The Cretan Greeks recognised the British efforts on their behalf. The archbishop and the Greek community communicated their thanks to Queen Victoria and the British Government. British Consul-General Biliotti reported: 'The feeling that settlement of Cretan question is due to Great Britain was manifested by acclamations of "Long Live England!" whenever British officers came in sight during Prince George's progress in town, and even later.'[85]

## Notes

1. Ayşe Nükher Adıyeke, *Osmanlı İmparatorluğu ve Girit Bunalımı (1896–1908)*, Ankara: Türk Tarih Kurumu, 2000, pp. 77–83. The Ottomans recorded population by religion. In any case, distinguishing the population of Crete by ethnicity or language would have made little sense, because there was little difference in either ethnicity or language between the two religious groups.
2. On the administration and history of the Crete Government, see Adıyeke, pp. 20–77, which is also the best description of the social and economic situation of the island. The 1868 Organic Statute, the Halepa Pact, the firman amending the Halepa Pact and the 1897 Peace Treaty are in Theodore George Tatsios, *The Megali Idea and the Greek-Turkish War of 1897: The Impact of the Cretan Problem on Greek Irredentism, 1866–1897*, Boulder, CO: East European Monographs, 1984, pp. 233–71. Sinan Kuneralp, ed., *Ottoman Diplomatic Documents on 'The Eastern Question': Crete and Turco-Greek Relations (1869–1896)*, Istanbul: Isis, 2012, pp. 442, 474 and 483.
3. Uğur Z. Peçe, 'An Island Unmixed: European Military Intervention and the Displacement of Crete's Muslims, 1896–1908', *Middle Eastern Studies*, vol. 54, no. 4 (2018), 575–91.

    Being primarily concerned with British machinations over the Cretan Question, I have not attempted to describe the particulars of the armed conflicts on the island. For detailed information see: Pınar Şenışık, *The Transformation of Ottoman Crete: Revolts, Politics, and Ideology in the Late Nineteenth Century*, London: I. B. Tauris, 2011. Mick McTiernan, 'A Very Bad Place for a Soldier: The British Involvement in the Early Stages of the European Intervention in Crete, 1897–1898', unpublished dissertation, King's College London, September, 2014. Robert Holland and Diana Markides, *The British and the Hellenes: Struggles for Mastery in the Eastern Mediterranean 1850–1960*, Oxford: Oxford University Press, 2006. Of these, Şenışık's volume is by far the most detailed and accurate.

    Published correspondence cited here, all Great Britain, Foreign Office: note that these 'blue books' were much more complete and reliable than many others, as seen below:

Turkey No. 4 (1897). *Notes Addressed by the Representatives of Great Britain, Austria-Hungary, France, Germany. Italy, and Russia, to the Turkish and Greek Governments in Regard to Crete*, London: Her Majesty's Stationery Office, March, 1897 (hereafter Turkey 4).

Turkey No. 5 (1897). *Replies of the Turkish and Greek Governments to the Notes Addressed to Them on March 2, 1897, by the Representatives of Great Britain,*

*Austria-Hungary, France, Germany, Italy, and Russia in Regard to Crete*, London: Her Majesty's Stationery Office, March, 1897 (hereafter Turkey 5).

Turkey No. 7 (1896): *Correspondence Respecting the Affairs of Crete*, London: Her Majesty's Stationery Office, 1896 (hereafter Turkey 7).

Turkey No. 9 (1897). *Reports on the Situation in Crete*, London: Her Majesty's Stationery Office, May, 1897 (hereafter Turkey 9).

Turkey No. 10 (1897), *Further Correspondence Respecting the Affairs of Crete*, London: Her Majesty's Stationery Office, July, 1897 (hereafter Turkey 10).

Turkey No. 11 (1897), *Further Correspondence Respecting the Affairs of Crete and the War between Turkey and Greece*, London: Her Majesty's Stationery Office, October, 1897 (hereafter Turkey 11).

4. FO 421/156, enclosure in Biliotti to Salisbury, 17 October 1896. FO 195/1960, 'Reconnaissance of Officers in the Districts around Candia to Ascertain the Existing State of the Moslem Property in the Interior', 20 August 1897. There are too many archival references on the Cretan warfare to describe here. See Turkey, 7, 9, 10 and 11 for reports of fighting, massacres and migration. Consul-General Biliotti's reports were fairly even-handed.

Examples, all in FO 421/156: Biliotti to Salisbury, 25 September, 3 October, 10 October, 17 October and 26 October 1896. Biliotti's reports did not spare either Muslims or Christians. He took pains to correct false or misleading reports, such as one on the supposed Muslim declaration of Holy War. (FO 421/156, Biliotti to Salisbury, Canea, 19 November 1896.) On Biliotti, see David Barchard, 'The Fearless and Self-Reliant Servant. The Life and Career of Sir Alfred Biliotti (1833–1915), an Italian Levantine in British Service', *Studi Micenei ed Egeo-Anatolici*, 48 (2006), pp. 5–53, especially pp. 22–50, on Biliotti's service in Crete.

Col. Chermside provided a fairly accurate list (because it was based on refugee and rations records) of the population of Candia in April 1897: Moslem Civilians 49,500, Greek Civilians 480, Turkish Garrison 3,432, Allied Garrison 1,343, Total 54,755. Of the Muslims, 31,900 were refugees from other parts of Crete. A total of 39,900 were receiving assistance (flour) from the Ottoman Government. (Chermside to Salisbury, Candia, 17 April 1897, in Turkey 9, pp. 39–40.)

Most of the extensive reports sent by the British ambassador in Istanbul, Philip Currie, have not been cited here. He could only be trusted as a source for British official positions when he was literally presenting orders from London. His valuable communications were mainly direct transmissions of reports from others, included unaltered, such as dispatches from Salisbury or the admirals. Those have been used considerably here. Currie's reports to London were often strangely at odds with the positions of the British Government, and his reports on the positions of his fellow Great Power ambassadors was often doubtful. For example, Currie wrote on 2 April 1897, that all the Powers' ambassadors in Istanbul agreed with him that Prince George must be appointed as governor of Crete. This was not at all the position of some of the Powers at the time. Were the ambassadors really opposing their own governments, or was Currie misrepresenting their statements? (FO 421/159, Currie to Salisbury, Constantinople, 2 April 1897.)

Currie's reports to London were often based on rumours for which he did not give sources. He reported what he could not know, such as secret meetings of the sultan. Currie believed the stories of Ottoman governmental manoeuvring told to him by those only described as 'my informants'. These included unbelievable and contradictory accounts of the sultan's intentions and cabinet meetings. At one point, Currie would state that the sultan was all-powerful, then later he would state that the sultan was forced to give way to the wishes of his ministers. On 14 April 1897, for example, Currie alleged that the sultan was in direct communication with the military forces, directing them and denying his ministers any information, causing 'great discontent'. Later the same day he telegraphed that the Council of Ministers was fully in charge of the Ottoman campaign. In some messages, Currie stated that the sultan was against the war, in others the sultan was leading the attack. (Among others in FO 421/159, see two communications in Currie to Salisbury, Constantinople, 14 April 1897, and Currie to Salisbury, Constantinople, 13 May 1897.)

5. See, for example, Biliotti to Salisbury, Canea, 21, 28 and 30 July 1896, in *Turkey 7*, pp. 211, 226 and 237. The Ottomans reported many incursions from Greece. These seem to have been accurate. For example, the Ottoman report of two ships delivering troops and munitions in August 1896 were substantiated by reports from the British ambassador in Athens. (Anathopoulo to Salisbury, London, 24 July, 8, 19 August 1896, in Turkey 7, pp. 16, 272 and 306. Egerton to Salisbury, Athens, 15 August 1896, in Turkey 7, pp. 305–6.)

6. Thomas W. Gallant, *The Edinburgh History of the Greeks, 1768–1913: The Long Nineteenth Century*, Edinburgh: Edinburgh University Press, 2015, p. 291.

7. Egerton to Salisbury, Athens, 12 June, 23, 28 July 1896, in Turkey, No. 7, pp. 121, 227–8 and 255. Herbert to Salisbury, Constantinople, 17 August 1896, in Turkey 7, p. 297. Biliotti to Salisbury, 17 August 1896, in Turkey 7, pp. 296–7. When tasked with the arrival of munitions from Greece, the Greek consul-general admitted it and said that they were necessary for Christian self-defence. (Egerton to Salisbury, Athens, 22 July 1896, in Turkey 7, p. 227.)

8. Herbert to Salisbury, Constantinople, 28 and 29 May 1896, in Turkey 7, pp. 87, 88 and 101. The British paid close attention to the troops the Ottomans sent to Crete from various parts of the Empire. See Herbert to Salisbury, Constantinople, 26 May, 1, 7 June 1896, in Turkey 7, pp. 87, 95, 100. Biliotti to Salisbury, Canea, 30 May 1896, 2, 4 June, 14 August 1896, in Turkey 7, pp. 91, 96, 99, 291.
9. Salisbury to Monson, Foreign Office, 19 June 1896, in Turkey 7, p. 126. Herbert to Salisbury, Constantinople, 21 June 1896, in Turkey 7, p. 128. Anthopoulo to Salisbury, London, 4 July 1896, in Turkey 7, pp. 161–2. Herbert to Salisbury, 4 July 1896, in Turkey 7, pp. 178–9. Herbert to Salisbury, 19 July 1896, in Turkey 7, pp. 195–6. Anthopoulo to Salisbury, London, 5 August 1896, in Turkey 7, pp. 263–4. Herbert to Salisbury, Constantinople, 21 August 1896, in Turkey 7, p. 301.
10. 'Dispositions que les Représentants des Puissances considèrent comme pouvant être proposées à la Porte', enclosure in Herbert to Salisbury, Therapia, 29 August 1896 in Turkey 7, pp. 343–6.
11. Herbert to Salisbury, Constantinople, 28 August 1896, in Turkey 7, pp. 334–5. Biliotti to Salisbury, Canea, 4 September 1896, in Turkey 7, p. 342. Salisbury to Herbert, Foreign Office, 6 September 1896, in Turkey 7, p. 342.
12. Biliotti to Salisbury, 16 September, 23 September, 9 October and 3 December 1896, in Turkey 8, pp. 10, 13, 49–50 and 114–15. FO 78/4841, Harris to Admiralty, 25 February 1897.
13. FO 421/158, 'Disposition of British Ships in Cretan Waters', 'Statement of Foreign Ships in Cretan Waters' and 'Minutes of Meeting of the Admirals' of the International Squadron', 4 February 1897, enclosure in Admiralty to Foreign Office, enclosures in Admiralty to Foreign Office, 8 March 1897.
14. FO 421/157, Salisbury initially approved the occupation of Canea and other towns and opposition to all Greek aggression. (Salisbury to Monson, Foreign Office, 15 February 1897; Sanderson to Admiralty, Foreign Office, 15 February 1897; Salisbury to Monson, Foreign Office, 16 February 1897, two messages). The Ottoman Government approved of the fleet occupying places, provisionally, as the admirals deemed necessary. (FO 421/157, Currie to Salisbury, Constantinople, 15 February 1897.) When the German *Kaiserin Augusta* arrived on 21 February, she landed an additional fifty men at Canea. Minutes of the Admirals Council are in FO 195/2003 and FO 78/4841–4837.
15. On the naval actions to bombard the insurgents and Greek soldiers, see the reports of Admiral Harris in FO 78/4841. The admirals' efforts and their problems are recorded in FO 421/156. See, for example, FO 521/156, Currie to Salisbury,

Constantinople, 26 November 1896 and enclosures, and 10 December 1896 and enclosure.

16. 'The Ministry of War to the Commander of the Body of Occupation of Crete, Colonel of Infantry, Timoleon Vassos', Athens, 13 February 1897, enclosure in Egerton to Salisbury, Athens, 16 February 1897, in Turkey 11, pp. 58–9 and p. 42. Biliotti to Salisbury, Canea, 9 and 11 February 1897, in Turkey 10, pp. 58 and 60. Vassos to Vice-Admiral Caneraro, Camp d'Atikianou, 18 (30) March 1897, enclosure in Harris to Hopkins, Suda Bay, 10 April 1897, in Turkey 9, p. 35.

    The actual numbers of Greek soldiers in the invasion force were subject to exaggeration: Admiral Harris estimated 5,000. Consul-General Biliotti more reasonably estimated 1,500 – 2,000, with nine mountain guns (small mobile cannons). (Harris to Admiralty, Canea, 17 February 1897, in Turkey 10, p. 80. Biliotti to Salisbury, Canea, 25 February 1897, in Turkey 10, p. 94) The British Military Intelligence report of 30 March 1897 was more reliable: Vassos had landed with 1,350 men, two Krupp 9-pounders, four mountain guns and three field guns.

    The insurgents had 7,500 with three guns. The Ottoman forces at the beginning of 1897 were 18,290. The Allies had landed 3,600. (FO 78/4843, Capt. H. A. Lawrence to War Office, 31 March 1897.)

17. FO 421/157, Lascelles to Salisbury, Berlin, 14 February 1897; Lascelles to Salisbury, Berlin, 14 February 1897; Monson to Salisbury, Paris, 15 February 1897; Monson to Salisbury, Paris, 14 and 15 February 1897. Duplicate dates here specify separate communications, which are only indicated if necessary. Note that many of the communications were sent to a number of ambassadors in the same form, and only one is listed in these notes.

18. German Chancellor von Hohenlohe to the German ambassadors in London, Vienna, Rome, Paris and St Petersburg, Berlin, 17 February 1897, in E. T. S. Dugdale, editor and translator, *German Diplomatic Documents 1871–1914*, vol. 2, New York and London: Harper, 1929 (hereafter GDD ii), pp. 452–3. FO 421/157, Lascelles to Salisbury, Berlin, 17, 18 and 19 February 1897; Monson to Salisbury, Paris, 16 February 1897. See also FO 421/157, Lascelles to Salisbury, Berlin, 18 February 1897.

19. FO 421/157, Salisbury to Lascelles, Foreign Office, 17 February 1897; Salisbury to Ford, Foreign Office, 19 February 1987; Rumbold to Salisbury, Vienna, 18 February 1897. See also Hatzfeldt to Foreign Office, London, 17 February 1897, in GP 12/2, pp. 331–3. Salisbury to Monson, Foreign Office, 29 July 1896, in Turkey 7, p. 230. Salisbury to Gosselin, Foreign Office, 29 July 1896, in Turkey 7, p. 231.

20. German ambassador in London Hatzfeldt remarked:

> Even today, the language used by the Prime Minister left me in no doubt that he is sticking to his fundamental aversion to Turkish rule and that he would not complain if it could be put to an end in Crete. Salisbury told Hatzfeldt that he knew that the loss of Crete might lead to the overthrow of the sultan, which he felt would be 'no particular misfortune'.

Hatzfeldt felt that Salisbury had always hated Abdülhamid II. (Hatzfeldt to Hohenlohe, London, 1 and 25 July 1896, in GP 12/1, pp. 170–1 and 184–7.)

21. FO 421/157, O'Conor to Salisbury, St Petersburgh, 19 February 1897 (O'Conor had relieved Currie as ambassador at Istanbul); Salisbury to O'Conor, Foreign Office, 22 February 1897; Lascelles to Salisbury, Berlin, 17 February 1897.
22. FO 421/157, Salisbury to Monson, Foreign Office, 24 February 1897.
23. FO 421/157, Lascelles to Salisbury, Berlin, 25 February 1897; Rumbold to Salisbury, Vienna, 25 February 1897; Ford to Salisbury, Rome, 26 February 1897; O'Conor to Salisbury, St Petersburgh, 25 February 1897; Salisbury to Lascelles, Foreign Office, 26 February 1897. Salisbury notified the Ottoman Government that, in view of the declaration of autonomy, the Ottomans and Greeks would have to withdraw all their troops from Crete. The notification stated that Crete would not be annexed by Greece 'in the present circumstances'. (Salisbury to Curry, Foreign Office, 27 February 1897, in Turkey 11, p. 87. Currie to Salisbury, Constantinople, 27 February 1897, in Turkey 11, pp. 87–8.)
24. FO 421/157, Gosselin to Salisbury, Paris, 26 February 1897; Salisbury to Currie, Foreign Office, 26 February 1897. FO 424/158, Rumbold to Salisbury, 24 February 1897. FO 424/158, Gosselin to Salisbury, Paris, 1 March 1897.
25. Turkey 4. The Ottomans were told the Powers expected Ottoman forces to be progressively evacuated, not all at the same time as the Greeks. See also FO 421/158, Salisbury to Monson, Foreign Office, 3 March 1897.
26. Turkey 5.
27. FO 421/158, Monson to Salisbury, Paris, 11 March 1897; Lascelles to Salisbury, 12 March 1897. FO 421/158, Salisbury to O'Conor, Foreign Office, 9 March 1897. Salisbury to O'Conor, Foreign Office, 16 March 1897, in Turkey 11, pp. 131–2. Ford to Salisbury, Rome, 17 March 1897, in Turkey 11, pp. 136–7. Salisbury to Ford, Foreign Office, 17 March 1897, in Turkey 11, p. 137. Rumbold to Salisbury, Vienna, 19 March 1897, in Turkey 11, p. 152.
28. Biliotti to Salisbury, Canea, 19 March 1897, in Turkey 10, p. 134. See also Salisbury to Biliotti, Foreign Office, 13 March 1897, in Turkey 10, p. 118. FO 195/2003, Greek Assembly Committee to 14 August 1897, and Savvakis

(Assembly President) to Chermside, attachments in Chermside to Harris, Candia, 14 August and 1 September 1897; Chermside to Harris, Candia, 15 and 16 August, enclosures. FO 78/4847, enclosures in Chermside to Harris, Candia, 1 September 1897.

29. FO 421/158, Biliotti to Salisbury, Canea, 11 March 1897. See the numerous reports of attacks on Muslims in FO 421/157 and 158. The numerous reports of British admirals made it plain that it was the Muslims that were being attacked. (CAB 37/44/12, 'Telegrams from and to Commander-in-chief, Mediterranean, and Rear-Admiral, Second in Command, in Cretan Waters', 1897, and CAB 37/44/13, 'Crete', 1897.

30. FO 421/159, Egerton to Salisbury, Athens, 17 March 1897; Admiralty to Harris, 26 March 1897. FO 421/158, Salisbury to O'Conor, Foreign Office, 9 March 1897; Lascelles to Salisbury, Berlin, 12, 13 and 17 March 1897; Rumbold to Salisbury, Vienna, 17 March 1897; Admiralty to Foreign Office, 13 March 1897; Ford to Salisbury, Rome, 11 March 1897. Harris to Admiralty, Suda, 5 April 1897, in Turkey 11, p. 175. Lascelles to Salisbury, Berlin, 30 March 1897, in Turkey 11, p. 163. Monson to Salisbury, Paris, 3 April 1897, in Turkey 11, pp. 170 and 173 (two communications). Radolin to Foreign Office, St Petersburg, 5 July 1896, in GP 12/1, pp. 174–5.

    Salisbury stated that Britain would agree to a blockade of Piraeus only if the other Powers agreed to the plan to send 10,000 troops to Crete (which the others would never do). Otherwise, he would only support a blockade of Crete. (Monson to Salisbury, Paris, 17 March 1897, enclosure, in Turkey 11, pp. 138–9.)

31. The British had the most powerful naval force in the Eastern Mediterranean, with five battleships in Cretan waters. The Russians were second in power, and they proved willing to cooperate with the British. Those who most wanted the blockade of Greek ports, the Germans and Austrians, had much more limited forces. (FO 421/158, 'Disposition of British Ships in Cretan Waters' and 'Statement of Foreign Ships in Cretan Waters' and 'Minutes of Meeting of the Admirals of the International Squadron', 4 February 1897, enclosure in Admiralty to Foreign Office, enclosures in Admiralty to Foreign Office, 8 March 1897. The Kaiser complained bitterly that the Germans did not have the ships themselves to enforce the blockade. (von Marschall to Hatzfeldt, Berlin, 24 March 1897, in GDD ii, pp. 456–7.) He was later to attempt to address the deficiency in the German navy.

32. FO 421/158, Rumbold to Salisbury, Vienna, 3 March 1897; 'Minutes of Meeting of the Admirals of the International Squadron', 4 February 1897, enclosure

in Admiralty to Foreign Office, 8 March 1897. FO 78/4843, 'March 18, 1897, To Admiralty and Commander-in-Chief'. In 'Copies of Telegrams'.

33. FO 421/158, Rumbold to Salisbury, Vienna, 22 March 1897; Mouvravieff to de Staal, St Petersburgh, 17 March 1897; O'Conor to Salisbury, St Petersburgh, 24 March 1897. The Italians stated that they would not cooperate with the blockade if Britain did not participate. On the German view, see von Marschall to Hatzfeldt, Berlin, 24 March 1897, in GDD ii, pp. 456–7. See also Hatzfeldt to Foreign Office, London, 4 August 1896, in GP 12/1, pp. 193–4, in which Salisbury stated that the British public and parliament were completely against a blockade.

(FO 424/158, Ford to Salisbury, Rome, 24 March 1897.) FO 421/158, O'Conor to Salisbury, St Petersburgh, 17 March 1897. See also FO 421/158, Monson to Salisbury, Paris, 24 March 1897; 'Verbal Communication made by Russian Ambassador', 27 March 1897, relaying a message from the Russian Government.

34. FO 421/158, O'Conor to Salisbury, St Petersburgh, 20 March 1897; Lascelles to Salisbury, Berlin, 30 March 1897.

35. FO 421/157, Lascelles to Salisbury, Berlin, 16 February 1897; Ford to Salisbury, Rome, 16 February 1897; Rumbold to Salisbury, Vienna, 26 February 1897; Salisbury to Monson, Foreign Office, 24 February 1897; Salisbury to Lascelles, Foreign Office, 24 February 1897.

36. FO 421/157, Lascelles to Salisbury, Berlin, 16 February 1897. (The Kaiser was citing the *Daily Chronicle*.) See also Hatzfeldt to Foreign Office, London, 8 March 1897, in GDD ii, p. 454.

37. There are far too many articles for consideration in a study on politics and diplomacy, not journalism. Some examples of what is described here: 'Massacres of Christians in Crete', *The Times*, 26 May 1896, p. 3; 'The Situation in Crete', *The Times*, 10 August 1896, p. 5; 'The Situation in Crete', *The Times*, 6 June 1896, p. 9; 'Massacres of Christians in Crete', 26 May 1896, p. 3. 'The Revolt in Crete: Riot at Heraklion', *Daily News*, 5 August 1896, p. 3; 'The Crisis in Crete', *Daily News*, 6 August 1896, p. 5. 'The Cretan Horrors: Six More Villages Destroyed', *Daily News*, 12 August 1896, p. 5. 'Turkish Atrocities in Crete', *Daily Telegraph*, 7 August 1896, p. 5. 'The Cretan Rising: Turkish Excesses', *Daily Telegraph*, 8 August 1896, p. 7. 'Crisis in Crete: Fresh Turkish Outrages', *Daily Telegraph*, 11 August 1896, p. 7. 'Crisis in Crete: More Turkish Atrocities', *Daily Telegraph*, 13 August 1896, p. 7. 'The Cretan Question', *Evening Standard*, 24 August 1896, p. 5. In one *The Times*' piece it was alleged that it was the Turks, not the Greeks, who had burned Muslim villages. ('The Situation in Crete', *The Times*, 3 August 1896, p. 5.)

Many of the reports in these newspapers came from the Reuters News Agency. They were also featured in provincial British newspapers, in the colonies and in America. Interestingly, the Ottomans, stung by press articles on Crete, paid the Reuters Agency to support a reporter who sent articles from Crete. Reuters took the money, then produced anti-Ottoman articles. (Servet Yanatma, 'The International News Agencies in the Ottoman Empire (1854–1908)', unpublished PhD dissertation, Middle East Technical University, Ankara: 2015, pp. 138–9.)

The most telling analyses were to be found in the *Pall Mall Gazette*, which reported that the newspapers had no idea what was actually transpiring in Crete or in the European Government deliberations. (See, for example, 'Occasional Notes', 14 August 1896, p. 2, 17 August 1896, p. 2 and 27 November 1896, p. 2.)

38. 'The Cretan Question', *The Times*, 11 August 1896, p. 10; 12 August 1896, p. 13; 25 August 1896, p. 10. 'The Anarchy in Crete', *Daily News*, 8 August 1896, p. 4. 'The Turk in Crete', *Daily News*, 20 August 1896, p. 4. 'Rebellion in Crete', *Daily Telegraph*, 5 August 1896.
39. See, for example, 'The Situation in Crete', *The Times*, 6 June 1896, p. 9. 'The Cretan Question', *The Times*, 18 August 1896, p. 3; 'The Powers and Crete', *The Times*, 14 August 1896, p. 3. Rear-Admiral Harris noted: 'No Greek reports are reliable. "Daily News" correspondent is a Philo-Greek, and "Times" correspondent was then a Greek named Kalopothakis.' FO 421/159, Harris to Admiralty, Suda, Canea, 1 March 1897.
40. 'London, Monday, August 3', *Daily News*, 3 August 1896, p. 4.
41. Papers of the Greek Committee. (New Series, 1897.) No. I: Crete and Greece, London, 1897, pp. 3–5. On the founding and earlier activities of the Greek Committee, see Pandeleimon Hionidis, 'Philhellenism and Party Politics in Victorian Britain: The Greek Committee of 1879–1881', *The Historical Review* (Greece), vol. 14 (2017), pp. 141–76.
42. All in *The Times*: 'The Radicals and Greece', 8 March 1897, p. 12. 'Sir W. Harcourt in Stepney', 5 March 1897, p. 11. 'The Radicals and Greece', 6 March 1897, p. 12. 'Mr. Asquith at Bradford', 2 March 1897, p. 11. 'Sir W. Harcourt at Norwich', 18 March 1897, p. 6. 'The Cretan Question', 25 March 1897, p. 6. I have only cited examples as described in detail in *The Times* in March 1897. There seemed no need for more. Some articles covered more than one meeting.
43. 'Class II. Crete', *Hansard*, House of Commons Debate, 7 May 1897, vol. 49, cc. 18–83. In the parliament elected in 1895, the Conservatives and their Liberal Unionist allies took 61 per cent of the seats.

44. See Gallant, pp. 294–9, Şenışık, pp. 160–1 and 171–2. The Ethnike Hetairia disclaimed responsibility for everything, including its actions in Crete (Şenışık, pp. 175–6).
45. FO 421/158. O'Conor to Salisbury, St Petersburgh, 20 and 24 March 1897; Rumbold to Salisbury, Vienna, 25 March 1897; Salisbury to Monson, Foreign Office, 23 March 1897; Rumbold to Salisbury, Vienna, 24 March 1897; Lascelles to Salisbury, Berlin, 26 March 1897.
46. FO 421/159, Egerton to Salisbury, Athens, 9 April 1897; Currie to Salisbury, Constantinople, 10 April 1897; Anthopoulo Pasha to Foreign Office, 17 April 1897; Skousès to Métaxas (Communicated by M. Métaxas), London, 17 April 1897; Currie to Salisbury, Constantinople, 17 April 1897; Currie to Salisbury, Pera, 17 April 1897; Anthopoulo Pasha to Foreign Office, 18 April 1897. The Greek Government contended that the Ottomans struck first, which was at odds with all other reports. (FO 421/159, Métaxas to Foreign Office, London, 20 April 1897). There are numerous reports on these initial Greek incursions in FO 421/159. Earlier, the Ottoman ambassador in London reported to the Foreign Office on 27 March that Greek forces had fired cannon shells into the tents of the Ottoman garrison at Fokonaria. (FO 421/158, Anthopoulo Pasha to Foreign Office, 27 March 1897).
47. The events of the war are not described here. See the history of the events of the war in Thessaly in FO 421/161, Merlin to Masse, Volo, 31 May 1897, enclosure in Egerton to Salisbury, Athens, 7 June 1897.
48. FO 421/160, Currie to Salisbury, Constantinople, 19 May 1897; enclosures in Currie to Salisbury, Constantinople, 24 May 1897.
49. Biliotti to Salisbury, 26 May 1897, in Turkey 11, p. 293. FO 78/4845, Harris to Hopkins, Suda, 23 May 1897. FO 78/4846, Harris to Hopkins, Suda, 7 June 1897. FO 78/4847 (Harris) 'To Admiralty', 12 September 1897; FO 78/4847, Harris to Hopkins, Suda, 17 September 1897. See the numerous examples of continuing troubles in FO 78/4846 and 4847.
50. Biliotti to Salisbury, Canea, 5 April 1897, in Turkey 10, p. 174. Harris to Admiralty, Suda, 9 April 1897, p. 176.
51. FO 141/160, Currie to Salisbury, Constantinople, 14 May 1897.
52. FO 421/160, Salisbury to Currie, Foreign Office, 13 May 1897; Salisbury to Lascelles, Foreign Office, 18 May 1897. Salisbury notified the Queen of this policy. (CAB 4/24, Salisbury to the Queen, 13 May 1897.
53. FO 421/160, Currie to Salisbury, Constantinople, 15, 16, 17 and 24 May 1897; Milbanks to Salisbury, Vienna, 18 May 1897; Egerton to Salisbury, Athens,

20 May 1897; Lascelles to Salisbury, Berlin, 25 May 1897; Currie to Salisbury, Constantinople, 24 and 29 May 1897.
54. FO 421/161, Currie to Salisbury, Constantinople, 12 June 1897 and enclosures.
55. FO 421/160/ Salisbury to O'Conor, Foreign Office, 15 May 1897. FO 421/162, Mouravieff to de Stall (communicated by M. de Stall), St Petersburgh, 21 July 1897. FO 421/161, Currie to Salisbury, Constantinople, 12 June 1897. FO 421/162, Currie to Salisbury, Constantinople, 15 July 1897; Currie to Salisbury, Constantinople, 15, 22 and 25 July 1897.
56. FO 421/160, Salisbury to Lascelles, Foreign Office, 18 May 1897; FO 421/162, Monson to Salisbury, Paris, 21 July 1897.
57. FO 421/163, Currie to Salisbury, Constantinople, 10 and 11 August 1897; Salisbury to Currie, Foreign Office, 15 August 1897; Salisbury to O'Conor, Foreign Office, 17 August 1897.
58. FO 421/163, O'Conor to Salisbury, St Petersburgh, 16 August 1897; Monson to Salisbury, Paris, 15 and 16 August 1897; Salisbury to Rumbold, Foreign Office, 16 August 1897; Milbanks to Salisbury, Vienna, 17 August 1897; Rumbold to Salisbury, Vienna, 20 August 1897. (There are multiple communications to and from these ambassadors on these dates.) Both Austria and Russia stated that the mistrust of Britain would be felt by 'some countries', but not them.
59. Salisbury's acceptance: FO 421/163, Salisbury to Monson, Foreign Office, 24 August 1897; Salisbury to Egerton, Foreign Office, 26 August 1897; Egerton to Salisbury, Athens, 28 August 1897. There are many documents on Salisbury's plans and the Powers' rejoinders in FO 421/163, too many to cite here. See, for example, 'Aide Mémoire Communicated by M. Geoffrey', Paris, 24 August 1897; Salisbury to Monson, Foreign Office, 24 August 1897; Salisbury to Monson, Foreign Office, 30 August 1897. The payments were fixed on 27 April 1898 by a European Commission in Paris. The final payments were contingent on the Ottoman evacuation of Thessaly. The British Treasury approved. (FO 421/171, Low to Gosselin, Paris, 27 April 1898; Treasury to Foreign Office, Treasury Chambers, 28 April 1898.) Various disagreements are in FO 421/171.
60. See the remarks of Count Goluchowski in FO 421/160, Rumbold to Salisbury, Vienna, 10 and 12 May 1897. The ambassadors of Russia, Britain, Italy and France notified the Ottomans of this in late May 1897. (FO 421/160, 'Draft of Memorandum' enclosure in Currie to Salisbury, Constantinople, 24 May 1897.)
61. FO 421/161, O'Conor to Salisbury, St Petersburgh, 16 June 1897. See also, Hohenlohe to Kaiser Wilhelm II, Berlin, 12 June 1897, and Holstein to Saurma, Berlin, 12 July 1897, in GP 12/2, pp. 423–4 and 427–9.

62. FO 424/160, Salisbury to Currie, Foreign Office, 13 May 1897. Stating the British position, Ambassador Lascelles in Berlin had told the German Foreign Minister, Adolf Hermann Freiherr Marschall von Bieberstein (Marschall): 'I could not believe that any civilized Power could consent, after having occupied Crete, to give it back to the Turkish Government.' (FO 421/157, Lascelles to Salisbury, Berlin, 19 February 1897.) Salisbury announced in the House of Lords that the Powers had decided that 'Greek communities which had not been under Turkish rule were not to be placed under Turkish rule.' Cited 'international arrangements (that is, the Treaty of Berlin.)' ('Turkey and Greece', House of Lords Debate, 2 August 1897, *Hansard*, vol. 52, cc. 49–53).
63. The various familial connections between the Greek and Russian royal families are documented in Coryne Hall, *Little Mother of Russia: A Biography of the Empress Marie Feodorovna (1847–1928)*, New York and London: Holmes and Meier, 2001.
64. Hall, pp. 182–3. Austrian Foreign Minister Goluchowski felt that the Russian proposal of Prince George had been initiated by the Russian Empress Dowager. (FO 421/168, Rumbold to Salisbury, Vienna, 5 January 1898.) On 25 April 1897, Queen Victoria telegraphed the Tsar. She asked him 'to agree to Lord Salisbury's proposal for joint action with you and France'. (Quoted in Friedrich von Holstein, *The Holstein Papers: Volume 4, Correspondence 1897–1909: The Memoirs, Diaries and Correspondence of Friedrich Von Holstein 1837–1909*, Cambridge: Cambridge University Press, 1963, p. 35.) The Russians brought the Queen's letter to the attention of the Germans (von Marschall to Tschirschev, Berlin, 31 May 1897, in GDD ii, p. 459.) See also, George Earle Buckle, ed., *The Letters of Queen Victoria*, vol. 4, London: John Murray, 1932, pp. 150–61. On British–Russian cooperation, see, for example: FO 421/ 178, Scott to Salisbury, St Petersburgh, 6 October 1898. See also George J. Marcopoulos, 'The Selection of Prince George of Greece as High Commissioner in Crete', *Balkan Studies*, vol. 10, no. 2 (1969), pp. 336–50. See also Radolin to Foreign Office, St Petersburg, 3 July 1896, in GP 12/1, p. 172.
65. FO 421/164, enclosure in Currie to Salisbury, Constantinople, 8 September 1897. FO 421/166, Gosselin to Salisbury, Paris, 5 November 1897; Salisbury to Currie, Foreign Office, 28 and 30 November 1897. The Ottoman officials were suggested as possibilities, surprisingly, by the Russians, almost surely with the knowledge that they would be rejected. (FO 421/166, Currie to Salisbury, Constantinople, 27 November 1897.)
66. FO 421/165, Monson to Salisbury, Paris, 2, 3 and 9 October and 29 November 1897; Milbanks to Salisbury, Vienna, 13 October 1897. Milbanks to

Salisbury, Vienna, 14 and 26 October 1897; Salisbury to Gosselin, Foreign Office, 30 October 1897. FO 421/166, Lascelles to Salisbury, Berlin, 29 October 1897; Salisbury to Currie, Foreign Office, 9 November 1897. FO 421/167, St John to Salisbury, Berne, 29 November 1897. The Germans said they only 'approved' the candidatures of Schaefer and Petrovich Bülow to Hatzfeldt, Berlin, 31 January 1898, in GP 12/2, p. 475.)

Salisbury either was confused as to his own intentions or was playing a diplomatic game: the British ambassador told Count Goluchowski of Austria that 'there was no question of the election of Prince George of Greece'. (FO 421/160, Rumbold to Salisbury, Vienna, May 6, 1897.) Salisbury stated that he would prefer a French, Austrian or Italian military officer for a short-term appointment as governor. (FO 421/160, Salisbury to Monson, Foreign Office, 10 May 1897.)

67. FO 421/167, Salisbury to Goschen, Foreign Office, 29 December 1897; Salisbury to Currie, Foreign Office, 31 December 1897. Zu Eulenburg to von Hohenlohe, Vienna, 2 January 1898, in GDD ii, p. 463. See also Salisbury to Goschen, Foreign Office, 31 December 1897. FO 421/168, Rumbold to Salisbury, Vienna, 5 January 1898. Hanotaux of France also accepted Prince George. (FO 421/167, Gosselin to Salisbury, Paris, 30 December 1897.) Marschall to Foreign Office, Pera, 26 January 1898, in GP 12/2, p. 474. The candidacy of Prince George was met with 'universal satisfaction' in Athens. (FO 421/167, Egerton to Salisbury, Athens, 31 December 1897.) Ambassador Currie was instructed to notify the sultan of Britain's support of Prince George. (FO 421/168, Salisbury to Goschen, Foreign Office, 17 January 1898; Salisbury to Currie, Foreign Office, 17 January 1898.)

68. FO 241/167, Currie to Salisbury, Constantinople, 24 December 1897; Rumbold to Salisbury, Vienna, 30 December 1897; Lascelles to Salisbury, Berlin, 30 December 1897. FO 421/168, Gosselin to Salisbury, Paris, 5 January 1898; Rumbold to Salisbury, Vienna, 3 and 5 January 1898; Currie to Salisbury, Constantinople, 29 January 1898.

69. FO 421/168, O'Conor to Salisbury, St Petersburgh, 19 January 1898; Currie to Salisbury, Constantinople, 22 January 1898; Salisbury to Currie, Foreign Office, 23 January 1898; Currie to Salisbury, Constantinople, 13 and 15 January 1898. FO 421/175, Goschen to Salisbury, St Petersburgh, 10 August 1898. FO 421/171, Salisbury to Currie, Foreign Office, 7 April 1898. German Ambassador Hatzfeldt in London felt that Salisbury did not particularly care for Prince George, but was convinced that local sentiment in Britain forced his hand. (Hatzfeldt to Foreign Office. London, 2 February 1898, and Radolin to Hohenlohe, St Petersburg, 13 March 1898, in GP 12/2, pp. 489–91.)

The French ambassador advised the sultan to himself put forward the name of Prince George, 'on the grounds that otherwise the appointment may be imposed on him, or the Prince may be invested with the Governorship without the consent of Turkey'. (FO 421/168. Currie to Salisbury, Constantinople, 28 January 1898.)

70. FO 421/173, 'Memorandum by Mr. Block', 30 May 1898, in de Bunsen to Salisbury, Constantinople, 31 May 1898.
71. FO 421/171, Tewfik Pasha to Anthopoulo Pasha (communicated by Anthopoulo Pasha, 13 April). FO 421/176, Tewfik Pasha to Anthopoulo Pasha (communicated by Anthopoulo Pasha, 13 September), Constantinople, 11 September 1898. Karatheodori had previously been suggested by the Ottoman Government, but rejected by the British.
72. FO 421/176, Rumbold to Salisbury, Vienna, 8 and 23 September 1898. Tschirsky to von Hohehlohe, St Petersburg, 1 May 1897, von Marschall to Hatzfeldt, Berlin, 24 March 1897, and von Holstein to von Saurma, Berlin, 12 July 1897, in GDD ii, pp. 456–62. Bülow to Marschall, Berlin, 15 March 1898, in GP 12/2, p. 494.
73. FO 421/171, Captain Craig to Admiralty, Suda Bey, 20 April 1898; O'Conor to Salisbury, St Petersburgh, 27 April 1898. FO 421/172, Chermside to Salisbury, Canea, 6 May 1898. FO 241/176, Scott to Salisbury, 21 September 1898.
74. FO 421/176, Salisbury to O'Conor, Foreign Office, 25 September 1898.
75. FO 421/178, Admiralty to Foreign Office, 17 December 1898, and enclosures. Şenışık, pp. 215–19. McTiernan, pp. 30–6.
76. FO 421/176, Salisbury to Bonham, Foreign Office, 14 and 22 September 1898.
77. FO 421/176, Salisbury to Scott, Foreign Office, 12 September 1898. FO 421/178, Salisbury to Scott, Foreign Office, 1 October 1898; Salisbury to Blunt, Foreign Office, 2 October 1898.
78. FO 421/171, Salisbury to Gosselin, Foreign Office, 28 April 1898. FO 421/176. Scott to Salisbury, St Petersburgh, 19 September 1898. See also, FO 421/176, Salisbury to Scott, Foreign Office, 17 September 1898.
79. FO 421/176, Biliotti to Salisbury, Candia, 30 September 1898. FO 421/178, O'Conor to Salisbury, Constantinople, 10 and 12 October 1898. Biliotti to Salisbury, Canea, 17 October 1898. There are numerous documents in FO 241/178 on the four Powers agreement with the ambassadors' statement. FO 421/178, Biliotti to Salisbury, Canea, 28 October 1898; Admiralty to Foreign Office, 5 November 1898 and enclosure. The British had demanded that the troops leave by 18 October, seven days after the Ottoman acceptance, a ridiculously short time.

80. FO 421/178, Biliotti to Salisbury, Canea, 18 October 1898; Salisbury to Monson, Foreign Office, 18 October 1898; Noel to Admiralty, Suda, 30 October 1898.
81. FO 421/178, 'Note Verbale', enclosure in O'Conor to Salisbury, Constantinople, 31 October 1898; Tewfik Pasha to Anthopoulo Pasha, enclosure in Anthopoulo to Salisbury, London, 5 November 1898; Monson to Salisbury, Paris, 21 October 1898; Scott to Salisbury, St Petersburgh, 26 October 1898; Currie to Salisbury, Rome, 27 October 1898. FO 421/166, Goschen to Salisbury, St Petersburgh, 5 November 1897. The Russians continued to attempt to convince the sultan to accept Prince George, but he would not yield. (FO 421/178, O'Conor to Salisbury, Constantinople, 23 October 1898.)
82. FO 421/178, Salisbury to Chermside, Foreign Office, 8 November 1898.
83. FO 421/178, Egerton to Salisbury, Athens, 26 November 1898; O'Conor to Salisbury, Constantinople, 1 and 11 December 1898; Tewfik Pasha to Anthopoulo Pasha (communicated by Anthopoulo Pasha, 19 December), Constantinople, 27 December 1898. The Ottoman Government had been notified informally earlier that Prince George would be named. (See, for example, FO 421/178, Scott to Salisbury, St Petersburgh, 17 November 1898.) The King of Greece was notified of Prince George's prospective appointment on 17 November. (FO 421/178, Egerton to Salisbury, Athens, 16 November 1898.) On Queen Victoria: Buckle, p. 328.
84. Marschall to Hohenlohe, Pera, 28 November 1898, in GP 12/2, pp. 310–12.
85. FO 421/178, Egerton to Salisbury, Athens, 8 December 1898; Biliotti to Salisbury, Canea, 21 December 1898. On Prince George's less than successful reign in Crete, see Robert Holland, 'Nationalism, Ethnicity and the Concert of Europe: The Case of the High Commissionership of Prince George of Greece in Crete, 1898–1906', *Journal of Modern Greek Studies*, vol. 17, no. 2 (October 1999), pp. 253–76.

# 4

# MACEDONIA

The Treaty of San Stephano that ended the Russo-Turkish War of 1877–8 created a Great Bulgaria that stretched far into the west of Ottoman Europe. The Russians, who had created the new country and whose troops remained in occupation, wanted a pliant Bulgaria, in effect a client state. Others opposed the Russian plan: Austria feared any Russian aggrandizement in the Balkans. A Bulgaria whose borders extended from the Black Sea to Albania would also stand in the way of Austrian hopes for their own expansion in the Balkans. The other Balkan nations – Serbia, Romania and Greece – opposed and feared the creation of a Greater Bulgaria. Britain opposed an extension of Russian influence and power that might ultimately lead to Russian control of the Straits.[1]

Reducing the large Bulgaria created in the Treaty of San Stephano, at the Congress of Berlin the Powers created two Bulgarias – an independent Bulgaria, in theory a tributary of the Ottoman Empire, and an autonomous Eastern Rumelia. Eastern Rumelia was theoretically a province of the Ottoman Empire, but with its own Christian governor and a native militia and gendarmerie, although Ottoman forces still defended the border with Bulgaria. In population, Eastern Rumelia was just as Bulgarian as was the Kingdom of Bulgaria – slightly less than 75 per cent. Bulgarians were left with two irredentist goals – unity of Eastern Rumelia with Bulgaria and taking the rest of what they had been awarded in the Treaty of San Stephano.

In 1885 a rebellion in favour of uniting Eastern Rumelia with Bulgaria broke out in Plovdiv and spread rapidly. Prince Alexander of Bulgaria, fearing that to do otherwise would cost him his throne, supported the rebels. Under the terms of the Berlin Treaty, the military border of the Empire was on the prime defensive position of the Balkan Mountains. Losing it would leave the Empire less protected from attack from the North. The Ottomans prepared for war, but the Powers stepped in and forced them to stand down. Most of the Powers, particularly Russia, opposed any Bulgarian unification that upset the terms of the Treaty of Berlin. Russian had found the new Bulgarian state to be anything but a pliant Russian client, and they disliked the Bulgarian prince, Alexander. Salisbury, stating he was driven by British public opinion in favour of the Bulgarians, proposed a compromise: Eastern Rumelia would theoretically remain part of the Ottoman Empire, but the Bulgarian prince would rule over both Bulgaria and Eastern Rumelia. The other Powers, fearing European conflict, reluctantly agreed. The Ottomans could not oppose the British plan when it was supported by the other Powers. The sultan was forced to agree to the plan, considerably damaging the Empire's defences. Something resembling a larger Bulgarian state had in fact been created, but Bulgaria had not yet reached the San Stephano borders.[2]

**Macedonia**

The region known to Europeans as Macedonia had no real physical boundaries (see Map 4.2). It stretched across mountains and rivers without taking any of them as political borders. By default, Europeans defined Macedonia as the Ottoman provinces of Selanik (Salonica), Kosova and Manastır, usually excluding Edirne (Adrianople) Province. For the Ottomans, these were purely administrative units that did not take into account ethnic groups.

The Ottoman Empire kept population records by religion, so ethnic groups cannot be properly enumerated. Among the Muslims, Albanian speakers predominated in Western Macedonia, and Turkish-speakers in the East. Among the Christians, the majority spoke Macedonian, with Greek speakers in the South and Serbian speakers in the Northwest. Another Christian group, the Romanian-speaking Vlach, made up less than 10 per cent of the Christian population (no one actually counted their numbers). However, the populations were very mixed in many parts of Macedonia.[3]

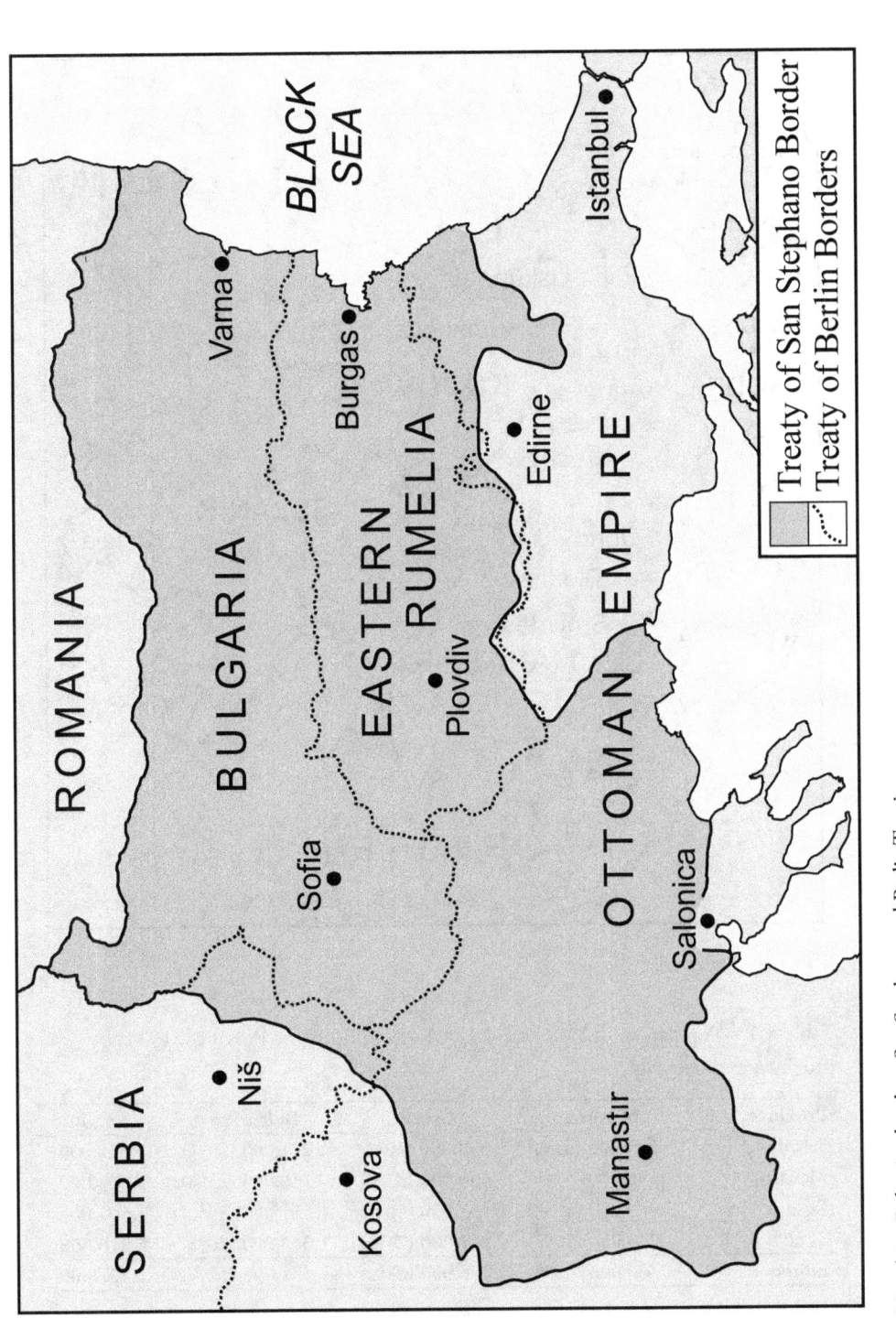

Map 4.1 Bulgarian borders. San Stephano and Berlin Treaties

Map 4.2  Macedonia

Table 4.1  Population of Ottoman Macedonia and Edirne Province, 1911, by province and religion[a]

| Province | Muslim | Greek | Bulgarian | Total[b] |
|---|---|---|---|---|
| Selanik | 605,000 (45%) | 398,000 (30%) | 271,000 (20%) | 1,348,000 |
| Manastır | 456,000 (43%) | 350,000 (33%) | 246,000 (23%) | 1,065,000 |
| Kosova | 959,000 (60%) | 93,000 (06%) | 531,000 (33%) | 1,603,000 |
| Total | 2,020,000 (50%) | 841,000 (21%) | 1,048,000 (26%) | 4,016,000 |
| Edirne | 760,000 (53%) | 396,000 (28%) | 171,000 (12%) | 1,427,000 |

[a] Rounded to the nearest thousand, with some rounding error.
[b] Includes groups not detailed in the table, such as Jews and Roman Catholics.

Source: McCarthy, 'The Population of Ottoman Europe'. The population numbers would have been somewhat different in 1903, but the Muslim to Christian proportion is essentially the same.[4]

## Creating a Macedonian Identity

Throughout Ottoman times, many administrative functions of government were assigned to religious communities (the *millet* system). Each had authority over churches, schools, charitable work and even many courts administered by religious leaders. For centuries, Christian Macedonians were all entered as 'Greeks', members of the Greek Orthodox Church. Macedonian Christian institutions were under control of the Greek Orthodox hierarchy. In 1872, however, a Bulgarian Orthodox autocephalous Exarchate was proclaimed with Sultan Abdülaziz's blessing. (The Greek Patriarchate immediately declared it schismatic.) The Ottomans recognised a separate Bulgarian Millet, with the right to its own schools, churches and ecclesiastical administration. Over the following years, many Christians in Macedonia joined the Exarchate. Greek priests were often evicted from churches, which came under Bulgarian bishops. Thus, the Macedonian Christians were divided into two religious 'nations', known as 'Patriarchists' and 'Exarchists', even though they shared the same language and culture.[5]

The Macedonian language was a close relative to Bulgarian, mutually intelligible, but with differences. To some who spoke Macedonian, the Macedonians and the Bulgarians were separate, albeit similar, peoples. Others who spoke Macedonian defined themselves as Bulgarian. The Bulgarians in Bulgaria and early twentieth-century newspapermen and diplomats called all the Macedonian Christians Bulgarians. Locals recognised the difference, however, and it affected their loyalties. As rebellion broke out in Macedonia, one group of rebels fought for an independent Macedonia, another for union with Bulgaria. Both groups aimed for an end to Ottoman rule, but they sometimes fought each other. They both agreed that Macedonian Greek Orthodox had to be 'convinced' that they must become real Macedonians/Bulgarians by adhering to the Bulgarian Exarchist Church.

Two organisations commanded the rebels in Macedonia: IMRO (Internal Macedonian Revolutionary Organization) was founded 1893. It spread through a network of Exarchate teachers and schools. IMRO's avowed aim was autonomy within the Ottoman Empire, although many of its members wished for eventual unison with Bulgaria. The other main organisation, the Supreme Macedonian–Adrianople Committee (SMAC), was formed in 1895 in Sofia, Bulgaria. It enjoyed more support from the Bulgarian Government, because its declared aim was uniting Macedonia with Bulgaria. Both groups, however, drew weapons and men from Bulgaria, which was home to a large number of Macedonians who had fled to Bulgaria after the Congress of Berlin returned Macedonia to the Ottoman Empire. Many of these migrants had taken official positions and had connections to the Bulgarian military.[6]

Although their memberships contained highly placed members of the Bulgarian state, the committees did not take orders from the Bulgarian Government. It was often rather the other way around. The Bulgarian Government feared them. Approximately 187,000 Bulgarians had migrated to Bulgaria and Eastern Rumelia after the 1877–8 War. They and their descendants formed a powerful lobby for Bulgarian action in Macedonia. What is certain is that the rebel communities could never have developed in Macedonia without Bulgarian assistance. The Bulgarian Government was sometimes forced by the Powers to publicly disavow the committees, but it never took effectual steps to stop them, because it agreed with their purpose. The Macedonian rebels were supplied with arms from Bulgaria. Sources disagree on how many were armed from stores in Bulgaria, but all agree that it was in the thousands. As the French ambassador in Istanbul, Jean Antoine Ernest Constans, asked: 'How do the bands get their supplies? How is the number of these bands constantly increasing despite the serious losses which have been inflicted on them? How do explosives, dynamite in particular, increase everywhere in the country?' How else but from Bulgaria? And the rebels were not only untrained peasants. Volunteers from Bulgaria, including regular army members and reservists, nominally resigning their posts, joined in the rebels' battles. Austrian observers believed that Bulgarian officers even directed rebel attacks. Bulgarian soldiers accompanied and safeguarded shipments of rifles and dynamite into Macedonia. Bulgarian 'trade representatives' coordinated with the committees.[7]

Concentrating on the British response to the troubles in Macedonia, I have not attempted to offer any detailed descriptions of the Macedonian/Bulgarian Committees' structures. British diplomatic reports from Sofia discussed the political effects of each committee, but concerning events in Macedonia itself, the British seldom acknowledged the difference between the two committees, referring only to 'the Committee' or 'the Bulgarian bands'. British proposals for Macedonia very seldom made note of any differences among the rebels. (Locals called the bands 'komitadjis', from the Turkish *komitacı*, 'committee man'.) Correspondingly, the British and other Europeans often described the

Muslims of Macedonia as Turks, even though most of the Muslims of Western Macedonia were ethnically Albanian.[8]

In many ways the actions of the Macedonian rebels were a textbook example of guerilla warfare: beginning at first in small bands, they attacked isolated Muslim and Patriarchist villages, collecting 'taxes' from villagers, enforcing 'revolutionary discipline' – adherence to the Cause and to the Bulgarian Church – by threats and violence, and sometimes murdering Ottoman officials and gendarmes. More positively, the rebels achieved some degree of loyalty by affording villagers protection from bandits and rapacious landlords. In general, however, they set upon their task of creating a revolutionary Macedonia by threat. As the Austrian consul-general in Salonica, Richard Hickel, stated: 'The Macedonian-Bulgarian villages are by no means self-motivated to subversion or inspired by lofty political ideals, but are enrolled with great and laborious persistence and terrorism.' Hickel noted that the penalty for opposing the rebels was death.[9]

In the first period of the rebellion, Muslim Albanian and Turkish villages were attacked, but the rebels concentrated many of their attacks on Christians that adhered to the Greek Orthodox Church, the Patriarchists, intent on forcing them to accept the Bulgarian Exarchate and the rebellion. Exarchist villages had no choice but to support the rebels. They were forced to provide food and shelter to the guerillas. Exarchists who openly opposed the rebels were murdered, convincing others to conform. Unless Ottoman forces were present, to oppose the bands might mean death, and the Ottoman forces were spread thin against a guerilla enemy. In standard guerilla practice, the rebels expanded their forces until they were able to fight pitched battles with Ottoman forces and eventually attempt to take cities. British diplomatic sources estimated 130 engagements between the bands and Turkish troops by 1903 – perhaps an exaggeration, but still an indication of significant guerilla activity.[10]

By 1902 the rebel bands were attacking Muslim villages, and the Muslims were fighting back in what amounted to a civil war. British Consul McGregor in Manastır wrote that rebels were killing Muslims across the region. Other Muslims were threatened with a similar fate if they did not contribute food and money to the rebels. Muslim villagers began to resist. Albanian chiefs organised to fight Bulgarians who were murdering Albanians. Armed Muslim villagers, sometimes, but seldom, aided by soldiers, fought battles with guerilla bands. Consuls recorded deaths in all communities – Patriarchists, Exarchists and Muslims. Muslims and Christians who had lived side by side for centuries were divided into warring camps. As was always the case in the Balkans and Middle East, conflict was accompanied by theft. All sides took advantage of fighting to seize the goods and flocks of the other.[11]

Ottoman forces responded to the rebels, but were obstructed by problems common to any counter-insurgency: the rebels could count on local support, forced or given willingly. Small bands could attack villages or gendarmerie outposts, then escape to the hills before the army could respond. By 1902, smaller army units were being attacked and even sometimes defeated by rebel bands. It was impossible to interdict the supply of arms from Bulgaria.

The Ottomans also suffered from a deficiency in manpower: sufficient regular troops were never available; they had to rely on local forces. Those who were called *ilave* ('additional') groups were under a military obligation, but had not served in the regular army or received proper training. They remained in their home provinces as part of the provincial reserves and could be called up temporarily as needed. As such, they were little different from the other Muslim villagers in their districts. British and other Europeans usually could not differentiate between them and other villagers. They used the pejorative description 'bashi bozuk' to describe Muslims who fought against rebels – an improper reference that had long been used in the British press to indicate murderous Muslims. While, as the consuls reported, the regular soldiers and reserves drawn from Anatolia kept to military discipline, the local levees did not. These were drawn from the same villages that had suffered from, and were fighting against, the Bulgarian bands. Moreover, battles with the rebels gave these irregulars the opportunity to engage in the same sort of plunder as the rebels.

Soldiers, themselves ill-fed and often unpaid, undoubtedly did steal from peasants. A particular excess arose when soldiers went to villages to search for arms and rebels. Propaganda from the British Macedonian Committee and European supporters greatly exaggerated these searches as tantamount to massacres, but there appear to have been many cases of maltreatment by soldiers searching for weapons and beating peasants until they produced them – particularly bad for those who did not have guns. However, as British

Consul Fontana in Üsküp and others noted, Ottoman soldiers, as opposed to local irregulars and villagers, did not take part in plundering whole villages or in wanton destruction.[12]

Much of the destruction and death in Macedonia, greatly exaggerated and called massacres of Christians in the British press, was actually the result of battles among villagers and between rebels and soldiers. Dislodging rebels in prepared defensive positions would have cost many military lives, and perhaps could not have been done at all. The Ottoman officers' solution was cannon. When rebels refused to surrender, they were bombarded from a distance. In the Ilinden Uprising (see below), for example, regular assaults on the rebel positions at Krushevo failed. Cannon dislodged them, but left the town in ruins. This situation was repeated in villages occupied by rebels. How much the destruction of those who would not surrender was a conscious plan to stifle the rebellion, rather than a tactic on the spot, is unknown. A myriad of documents attests that Bulgarian villagers and komitajis were surrendering their weapons and accepting an Ottoman amnesty in fear of the bombardments.[13]

## The Ottoman Response to Muslim Offences

Importantly, British consuls documented the government reaction to Muslim offences. For example, offences against Christians were reported by Consul Fontana in Üsküp, but also Ottoman punishment, including capital punishment, of the Muslim offenders. Even government officials accused of offences were arrested. Consul McGregor also wrote of individual instances of punishment of Muslims: 'Three days ago nineteen Mussulman Beys and Aghas from the Okhrida and Kyrchevo districts, some of whom had been denounced to Hilmi Pasha by myself as notorious evil-doers and tyrants, were exiled to Adana.' Thirty Muslims whom McGregor called 'petty tyrants' had similarly been exiled in October. He reported that local Muslims were being arrested and punished by the government. When officers were put on public trial, McGregor forwarded reports on convictions.[14]

Consul Fontana wrote that Hilmi Paşa, the governor-general of Macedonia (see below), was proving an energetic and successful governor. In a short time after his arrival, he had arrested 208 Muslim and twenty Christian 'brigands and others'. Hilmi, he wrote, was unafraid to use imperial troops to fight both Muslim and Bulgarian troublemakers. The relative numbers of Christians and Muslims arrested is worth note. When rebels set off a massive bomb in Salonica, the bombings caused a reaction in Manastır, where sixteen Bulgarians were killed. McGregor reported that the governor had taken prompt action, sending soldiers to cordon off the Muslim and Bulgarian quarters to keep the violence from spreading.[15]

In a battle between soldiers and a large rebel band at the village of Smyrdesh in April 1903, soldiers had used cannon to reduce the rebels. After the insurgents had been defeated, with 105 dead and eighty-seven wounded, and the remainder had fled, local Muslims looted the village. An Ottoman commission investigated, found the rebel guerillas and Muslim villagers guilty, and returned 90 per cent of the stolen property. (On 10 July 1903 the band of rebels primarily involved in Smyrdesh returned to the village and murdered those who had given testimony against them to the commission.)[16]

When local Muslims destroyed villages after the Ilinden Rebellion, Hilmi Paşa, the governor-general, arrested thirty-six immediately and scores more, including Muslim leaders, were arrested soon after.[17]

One report showed conclusively that the Ottoman response was against rebels, not directed against Christians. The greatest mortality in an engagement with rebels was not of Christians: when Albanian Muslim bands attacked Mitrovitza in March 1903, Ottoman soldiers repulsed them with cannon fire, leaving an estimated 250 dead and 150 wounded Albanian Muslims. This toll was far greater than any mortality in battles against Bulgarian rebels.[18]

**An Accurate Assessment**

Britain was fortunate to have one of the most able diplomats of the nineteenth century, Sir Alfred Biliotti, as its consul-general in Salonica from 1899 to 1903. Biliotti brought to his position a lifetime spent in the Middle East and Balkans and an extensive knowledge of the peoples of the Ottoman Empire. Perhaps because of this, his reports on Macedonia were remarkably impartial, or at least much more so than those of most diplomats. Biliotti accurately warned that there would be a major Bulgarian revolt in spring of 1903. He also stated that Muslims, not only Christians, were being killed in Macedonia.[19]

Biliotti reported that Ottoman officials were doing all they could, with a good degree of success, in keeping in check Muslim reprisals for the actions of the rebels. At the beginning of May 1903, Bulgarian agents in Salonica blew up gas mains, threw bombs and shot and killed innocent Muslims and Christians. A bomb manufactory was discovered by the authorities. Biliotti reported: 'The police and military authorities have shown the greatest activity and courage in looking for and arresting all suspicious characters, many of who offered a desperate resistance, and in searching for bombs.' He stated that the authorities had kept absolute calm, and that, despite Bulgarian Committee reports to the contrary, there had been no massacres. 'I have great pleasure in reporting that everyone is unanimous in praise of the Vali (governor).'[20]

Biliotti forwarded to the embassy lists of Muslims and Greeks killed by Bulgarian bands, often with considerable brutality, such as beheadings, the heads thrown to the dogs. He wrote that Muslim peasants were terrified. The Muslims felt that Bulgarian actions were intended to draw reprisals, followed by European intervention. Biliotti agreed. He felt that Bulgarian murders of Muslims were causing Muslim hatred.[21]

A set of the rules of the Macedonian Revolutionary Committee were discovered and found their way to Biliotti in June 1903. These were detailed plans for rebellion that were soon to be carried out. Biliotti commented:

> The general ideas of these 'Regulations' are: to accuse the troops of offenses they did not commit; to exaggerate such offenses as they may have committed; to colour their actions as to make them appear as offenses; to persuade or force the villagers to go en masse and lay complaints first before the Consuls, afterwards before the Vali.

He had no doubt that the European consuls were intended to be unwitting agents of the Bulgarian revolution. His sources revealed that the Bulgarian Committee was resolved to organise attacks on Muslims in order to provoke reprisals, leading to European intervention.[22]

Consul-General Biliotti's reports to the embassy in Istanbul were full of incidents of Bulgarian guerillas' attacks on Christians and Muslims alike – many hundreds of pages of them – and of attacks on gendarmes and soldiers. There are far too many of these to refer to them here. The bands particularly targeted Muslims and Greek Orthodox, especially the latter, attempting to force them to accept the Bulgarian Exarchate. *Muhtars* (mayors), schoolteachers and priests suffered most. Entire villages were forced at gunpoint to go to the mountains and join the rebels.[23]

Perhaps due to his long-term association with the Balkans, Biliotti was able to develop a network of informants (what today would be called spies). Other consuls all too often relied on the word of those who came to them with tales. Biliotti relied on those he himself sent out to investigate:

> I have just obtained a number of details, some of them hitherto unknown to me, that go to prove in a yet more conclusive manner that not only are the Christians of Macedonia suffering more from the Bulgarian bands than from the Turkish authorities, but that they are suffering just now exclusively from the action of the Committee and that the Moslems also have during the past few weeks been murdered in not inconsiderable numbers.

Biliotti's sources told him that Bulgarians were being compelled by the committee to accuse Muslims and Greeks of murders done by Bulgarians. Villagers were being made bankrupt and were close to starvation not because of taxes, but because of extortion and destruction by the bands. Anyone who denounced a Komitaji for his crimes was killed.[24]

The Ottoman Government was not excused in Biliotti's reports. He particularly felt that officials were not sufficiently active in countering the rebels, allowing them to organise and recruit.[25] He reported that soldiers were guilty of beating peasants when searching for arms, but said that the stories of soldiers' 'excesses' were much exaggerated, the product of rebel committee propaganda. In general, however, he described the traditional Ottoman administration in Macedonia as incompetent and corrupt. Biliotti was not against aspects of European control in Macedonia. He felt that the reforms instituted by Hilmi Paşa were having good effect, but European supervision of the gendarmerie and the financial system were needed. His criticisms of the Ottoman system and preference for European control made Biliotti's sympathetic treatment of Ottoman problems and the sufferings of Muslims all the more believable.[26]

## The Ilinden Revolt

Proving that the Bulgarian Government would not or could not deter the Macedonian rebels, in October of 1902, Bulgarian General Ivan Tzontcheff, the leader of SMAC, led an armed force from Bulgaria to Cuma-ı Bala (Gorna Dzhumaya), a town with a large Muslim majority within the region of Razlog, which had a Christian majority – the Gorna Dzhumaya Uprising. The revolt was poorly prepared and relied on the expectation that local Macedonian Christians would join it. Few did so, and the Ottoman army put the revolt down easily. The SMAC fighters were forced to flee back into Bulgaria, but during the fighting, villages were razed and a large number of Macedonians also fled to Bulgaria, many of whom returned when the sultan granted an amnesty.[27]

A much larger revolt in 1903 was more successful, although ultimately it also failed.

The rebellion known as the Ilinden Revolt is considered to have begun with the seizure of the town of Krushevo by IMRO on 2 August 1903 and proclamation of a Macedonian Republic there, although the revolt had actually been developing for months and extended well beyond Krushevo. The rebels were joined by officers and men from the Bulgarian army. Following committee orders, Exarchists and dragooned Patriarchists joined the fighting; women and children took to the hills. By 4 August, there was severe fighting in the region. Ottoman officials were murdered. Government buildings and Patriarchist and Muslim houses and shops were sacked and burned down. British Consul McGregor reported: 'In certain villages, the departure of the inhabitants was preceded by sanguinary excesses committed on the Turks.' MacGregor's was a great understatement: Muslims' villages all over the region were attacked and plundered. Muslims were killed in great numbers. The rebel committee stated to the British consul that it was attacking Muslims, burning their villages and driving them out.[28]

The rebels were never in sufficient numbers to hold out against the Ottoman army. Their intention was to spark counter-massacres that would be portrayed in Europe solely as Muslim atrocities against Christians. European observers understood that this was the rebels' intent. In this they were successful, but the Powers did not act as the rebels wished.[29]

Eight hundred troops who tried to dislodge the rebels were at first repulsed. Artillery then bombarded the town, forcing surviving rebels to flee. The troops entered the town on 13 August. Artillery fire surely accounted for much of the destruction and the dead. Estimates of the dead are extremely unreliable. McGregor stated that twenty-two Muslims had been killed when the insurgents took Krushevo, forty-four Christians had died in the battle and thirty-five Muslims had been killed or wounded in the battle. Numbers must have been higher; and they do not count Muslim or Christian deaths in the countryside. Just before the rebels were defeated in Krushevo, the French consul in Istanbul, Jean Antoine Ernest Constans, predicted: 'The Porte has, to date, made laudable efforts to constrain the Muslims, and I believe it will continue along this path. But if the crimes committed in recent days by the gangs repeat, will it not be powerless?' That was so. Before order was restored in Krushevo, local Muslims who had fled the town and returned and others from the region sacked Christian houses and shops. Fighting and reprisals continued for some time in the countryside.[30]

An interesting facet of the Krushevo incident was that Christian refugees from the region said that regular and auxiliary troops from Anatolia did not take part in pillage:

> It is said that the Anatolian troops took very little part in the work, and that in many cases they showed kindness to the women and children who took refuge in the forest, bringing them water and otherwise attending to their needs.

Those who pillaged the town were local Muslims, the same group that had suffered murders and burnings from the Bulgarians in Krushevo and its region.[31]

In a military sweep of the region after the uprising had been defeated, Ottoman forces confiscated between 1,200 and 1,400 rifles (numbers in sources differed).[32]

It is possible to tentatively analyse the history of the events of 1903 from the consular documents.

- The Bulgarian revolt was based on attacks on Ottoman soldiers and officials and on Muslims living in villages. The attacks preceded the 'official' beginning of the revolt in August 1903 and continued during that revolt.
- Bulgarian villagers joined the rebels. Many joined the komitajis out of belief or the simple desire to plunder Muslim property and settle old scores. Many others were forced to take part, as witnessed by the many documents that described rebels occupying both Exarchist and Patriarchist villages and forcing the villagers to join them.

- Although they were much exaggerated, there were indeed massacres of Christians. Very seldom were these committed by regular Ottoman soldiers, who usually seem to have done what they could to stop attacks on the innocent. There can be no question, however, that Macedonian rebels were treated harshly, and that artillery was used in fighting rebels in villages, with attendant civilian deaths.
- Muslims were also massacred during and before the revolt. The rebel intent was to draw European intervention by causing reprisals from Muslims for massacres of Christians.
- The rebels began the attacks on Muslim villages, but both rebels and Muslim villagers under no military control engaged in plunder and sometimes murder of their enemies. It is important to note that few actions of these villagers came until after the attacks of Bulgarian bands. Revenge must have been a primary motivation for attacks on Christians.
- Ottoman officials prosecuted guilty Muslims, including officers and soldiers, in large numbers. If, on the other hand, rebels or the Bulgarian Government ever punished their fellows for misdeeds, such actions do not appear in the record. Both Muslim and Bulgarian villagers and combatants benefitted from general amnesties. The amnesties were a governmental gesture towards peace and reconciliation, often influenced by European pressure, but they meant that the guilty escaped.[33]

This was not the story that appeared in the British press, nor did the politicians who began deliberations on Macedonia take into account the actual events there.

**Revolt in Edirne Province**

Soon after it broke out in Manastır Province, the 1903 Bulgarian uprising spread far to the East into Edirne (Adrianople) Province. It was hampered by the fact that the Christian population of the province was more than two-thirds Greek, and the Greeks wanted no part of a Bulgarian revolt (Table 4.1). Those who took part were either Bulgarian nationals, Macedonian refugees in Bulgaria or Ottoman Bulgarians living in the districts on the Bulgarian border or in the mountains. What was styled as an uprising in Edirne Province is more accurately described as an invasion from Bulgaria that gathered local supporters.

Preparations for the uprising in Edirne were either facilitated or at least tolerated by the Bulgarian Government: rebel bands gathered in Bulgaria near the Ottoman border. Bombs were openly prepared in factories in Bulgaria (one of the factories exploded, killing the rebels), then smuggled across the border. Bulgarian army officers openly sold rifles to the komitadjis. Committee bands gathered openly in Plovdiv (Philippopolis, Filibe), then crossed into the region south of Edirne and into the Stranja (Strumica, Üstrümce) Mountains, where rifles and bombs had already been stored. The British vice-consul at Varna in Bulgaria, Alfred Gardner Brophy, reported that hundreds of men had left the Varna region by rail for Edirne Province, and that the border was open to them.[34]

Expecting troubles, the Ottomans began a sweep for arms in August 1903. They obviously were not completely successful. Substantial stored caches of rifles, ammunition and bombs awaited the rebellion.[35]

Officers from Bulgaria became the leaders of bands of the local Bulgarians that joined the revolt. British Ambassador Nicholas O'Conor stated that the Bulgarians in the border region joined in the rebellion and burned Turkish and Greek villagers' crops, killed village guards and pillaged. Lieutenant-Colonel Francis Richard Maunsell, the British Military Attaché, described the events: 'The insurrection was led by men who came across the frontier, and roused the population of the Bulgarian villages, who appeared thoroughly organized and ready for the signal.' Fighting broke out between soldiers and rebels in various regions from 12 to 16 August. The government building at Kırk Kilisse was burned. Soldiers were attacked by large bands, and military outposts were taken. On 20 August, villages in Northeast Edirne Province were burnt out by the rebels. Dynamite smuggled from Bulgaria was used to destroy Turkish and Greek villages. Guerillas attempted to blow up bridges and tunnels on the Dedeağaç–Edirne rail line, which were used by troops going to fight the rebels, but their attack was defeated by Ottoman defenders.[36]

By 22 August, rebel bands driving up the Black Sea Coast reached Midye, 50 miles from Istanbul, driving before them Turkish and Greek refugees from destroyed villages. Further revolts had broken out in the Strumja Mountains and in Salonica Province. The Ottomans called up all the men they could, including both the reserves and ilave battalions. Ottoman forces were at first forced to withdraw from the northern districts of Edirne Province, but by the end of August they had begun to clear the insurgents from the Northeast, the Strumja Mountains and Salonica Province. Ottoman combat forces had risen to 72,000 men.[37]

By the end of September, the Bulgarian forces had been driven across the border, accompanied by Bulgarian villagers fleeing from indiscriminate Turkish and Greek revenge. As was always the case, the Bulgarian Government denied it had any part in the invasion. Confronted on Bulgarian support of the rebels by the British consul-general in Sophia, Francis Elliot, the Bulgarians disavowed all.[38]

## The Domestic Force behind British Policy in Macedonia

Judged only by Great Power politics of the time, one might question why Britain was concerned with Macedonia. Russia feared an expansion of a Bulgaria that had ceased to be its ally. Austria was concerned over warfare on its borders. In addition, as many suspected, Austria might have planned ultimately to claim Macedonia for itself. Each country had a great army that could have enforced its will, but each feared the other, and thus they cooperated. The Austrian and Russian actions in Macedonia, if misguided, were nevertheless understandable. But what of Britain? What were the British geopolitical or financial interests in Macedonia? Militarily, there was no way Britain could have played a part in Macedonia. All she could do was to use her fleet to threaten the sultan. And what was there about Macedonia that would cause her to do so?

The main reason for British interest in Macedonia was domestic, not international.

On the issue of Macedonia, the opinions of the British press and political pressure groups and British politicians were symbiotic. Each fed the other. Politicians such as Lord Lansdowne and Sir Edward Grey intended to force the Ottomans to abandon control of Macedonia, and the press and the political groups pressured them to do so. Few voices were raised in Great Britain in defence of the Turks. Newspapers and members of parliament joined in partisan attacks on the Ottomans — attacks that relied on questionable reports and often outright misinformation and lies. Politicians complained that they were constrained by Great Power dissension, but any actions against the Ottomans were supported by the public, or at least by the members of the public that were concerned with Macedonia.[39]

## The Balkan Committee

The Balkan Committee shared the anti-Turkish philosophy and many of the members of the Anglo-Armenian Association. The committee was founded by Liberal members of parliament in 1903, under the guidance of James Bryce, who had also founded the Anglo-Armenian Association. Bryce became the first president of the committee. Members included prominent Britons such as George Macaulay Trevelyan, Ramsay Macdonald, Arthur Ponsonby, George Cadbury, G. K. Chesterton and the editor of the *Daily News*, A. G. Gardiner, as well as churchmen, noted professors, MPs and journalists. The Balkan Committee was nominally led by a president and an executive committee, but its affairs were mainly directed by the Liberal MP Noel Buxton, Chairman of the Executive Committee.[40]

Soon after the Balkan Committee was formally founded in 1903, Bryce and Buxton issued a manifesto outlining the committee positions. It attacked the Treaty of Berlin for leaving territory in Europe to the Ottoman Empire. By doing so, it stated, the Powers now had responsibility for Ottoman Europe. For many years, they alleged, the Turks had been oppressing the Christians of Macedonia. Landlords and tax collectors were brutal in their exactions. There was no law to defend Christians: 'Any outrage committed by a Turk against a Christian goes unpunished.' Unaided by the Powers, who should have defended them, the Bulgarians of Macedonia had taken action and revolted. The Turks had reacted with inhumane violence. The only solution was for Britain to do its duty – force all Turkish troops from Macedonia and put complete power in the hands of a Christian governor, answerable only to the Powers, not the Ottoman Government.[41]

Bryce felt that it was best not to disclose the real purpose of the committee, which was to end the Ottoman Empire. He wrote to Buxton: 'I personally want to see Turkish rule removed out of existence altogether, in Asia as well as in Europe, and the sooner the better.'[42]

Further manifestos followed. The committee addressed an open memorandum to the Powers that depicted conditions in Macedonia in bleak terms: it was alleged that 10,000 Christians had been murdered in 1903–4 alone, and the numbers of murders were increasing. Past reforms, for which the Ottoman Government supposedly gave no support, had failed because they left much power in the hands of the Turks. The Powers should intervene and take over. If this was done, the Albanians and Slavs would unite in a 'simultaneous movement against the common oppressor (the Turks)'. Unless the Powers intervened, 'it is impossible to entertain any hope that the anarchic degeneration of the country will be checked'. It is doubtful if the committee believed that the Powers, other than perhaps Britain, would pay attention to this manifesto, but the real intended audience was the British public. Copies were distributed to the press and were published in newspapers. Newspapers in Britain printed hundreds of articles on the Balkan Committee from 1903 to 1913.[43]

The Balkan Committee uniformly favoured the Bulgarians and, to a lesser extent, the Serbs. It indicated that it was in touch with the Macedonian rebels. The committee was generally unsympathetic to the Greeks. Their descriptions of Greek actions in Macedonia were as absurd as their depictions of Turkish deeds. At one point, for example, the Balkan Committee alleged that mixed Greek–Turkish bands were slaughtering Bulgarians with the encouragement of the Greek Bishop of Manastır. Committee member Henry Noel Brailsford wrote: 'It is true that the Bulgarians were fighting for liberty, while the Greeks had allied themselves with the tyrant.' Greece and its supporters naturally considered the Balkan Committee to be an enemy.[44]

Some Balkan Committee members reported on massacres they had heard of during their journeys to Macedonia, almost all of which were stories they had heard from local Christians, not what they had seen themselves. The other reports of the committee were without real attribution of sources – 'a priest', 'a peasant', 'a letter from a respected resident in Macedonia, for whose accuracy it (the Balkan Committee) can vouch'. The stories were duly reported in the press. They read like the massacre stories told everywhere in the time of 'yellow journalism'. For example, the 'respected resident' reported:

> A peasant from the burned village of Armensko tells a horrible story, which I have reason to believe is true. His own brother was massacred among the first, and his brother's wife, while holding her infant to her bosom and resisting outrage, had both her arms cut off, also her breasts, while her head was slashed open on one side. The little child was cradled in her arms.[45]

The Balkan Committee began what were to become a series of public meetings on the Macedonian Question with a mass meeting in the 2,000-seat St James's Hall on 29 September 1903. On the platform were James Bryce,

President, Noel Buxton, Chairman of the Executive Committee, R. A. Scott, Treasurer, and H. N. Brailsford. There were also members of parliament, bishops and other clergy, and lords. Various worthies, including the Archbishop of Canterbury, the Bishop of London, the Bishop of Durham, Herbert Asquith (later prime minister), Henry Campbell-Bannerman (later prime minister), Richard Haldane (later war secretary and Lord Chancellor) and many others wrote letters of support.

The topics of the September 1903 meeting were to become common features of subsequent Balkan Committee public meetings:

- A catalogue of Turkish wrongs, with graphic details.[46]
- An appeal to common Christianity. 'England had a right, and something which was much greater than a right, it had a most solemn duty to intervene.'
- Britain had 'put its money on the wrong horse' in the Crimean War and in 1878. It should always have opposed the Turks. Because it had supported the Turks in their iniquity, Britain now had the duty to make things right.
- The Turks had done nothing since 1878 to improve their Empire, nor to ameliorate the conditions of Ottoman Christians. Instead, the Ottoman Government sponsored attacks on Christians. It was not only the right of the Macedonian rebels to rebel; it was their duty.[47]
- The Turks would eventually leave Europe, even Istanbul, no matter how much they were temporarily propped up by European politics: 'Why should we protract the agony?'
- Britain must press the Powers to immediately intervene in Ottoman Europe. Macedonia must be ruled by a Christian governor, answerable to the Christian Powers, not in any way to the sultan (that is, it should be effectively removed from the Ottoman Empire). Once this had been done, Macedonia would be at peace and would prosper. The differences in belief among the Macedonian Christians and 'racial differences' were minor and would present no problem to Christian unity against the Turks.
- The world would be much the better if the Ottoman Empire ceased to exist. 'The rule of the Turk was an abomination and an anachronism in Europe, and there was no man in that assembly who would not be glad to hear that an end had been made of the Sultan and his rule.'[48]

Little changed in the Balkan Committee meetings and propaganda that followed after 1903. The committee's pressure on the British Government continued to 1908 and beyond. At a meeting on 27 January 1908, the committee once again called for European governance in Macedonia, asserting that there had been 10,000 murders there, a ridiculous figure many times the actual number. A request for immediate action was sent to the prime minister and foreign secretary.[49]

In a meeting in 1908, again at St James Hall and again filled with more than 2,000 listeners, speakers stressed the same topics as they had five years earlier. In 1903, the Balkan Committee had offered only stories of Turkish atrocities that drove the Bulgarians to revolt. By 1908, when new troubles threatened, they were forced to admit that Christian Greeks and Christian Bulgarians were killing each other. This was also blamed on the Turks. The report of one Balkan Committee meeting, at the Westminster Hotel in London on 28 January 1908, was typical of the Balkan Committee meetings of the time. Its main points:

- 'The massacres of Christians by Christians occurred nowhere but under the Turk. Whenever a man had been freed from Turkish rule these things ceased. They were there because the Turk was there, and as long as the Turk was there so long would these outrages be there.' (Given European history, this was a very odd opinion.)
- The Turks benefitted from fighting and division among the Christians. 'It was part of his business to promote it.'
- 'Massacres and outrages on women and children by Turkish soldiers' were continuing.
- 10,000 Christians had been murdered in the last four years, as reported in *The Times*. (Actually, the figure had been given to *The Times* by the Balkan Committee itself, which then reported it as being *The Times*'s own report. Presumably the figure was to be added to the 10,000 that the committee had reported as being killed earlier.)
- Limited reforms forced on the Ottomans by the Austrians and Russians had been failures.
- 'There would never be full security and peace in the regions of Macedonia until the Turk had left them for good.' All power should be transferred immediately to Europeans.[50]

Other meetings of the Balkan Committee, always well-reported in the press, stated the committee's views in much the same terms as did the 1903 and 1908 meetings cited above: Turks were massacring Macedonian Christians. The Turks were even at fault if Christians were killing each other. The Ottomans had to go. It was the duty of the British to remove them.[51]

Meetings quoted the newspapers. The newspapers then reported what was said in the meetings. Newspapers routinely printed summaries of the meetings of the Balkan Committee. Even *The Times* devoted much space to lengthy press releases from the committee, printed in their entirety. These contained the usual horror stories of rape, murder, destruction and pillage.[52]

The committee sent out materials and instructions on what should be included in meetings that excoriated the Turks. It was active in providing speakers on Balkan issues to churches and civic groups, complete with 'lantern slides'. In particular, the committee wrote, meetings should always call for European governance in Macedonia. The committee organised more than 300 public meetings in 1903 alone. Some of these were large gatherings, with audiences in the thousands. Others were small meetings in churches and civic buildings. In one such meeting in Cambridge, for example, Noel Buxton, the Bishop of Ely, and others told the audience: 'The people of Macedonia had suffered oppression for 25 years, and in this matter a national obligation rested upon this country (Britain), in which also her honour was involved.' *The Times*, which reported the meeting at length, wrote that there was 'a large attendance'.[53]

Civic organisations and politicians were enlisted in the cause. In Glasgow, 'influential citizens' petitioned the Lord Provost for a meeting on the Macedonian Question.[54] The meeting passed a resolution 'expressing horror, indignation, and sorrow at the ruthless massacres and outrages being perpetrated in Macedonia and other provinces under Turkish rule'. Speakers described the Turks as 'essentially uncivilized', the Ottoman Empire as deserving of destruction and the sultan as a terror-stricken coward who would be easily dealt with by 'a British squadron passing the Bosporus'. A similar meeting, 2,000 attendees reported, was called by the Lord Mayor of Birmingham, 'in compliance with an influentially signed requisition'. As in the Glasgow meeting, a motion was passed demanding that the Turks be removed from rule in Macedonia. Rebellion there was understandable and completely justified.

The British, it was declared, had made a mistake in supporting the Turks in the Crimean War and after.[55]

The Balkan Committee had extensive ties with the British Labour movement. Union representatives tied to the committee sent out committee propaganda to all the chief labor organisations.[56]

The tenor of the image of the Turks brought to the British public by the Balkan Committee is exemplified by two books written by officials of the Balkan Committee.[57]

Noel Buxton made plain his feelings about the Turks in his *Europe and The Turks*. He headed one chapter on the Turks as 'the Cause of the Trouble' and included a basic depiction: 'His (the Turk's) government is based on barbarous ideas—Inefficiency, corruption, inequality, cruelty.'[58]

The Turk, whom Buxton called 'the Interloper', was doomed to be driven from Europe, which even the Turks themselves allegedly accepted:

> The Turk himself admits that he is but a stranger and an interloper in Europe. It is a saying with him that here he has not come to settle, and to Asia he will return, though, as he came in blood, so in blood will he go out.[59]

Buxton felt that it was time to make sure that the supposed prophecy came true. He believed that, because they were Muslims, the Turks were incapable of civilisation and good government.

Buxton's book was filled with pejorative references to Turks, detailing their cruelty and what he called their 'stupidity'. 'It is one of the strangest vagaries of the Creation that anyone so disqualified for ruling was made a conqueror and a sovereign ... Where the Turkish hoof treads the grass never grows.' Islam was to blame for such a 'race' of poor governors: 'Mahomedanism has in one respect at least been an affliction to the world, for it instilled a spirit of conquest, and the power to conquer, into nations unfit to govern.'[60]

Given his characterisation of Ottoman rule, it is not strange that Buxton planned to end it. In his plan, Macedonia was effectively to be removed from Ottoman jurisdiction and placed under the control of European commissioners and a Christian governor. According to Buxton's plan, however, 'reforms' forced by Europeans would not stop there. Macedonia would eventually be removed from the Ottoman Empire, followed by other Ottoman territories. Buxton's solution to the problems of the Ottoman Empire was to dissolve it.

The methods of destruction were unimportant, '[a]ny plan is right that removes the supreme Turkish authority'. He was not content with Macedonia. Iraq, Libya, Eastern Anatolia and Palestine were also to be taken from the Ottomans. He was quite willing for war to be fought to gain those ends.[61]

H. N. Brailsford was the first Honorary Secretary of the Balkan Committee and later a member of the committee's Executive Committee. He had a long history of antipathy toward the Turks as a writer for the *Manchester Guardian* and the *Fortnightly Review*, and as a pamphleteer on the Macedonian Question. He had even enlisted to fight against the Turks in the 1897 War with Greece as a member of the British Philhellenic Legion, receiving a minor wound.[62]

Brailsford's book, *Macedonia: Its Races and their Future*, was a polemic from start to finish. The Turks, he believed, had no concept of civil order, and thus provided no security in Macedonia. The only interest of the Turks was to live off the Christians of the Empire, contributing nothing themselves: 'Turks have become a parasitic race.' The Bulgarians of Macedonia, on the other hand, were a 'democratic organization' in which all Macedonians believed and trusted. Any Ottoman effort to quell disturbances or reform Macedonia were necessarily futile, because the Turks could not govern properly.[63]

Brailsford held the racialist beliefs that were not uncommon at the time. His book contained much consideration of the 'racial' composition of Macedonian peoples, and assertions of 'Aryan' and 'non-Aryan' descent. Albanians were 'by no means clever'. He repeated the common European prejudices about Jews – that they were crafty merchants whose outlook on life was 'Oriental', and 'whose culture was the lore of the Talmud' – but his most complaint was that the Jews were 'stubbornly Turcophile'. The Jews, according to Brailsford, had a far-reaching effect:

> This attitude of the Turkish Jews has serious political consequences, since it goes far to influence the sympathies of the great newspapers and press agencies of the West, which are owned and managed by Jews, and thus delays and distorts the working of European opinion.

(The editors of all the large London newspapers were Christians.)[64]

Brailsford set forth an analysis and plan identical to that of the Balkan Committee: all would have been better if the British had let stand the 1878 San Stephano Treaty, leaving Macedonia to the Bulgarians. Past programmes of reform were complete failures, as would be any programme that left Turks in charge to any degree. The only solution was 'to withdraw the actual government of Macedonia from Constantinople', and to place it in the hands of Europeans. Britain had the duty to intervene to accomplish this.[65]

The acceptance of the positions of the Balkan Committee were greatly aided by its ties to the British Government, especially the Liberals. Members of the committee were prominent members of parliament. Meetings of the Balkan Committee were commonly held in the House of Commons. In 1906, sixty-four members of the House of Commons petitioned the Secretary of State for Foreign Affairs (Grey) to undertake the actions requested by the Balkan Committee. Their memorial was also forwarded to the prime minister (Campbell-Bannerman). A uniform theme was that Britain had been wrong in standing against the Treaty of San Stephano in the Congress of Berlin. There would be no troubles in Macedonia, the committee asserted, if Bulgaria had been given it all, as the San Stephano Treaty had demanded.[66]

The committee pressured the government with 'memorials' – lengthy statements of principle and assertions of supposed facts – in which they blamed everything on the Ottomans and demanded that Europeans take over the government, security forces, finances and judiciary in Macedonia. Deputations from the committees met with prime ministers and foreign secretaries to press their case against the Ottomans. The deputations, as seen above, included prominent men, many of them members of parliament. All the deputations and memorials were well-reported in the press.[67]

When Macedonian reforms were instituted by Austria and Russia (described in the next chapter), the Balkan Committee responded that they never went far enough. They demanded complete autonomy for Macedonia under a European governor, and effective European control of the region. The committee objected to control by Austria and Russia alone. British control was needed, but was not present.[68]

## The Churches

Both the Established and Nonconformist churches in Britain were firmly and vocally behind the programme to evict the Ottomans from Macedonia. The weapons that the churchmen proposed to be used against "The Turk" were spiritual, political and even military.

The Bishops of London and Exeter sanctioned a prayer for use in their dioceses. The prayer called upon God to 'Deliver them (the Macedonian Christians) from the hand of the oppressor'. The Archbishop of Canterbury wrote to the Anglican churches asking for prayers until Turkish tyranny had passed. Also calling for prayers, the Bishop of Winchester told his diocese:

> We are witnesses of a terrible spectacle, not of a war with rebels, which is terrible enough, but of a campaign of extermination organized and carried out against the Christian inhabitants of Macedonia upon a scale of barbarity and ferocity which recalls the days of Timur and Jenghis Khan.

The bishop said that the Turks could never reform.[69]

The Bishops of Rochester and Ripon called on the government to take action against 'Turkish misrule'. The Bishop of Wakefield preached that 'the angels were looking down on the great theatre and were witnessing the tragedy in Macedonia carried out with such calculated ferocity against helpless Christian women and children'. In a 'service of intercession' at St Mathews Church, Westminster, the congregation was asked 'to remember what the Turkish Empire was and had been throughout history, a tyranny founded on slavery and polygamy, a tyranny operating by rape and massacre'. Descriptions of Turkish 'satanic crimes' followed.[70]

Presbyterian and Wesleyan synods called on the British Government to take action to relieve the Christians from the atrocities inflicted on them. The general committee of the Congregational Union of England and Wales passed a resolution calling on the British Government 'to save our fellow Christians in South-East Europe from the intolerable evils of internecine strife and of Turkish rule'. Nonconformist churches and church unions all over Britain passed resolutions calling on the British to act to end Ottoman rule in Macedonia. The *Daily News* began printing lists of them, which ran into the hundreds, but there were soon too many to print; after beginning one such long list it gave up and simply wrote, 'and many others'.[71]

The churches organised mass meetings, opening with hymns and prayers, at which the Turks were excoriated and the British Government called on to act. At one, organised by the Metropolitan Free Church Association, an overflow audience was told by ministers: 'The sultan aimed at the extermination of the Christian races in his domains.' The government, Conservative at the time (1903), was damned for its lack of courage and morality. ('O that now we had but one hour of William Ewart Gladstone.') Speakers, although men of religion, were nevertheless bloodthirsty: 'If the Sultan will not heed the articulate conscience of Europe, then I would have him brought to reason by the thunder of British artillery. (Loud Applause.)' One minister described the sultan as a mad dog who must be put down: 'Some men were not fit to live'; 'The meeting was closed with the Doxology and the Benediction.' It was not a gathering of religious pacifists.[72]

Like other Britons, the clergy received their information from the press.[73]

## The Press

Hundreds of British newspaper stories featured descriptions of the sufferings of Macedonian Christians, almost none described the losses of Turks and Albanians. In fact, Muslims in Macedonia were victims of attacks by the bands, but readers in England would never have known it. What was primarily missing from the press reports was any mention of the attacks by the Macedonian rebels on Muslim villagers and Ottoman officials. When Muslim deaths were sometimes presented, they were described as justified acts of revenge. The great number of attacks by rebels of the Bulgarian Orthodox denomination on those who espoused the Greek Orthodox faith also were seldom mentioned. The result was the appearance of one-sided Bulgarian suffering.

British readers would have believed that the rebels were winning against the Ottoman army, and that the Ottomans would soon be driven from Macedonia. The *Daily News*, obviously hoping for victory by the Macedonian rebels, printed articles showing rebel successes. For example, it reported in August 1903: 1,000 men from Manastır City alone had left to join the rebel fight. In the field there were 20,000 to 30,000 rebels, and more would soon join them. Salonica was in a state of siege. The garrison at Ohrid, surrounded by rebel forces, was unable to leave to join the fight. The Ottoman army was defeated in numerous battles. Ottoman soldiers were deserting in large numbers. A general rebellion would break out in the other regions of Macedonia within a month. None of this was true.[74]

The newspapers made no attempt to hide their sympathies. The *Daily News* expressed its wish for the rebel's success: 'May Providence grant them (the rebels) further measure of success.' 'No English lover of freedom can do otherwise than wish them well.' The *Daily News* was particularly intemperate in its descriptions of the hated Turk: 'barbarian'; 'a great terror'; 'wholesale plunder'; 'wolves that have torn and harried'; '[t]he Turk means to exterminate the Macedonian Bulgars'; '[t]hey are ferocious brutes in human shape'; 'their black ignorance, their blind fanaticism'; 'Bestial Turk'; 'Butcher Abdul (Abdülhamid)'.[75]

Quotes from rebel leaders and the Bulgarian Government were ubiquitous. *The Times*, which printed 622 articles on Macedonia in 1903 alone, published extensive interviews with the leaders of the rebel committees, as did other newspapers. Very little was seen from Ottoman representatives or Macedonian Muslims. A few lines from statements of the Ottoman ambassador in London were sometimes included in articles otherwise attacking the Turks.[76]

As was the journalistic custom of the time, gross exaggerations were printed as fact. It was reported, for example, that 30,000 to 50,000 Christians had been massacred in Manastır Province alone. *The Times* reported that by Ottoman Government order all Bulgarians thought to be committee members were to be shot, whether or not they were armed. Ambassador O'Conor protested that no such orders had ever been issued. The *Daily News* 'Special Commissioner' reported from Sofia: 'The revolutionary leaders, I learn, have at the present in their possession a large quantity of Indian plague bacillus, with the dire determination to infect Constantinople, Salonika, and even Berlin.'[77]

According to the *Daily News*, the only solution for Macedonia was European control, although this remedy had been thwarted by Austria and Russia, who planned to divide Macedonia and Istanbul among themselves, as they had Poland. Thus, the Austrians and Russians had initiated 'useless, insincere sham reforms', whereas the only real solution was to free Macedonia from 'the Turk's misrule'. The *Daily News*, confirmedly Liberal, blamed the Conservative Balfour administration for inaction on Macedonia. It stated the Russians and Austrians could not be trusted. It wanted British 'direct action'. Macedonia must come under European power. 'Now again we have the proof that the governing Turk—in normal times an indolent brigand—is, in times of convulsion, an enemy of the human race.'[78]

**The Journalists**

The remedies for the Macedonian troubles advanced by the newspapers might have been written by the Balkan Committee, as they perhaps were.

Two journalists who reported on Macedonia were members of the Executive Committee of the Balkan Committee – Henry Wood Nevinson for the *Daily Chronicle* and Henry Brailsford for the *Manchester Guardian* and *Daily News*. Brailsford's book, *Macedonia: Its Races and their Future*, was serialised in both the *Manchester Guardian* and the *Fortnightly Review*.[79]

Walter Crawfurd-Price of *The Times* reported that he had travelled for a month through the war-torn region near Manastır, but his reports of destroyed villages raise questions. He reported that small villages supposedly had up to 700 destroyed houses each. These were levels of destruction that the consuls seem not to have noticed. He was more likely to have reported what was told to him, rather than what he saw. (*The Times* reported that 700 houses in one village, 'Aposhepo', had been destroyed; the *Daily News* reported 126 houses in the same village. Neither was likely correct.) Crawfurd-Price routinely damned all Ottoman administration. For example, he blamed the Ottoman governor-general, Hilmi Paşa, for supposed massacres ('an instrument of butchery'). In fact, even those consuls and other European officials who disliked the Turks praised Hilmi Paşa. The European diplomats felt him to be the best Ottoman administrator.[80]

John M. Macdonald began to write reports for the *Daily News* in January 1903. He toured some of Macedonia with a translator, but most of his information came from Salonica and Bulgaria, where he collected stories from Macedonian rebels and refugees. Macdonald stated that he was privy to consular documents regarding Bulgarian (he described all Macedonians as Bulgarians) suffering, but his reports bore little relation to real consular reports: 'In Macedonia there are more than a hundred and sixty thousand Bulgarian houses.' 'The "Komitadjis" have stringent orders never to fight except in self-defense.' Macdonald invented or repeated false information on atrocities. One village in which he reported 'atrocities' was, according to the British Foreign Office, in fact in Bulgaria, not, as Macdonald reported, in Macedonia. There had been no atrocities there.

The *Daily Telegraph*'s unnamed 'Special Correspondent' on Macedonian affairs quoted what amounted to press releases on Macedonia by the Bulgarian Government. He even stated that he had been authorised by the Bulgarian Government to send his reports. For example, in a long 'interview' with an unnamed Bulgarian rebel, he supposedly quoted the rebel. The rebel, described as a peasant from a village, gave a remarkably coherent and detailed account of political and military affairs well beyond his ken.[81]

Neutrality was not expected of the correspondents, quite the contrary. The *Daily News* even chose as its correspondent in Macedonia Alfred Arthur Greenwood Hales. Hales did indeed have knowledge of the guerilla war in Macedonia – he had been a member of a SMAC band fighting against the Ottomans. There is even a photograph of him swearing allegiance to the rebel cause, kissing the rebel flag as he did so. As the *Daily News* editors must have expected, Hales produced heart-rending stories of Bulgarians driven from their homes and tortured by the forces of the sultan ('Abdul the despot, Abdul the accursed').[82]

The *Daily Mail* correspondent in the Balkans, Reginald Wyon, contributed renditions of massacres carried out by Turks, relating what he had been told by single persons. The stories were horrifying. Wyon never wrote of any Muslims who were killed by Christian Macedonians. His primary source of information was the rebel committees (he did not distinguish which rebel group), usually reported from Sofia. He seems to have believed, or at least reported as fact, the statements from the rebel committees, such as that 60,000 Bulgarians were homeless and that the Turks planned to kill all Bulgarians in Macedonia. 'The district of Ohrid was destroyed, and, at the present rate of devastation, there will not be a human being left alive in two weeks' time.' According to him, all the villages in the district of Kastoria had been 'laid waste' and Kastoria itself plundered and seventy Christians killed. The standard fabrications of yellow journalism were not neglected: women and children were slaughtered, mercilessly. Children were baked in ovens; Bulgarians were sent out from Salonica by boat, supposedly to safety, but instead were thrown overboard and killed: 'The Porte is systematically devastating Macedonia and massacring the Christian population.'[83]

Wyon did not hide his sympathy for the rebels and detestation of the Turks: 'The insurrectionary movement can never be crushed by the Turks except by the utter extermination of every living soul in the country. And this, even for such experienced butchers, is rather too formidable an undertaking.' Wyon's solution to the problems of Macedonia was the standard one – European intervention – the need of which he put in graphic terms: 'When will Europe intervene? is the cry constantly made to me when I visit the few stragglers who reach here. But it seems as though, when Europe at last intervenes, there will not be a Christian left alive.'[84]

**Press Agencies**

Although they also excerpted items from the London dailies, provincial newspapers were dependent on press agencies for international news, particularly Reuter's (later Reuters) and the Press Association. Most of the press agencies' accounts that appeared in both the London and the provincial press were printed without sources or attributions. Statements such as '[a] reign of terror is reported to be prevailing at Uscub' were simply presented as fact, without attribution.[85]

The most common press agency stories of Christian Macedonian suffering and atrocities committed by Turks originated in Sofia, Bulgaria. One story, reported by the Press Association, stated: 'In the vilayet (Manastır) unimaginable atrocities were committed daily by the Turkish soldiers, who were pillaging and murdering everywhere. Young girls were dishonoured before the eyes of their fathers and mothers.' The only source given was 'a European merchant'. Another Press Association report from Sofia spoke of 'women, children, and old men massacred indiscriminately', that soldiers murdered prisoners, that women were repeatedly raped by soldiers and that '[i]n the repressive measures adopted by the Turkish authorities the utmost limit of barbarism has been reached'. The source of this information was identified as 'one of the best-informed consulates in Macedonia'. Press Association information was often unbelievably detailed – how many were murdered, details of actions by individual Turks, which houses were robbed, etc. – as if the reporter, writing from Bulgaria, had seen the events. What was reported did not appear in consular reports from the same period.[86]

The Press Association routinely reprinted absurd allegations from the Bulgarian press as facts, such as that the hands of Bulgarian merchants were cut off and carried on poles to be exhibited in Manastır City, outnumbered insurgents nevertheless killed hundreds of Turks, cities such as Razlog were completely destroyed (it was still there long after), a small group of insurgents held off thirty attacks by soldiers, etc. The articles from Sofia could rise to the absurd: the Press Association reported that the Turks planned to exile all the Bulgarians from Macedonia to Anatolia. It printed, without comment or criticism, the assertion that Turks had burned *all* (emphasis added) the villages in Manastır Province in the midst of a general massacre.[87]

The Reuter's agency, the most quoted press agency, was no better. In general, Reuter's saw no difficulty in printing the assertions of the Bulgarian rebel committees and the Bulgarian Government as fact. Reuter's provided extensive 'circulars' (releases sent to embassies and the press) from the Macedonian Committees, detailing victories over the Ottoman army, the failure of European plans for reform as well as murders and destruction by the Turks. Although sources were seldom given, it is obvious that the main sources of the Reuter's articles were the Macedonian Committees' leaders and membership.[88]

Reuter's sources were uniformly one-sided, drawn from rebels, Bulgarians and unidentified informants. Although a small number originated in Vienna or Istanbul, most of the Reuter's articles came from Sofia. One set of Reuter's dispatches from Sofia, for example, cited reports of the Macedonian Rebel Committee, 'private advices', and 'a private dispatch from Rila Monastery'. Reuter's reported from Sofia a Bulgarian Government claim that: 'The Porte is systematically devastating Macedonia and massacring the Christian population.' Reuter's also reported that, '[a]ccording to an official statement, 15,000 Bulgarians have been killed in the disturbances in European Turkey since April 15 (1903)'. The 'official statement' authorship was unnamed. The same article quoted that 130 villages had been burned to ashes by troops and local Muslims, according to an unnamed leader of Macedonian rebels. (The Press Association, reporting from Sofia, increased the death toll. It quoted the Macedonian Rebel Committee's statistics of between 30,000 and 50,000 Christians killed by Turks and 150,000 Macedonians hiding in forests and mountains. The author stated categorically that these statistics were true, agreed upon by 'all the reports received from the vilayet of Monastir.')[89]

Reuter's reported information was supposedly drawn from consular dispatches on massacres and consular fears of massacres, although reporters should not have seen those dispatches, and probably invented them, because they did not correspond to actual consular reports. One Reuter's report included information that the British were financing the revolution in Macedonia, a statement that would have surprised and dismayed the Foreign Office.[90]

There were press voices that opposed the routine vilification of the Turks: the *Daily Telegraph* printed some reports from its unnamed Constantinople Special Correspondent that included mention of Macedonian rebel attacks.

Most of the few even-handed articles, however, were not in the popular press. Thoughtful, often critical of the British Government, editorials in smaller London newspapers sometimes questioned the one-sided portrayals of events in Macedonia, but, because they were dependent on the press services for news, they printed the same sort of Turkish atrocity stories seen in other newspapers in their news sections, which were more likely to be read than editorials. For example, the *St James's Gazette* accurately editorialised that all sides in the conflict had committed atrocities, and cautioned against British interference. In the same issue, however, the *Gazette* published the same false Reuter's report on 50,000 massacred by Turks that appeared in other papers. The *Gazette* reported, based on a ridiculous statement from the Bulgarian Foreign Office, that the Turks had destroyed Kastoria and massacred the entire population of 10,000, an event that never happened.[91]

British consuls had their own prejudices, often displayed in their reports. Diplomatic reports were nevertheless valuable in judging the journalistic reports that have all too often been a staple of the nationalist histories of Macedonia. They contained refutations of the tales printed in the British press, which Ambassador O'Conor called 'exaggerated and sensational'. O'Conor was a constant critic of the British reporting on Macedonia, and was generally sympathetic to the plight of the Ottoman Government. Reports such as destruction of a monastery, that 5,000 rifles were being distributed to the Muslim population and that all Bulgarians taken as prisoners were shot were all identified as false by British diplomats in Macedonia. Consul-General Biliotti complained of

> the systematic course pursued by the greater part of the Press and some Consuls, who never cease finding fault with the Turkish government, whatever it did, thus encouraging the bands beyond all measure. In fact some of the Consuls do not appear to have ever heard of or at least do not appear to have ever reported Bulgarian atrocities, while they never fail to raise an outcry on every occasion against 'Turkish atrocities,' which, such as they were, had their origins in the actions of the Committees and their supporters.[92]

Consul-General Biliotti was a consistent critic of newspaper reports and journalists sent to report on Macedonia. He complained to his superiors of the 'anti-Turkish bias of foreign correspondents'. He stated that the journalists went so far as to take insurgents as their guides in the region. The consul-general who replaced Biliotti, Robert Graves, however, readily accepted journalists and their accounts. He took credit for assisting them and proudly proclaimed that they were his friends.[93]

The Macedonian nationalists understood and appreciated the British journalists. The Macedonian Committee's newspaper, *Reformi*, described them as such: 'These gentlemen are impressed by the courage and perseverance of the Macedonians and love Macedonia like their own homeland.' Macedonian refugees in Bulgaria passed a resolution thanking the Russian and British press 'for their sympathy towards our compatriots'.[94]

Perhaps the best description of the appreciation of the Macedonian rebels for the British press was in a letter sent to the *Daily News* by the rebel leader General Ivan Tzontcheff:

> To the Honourable Editor of 'The *Daily News*,' London.
>
> Dear Sir, — True to its noble tradition to be everywhere the defender of the oppressed, 'The Daily News,' as in the time of the Turkish atrocities in Bulgaria, has taken up the cause of the Macedonians. After Mister John Macdonald, for whom we keep good memory, you have sent for your correspondent a noble man, who became our brother of arms, and fought in the fields of Macedonia with the greatest courage. The letters of Mister A. Hales, like the famous letters of MacGahan (on the 1876 troubles), stir up the conscience of the English nation for the Macedonians fighting for their liberty.
>
> It is a high pleasure for me and for my comrades that we had in the midst of us a man of 'The *Daily News*,' an Englishman, who made the cause of the Macedonians his cause, and was ready to sacrifice his life for their liberty.
>
> The subscription raised by your journal is another prove (sic) of your warm sympathy for the Macedonians, and we have the hope that you will continue to defend our cause until the dawn of liberty and justice in our country.
>
> Full of gratitude, I, in the name of the Macedonian organization, and in the name of my comrades, cry: Long live 'The *Daily News*,' the defender of liberty and justice.
>
> Yours respectfully,
>
> Sub-President of the Committee, TZONTCHEFF
> Haut Comité, Macéde-Adrinopolitain
> No. 945, 5th Novembre, 1903.[95]

# Notes

1. On the history of the rebellion in Macedonia, see: the most complete history is Fikret Adanır, *Die Makedonische Frage: Ihre Entstehung und Entwicklung bis 1908*, Wiesbaden, Steiner, 1979. See also İpek Yosmaoğlu, *Blood Ties: Religion, Violence, and the Politics of Nationhood in Ottoman Macedonia, 1878–1908*, Ithaca: Cornell University Press, 2014. Duncan M. Perry, *The Politics of Terror: The Macedonian Liberation Movements, 1893–1903*, Durham, NC: Duke University Press 1988. Nadine Lange-Akhund, *The Macedonian Question 1893–1908 From Western Sources*, translated by Gabriel Topor, Boulder, CO: East European Monographs, 1998. Gül Tokay, *Makedonya Sorunu: Jon Turk İhtilali'nin Kökenleri, 1903–1908*, Istanbul: AFA Yayınları, 1996. Douglas Dakin, *The Greek Struggle in Macedonia*, Thessaloniki: Institute for Balkan Studies, 1966. Julian Brooks, 'Managing Macedonia: British Statecraft, Intervention, and "Proto-peacekeeping" in Ottoman Macedonia, 1902–1905', unpublished PhD dissertation, Simon Fraser University, 2014. Brooks provides excellent detailed information on the workings of the rebel groups, the Bulgarian Government and the British press and parliament, as well as containing an extensive English-language bibliography. I have cited it here for some documents that I have not been able to access. The work is less reliable on the details of the actual conflicts in Macedonia, because Brooks seems to have taken all consular reports indiscriminately as accurate. Angelos A. Chotzidis, 'A Re-appraisal of the Austro-Hungarian Reform Policy in Macedonia (1903)', *Balkan Studies* (Greece), vol. 37, no. 2 (1996), pp. 257–69. Christopher Psilos, 'The Young Turk Revolution and the Macedonian Question 1908–1912', unpublished PhD dissertation, University of Leeds, 2000. While valuable for its use of Greek archival material, this study suffers from a lack of Turkish materials, consideration of which should have been expected in a study of the Committee of Union and Progress. Andrew Rossos, *Macedonia and the Macedonians: A History*, Stanford, CA: Hoover Institution, 2008, pp. 69–124. For a brief study of the effect of the Macedonian rebellion on Turks, see George W. Gawrych, 'The Culture and Politics of Violence in Turkish Society, 1903–14', *Middle Eastern Studies*, vol. 22, no. 3 (July 1986), pp. 307–30. On the motivations and loyalties of the Macedonian rebels, see Keith Brown, *Loyal unto Death: Trust and Terror in Revolutionary Macedonia*, Bloomington: Indiana University Press, 2013.
2. On the unification, see: Yasamee, *Ottoman Diplomacy*, pp. 153–78. W. N. Medlicott, 'The Powers and the Unification of the Two Bulgarias, 1885', *The English Historical Review*, Part I, vol. 54, no. 213 (January 1939), pp. 67–82; Part II, vol. 54, no. 214 (April 1939), pp. 263–84, and Richard J. Crampton, *Bulgaria 1878–1918*, Boulder, CO: Eastern European Monographs, 1983, pp. 85–103. Gordon Martel,

'Liberalism and Nationalism in the Middle East: Britain and the Balkan Crisis of 1886', *Middle Eastern Studies*, vol. 21, no. 2 (April 1985), pp. 172–91. On the development of Bulgarian separatism in the Ottoman Empire, see Denis Vovchenko, *Containing Balkan Nationalism: Imperial Russia and Ottoman Christians, 1856–1914*, Oxford: Oxford University Press, 2016, pp. 108–90. The solution for Eastern Rumelia was not well received in Bulgaria, and Prince Alexander was ousted in a military coup in 1886. European diplomacy for the period is described in F. R. Bridge, and Roger Bullen, *The Great Powers and the European State System, 1814–1914*, Toronto: Pearson Longman, 2005, pp. 233–41 and 260–6. Bridge and Bullen accurately describe the machinations of the Europeans, but they consider the Ottoman Empire only as the pawn in the European diplomatic chess game.

3. On the Vlachs, see: T. J. Winnifrith, *The Vlachs: The History of a Balkan People*, London: Duckworth, 1987.
4. Justin McCarthy, 'The Population of Ottoman Europe Before and After the Fall of the Empire', in Heath W. Lowry and Ralph S. Hattox, eds, *Proceedings of the Third Conference on the Social and Economic History of Turkey*, Istanbul: Isis, 1990, pp. 275–98. The figures in the table are drawn from Ottoman population registration statistics, adjusted for undercounts of women and children, as described in the article. See also Daniel Panzac, 'La population de la Macédoine au XIXe siècle (1820–1912)', *Revue du monde musulman et de la Méditerranée*, no. 66 (1992), pp. 113–34. Note that the distinction between Greek and Bulgarian is not reliable. See İpek K. Yosmaoğlu, 'Counting Bodies, Shaping Souls: The 1903 Census and National Identity in Ottoman Macedonia', *International Journal of Middle East Studies*, vol. 38, no. 1 (February 2006), pp. 55–77. Yosmaoğlu, *Blood Ties*, pp. 131–68. Dakin offered different statistics, from Greek sources, and did not include the Muslim population (Dakin, *Greek Struggle*, p. 20). The incredibly varying list of Greek and Bulgarian statements on population would fill a chapter by themselves. See Justin McCarthy, *The Ottoman Peoples and the End of Empire*, London and New York: Arnold and Oxford University Press, 2001, pp. 53–60.
5. See Yosmaoğlu, *Blood Ties*, pp. 53–65, and her excellent analysis of the creation of 'Macedonia' (İpek K. Yosmaoğlu, 'Constructing National Identity in Ottoman Macedonia', in I. William Zartman, ed., *Understanding Life in the Borderlands: Boundaries in Depth and in Motion*, Athens, Georgia: University of Georgia Press, 2010, pp. 160–88.)
6. IMRO (Vatreshna Makedonska Revolyutsionna Organizatsiya.) SMAC (Varhoven makedono – odrinski komitet.) The names of the organisations changed slightly over time. SMAC was often called the External Macedonian Revolutionary

Organization (EMRO) in the literature. The most complete description of the Macedonian Committees and their politics are in Adanır's *Die Makedonische Frage*, pp. 100–33, Yosmaoğlu, *Blood Ties*, pp. 209–87, Lange-Akhund, pp. 34–54, and Perry, pp. 31–104 and 144–83. Jean Ganiage ('Terrorisme et Guerre Civile en Macédoine (1895–1903)', *Guerres mondiales et conflits contemporains*, no. 201 (Janvier 2001), pp. 55–81) provides excellent descriptions of early rebel activities and organisation and a bibliography, but a lack of listed sources makes some of his judgements questionable. Stephen Fischer-Galati, 'The Internal Macedonian Revolutionary Organization: Its Significance in "Wars of National Liberation"', *East European Quarterly*, vol. 6, no. 4 (1973), pp. 454–72. Fischer-Galati believed he knew what was in the minds of both the people of Macedonia and the Ottomans, without demonstrating the sources of his knowledge.

7. Constans to Delcassé, Therapia, 22 August 1903, in France, Ministère des Affaires Étrangères, *Documents Diplomatiques: Affaires De Macédoine, 1903–1905*, Paris, Imprimerie Nationale, 1905 (hereafter Affaires 1903–5), no. 22. Ritter von Stepski to Goluchowski, Monastir, 10 January 1903, HHStA PA XXXVIII/Konsulat Monastir 1903, vol. 392, no. 1. Hickel to Goluchowski, Salonica (Saloniki), 21 February 1903, HHStA PA XXXVIII/Konsulat Salonica 1903, vol. 407, no. 7. Kral to Goluchowski, Monastir, 17 April 1903, HHStA PA XXXVIII/Konsulat Monastir 1903, vol. 392, no. 44. I have not seen the original of these Austrian documents, which are reproduced in Macedonian Heritage (http://www.macedonian-heritage.gr/OfficialDocuments/events.html, hereafter MH). Even though the compilers, from Thessaloniki, have a definite point of view, I believe the documents are genuine. I have checked a number of their documents from the British Foreign Office and found them to be exact. On the Greek officers, see Reverseaux to Delcassé, Vienna, 20 November 1902, in DD, no. 38, and descriptions below.

The French Chargé d'Affaires in Istanbul mentioned briefly that in the first stage of their rebellion the Macedonian rebels had smuggled rifles across the Greek border, but given the interests of the Greek Government, this must have been minimal. (Bapst to Delcassé, Therapia, 29 July 1902, in France, Ministère des Affaires Étrangères, *Documents Diplomatiques: Affaires De Macédoine, 1902*, Paris: Imprimerie Nationale, 1903 (hereafter Affaires 1902), no. 22.)

On Bulgarian promises and efforts to restrain the Macedonian rebels, see Boulinière to Delcassé, Sofia, 3 March 1902, and Delcassé to Boulinière, Paris, 3 October 1902, in Affaires 1902, nos. 10 and 34, and Crampton, pp. 271–93. In February of 1904, bowing to further pressure from the Powers, the Bulgarian Prime Minister Stoyan Danev officially closed the Macedonian Committees' offices and arrested some committee members. He promised a closer watch on the border to interdict the bands. Little came of it, because Danev, who may or may not have been sincere, had little actual control of the situation. His actions had no real effect. Lower officials warned committee members of impending arrests so that they could escape. Bands still crossed the border, aided by officials and soldiers. Even so, Danev's actions prompted popular demonstrations and problems in the Bulgarian Parliament. (Bourgarel to Delcassé, Sofia, 14 February 1903, in France, Ministère des Affaires Étrangères, *Documents Diplomatiques: Affaires De Macédoine, Janvier-Février 1903*, Paris, Imprimerie Nationale, 1903 (Affaires 1903), nos. 10 and 16. Brooks, pp. 235–7.)

8. The consular reports on events in Macedonia have been considered in some detail in Justin McCarthy, 'British Diplomacy and the Ottoman Balkans', in *The Balkans and the Balkan History from the 14th Century to the Present*, Ankara: Genelkurmay Basımevi, 2014, pp. 309–30. Some of the material in this and the next chapter first appeared in that article.

    On the Bulgarian refugees, see Justin McCarthy, 'Ignoring the People: The Effects of the Congress of Berlin', in Hakan Yavuz and Peter Sluglett, *War and Diplomacy: The Russo-Turkish War of 1877–1878 and the Treaty of Berlin*, Salt Lake City: University of Utah Press, 2011, pp. 429–48. Anna M. Mirkova '"Population Politics" at the End of Empire: Migration and Sovereignty in Ottoman Eastern Rumelia, 1877—1886', *Comparative Studies in Society and History*, vol. 55, no. 4 (October 2013), pp. 955–85.

9. Hickel to Goluchowski, Salonica, 21 February 1903, in HHStA PA XXXVIII/Konsulat Salonica 1903, vol. 407, no. 7, MH. See also Kral to Goluchowski. Monastir, 11 March 1903, in HHStA PA XXXVIII/Konsulat Monastir 1903, vol. 392, no. 22, MH. On the detailed committee regulation for the creation and governance of bands, see FO 421/199, 'Instructions for the Interior' and 'Regulations for Village Bands', enclosures in O'Conor to Lansdowne, 11 November 1903.

10. There are numerous documents on the rebels' attacks and extortions. Among many others, see, for example: 'Extract from Annual Report for Bulgaria for the Year 1906 (Enclosure in Despatch from Sir G. Buchanan, No. 1 of January 1, 1907)', in BDOW 5, pp. 100–3. FO 195/2156, Biliotti to Whitehead, Salonica, 26 and 31 January 1903. FO 294/28, Pissurica to Biliotti, Monastir, 2, 6 and 31 January, 2 and 21 February, 5 March 1903. FO 421/198, Fontana to Biliotti, Uscub, 2 July 1903.

11. See, for example: FO 195/2157, Fontana to Graves, Uscub, 28 August 1903. FO 294/28, McGregor to Biliotti, Monastir, 15 July, 2 and 22 August 1903. FO 195/2157, McGregor to Biliotti, 10, 13, 22 and 27 July 1903; Graves to

O'Conor, Salonica, 22 August 1903. McGregor noted that the government was trying to stop the Albanians from taking action, but doubted it would work. He felt the Muslims and Bulgarians were taking sides against each other. (FO 294/28, McGregor to Biliotti, Monastir, 19 April 1903.) Muslim villagers were surely resisting the Bulgarian attacks, fighting back against the bands (FO 294/28, McGregor to Biliotti, Monastir, 19 April 1903). See also FO 294/28, Pissurica to Biliotti, Monastir, 13 March 1903. In one instance, Bulgarians robbed and killed a Muslim. Muslims in revenge killed Bulgarians (FO 294/28, Pissurica to Biliotti, Monastir, 11 March 1903). In another, local Muslims fought a band and both Muslims and Bulgarians, including women, died (FO 294/28, Pissurica to Biliotti, Monastir, 1 February 1903). I have concentrated on the pivotal year of 1903. For troubles in 1904, see FO 195/2182 and 2183.

Some of the reports were gruesome, but demonstrate why the Muslims began to fight:

> The Turkish population has been subjected to severe provocation, as in the case of Vefssel Agha, where the assassins, not content with murdering and robbing an inoffensive man who had happened to have lent them a few liras, killed his mother and mutilated her dead body with revolting barbarity.

(FO 294/28, McGregor to Biliotti, Monastir, 5 April 1903.)

12. Steeg to Delcassé, Salonika, 15 October 1902, in Affaires 1902, no. 28. FO 195/2157, Graves to O'Conor, Salonica, 1 September 1903; Graves to O'Conor, Salonica, 16 September 1903. Fontana identified some plunderers and killers as 'the Turkish (that is, Muslim) villagers of the neighbourhood, at Armensko and Rokovo, the Turks of Florina, and at Mokreni (Klissura) the Turkish Beys of Kaïlar'. He described the irregulars as 'simply straggling crowds of armed irregulars who refuse to obey their officers and of whom their officers are afraid'. He added that they were responding to Bulgarian attacks. (FO 195/2157, Fontana to Graves, Uscub, 31 August 1903.) FO 294/28, McGregor to Biliotti, Monastir, 20 April 1903. Both Fontana and McGregor reported beatings. (See, for example, FO 195/2157, Fontana to Biliotti, Uscub, 2 July 1903; McGregor to Graves, Monastir, 24 July 1903.) It is difficult to tell how many incidents reported were actually occurred and how many committee-based propaganda.

On the sad state of the Ottoman army in Macedonia and its relations with the populace, see: İpek K. Yosmaoğlu, 'Marching on an Empty Stomach', in Lorans Tanatar Baruh and Vangelis Kechriotis, eds, *Economy and Society on Both Shores of the Aegean*, Athens: Alpha Bank, 2010, pp. 277–96. Tokay, *Makedonya Sorunu*, pp. 105–16.

13. See, for example, FO 195/2157, McGregor to Graves, Monastir, 29 September 1903. McGregor included reports on this from the vilâyet government. See also FO 195/2157, Graves to O'Conor, Salonica, 5 September 1903; McGregor to Graves, Monastir, 13 October 1903, which also includes Ottoman reports on the situation. See the description of the use of cannon in the report of the Bishop of Florina. (FO 195/2157, Graves to O'Conor, Salonica, 22 August 1903.)
14. FO 195/2157, Fontana to Graves, Uscub, 19 September and 3 October 1903. FO 294/28, McGregor to Graves, 30 December and 19 October 1903. FO 195/2157, McGregor to Graves, Monastir, 27 September 1903. There were numerous arrests in connection with the events at Smyrdesh (FO 195/2156, McGregor to Biliotti, Monastir, 24 April 1903.) On the trials, see, for example, FO 294/28, McGregor to Graves, Monastir, 15 October 1903. There are many examples in the consular correspondence.
15. FO 195/2156, Fontana to Biliotti, Uscub, 19 January 1903. FO 294/28, McGregor to Biliotti, 7 May, and McGregor to Biliotti, 10 May 1903. On the Salonica bombings, see Steeg to Delcassé, Salonika, 3 April 1903, Affaires 1903–5, no. 10.
16. FO 294/28, McGregor to Biliotti, Monastir, 14 April 1903; McGregor to Biliotti, Monastir, 14 April 1903. FO 195/2156, McGregor to Biliotti, Monastir, 25 June 1903; FO 195/2156, McGregor to Biliotti, Monastir, 3 July 1903. On the rebel murders of the witnesses, see FO 195/2156, McGregor to Biliotti, Monastir, 19 July 1903. For similar cases, see FO 195/2156, McGregor to Graves, Monastir, 27 July 1903.
17. FO 195/2157, McGregor to Graves, Monastir, 27 September 1903.
18. FO 195/2156, Biliotti to O'Conor, Salonica, 31 March 1903. Fontana to Biliotti, 4 April 1903. Constans to Delcassé, Pera, 7 April 1903, in Affaires 1903–5, no. 4. For other regular army battles with Albanians, see: Vauvineux to Delcassé, Belgrade, 1 March 1902, in Affaires 1902, no. 2. FO 195/2182, Fontana to Graves, Uskub, 15 February 1904.
19. It is unfortunate for the historical record that Sir Robert Wyndham Graves took Biliotti's place as consul-general at Salonica (21 July 1903). Graves came to Salonica after appointments in Crete and Erzurum. Perhaps influenced by his own background (his father was Anglican Bishop of Limerick), Graves showed a marked partiality toward Christians and a dislike for Muslims. Graves paid little attention to reports of his consuls. He preferred the accounts of the rebel committees, what he heard from one of his friends, the Bulgarian consul, and individual Bulgarians. The opinions he forwarded often had no relation to reality. Graves was proud of his association with members of the British Balkan

Committee and others who were sponsoring propaganda against the Turks in London. (FO 195/2157, Graves to O'Conor, 21 July 1903. For more detail on Graves, see: McCarthy, 'British Diplomacy', Justin McCarthy, Cemalettin Taşkıran and Ömer Turan, *Sasun*, Salt Lake City: University of Utah Press, 2014, pp. 100–15. Robert Graves, *Storm Centres of the Near East*, London: Hutchinson & Co., 1933, pp. 197–9, 209–10, 213–25, 221.) On Biliotti, see Barchard.

On the reliability of the various British consuls in Macedonia, see McCarthy, 'British Diplomacy'.

20. FO 195/2156, Biliotti to O'Conor, Salonica, 2, 3 and 7 May 1903. Consul Fontana in Üsküp reported that authorities had kept in check Muslims who wanted to take revenge for the Salonica bombings. (FO 195/2156, Fontana to Biliotti, Uscub, 6 May 1903.)
21. FO 195/2156, Biliotti to O'Conor, Salonica, 28 February 1903; Biliotti to Whitehead, Salonica, 6 February 1903.
22. FO 195/2157, Biliotti to O'Conor, Salonica, 27 June 1903, underlining as in the original. Biliotti went on to describe the pamphlet's instructions on murder, terror and extortion. FO 195/2157, Graves to O'Conor, Salonica, 23 July 1903, a report of one of Biliotti's 'trustworthy confidential sources' that arrived after Biliotti had left Salonica.
23. For typical reports, see FO 195/2156, Biliotti to O'Conor, Salonica, 28 February and 3 April 1903, and FO 195/2157, Biliotti to O'Conor, Salonica, 25 June 1903.
24. FO 195/2156, Biliotti to Whitehead, Salonica, 15 February 1903.
25. FO 195/2156, Biliotti to O'Conor, Salonica, 16 May 1903.
26. FO 195/2157, Biliotti to O'Conor, Salonica, 9 July 1903.
27. 'Extract from Annual Report for Bulgaria for the Year 1906 (Enclosure in Despatch from Sir G. Buchanan, No. 1 of January 1, 1907)', in BDOW 5, pp. 100–3. Steeg to Delcassé, Salonika, 3 December 1902, in Affaires 1902. Adanır, pp. 150–2. Perry, pp. 116–19. There had been a previous SMAC uprising in 1895, easily put down. The numbers who fled were reported widely differently: Adanır (p. 152) reported 200, Lange-Akhund an incredible 3,000 (pp. 113–15).
28. Adanır (pp. 185–6) gives a number of examples of the attacks. See also: Gauthier to Constans, Monastir, August 1903, in AMAE/NS Turquie-Macedoine, vol. 35, f.175r, no. 36, MH. Vernazza to Delcassé, Salonique, 6 August 1903, in AMAE/NS Turquie-Macedoine, vol. 35, ff.193r-195r, no. 35, MH. On the politics of the revolt, see Adanır, pp. 179–99. FO 195/2157, Graves to O'Conor, Salonica and McGregor to Graves, Monastir, 4 August 1903. One

month later, on the strength of reports he received from the Macedonian Committee, Graves reported that all had been orderly in the rebels' occupation, with no troubles except forced 'contributions', no excesses were committed and local administration was carried on without a hitch. (FO 195/2157). His later report contradicts all other evidence. Graves had decided he supported the rebels and became a conduit for their propaganda. (See McCarthy, 'British Diplomacy'.) See also Perry, pp. 133–40. Lange-Akhund (pp. 118–29) gave an account of the uprising that included few Muslim deaths and only offered a greatly exaggerated number of Christian deaths.

29. On the rebel expectation of intervention, see Adanır, pp. 187–9, and Steeg to Delcassé, Salonique, 12 August 1903, in AMAE/NS Turquie-Macedoine, ôïi.35, ff.254r–259r.
30. Constans to Delcassé, Therapia, 11 August 1903, in Affaires 1903–5, no. 16. FO 294/28, McGregor to Biliotti, Monastir, 4 and 8 August 1903. FO 195/2157, McGregor to Graves, Monastir, 4, 5, 8 12, 16 and 19 August 1903. FO 195/2147, Pissurica enclosure in McGregor to Graves, Monastir, 24 August 1903. It should be noted that neither McGregor nor Pissurica were in Krushevo and had made no personal investigation there. The first Briton to see Krushevo was the British military attaché, Colonel F. R. Maunsell, who reported:

> The principal fighting continues to be centered round Krushevo, which was re-occupied by Turkish troops on the 13th instant, after several assaults had been repulsed and a bombardment by four batteries of artillery had been carried out. The insurgents drew off to a strongly entrenched position outside the town, where fighting still continues. In the village, the church and an adjoining part of the village held out after the rest, and, although completely surrounded and offered the sultan's pardon, they refused, and managed eventually to cut their way out.

(FO 421/198, Maunsell to O'Conor, Therapia, 19 August 1903. Maunsell's military reports would be important to a history of the military events of the insurrection.)

31. FO 195/2157, Graves to O'Conor, Salonica, 30 August 1903.
32. Kral to Goluchowski, Monastir, 28 September 1903, HHStA PA XXXVIII/ Konsulat Monastir 1903, vol. 393, no. 127, MH.
33. Not all the consular officials would have been in agreement with this presentation. Some, such as Graves and MacGregor, were willing to accept the assertions of the Balkan Committees. See the analysis in McCarthy, 'British Diplomacy and the Ottoman Balkans'.

34. FO 421/198, du Vallon to Elliot, Philippopolis, 9, 14 and 16 August 1903; Brophy to Elliot, Varna, 19 and 24 August 1903.

    I have not considered here the murder of a Russian consul on 8 August 1903, because it had little effect on the events, although the rebels thought it might lead to Russian support of their cause. The Russians sent a fleet to İğneada to threaten the Ottomans over the matter, but it was peacefully settled when the Ottomans hanged soldiers, most of whom were surely innocent. See Duncan M. Perry, 'Death of a Russian Consul: Macedonia 1903', *Russian History*, vol. 7, no. 1/2 (1980), pp. 201–12, and Constans to Delcassé, Therapia, 15 August 1903, in Affaires 1903–5, no. 18.
35. FO 421/198, du Vallon to Elliot, Philippopolis, 14 August 1903.
36. FO 421/198, O'Conor to Lansdowne, Constantinople, 18 and 22 August 1903; Missir to Eyres, Dedeagatch, 12 August 1903; Maunsell to O'Conor, Therapia, 19 August 1903. Constans to Delcassé, Therapia, 22 August 1903, in Affaires 1903–5, no. 22. The uncompromising violence of the Macedonian insurgents and the response of Ottoman forces and local Muslims in 1903 are catalogued and described throughout FO 421/196, 197, 198, 199, and to a lesser extent in documents in later volumes of FO 421.
37. FO 421/198, Maunsell to O'Conor, Therapia, 28 August and 10 September 1903; Elliot to Lansdowne, Sophia, 30 August 1903; FO 421/198, O'Conor to Lansdowne, Therapia, 28 August 1903; Maunsell to O'Conor, Therapia, 25 August 1903. See also FO 421/198, Massy to O'Conor, Therapia, 10 September 1903. On the expansion of the rebellion to Salonica Province, see FO 421/198, 'Report on Eastern Cazas of Salonica Vilayet', enclosure in Graves to O'Conor, Salonica, 11 August 1903; Graves to O'Conor, Salonica, 13 August 1903. FO 421/198, O'Conor to Lansdowne, Therapia, 24 August 1903. Note that these refugees were ethnic Greeks and Turks, not the Albanian Muslims and Patriarchists in Western Macedonia. See also, FO 421/198, Maunsell to O'Conor, Therapia, 25 August 1903.
38. FO 421/198, Elliot to Lansdowne, Sophia, 19 and 26 August 1903. Because Bulgaria was theoretically part of the Ottoman Empire, it rated only a consul-general. Elliot in fact acted as an ambassador.
39. See K. G. Robbins, 'Public Opinion, Press, and Pressure Groups', in F. H. Hinsley, ed., *British Foreign Policy under Sir Edward Grey*, London: Cambridge University Press, 1977, pp. 70–88. On the European concepts of the Balkans, see Maria Todorova, 'The Balkans: From Discovery to Invention', *Slavic Review*, vol. 53, no. 2 (Summer 1994), pp. 453–82. Eugene Michail has provided a theoretical analysis of the British image of the Balkans that has generally informed

some of the descriptions here. (*The British and the Balkans: Forming Images of Foreign Lands, 1900–1950*, London: Continuum, 2011.)

40. The Balkan Committee, like the Armenian Association, was led by Liberal Party members, supported by the general sentiment of the party. The National Liberal Federation passed a motion claiming the Turks were engaging in wholesale massacre of Christians and the sultan had to be ejected from control of Macedonia. ('Intercession Services', *The Times*, 8 October 1903, p. 6.)

    As was the case with the Anglo-Armenian Association, I have not attempted to describe the philosophical bases of the Balkan Committee's plans. These are considered in detail by James Andrew Perkins, 'British Liberalism and the Balkans, c. 1875–1925', unpublished doctoral dissertation, University of London, 2014, especially pp. 36–58, 143–52 and 159–61, Maria Todorova, *Imagining the Balkans*, Oxford: Oxford University Press, 2009, pp. 116–26, and Davide Rodogno, *Against Massacre: humanitarian Interventions in the Ottoman Empire 1815–1914*, Princeton: Princeton University Press, 1912, pp. 18–35 and 234–8.

    On the Balkan Committee see: Michail, pp. 11–17 and 30–42. Barry Patrick Dackombe, 'Single-Issue Extra-Parliamentary Groups and Liberal Internationalism, 1899–1920', unpublished PhD dissertation, Open University, 2008, pp. 106–20. The outdated article by Leften S. Stavrianos ('The Balkan Committee', *Queen's Quarterly*, vol. 48 (Autumn 1941), pp. 258–67) is of little use, especially because he identified none of his sources. On Buxton, see H. N. Fieldhouse, 'Noel Buxton and A. J. P. Taylor's "The Trouble Makers"', in Martin Gilbert, ed., *A Century of Conflict 1850–1950*, New York: Atheneum, 1967, pp. 175–98. David Rodogno considers French attitudes on Macedonia, which have not been considered here, as well as the Balkan Committee, but his study is not accurate on the events of the rebellion. ('The European Powers' Intervention in Macedonia, 1903–1908: An Instance of Humanitarian Intervention?', in Brendan Simms and D. J. B. Trim, eds, *Humanitarian Intervention: A History*, Cambridge: Cambridge University Press, 2011, pp. 205–25.) The quasi-biography of Buxton (T. P. Conwell-Evans, *Foreign Policy from a Back Bench: A Study Based on the Papers of Lord Noel-Buxton*, London: Oxford University Press, 1932) contains very little of value.

41. 'Statement by the Balkan Committee', *The Times*, 18 September 1903. Bryce retired from the Balkan Committee in December of 1905. He was taking up a position in the government and felt the committee should be independent, the better to criticise government actions. He took the opportunity of his farewell speech to complain of the situation in Macedonia, advocating European

control of all major institutions there, including the gendarmerie, the courts and finance. He praised the Bulgarians and described the Ottomans as 'the common enemy'. ('The Balkan Committee: Farewell Speech by Mr. Bryce', *The Times*, 25 December 1905.)

Other committees and 'experts' on Macedonia existed and had some effect on British policy and public opinion, although nothing like that of the Balkan Committee. The Balkan Committee was supported by those who advocated the Armenian Cause. The 'Friends of Armenia' wrote Grey that they hoped he would persevere in coercing the Ottomans despite objections from other Powers. (FO 421/241, Friends of Armenia to Grey, London, 1 April 1908.) 28,000 British women sent a petition to the Queen and another 23,500 a petition to the government. They asked for a 'Christian Governor responsible to the Powers'. ('Macedonia', *The Times*, 3 December 1903, p. 9.)

42. Bryce to Buxton, 15 July 1903, quoted in Taylor, 'Noel Buxton', p. 180.
43. For example, 'The Balkan Question', *The Times*, 3 February 1908, p. 4. In that time period, computerised searches reveal that *The (London) Standard* printed sixty-four articles that included the words 'Balkan Committee', *The Times* 162 articles (although, for *The Times* these included letters to the editor and a small number of indexes). The British Library's British Newspaper Archive listed 440 pieces on 'Balkan Committee', almost all of them actual articles. These figures do not include the many articles that mention the words of members of the committee, but not necessarily the name 'Balkan Committee'. For example, the British Newspaper Archive listed 113 articles under 'Noel Buxton AND Macedonia' and 344 articles under 'Bryce AND Macedonia'. (There obviously is some overlap in articles with these names and those including 'Balkan Committee'.)
44. FO 421/202, Balkan Committee to Lansdowne, London, 29 April 1904. 'The State of Macedonia', *The Times*, 21 December 1906, p. 12. H. N. Brailsford, *Macedonia: Its Races and their Future*, London: Methuen, 1906. p. 130. See also pp. 191–220. On the Balkan Committee support of Bulgaria, see Keith Robbins, *Politics, Diplomacy and War in Modern British History*, London: Hambledon Press, 1994, pp. 143–4 and 217–23. Robbins (Chapter 11) also considers the effects of public opinion on Edward Grey's policies. See the reviews of Balkan Committee publications in *The Hellenic Herald*, vol. 1, no. 12 (October 1907), pp. 172–5. Although it favoured the Bulgarians, the Balkan Committee did attract the attention of the Greeks and Serbs. The Serbian and Bulgarian ambassadors and the Secretary of the Greek Legation attended at least one committee meeting. 'Turkish Reforms', *The Times*, 19 July 1910, p. 14.

45. 'Macedonia', *The Times*, 1 October 1903, p. 10.
46. James Bryce, speaking of an article in *The Times*: '[A] document which was purloined from Hilmi Pasha's archives supposedly showed 93 villages destroyed.' The speaker said that evidence in *The Standard* showed 111 villages destroyed, 9,700 houses burned and 50,000 refugees – 'all homeless, all starving, because the policy of the Turks was not only to kill by the sword, but kill by famine'. The Macedonian Committee itself had alleged twenty-two destroyed villages and towns, and they were not given to understatement. (FO 195/2157, McGregor to Graves, Monastir, 27 September 1903.)
47. It was alleged in the meeting that Hilmi Paşa, the governor-general of Macedonia, was in fact responsible for the massacres of Christians.
48. 'Meeting in St. James Hall', *The Times*, 30 September 1903, p. 4. *The Times* devoted columns to its reporting of the meeting, with extensive quotes from the speakers, and repeated the message of the speakers in two editorials (p. 7). Other London and provincial newspapers also covered it in detail. See, for example, 'Turkish Misrule: London Protest Meeting', *Daily Telegraph*, 30 September 1903, p. 9.
49. FO 421/240, Balkan Committee to Grey, London, 31 January 1908. O'Conor commented that the committee's memorandum was nonsense. (FO 421/240, O'Conor to Grey, 4 February 1908.)
50. 'The Macedonian Question', *The Times*, 28 January 1908, p. 8. At the meeting, Lord Lansdowne and his plan were praised.
51. For a summary and analysis on popular opinion and the British press on the Macedonian Question, see Ryan Gingeras, 'Between the Cracks: Macedonia and the "Mental Map" of Europe', *Canadian Slavonic Papers*, vol. 50, nos. 3/4 (September–December 2008), pp. 341–58. For example, in the press, see: 'The Macedonian Question: Conference of the Balkan Committee', *The Times*, 14 February 1905, p. 5; 'Turkish Reforms', *The Times*, 19 July 1910; 'Protest by the Balkan Committee', *The Times*, 5 July 1911. At the 14 February meeting, Herbert Gladstone falsely stated that the Turks had not carried out one reform in seventy years. ('The Condition of Macedonia', *The Standard*, 14 February 1905, p. 6.)
52. See, for example, 'The Situation in Macedonia', *The Times*, 25 October 1906, p. 9.
    The *St James's Gazette* printed a small number of articles explaining that evidence in favour of the Ottoman and against the Bulgarian rebels was ignored, and that Bulgarians were killing Muslims indiscriminately (for example, 'Tumult and Shouting', 20 August 1903, p. 3; 'Balkans Peril', 10 August 1903, p. 11).
53. 'The Balkan Committee', *The Times*, 11 March 1904, p. 7. 'Macedonia', *The Times*, 29 October 1903, p. 4. ('Notice to the Organizers of Meetings.') The meeting on the Macedonian Question of the Literary Society of the King's

Weigh Church (a Congregational church in London), sponsored by the Balkan Committee. Even such small meetings were reported in *The Times* and local papers. ('Macedonia', *The Times*, 18 November 1903, p. 5. 'Macedonia', *The Times*, 11 December 1903, p. 6. There were too many meetings, large and small, to cite here. For example, see these from *The Times* in 1903: Glasgow ('Macedonia', 21 October 1903, p. 8.) Liverpool ('Macedonia', 23 October 1903, p. 9.) Birmingham ('Meeting in Birmingham', 10 October 1903, p. 10.) Nottingham ('Public Meeting at Nottingham', 2 October 1903, p. 9.).

54. The Lord Provost, elected by the city council, held an office somewhat comparable to mayor in other cities.
55. 'Macedonia: Public Meetings', *The Times*, 21 October 1903, p. 8. 'Meeting in Birmingham', *The Times*, 10 October 1903, p. 10. How the British were to pass through the Bosporus from the Black Sea was not explained. Perhaps they meant the Dardanelles.
56. 'The Balkan Committee', *The Times*, 18 April 1904, p. 7.
57. In the interest of brevity, I do not describe at any length another book, edited by a member of the Balkan Committee, Luigi Villari (*The Balkan Question*, seen in the American edition, New York: Dutton, 1905.). Contributors included Bryce and other members of the Balkan Committee, as well as the London representative of the Bulgarian rebels. The book contained attacks on subjects such as polygamy and the Caliphate that had nothing to do with the Balkan Question, but portrayed the Turks in a bad light. Albanians were 'savages', Turks ('essentially nomads') were always bad rulers, the Turkish population was decreasing because of the effects of syphilis, etc. Bulgarians were portrayed as hard working and honest people who love education. Arguments for Bulgarian dominance were bolstered by completely false statistics on population. The solution offered for the Macedonian problem was European control, of course.
58. Noel Buxton, *Europe and the Turks*, London: Murray, 1907. Those interested in Buxton's opinions on the Ottoman Empire should also see Noel Buxton and Harold Buxton, *Travel and Politics in Armenia*, New York: Macmillan, 1914.
59. Buxton, pp. 60–1.
60. Buxton, pp. 61–2 and 69.
61. Buxton, p. 100–1 and 112. His plan for changes was delineated in Buxton, pp. 98–118.
62. F. M. Leventhal, *The Last Dissenter: H. N. Brailsford and His World*, Oxford: Clarendon Press, 1985, pp. 29–60.
63. London: Methuen, 1906, pp. 26, 30–3 and 111–33. Brailsford's depictions of the Ottoman Government were often simply wrong. He alleged, for example,

that no Christian was allowed to hold an executive or administrative post in the Ottoman Government (Brailsford, p. 26). Two books by Carter Vaughn Findley demonstrate the absurdity of this: *Bureaucratic Reform in the Ottoman Empire*, Princeton: Princeton University Press, 1980, and *Ottoman Civil Officialdom*, Princeton: Princeton University Press, 1989.

64. Brailsford, pp. 28–9 and 82–3. I have not tried to find the religions of editors of the main Continental newspapers, but I doubt if many were Jewish.
65. Brailsford, p. 322. Brailsford broke with the general Balkan Committee sentiment, however, in that he believed the governor-general of Macedonia should be a Muslim, although not an Ottoman subject. This, he felt, would assuage Muslim feelings. On reform, see pp. 290–322.
66. 'The Balkan Committee', *The Times*, 7 April 1906, p. 12. 'Statement by the Balkan Committee', *The Times*, 18 September 1903, p. 10.

    An example of the stance of the committees: Samuel Smith, MP, a member of the Anglo-Armenian Association, rose in the House of Commons to condemn the Turks for the deaths of 200,000 Armenians. All, he said, had been ordered by the sultan. Britain was also at fault for opposing the Treaty of San Stephano, and he favoured Russian occupation, including a Russian port on the Mediterranean. Smith was in favour of the dismemberment of the Ottoman Empire. ('Armenian Christians', House of Commons, 3 March 1896, *Hansard*, vol. 38, cc. 37–125; 'House of Commons: The Armenian Question', *The Times*, 4 March 1896, p. 6.) Except in the case of *Hansard* being cited in another source, reference here is to the online *Hansard*, http://hansard.millbanksystems.com.
67. Some of these are mentioned above. See also 'The Situation in the Balkans', *The Times*, 17 January 1905; 'Armenian Reform', *The Times*, 27 November 1913, p. 7; 'Reforms in Armenia', *The Times*, 15 August 1913, p. 5); 'Armenian Reform', *The Times*, 27 November 1913, p. 7; 'To-Day', *The Times*, 13 May 1896, p. 6.
68. FO 421/199, 'Notes by Balkan Committee on New Austro-Russian Reform Scheme. (Communicated by Mr. N. Buxton, November 5. Issued by the Balkan Committee, November 3, 1903.)'
69. 'Macedonia', *The Times*, 4 December 1903, p. 5. 'Macedonia', *The Times*, 3 October 1903, p. 8. 'Macedonia: Letters from the Primate and Bishop of Winchester', *The Times*, 2 October 1903, p. 9. The Bishop of Winchester believed that the Christians were all 'members of the Greek Church'.
70. 'Macedonia: Letter from the Bishop of Rochester', *The Times*, 13 October 1903, p. 8. 'Macedonia', *The Times*, 2 October 1903, p. 10. 'Macedonia', *The Times*, 1 October 1903, p. 10.

71. 'The Situation in Macedonia', *The Times*, 17 September 1903, p. 10. 'The Situation in Macedonia', *The Times*, 16 September 1903, p. 4. For the lists, see, for example, 'Macedonia's Cry', *Daily News*, 24 September 1903, p. 12. See the other lists printed under the same title in many issues of the *Daily News*, and 'The Balkan Horrors: Free Church Action. Intervention Demanded. Pulpit References', *Daily News*, 14 September 1903, p. 4.

72. 'Turkish Outrages: City Temple Gathering. Eloquent Protests', *Daily News*, 25 September 1903, p. 12.

73. The newspapers cited below, especially the *Daily Telegraph*, the *Daily News* and the *Daily Mail* were most often mentioned, but even when no sources for the clergy's belief were cited, the sources for their assertions were obvious. There were almost no other sources of information. See, for example, 'Free Church Ministers' Protest', *Daily News*, 10 September 1903, p. 7.

74. 'Balkans Aflame' and 'Active Revolt: "*Daily News*" Predictions Fulfilled', *Daily News*, 13 August 1903, p. 7.

75. Among many other examples, see 'Macedonia Again', *Daily News*, 8 August 1903, p. 6. 'Exterminating a People', *Daily News*, 27 August 1903, p. 7. The author of the latter article, John Macdonald, added that British policy was 'an indelible disgrace'. 'Macedonia', *Daily News*, 29 September 1903, p. 6. 'Macedonia in Arms', *Daily News*, 10 August 1903, p. 6.

76. See, for example, 'Macedonia: Interview with Saranoff', *The Times*, 18 November 1903, p. 5. 'Macedonia: Statement by General Tzontcheff', *The Times*, 16 December 1903, p. 7. It should be noted that the 622 articles were all the ones that included the word 'Macedonia' in *The Times*' historical data base. Some of these were short mentions, and many were on political machinations in Istanbul and among the Powers.

For interviews with Bulgarian and Macedonian rebel leaders, see, for example: John Macdonald's long interview with the Bulgarian 'Minister-President'. ('Mr. Daneff on "The *Daily News*," an Interview. Bulgarian Manifesto (From Our Special Commissioner').), Sofia, 6 May 1903, *Daily News*, 14 May 1903, p. 8.) 'Gallant Macedonia: Aims of the Insurgents. Interview with (Rebel Leader) Boris Saranoff', *Daily News*, 17 December 1903, p. 10, complete with a portrait of Saranoff. 'The Crisis in the Balkans: Macedonian Testimony. (By John Macdonald)', *Daily News*, 27 July 1903, p. 7.

77. 'Thirty Thousand Massacred', *Daily News*, 9 September 1903, p. 7. FO 421/199, O'Conor to Lansdowne, Therapia, 28 September 1903. See also FO 421/198, Lansdowne to O'Conor, 30 September 1903. 'Macedonia's Despair: Leaders'

Terrible Resolve', *Daily News*, 1 June 1903, p. 5. 'Balkan Terror: Macedonian's Frightful Plan, Destruction by Plague', *Daily News*, 6 June 1903, p. 7.

78. 'In the Balance', *Daily News*, 27 August 1903, p. 6. See also 'Why Not a Concert?' *Daily News*, 11 August 1903, p. 6. 'Aims of the Macedonians: A European Misconception', *Daily News*, 12 August 1903, p. 12. 'Turkey and Macedonia', *Daily News*, 28 February 1903, p. 7. 'Notes on the Situation', *Daily News*, 11 August 1903, p. 7. 'Outlook in Macedonia', *Daily News*, 28 February 1903, p. 7.

79. Despite its title, a valuable source on the journalists is Peter Kardjilov, *The Cinematographic Activities of Charles Rider Noble and John Mackenzie in the Balkans*, vol. 1, translated from the Bulgarian by Ivelina Petrova, Newcastle upon Tyne: Cambridge Scholars Publishing, 2020, pp. 26–43.

80. 'The Condition of Macedonia', *The Times*, 2 December 1903, p. 8. 'Suffering Macedonia', *Daily News*, 9 December 1903, p. 9. 'Macedonia—A Suggestion', *The Times*, 2 September 1903. 'The Turks in Macedonia', *The Times*, 10 February 1903, p. 5. The *Daily Telegraph* noted: 'Hilmi Pasha, who was formerly governor-general of Adana, and later on of the Yemen, ranks as an energetic and intelligent statesman, not open to corruption, and gained great esteem from his previous services.' ('Balkan Troubles', 2 March 1903, p. 9.) Lionel James seems also to have been a correspondent for *The Times*, but I have not been able to ascertain which articles may have been his.

81. 'Balkan Crisis: Bulgarian Demands on Turkey', *Daily Telegraph*, 23 September 1903, p. 10. 'Macedonia: A False Truce', *Daily Telegraph*, 19 August 1903, p. 11. The *Daily Telegraph* at first was content to only report political events, but by 1903 it was printing the most prejudiced Reuter's reports. (For the earlier reports, see, for example, 'Macedonia and the Macedonians', *Daily Telegraph*, 20 February 1903, p. 11. Examples of Reuter's reports in the *Daily Telegraph*: 'The Russian Fleet', *Daily Telegraph*, 22 August 1903, p. 9. 'Critical Situation at Salonica', *Daily Telegraph*, 20 August 1903, p. 7. 'Balkan Crisis', *Daily Telegraph*, 15 August 1903, p. 7. 'Terrible Reports from Sofia', *Daily Telegraph*, 9 September 1903, p. 9. See also 'Turkish Methods', *Daily Telegraph*, 28 September 1903, p. 7, among others.) 'Among the Macedonian Revolutionists: Interviews by Moonlight', *Daily Telegraph*, 20 October 1903, p. 7.

82. 'Suffering Macedonia: Among the Refugees. Appeal to the Jews (By A. G. Hales)', *Daily News*, 23 November 1903, p. 10. Hales wanted 'the wealthy Jews' of England to help the Macedonians.

83. All Reginald Wyon, *Daily Mail*: 'Turkish Inhumanity', 7 September 1903, p. 3. 'Reprisals Threatened', 9 September 1903, p. 5. 'Balkan Horrors', 10 September

1903, p. 5. 'Eve of War', 15 September 1903, p. 5. '"Unspeakable" Turks', *Daily Mail*, 12 September 1903, p. 5. 'Surrounded by Spies', 19 September 1903, p. 5. Reginald Wyon, 'Exile or Death', *Daily Mail*, 10 October 1903, p. 5. 'Sacking of Kastoria', *Evening News and Mail*, 19 September 1903, p. 2. Wyon wrote a book on his adventures in the Balkans, published in 1904. The book was full of anecdotes and sympathy for the rebels, and dwelt on Wyon's troubles as a traveller. In general, it was considerably more temperate than his newspaper articles. (Reginald Wyon, *The Balkans from Within*, London: Finch, 1904.)

84. Reginald Wyon, 'Why the Powers Must Intervene', *Daily Mail*, 26 September 1903, p. 4. 'Turkish Inhumanity', *Daily Mail*, 7 September 1903, p. 3. The rebel's magazine described Wyon as 'particularly devoted to the Macedonian cause'. (*Reformi*, vol. 6, no. 12 (14 February 1904), p. 4, in Kardjilov, p. 238.)

85. No heading, *Sheffield Daily Telegram*, 20 August 1903, p. 5. I have taken examples of press agency articles primarily from provincial newspapers to demonstrate the scope of their influence. For the Ottoman Government's views and concerns on press agency reporting, see Servet Yanatma, 'The International News Agencies in the Ottoman Empire (1854–1908)', unpublished PhD dissertation, Middle East Technical University, 2015.

86. 'Balkan Atrocities', *The Dundee Courier*, 11 September 1903, p. 5. See also, 'Turkish Methods in Macedonia', *The Dundee Courier*, 12 September 1903, p. 5. 'The Macedonian Revolt: Barbarous Methods of Repression', *Manchester Courier*, 26 August 1903, p. 10. See also, for example, 'More Alleged Atrocities', *Sheffield Daily Telegram*, 30 September 1903, p. 7.

87. 'Turks and the Bulgarian Rebels: Tales of Fiendish Cruelty', *The Evening Post*, 23 May 1903, p. 5. 'Macedonia: Terrible Massacres', *Western Daily Press (Bristol)*, 26 August 1903, p. 10; 'Macedonia', *Manchester Evening News*, 3 October 1903, p. 5.

88. See, for example, 'Devastation in Monastir: Bulgarian List of Destroyed Villages', *Manchester Courier*, 1 October 1903, p. 7; 'Bulgarian Appeal to the Powers: Statement of a Revolutionist', *Sheffield Daily Telegram*, 11 August 1903, p. 5, in which Ottoman repression and massacres were given as the cause of revolt. 'Balkan Rising: The Act of Despair. Appeal of the Macedonian Committee', *Daily News*, 11 August 1903, p. 7.

89. 'Balkan Fights', *Daily News*, 11 September 1903, p. 7. 'Macedonian Revolution: Heavy Death-Roll', *The Dundee Courier*, 16 November 1903, p. 5. 'Indictment of Turks', *The Dundee Courier*, 15 September 1903, p. 5. Reuter's stories, again from Sofia, told the same accounts of Turkish actions in Edirne ('Macedonian Situation', *Sheffield Daily Telegram*, 15 June 1903, p. 6.) 'Famine, Fire, and the

Sword: Appalling Stories from Monastir', *Manchester Courier*, 9 September 1903, p. 10. Of course, the stories were actually from Sofia, not Manastır.

90. 'Consular Advices: Fears of a Great Massacre at Monastir', *Manchester Courier*, 15 August 1903, p. 8. 'Balkan Peril' and 'Power of the Committees', *Daily News*, 17 April 1903, p. 7.

91. 'The Sacred Right to Murder', *St James's Gazette*, 9 September 1903, p. 3. 'Balkan Crisis', *Daily Telegraph*, 8 May 1903, p. 9. 'Bulgaria Warned', *St James's Gazette*, 9 September 1903, p. 8. The *St James's Gazette* routinely printed Reuter's stories, along with many unattributed articles obviously taken from press agencies and other newspapers. These were uniformly anti-Ottoman.

92. John Burman, *Britain's Relations with the Ottoman Empire during the Embassy of Sir Nicholas O'Connor to the Porte, 1898–1908*, Istanbul: Isis, 2010, pp. 212–15. FO 421/199, O'Conor to Lansdowne, Constantinople, 8 October 1903. See also FO 421/198, Elliot to Lansdowne, Sophia, 22 August 1903. FO 195/2156, Biliotti to O'Conor, Salonica, 9 March 1903. FO 421/198, O'Conor to Lansdowne, Therapia, 18 August 1903. FO 421/198, O'Conor to Lansdowne, Therapia, 30 September 1903; FO 421/198, Fontana to Graves, Uscub, 8 September 1903; FO 195/2157, Fontana to Graves, Uscub, 8 September 1903. Musurus Paşa, the Ottoman ambassador in London, identified as absolute nonsense the report in *The Times* on Turks massacring all the women and children in twenty-two villages in Florina and Monastir districts. (FO 421/198, Musurus to Lansdowne, London, 27 August 1903.) See also FO 421/198, Musurus Pasha to Lansdowne, London, 14 August 1903.

93. FO 421/196, O'Conor to Lansdowne, Constantinople, 25 March 1903: 'Summary of Consular Despatches concerning Affairs in Macedonia'. Robert Graves, *Storm Centres of the Near East: Personal Memories, 1879–1929*, London: Hutchinson, 1933, pp. 199–202, 206, 212–13, 225 and 239.

94. *Reformi*, vol. 5, no. 40 (September 1903), p. 4, quoted in Kardjilov, p. 32. FO 421/241, 'Resolution Passed at the Macedonian Meeting held in Sophia on February 19 (March 3), 1908', enclosure in Barclay to Grey, Sophia, 1 April 1908.

95. 'General Tzontcheff Thanks "The Daily News"', *Daily News*, 11 November 1903, p. 9.

# 5

# BRITISH POLITICIANS AND MACEDONIA

Analysts have disagreed on the effect of the Balkan Committee and the press on British foreign policy. Unquestionably, British foreign secretaries cited the pressure of British public opinion on their decisions. They forwarded the statements of the committee to the embassy in Istanbul. It is most important to note that the proposals of the British Government coincided with those of the committee, but it is also true that the British politicians themselves held the same views toward the Ottoman Empire as the Balkan Committee.[1]

## Lord Lansdowne

Henry Charles Keith Petty-Fitzmaurice, Fifth Marquess of Lansdowne, Conservative foreign secretary from 1900 to 1905 was particularly affected by the Balkan Committee. He has been described as 'living in terror of the Committee'.[2]

Lansdowne attempted to convince the Powers to put into effect a programme that was an almost exact duplicate of that of the committee – a European governor and European Commission were to rule over Macedonia. Organs of security and the judiciary were to be put under overall European control. Oddly for a Conservative, the party of Disraeli, Lansdowne echoed the Balkan Committee in saying that Britain was ultimately responsible for the troubles in Macedonia, because Britain had been the main force in supplanting the Treaty of San Stephano with the Treaty of Berlin.[3]

Lansdowne made his feelings on Macedonia and the Turks plain. Speaking in the House of Lords, he described the Ottoman Government as 'chronic and grievous mismanagement'. He made reference to the failing of the Ottomans to carry out reforms envisaged in the Treaty of Berlin, neglecting, of course, to mention the more egregious British violations of that treaty by not protecting the Muslim populations of Serbia, Bulgaria and Romania, as had been stipulated in the treaty. In another speech before parliament, Lansdowne admitted that some of the problems in Macedonia had been caused by Christian rebel bands, but said that the bands' actions were understandable, because they were reacting to 'the long-standing misgovernment and maladministration of the Turkish Government'. He was sure the Bulgarian Government would keep the bands in check in the future.[4]

The Balkan Committee and the foreign secretary worked to the same ends, the one politically supporting and drawing public support for the plans of the other, which were also the committee's plans. Lansdowne's sentiments and attempts at removing Turkish control over Macedonia were well received by the Balkan Committee. Both Buxton and Bryce praised him. At various times, members of the Balkan Committee spoke in both the Lords and the Commons in support of Lord Lansdowne's proposals.[5]

During Lansdowne's tenure in office, parliament was deliberately kept in the dark by the government. The Parliamentary Papers, known as the 'Blue Books', provided to the parliament and the public and quoted by Lansdowne, his supporters and the Balkan Committee, were deliberate 'falsifications by omission'. British consuls in Macedonia were by no means unprejudiced, and they tended to provide the government in Westminster with what it wanted to hear. Nevertheless, they did forward extensive reports on attacks on Muslims and ill deeds by the insurgents. Ottoman attempts at fairness and restoring order were often noted. Hilmi Paşa, the inspector-general of Macedonia, was especially praised. Collectively, these consular reports cast real doubt on the image of the Macedonian troubles portrayed by the British Government. They were not to be seen until archives were opened many decades later. Instead, the government printed a Blue Book that omitted anything that would cast doubt on its policies. For the period of the most intense combat in Macedonia, August of 1903, for example, the Blue Book contained only fourteen documents. Five of these were on 'Turkish excesses', the rest mainly straightforward reports on military engagements. There was nothing on Muslim suffering or the very real massacres of Muslims committed by the rebels.[6]

While Lord Lansdowne was in command of British decisions on Macedonia, he had the public support of his prime minister, Arthur Balfour. Although he did not think much of any of the Balkan Christians or Muslims, Balfour preferred the Bulgarians to the others. He would have been willing to see a Bulgarian Macedonia, but he realised that the other Powers would not accept that, so he supported Macedonian autonomy.[7]

**Sir Edward Grey**

Edward Grey, foreign secretary from 1905 to 1916, had been a committee member of the Anglo-Armenian Association. His views of the Ottomans echoed those of the association. In 1896, Grey spoke in parliament against the Turks, blaming the Ottoman Government for troubles in Eastern Anatolia. He described that government as a 'system of misgovernment under which such cruelty (against Armenians) has been possible'. He described the Ottomans as 'bad government', guilty of forcing 'exceptional persecutions and massacres' on the Armenians. He was in favour of the British Government taking 'independent action', and lamented that the (Conservative) government had not considered it. Although he was weak on specifics, he promised that a Liberal government would force the Ottomans to change.[8]

Once he became foreign secretary, Grey consistently tried to apply 'coercive measures' to the Ottomans to facilitate the dismemberment of the Ottoman Empire. Grey was particularly inimical to Sultan Abdülhamid II. He felt that '[h]is rule has been bad for his country in every way, materially and morally". The sultan's government was 'a clique of scoundrels', a 'corrupt misgovernment'.[9]

Grey wrote to the Balkan Committee's great St James's meeting in 1903, indicating his support for the efforts of the Balkan Committee. He was a particular favourite of the committee: 'The Balkan Committee desires to express to Sir Edward Grey its sincere gratitude for the policy which he is now pursuing in the question of Macedonian reform.' Like Lansdowne's plans, Grey's proposals for Macedonia followed closely the designs of the Balkan Committee.

The Balkan Committee praised Grey's initiatives in the Balkans, which were in line with the committee's own views. Like Grey, they held that limiting the Ottoman gendarmerie in Macedonia and putting everything under the ultimate control of a European Commission was the solution to the problems of Macedonia. For his part, Grey admitted that he was mindful of the Balkan Committee's influence.[10]

Sir Henry Campbell-Bannerman, Grey's prime minister from 1905 to 1908 had declared publicly his support of the Bulgarian insurgents and animosity toward the Turks in 1903:

> ... The Turk, who after generations of cruel mismanagement, has at last goaded the subject race in that country (Macedonia) into desperation, and the Christians, who, having been the victims of those cruelties, has risen at last in a frantic attempt to emancipate himself (sic).

Campbell-Bannerman praised the Treaty of San Stephano and damned the Treaty of Berlin. He pronounced that Gladstone's old policy of evicting the Turk, 'bag and baggage', from Europe had been correct.[11]

Herbert Henry Asquith, who became prime minister in 1908, had also made his judgements on Macedonia known. Speaking before his constituents in East Fife, he attacked the Treaty of Berlin, which had left Macedonia to the Ottomans; the Macedonians were paying for that mistake:

> The facts are familiar and undisputed. The system of Government which prevails there—if government it can be called—is a system of organized inequality and tyranny. Turkish landowners and Turkish officials drain the centre of its wealth. The courts are corrupt; justice is a mockery. The evidence of a Christian is not received, police are licensed oppressors of the poor; neither life, nor property, nor honour is in security.

Asquith declared that 'if any insurrection was justifiable it was justified there'. The only solution was to remove Macedonia from Ottoman power. If the sultan did not agree, force should be used.[12]

Politics among the Great Powers were to continue to frustrate British attempts to deal harshly with the Turks. On 9 July 1907, a high-level deputation, organised by the Balkan Committee, met with Sir Edward Grey at the Foreign Office. It was led by the Archbishop of Canterbury and included bishops and other clergy, lords, labour leaders and twenty-three members of parliament (nearly all from Grey's Liberal Party). The deputation advanced all the points made often by the committee – massacres, Ottoman Government failures and oppression of Christians, the failure of past reforms, which did not go far enough, and the need to have Christian and Great Power control over Ottoman Europe. Grey responded that conditions had improved in Macedonia, but that he wished for a Macedonian Government answerable only to the Powers. He said, however, that the other Powers would not support it, and Britain could not enforce it in the face of their opposition. When Grey put forward his 1908 proposal for autonomy in Macedonia, the Balkan Committee praised him for putting into effect the committee's proposal of 1903. Like Lansdowne, he was unsuccessful in his plans, due to opposition by the other Powers. He told the Balkan Committee of his disappointment, and promised to keep trying.[13]

The relationship of the Balkan Committee and the British Government, and in particular Foreign Secretary Grey, was not lost on Europeans. The Continental press commented that Grey's proposals on the Balkan Question were decided by political pressure from the Balkan Committee, or were at least directed at appeasing the sentiments of the committee. The Austrians, in particular, felt that the British Balkan Committee had interfered in a Balkan settlement, with negative results.[14]

In his memoirs, Grey indicated the importance of the Balkan Committee and public pressure in deciding foreign policy, and his frustration at not being able to carry out their plans:

> Had we considered our political interest, we should have left the (Macedonian) question alone. As I have already explained, our activity in protesting against Turkish misrule diminished our influence and was therefore adverse to British commercial interests in Turkey. But humanitarian feeling in Britain and the persisting sympathy for Christian populations under Turkish rule was so strong that British political and material interests were overborne by it. All the sympathy of British Secretaries for Foreign Affairs was with this sentiment, and their action was inspired by this motive, though each successive occupant of the Foreign Office may well have felt choked by despair of achieving any measure of success. Macedonian Reforms could be dealt with only in concert with other Powers. Not one of the other Powers was disinterested; not one of them believed that Britain was disinterested. Each was conscious of some political motive of its own, and they all invented some political motive that was attributed to us.[15]

## The Powers Intervene

The questions for the two Powers closest to Ottoman Europe was how to deal with the Ottoman Empire and avoid war among themselves. Russia and Austria–Hungary considered what they felt was soon to be the demise of the Ottoman Empire in Europe. One possibility was that Russia would fulfill its long-held ambition to take Istanbul and the Straits. Austria might take Macedonia, including its port of Salonica. It was a solution that appealed to neither power.[16]

The government of Austria–Hungary firmly opposed Russian occupation of Istanbul. They feared, probably correctly, that Russian control of the Balkans would follow. Austrian Foreign Minister Agenor Maria Goluchowski stated:

> If the Russians possessed Constantinople, the Russian Czar would very soon be regarded as the head of the Eastern Orthodox Church, and he would have authority over all peoples from the shores of the Bosphorus to the banks of the Danube.

The Russian threat to Austrian domains would markedly increase. Moreover, Austrian conquest of Macedonia might come only at a significant loss of men and treasure, and Russia's new position on the Straits would inevitably lead to conflict with Austria, a conflict driven by Russia's pan-Slavism. Austria did not abandon its dream of taking Salonica, but times were not ripe for that.[17]

The Austrians placed no faith in Britain's traditional commitment to keep Russia from Istanbul. They felt that Britain's position on protecting Istanbul and the Straits was weak. The British could not be relied on to oppose a Russian takeover. The French were in effect allied with the Russians and would support them. This meant that there was all the more reason to come to an arrangement with the Russians to keep Russia from the Straits. Joint Russian–Austrian action in the Ottoman Empire was necessary, freezing out the British and French.[18]

The Russians were not the threat to the Straits that the Austrians imagined. By 1895 Russia was beginning to take action in the Far East that would culminate in the Russo-Japanese War of 1904–5. Russia needed no problems in the Near East. Since they were not yet militarily or politically prepared to take and hold the Straits themselves, the Russians needed the Ottomans to control them, because the Ottomans would not allow any foreign navies through to the Black Sea to attack Russia. As long as the Straits remained open to Russian merchant shipping, especially grain exports, they would be satisfied. The Russians were building up their military forces. Eventually, they felt, the Bosporus and Dardanelles would become Russian. They had only to be patient, and to ensure that no one else took them.[19]

If the Ottoman Empire were to be protected, it was also in Russia's interest to keep the peace in Ottoman Europe, where the greatest threat was Bulgarian irredentism. Whereas Russia had once treated Bulgaria almost as a client state, Bulgaria has changed. It had begun to act independently, often unwilling to follow the lead of Russia. It was in Russia's interest to keep Bulgarian aspirations in check, protecting the Ottoman Empire, at least for a while.[20]

Neither Russia nor Austria wanted Britain to be involved in Macedonia. When Ottoman forces defeated Greece in the 1897 War, Salisbury had wanted a European conference that might radically alter the status of Ottoman Balkans. The other Powers refused to consider his proposal. Instead, the Russians and Austrians came to an agreement in April 1897, when Austrian Emperor Franz Joseph visited Tsar Nicholas II in St Petersburg. While not a permanent treaty, and with disagreements on eventual plans, especially in Bosnia, the Austro-Russian Agreement of May 1897 did pledge the two to support the status quo in Ottoman Europe, to resist any enlargement of Bulgaria into Macedonia and to resist any agitation in the Balkans. It was further agreed that Russia would not take Istanbul.[21]

Russia and Austria were therefore committed to end any situation that threatened the peace in Ottoman Europe. The outbreak of internal conflict in Macedonia was surely that. The options in dealing with Macedonia were limited. The most obvious should have been to not interfere at all with Ottoman pacification efforts and to stop Greece, Serbia and especially Bulgaria from interfering. This was politically impossible. Public opinion in Europe was firmly against Ottoman action in Macedonia which, even though greatly exaggerated in the European Press, could indeed be brutal, matching violence with violence. As for putting the necessary pressure on Balkan States to end their support of Macedonian rebellion, European Powers simply would not coerce Christian states as they would the Muslim Ottoman Empire. Led by Austria and Russia, the Europeans proved willing to coerce only the Ottomans, demanding reforms that they claimed would pacify the situation.[22]

Throughout the Macedonian Crisis, the European Powers were unwilling or unable to restrain Bulgaria, Greece and Serbia from supporting the rebels in Macedonia. Arms and men flowed across the borders into the Ottoman Empire. Rebel committees met and organised in Bulgaria, only occasionally hampered when the Bulgarian Government briefly acted to curry favour with the Powers, then allowed once again.

In early 1902 the Powers, led by Russia and Austria, made 'representations' to Bulgaria concerning its support for the Macedonian guerillas. Despite the fact that British diplomats had reported the importation of arms from Bulgaria to Macedonia, Foreign Secretary Lansdowne did not wish these complaints to be made, because he stated he was satisfied with the patently false Bulgarian statements that the Bulgarians were stopping the aid to the rebels. He nevertheless felt the need to cooperate with the other Powers, so acquiesced to the Powers' statement.[23]

When rebel bands invaded the Ottoman Empire from Bulgaria in the 1902 Gorna Dzhumaya Invasion, the Powers, including the British, complained to the Bulgarian Government, which refused to consider any protests. No real pressure was put on Bulgaria. Instead, the Powers put pressure on the Ottomans. In November of 1902, the Austrian and Russian ambassadors in Istanbul notified the Ottoman Government that it would have to make reforms, directed by Austria and Russia, or risk losing Macedonia. The Ottomans responded with a reform plan of their own: the administration of Macedonia would be reformed. Christians would be taken into the police and gendarmerie, and half the new judges would be Christians. Inspectors would be named to fire deficient officials. The sultan named the extremely competent Hüseyin Hilmi Paşa as inspector-general of the three provinces. The Powers were not satisfied. They demanded more.[24]

## The Austrian–Russian 'Vienna Plan'

Declaring accurately that they were the Powers most concerned with the Ottoman Empire in Europe, the Austrians and Russians prepared a joint plan of reforms in Macedonia (17 February 1903). The plan assumed that the troubles in Macedonia had been the result of poor Ottoman administration.

- An inspector-general would be appointed for a period of three years. He could only be dismissed after consultation with the two Powers. He was to have full powers.

- Foreign specialists would reorganise the gendarmerie, but would be under the orders of the Ottoman Government. Christians would make up 20 per cent of the gendarmes, with more to be added later.
- Village policemen would be drawn from their own village. Christian villages would have Christian police.
- Amnesty would be granted for all 'political crimes', unless prisoners had been convicted of crimes such as murder and robbery ('crimes at common law').
- Tax revenues of each province would be paid into an account held by the Ottoman Bank (a European institution). Taxes would be first dedicated to local expenses.
- Regulations on government expenditures would be created. (Although not stated, these would obviously be set by the two Powers.)[25]

The Russians and Austrians acknowledged that the sultan had the right to put down rebellion in his dominions. They assumed, however, that rebellions would not take place if reforms were made. Their assumptions on the need for Ottoman reforms were seconded by the British, with the exception that the British wanted the reforms to be much more onerous for the Ottomans.

The Russian–Austrian plan had difficulties: it gave very little weight to the force of Macedonian/Bulgarian nationalism and irredentism. The insurgents desired an end to Ottoman rule, not reforms with the Ottoman Empire. The plan did not consider how the Ottomans would pay for it. Its greatest flaw was the common imperialist assumption that the Powers always knew better than the local rulers regarding what was needed.[26]

The sultan accepted the Russian–Austrian proposal and sent instructions for its implementation on 2 April 1903.[27]

The British obviously resented the dominance of Austria and Russia in the Macedonian Question. As long as the two Powers closest to Macedonia agreed upon actions, however, they could assert little pressure to affect their plans. Lansdowne accepted the two Powers' plan because he felt he had no choice – he believed it was essential to do something quickly, and the Austrian–Russian plan was the utmost the other Powers would support. All he could do was to offer futile suggestions to make the Vienna Plan more onerous to the Ottomans. He stated the plan was not enough, and he left open the possibility that the British would later propose modifications in the administration of Macedonia. He particularly wished that the governor-general of Macedonia be named by the Powers, and be responsible to them. The British policy was to be constant under both Conservative and Liberal governments. Lansdowne and his successor as foreign secretary, Edward Grey, were to continue to press for 'reforms' that would remove Ottoman control over Macedonia.[28]

Two months after the reform plan was presented, the Ottomans were complying, but not at a fast enough pace for the Europeans. The Russians reported that the reforms were being put in place: Christians were being enrolled in the gendarmerie, and Christian guards (*bekçi*) were being put in place in Christian villages. Half the judges in criminal and civil courts were to be Christians. The Ottoman Governor-General Hilmi Paşa was reorganising the administration. This was not enough for the Powers. The Ottomans were, it seems, to have changed and pacified Macedonia in two months. Lansdowne complained that the Ottomans were too dilatory in naming new gendarmes and employing foreigners. The Austrians and Russians threatened that they would not hold back the Balkan states from interfering if the Ottomans did not act more quickly.[29]

The rebels in Macedonia saw the actions of the Powers as the first step toward achieving their goals. They needed to demonstrate that reforms under Ottoman control would always be insufficient, and unrest would continue unless Macedonia were cut free from the Ottoman Empire. They envisaged armed intervention by the Powers if their revolt expanded into a greater war. The Ilinden Revolt was the result. The rebels never had a chance of defeating the Ottoman Army in open battle, but that was not their intention. They hoped through massacre of Muslims and counter-massacre of Christians to elicit the sympathy of Europe, leading to intervention against the Ottomans.

British newspapers began to publish exaggerated and fabricated reports of the Ilinden Revolt, which extended from August to October 1903, as seen in the previous chapter. The British Government felt forced to act. On 19 September 1903, seven months after the Austrian–Russian plan had been first considered and while the Ilinden Revolt was in progress, Lansdowne notified the Russians and Austrians that he did not believe the plan had worked. He told the two Powers that the British had always reserved the right to end their support of the proposals if they proved inadequate. What was needed was that the Ottomans must be forced to accept 'measures of a more thorough and practical kind, enforced by pressure of a more direct and convincing character'. A foreign governor was necessary, as no Muslim could effectively function as governor or inspector-general of Macedonia. A large number of European officers must be delegated to accompany the Ottoman army (a policy that Austria and Russia had repeatedly rejected as impractical). The other Powers politely declined to consider the British proposals. On 24 April the Austrian and Russian ambassadors presented the Ottoman Government with a memorandum stating that the two governments continued to support the Vienna Plans, with no mention of the British proposals.[30]

Lansdowne did not abandon his project. In a useless gesture, because he had no support from other Powers, he notified the Ottomans that radical reforms were needed. In Istanbul, Ambassador O'Conor wrote to Lansdowne that it was unwise to present the British plan to the Ottomans, because it showed a separation among the Powers. Lansdowne sent the message anyway, and it accomplished nothing.[31]

On 29 September, Lansdowne once again recommended to Austria and Russia that they widen the scope of the reforms: 'In our view, no scheme is likely to produce satisfactory results which depends for its execution upon a Mussulman Governor entirely subservient to the Turkish Government and independent of foreign control.' Therefore, it would be necessary to appoint a Christian Governor unconnected with the Ottoman Empire or a Muslim Governor 'assisted by European Assessors'. European officers and non-commissioned officers should be appointed immediately to the gendarmerie. Turkish reservist troops should be immediately withdrawn from Macedonia. Lansdowne acknowledged that the two Powers did not wish military attachés to be assigned to the Ottoman troops, but he still wished them to be accepted – six officers from each of the Powers – 'with the object of exercising a restraining influence upon the Turkish troops'. Lansdowne's proposals were again rejected, although they may have had a slight effect on the Austrian–Russian project that was to come.[32]

## The Mürzsteg Proposals

Through September of 1903, much to the chagrin of the British, the Austrian and Russian governments kept to the Vienna Proposals. Then the emperors stepped in. When Russian Tsar Nicholas II visited Emperor Francis Joseph of Austria–Hungary in Mürzsteg, Austria, in September 1903, the two agreed to a new set of proposals. The proposals, signed on 2 October 1903, were essentially emendations to the Vienna reforms.

- Civilian advisors ('agents civils'), appointed by Austria and Russia, would look to the needs of the Christian population, advise the governor-general and report to their embassies.
- The gendarmerie would be reorganised by a European general and his deputies, also foreigners.
- The administration and judiciary would be reorganised, and local autonomy encouraged.
- Once Macedonia had been pacified, the Ottomans would redistrict the provinces along ethnic lines.
- A commission made up of an equal number of Muslim and Christian delegates would examine political and other crimes. Consular representatives of Austria and Russia would take part in the commissions.
- The Ottoman Government would allocate special funds to aid Christian refugees and rebuild destroyed Christian homes. The aforementioned commission, aided by 'Christian Notables', would decide payments. Christian refugees and Christians whose homes had been destroyed would pay no taxes.
- Because most of the excesses and cruelties had been committed by irregular troops and 'bashi-bozuks', these would be disbanded.[33]

Like the earlier reform scheme, the Mürzsteg Proposals offered few specifics. They created new systems of European control, leaving the details to be considered later, probably by ambassadors in Istanbul. The proposals were notable in their concern solely for Christian suffering and Christian needs. Destroyed Muslim homes and Muslim refugees were ignored. And the statement that most 'excesses' had been committed by Ottoman irregular troops, ignoring the insurgents' 'excesses', was either ignorance or deliberate obfuscation. The plan to divide the region along ethnic lines indicates how little the actual situation in Macedonia was understood: the population was so mixed down to the village level that no division by ethnicity would have been possible without massive population transfers.

The Ottoman Government objected to the Mürzsteg Proposals as unneeded and denying Ottoman sovereign rights. The sultan attempted to have the proposals modified, writing to the Tsar for consideration. He even asked for help from the British, although he acknowledged the force of British public opinion was against him: 'The Sultan implored His Majesty's Government not to encourage a policy based upon hostility to the Moslem race.' All was to no avail. On 25 November, the Ottomans accepted the Mürzsteg Proposals, although they reserved the right to negotiate changes later, which the Powers were never to allow. Russian and Austrian 'civil agents' were appointed to advise and watch over the government in Macedonia. A European general and his subordinates were named. Irregular troops were no longer used. Other parts of the project were little implemented, because they could not be afforded (see below).[34]

The British, while they were forced diplomatically to give grudging assent to the Mürzsteg Proposals, found them to be deficient. Lansdowne did not support any reforms that allowed the Ottomans to retain control in Macedonia. He wrote: 'There seemed to me to be only two possible solutions of the Macedonian difficulty. Macedonia might be either joined to Bulgaria, or given an autonomous regime under a Governor virtually independent of the Sultan.' Lansdowne's problem was that neither Russia nor Austria would support either.[35]

Lansdowne soon was telling parliament he was disappointed with the progress of Macedonian reforms, which he blamed on the Ottomans:

> We all know that, however promising may be the measures of reform put forward for the acceptance of the Turkish Government, and however readily those reforms may he accepted, there is always left a great deal of room for the exercise of those arts of delay and obstruction in which, I am afraid, it must be said, Turkish officials are usually found to excel.[36]

Lansdown continued to press the other Powers to stiffen the Mürzsteg Proposals, which he stated were a failure even before they were implemented. He wanted active European intervention in Macedonia, forcing the Ottomans to make the region autonomous. Furthermore, as Lansdowne announced to the French ambassador, he wanted European control to be extended from the three Macedonian provinces to include the provinces of Edirne and Yanya (Yanina), covering all but the Northwestern province of Üsküdar, which he probably had simply neglected to mention. Lansdowne later decided that Edirne Province would be excluded. (This would have led to an interesting situation, in which Ottoman control would remain to the West and East of the area under European control.) The other Powers once again rebuffed Lansdowne's recommendations.[37]

Lansdowne told the other Powers that it was essential for the Ottoman army in Macedonia to be greatly reduced. Could he not have understood that this would encourage the rebels to take an even more active part in the disorders? His plan seemed to assume that the army was at fault, and removing it would bring peace. The numbers of what military forces remained in place, he proposed, would be allowed for only a limited period, and would be under sole command of the inspector-general. The inspector-general, moreover, would be overseen by a committee named by the Powers. The Powers would guarantee that Bulgaria would stop the rebel gangs and not occupy any Ottoman territory once the Ottoman soldiers were gone (despite all evidence that the Bulgarians had never cooperated in this before). By reducing Ottoman forces in Macedonia, the Lansdowne proposals would have made the situation worse, especially as Greek and Serbian bands joined Bulgarians and Muslims in a four-way civil war.[38]

## The Chance for Success

The Powers' plans for Macedonia never stood a chance of success. In a discussion with Alan Johnstone, the British Chargé d'Affaires in Vienna, the Russian ambassador, Count Pyotr Kapnist, showed real understanding of the problem that would keep any reforms from success:

> Count Kapnist added that in his personal opinion the danger of the future lay, not so much in the refusal of the Sultan to introduce reforms—His Majesty would, he thought, always yield to pressure—as in the difficulty of controlling or suppressing the Bulgarian Committees, who terrorized the Macedonians far more than did the Turks. I (Johnstone) said that it was the very object of the reforms to pacify the disaffected districts, and allay the discontent which had led to the revolt. The Ambassador replied that he feared the Committees had really no wish to see any improvement in Macedonia, their object being to create a state of things which would lead to an attack on Turkey, if not by the Great Powers, at any rate by one of the smaller nations.[39]

The European projects were flawed in their basic assumption – that reforming the Ottoman administration of Macedonia would end the troubles. They consciously or unconsciously accepted the declarations of the rebel committees that all they wanted was good government. This was not true, as Count Kapnist understood. What the rebels wanted was to detach Macedonia from the Ottoman Empire, either as a separate state or as part of Bulgaria. Insofar as they were able, they would continue their agitation until they reached their goals. They would never accept reforms that kept Macedonia within the Ottoman Empire.

The need for better administration of Macedonia was clear. Both Muslims and Christians needed improved taxation, judicial systems and government administration. But all of this depended on peace and civil order, which could not be attained in the midst of a war. The rebel insurgents, who had no desire for peace or effective reform, had to be put down before Macedonia could be reformed. As has been proven in numerous successful and unsuccessful campaigns throughout history, the only way to end a guerilla campaign is with overwhelming force coupled with transition to good government. The morality of the various wars against guerillas can be debated, but the need for armed opposition to defeat insurgents is undeniable.

The Ottomans put down the Gorna Dzhumaya Uprising and the great Ilinden Revolt militarily. If they had not done that, there would never have been any chance of reforms within Macedonia. After that, however, the actions of the Powers kept them from continuing successful military opposition to the rebels. European pressure and European public opinion restrained them. The Ottomans understood that they were hamstrung by the Europeans. The sultan felt that his forces were kept from effective action against the bands by European public opinion, which in turn affected the European governments. He complained that '[h]is troops were precluded from searching for hidden arms and acting energetically as their conduct might be open to misconstruction and they would be represented by the European press as having been guilty of barbarities, etc.'. The press, he protested, especially in Britain, magnified the real and invented crimes of Ottoman soldiers and generally ignored the horrific acts of the insurgents.[40]

Nationalists in Bulgaria, Greece and Serbia argued at the time, and argue still, that the problem was that the Ottomans were wrong in opposing what they called the legitimate national aspirations of the Christian peoples. Rather than fighting in Macedonia, the Ottomans should have simply abandoned this course of action. Such claims rest, of course, on the assumption that the nationalists understood the wishes of the people. There also is the problem that 'the people' were not what each group of nationalists alleged. Macedonia was portrayed by the rebel nationalists and the British press as a Christian place ruled over by Muslims. The plans of the Powers uniformly spoke of the needs of Christians. But the population was not made up of what they portrayed. Muslims constituted half of the population and the largest single group in the provinces that the Powers defined as Macedonia (Table 4.1).

Searching through the diplomatic literature and the British popular press, one finds little evidence that the Great Powers took the actual population of Macedonia into consideration in their various plans and demands. This was despite the Powers' knowledge of the Muslim preponderance in the population.[41]

The sultan was rightly concerned that the European proposals would diminish Ottoman power and might lead to the Empire's loss of Macedonia, but there were also fears for the Muslims of Macedonia. Had the Ottomans abandoned Macedonia, they would have been denying the demographic realities and, in fact, would have been abandoning the majority of the population. This, not only imperial prestige, goes far to explain why the Ottomans determined to keep Macedonia, despite all the pressures to relinquish it.

The European Powers, publicly even Britain, asserted that they wanted Macedonia to remain in the Ottoman Empire. If one accepts the highly questionable idea that European Powers should have intervened in Macedonia, their only possible successful policy of the Powers in Macedonia should have been:

- Forcing the nations surrounding Macedonia to end their support of rebel bands and close their borders to them.
- Allowing the Ottomans to defeat the rebels militarily.
- Forcing reforms in the Ottoman military response, such as restricting the use of local levies and increasing the numbers of regular troops.
- Forcing administrative reforms in Macedonia.

- Facilitating financial and economic reforms in the Ottoman Empire, such as allowing the Ottomans to set their own customs duties, which they were not allowed to do without the approval of all the European Powers.
- Accepting the demographic realities in Macedonia – not portraying it falsely as a Christian region where Christian nationalism was opposed only by a Muslim government in Istanbul.

None of this happened. The Europeans would never have relaxed their financial hold on the Ottoman Empire; there was too much to gain by merchants' interests from restricting the Ottomans financially. Throughout the conflict, the Powers proved unwilling to take any real action against Bulgaria and later Greece; to them, it would have been unthinkable to apply to Christian states the military threats applied to the Ottomans. The Powers were willing only to restrict the Ottomans. And the Ottomans were not allowed to deal with the situation themselves. Ottoman mobilisation on the Bulgarian border, intended to end Bulgarian support for the rebels, even if it meant war with Bulgaria, was stopped after mobilisation was well underway.[42]

## Paying for It All

The gravest problem for the Ottoman Government was financial. The cost of defending the Empire was ruinous. (In 1903–4, Ottoman expenditure on the army, navy and police/gendarmerie was 76 per cent of total revenue of the Empire.) There was no money, but the Powers expected the Ottomans to pay for all of the reforms. The financial demands of the European reforms project put an impossible strain on the Ottoman Government. Ambassador O'Conor reported the situation: salaries of troops and officials throughout the Empire had not been paid, in some cases they were in arrears for years. The revenues of the three Macedonian provinces were roughly £T 1,600,000 a year, and the cost of the military needed to fight the insurgents (200,000 men) and keep the peace was £T 1,200,000 a year. (1.1 Ottoman Lira, £T, equalled 1 Pound Sterling.) Yet under the new scheme, the Austrian and Russian agents estimated that after the new expenses in the reform proposal, there would be only 600,000 left for the military in Macedonia – half of what was needed. But the soldiers were essential to defend against possible attack from Bulgaria, not to mention in Macedonia itself. If the Ottoman Army were drastically reduced, the Powers would only promise that an attack by Bulgaria 'would be seriously resented'. Such resentment would not defend the Empire. In addition, the traditional income to the government from Macedonia after military expenditures would be lost.[43]

The Austrians believed that no improvements could be expected in Macedonia without the funds that would be provided by a 3 per cent increase in Ottoman customs duties. The other Powers, except Britain, agreed that the customs duties increase was essential. The British long held out against any agreement to increase customs duties. They had a practical reason – opposition from British merchants, who wished to pay no more in duties. In addition, Lansdowne told the Ottomans that he would not approve any increase unless 'abuses' that had hurt British trade were improved. But the ostensible reason for British refusal was lack of progress in Macedonian reforms. This was unreasonable, because the funds from customs collections were needed precisely for the Macedonian reforms. Without funding for the gendarmerie and civil administration, the state of Macedonia could only become worse. The other Powers were incensed by the British non-cooperation. When British Ambassador Charles Hardinge in Vienna discussed the issue with the Austrian foreign minister,

> Baron Aehrenthal replied that the isolated action of Great Britain in withholding for several months her consent to the increase of the Turkish customs dues had jeopardized the Concert of the Powers in Macedonia, and had had the appearance of a selfish policy dictated by the advantages to be obtained for British trade in the Near East.

Despite their protests that they were only looking out for the success of reform, it is obvious that the British only wanted reform in Macedonia on their own terms and in their own interests.[44]

The Ottomans tried to deal with their financial problems and European pressure by disbanding what military units they could. By August 1904, thirty-three battalions of reserves in Macedonia had already been disbanded and two more divisions would soon follow. The insurgent bands responded by increasing their attacks.[45]

In April of 1907 the British, under intense pressure from Austria, finally consented to a 3 per cent customs duty increase for seven years: 25 per cent of the receipts of the increase would be applied to past Ottoman debts,

75 per cent to Macedonia. The European-controlled Public Debt Administration would control administration and distribution of the new customs receipts. Needed additional expenses for Macedonia would be met by the Public Debt Administration, recompensed by tax revenues consigned to it by the Ottoman Government. The British also applied certain conditions: the British must be satisfied with the fulfillment in 'the conditions laid down in regard to the Civil Budget of the three Vilayets, the Macedonian Gendarmerie and the other kindred subjects in Macedonia'. The 3 per cent increase depended on these undefined stipulations being fulfilled. The British later were to use this stipulation to gain their aims.[46]

An important point was that the Europeans, who could afford to pay for reforms, would not do so. The Ottomans, who could afford nothing, were expected to pay for everything. The British Treasury even refused to pay a salary supplement to British gendarmerie officers in Macedonia so that good men could be enrolled. The Ottoman Government was expected to pay a considerable sum for the Macedonian reforms, including the salaries of foreign officials and gendarmerie leaders. The Ottomans made an initial payment of £T 60,000 for the Europeans' initial expenses and £T 250,000 annual payments. Because the Ottoman Government could not pay, it had to borrow the money. Various future tax collections were signed over to Europeans as security for the loans.[47]

On 8 May 1905, the Six Powers (Britain, France, Russia, Austria, Germany and Italy) presented a collective note to the Ottoman Government demanding the creation of a Financial Commission, made up of delegates named by France, Germany, Britain and Italy. The commission would control Macedonian finances. The Financial Commission would act in concert with the governor-general and the Austrian and Russian civil agents. The Ottoman Government did not reply, and another note was sent on 24 June. When the Ottomans finally did reply on 12 July, the Europeans found their reply unacceptable. After another Powers' note, the Ottomans again did not reply. The Powers then named the four delegates to the commission and sent them off to Macedonia. The Ottomans refused to accept them. The Powers decided on a military threat, a 'naval demonstration', first suggested by the Austrians and Russians. The British suggested an occupation of the island of Mytilene, which other Powers, but not the Germans, accepted. On 27 November the

Powers' squadron arrived at Mytilene, landed forces and occupied the customs house and telegraph office. On 5 December, the Ottomans accepted the demands in principle. They agreed to the Financial Commission. The British, however, were to remain unconvinced by the financial reforms, as well as the success of the reforms in general.[48]

**Greeks, Serbs and Bulgarians**

Greek interests in Macedonia had lost steadily through the actions of the Bulgarian rebels. Patriarchist villages had joined the Exarchist Church through threats by the bands and an affinity with their language brothers. In response, Patriarchists had generally sided with the Ottomans, who were protecting them from Bulgarian bands. Small groups of Patriarchists, accepted by the Ottomans, organised into bands, fought the Exarchist guerillas and even accompanied Ottoman forces, armed by the Ottomans.[49]

At the end of 1902 local Patriarchists and the Greek Government began to act on their own, at first arming Patriarchist villages. Though the Bulgarians had dominated the conflicts in Macedonia, the Greeks had distinct advantages when they began to organise their own cadres there: the first was financial. Greek partisans were able to draw on extensive funds from Greek merchants, the Greek Government and even the Greek Church. The Greek Government could openly support them, confident that the European philhellenes would not exert on them even the very limited pressure they put on Bulgaria. The Greeks also had a group of dedicated and trained fighters to match those of the Bulgarian bands – the veteran guerillas from the war in Crete, whom the Greek Government transferred to Macedonia.[50]

Greek guerilla action in Macedonia began in earnest in 1904. A Greek 'Macedonian Committee', founded in 1905, was in charge in Western Macedonia and an organisation led by the Greek consul-general in Salonica, Lambros Koromilas, controlled the Greek bands in Central and Eastern Macedonia. Both groups were supported by military officers, politicians and influential businessmen, who disseminated propaganda and sent arms to Greek fighting bands. Many supporters had been in the National Society (Ethniki Etaireia) that had acted in Crete. Bulgarian bands had long passed into Macedonia to and from Bulgaria. Greek bands now passed into Macedonia both by land and sea. The Greek Government facilitated supplies and ammunition passing over the border. The Ottomans found it impossible to interdict arms and men in mountainous terrain and on long coastlines.[51]

The Greek bands in Western Macedonia operated under a detailed organisational plan that stated that all Patriarchists were under the command of the Greek Committee. The plan created a governing structure, with elections, taxes and support for bands, judges and fines and penalties for non-compliance with orders. The blueprint of the quasi-government can only have been put into effect in some areas, but the intent was to create a Greek Government in Macedonia.[52]

By 1907, the situation in Macedonia had worsened considerably. Greek bands became much more active, organising and operating from Thessaly. The Greek Government, although it made promises to stop the bands' incursions, did nothing. Indeed, Greek consuls in Macedonia aided the bands. Conflicts between Greeks/Patriarchists and Bulgarians/Exarchists increased exponentially, with the Greeks in the ascendancy. Muslim villagers became less likely to be the targets of the bands, which concentrated on killing other Christians. The Ottoman Army, its strength in Macedonia diminished through European pressure and financial necessity, fought both. The European-led gendarmerie had little effect on the bloodshed. In one way, the new gendarmerie was working well; it had greatly reduced the number of ordinary crimes such as burglary, but it very seldom dealt with the Bulgarian and Greek bands. Bulgarians and Greeks were each killing the adherents of the other group. Both the Greek and the Bulgarian Governments reported large numbers of murders by the other's surrogates. Each accused the other of extermination policies. Neither admitted supporting the bands in Macedonia.[53]

Initially, small bands of Serbian guerillas in Northwestern Macedonia had fought alongside Bulgarian bands, but soon broke with both. In Northern Kosova Province, Serbian bands began to be active, opposing both the Bulgarian bands and Ottoman soldiers. In one battle, for example, two Bulgarian bands who planned an attack on a Serbian town were met by a Serbian band, who pushed them back. As they retreated, they were met by an Ottoman Army detachment, which wiped them out. In the village of Pesca, Serbian and Bulgarian bands fought for several hours, until Ottoman troops dispersed both. In the villages, Serbs and Bulgarians were murdering each other. In general, the Serbs, operating to the North of most of the Patriarchist population, did not come into conflict with Greek bands.[54]

Like Greece and Bulgaria, Serbia denied that it was supporting the Serbian bands in Macedonia, but in August of 1903 agitation for raising and financing Serbian bands in Macedonia had become widespread in Serbia. Subscriptions were raised to finance bands, with the tacit approval of the Serbian Government. The Secret Service, a unit of the Foreign Office, further financed the bands. The Russians and Austrians approached the Serbian Government on 'the formation on the Serbian territory of armed bands which entered Macedonia, where they had bloody conflicts either with Turkish troops or with Bulgarian gangs'. They accused the Serbian Government of sponsoring the gangs and not stopping them from entering Macedonia. Like the Bulgarian and Greek Governments, the Serbian Government denied responsibility, but 'undertook to oppose them in the future by all means in its power'. That was the extent of the Powers' pressure on Serbia.[55]

Muslim villagers still suffered from attacks by the Christian bands, and there was some organisation of Muslim, particularly Albanian, bands. The deaths of Muslims, however, while significant, were less than they had been previously. The conflicts were now primarily among the Christian groups, with better led and financed Greek bands the more effective.[56]

The Austrian and Russian ambassadors noted the increase of violence among the Christian communities. In a notice to the Ottoman Foreign Ministry, they blamed the Ottomans for the 'state of anarchy'. French Charge d'Affaires Auguste Boppe described the situation: 'The antagonism between the different Christian races is getting worse every day, and its deplorable effects only increase with the ever-increasing strength and boldness of the gangs.' Murders were increasing daily. The Greek gangs had adopted the tactics previously used by the Bulgarian gangs, forcing Exarchist villages to decide they were Patriarchists. Boppe noted that, under such conditions, the Macedonians were little concerned with the Powers' reforms.[57]

British Consul-General Lamb at Salonica reported extensive 'Political Murders and Crimes'. Lamb did his best to compile the incidents of murder committed by the bands, providing month-by-month accounts of the violence. He reported that the murders in 1907 were worse than they had been in 1906. He listed the number of 'political assassinations' in 1907 in the area covered by the reforms and the European-led gendarmerie:

| | |
|---|---|
| Bulgars | 991 |
| Greeks and Patriarchists | 319 |
| Serbs | 155 |
| Vlachs | 40 |
| Moslems | 128 |
| Soldiers, Gendarmes, etc. | 135 |
| Total | 1,768 |

It should be noted, as Lamb stated, that these were only the murders that had been reported to him. Other British and French consuls also sent in long lists of murders and pillage.[58]

Following the attitude of his government, in December of 1904, the British Chargé in Istanbul, Walter Townley, told the Ottomans the blame was theirs. The Grand Vezir stated that nothing could be done unless the Powers suppressed the support the gangs received from the neighbouring states. Townley responded:

> Whatever foundation there might be for his assertion that the countries he had mentioned did not do their duty in restraining their bands, it seemed to me clear that Turkey must be held responsible for maintaining order within its own territories.

He threatened the Grand Vezir with an even more extensive list of reforms than the Mürzsteg Proposals.[59]

For the Ottomans, the situation was impossible. If they were to retain Macedonia, the only solution to the anarchy there would have been two-fold: European pressure on Serbia, Bulgaria and Greece to end their support of the bands – pressure of the sort that the Powers were exerting on the Ottomans – and an increase in Ottoman military force, even with the dangers of its harsh tactics, to defeat insurgents. But the Powers steadfastly refused to pressure the Christian nations of the Balkans with anything but 'strong representations'. Led by the British, using political and economic force, the Powers even caused the Ottomans to diminish their military commitment in Macedonia – the opposite of what was needed. So perhaps the only solution was for the Ottomans to leave, aborting a hopeless effort that was costing them soldiers' lives and bankrupting the state. Yet if the

Ottomans abandoned Macedonia to Serbs, Bulgarians and Greeks, there can be no doubt that they would continue dispossessing and killing each other, and that the Muslims, without protectors, would suffer worst of all. Indeed, that was what was to happen when the Ottomans were driven out in 1912.

**Foreign Secretary Grey**

The British Government changed when the Liberal Party won the election of 1905, but the British policy toward the Ottoman Empire remained the same. The British response to the increase in violence in Macedonia was typical of the British approach throughout the troubles. British representatives in Macedonia correctly stated that the disruptions in Macedonia were the result of bands that were supported by Greece, Bulgaria and Serbia. The only solution to the support that those governments gave to the guerilla bands, the British suggested, was, once again, that 'strong representations' be made at Athens, Belgrade and Sophia. At no time did the British or the other Powers apply to Greece or Bulgaria the sort of threats and coercion applied to the Ottomans. No one proposed sending European gendarme officers or 'civilian control officials' to guard against armed incursions into the Ottoman Empire. There was no lack of information on the support the guerilla bands were receiving from Greece and Bulgaria; the British consuls reported on it extensively. Yet nothing was done to affect the Greeks or the Bulgarians – nothing, that is, except 'strong representations'. Instead, the British proposed that more changes be forced on the Ottomans, not on Greece, Bulgaria or Serbia: the Ottomans would have to make changes in the judiciary and the gendarmerie. This was based on the faith that substituting Europeans for Ottomans would end all conflicts. Why this would stop the attacks by the bands was never explained or understood. Foreign Secretary Grey believed a gendarmerie completely under the control of European officers would easily put down the bands. (He obviously did not have a military mind.)[60]

The Russians understood that domestic pressure was forcing Grey's hand. The also said they felt no obligation to comply with British domestic politics.[61]

Grey worried that Britain was continuing to be frozen out of its place in negotiations on Macedonia by Russia and, particularly, Austria. He planned to renew British influence with a new set of proposals that enlarged upon those originally put forth by Lansdowne. On 18 December 1907, Grey made his proposal to the other Powers: a greatly increased gendarmerie would oppose the bands, taking the place of the Ottoman Army. The force would be under European command. A governor of Macedonia would be appointed for a term of seven years. He would have complete powers and could only be removed by the Powers. In effect, Macedonia would be removed completely from Ottoman control. The governor's salary, and those of his subordinates in the administration and the gendarmerie, would be set by the agents of the Powers. The Powers were to force the Ottomans to accept the plan. As always, the Ottoman Government would pay for it all. Grey planned for the Ottomans to pay the expenses through a large decrease in the numbers in their army.

Grey recognised that the Ottomans would object to a decrease of their army, which was needed to defend the Empire. In response, he stated that the Powers 'should guarantee the integrity and external security of this part of the Sultan's dominions as long as the arrangement continued, and proved effective in securing reform satisfactory to the Powers'. Others, Grey acknowledged, believed that a large force of Turkish gendarmes officered by Europeans with no knowledge of the territory or the local languages would be unworkable. Up to that time, the gendarmes had only dealt with ordinary crimes, not guerilla warfare. Grey answered with faith. He asserted that there would be no insuperable problems with European officers leading Turkish gendarmes. 'With the exercise of tact and discretion on the part of the officers, it should be possible to avoid friction and insure harmonious working.' When the German ambassador, Count Paul Wolff Metternich, remarked to Grey that, '[s]uch an arrangement would practically amount to taking control of a part of the Sultan's territory out of the Sultan's hands', Grey responded that was exactly what he wished.[62]

The British plan for what would in effect be an independent Macedonian army was understandably unacceptable to the Ottomans. They correctly regarded it as a step in the dismemberment of the Ottoman Empire. The Ottoman Government openly stated that Britain's intention was to create an autonomous Macedonia, in line with the plans of the British Balkan Committee and the Bulgarian Government.[63]

Grey delivered a speech in parliament on 25 February 1908 that incensed his foreign colleagues. He began by stating that the British had been most responsible for improvements in Macedonia, but that the other Powers had refused to go far enough in fulfilling British plans. The British had been forced to go along with the others so as not to destroy the unity of the European Concert. Despite great opposition from the other Powers, Britain had delayed approving a 3 per cent customs increase until there were judicial and other reforms. The other Powers had finally agreed, and the 3 per cent increase was approved, but Austria and Russia had been dilatory in supporting British plans for necessary reforms of the judiciary. Grey told parliament of his plan for an independent governor and gendarmerie under European control. The other Powers would have to support his plans, not make only small changes to the Mürzsteg Programme, if they wanted success in Macedonia. Moreover, failure to enact the British proposals would lead to the weakening of the European Concert and perhaps its dissolution, with disastrous consequences. Grey's words might have been pleasing to the Balkan Committee, but the speech was not one that appealed to the other Europeans.[64]

The other Powers wanted none of it. Although some said they agreed idealistically with Grey's plan, they thought it unworkable. For the Ottomans, the ultimate effect of the British proposal would have been obvious – the loss of an 'autonomous' region, just as they had lost Eastern Rumelia and Crete. The other Powers believed the sultan could never accept that. He would have to be forced, perhaps by military action, to accept what was in fact an excision of Macedonia from his Empire, and the Powers would not agree to military action. British Ambassador O'Conor wrote to Grey that the other Powers would never accept his plan. The Austrians were especially strong in what amounted to a condemnation of Grey's interference in Macedonia. Baron Aehrenthal told the British ambassador in Vienna that the British could easily propose idealistic and impractical plans, because they knew they would not suffer the consequences, 'sitting quietly at home in their island'. Austria, however, would suffer from the conflicts that would come. Germany agreed with Austria. The French and Italians offered Grey no support. The Greeks objected that creating an autonomous Macedonia would eventually lead to it becoming part of Bulgaria. Not all were against Grey's plan – the Bulgarians were very happy with it.[65]

Interestingly, in his speech to parliament of 25 February 1908, Grey mentioned only bands from Bulgaria and Serbia. Those governments, he said, must stop the bands at their borders. However, he made no mention of the Greek bands that were equally causing havoc.

The Russians stated with regret that they could not accept Grey's plan. They proposed a more limited reform scheme of their own: the general leading the gendarmerie would sit as an advisor on the Financial Commission, which would improve coordination in administration. There would be no reduction in the Ottoman Army, and thus no need for any guarantee of Ottoman security by the Powers. Gendarmerie numbers might be increased. Villager defenders would be armed and organised in each village as a sort of communal guard ('gardes-champêtres'). These would be able to defend against bands. The Russians agreed with the British that the governor-general should have a fixed term, but stated he would not be autonomous. The Financial Commission would include members from each of the six Great Powers, a sop to British sensitivities over Austrian–Russian control. The Russians included undefined plans for cooperation between the Financial Commission and the Ottoman Government. In general, little was changed from the status quo. The British plan for Macedonian autonomy was categorically rejected, although the Russians diplomatically said the British proposal could be considered as a basis for further discussion. The Austrians notified the British that they agreed with the Russian proposal.[66]

Grey voiced his disappointment in his response to the Russians. He maintained that a great reduction in the Ottoman Army was essential, and the Ottomans could count on the Powers to defend them. He added a new proposal: the Ottomans were then collecting the taxes from Macedonia and forwarding, he believed in a laggard fashion, what was needed to the Financial Commission. Grey proposed that the Financial Commission would collect the taxes in Macedonia and send to the Ottoman Central Government Treasury whatever the commission wished. The Ottomans would pay for the army from what they were sent and from the general treasury. (It cannot have escaped Grey that this would be a significant loss of Ottoman sovereignty.) Grey still insisted that the governor and the gendarmerie general be independent of the Central Government.[67]

There was much communication between the British and the Russians. The British accepted many of the Russian proposals, but insisted that the inspector-general should have independent power to hire, fire and control officials in the civil administration, as well as independent authority over the budget. Grey also wanted a greatly increased force of rural guards, under the control of the European-led gendarmerie. The Russians were conciliatory over the powers of the European leaders of the gendarmerie, but added: 'It would be essential condition that foreign officers should not assume responsibility of repressing bands or expose their lives.' This was in complete opposition to Grey's plans for the gendarmerie. The British plan for Macedonian autonomy had once again failed.[68]

**The Macedonian Issue Abandoned**

The 1897 agreement between Austria and Russia broke down in 1908, when Austria–Hungary received a concession (developmental permission) from the Ottoman Government to conduct surveys for a railway in the Sancak of Yenipazar (Novi Bazar), connecting Austria to the Ottoman railway system. The only Austrian rail connection to the Ottoman Empire was through the trunk line that ran from Vienna through Belgrade and Sofia. It was obviously insecure for the Austrians. Moreover, the only Austrian rail path to Salonica, the commercial entrepot for Macedonia, was a long route through Serbia, Bulgaria and Edirne. The planned new route would have commercial and possibly military benefit for the Austrians and Hungarians, if it could be completed (there were significant engineering challenges, and the line was never completed).[69]

To the Russians, the plan was an attempt to increase Austrian power in the region. The railway would be a boon to commerce, but it could also swiftly deliver Austrian soldiers. The Russians viewed it as upsetting the status quo that the two powers had agreed to in 1897. Russian popular opinion and the press portrayed it as an attack on the interests of Russia and Serbia, and defending their fellow Slavs in Serbia was always important to the Russians. The only British concern was not the railway plan itself, but the effect they believed it had on Grey's plans for Macedonia. Ambassador O'Conor and the Foreign Office believed that the price the Austrians had paid for Ottoman acceptance of the railroad scheme was an agreement not to coerce the Ottomans on reforms. Grey asserted that no railroad schemes should be accepted until the Ottomans had agreed to Grey's reform plans. The Austrians protested that they had made no such arrangement with the Ottomans, but refused to back down and completed the survey for the new line.[70]

Whether or not the Austrians made an arrangement with the Ottomans to ease pressure over Macedonia, and this is unclear, it was obviously to the Ottomans' advantage to drive a wedge between Russia and Austria. The Austrians were willing to act in their own perceived interest, as was to be shown when they annexed Bosnia (to be seen in the following chapter).

## 1908 Revolution

The Powers had sickened of Macedonia. The initial unison of the Powers over Macedonia had always been illusory. The unity between Russia and Austria had dissolved. Now the Young Turk Revolution of 1908 afforded the Powers the chance to wash their hands of the Macedonian problem. They stated, disingenuously or not, that they would see if the new Ottoman Government would reform Macedonia. Grey was notified by the other Powers that the Macedonian reforms were in effect dead. Russian Foreign Minister Alexander Petrovich Isvolsky told the new British ambassador in St Petersburgh, Arthur Nicolson, that he was sorry to have to suspend further consideration of Macedonian reforms, but he was not at all sure that Austria and others would have agreed to them. Better to wait and see how the new Ottoman Government turned out.[71]

The Powers' commitment to a European-led gendarmerie soon dissolved. The Austrian gendarmerie officers were given 'unlimited leave of absence'. The other European officers soon followed. A collective note from the Powers to the Ottoman Government stated that the employment of the European officers was 'temporarily suspended'.[72]

The fate of Ottoman Macedonia would be decided four years later in the Balkan Wars.

## Notes

1. For Balkan Committee material sent to the Istanbul embassy, see, for example: FO 421/189, 'Notes by Balkan Committee', 5 November 1903. FO 421/202, Balkan Committee to Lansdowne, London, 29 April 1904. FO 421/206, Balkan Committee to Lansdowne, London, 28 and 29 December 1904.
2. F. R. Bridge, 'Relations with Austria-Hungary and the Balkan States, 1905–1908', in Francis Harry Hinsley, ed., *British Foreign Policy under Sir Edward Grey*, Cambridge: Cambridge University Press, 1977, p. 167. See also, FO 800/143, Lansdowne to O'Conor, private, Foreign Office, 18 October 1903, and Michail, p. 14. Lansdowne's brother, Lord Edmond George Petty-Fitzmaurice, was also a

supporter of the Macedonian cause, lending his name to the Macedonian Relief Fund of the Balkan Committee.
3. 'The Affairs of South-eastern Europe', House of Lords, 28 March 1905, *Hansard*, vol. 143, cc. 1314–50. Lansdowne had proposed in 1903 and 1905 that a European Commission and Christian governor be put in place in Macedonia.
4. 'Imperial Parliament: House of Lords', *The Standard*, 16 February 1904, p. 6. See also, 'Parliament: House of Lords', *The Times*, 26 February 1908, p. 6. 'Affairs in Macedonia', House of Lords, 13 March 1903, *Hansard*, vol. 119, cc. 706–23. In a draft of a letter to Ambassador O'Conor in Istanbul, Lansdowne once cited 'the working of his (the sultan's) crafty but crooked mind'. 'Crafty but' was crossed out in the final letter. (FO 800/143, Lansdowne to O'Conor, Foreign Office, 30 August 1904.)
5. 'The Balkan Committee: Farewell Speech by Mr. Bryce', *The Times*, 25 December 1905. 'The Balkan Situation', *The Times*, 7 March 1904, p. 4. A Parliamentary White Paper of 1903, 'Turkey No. 4', included a statement from Lansdowne that no Muslim should ever be governor or inspector-general of Macedonia and that European officers should be in charge of gendarmerie. ('The Balkan Troubles: Official Despatches', *The Standard*, 17 October 1903, p. 5.) See also 'The Situation in the Balkans', *The Times*, 18 January 1905, p. 10. On the general effect of the Balkan Committee on British politics, see Perkins, pp. 143–61.
6. *Turkey No. 1 (1904): Further Correspondence respecting the Affairs of South-Eastern Europe, March–September, 1903, Presented to Both Houses of Parliament by Command of His Majesty, January, 1904*, London: HMSO, 1904 (Cd. 1875); *Turkey No. 2 (1904): Further Correspondence respecting the Affairs of South-Eastern Europe, in Continuation of 'Turkey No. 1 (1904), Presented to Both Houses of Parliament by Command of His Majesty, February, 1904'*, London: HMSO, 1904 (Cd. 1879).

   This is perhaps the best place to issue a caveat about British governmental sources. Scholars have long relied on the dubious information in the Blue Books. Often this was necessitated by the lack of original diplomatic records (a good example of this is William L. Langer, *The Diplomacy of Imperialism, 1890–1902*, New York: A. A. Knopf, 1935 and 1951.) These records have now long been opened, however, and they often tell a very different story than that of the much-vetted government publications. G. P. Gooch and Harold Temperley's *British Documents on the Origins of the War, 1898–1914* (11 vols, London: H. M. Stationery Office, 1926–38) has been particularly quoted by scholars, perhaps because its eleven large volumes seem encyclopaedic. It is not, although it is of great value, and I have used it extensively. But its compilers had a definite bias, and it is instructive that Gooch

was a board member of both the Balkan Committee and the British Armenia Committee. Temperley was a longtime Liberal apologist for British policy and, as the *Oxford Dictionary of National Biography* put it, the Turks were his *bêtes noires*.
7. Frances A. Radovich, 'Britain's Macedonian Reform Policy, 1903–1905', *The Historian*, vol. 43, no. 4 (August 1981), pp. 501–2. Balfour's public views were moderate: in 1903, he blamed the Macedonian unrest on the Turks, the Bulgarians in Bulgaria and the rebels in Macedonia. He truthfully commented that the rebels were drawing reprisals from the Turks in order to draw Europe into the conflict on their side. For this, he was roundly castigated in the press and by the Balkan Committee. (See 'Macedonia and Britain', *Spectator*, 3 October 1903, p. 22; 'Mr. Balfour at the Albert Hall', *Spectator*, 14 May 1904, p. 7; 'Macedonian Atrocities', *Daily Mail*, 27 August 1903, p. 5; no title, *Spectator*, 15 August 1903, p. 1.)
8. 'Armenian Christians', House of Commons, *Hansard*, 3 March 1896, vol. 38, cc. 37–125. See also the extended report on this debate in 'House of Commons', *The Times*, 5 March 1896, p. 6, and Grey's speech in 'Armenian Christians', House of Commons, *Hansard*, 3 March 1896, vol. 38, cc. 37–125.

Anne Louise Antonoff contended that Grey was also a member of the Balkan Committee, but I have found no proof of this. It is possible that he met with the original parliamentary group. (Anne Louise Antonoff, 'Almost War: Britain, Germany, and the Bosnian Crisis, 1908–1909', unpublished PhD dissertation, Yale, 2006, p. 309.) On Grey, see Keith Robbins, *Sir Edward Grey: A Biography of Lord Grey of Fallodon*, London: Cassell, 1971, although it contains little on Grey's dealings with the Ottoman Empire. Christopher Clark described Grey:

> [H]e had long been a Liberal MP, yet he believed that foreign policy was too important to be subjected to the agitations of parliamentary debate. He was a foreign secretary who knew little of the world outside Britain, had never shown much interest in travelling, spoke no foreign languages and felt ill at ease in the company of foreigners.

(*The Sleepwalkers: How Europe Went to War in 1914*, New York: Harper, 2012, pp. 200–1)
9. FO 800/79, Grey to O'Conor, 17 December 1907. FO 800/143, Grey to Lowther, Constantinople, 30 April 1909.
10. CAB 37/91/5, Grey to Cabinet Memorandum, January 1908. 'Macedonia's Cry', *Daily News*, 1 October 1903, p. 4. 'Macedonian Reform', *The Times*, 11 April 1908, p. 3. No Heading ('At a Meeting of the Balkan Committee, Held at the

House of Commons Yesterday, . . .'), *The Times*, 7 February 1908, p. 12. Letter from the Balkan Committee, *The Times*, 6 March 1908, p. 6. FO 800/79. Grey to O'Conor, 8 February 1908. The Balkan Committee, however, was frustrated that Grey's good intentions did not bring results, and that he was forced to defend his policies that had been affected by the Powers' politics. (FO 800/79, Grey to O'Conor, private, London, 11 July 1907.)

11. 'Sir H. Campbell-Bannerman at Stirling', *The Standard*, 23 October 1903, p. 4. In 1903, Campbell-Bannerman declared himself fully sympathetic with the goals of the Balkan Committee (no title, *The Times*, 10 October 1903, p. 10.)

12. 'Britain and Macedonia: Mr. Asquith's Declaration', *Daily News*, 15 October 1903, p. 6.

13. 'Sir E. Grey on Macedonia', *The Times*, 10 July 1907, p. 4. Balkan Committee, *Sir Edward Grey's Proposal in 1908*, London: the Balkan Committee, no publication date listed, probably 1908. 'Turkish Misrule: Sir E. Grey and Reform Schemes', *The Standard*, 9 April 1906, p. 9.

14. 'The Balkan Problem', *The Times*, 2 April 1909, p 5. The *Neue Freie Presse*, quoted in 'From Our Own Correspondent, Vienna', *The Times*, 9 April 1908, p. 5; Antonoff, pp. 309 and 367, note 85. The Ottomans surely felt committee interference to be the case. See 'The Situation in Turkey', *The Times*, 11 February 1911, p. 5.

15. Viscount Grey of Fallodon, *Twenty-Five Years: 1892–1916*, London: Hodder and Stoughton, 1926, vol. 1, pp. 172–3.

16. For excellent descriptions and analyses of the situation in Macedonia and the European reforms, see Ahsene Gül Tokay, 'Macedonian Reforms and Muslim Opposition during the Hamidian Era: 1878–1908', *Islam and Christian–Muslim Relations*, vol. 14, no. 1 (2003), pp. 51–65, and 'The Macedonian Question and the Origins of the Young Turk Revolution, 1903–1908', unpublished PhD dissertation, University of London, 1994. Tokay is almost unique in her consideration of the Muslim populations of Macedonia. See also Julian Brooks, 'Managing Macedonia: British Statecraft, Intervention, and "Proto-peacekeeping" in Ottoman Macedonia, 1902–1905', Simon Fraser University, 2014, pp. 581–602. The Foreign Office summarised diplomatic events in Macedonia in FO 881/8555, 'Memorandum Respecting the Progress of Macedonian Reform', Foreign Office, January 1906 (no other date given), FO 881/8294, 'Memorandum Respecting the Progress of Macedonian Reform', Foreign Office, 14 December 1904, and FO 881/8555, 'Memorandum Respecting the Progress of Macedonian Reform', Foreign Office, January 1906 (no date given).

17. 'Aufzeichnung einer Unterredung des Grafen Goluchowski mit dem deutschen Reichskanzler Fuersten Hohenlohe, December, 1895', and 'Der Botschafter in Konstantinopel, Freiherr von Galice an den Österreich-ungarischen Minister des Auessern, Graf Goluchowski', Pera, 20 February 1896, in Eurof Walters, 'Austro-Russian Relations under Goluchowski, 1895–1906', *The Slavonic and East European Review*, vol. 31, no. 76 (December 1952), pp. 212–31 – a document collection.
18. 'Résumé der Unterredungen des Grafen Goluchowski mit Seiner Majestaet dem deutschen Kaiser, dem Fuersten Hohenlohe und Baron Marschall waehrend seines Besuches in Berlin', March 1896, and 'Résumé der Unterredungen des Grafen Goluchowski mit Kaiser Wilhelm waehrend seines letzten Besuches in Berlin', January 16–19 1897, in Eurof Walters, Austro-Russian Relations under Goluchowski, 1895–1906, *The Slavonic and East European Review*, vol. 31, no. 77 (Jun 1953), pp. 503–27.
19. 'Der Botschafter in St Petersburg, Prinz Liechtenstein an Goluchowski', St Petersburg, 18 May 1897, in Eurof Walters, Austro-Russian Relations under Goluchowski, 1895–1906, *The Slavonic and East European Review*, vol. 31, no. 77 (Jun 1953), pp. 503–27. On Russian perceptions of their weakness and need for time, see Kurat, pp. 136–7, describing the situation in 1908.
20. Denis Vovchenko, *Containing Balkan Nationalism: Imperial Russia and Ottoman Christians, 1856–1914*, Oxford: Oxford University Press, 2016, pp. 229–41. Crampton, pp. 59–175.
21. Alfred Franzis Pribram and Archibald Cary Coolidge (English Edition), *The Secret Treaties of Austria-Hungary*, vol. 1, Cambridge, MA: Harvard University Press, 1920, pp. 185–95. 'Goluchowski an Kaiser Franz Joseph', Schoenbrunn, 20 October 1898, ‚Denkschrift des neuernannten Botschafters in Petersburg, Freih. von Aehrenthal an Graf Goluchowski', 31 December 1898, 'Goluchowski an Aehrenthal', Vienna, 2 March 1899, in Eurof Walters, 'Austro-Russian Relations under Goluchowski, 1895–1906', *The Slavonic and East European Review*, vol. 32, no. 78 (December 1953), pp. 187–214. William L. Langer, *The Diplomacy of Imperialism*, 2d edn, New York: Knopf, 1951, pp. 371–5. Langer's monumental work has unfortunately been of little use here, because it was written before most archival documents were available. It has been consulted, but has only occasionally been useful, such as in this subject.
22. The Europeans gave Article 23 of the Treaty of Berlin as justification for Great Power intervention in Macedonia. The treaty had committed the Ottomans to reforms and new laws. The Powers now stated that the stipulations had not been carried out, and the treaty gave them the right to intervene.

23. FO 421/193, Lansdowne to Monson, 9 April 1902, and FO 421/193, Lansdowne to Elliot, 12 April 1902, Brooks, pp. 133–5 and 144–7. Brooks cites FO 65/1664, Scott to Lansdowne, 1 March 1902, which I have not seen.
24. The sultan's detailed instructions are quoted in Bapst to Delcassè, Pera, 1 December 1892, in Affaires 1902, no. 41.
25. FO 421/196, M. Zinovieff to Benckendorff (Communicated by Count Benckendorff, 17 February 1903), Pera, 6 February 1903. The French had notified the Russians that they agreed perfectly with Russian plans. (Delcassé to Montebello, Paris, 3 January 1903, in France, Ministère des Affaires Étrangères, *Documents Diplomatiques: Affaires De Macédoine. Janvier-Février 1903, no. 1*, Paris: Imprimerie Nationale, 1903.)
26. See FO 421/196, Scott to Lansdowne, 21 January 1903.
27. Constans to Delcassé, Pera, 2 April 1903, in France, Ministère des Affaires Étrangères, *Documents Diplomatiques: Affaires de Macédoine, 1903–1905*, Paris: Imprimerie Nationale,1907, no. 3, which contains the government's detailed instructions to provincial officials on the reforms.
28. FO 421/196, Lansdowne to Plunkett, Foreign Office, 12, 17 and 20 February 1903.
29. Tokay, 'Macedonian Reforms', pp. 57–8. FO 421/197, 'Report of the Russian Consular Representative in Uskub as of April 3, 1903'. FO 421/197, O'Conor to Lansdowne, Constantinople, 4 April 1903; Lansdowne to O'Conor, Foreign Office, 11 April 1903. It was difficult to retain Christians in the gendarmerie, because of poor and dilatory pay. (Tokay, *Makedonya Sorunu*, pp. 117–18 and 121.
30. FO 421/198, Lansdowne to Mensdorff and Lansdowne to Graevenitz, 19 April 1903; Lansdowne to O'Conor, Foreign Office, 23 September 1903; O'Conor to Lansdowne, Therapia, 25 September 1903. On opposition to the British plan and any suggestions of autonomy in Macedonia, see FO 421/198, Plunkett to Lansdowne, Vienna, 25 September 1903; Lascelles to Lansdowne, Berlin, 25 September 1903; Plunkett to Lansdowne, Vienna, 27 September 1903.

    The Ottoman Government thanked the Austrians and Russians for their continued commitment to the reforms. It reiterated that it also was committed to them, but there were two difficulties: the continuing revolt had made it impossible to implement the reforms completely at present. Ottoman army units needed to bring peace to Macedonia instead had to be placed on the Bulgarian border, because of Bulgarian military mobilisation. The Ottomans hoped that the continuing efforts of the two Powers would cause Bulgaria to end support of the insurgent bands. (FO 421/198, Lansdowne to O'Conor, 30 September 1903.)

31. FO 421/198, O'Conor to Lansdowne, Constantinople, 26, 27 and 28 September 1903; Lansdowne to O'Conor, Foreign Office, 26 September 1903.
32. FO 421/198, Lansdowne to Plunkett, Foreign Office, 29 September 1902. On the same day, the Austrians told the British that they would not put forward any new programme, refusing the British request. Despite British insistence, the two continue to reject them. (FO 421/198, Lansdowne to Plunkett, Foreign Office, 29 September 1902. FO 421–199, Lansdowne to Lascelles, Foreign Office, 7 October 1903.

   The sultan was pleased that the Russians and Austrians had not listened to the British and demanded a Christian governor-general for Macedonia, named by the Powers, instead of a Muslim inspector-general. He noted the domestic pressure on the British Government. (O'Conor to Lansdowne, Constantinople, 19 November 1903, in BDOW 1, pp. 303–5.)
33. FO 421/199, 'Identic Instructions Sent by the Austro-Hungarian and Russian Governments to their Ambassadors at Constantinople. (Communicated to the Foreign Office by Austro-Hungarian Chargé d'Affaires, October 24, 1903)', signed at Mürzsteg, 2 October 1903. On the Mürzsteg Agreements, see Nadine Akhund, 'Stabilizing a Crisis and the Mürzsteg Agreement of 1903: International Efforts to Bring Peace to Macedonia', *The Hungarian Historical Review*, vol. 3, no. 3 (2014), pp. 587–608. The Proposals were renewed in 1905.
34. FO 421/199, O'Conor to Lansdowne, Constantinople, 5, 19, 24 and 25 November 1903; Spring-Rice to Lansdowne, St Petersburgh, 24 November 1903.
35. Lansdowne to Monson, Foreign Office, 25 February 1904, in BDOW 5, pp. 68–9. CAB 38/75/52 and 68, draft dispatches from Lansdowne, 25 March and 17 April 1905.
36. 'Macedonia', House of Lords debate, 5 May 1904, Hansard, vol. 134, cc. 499–515.
37. There are many examples of this. See, for example, Cambon to Delcassé, London, 9 January and 29 March 1905, in Affaires 1903–5, nos. 97 and 128. Lansdowne to Scott, Foreign Office, 4 March 1904, in BDOW 5, p. 73; Lansdowne to Plunkett, Foreign Office, 25 January 1905, in BDOW 5, p. 76.
38. Lansdowne note to the other Powers, 11 January 1905, enclosure in Cambon to Delcassé, 13 January 1906, in Affaires 1903–5, no. 99.
39. FO 421/199, Johnstone to Lansdowne, 4 November 1903. See also: Consul-General Biliotti's complete agreement with this assessment. (FO 195/2156, Biliotti to O'Conor, Salonica, 11 March 1903. Tokay, 'Macedonian Question', pp. 52–5.
40. O'Conor to Grey, Pera, 7 December 1907, BDOW 5, pp. 217–19.

41. In 1903, the Austrian Foreign Office listed a population that was 52 per cent Muslim, 45 per cent Orthodox and 3 per cent Catholic. The numbers are not strictly comparable to those in Table 4.1, because the Austrians included the Yanya and Üsküdar Provinces in their figures. (Austria–Hungary, HHStA PA XII/319, Liasse XXXV, Entwurf einer neuen Abgrenzung der Balkan Vilajets mit Ausnahme des Vilajets Adrianopel, mit besonderer Berücksichtigung der in denselben obwaltenden nationalen Verhältnisse, August 1903, cited in Chotzidis, p. 265).
42. FO 421/198 and 199 contain numerous documents of mobilisation and preparation for war. See especially Lt Col. Maunsell's evaluation of the Ottoman plan of attack. (FO 421/198, Maunsell to O'Conor, Therapia, 15 September 1903.)
43. FO 421/204, O'Conor to Lansdowne, Constantinople, 12 July 1904. Tokay, 'Macedonian Question', p. 49. Stanford J. Shaw, 'Ottoman Expenditures and Budgets in the Late Nineteenth and Early Twentieth Centuries', *International Journal of Middle East Studies*, vol. 9, no. 3 (October 1978), pp. 373–8. On British deliberations on the customs issue, see CAB/37/75/ 35, 37, 38, 39 and 42. On pay in Macedonia, see Tokay, *Makedonya Sorunu*, pp. 112–13.
44. Grey to Goschen, Foreign Office, 9 January 1907, in BDOW 5, p. 196. O'Conor to Tewfik Pasha, Constantinople, 25 April 1907, in BDOW 5, p. 199. 'Extract from the Memorandum by Sir C. Hardinge', 19 August 1907, in BDOW 5, pp. 208–11. Secretary of State to Musurus Pasha (Ottoman ambassador), Foreign Office, 27 February 1905, enclosure in Cambon to Delcassé, London, 1 March 1905, in Affaires 1903–5, no. 114. Yosmaoğlu, *Blood Ties*, pp. 41–4. A reason offered by the British to refuse the increase was inadequacies in Ottoman customs administration, but even the British had to ultimately admit that the Ottomans had greatly improved this. It was, after all, in their own interest.
45. FO 421/204, O'Conor to Lansdowne, Therapia, 2 August 1904.
46. 'Customs Increase Negotiations', enclosure in Barclay, 'Annual Report for Turkey for the Year 1906: January 18, 1907', in BDOW 5, pp. 168–74. O'Conor to Tewfik, Constantinople, 25 April 1907, in BDOW 5, p. 199.

    The history of the negotiations on the customs increase is described in detail in Donald C. Blaisdell, *European Financial Control in the Ottoman Empire*, New York: Columbia University Press, 1929, pp. 156–76.
47. FO 421/202, Treasury to Foreign Office, 2 March 1904; Foreign Office to War Office, 3 March, 18 April 1904; Foreign Office to Treasury, 12 April 1904. FO 421/203, Treasury to Foreign Office, 2 May 1904. FO 421/205, Foreign Office to Treasury, 6, 22 and 23 October 1904. The Foreign Office begged the Treasury

for the small sums involved, to no avail. FO 421/203, O'Conor to Lansdowne, Constantinople, 3 and 24 May 1904.
48. 'Note Verbale of Sublime Porte to Representatives of Six Great Powers', 20 October 1905, in BDOW 5, pp. 81–2. O'Conor to Lansdowne, Therapia, 27 October 1905, in BDOW 5, p. 85. Lansdowne to O'Conor, Foreign Office, 24 October 1905, in BDOW 5, p. 89. Lansdowne to Goschen, Foreign Office, 28 October 1905, in BDOW 5, pp. 82–3. Lansdowne to Spring-Rice, Foreign Office, 6 November 1905, in BDOW 5, p. 91. O'Conor to Lansdowne, Pera, 27 November 1905, in BDOW 5, p. 98. Lansdowne to O'Conor, Foreign Office, 6 December 1905, in BDOW 5, pp. 98–9. Rouvier to Boppe, Paris, 28 October and 8 November 1905, in Affaires 1903–5, nos. 164 and 165. Boppe to Rouvier, Pera, 14 November 1905, which contains the proposed financial regulations and the Powers' note to the Ottoman Government. See also, Brooks, pp. 631–9.

There were negotiations over the final plan, not described here. See: Boppe to Rouvier, Pera, 5 and 8 December 1905, in Affaires 1903–5, nos. 174 and 175. Ambassador O'Conor provided a detailed summary of the negotiations in FO 78/5395, O'Conor to Lansdowne, Therapia, 25 July 1905. The French, with their extensive financial interest in the Ottoman Empire, considered the customs increase and financial regulation so important that they devoted an entire book of documents to it. (France, Ministère des Affaires Étrangères, *Documents Diplomatiques: Affaires De Macédoine, Élévation des Droits de Douane en Turquie, 1906–1907*, Paris: Imprimerie Nationale, 1907.) I have not considered it necessary to refer to it here.
49. McGregor to Graves, Monastir, 31 July 1903. Kral to Goluchowski, Monastir, 1 August 1903, in HHStA PA XXXVIII/Konsulat Monastir 1903, vol. 392, no. 87, MH. Tokay, 'Macedonian Reforms', pp. 54–7.
50. The most complete study of Greek activities in Macedonia is in Dakin, *Greek Struggle*, pp. 117–45, 162–237, 252–87, 306–20 and 360–74. See also: Basil C. Gounaris, 'Social Gatherings and Macedonian Lobbying: Symbols of Irredentism and Living Legends in Early Twentieth-Century Athens', in Philip Carabott, ed., *Greek Society in the Making, 1863–1913: Realities, Symbols and Visions*, London: Routledge, 1997, pp. 98–112 in Kindle Edition. Tokay, 'Macedonian Question', pp. 76–80. Yosmaoğlu, *Blood Ties*, pp. 40–1. Lange-Akhund, pp. 54–7.
51. Steeg to Delcassé, Salonica, 3 December 1902, in France, Ministère des Affaires Étrangères, *Documents Diplomatiques: Affaires De Macédoine 1902*, Paris : Imprimerie Nationale, 1903, no. 42. FO 421/240, Merlin to Elliot, Volo, 24 December 1907. FO 421/241, Merlin to Elliot, Volo, 25 February 1908. Munir Paşa to Delcassé, Paris, 5 April 1905, in Affaires 1903–5, no. 136.

52. FO 421/241, 'Regulations for the National Organization of Greek Population in Macedonia', enclosure in Barclay to Grey, Constantinople, 18 March 1908.
53. See the detailed report in FO 421/240, 'Report by Lieutenant-Colonel Bonham on the Working of the Gendarmerie during the Year 1907', enclosure in O'Conor to Grey, Pera, 21 January 1908. F. Elliot, 'Extract from the Annual Report for Greece for the Year 1907', in BDOW 5, pp. 119–21. Adanır, pp. 217–22. Delcassé to d'Ormesson (ambassador at Athens), Paris, 3 April 1905, in Affaires 1903–5, no. 137.

   On the Ottoman gendarmerie, see: Nadir Özbek, 'Policing the Countryside: Gendarmes of the Late 19th Century Ottoman Empire (1876–1908)', *International Journal of Middle East Studies*, vol. 40 (2008), pp. 47–67. Yosmaoğlu, *Blood Ties*, pp. 36–9. Tokay, *Makedonya Sorunu*, pp. 117–30.
54. FO 421/198, Thesiger to Lansdowne, Belgrade, 20 August 1903. Steeg to Delcassé, Salonika, 10 October 1904, in Affaires 1903–5, no. 89. Benoit to Delcassé, Belgrade, 19 April 1905, in Affaires 1903–5, no. 135. Satow report, Uskub, 28 November 1904, enclosure in Townley to Lansdowne, Constantinople, 29 November 1904. Lange-Akhund, pp. 58–61.
55. Tokay, 'Macedonian Question', pp. 82–6. Dakin, *Greek Struggle*, pp. 171–3 and 241–2. Benoit to Delcassé, Belgrade, 1 February 1905, in Affaires 1903–5, no. 106.
56. Tokay, 'Macedonian Reforms', pp. 59–63. Tokay pointed out the influence of Muslim discontent on the 1908 revolution.
57. Enclosure in Constans to Delcassé, 1 December 1904, in Affaires 1903–5, no. 93. Boppe to Rouvier, Therapia, 10 August 1905, in Affaires 1903–5, no. 150.
58. FO 421/240, 'Memorandum by Consul-General Lamb on the Course of Events in Macedonia during the Year 1907', enclosure in O'Conor to Grey, Pera, 18 February 1908. For other examples of Lamb's extensive and detailed reports on Macedonian violence, see, among others, FO 421/240, Lamb to O'Conor, Salonica, 16 January 1908; FO 421, Lamb to Barclay, Salonica, 20 March and 14 April 1908. See also FO 78/5338, Satow to du Vallon, Uskub, 12, 16 and 22 December 1904; numerous examples in FO 195/2297 and 2298. On the murders, see also, for example, FO 421/240 enclosure in Buchanan to Grey, Sophia, 24 January 1908; Heathcote to O'Conor, Monastir, 19 and 24 January 1908; Satow to Lamb, Uskub, 21 January 1908; enclosure in Lamb to O'Conor, Salonica, 12 February 1908.
59. FO 78/5338, Townley to Lansdowne, Constantinople, 13 December 1904. Townley himself recognised that the main problem was not with the Ottomans, but with 'race hatred'. As a good officer of the Crown, however, he carried out

his orders. (FO 78/5338, Townley to Lansdowne, Constantinople, 19 December 1904.)
60. Grey to O'Conor, FF, 11 July 1907, in BDOW 5, pp. 205–6. 'Extract from the Memorandum by Sir C. Hardinge', 19 August 1907, in BDOW 5, pp. 208–11. Grey to Goschen, FF, 13 December 1907, in BDOW 5, p. 219.
61. Grey to Nicolson, Foreign Office, 7 March 1907, in BDOW 4, pp. 277–9. Goschen to Grey. Marienbad, 5 September 1907, in BDOW 4, pp. 582–4.
62. Grey to Goschen, Foreign Office, 29 May 1907, in BDOW 5, pp. 201–2. FO 421/241, Grey to Bertie, Foreign Office, 3 March 1908. The same message was sent to other ambassadors, with instructions to relay it to the respective governments. FO 421/241, Grey to Lascelles, Foreign Office, 31 March 1908. Grey to O'Conor, Foreign Office, 17 December 1907, in BDOW 5, pp. 219–21. See also CAB 37/91/19, Grey, 'Memorandum Communicated to Count Mensdorff', 18 December 1907.
63. FO 421/243, O'Beirne to Grey, St Petersbourgh, 10 July 1908. The Italians believed that the Ottomans would never accept the new army unless forced militarily, which the Powers would not do. (FO 421/243, Erskine to Grey, Rome, 14 July 1908. Fitzmaurice Memorandum, 9 August 1907, in BDOW 5, p. 207.
64. 'Macedonia', House of Commons Debate, 25 February 1908, *Hansard*, vol. 184, cc. 1663–1708.
65. FO 421/241, Barclay to Grey, Sophia, 18 March 1908; Goschen to Grey, 3 April 1908; Lascelles to Grey, Berlin, 9, 13 and 18 March 1908; Barclay to Grey, Pera, 1 April 1908. There are many documents on the rejection of Grey's proposal. See, for example, FO 421/241, Goschen to Grey, Vienna, 6, 9, 14 and 16 March and 3 April 1908. Bertie to Grey, Paris, 9 March 1908. 'Aide-Memoire Communicated by the Austrian Ambassador', 6 April 1908; Elliot to Grey, Athens, 12 March 1908. O'Conor to Grey, Constantinople, 18 February 1908, in BDOW 5, pp. 219–30. See also Schöllgen, pp. 197–205.
66. FO 421/241, 'Aide-Mémoire Communicated to Sir E. Grey by Count Benckendorff, March 31, 1908', St Petersburg, 26 March 1908; 'Aide-Memoire Communicated by the Austrian Ambassador', 6 April 1908. The date on the Austrian note was 30 March 1908; Isvolsky to Benckendorff (Communicated by the Russian ambassador), 29 April 1908.
67. FO 421/241, 'Memorandum Communicated to the Russian Ambassador in Reply to his Excellency's Communication of March 31, 1908'. Note a discrepancy in listed dates of the Russian message. See also FO 421/241, Grey to Barclay, Foreign Office, 1 May 1908.

68. FO 421/242, 'Memorandum Communicated by Sir Edward Grey to Count Benckendorff', Foreign Office, 15 May 1908; O'Beirne to Grey, St Petersburgh, 4 June 1908; Grey to O'Beirne, Foreign Office, 17 June 1908. See also Ambassador Gerald Lowther's short, and unsatisfactory, summary of British–Russian negotiations in 'Extract from Annual Report for Turkey for the Year 1908', in BDOW 5, pp. 230–1.
69. F. R. Bridge, *Great Britain and Austria-Hungary 1906–1914: A Diplomatic History*, London: Weidenfeld and Nicolson, 1972, pp. 77–93. Arthur J. May, 'The Novibazar Railway Project', *The Journal of Modern History*, vol. 10, no. 4 (December 1938), pp. 496–527. Tokay, 'Macedonian Question', pp. 118–19.
70. O'Conor to Grey, Constantinople, 4 and 5 February 1908, in BDOW 5, pp. 225–6 and 330. Grey, 'Memorandum Communicated to Count Benckendorff', 4 March, in BDOW 5, pp. 347–8. Grey to Goschen, Foreign Office, 4 March 1908, in BDOW 5, pp. 348–9. Bridge and Bullen, pp. 287–94.

    On Russian popular and official feeling against the scheme, see Nicolson to Grey, St Petersburgh, 30 January and 13 February 1908, in BDOW 5, pp. 328–9 and 336.
71. FO 421/243, Nicolson to Grey, St Petersburgh, 13 and 22 August 1908. On the end of the reform proposals, see Steven W. Sowards, *Austria's Policy of Macedonian Reform*, Boulder, CO: East European Monographs, 1989, pp. 74–88.
72. FO 421/243, Nicolson to Grey, St Petersburgh, 19 August 1908; Grey to Nicolson, Foreign Office, 31 August 1908. The Russians vacillated (FO 421/243, Nicolson to Grey, St Petersburgh, 26 August 1908), but eventually agreed. FO 421/244 includes much debate on the question of retention of the European officers. FO 424/244, enclosure in Lowther to Grey, Therapia, 8 September 1908.

# 6

# OTTOMAN REVOLUTION, ITALIAN WAR

Driven by years of unpaid salaries, failures in Macedonia and European actions against the Ottoman Empire, in July of 1908 the Ottoman army in Europe revolted in favour of a new constitutional government – the so-called Young Turk Revolution. Although led by the army, the revolt had long been the aim of the nationalist reformers of the Committee of Union and Progress (İttihad ve Terakki Cemiyeti, CUP) that had organised revolutionary cells within and without the Empire. Faced with the rebellion, Sultan Abdülhamid II, ever an accomplished politician, yielded. He revoked his suspension of the Ottoman Parliament, which had never theoretically been abolished, only prorogued for thirty years.[1]

The secret organisation of the CUP did not formally take part in the elections of November to December 1908. The revolutionaries did not have any experience in governing, so they at first selected established politicians to operate the organs of the state. Men who had risen during Abdülhamid's reign remained as Grand Vezirs – first Mehmed Sait Paşa, followed by Mehmed Kâmil Paşa and Hüseyin Hilmi Paşa.[2]

The CUP, though not yet officially a political party, remained the real power in the state. Kâmil Paşa attempted to assert his own authority over that of the CUP but failed, becoming the committee's greatest enemy. Abdülhamid remained as a constitutional monarch, but in April 1909 he was believed to have supported a counter-revolution, intended to return him to power. The revolt was swiftly put down by the army and Abdülhamid deposed. The army retained much power, but the CUP emerged from its secrecy to become a secularist and reformist political party which took control of parliament.

The Italian War (see below) damaged the authority of the CUP and led to defections in parliament and dissensions within the party. Nevertheless, in April 1912 the CUP won an unfair election in which it used all the power of the state to insure victory. The opposition Liberal Entente Party (the Freedom and Accord Party, Hürriyet ve İtilâf Fırkası) protested the results. A group of army officers, the Saviour Officers (Halâskâr Zabitan), threatened armed action unless the CUP-dominated cabinet resigned, which it did. A Government of National Unity was formed which included enemies of the CUP, Kâmil and Mehmed Ferid. The new government began immediately to persecute leaders of the CUP. Parliament was dissolved and new elections were begun in which state power was now used against the CUP, but the elections were disrupted by the beginning of the Balkan Wars.

Democracy had turned out to be a messy business.

The British Foreign Office initially approved of the 1908 revolution and the new government. A government that espoused democratic principles and had a constitution and a parliament naturally appealed to a British public that had been fed a steady diet of vilification of Abdülhamid – 'the Red Sultan'. The revolution also allowed Britain to extricate herself from an intractable situation in Macedonia; the Europeans could pretend that the new Ottoman government would solve the Macedonian problem through democratic methods. Foreign Secretary Grey at first promised nothing but good wishes toward the new Ottoman Government. He pledged support and what he called a 'benevolent attitude' toward the Ottomans. At first, Grey's only worry was that, if the Turks should succeed in creating a working constitutional government, the Egyptians would also want one, putting the British in a very awkward position. Grey, however, was not sure that all would be well in the Ottoman Empire: 'It may well be that the habit of vicious and corrupt government will be too strong for reform and that animosities of race and religion will again produce violence and disorder.'[3]

Grey had no affection for the Ottomans. He saw them as pieces in the delicate game of Great Power politics. His initial hope for the Ottoman Empire was simply that it would cause no trouble among the Great Powers. He had to contend with German and Russian plans for the Ottoman Empire. Grey had the nearly impossible task of placating the Ottomans, while at the same time supporting the Russians. Grey needed accurate information on Ottoman politics and the schemes of the other Powers in Istanbul. He did not get that information from his ambassador to the Ottoman court.

## Ambassador Lowther

The British were unfortunate to have appointed Gerard Augustus Lowther as their ambassador to the Ottoman Empire in 1908. Lowther had been born into a wealthy noble family with strong connections to the Foreign Office. His father, William Lowther, brother of the Earl of Lonsdale, had been an ambassador and member of parliament. His brother James was Speaker of the House of Commons from 1905 to 1921. Lowther entered the diplomatic service in 1879. He served as second secretary in Istanbul from 1884 to 1891. He thus had experience serving in the Ottoman Empire, and might have been seen as a good choice to succeed Nicholas O'Conor, but he was not a good choice.

At first Ambassador Lowther supported the revolution, especially because '[t]here should now be great opening for bona fide British business'. He only mildly disparaged the CUP, calling them 'good intentioned children'. He felt they could not last and would be soon be replaced by unspecified 'better men'. When they were not replaced by old Ottoman aristocrats of whom he approved, he began to take a darker view of those whom he consistently referred to as 'The Committee'. He became increasingly incensed that Jews and Freemasons were prominent in the CUP.[4]

Lowther exhibited the prejudices of many in his aristocratic class. He particularly disliked Jews, Freemasons and what he always called 'crypto-Jews', members of the Ottoman Dönme community whose Jewish ancestors had converted to Islam. Lowther was what a later age would call a conspiracy theorist. He believed that a cabal of Freemasons and Jews secretly guided the politics of the Ottoman Empire, and that the Jews, both within and without the Ottoman Empire, plotted with the CUP to keep down their rivals – the Greeks, Armenians and Bulgarians. Lowther's portrayal of the Jews could have come from any screed of European antisemitism. To Lowther, the Jews and Dönmes, whom he falsely believed were cooperating conspirators, were rich bankers who used their wealth and financial acumen to direct political affairs.

Lowther saw the Jewish conspiracy everywhere: 'Jews of all colours, native and foreign' seemed to be potential spies for the 'occult Committee (the CUP)'. Lowther reported that 'people' were remarking that the CUP revolution was a Jewish, not a Turkish, revolution. Lowther saw it as significant that both Italy (Primo Levi) and America (Oscar Strauss) had appointed Jews as ambassadors to the Ottoman Empire. The Turks, Lowther asserted, needed the financial skills of the Jews. The Jews, for their part, planned to reward unrestricted Jewish immigration into Palestine or perhaps Iraq by paying off all the Ottoman debt.[5]

According to Lowther, the Ottoman attempts to create some form of democracy had no chance of success, because of the Jews:

> A constitution in a way implies economic progress, but the economic organism of the Turk is of the feeblest kind, and, unsupported, could not stand alone a week. It was hoped in the beginning that the Armenians, Bulgarians, Greeks and the Ottoman Jew would serve as economic props, but the Young Turk seems to have allied himself solely with the Jew, Ottoman and foreign, and to have estranged the other races. The same result has been witnessed in Hungary, where the Hungarian, who is of Turkish stock and is similarly devoid of real business instincts, has come under the almost exclusive economic and financial domination of the Jew. The latter seems to have entangled the pre-economic-minded Turk in his toils, and as Turkey happens to contain the places sacred to Israel, it is but natural that the Jew should strive to maintain a position of exclusive influence and utilize it for the furtherance of his ideals, viz. the ultimate creation of an autonomous Jewish state in Palestine or Babylonia.[6]

While it is true that leading members of the Committee of Union and Progress were also members of Freemason lodges, the theories of Lowther made the sort of leap of illogic that characterises conspiracy theories: to him, the fact that there were Masons in the government meant that a Masonic conspiracy ran the government. The fact that there were Jews among the members of the CUP meant the Jews were behind all. In fact, the revolutionaries who coalesced into the CUP had used Freemason organisations to gather together, as had revolutionaries in other countries. There is absolutely no evidence that they ever followed a supposed Freemason plan, either before or after they took power.[7]

Lowther's prejudices were best exemplified in a long letter he sent to Charles Hardinge, Permanent Under-Secretary of State, leader of the Foreign Office.

Most of the points in the letter were the same as those cited above. In particular, the Turks allegedly knew that they needed the Jews for their supposed financial and conspiratorial abilities. ('The Oriental Jew is an adept at manipulating occult forces, and political Freemasonry of the continental type has been chosen as the most effective bond and cloak to conceal the inner workings of the movement.') The Turks knew they were incapable of succeeding on their own. Lowther's letter showed only contempt for the Ottoman Government. ('At present the Turkish constitutional régime is a sham.') The Turks knew that the army had to be in charge of the country, because otherwise the Turks would be overthrown by the other 'races' in the Empire, 'as it (the Turkish race) is inferior to the majority (Arabs, Greeks, Bulgarians, etc.), in intelligence, instruction and business qualities'. The Arabs, he declared, 'hate and despise the Turk'. Many Arabs, Lowther hopefully believed, looked for a new Arab government, led by the Khedive of Egypt, 'under British auspices'.

Many of Lowther's assertions in the letter were plainly ridiculous: every Jew was a spy for the CUP. The Jews or the 'crypto-Jews' were in charge of the press and the telegraph system. Freemasons, who were led by the Jews, controlled the police and gendarmerie. Officials all over the Empire were told that they could only keep their positions if they became Freemasons. The Jews were conspiring to end British rule in Egypt. Even though Catholics were forbidden to become Freemasons by the Pope, 'large numbers' of Catholics had become Masons. Lowther believed that 'Liberté, Egalité and Fraternité', had been adopted as the motto of the Young Turks only because it was the motto of the Italian Freemasons. But, although his knowledge of French Revolution slogans was weak, he did fear the effect of French traditions of revolution:

> The Young Turks, partly at the inspiration of Jewish Masonry, and partly owing to the fact that French is the one European language extensively spread in the Levant, have been imitating the French Revolution and its godless and levelling methods. The developments of the French Revolution led to antagonism between England and France, and should the Turkish revolution develop on the same lines, it may find itself similarly in antagonism with British ideals and interests.[8]

How much Lowther's letter affected the British Government cannot be known for sure. It is instructive, however, that Lowther's letter was forwarded by the Foreign Office to British ambassadors and representatives in Europe and the Middle East for their information.

His prejudices did not inure Lowther to the new government of soldiers and intellectuals who had revolted against the rule of Sultan Abdülhamid II and created a new government just before Lowther's arrival. Their numbers and supporters included some from the very groups Lowther despised – Freemasons, Dönmes and Jews. Like it or not, and whatever his prejudices, Lowther should have shown a friendly face to any Ottoman government and at least pretended to be neutral in domestic politics. For Lowther, this was impossible. Given the propensity of British officials to interfere in domestic matters, it would always have been difficult, but Lowther was incapable of wielding British power strategically or diplomatically.

Lowther never appreciated the CUP and the parliament for the reformers they were. While in power the CUP proposed major reforms: constitutional changes, allowing labour organisations, press freedom (at least in theory), compulsory primary education, reformed finance and taxation, great restriction on the sultan's power in favour of the cabinet and great increases in funds for the army and navy, which Abdülhamid had neglected. By no means were all of these successfully implemented, in part because wars from 1911 on consumed the government's resources, but they were the most significant reforms ever attempted in the Ottoman Empire. Lowther either did not understand these efforts, or perhaps did not care. If the British Government had depended on Lowther's reports, they would have known little of the modernisation plans of the CUP – the sort of modernisation they in theory supported.[9]

Much of what can be attributed to Lowther, for good or bad, was written by his Chief Dragoman, Gerald Henry Fitzmaurice. The title dragoman (from the Turkish *tercüman*, translator) belied the importance of the office. Dragomans, who spoke fluent Turkish, were important representatives of ambassadors, who did not. Fitzmaurice was constantly in touch with Turkish politicians and cabinet members until the CUP Government, which disapproved of him, limited his access. Despite that, Fitzmaurice was the constant source of information for Lowther. More than that, he made use of his position at the ambassador's side to affect Ottoman politics. He often spoke to the Ottomans as the voice of British policy. It was sometimes Fitzmaurice's own policy, not necessarily that of Whitehall. As will be seen in the next chapter, this resulted in rebukes from the Foreign Office.[10]

Fitzmaurice's opinions echoed those of Lowther. Indeed, he was probably the force behind many of Lowther's conspiracy theories. Like Lowther, he disliked and feared the Jews and Freemasons. He felt that the Jews had profited immensely from support of the CUP, so much so, he wrote, that Armenians and Greeks feared that Jews would take over the entire Ottoman economy. Fitzmaurice admitted he was the author of the infamous letter on the Jews and Freemasons sent under Lowther's name.[11]

When Turkish and European newspapers printed articles accusing him of a mania on the supposed power of the Jews and Freemasons, Fitzmaurice responded in a letter to the Foreign Office, attacking those same Jews and Freemasons. Fitzmaurice accused them of conspiracies and political assassinations, with no proof offered. Ambassador Lowther wrote that he quite agreed with Fitzmaurice.[12]

**The Counter-revolution**

As Lowther's relations with the CUP deteriorated, he began openly to meet with representatives of the Liberal opposition, such as İsmail Kemal and Prince Sabahattin, and not with pro-government advisors. Their influence reinforced Lowther's animosity toward the CUP and his feeling that the country was against CUP rule.[13]

In April of 1909, those who opposed the CUP, supported by soldiers from the ranks, Liberal Party members and religious leaders opposed to CUP secularism, rose in Istanbul, taking over the city and overturning the government. The sultan, whether or not he had instigated the revolt, took power once again, naming his supporters to the cabinet. The degree to which the British Embassy supported the Istanbul revolution of 13 April 1909 is debated. Unquestionably, Lowther and Fitzmaurice were in close contact with forces opposing the CUP. Lowther's confidants, Kâmil Paşa, Lowther's favourite, and İsmail Kemal, were a part of the revolt. The ambassador was pleased with the insurrection, calling it 'a distinct defeat of the Committee of Union and Progress and their ultra-liberal ideas, for which the country as a whole is not ripe'. When army forces in Macedonia began to organise to march against the counter-revolution, Lowther instructed his consuls in Macedonia to exert themselves to discretely oppose the 'malcontents' and to convince them to negotiate with Abdülhamid's Government in Istanbul. He attempted without success to have Fitzmaurice accompany a delegation from Istanbul to meet with the Macedonian army, then at the gates of Istanbul, heedless of the fact that this would at least have the appearance of Britain supporting the counter-revolutionaries. Surely the CUP and the forces that had defeated the counter-revolution believed that Lowther had supported the revolt.[14]

The Macedonian army set out by train to put down the counter-revolution. It was met at Yeşilköy, near Istanbul, by members of the parliament that showed their support. The army occupied the capital on 24 April, meeting little resistance. On 26 April the parliament deposed Abdülhamid II, the deposition approved by the Şeyhülislam the following day. (Lowther said the deposition had been driven 'by the younger men and irresponsible hot-heads.')[15]

Perhaps because of his own aristocratic upbringing, Lowther was always unsympathetic to the 'new men' who had supplanted the old Ottoman aristocracy in power. He was particularly revolted by the deposition of Abdülhamid. It was surely true that Lowther was very sympathetic to those who tried to return Abdülhamid II to power, and was opposed to those who stopped them. According to Lowther, Jewish and 'crypto-Jewish' Freemasons had been the driving force behind the deposition of Abdülhamid II and creation of the new government in 1908. The Ottoman army, which had put down the counter-revolution, was led by Freemasons; junior officers were enrolled in Masonic lodges by their superiors. 'The Jews, Socialists, and Freemasons are all supreme, latter making great strides.'[16]

When Lowther made his sympathy for Abdülhamid known to London, Grey wrote to him that he himself had no sympathy for Abdülhamid and had more hope than did Lowther for the new regime. Obviously affected by Grey's criticism, Lowther wrote back, reversing his opinion and stating that Grey was correct about Abdülhamid, but went on to say the new government was just as bad. In his response to Grey, Lowther did not hesitate to put the blame on the Jews, among other 'extremists'.[17]

The opinion of the CUP toward Lowther and Britain could not have been helped by the ambassador's well-known sympathy for the CUP's political enemies. Lowther showed special support for Mehmed Kâmil Pasha, Abdülhamid's longtime Grand Vezir, who had joined the main political opposition to the CUP, the Liberal Entente. Lowther felt that Kâmil relied on Lowther's advice. (Kâmil became known in Istanbul as 'English Kâmil'.) Lowther also took the counsel of, and believed what he was told by, people like Ferid Paşa and İsmail Kemal, bitter opponents of the CUP. When the CUP Government was overthrown in 1912 and Kâmil once again became Grand Vezir, Lowther was overjoyed. He observed: 'There is certainly a much more friendly and moderate attitude observable toward us in particular in this new Government than in the old.' But the Balkan Wars brought to an end the rule of Kâmil and his party. Lowther was forced to deal once again with his enemies, the CUP, now even more entrenched in power. The new CUP Government, led by the triumvirate of Cemal, Enver and Talat (Lowther's 'leading Freemason'), had correct relations with the English, but Lowther was no respected confidant.[18]

Had they been heeded, the reports Lowther sent to London would have created an odd picture of the Ottoman Empire. Much of what Lowther reported to London was little better than political gossip, always prejudiced against the CUP. A typical letter from Lowther to Arthur Nicolson (Permanent Under-Secretary for Foreign Affairs – head of the Foreign Office) began, '[t]here is little to record this week', and then went on to write a lengthy complaint on the CUP. He described the counter-revolution as a justified reaction to the CUP and condemned the suppression of the revolt as an over-reaction: 'I am convinced that the so-called reactionary movement could have been dealt with in a milder and yet more satisfactory manner.' He did not hesitate to let London know his opinion of Ottoman politicians. Ahmed Riza, president of the Ottoman Parliament, was 'a hopeless ass'. The minister of the interior was 'that fool Talaat'.[19]

Instead of accurate analyses, Lowther often relayed to the Foreign Office the rumours he or his agent Fitzmaurice had heard and believed. He sent his convictions to London: the CUP were planning to murder the sultan and declare a republic. Furthermore, under the influence of Masonic ideology, the CUP intended to destroy the Sharia (Islamic Holy Law). They had persuaded many members of the Islamic religious establishment, the Ulema, to become Masons. These were used to bring around the Muslims to the Masonic plans. Lowther quoted an unidentified Turk who called this 'drugging the (Muslims) with Jewish hashish'. Lowther was sure that 80 to 90 per cent of the people of the Ottoman Empire opposed the CUP. To him, one thing was sure, the government would never be able to unite the people behind it: 'How can we expect Jews and Freemasons to work harmoniously with the Moslems? It is as unnatural as Moslems and Christians working harmoniously here.'[20]

As troubles were beginning between the Ottomans and Italians in Libya, Lowther did mention Tripoli in a 20 September report, but only to complain of actions of the Ottoman government. In October of 1911, when Italy invaded Libya, Lowther wrote little on the Ottoman reaction to those events, but he did report that he had undiplomatically told the Grand Vezir that the Ottomans had not shown themselves to be friends of Britain, implying that this was why the Ottomans could expect no help from the British.[21]

## Bosnia and Eastern Rumelia

In 1908, two events overcame the new Ottoman Government: Austria annexed Bosnia–Herzegovina, which it had occupied since 1878, and Bulgaria declared its independence, combining Bulgaria and Eastern Rumelia into one kingdom. Both were direct violations of the Treaty of Berlin, and the Austrian annexation nearly caused a European war. Ottoman protests were futile. In the end the Ottomans were forced to be satisfied with monetary compensation. The losses were intensely lamented by the Ottoman populace, but these were one of the only times the Ottomans received anything for lands taken from them.[22]

Even though the Prince of Bulgaria already had been made governor of Eastern Rumelia, joining the Ottoman province in a personal union with Bulgaria, Eastern Rumelia remained in theory a tax-paying part of the Ottoman Empire. Bulgaria itself theoretically was still a part of the Empire, albeit a totally autonomous part. The disarray of the 1908 Young Turk Revolution created an opportunity for real unification and a declaration of independence on 5 October 1908. Ferdinand, who had previously only been styled as Prince of Bulgaria and governor of Eastern Rumelia, became the King of Bulgaria. At first there was real possibility of war, although neither the Bulgarians nor the Ottomans were ready for one.[23]

On 7 October 1908, Austria–Hungary officially announced the annexation of Bosnia. Short of an unthinkable war with Austria, there was little the Ottomans could do. Ottoman proposals, such as creating an independent or autonomous Bosnia, were ignored. Ottoman war with Austria was never seriously considered. A boycott of Austrian commerce with the Ottoman Empire

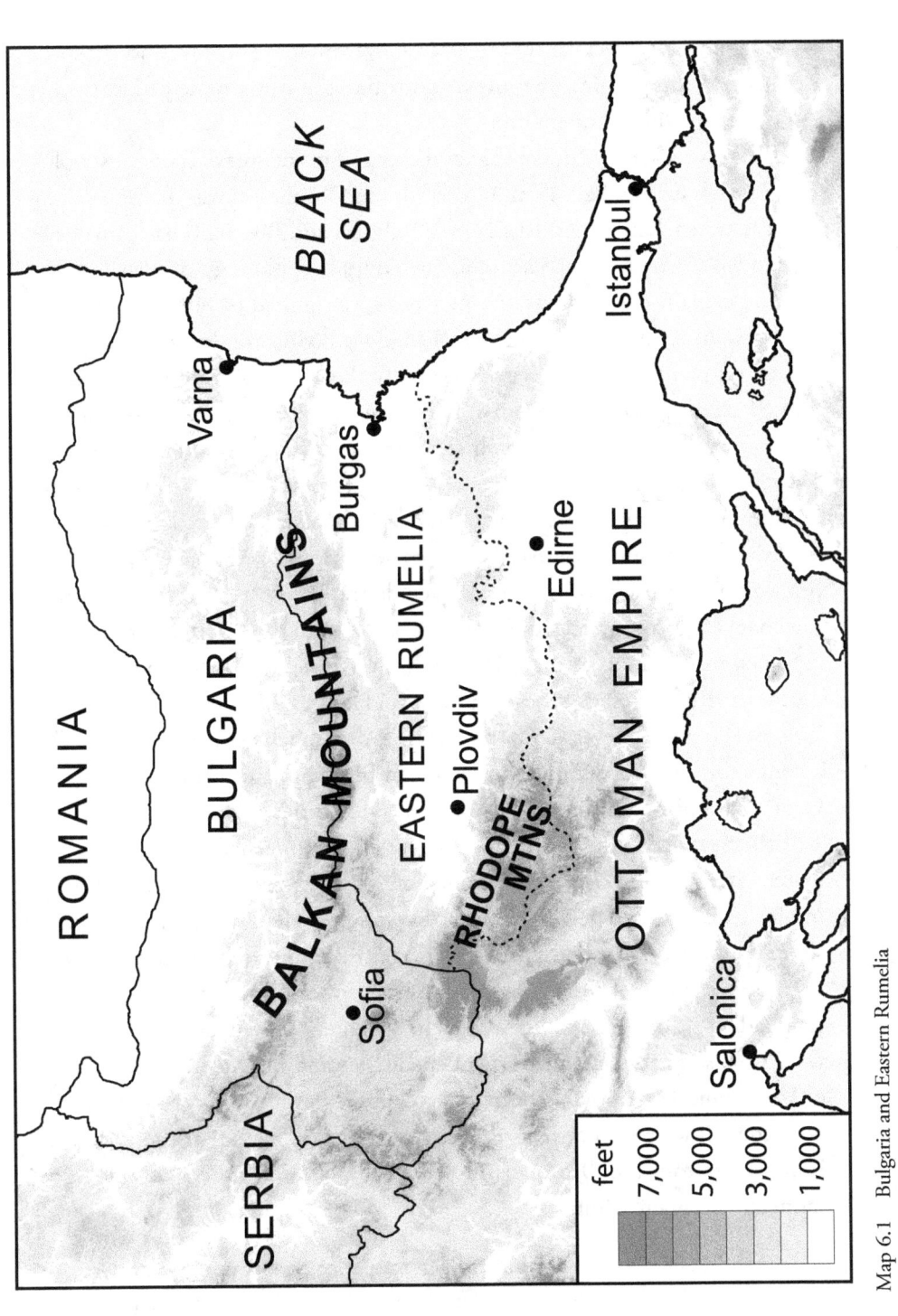

Map 6.1  Bulgaria and Eastern Rumelia

had a significant effect on the Austrian Government. There was no prospect of Austria relinquishing the annexation, but the boycott helped convince Austria to provide compensation.[24]

The Powers competed, debated and engaged in the sort of ludicrous diplomatic manoeuvring that might have led to war. The danger was that war might erupt between Austria and Russia over Bulgaria and Bosnia. (Historians have contended themselves with detailing the complex diplomacy of the time. No one can explain the madness of a European war ignited by either annexation of Bosnia or creation of a Bulgarian Kingdom.) Much diplomatic effort was wasted on plans for a conference to modify the Treaty of Berlin, but Austria refused to allow consideration of the status of Bosnia in any conference. Russia wanted the prospective conference to consider the status of the Straits. However, despite the British détente with Russia (see Chapter 7) and membership of the Triple Entente with France and Russia, Grey could not agree with the Russian proposal that the Straits be completely opened only to Black Sea littoral countries, which would exclude the British navy and put British merchants at a commercial disadvantage. Moreover, the Ottomans refused to consider any opening of the Straits, and Grey believed that forcing them to accept the Russian plans for the Straits would lead to disorder in the Ottoman Empire and perhaps even a new revolution. After much deliberation, plans for a conference were abandoned in favour of bilateral agreements between the Ottomans and Bulgarians and Ottomans and Austrians.[25]

British advice to the Ottomans was initially rational. In the period immediately after the Turkish Revolution, Foreign Secretary Grey was still hoping for success of the new Ottoman Government. He particularly wanted to shore up the pro-British Grand Vezir, Kâmil Paşa. Grey felt, quite accurately, that the real need of the Ottomans was money, not territory, which in any case had already been lost. Grey told the Ottoman Government that Britain would refuse to accept Bulgarian independence and the Austrian annexation of Bosnia and Herzegovina, because no changes in the Treaty of Berlin could be made without the consent of all the signatories, including the Ottoman Empire. He told the Ottomans, however, that all they could hope for was monetary compensation:

> The independence of Bulgaria and annexation of Bosnia were no material loss to Turkey, though injurious from the point of view of sentiment and

prestige; if Turkey protested and eventually asked for compensation we should support any proposals which seemed fair consideration for her.

The compensation, of course, would be set by the Powers.[26]

Grey's support for the Ottomans would only go so far. They suggested, since the Treaty of Berlin was to be altered, that Articles 23 and 61 of the treaty, which specified that the Ottomans would make reforms in Europe and Anatolia and had been used by the Powers as justification for intervention in Macedonia and Eastern Anatolia, should be abrogated. Grey refused to consider it. In fact, the Treaty of Berlin, which had guaranteed Ottoman sovereignty over Bosnia and Bulgaria and the separation of Eastern Rumelia from Bulgaria, had already been scrapped. While accepting that others could negate the treaty's provisions at will, Grey asserted that the Ottomans could not. Also, while he had acknowledged the Ottoman need for financial help, he was absolutely against any increase in Ottoman customs duties.[27]

The Ottomans, prevented by the Powers from acting militarily, demanded compensation for the loss of Eastern Rumelia, 125 million francs. Bulgaria refused to pay so much, but in 1909 Russia stepped in and brokered an arrangement in which a Russian loan allowed the Bulgarians to pay 82 million francs to the Ottomans. In payment for the remainder of the 125 million the Russians forgave payments on the Ottoman's debt to Russia from the 1877–8 War indemnity.[28]

A preliminary settlement between the Austro-Hungarian and Ottoman Empires was agreed on 11 January 1909, and the final Austro-Turkish Protocol signed on 12 February 1909. The protocol specified, among other stipulations, that Austria would pay 2.5 million gold Turkish Liras to the Ottomans. Some articles of the protocol were declarations of intentions: Austria would support the increase of Ottoman customs duties from 11 to 15 per cent and the abolition of the Capitulations. As such changes had to be agreed by all the European Powers, the articles were dead when they were written, because Britain would not agree to either.[29]

Grey was able to portray Britain as the friend of the Ottomans – one who had secured them at least compensation when they might not have gained even that. The British had forestalled Russian plans to open the Straits, supporting the Ottomans. The impression of British friendship was to be short-lived.

## The Italian War

Only unified as a state in 1870, Italy was a latecomer to imperialism, and it found that little was left for it. More powerful nations, France and Britain, had taken the choicest morsels in Africa, leaving Italy with only the possibility of taking backwaters like Eritrea and Libya. In Eritrea, Italian expansion plans had met defeat by Ethiopian forces in 1896. Libya, a little-populated region that was mostly desert, was not worth much. Libya had a population of only half a million, poor ports and limited commerce. It had been a constant financial loss to the Ottomans. However, France had taken, or controlled, Morocco, Algeria and Tunisia; Britain had taken Egypt. Italy wanted its share of the spoils, and Libya was all that was left for them.[30]

The initial Italian penetration of Libya was financial. Italian financial interests were deeply involved in coastal Libya – the Ottoman province of Tripoli (Trablusgarp). These investments had not provided the expected revenues, which the Italians blamed on the Ottomans, but which were actually the result of a poor and unproductive land. Italian banks had lost a fortune in Libya, and the banks felt, unrealistically, that Italian control of Libya and its finances would allow them to recoup their losses. France was to take control of Morocco, and the Italians believed this upset the balance of power in the Mediterranean, demanding a corresponding Italian occupation on the African coast. The main reason for Italian action, however, can be called emotional. Italy did not feel that the Ottomans had given them the same status and benefits accorded to France, Britain and Germany.

The Italians had protested in December of 1910 that they had no designs on Tripoli, that all they wanted was a commercial opening for their merchants and banks, but the Ottomans knew the protests were duplicitous. The Ottomans feared, with much justification, that Italy was preparing commercially for the ultimate takeover of Libya. Italian newspapers and politicians had asserted exactly that. While they did not actively coerce Italian merchant ventures in Libya, they surely did not shine on them. The interests of other European countries in matters such as the construction of new ports were favoured over Italy's.[31]

The Italians had reason to be confident that the European Powers would not stand in their way over Libya. The Germans and Austrians were their allies and, although neither would like the Italian plans, they would be unlikely to stop them. (To be sure, the Italians did not share their plans with either of their allies.) The French had accepted, in a series of deliberations with Italy in 1902, that Italy would have the right 'to extend its influence' in Libya if France did so in Morocco. In 1902, the British had made it plain that they looked favourably on Italian 'interests' in Libya, but never actually declared they supported Italian conquest there. Nevertheless, it was obvious to the Italians that there would be no British opposition to an attack on Libya. Before the Italian invasion began, Foreign Secretary Grey told the Italian ambassador that Britain would not intervene in an Italian–Ottoman war. He assured the Italians of Britain's sympathy with their aims, although he opposed outright Italian annexation of Libya, preferring that the sultan kept a nominal sovereignty.[32]

The British hoped to separate Italy from its lukewarm adherence to its alliance with Germany and Austria. On 19 September 1911, Grey instructed Arthur Nicolson: 'It is most important that neither we nor France should side against Italy now.' Recognising that the British press was against the Italian claims, Grey wanted the Turks to be blamed for Italian actions. He told Guglielmo Imperiali, Italian ambassador in London, that he hoped that the Ottomans would do something to enable Britain to tell the Ottomans that 'any action Italy took to defend her interest had been brought by the Turks upon themselves'. Grey said the Turks, if they wished, could appeal to the Germans and Austrians, not the British, a statement that was relayed to the Ottoman Grand Vezir. As the Italians were German and Austrian allies, this was an unlikely plan. The Ottomans asked the British for at least a 'friendly word' to the Italians:

> He (the Ottoman Embassy Councilor) pressed Sir A. Nicolson hard to say that His Majesty's Government would say a friendly word at Rome in favour of moderation. Sir A. Nicolson told him that we could not do so and it was none of our business.

(Given past British intervention in the Ottoman Empire, an astounding observation.)[33]

For the Italians, British neutrality in the upcoming war was essential. Grey declared British neutrality on the same day that Italy announced war with the Ottoman Empire. He told the Italian ambassador that his sole concern was that Italy do nothing that would draw other European Powers into conflict. Grey assured the Italians that Ottoman troops would not be allowed to cross Egypt to fight the Italians in Libya.[34]

**War**

When the Italians threatened the Ottomans, the British Government did not officially admit that Italy would go to war. Foreign Secretary Grey remarked: 'I cannot believe that Italy is going to occupy Tripoli by force. She probably wants to satisfy her own public opinion and to frighten the Turks by a demonstration.' Six days after Grey's statement, the Italians declared war.[35]

The Italian Chargé d'Affaires in Istanbul presented an ultimatum to the Ottoman Government on 28 September 1911. It stated that due to Ottoman neglect of Italian interests, the Italians would occupy Tripoli immediately. They asked the Ottomans to accept the occupation. The Ottomans were given twenty-four hours to reply. In its immediate response, the Ottoman Government declared that it did not believe that Italians had been discriminated against in Tripoli, but they were willing to grant commercial concessions to Italian merchants in order to have peace. The Ottoman response was ignored. The Italian fleet bombarded Tripoli on 3 October 1911; marines landed on 4 October and the main body of troops on 10 October.[36]

Britain could have kept its promise to defend Ottoman territorial integrity without firing a shot. British-occupied Egypt, in theory still a part of the Ottoman Empire, stood between Libya and the Ottoman army. Britain would only have had to allow Ottoman troops to pass through Ottoman territory, even if it was territory 'protected' by the British. But 'strict neutrality', as defined by the British, meant that no territory under British control could be used by the warring parties. In practice, this was a great disadvantage to the Ottomans and very little to the Italians. The Italians brought their troops and supplies on the short sea route from Italy. Their weak navy having no control of the sea, the Ottomans could only reinforce their garrison by land. The British made this impossible. Not only did they forbid any Ottoman troop movements across Egypt, they arrested Ottoman officers and soldiers who attempted to cross surreptitiously. The Ottomans initially smuggled some men, primarily officers, across the Sinai, then through the Egyptian desert, but many were captured by the British, and only a small number managed to reach Libya. By January of 1912 the Ottomans had largely abandoned the effort. (Those who arrived in Libya, however, proved to be of great use in organsing Arab tribal forces and directing attacks on the Italians.)[37]

At least one British official showed concern over Britain's failure to honour its commitments to the Ottoman Empire. Ambassador Francis Bertie in Paris commented on the agreements to defend the territorial integrity of the Ottoman Empire. He wrote to Nicolson that the British were 'in an awkward position as regards our Paris or Berlin Treaty engagements towards the Porte'. Bertie seems to have been the only one who even considered the issue.[38]

**The Press and Parliament**

The reports and editorials in the British press, whose members could have been expected to oppose the Ottomans at most times, adopted a quite different stance on the Italian War. The Italian invasion, and especially the mass murder of Libyan Arabs by Italians, were well-known. Both Liberal and Conservative newspapers condemned the Italians. Newspapers printed stories of the murders of men, women and children by the Italian forces. The *Daily News*, *The Times* and other papers published editorials against the Italians. The *Illustrated London News* even printed a number of full-page pictures of Italian soldiers massacring defenceless Arabs.[39]

Although they could not compare in number to the meetings held by the Anglo-Armenian Association or the Balkan Committee, there were protest meetings directed against the Italian invasion reported by the newspapers. Twenty MPs sent a resolution to Grey 'deploring the savage and inhuman atrocities committed by the Italian troops'.[40]

British leaders' standard excuse that they were acting against the Ottomans because of public opinion could not be used to justify British policies in Libya. Public opinion, while not quite on the side of the Ottomans, was against the Italians. Faced with such opposition, the British Government did not change its policies. It still stood against the Ottomans. It was necessary, however, to be circumspect. The government was not about to admit its place in the Libyan War. The British Government's official position, much questioned in parliament, was that it had been in complete ignorance of what Italy would do in Libya. The government told parliament in a number of debates that it had known nothing of a planned Italian invasion until the declaration of war on 30 September 1911. This was untrue. The foreign secretary had not only known the Italian plans, but had counselled the Italians to make sure blame would be put on the Turks. The continued assertion that the British had known nothing of Italian plans to attack before the declaration of war became an embarrassment when the Italian prime minister told the press that Britain had known of Italian intentions and approved of them before the invasions. When reminded of that in parliament, Grey did not respond.[41]

Members of parliament could learn nothing of the government's attitude on past promises in the Treaties of Paris and Berlin. When questioned on how Britain could avoid its commitments to the integrity of the Ottoman borders, Grey said he could not say anything without consultation with the other Powers. The consultation on those treaty obligations never took place. Nor could the MPs learn of events after the invasion. When asked about matters such as the Italian murders of Arab civilians, both Grey and Prime Minister Asquith responded either that they had no information on that or they simply refused to answer, despite the fact that the newspapers were full of the atrocity reports. Instead, Grey told parliament that he thought such questions should not be asked in the House of Commons, because they were offensive to a foreign government (Italy). On that and all other matters concerning the war, the government refused to release consular reports.[42]

## Mediation

The Ottomans appealed to the British Government to intervene with the Italians, because of British 'humanitarian feelings' and friendship with the Ottomans. They did not attempt to ask for British military intervention under the terms of the Treaties of Paris and Berlin. They only asked for British assistance in coming to terms with the Italians. On 21 October 1911, Grand Vezir Said Paşa asked Great Britain to intervene diplomatically with Italy. The Ottomans reminded the British that they were bound by treaty to guarantee the integrity of the Ottoman Empire. Said offered financial benefits to Italy. He offered an alliance between Britain and the Ottoman Empire, and eventually with the other Powers in the Triple Entente. But the British refused to even enter into negotiations between the Ottomans and Italians, stating their strict neutrality kept them from entering into any negotiations. Why neutrality kept the British from mediating with both sides was not explained to the Turks. In fact, British officials told parliament the complete opposite. Parliament was told that nothing in the declaration of neutrality kept the British from mediating, but that they had not tried because the warring parties were too far apart.[43]

After their initial success in taking coastal towns, the war began to go badly for the Italians. Although they were greatly outnumbered, Turkish troops and local Senussi tribesmen kept the Italians to fortified coastal towns, where they could be defended by naval gunfire. The interior of Libya was never in the Italians' grasp. Neither the local Turkish soldiers and Arabs who fought the Italians nor the Ottoman Government yielded to them.

As the war continued without resolution, the Ottomans repeatedly requested mediation by the Powers. Other European governments wished to consider it, but Britain continued to oppose it. Instead of mediation and compromise between the combatants, Grey felt that the only solution to the Libyan problem was to pressure the Ottomans to give way to the Italians, but Ottoman officials would not cooperate. (Nicolson called those who wanted to give in to the Italians 'moderates'. The others were 'hotheads'.)[44]

## Expanding the War

Utilising their naval superiority, the Italians expanded the conflict in an attempt to force the Ottomans to negotiate peace. They bombarded coasts on the Red Sea, in Syria and in Anatolia, attacking and sinking coastal ships. Italians seized the poorly defended Dodecanese Islands from 28 April to 21 May. In a desperate move that was sure to draw the Powers into the conflict, the Italian navy blockaded the Dardanelles.[45]

The British only changed their minds about mediation when it came to a matter that was important to them – Italian possession of the Dodecanese and the subsequent blockage of commerce through the Straits. Britain was especially concerned that Italian action in the Dodecanese might cause the Ottomans to close and possibly mine the Dardanelles, which in fact took place. Arthur Nicolson reported that British ships with cargoes worth more than ten million pounds were stranded in the Black Sea. Russian grain shipments were similarly trapped. The British Admiralty was against any Italian occupation of the islands, fearing their possible use as a naval base. The British finally admitted that they could mediate, but British attempts to mediate over the Dodecanese foundered upon Italian refusal to consider evacuation of the islands.[46]

The Ottomans were forced to make a disadvantageous peace with Italy (the Treaty of Ouchy, also called the Treaty of Lausanne, 16 October 1912) when an alliance of Greece, Serbia, Montenegro and Bulgaria attacked the Ottoman Empire in Europe. Faced with a larger war, the Ottomans were forced to give way. The treaty specified that the Ottomans lost Libya and that the Dodecanese would be returned to them. However, there was a problem that was to cause difficulties in the coming years: Italy pledged to leave the Dodecanese only after all Ottoman forces and officials had left Libya, but the Ottomans had left 300 men, along with heavy weapons and ammunition, behind, in anticipation of later fighting after the Balkan Wars. Citing this, and probably because they had never planned to leave the islands, the Italians remained. Despite pressure from all sides, they remained until after World War II.[47]

## Ottoman Understanding

From the 1890s, the British had acted against the interests of the Ottomans. Only the opposition of other Powers had kept Salisbury from attacking and dividing the Ottoman Empire. Britain had worked against Ottoman interests in Crete, Macedonia and Thessaly. Now Britain had supported Italy in Libya and, by denying transit through Egypt, had done all she could to ensure Ottoman defeat. The Ottomans very well understood the British position. In an interview with the British military attaché, G. E. Tyrrell, War Minister and later Grand Vezir Mahmud Şevket Paşa indicated he knew what Britain had done, or not done, for the Ottomans:

> I have the honour to inform you that I saw Mahmud Shevket Pasha (the Grand Vezir) this afternoon. His Excellency appeared to be in an irritable and nervous frame of mind and was at first inclined to be sulky. However he brightened up after a little, and said that it was as clear as daylight that the present situation was due to England and France, and that it was our fault that Italy had to all intents and purposes blockaded the Dardanelles, for that was what her presence in the Aegean amounted to. He went further, and said that England and France were primarily responsible for the war.
>
> I expressed my surprised at hearing him talk like thus, remarking that during all these months he had never taken this line, and that it was more generally considered that if any foreign Powers were to be blamed for Italy's action in attacking the Tripolitaine, those Powers were Italy's allies.

He said: No, England and France were the two great Mediterranean Powers. Italy would not have dared to do anything in the Mediterranean without their permission, England had only to hold up her finger and Italy would not have stirred. It was all a question of the equilibrium of the Mediterranean. What we were doing to allow Italy to establish herself, first on the African coast and then in the Aegean, he could not imagine,

Mahmud Pasha, the sous-chef of the General Staff, who was present at our interview, recalled that many years ago when Italy proposed to take Tripoli, it had merely been necessary for Lord Beaconsfield to forbid it, and nothing happened. Exactly the same conditions obtained to-day. If England chose to forbid Italy to do this or that in the Mediterranean or elsewhere, she would have to obey, and there would be no question of a war with her.

With this Mahmud Shevket Pasha agreed. He said that the Triple Alliance did not bind either of the other contracting parties to intervene on Italy's behalf if a war with England arose from her wanton attack on Turkey or from her action in forcing the closing of the Dardanelles. On the contrary, Austria at least would be delighted to see Italy get a good beating.

Tyrrell was forced to admit that the description of Austrian feelings was accurate. Mahmud Şevket went on to state that the Ottomans had granted commercial concessions to the British in hopes of British friendship and support. Instead, Britain had shown the Ottomans 'a consistently unfriendly attitude from the beginning of the war with Italy'.[48]

## The Source of the British Position

The status quo of the Ottoman Empire was theoretically supported by all. Britain gave lip service to the continuation of the Ottoman Empire, but its actions were the opposite. In North Africa, the Aegean, the Balkans and Anatolia, Britain supported the dismemberment of the Ottoman Empire.

Public opinion had been a significant factor in past British actions against the Ottomans, often cited by the British and other Europeans as the reason for British plans. However, the antipathy of British leaders had been at least as important as public opinion. In the Italian Crisis, the British proved that they were capable of acting against the Ottomans even in the face of popular opposition. Unlike other times in which the British leaders could cite public opinion as justification for its actions against the Ottoman Empire, British public opinion was against the Libyan War. The reason predominently cited for the British support of the Italians was that Britain wanted to seduce the Italians from their loyalty to the Triple Alliance. British documents do not indicate that they ever thought at the time that this was a significant possibility. No one believed that Italy would ever be anything but an independent player in diplomacy and war.

A more basic reason should be considered – the British leaders wanted, or at least were very willing, for the Turks to lose. Italy was one of the six Great Powers, albeit the least of them. It would not do for a Great Power, a Christian state, to fail against a Muslim state. Arthur Nicolson, the head of the Foreign Office, made no secret of his personal feelings:

> It seems to me exceedingly foolish that we should displease a country with whom we have always been on the most friendly terms and whose friendship to us is of great value, in order to keep well with Turkey, who has been a source of great annoyance to us and whose Government is one of the worst that can well be imagined. I should far prefer having Italy as a neighbor to Egypt than the Turks.[49]

Nicolson's only objection to Italian invasion of Ottoman Libya was that the Italians had done it so badly. He wrote that he was 'anxious that in all conflicts between the West and the East that the former should be successful'. It might have been a description of continuous British foreign policy.[50]

The only serious concern for the British was not any effect of the Libyan War on the Ottoman Empire, but on implications for the rest of the Ottoman Europe, which might lead to a greater war that might draw in the Powers, but they doubted that would happen. Nicolson wrote on 17 January 1912:

> I am afraid the (Libyan) war will drag on for some time to come, and of course there is always the danger that It may give rise to complications in the Balkans, though I think that the risk of these is somewhat exaggerated, as no one, as far as I am aware, is at all desirous of seeing any serious complications arise.

'Serious complications' did arise. Nine months after Nicolson's confident statement, the Balkan Wars erupted.

## Notes

1. On the 1908 revolution and on the CUP, see: Feroz Ahmad, *The Young Turks: The Committee of Union and Progress in Turkish Politics 1908–1914*, Oxford: Clarendon,

1969. Sina Akşin, *Jön Türkler ve İttihat ve Terakki*, İstanbul: Remzi, 1987. Yusuf Hikmet Bayur, *Türk İnkılâbı Tarihi*, vol. 1/2, third printing, Ankara: Türk Tarih Kurumu, 1983, pp. 59–101. M. Şükrü Hanioğlu, *A Brief History of the Late Ottoman Empire*, Princeton: Princeton University Press, 2008, pp. 150–67. Stanford J. Shaw and Ezel Kural Shaw, *History of the Ottoman Empire and Modern Turkey*, vol. 2, Cambridge: Cambridge University Press, 1977, pp. 273–92. Sina Akşin, *Turkey from Empire to Revolutionary Republic*, New York: New York University Press, 2007, pp. 53–70. On the elections, see Hasan Kayalı, 'Elections and the Electoral Process in the Ottoman Empire, 1876–1919', *International Journal of Middle East Studies*, vol. 27, no. 3 (August 1995), pp. 265–86.
2. Akşin, *Jön Türkler*, pp. 86–7 and 89.
3. FO 800/79, Grey to Lowther, Foreign Office, 31 July and 11 August 1908. Feroz Ahmad, 'Great Britain's Relations with the Young Turks 1908–1914', *Middle Eastern Studies*, vol. 2, no. 4 (July 1966), pp. 302–29.
4. FO 800/79, Lowther to Grey, Therapia, 11 and 25 August 1908. Lowther's views are well summarised in Elie Kedourie, 'Young Turks, Freemasons and Jews', *Middle Eastern Studies*, vol. 7, no. 1 (January 1971), pp. 89–104.
5. Lowther to Hardinge, Constantinople, 29 May 1910, in Sinan Kuneralp and Gül Tokay, *The Private Correspondence of Sir Gerard Lowther, British Ambassador to Constantinople (1908–1913)*, Istanbul: Isis, 2018 (hereafter Kuneralp and Tokay), pp. 227–40.
6. Lowther to Grey, Constantinople, 25 August 1908 and 5 May 1909, pp. 21–3 and 107–8. Lowther to Hardinge, Constantinople, 29 May 1910, in Kuneralp and Tokay, pp. 227–40. Why Lowther felt the Zionists wanted to go to Iraq was not described.
7. The best description of the Ottoman Freemasons is M. Şükrü Hanioğlu, 'Notes on the Young Turks and the Freemasons, 1875–1908', *Middle Eastern Studies*, vol. 25, no. 2 (April 1989), pp. 186–97. Hanioğlu demonstrates that after the revolution, when Lowther was writing, it was the Freemasons who conformed to the CUP plans, not the CUP to the Freemasons. See also, Ozan Arslan and Cinar Ozen, 'The Rebirth of the Ottoman Committee of Union and Progress in Macedonia through the Italian Freemasonry', *Oriente Moderno*, Nuova serie, Anno 24 (85), Num. 1 (2005), pp. 93–115.
8. The complete letter is published in Kedourie, pp. 94–103.
9. Shaw, pp. 282–7. Akşin, *Jön Türkler*, pp. 63–70.
10. Fitzmaurice's biography is G. R. Berridge, *Gerald Fitzmaurice (1865–1939), Chief Dragoman of the British Embassy in Turkey*, Leiden: Nijhoff, 2007.
11. FO 800/79, Fitzmaurice to Tyrrell, Constantinople, 27 June 1909. Berridge, pp. 145–52. I feel that Berridge is much too sympathetic to Fitzmaurice.

12. Lowther to Nicolson, Pera, 26 April and 3 May 1911, and enclosures, in Kuneralp and Tokay, pp. 301–2 and 304–6.
13. Ahmad, 'Relations', p. 312.
14. Akşin, *Jön Türkler*, pp. 135–40. Ahmad, 'Relations', pp. 312–14. Berridge, pp. 131–7. On the politics and events of the counter-revolution, see Ahmad, *Young Turks*, pp. 34–43. Bayur 1/2, pp. 182–95 and 204–17. CAB 37/99/62, Lowther to Grey, Pera, 14 April 1909. For a divergent view on which I have many disagreements, see Hasan Ünal, 'Britain and Ottoman Domestic Politics: From the Young Turk Revolution to the Counter Revolution, 1908–9', *Middle Eastern Studies*, vol. 37, no. 2 (April 2001), pp. 1–22.
15. CAB 37/39/72, Lowther to Grey, Pera, 28 April 1909, which contains Lowther's complete report of events.
16. Lowther to Hardinge, Pera, 25 April 1909, in Kuneralp and Tokay, p. 101. Lowther doubted if the sultan had supported the counter-revolution. (FO 371/772, Lowther to Grey, Pera, 5 May 1909. CAB 37/99/65, Lowther to Grey, Pera, 21 April 1909. See also: CAB 37/99/75, Lowther to Grey, Pera, 5 May 1909. Lowther to Hardinge, Pera, 19 April 1909, in Kuneralp and Tokay, pp. 215–16.)
17. FO 800/79, Grey to Lowther, Foreign Office, 30 April 1909. Lowther to Grey, Constantinople, 12 May 1909, in Kuneralp and Tokay, pp. 110–15.
18. Lowther to Hardinge, Constantinople, 10 November 1908, and 29 July 1919, in Kuneralp and Tokay, pp. 39–40 and 142–4. Lowther to Nicolson, Pera, 1 March 1911, in Kuneralp and Tokay, pp. 282–4. Lowther to Hardinge, Pera, 2 March 1909, in Kuneralp and Tokay, pp. 83–4. On Lowther's approval of Kâmil, see also FO 800/79, Lowther to Grey, Constantinople, 29 December 1908. Lowther recommended that Kâmil be made an honourary Knight Grand Cross of the Order of the Bath. (FO 800/79, Lowther to Grey, Constantinople, 12 January 1909.) Fitzmaurice described Kâmil as 'pro-English to infatuation'. (Fitzmaurice to Tyrrell, Constantinople, 11 January 1909, in BDOW 5, p. 272.) See Kâmil's long justification and plea for British protection in FO 800/79, M. Kiamil to Grey, Constantinople, 12 June 1909. Lowther to Nicolson, Pera, 1 November 1911, in Kuneralp and Tokay, pp. 337–9. For a supportive view of Kâmil, see Hilmi Kâmil Bayur, *Sadrazam Kâmil Paşa*, Ankara: Sanat, 1954.
19. FO 800/351/2, Lowther to Nicolson, Therapia, 25 October 1911. FO 800/355/1, Lowther to Nicolson, 15 May 1912, in Kuneralp and Tokay, p. 394. FO 800/192, Lowther to Hardinge, 25 April 1909. For typical Lowther reports, see: CAB 37/100/93, Lowther to Grey, Pera, 25 May 1909, and FO 800/350/2, Lowther to Nicolson, Therapia, 30 August 1911.

20. Lowther to Hardinge, Constantinople, 29 May 1910, in Kuneralp and Tokay, pp. 227–40. FO 424/235, Lowther to Grey, Constantinople, 26 November 1912. Lowther to Hardinge, Pera, 2 March 1909, in Kuneralp and Tokay, pp. 83–4. See also, Lowther to Hardinge, Therapia, 27 July 1909, in Kuneralp and Tokay, pp. 147–8. Lowther to Nicolson, Pera, 1 March 1911, in Kuneralp and Tokay, pp. 282–4. See also Lowther's long letter (FO 800/79, Constantinople, 12 May 1909), which does not read as if Lowther himself wrote it. It may have been the work of Fitzmaurice.
21. FO 800/350/2, Lowther to Nicolson, Therapia, 20 September 1911; Lowther to Nicolson, Therapia, 27 September 1911.
22. On the Bosnian and Bulgarian crises, see: F. R. Bridge, *Great Britain and Austria-Hungary 1906–1914: A Diplomatic History*, London: Weidenfeld and Nicolson, 1972, pp. 111–38. Eber Harold Rice, 'British Policy in Turkey: 1908–1914', unpublished PhD dissertation, University of Toronto, 1974, pp. 26–48. BDOW 5, pp. 356–819. GP 26. Anne Louise Antonoff, 'Almost War: Britain, Germany, and the Bosnia Crisis, 1908–1909', unpublished PhD dissertation, Yale, 2006. Bernadotte E. Schmitt, 'The Bosnian Annexation Crisis', *Slavonic and East European Review*, four parts: vol. 9, no. 26 (December 1930), pp. 312–34, vol. 9, no. 27 (March 1931), pp. 650–61, vol. 10, no. 28 (June 1931), pp. 161–71, vol. 10, no. 29 (December 1931), pp. 408–19, vol. 10, no. 30 (April 1932), pp. 641–57. Crampton, pp. 307–14.
23. See the long description of the events of Bulgarian declaration in FO 371/553, Buchanan to Grey, Sophia, 14 October 1908. The diplomatic literature contains many documents on Bulgarian and Ottoman mobilisations, as well as contentions by both side that they did not war. See FO 371/553, FO 421/244 and FO 421/245 for the many reports, especially: FO 371/553, Bertie to Grey, Paris, 17 October 1908; Lowther to Grey, Therapia, 13 October 1908; Buchanan to Grey, Sophia, 12 October 1908; Grey to Lowther, Foreign Office, 15 October 1908; Lowther to Grey, Constantinople, 20 October 1908. FO 421/244, Grey to Bertie and others, Foreign Office, 16 October 1908; Lowther to Grey, Constantinople, 20 October 1908; Surtees to Lowther, Constantinople, 20 October 1908. FO 421/245, Buchanan to Grey, Sophia, 5 November 1908. The documents seem to indicate that the Ottomans, although preparing to fight, did not seriously intend to go to war, but were using the threat of war as a bargaining chip. The British War Office did not think the Ottomans could easily triumph in a war with Bulgaria. (FO 424/244, 'Notes on the Present Military Position in the Balkans', enclosure in War Office to Foreign Office, War Office, 9 October 1908.) The Bulgarians wanted to avoid conflict, because they had succeeded already and could only lose

from a war, and the Bulgarian economy was a shambles. (FO 421/244, Buchanan to Grey, Sophia, 10 October 1908.)

24. On the boycott, see: FO 421/244, Eyres to Grey, Constantinople, 10 October 1908. FO 371/553, Lowther to Grey, Therapia, 13 October 1908; Goschen to Grey, Vienna, 16 October 1908. FO 424/245, Lamb to Lowther, Salonica, 26 October 1908.

25. 'Memorandum by Sir E. Grey', 14 October 1908, in BDOW 5, p. 441. Lowther to Grey, Therapia, 15 October 1908, in BDOW 5, p. 447. Grey to Iswolsky, Foreign Office, 15 October 1908, in BDOW 5, pp. 451–2. On Russian demands to the Ottomans, see Kurat, pp. 161–7.

26. Grey to Nicolson, Foreign Office, 6 October 1908, in BDOW 5, pp. 395–6. Grey to Lowther, Foreign Office, 5 and 13 October 1908, in BDOW 5, pp. 388 and 433. See also, Grey to Bertie, Foreign Office, 9 October 1908, in BDOW 5, p. 410. Britain told Bulgaria that it did not accept the Bulgarian declaration. (FO 421/244, Grey to Buchanan, Foreign Office, 6 October 1908.) Neither Bulgaria not Eastern Rumelia had often paid their taxes or tribute. For Ottoman acceptance of the Bulgarian compensation plan, see FO 371/554, Grey to Lowther, 26 October 1908.

27. Grey to Lowther, Foreign Office, 14 and 19 November 1908, in BDOW 5, pp. 497–8 and 502.

28. Lowther to Grey, Constantinople, 6 February 1909, in BDOW 5, pp. 593–4. The Ottoman–Bulgarian Agreement is in Lowther to Grey, Pera, 24 April 1909, in BDOW 5, pp. 791–8. The Russians acted primarily out of the desire to draw Bulgaria to their side and out of the orbit of Austria. FO 421/245 contains very extensive documents on the deliberations that set the Bulgarian payments. For a detailed description of the Bulgarian economic situation and tribute, see FO 421/245, Buchanan to Grey, Sophia, 10 November 1908; Carnegie to Grey, Vienna, 24 November 1908.

29. 'Protocol between Austria-Hungary and Turkey', *The American Journal of International Law*, October 1909, vol. 3, no. 4, Supplement: Official Documents (October 1909), pp. 286–9. The 2.5 million was nominally payment for Ottoman governmental properties in Bosnia. See also Lowther to Grey, Constantinople, 11 January 1909, in BDOW 5, p. 562.

30. On the Italian motives and decisions to declare war, see: the summary of Italian politics and aims in Libya in

'Extract for the Annual Report on Italy for the Year 1911', in BDOW 9/1, pp. 259–92, and Rodd to Grey, Rome, 1 October 1911, in BDOW 9/1, pp. 292–4 (a very good explanation of the reasons Italy went to war). Salt, *Last Ottoman Wars*, pp. 114–24. R. J. B. Bosworth, *Italy, the Least of the Great*

*Powers: Italian Foreign Policy before the First World War*, London: Cambridge University Press, 1979, pp. 127–95. R. J. B Bosworth, 'Italy and the End of the Ottoman Empire', in Marian Kent, ed., *The Great Powers and the End of the Ottoman Empire*, second edition, London: Cass, 1996, pp. 52–75. C. J. Lowe and F. Marzari, *Italian Foreign Policy 1870–1940*, London: Routledge & Kegan Paul, 1975, pp. 51–4, 86–90 and 112–32. Timothy W. Childs, *Italo-Turkish Diplomacy and the War over Libya*, Leiden: Brill, 1990. Luca Michelleta and Andrea Ungari, *The Libyan War 1911–1912*, Newcastle: Cambridge Scholars, 2013, pp. 1–90 and 128–30, contains a number of informative articles on the Italians and the war. Richard Bosworth's article ('Britain and Italy's Acquisition of the Dodecanese, 1912–1915', *The Historical Journal*, vol. 13, no. 4 (December 1970), pp. 683–705) barely mentions the effects of the war on the Ottoman Empire nor diplomacy with the Ottomans. It is, however, a good summary of the relations between Britain and Italy.

31. FO 424/226, Rodd to Grey, Rome, 31 December 1910. The British ambassador in Rome, Rennell Rodd, felt that none of the Italians' perceived grievances were a justification for war. Italian Foreign Minister Giulio Prinetti, speaking of the 1902 Italian–French Agreement, said he wanted a political arrangement like the one that the British had in Cyprus and Egypt. He thought Tripoli would be an outlet for Italian emigration! (Currie to Lansdowne, Rome, 1 January 1902, in BDOW 8, p. 20.)

32. Ministère des Affaires Étrangères, *Documents Diplomatiques: Les Accords Franco-Italiens de 1901–1902*, Paris: Imprimerie Nationale, 1920, pp. 1–5. Grey to Rodd, Foreign Office, 29 September 1911 (two documents), in BDOW 9/1, pp. 284–5. F. 63. CAB 37/107, Grey to Sir R. Rodd, Foreign Office, 28 July 1911; Grey to Lowther, Foreign Office, 22 September 1911.

    The Germans, Italy's ostensible allies, had remarkably little effect on the diplomacy of the Italian War. See W. David Wrigley, 'Germany and the Turco-Italian War, 1911–1912', *International Journal of Middle East Studies*, vol. 11, no. 3 (May 1980), pp. 313–38. Wrigley demonstrates how internal conflict among German politicians and diplomats kept the Germans from playing a significant role.

    In 1899, the British had refused to give Italy any guarantees for Tripoli. In 1902, Foreign Secretary Lansdowne had made a declaration to Italy that Britain had no interest in taking Libya. The rest of the message was ambiguous:

    > If at any time an alteration of the status quo should take place, it would be their (the British Government's) object that, so far as is compatible with the obligations resulting from the Treaties which at present form part of the public law of Europe, such alteration should be conformity with Italian interests.

The guarantee of Ottoman borders in the Treaty of Berlin was 'part of the public law of Europe'. Lansdowne had also written:

> It has always been given to understand that it was the desire of His Majesty's Government to maintain the status quo on the shores of the Mediterranean, and that it would take no part in any attempt to alter the position of Tripoli to the detriment of the Turkish Government.

(Salisbury to Currie, Foreign Office, 13 May 1899, BDOW 1, pp. 206–7. Lansdowne to Currie, Foreign Office, 8 February 1902 and 7 March 1902, BDOW 1, pp. 277–91.)

One potentially important document – 'Correspondence on the Anglo-Italian Agreement. Future of Tripoli' (FO 881/8581X) never reached the National Archives from the Foreign Office, either lost or destroyed.

33. Grey to Nicolson, Fallodon, 19 September 1911, in BDOW 9/1, p. 274. Lowther to Grey, Constantinople, 25 September 1911, in BDOW 9/1, pp. 276–7. Gianpaolo Ferraioli, 'Italian Diplomacy and the Libyan Enterprise', in Micheleta and Ungari, p. 81. See also FO 800/350/2, Nicolson to Grey, Foreign Office, 27 September 1911.
34. FO 371/1252, Grey to Rudd, Foreign Office, 29 and 30 September 1911.
35. FO 800/350/2, Grey to Nicolson, Fallodon, 23 September 1911.
36. Lowther to Grey, Constantinople, 28 September 1911, in BDOW 9/1, pp. 287–8. FO 371/1252, Sublime Porte to Italian Ambassador (Communicated to Foreign Office by Tewfiq Pasha), 30 September 1911.)
37. Mesut Uyar and Edward J. Erickson, *A Military History of the Ottomans*, Santa Barbara, CA: Praeger/ABC-CLIO, 2009, pp. 223–4. Grey to Rodd (ambassador in Rome), Foreign Office, 29 September 1911, BDOW 9/1, p. 284; Grey to Bertie, Foreign Office, 30 September 1911, BDOW 9/1, p. 286; Grey to Rodd, Foreign Office, 2 October 1911, BDOW 9/1 p. 296. FO 424/230, Lowther to Grey, Constantinople, 9 January 1912; Grey to Rodd, Foreign Office, 30 September 1911, BDOW 9/1 p. 287. FO 424/230, Satow to Lowther, Jerusalem, 26 January 1912. Grey to Rodd, Foreign Office, 30 September 1911, in BDOW 9/1, p. 287. See also FO 424/230, Lowther to Grey, Pera, 4 January 1912.
38. FO 800/351/1, Bertie to Nicolson, Paris, 8 November 1911.
39. It is only possible here to give examples of the many articles and editorials: 'The War in Tripoli (editorial)', *The Times*, 1 November 1911, p. 9. 'The Slaughter at Tripoli (editorial)', *Daily News*, 6 November 1911, p. 6. 'Tripoli Slaughter:

British Officer's Sever Indictment, Women Mutilated, Appeal to England to Stop the Horrors', *Globe*, 4 November 1911, p. 10. 'The Turco-Italian War' and 'The Massacre of Arabs', *The Times*, 6 November 1911, p. 5. *Illustrated London News*, 11 November 1911, pp. 5, 17–19 (artists' renditions, not photographs). 'An Execution', *Daily News*, 18 November 1911, p. 1. 'The Truth about Tripoli', *Daily News*, 21 November 1911, pp. 1 and 2.

40. 'Seizure of Tripoli: London Protest Meeting', *Daily Telegraph*, 8 November 1911, p. 4. 'The Alleged Atrocities in Tripoli: Noisy Protest Meeting', *The Times*, 21 November 1911, p. 5. 'The War in Tripoli: Meeting of MPs', *Westminster Gazette*, 8 November 1911, p. 11.

41. 'Italy and Turkey', House of Commons Debate, 2 November 1911, *Hansard*, vol. 30, cc. 981–6. 'Italy and Turkey', House of Commons Debate, 22 November 1911, *Hansard*, vol. 31, c. 1172. 'Italy and Turkey', House of Commons Debate, 14 December 1911, *Hansard*, vol. 32, cc. 2500–1.

42. 'Italy and Turkey', House of Commons Debate, 22 November 1911, *Hansard*, vol. 31, c. 1343W. See also 'Italy and Turkey', House of Commons Debate, 24 October 1911, *Hansard*, vol. 30, c. 5. 'Italy and Turkey', House of Commons Debate, 9 November 1911, *Hansard*, vol. 30, cc. 1786–9. 'Italy and Turkey', House of Commons Debate, 2 November 1911, *Hansard*, vol. 30, cc. 981–6.

43. FO 371/1252, Grand Vezir to Tewfik Pasha, Communicated to the Foreign Office, 30 September 1911. FO 800/180, 'Communicated by the Turkish Ambassador', 31 October 1911; 'Communicated to the Turkish Ambassador', Foreign Office (Arthur Nicolson), 2 November 1911. Nicolson said that an Ottoman alliance with Britain would never happen. (FO 800/351/3, Nicolson to Hardinge, Foreign Office, 2 November 1911.) Grey: 'Our attitude will be one of neutrality, and we have declined to meet a request which was made to us by the Turkish Embassy to intervene in the matter.' (FO 800/350/2, Grey to Goschen, Foreign Office, 25 September 1911.) Speaking for the government, Francis Acland stated in parliament that the British could have mediated, but the two sides were too far apart for that. ('Italy and Turkey', House of Commons Debate, 8 November 1911, *Hansard*, vol. 30, cc. 1630–1.)

44. FO 800/352/1, Cartwright to Nicolson, Vienna, 26 October 1911, commenting on Grey's letter to ambassadors. FO 800/351/3, Nicolson to Hardinge, Foreign Office, 12 October 1911.

   On the interminable and fruitless deliberations of the Powers before the Italian action in the Aegean, see the many documents in DD 2. Both the Italians and the Ottomans refused to allow the Powers to set the peace terms. (See especially

Barréew to Poincaré, Rome, 15 March 1912, Poincaré to ambassadors in European capitals, Paris, 4 April 1912, and Bompard to Poincaré, Constantinople, 29 April 1912, in DD 2, nos. 208, 299 and 378.)

45. On the military events of the war, see the short description in Uyar and Erickson, pp. 222–5.
46. Cambon to Poincaré, London, 20 April 1912, in DD 2, no. 368. Admiralty to Foreign Office, 29 June 1912, in BDOW 9/1, pp. 413–16. Bosworth, *Italy*, pp. 688–9. The French and British agreed that Italy should give up the islands. (FO 424/232, Dering to Grey, Rome, 17 September 1912.) A French suggestion, supported by Britain, for a joint communication on the Dodecanese by the Powers to Italy foundered when Germany, Russia and Austria–Hungary refused. FO 424/233, Bertie to Grey, Paris, 9 October 1912; Grenville to Grey, Berlin, 10 October 1912; Buchanan to Grey, 10 October 1912. See the many references to mediation in BDOW 9/1, pp. 298–315. See also Childs, *Italo-Turkish Diplomacy*, pp. 143–54.

    The Italian action in the islands and the Dardanelles came as a surprise to the British. Nicolson doubted that the Italians would take any action against the Turkish islands or of blockading the Dardanelles. (FO 800/352/2, letters from Nicolson to that effect to various ambassadors, 1912.)
47. Rodd to Grey, Rome, 2 December 1912, in BDOW 9/1, pp. 438–41. Uyar and Erickson, p. 225. Britain and the other powers recognised Italian sovereignty over Libya immediately. See the various documents to that effect in BDOW 9/1, pp. 430–44. The secret and official peace treaty documents are in Childs, pp. 106–31, 137–41 and 243–53.
48. Tyrrell to Lowther, Constantinople, 29 April 1912, in BDOW 9/1, p. 392. Meeting with Ambassador Lowther, Mustafa Asım Bey, Ottoman Foreign Minister, complained that he had been bitterly reproached for his pro-British policy, but his policy had resulted in 'no good whatever'. (FO 800/355/1, Lowther to Nicolson, 29 May 1912.) Even Lowther had to admit that Britain had lost much public sympathy in the Ottoman Empire. (FO 424/250, Lowther, 'Annual Report for 1911', pp. 7–9.) See also FO 800/357/2, Lowther to Nicolson, Pera, 12 June 1912.
49. Nicolson to Grey, Foreign Office, 2 October 1911, in BDOW 9/1, pp. 297–8.
50. FO 800/351/3, Nicolson to Goschen, Foreign Office, 7 November 1911, F. 51.

# 7

## THE BALKAN WARS

By 1912 the diplomatic situation in the Balkans had changed considerably. Russia had regained much of the confidence it had lost in the debacle of the war with Japan. One of the effects of that war was a renewed Russian concentration on Europe, rather than the Far East. The 1897 Russian agreement with Austria on the status quo in the Balkans had foundered on the failure of the Russian–Austrian Macedonian reform agreement and the Austrian annexation of Bosnia. The greatest effect on Ottoman–British relations came from the British rapprochement with Russia. An Anglo-Russian Convention on Iran, Afghanistan and Tibet was signed on 31 August 1907. It ended Russian and British competition in Iran, dividing the country into 'zones of interest', and guaranteed Britain a protectorate in Afghanistan. The 'Great Game' in Asia was over.[1]

Although it ostensibly only related to Iran, Afghanistan and Tibet, the implications of détente between Britain and Russia went beyond those regions. Although no formal defensive alliance between the two had been signed, the direction of British and Russian policy against the Germans was set. In its intentions, Britain had actually joined the existing alliance between France and Russia, the Triple Entente. For the Ottomans, both Britain and Russia had been, to varying degrees, against Ottoman interests. While Britain and Russia had often been at odds in Macedonia and elsewhere, they could now be expected to take concerted action in the Ottoman Empire. The convention was a signal to the Ottomans of what could be expected from the British and Russians in the future. Iran had been divided without the consent of the Iranians. The Iranians were only notified of the agreement to take over their country a month after the Russians and British had signed the agreement to do so. It was doubtful if the Ottoman Empire would be treated differently, unless politics among the Powers somehow intervened to protect them.[2]

Until the Austrian takeover of Bosnia and her loss to Japan, Russia had often played a somewhat moderating role in the Balkans and Anatolia. Russian interest had been to avoid conflict in the Balkans – conflict that might have led to war with Austria and perhaps Germany – a war Russia could not win. She had stood in the way of British plans to deal harshly with the Ottoman Empire. After the Bosnian Crisis, Russia feared Austrian expansion, including possible Austrian conquest of Serbia. Pan-Slavist propaganda intensified Russia's perceived need to do something to increase her own power in the Balkans, advance the cause of the Balkan Slavs and oppose Austria. Public opinion and the press affected even the Tsar's government to adopt a policy in favour of the Balkan Christian nations. The new goals were to be advanced by the creation of larger, stronger Balkan Christian states at the expense of the Ottoman Empire.[3]

In the spring of 1912, Russia brokered offensive alliances directed against Ottoman Europe: Bulgaria and Serbia in March, Greece and Bulgaria in May and Montenegro with Serbia and Bulgaria in October. That Russia was behind the Balkan Alliance was no secret. Russian Foreign Minister Sergei Dmitriyevich Sazonov told British Chargé d'Affaires Hugh James O'Beirne that the treaty between Serbia and Bulgaria was originated by Russia and negotiations conducted under her aegis. Sazonov later related that Russia had acted out of its duty as Protector of the Slavs. The British Foreign Office recognised the Russian machinations, but voiced no objections to the actions of Britain's Russian ally.[4]

As war threatened in the Balkans, the great British fear was that a conflagration there might spread to the rest of Europe. The fear was that war between the Triple Alliance and the Triple Entente might be sparked by the Great Powers supporting sides in the Balkans: Austria was committed to not allow Serbia to take Ottoman lands that would give it access to the Adriatic. Russia supported the Serbs. Germany and Austria feared that a

Balkan Alliance, brokered by Russia, would greatly increase Russian influence in the Balkans, a position with which Russia increasingly agreed.[5]

The British publicly supported an Austrian plan for the maintenance of the status quo in the Balkans, accompanied by reforms for Ottoman Balkan Christians. The proposals of Britain and the other Powers to prevent a Balkan war were incredibly naïve. Their plan was that if the Ottomans implemented undescribed reforms in Europe, the Balkan States would not go to war. As always, all actions were to be on the part of the Ottomans. The reforms the British wanted from the Ottomans were to be based on Article 23 of the Treaty of Berlin. It was a strange choice. Article 23 referred to reforms in Ottoman Crete, instituted by the Ottoman Organic Law of 1868. They had basically divided the Ottoman bureaucracy in Crete between Muslims and Christians. Administrative councils and the judiciary were similarly divided, and mixed Christian/Muslim courts adjudicated disputes between Muslims and Christians. Much power was devolved to the Christian population, especially in districts that were mainly Christian in population. Greeks in Crete had still revolted, and Greece had intervened, leading to the 1897 War and the Ottoman loss of Crete. Yet this was the system recommended by the British. Of course, the Balkan Allies wanted nothing to do with power-sharing with Muslims. They would never have accepted the reform scheme, and the Ottomans thought Grey's plan ridiculous.[6]

In fact, the Balkan Allies had already decided to go to war. The Russians, coming to the realisation that a Balkan war might expand into a European war, now tried to dissuade the Balkan countries from attacking, but it was too late to stop the process they had begun. As the British well knew, the Balkan Allies had met to decide to attack, despite the fact that they could not agree on how they would divide Ottoman Europe if they were successful. British representatives in the Balkan capitals had notified London of the Allies' plans: for example, writing from Sofia, British Ambassador Colville Barclay had informed the British Government that the alliance of Bulgaria, Serbia, Montenegro and Greece was set upon demanding 'decisive action'. They had decided that the Powers would not intervene: although not pleased that they were going to war at that time and without asking for Russian counsel, Russia was sympathetic to them, Italy was completely occupied with her war with the Ottomans and Austria was revamping her military.

Those situations would soon change, and now was the time to strike. The Balkan Allies refused to consider even the toothless warning from the Powers. They had already decided on war. The Balkan Allies presented an ultimatum with impossible terms for reforms, but their troops were already crossing the Ottoman borders.[7]

Serbia, Bulgaria, Montenegro and Greece attacked the Ottoman Empire in October 1912. By the spring of 1913 the Ottoman armies in the Balkans had been defeated. The Greek navy had taken all the Aegean Islands that were not occupied by Italy. Ottoman forces still held the Gallipoli Peninsula and the defences of the Çatalca Line near Istanbul, where fierce fighting continued, with Bulgarian forces intending to occupy the Ottoman capital.[8]

As they had in the Italian War, the British refused to keep their treaty commitments to defend the territorial integrity of the Ottoman Empire. Britain's ally, Russia, had been instrumental in creating the Balkan Alliance. She told the British that she wanted the European Powers to stay out of the conflict. It was to be up to the combatants to settle matters on their own, on the battlefield.[9]

Not expecting the British would keep to their commitments, on 5 November 1912 the Ottomans instead asked the British only to intervene with the other Powers to mediate immediately to bring an end to hostilities and fix the conditions of a peace. They said they would open the Straits to ships of the Powers. The British refused the Ottoman offer. Grey instead solicited the Balkan Allies as to what they wanted from a peace. The Ottomans asked on 11 November why they had received no response to their request from Britain. But the British had gone over completely to the side of the Balkan Allies. The only mediation they planned was to ensure that the Allies retained all they had conquered. Already in October of 1912 Grey had told the other Powers that, while he was still personally in favour of the status quo, he could not countenance denying the Balkan Allies any of the lands they had conquered. Once again, the principle held that no lands that had been taken by Christians could ever be returned to Muslims.[10]

## British Sympathies

The stated intentions of the British and other Powers for preservation of the status quo in the Balkans were quickly forgotten. Russian Ambassador

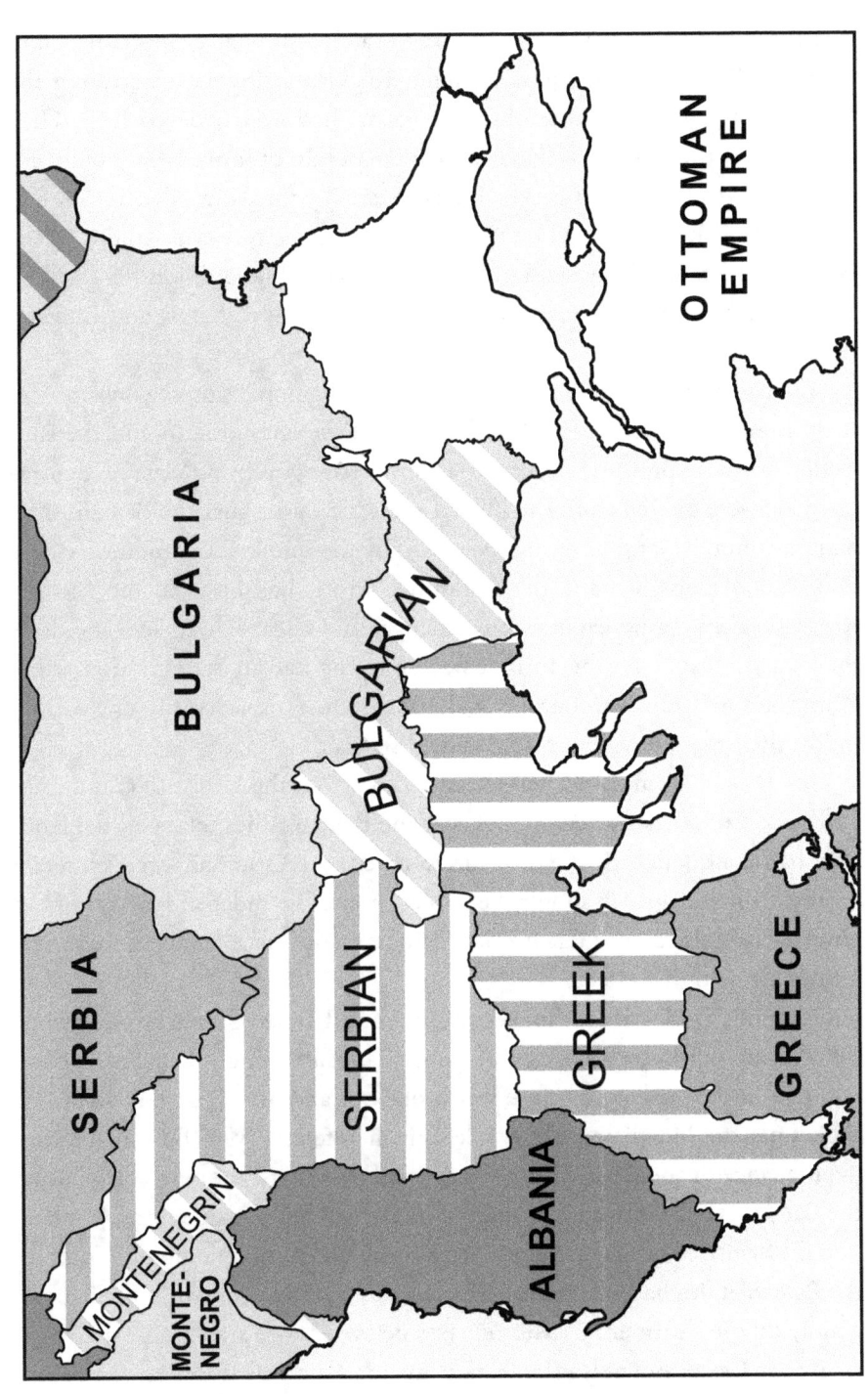

Map 7.1 Balkan War conquests

Alexander von Benckendorff told Grey that Russia had changed its mind on upholding the status quo, although Russia's assistance in creating the Balkan League made it doubtful that Russia had ever believed in it. Grey agreed with the Russians: 'I observed that public opinion here would not side with any attempt to turn the Balkan States by force out of what they had conquered'. The British public and most politicians were sympathetic to the Balkan Christians. Grey stated: 'I am sure that public opinion here will be cordially and entirely in favor of contemplated gains to Servia and Bulgaria (the "fruits of victory").'[11]

The Balkan Committee published a series of pamphlets on the Balkan War. It declared on 12 October 1912 that '[t]he time has come to end the subjection of these promising races to an unworthy governing class'. Extensive citations were offered from the Liberal press, declaring that the Balkan Allies had not wanted war, but were driven to it by the intolerable condition of the Balkan Christians. Britain, the committee wrote, had been far too friendly toward Turkey – a policy that must change. The Great Powers had not done their duty in expelling the Turk; it was up to the Balkan States to do so. The Christians in Ottoman Europe had shown their capacity for civilisation, unlike the people in 'uncivilized Asiatic districts'.[12]

The Balkan Committee met in January 1913 in the House of Commons, and passed resolutions demanding that the Balkan Allies retain all the lands they had conquered. If, the committee stated, the Ottomans were to retain any land in Europe, it should be placed under an independent European governor and effectively taken from Ottoman control. A memorandum was sent to Grey to that effect.[13]

The policies of Prime Minister Asquith and Foreign Secretary Grey when the Balkan Crisis began were the subject of surprisingly little parliamentary debate. Immediately before war broke out and as it began, government spokesmen told parliament the sole British interests were Balkan reforms, maintenance of the territorial *status quo* and avoiding European war. During the Balkan Wars, Grey and the other officials offered parliament no justification for British neutrality. MPs did not pressure them on that point. Not until the Balkan Allies had triumphed were serious questions raised in parliament, mainly on the treatment of Muslims (see below).[14]

British Government leaders openly favoured the Balkan Allies. The Financial Secretary of the Treasury, Charles Mastermann, spoke on 18 October at

Bethnal Green: 'I ask you to take a sympathetic view towards those fighting in the cause of liberty and progress and who have been suffering for years owing to the murders and pillage of the Turks.' Winston Churchill, First Lord of the Admiralty, addressed the Balkan War in a speech on 30 October 1912. He defended the attack of the Balkan Allies who, he said, were fighting to adjust old wrongs and to fulfill their destinies. Prime Minister Asquith, in a speech at the Guildhall on 9 November 1912, declared: 'The victors are not to be robbed of the fruits which cost them so dear.' Asquith expected the Bulgarians to break the Çatalca Line and reach Istanbul. He welcomed the upcoming fall of Edirne (see below), because it would bring the war to an end with Bulgarian victory.[15]

**Edirne and the Çatalca Line**

Ambassadors of the six Great Powers (Great Britain, France, Germany, Austria–Hungary, Russia and Italy) assembled in London in December 1912 to decide on joint action in the Balkan conflict. Britain took charge of the meetings; Grey was the only foreign minister to attend, and he and the Foreign Office head of administration, Arthur Nicolson, were the *de facto* chairs. From the first, the intention of Britain, France and Russia – the Triple Entente – was favourable to the Balkan Allies. Germany and Austria–Hungary generally attempted to lessen the blow on the Ottomans from their defeat. Italy vacillated, especially on questions of the Adriatic and the Aegean. The spectre of possible European war hung over the deliberations and affected the decisions of the ambassador's conference. Participants spoke of the need to retain the Concert of Europe, in which European Powers acted as one, although the alliance system had destroyed the ideal of any real concert. Nevertheless, none of the Powers wanted the Balkan War to expand to the rest of Europe.[16]

The swift Ottoman defeat had brought Bulgarian forces nearly to Istanbul. Ottoman forces held the fortified Çatalca Line, their last redoubt before Istanbul, against fierce Bulgarian attacks. The Ottomans also continued to hold Edirne (Adrianople) against Bulgarian siege, but they had lost the Aegean Islands, Chios (Scio), Samos and Mytilini (Lesvos), that commanded the Anatolian coast to Greek naval invasion. There was nothing the Ottomans could do about the lost territories far from Istanbul. Their concern was for Edirne Province, which they hoped to retain and to protect its Muslim population. (The population of Edirne Province before the war had been 51 per cent Muslim, 25 per cent Greek Orthodox and 19 per cent Bulgarian Orthodox, the remainder other religious groups; see Table 4.1.)[17]

The British took the lead in proposing that the Ottomans capitulate to the demands of the Balkan Allies. Grey proposed to the meeting of ambassadors that the Ottomans (not the Balkan Allies) be told there would be 'consequences' for them if hostilities resumed: 'The Powers would be obliged to consider the future situation of Constantinople and the developments of the war in Asia Minor. The Powers will be obliged to intervene in Turkey for the protection of their financial interests.' If peace were concluded, however, financial assistance might be available to the Ottomans. No actual assistance was ever actually promised or delivered.[18]

The ambassadors finally decided on a diplomatic demand (*démarche*) to the Ottomans that corresponded to the British and French wishes: the Ottomans were told that if they did not abandon Edirne and accept the Powers' decision to relinquish any claim to the Aegean Islands in favour of Greece, the status of Istanbul and Asia Minor would be called into question. If they did abandon them and signed a peace treaty, the Powers would give them 'moral and material support'. The Powers would guarantee that the Muslim Holy Places in Edirne would be protected and that Great Power guarantees on the Aegean Islands would ensure that they would be no danger to Ottoman security.[19]

Russia, supported by Britain, was adamant that the Ottomans give up Edirne to the Bulgarians. The Russians proposed military intervention by the Powers to force the Ottomans to give way, but the Germans and Austrians refused. The Germans correctly declared: 'It cannot be the duty of the Powers to substitute themselves for the Balkan States in their dispute with Turkey.' The Russians suggested that Britain, France and Russia act independently, but Grey felt this would only encourage the Turks by showing division among the Powers. Instead, Grey threatened the Ottomans with even greater loss if they did not abandon Edirne. Grey told the Ottoman ambassador in London that the Turks could expect nothing from the Powers but pressure 'to compromise about the town of Adrianople'. It was obvious that the compromise he intended was Ottoman abandonment of the city.[20]

The Germans suggested that the Ottomans might relinquish Edirne if they gained a customs increase and assurances on the Aegean Islands. Grey said no to both. He said he could never justify a customs increase to parliament, because by paying increased duties British merchants would in essence be paying a price for Edirne.[21]

The Ottoman Cabinet agreed on 22 January to accept the Powers' demands on Edirne and the Aegean Islands, but Enver, Talat and forty armed men appeared on 23 January and forced the cabinet to resign. The new government of the Committee of Union and Progress nevertheless found it impossible to save Edirne. They attempted a futile compromise: they notified the British on 26 February 1913 that they were willing to cede Edirne and accept a reduced border in Thrace, leaving the region north of Lüleburgaz to the Bulgarians. They asked that soldiers (with their cannon, etc.) and civilians be allowed to leave the city. The Bulgarians did not accept the offer.[22]

**Forcing the Ottomans to Comply**

None of the Powers was willing to militarily attack the Ottoman Empire to enforce their demands to sign a European-brokered peace. To do so might provoke a war between the Triple Alliance and the Triple Entente. The weapon proposed to force the Ottomans to comply with the European demands was a 'naval demonstration'. There was much disagreement on what was meant by this term. To some it was sending battleships to Istanbul to threaten the Ottomans, ships which would have to pass through the defended Straits. To others it included landing troops, especially landing marines from naval vessels. The term 'naval demonstration' implied that the ships or land forces would not remain after the Ottomans had acquiesced to the Powers' plans. No one could be sure of the outcome of a demonstration, however, and it was full of potential dangers of starting larger wars. The French and Russians nevertheless wanted a naval demonstration at Istanbul. The Italians, Germans and Austrians were against it. Assuming that negotiations with the Ottomans would not have a satisfactory conclusion for them, the Bulgarians also wanted a demonstration; for them, anything that drew Ottoman forces away from the front line would be valuable. Grey was opposed. In theory, he had nothing against a demonstration, but he felt there would be practical difficulties in carrying it out. Instead, he decided that the ships of the Powers should go to Besika (Beşik) Bay, in the Dardanelles, within striking distance of Istanbul, where they could threaten, but not yet advance to Istanbul.[23]

Despite the objections raised by the Ottomans and the Germans, the British position won out.

Many suggestions were debated among the Powers, including, in exchange for two Aegean Islands the Ottomans needed for their defence, Italy giving Greece some islands when they turned over the Dodecanese to the Ottomans. (Of course, Italy had no such plan.) The debates among the Powers on the islands possessed by the Italians were seemingly endless. Positions changed; the other Powers sometimes did what they could to pressure the Italians to give them up, sometimes accepted that the Italians would never do so. The Turks were very concerned on the issue. Both Ambassador Mallet and Nicolson feared that the Ottomans, perhaps in alliance with Bulgaria, would go to war with Greece. (Nicolson thought that the Italians would never agree to the above plan, nor that Greece would ever agree to exchange Chios and Mytilini for Italian islands.)[24]

## Threats and Mediation

Grey notified the Ottomans that if they did not cooperate with the Powers' plan they would suffer. A collective note addressed to the Ottomans, dictated by Grey, threatened the position of the Ottoman capital and the possible extension of the war into Anatolia. The Ottomans would have to accept the loss of Edirne and leave the question of the islands to the Powers. If they did so, they could expect 'the moral and material support of the Great European Powers', but no specific European aid was offered. The Ottoman response was that they could not abandon Edirne, which was an overwhelmingly Muslim city, although they were willing to give up part of the city. They also could not cede the Aegean Islands that were close to the Anatolian mainland and were necessary for the defence of Anatolia. It was essential that they be allowed to raise their customs duties by 4 per cent, end foreign post offices and terminate the Capitulations.[25]

Grey's reply to the Ottoman note stated that it was unacceptable. The Powers could only mediate 'if it (the Ottoman Government) shows itself disposed to accept their (the Powers) opinions'. Neither the Ottomans nor the Balkan Allies had yet accepted the mediation of the Powers on the Powers' terms, so negotiations for peace were only carried on between Bulgaria and the Ottomans. Grey told the Bulgarians not to accept the Ottoman proposals.[26]

Grey was especially bothered by the Ottoman proposals for the customs duties and the end to the Capitulations, but stated he would not even consider them with the other Powers until peace was settled. Ultimately, the British were to accept neither.[27]

The question of Edirne was closed, at least temporarily, when the city finally fell to the Bulgarians on 26 March 1912. An armistice was signed between Bulgaria and the Ottoman Empire on 3 December 1912. Peace negotiations were to begin in London.

Once the Ottomans had lost Edirne, the British, in concert with the other Powers, agreed to arrange a peace, but they demanded that the Ottomans first accept binding mediation before the Powers approached the Balkan nations. The Ottoman Government presented a plan requesting Great Power mediation on the basis of five points:

1. The Powers guarantee that the Ottomans would pay no indemnities to the Balkan Allies.
2. The Powers guarantee that the new Ottoman border would pass near Edirne ('près d'Andrinople').
3. Decisions on the public debt, concessions and railways would be satisfactory for the Ottomans.
4. The Powers agree to a 4 per cent increase in Ottoman customs duties.
5. The Balkan States would not be given Capitulations in the Ottoman Empire.

Grey said these points were reasonable, with the exception of the 4 per cent duties increase, but supplied his own interpretation: the Ottoman–Bulgarian border would be a line from Enez (Enos) to Midye (Kıyıköy), not nearly close to Edirne (Map 7.2). The Public Debt, railways, etc. issues would be decided in an 'equitable' manner (not necessarily satisfactory to the Ottomans). Also, the question of the Aegean Islands, not mentioned in the Ottoman proposals, would be left to the Powers. The Ottomans responded that the border should at least leave them half of Eastern Thrace, needed to protect Istanbul, which was not what Grey had in mind. The British told them that they would have to accept the decisions of the Powers, which might not be what the Ottomans wanted: 'What was desired was a simple affirmative or negative from the Porte as to whether the Turkish Government were prepared to accept the advice of the Powers.' On 28 February 1913 the Ottomans, having no choice, consented to Great Power mediation, accepting that the Powers would decide the terms of peace.[28]

The Balkan Allies prevaricated. They brought up many reasons not to engage in peace talks, including the need for the Ottomans to first agree to pay indemnities, which the Ottomans could not pay. The Balkan Allies submitted a bill for indemnities to the Financial Commission the Powers had created in Paris to deal with financial matters arising from the war – 1,842,603,560 Francs to cover their wartime expenses. The Financial Commission estimated this as the equivalent of 73 million Ottoman Lira (and 80 million was more accurate), a colossal sum. The entire Ottoman state revenues in 1912 had been only 30 million Lira.[29]

On 14 March 1913, the Balkan Allies responded collectively to the Powers' suggestion of mediation. They demanded that the Ottomans relinquish Crete, still theoretically an autonomous Ottoman province, and the Aegean Islands and that an indemnity be paid. The Ottoman border would be from East of Tekirdağ to Midye. Edirne and Scutari (Üsküdar) in Albania would go to the Allies. They also demanded that any peace treaty guarantee the privileges and right of the religious/national fellows (*congénères*) in the Ottoman Empire.[30]

The British presented a draft treaty to the conference of the Powers' ambassadors:

- The Ottoman border with Bulgaria was to be the Enez–Midye Line. The rest of Ottoman Europe was to be ceded to the Balkan Allies.
- All questions on Albania would be settled by the Powers.
- Crete would pass from theoretical Ottoman sovereignty to Greek rule.
- Disposition of the Aegean Islands would be left to the decision of the Powers.
- Financial questions, such as distribution of the Ottoman Debt would be settled by an international commission at Paris.[31]

Any promises of the integrity of the Ottoman borders had been completely abandoned. The one allowance for the Ottomans was the exclusion of huge indemnities to be paid by the Ottomans to the Balkan Allies. The Russians

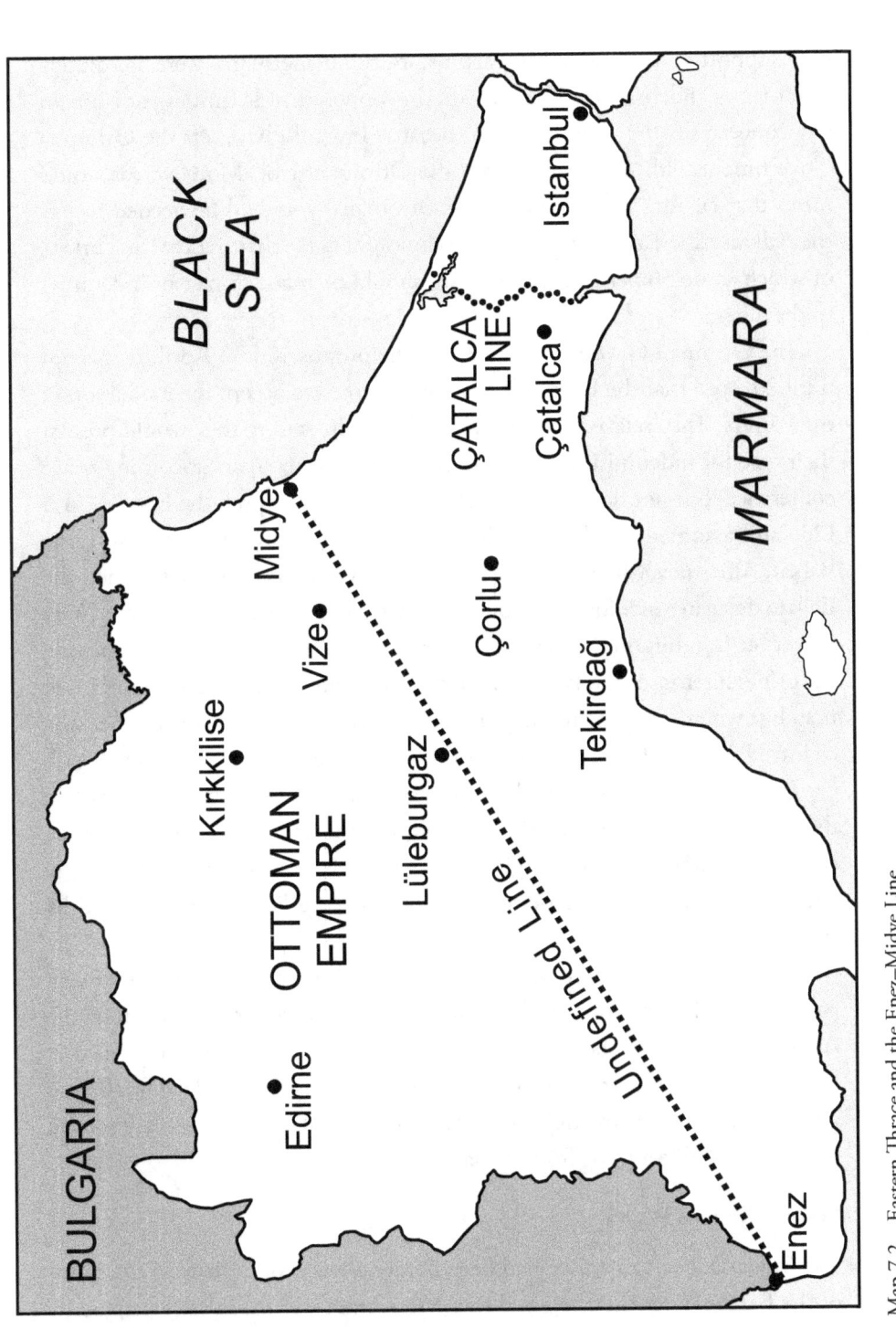

Map 7.2  Eastern Thrace and the Enez–Midye Line

had supported the indemnity claims, but the Germans were absolutely against any indemnities. The British also opposed indemnities, not out of any concern for the Ottomans, but because it would have left the Ottoman Government with no means to pay the Ottoman debt. Moreover, it would mean that custom duties paid to the Ottomans would all be needed to pay the Balkan Allies, as Grey stated: 'We could not agree that trade with Turkey, of which some 60 per cent was British, should be made to pay an indemnity to the allies.'[32]

The Ottoman Government accepted the proposals on 3 April. It was not until 20 April that the Balkan States finally agreed to accept the mediation of the Powers. They relaxed their previous demands, stating they would present their case for indemnities and the frontiers of Albania to an upcoming peace conference, but not demanding indemnities. They accepted the Enez–Midye Line and assumed the Aegean Islands would be lost by the Ottomans. The Balkan Allies never had the chance to formally state their wishes. When the Balkan delegates met for the second time with the representatives of the Great Powers at London on 20 May, they were presented with a treaty embodying the original terms of the Powers, all ready for them to sign. They demurred at first, but when, on 27 May, Grey frankly told them that they must either sign or leave London, they signed without much further delay on 30 May 1913.[33]

The subsequent Treaty of London (30 May 1913) followed the British draft almost exactly, except that the status of Crete was to be decided by the Powers, not immediately given to Greece. It was not so much a treaty among belligerents as a settlement imposed by the Powers, as proposed by the British.[34]

The Treaty of London was one of the least successful treaties in European history. It contained no division of the conquered territories among the Allies, leaving that to be settled in a subsequent war. None of the considerations brought up by the Ottomans were even considered. No thought was given to the status or the rights of the affected populations. The treaty proved to be unworkable almost from its date of signing.

**Second Balkan War**

The Bulgarians felt that they had been denied their proper share of the spoils of the Balkan War; they believed that Macedonia and Salonica, occupied by

Serbia and Greece, should have been theirs. On 29 June 1913, the Bulgarians attacked their allies, and lost. Romania entered the war against them on 10 July. After much deliberation in the Ottoman Cabinet, Ottoman forces advanced from the Çatalca Lines, first to the Enez–Midye Line (12 July), then on into Thrace (20 July). They retook Edirne on 22 July, and elements of the army even moved briefly into Bulgaria proper.[35]

When the Turks defeated Bulgaria in the second Balkan War, retook Thrace and returned to Edirne, Grey did all he could to force them to abandon it.[36]

On 15 July Grey advised the Ottomans not to go beyond the Enez–Midye Line. He told them of disastrous consequences if they advanced, because '[a] Power' (Russia) might intervene and take Istanbul. When the Ottomans ignored his warning, Grey once again threatened the Ottomans with 'consequences' on 26 July and again in August. He told the Ottoman negotiator, İbrahim Hakkı Paşa, that the Powers would agree 'to secure her possession of Constantinople and Asiatic Turkey in return for withdrawal from Adrianople'. The threat was apparent. Hakkı Paşa was advised that Ottoman persistence would 'endanger her future as an independent state'. Grey was being duplicitous. No matter what he told the Ottomans, he had actually decided that he was not in favour of giving the Ottoman Empire any guarantee for its possessions in Asia Minor, because it might be construed as directed against Russia.[37]

The Ottomans ignored Grey's advice.[38]

Russia, for its part, did not hesitate to use the always-present appeal to Christianity: Sazanov declared of the Ottomans retaining Edirne: 'It is impossible. It would be the first time that a Christian country would be allowed to fall back under Muslim rule.'[39]

Russia did indeed want military intervention. The Russians had vacillated throughout the Balkan Crisis – first organising the Balkan Alliance, then opposing war and finally opposing Ottoman reconquest. In November 1912, the French foreign minister said that the Russians had made a proposal that Russia, France and Britain should notify the Bulgarians that they would not be allowed to permanently retain Edirne. The French refused. On 3 November the Russians changed their minds and decided Bulgaria could keep Edirne. Russia suggested a combined 'naval demonstration' by Britain, France and Russia against the Ottomans. The Russians suggested an occupation of the Enez–Midye line by the Powers, and even threatened that unless the Powers intervened to force Turkey to accept the Enez–Midye line, Russia would act alone. Foreign Minister Sazonov threatened that Russia would occupy an Ottoman Black Sea port. All the Russian plans foundered, however, when Germany and Austria categorically refused to participate. The Germans announced they were 'strongly opposed both to collective and individual action (against the Ottoman Empire)'. The French also declined to join any demonstration, not wanting a conflict between the Triple Entente and the Triple Alliance. Conflict with Germany and a possibly expanded war was too serious a possibility for the others to act. Russia ultimately was also too worried of European war and abandoned plans for military action.[40]

Defeated in their wish for military intervention, the Russians proposed 'financial pressure' to force the Ottomans to abandon Edirne. If the Ottomans did not do so, they would receive none of the loans they needed for reconstruction. Grey agreed to try this:

> I said that there was not, nor was there likely to be, any disposition to lend money to Turkey. I could not control financiers here, but would join in any declaration to which other Powers agreed, as I thought that the financial lever was the one most likely to be effective.

In other words, the Ottomans would not receive loans, no matter what they agreed to, but Grey was willing to lie to them.[41]

The one good card the Powers had to play was a potential increase in Ottoman customs duties. The dues had been set at 11 per cent, and, according to the financial Capitulations, the Powers needed to approve any increase. None had been granted, due to British opposition. The case for an increase was obvious: the Ottoman Empire, a net importer, badly needed the funds. The Balkan Allies all applied much larger duties (Greece: 20–27 per cent, Bulgaria: 14–21 per cent, Serbia: 42–57 per cent). But the British were adamant. Grey had even refused to accept an increase as an inducement for the Ottomans to abandon Edirne. Britain had the largest share of Ottoman imports and thus had the most to lose from any increase in customs duties.[42]

When asked in parliament why the British objected to a Turkish reconquest of Thrace, Grey gave an answer that defined *realpolitik*:

Mr. WALTER GUINNESS

    May I ask. whether, in view of the Powers having allowed the former Allies to indulge in a naked war of conquest, there is any reason to object to the reoccupation of former Turkish territory in accordance with the principles of nationality, which the right hon. Gentleman formerly supported?

Sir E. GREY

    These questions are really based on the assumption that the action of the Powers is regulated by logic and international law. The action of the Powers seems to me to have been influenced in the case of each individual Power, first, by the view of what its own interests require, and, in the case of all the Powers, by a common desire to preserve the peace of Europe. I imagine that their action will continue to be regulated by those influences.[43]

The Powers arrived at various schemes to force the Ottomans out of Edirne, but Germany and Austria, while giving lip service to Ottoman abandonment of Eastern Thrace, frustrated any real combined Great Power intervention. The Germans were unwilling to take any military action against the Ottoman Empire. The German foreign minister advocated 'diplomacy not force' in dealing with the Turks. The Germans correctly believed that a settlement could only be reached when the Ottomans negotiated directly with the Bulgarians. When ambassadors of the Powers at Istanbul wanted to warn the Ottomans of financial consequences if they did not retreat to the Enez–Midye line, the German ambassador said he would only mention it in conversations. The Germans knew that a call to the Ottomans to abandon their reconquest was futile, because the Turks knew that no combination of Powers would agree to stop them, and no single Power would do so, because it would break up the European Concert.[44]

The Ottomans refused all the plans to abandon their reconquest. They notified the Powers that they needed Thrace to defend Istanbul and the Straits.[45]

Hakkı Paşa, ex-Grand Vezir and special Ottoman representative to London, advanced cogent arguments for leaving the Ottomans in Edirne Province:

- The Europeans had never previously considered that Edirne Province should be part of Bulgaria. In all the deliberations on reforms or autonomy of Macedonia, Ottoman loss of the province had never been considered.

The Balkan Allies had not considered Thrace in their demands that led to the Balkan War, only Macedonia. Even the San Stephano Treaty, which had created a Great Bulgaria, had never denied the province to the Ottomans.
- Two-thirds of the population of Edirne Province was Turkish Muslims.
- Those who believed that Bulgaria must not be humiliated should also consider the danger of useless humiliation of Turkey. Muslims will know that the Ottoman Empire has been denied the rights afforded to the other Balkan States because it is a Muslim state.
- European interests in the Empire will suffer.
- The London Agreements were not ratified by Bulgaria, and thus were not binding. In any case, the agreement left Ottoman Europe to the Balkan Allies as a group – an association that no longer existed. Other 'solemn agreements' had been violated without Great Power complaint, such as the violation by Romania in attacking Bulgaria and violations of the Treaty of Berlin.
- The Europeans had originally supported the *status quo* in Ottoman Europe, but abandoned that idea for *de facto* considerations when the Balkan Allies triumphed. That same principle should be applied to the Ottoman reconquest of Edirne.
- 'The so-called principle that a Mohammedan State must never recover territory lost to the benefit of Christian people is a shame for those who think so in the twentieth century'.[46]

Hakkı Paşa was of course correct in stating that the principle that no land once conquered by Christians must ever revert to Muslim rule was shameful. At its heart, the demand that the Ottomans give up Edirne was irrational. What benefit was it to any of the European Powers if Bulgaria held Eastern Thrace? None of the voluminous documents on the question seem to have considered any economic benefit for the Powers. For the British this was especially true, because British goods imported into Bulgaria paid higher customs duties than goods entering the Ottoman Empire. Istanbul was the natural entrepot of goods from Eastern Thrace, and this trade would suffer or end completely if Thrace was Bulgarian.

The Foreign Office was by no means unanimous in supporting Grey's demands on the Ottomans. Louis Mallet, the Foreign Office Under-Secretary, wrote: 'I must say that there is a great deal in Hakkı Pasha's argument—we have no interest in turning Turkey out of Adrianople.' Grey's advisor Alwyn Parker wrote that the British had nothing to gain by expelling the Turks. The only possible benefit might have been to keep the Russians from intervening, but all indications were that they would not do so. Russia feared both conflict with Germany and Austria and the closing of the Straits by the Turks. Moreover, 'Russian sympathy for Bulgaria is at a low ebb.' Parker felt no sympathy for the Bulgarians ('[t]he most barbarous in Europe'), because '[t]he Bulgarians had shown themselves guilty of the worst atrocities perpetrated in the whole war'. Even Arthur Nicolson, the head of the Foreign Office and no friend of the Ottomans, wrote: 'I am really pleased that Turkey has been able to retain Adrianople.'[47]

In an interview with Grey, Francis Bertie, the British ambassador to France, had the temerity to suggest to the foreign secretary that it was not wise policy to deny Edirne to the Ottomans. Grey stated that the Ottomans were bound by their promises in the Treaty of London, and they would have to withdraw from Thrace. Bertie said 'that the present is a Treaty-breaking age', and Britain was itself breaking treaty pledges. Grey's response to this was incredible, given Britain's past pledges to preserve Ottoman territorial integrity:

> I (Bertie) said that everybody seemed to kick against inconvenient obligations but the Englishman's word used to be considered his bond.
>
> Sir E. Grey replied that his wish is to preserve the sacred character of England's word, written or said.[48]

Perhaps Grey meant that the sacred character of England's word only as it applied to European Christians.

As had been the case for the other borders in Southeastern Europe, the borders of Ottoman Thrace were decided in war. In this rare case the Ottomans had won, and the Ottomans and Bulgarians proved able to settle the question without Great Power intervention and despite British wishes. The Ottoman reconquest of Eastern Thrace was recognised in the Ottoman–Bulgarian Treaty of Constantinople of 29 September 1913.[49]

## The Aegean Islands

Greek naval forces conquered the Ottoman Aegean Islands in the first Balkan War. The other islands, the Dodecanese, were under Italian occupation.

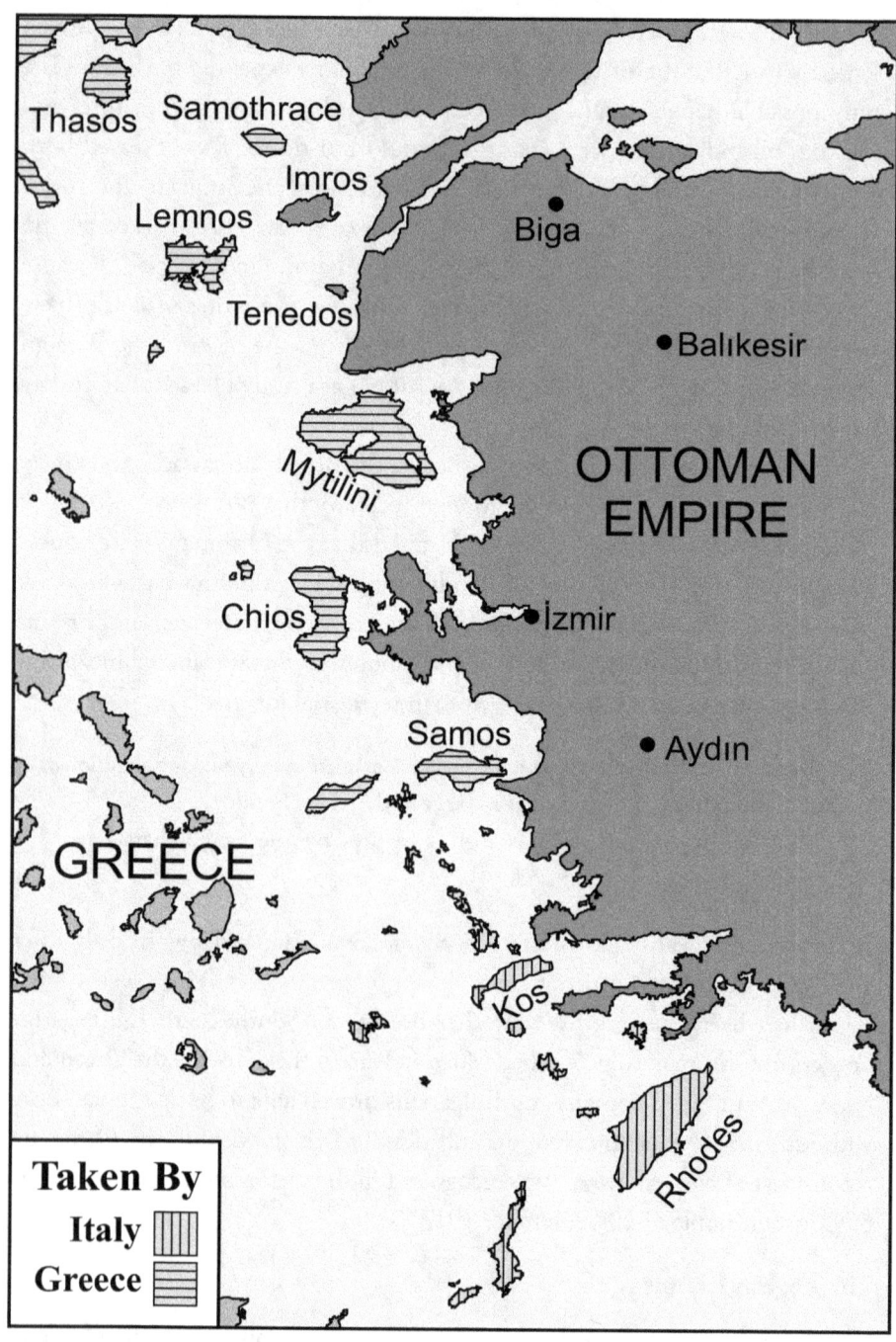

Map 7.3  The Aegean Islands

Five months before the Treaty of London was signed, the British had already told the Greeks that they favoured Greek retention of the Aegean Islands. Britain, however, was not able to formally insert Greek ownership of the islands into the London Treaty, which left the question of the Aegean Islands in abeyance, stipulating that the Powers were to decide. The Greeks opposed the treaty provision on the islands, stating that they should be awarded to Greece. Britain agreed with them, but felt other Powers would initially have a problem with that. Grey promised the Greeks, however, that all would work out well for Greece, because Britain would ensure that it did.[50]

Everyone, including the Ottomans, seems to have agreed that most of the islands that had been taken by Greece would remain with Greece. However, about two of them, Chios and Mytilini, which were extremely close to the mainland of Anatolia, there was disagreement. The Ottoman argument for keeping the islands was strategic – islands so close to the mainland would be a military threat and a haven for smugglers. They offered complete autonomy in all domestic matters to the islands that lay close to the mainland, as well as the islands (Imbros and Tenedos) that were close to the Dardanelles. The Germans and Austrians agreed; they wanted the islands near the Dardanelles and Chios and Mytilini to be returned to the Ottoman Empire.[51]

The counter-argument was demographic – a large majority of the islands' population was Greek and Christian. (It should be noted, however, that no one had considered the demographic argument when majority Muslim territories in the Balkans were given to Christian countries.) The British wanted both islands to go to Greece. Arthur Nicolson described the position of his political superiors on the islands, which Nicolson admitted he only accepted reluctantly: all the Aegean Islands should be given to Greece. Those that had 'strategic importance' or lay close to the Turkish mainland should be neutralised, with no fortifications or naval bases, but ruled by Greece. Nicolson stated that public opinion in Britain would not support leaving any of the islands within the Ottoman Empire.[52]

The British declared that the Turks would only be able to reclaim Chios and Mytilini by force, which was unacceptable. They had not thought it unacceptable when those islands were taken from the Ottomans by force. The British theoretically justified the Greek position of the islands close to the Anatolian coast by citing a 'principle of nationalities'; the population was mainly Greek, so the islands should belong to Greece. Such a position did have moral force, if such a principle was truly believed. But how could the British under that principle accept the award of majority Albanian lands to Serbia, Montenegro and Greece? How could they include award of majority Turkish Western Thrace to Bulgaria? Indeed, how could a colonial power speak of national self-determination at all? What was really at play was the old principle that no land that had been taken by Christians should ever be returned to Muslim rule.

The question of the Aegean Islands brought forth a division between the Triple Entente and the Triple Alliance. The Italians, Germans and Austrians wanted the Ottomans to be given the six Greek-occupied islands if they relinquished Edirne. Grey said that the Turks would have to take the islands only by force, and that they would then oppress the natives. The Powers would then have to intervene, which the European public did not want. If the islands were granted autonomy, they would decide to go to Greece anyway, and the Powers did not want to enforce their retention by the Ottoman Empire. In any case, the British would not be willing to use force to stop their annexation by Greece. The British made it clear that the islands, except perhaps Imbros, Tenedos and Thasos (near the Dardanelles opening), should be given to Greece, but Grey told Greek Prime Minister Venizelos that Britain would have preferred that Greece retain all the islands.[53]

The question of the islands was to be inextricably tied with that of Southern Albania. During the war, Greece, Serbia and Montenegro had occupied parts of Northern, Western and Southern Albania. Italy and Austria demanded that the invaders not possess the Albania coastline and its ports. Possessing the Adriatic coast would give Serbia access to the sea and provide new bases for the Greek navy. Italy demanded that Greece relinquish the Southern Albanian region she had conquered in the war. There was danger of another war over Albania.[54]

Grey arrived at a solution, not out of concern for the Albanians or because he wished Greece to lose South Albania, but, as always, for fear of complications among the Powers. Greece did not want to surrender either South Albania or the Aegean Islands, both of which it had occupied in the war. However, the Triple Alliance Powers – Italy, Germany and Austria – were unwilling to leave South Albania to Greece. Both Italy and Austria feared that a Greek naval base in Epirus would allow the Greeks to restrict access to the Northern Adriatic. They were willing to give Greece most, not all, of the Aegean Islands, not necessarily to include those occupied by Italy.[55]

On 12 December 1913, Grey presented his plan for Southern Albania and the Aegean Islands. British ambassadors were instructed to convey the plans to the Powers' governments. It had been decided to leave within Albania the southern districts of Koritza (Korçë) and Stylos. The conference of ambassadors in London had linked this to the award of the Aegean Islands, except Imbros and Tenedos, to Greece, a *quid pro quo*. The Greeks should evacuate Southern Albania and, to facilitate the evacuation, they should be told they would get the islands. The Ottomans would have to accept this, but would be told the islands would be demilitarised. Italy would be told that as soon as the last Ottoman soldiers left Tripoli, the Dodecanese would become autonomous under the sultan's sovereignty. Grey justified the award of Chios and Mytilini to Greece, which he had always intended to do, on the basis of political necessity.

> If any attempt was now to be made to modify this settlement so far as the islands were concerned, it would be open to any of the six Powers to demand the reopening and reconsideration of their decision as regards the Southern Albanian frontier.[56]

Grey's plan ignored the fact that Italy had no desire to leave the Dodecanese. When presented with the plan, the Italian Minister of Foreign Affairs stated that Italy would not agree. Under the Treaty of Lausanne, the Italians had agreed to leave only when the last Ottoman soldiers were gone. The Italians said that public opinion would not allow them to relinquish the islands. Instead, the Italians presented new demands before they would leave the Dodecanese:

1. That all Turkish officers and men, they alleged over 220–30 in number, should withdraw from Cyrenaica. (This was nonsense. The last Ottoman soldiers in Libya, perhaps forty in all, were captives of the Senussi and could not leave. When asked to rescue them, the Italians had refused.)
2. That the Turkish Government should take back from the Arabs the arms which the Porte had furnished them during the war (an obvious impossibility).
3. That the Greeks should first evacuate the islands of which they were in occupation (which the Greeks would never do).

The Italians had no wish to leave. However, the Italian Government intimated that they would be willing to exchange the Dodecanese in exchange for commercial rights in Southern Anatolia, including building a railroad from Antalya. The British blocked this, because it would compete with British interests, in particular the British-owned Smyrna to Kasaba Railway.[57]

The Ottomans, as might have been expected, objected to Grey's proposal, of which they had heard nothing until it had been published. The Ottomans reserved the right to go to war with Greece over the islands. Ambassador Mallet told the Grand Vezir that the fact that the Ottomans were to be given Imbros and Tenedos proved British friendship, which did nothing to appease the Grand Vezir on the loss of Chios and Mytilini. He bitterly told Mallet that the British did not want regeneration of the Ottoman Empire: 'They wanted the destruction of Turkey.'[58]

Mallett said he regretted that the Grand Vezir might think England was unfriendly, but what else could the Turks think? The Ottoman feeling was soon to reverberate when World War I began.

Grey wanted military coercion to force the Ottomans to accept the islands settlement. He at first refused to send a note on the Powers' proposal to the Ottoman Government unless it included a military threat, but he was thwarted by opposition from other Powers. Germany refused to militarily coerce the Ottomans. The other Powers also refused Greek Prime Minister Venizelos's proposal, supported by Britain, that the Powers send ships to protect the islands from Turkish attack. Grey accepted defeat and dropped his plan. He told the German ambassador that Britain had no real concern on the islands; he did not care whether Greece or Turkey controlled them – given all that Grey had done, a more than doubtful statement.[59]

The question is why was Grey concerned at all with the feelings of Greece? Greece was already taking a vast amount of territory. Why should Greece receive either Southern Albania or all the Aegean Islands? The political necessity behind keeping Greece out of Southern Albania was real. Italy and her ostensible allies, Austria and Germany, would not accept it. (Southern Albania also had an Albanian majority, not that any of the Powers cared.) But what of the Aegean Islands, particularly those very close to the Anatolian mainland? No argument could be made that the Greeks needed them for defence, whereas the Ottomans obviously did. A demographic argument could surely be made – the islands' populations were Greek – but the demographic argument had not held when majority Muslim populations had been dispossessed. The islands were a Greek–Ottoman conflict waiting to happen, and the Ottoman Government was under intense domestic pressure to reclaim them.[60]

There was no need to combine the Albanian and Aegean Islands questions together. War might conceivably erupt over Southern Albania, but no one threatened it over the islands. Germany, Austria and Italy were willing to use military force to eject Greece from Albania, but Grey refused to sanction the use of force against Greece unless it was also applied to the Ottomans to pressure them to accept Greek annexation of the islands. Grey told the other Powers that if the Greeks, despite gaining the islands, refused to leave Albania, he would only accept military action against them if all the Powers agreed to it. Russia refused to do it, as Grey surely knew. The Powers might have put diplomatic, commercial and military pressure on the Greeks – the sort of pressure that had been used so often against the Ottomans. No such pressure was ever applied. The only British pressure was applied to the Ottoman Government, to make sure that the Ottomans did not go to war with Greece. The fact was that the old principle held – no land that had been under Christian rule, no matter how briefly, should be returned to Ottoman rule. That had been the principle in 1897 and in the attempts to expel the Ottomans from Edirne. It applied to the Aegean Islands.[61]

The Powers decided definitively on 9 February 1914 that Greece would retain the islands.[62]

## The Embassy

As it always had been during the ambassadorship of Gerald Lowther, the embassy was a poor source of information for the British Government, as well as a poor diplomatic resource.

The British seem to have been surprised by the outbreak of the Balkan War. The advice they had received from the Istanbul embassy was completely wrong. Lowther showed little understanding of present or future problems in the Balkans. Writing on the situation in the Balkans, he told Grey in 1908 that 'if trouble is to come, it will be between the different sections of Christians, and not so much between Christians and Turks'. Nicolson wrote on 19

February 1912: 'Lowther is still fairly convinced that there will be no troubles in the Balkans, and indeed that the likelihood of a rising in Albania is very remote.' Nicolson thought Lowther was 'a little too optimistic'.[63]

When the CUP returned to power in 1913, Lowther had lost none of his animosity toward them:

> We have returned to reach the same condition of affair that existed in 1908 namely that the Government is no Government at all but is being run by a handful of desperados and an explosion may occur at any moment.

According to Lowther, the 'desperadoes' were encouraged by the Jews, but most of the population hated them. The CUP Government did not like Britain (perhaps understandably, given that Lowther was Britain's representative).[64]

Ambassador Lowther was usually content to let sensitive negotiations with Ottoman officials on the wars be conducted by Gerald Fitzmaurice, on agendae set by Fitzmaurice. For example, on the outbreak of the first Balkan War, Lowther sent Fitzmaurice to confer with the Grand Vezir. He did not go himself, and it was Fitzmaurice's report of the meeting that Lowther forwarded to London. Once the first war was lost, Fitzmaurice again was the British representative to the Ottoman Government. It is difficult to imagine the Ottomans appreciated his preaching to them like a teacher to students ('I told him it was a moment for pocketing national pride and sentiment and being guided by reason'). Fitzmaurice told Grand Vezir Kâmil that the reason the Balkan Allies did not listen to the advice of the 'elder states' was that they 'had been imitating the contagious example of the younger Turks in not heeding their elders'. According to Fitzmaurice's own words, he complained to Ottoman officials, themselves politicians, that the politicians had ruined the Turkish military. He told them, amazingly, how satisfactorily negotiations had worked out for the Ottomans in the loss of Bosnia in 1908 and in the loss in the Italian War, and thus they should accept their losses once again, this time losses to the Bulgarians, Greeks and Serbs. All would be well if the Ottomans took his advice. He proceeded to present detailed plans for how the Ottomans should negotiate with the Balkan Allies, what they should do in the present situation and what Britain's position would be.

Fitzmaurice announced how pleased he was with his efforts, which he credited for upcoming negotiations between the Ottomans and the Bulgarians (which failed at the time). When Foreign Office officials learned of Fitzmaurice's negotiations on their behalf, which they had not approved, it did not have a calming effect on them. Nicolson and Grey both commented that they had not been aware of what Fitzmaurice had done. Nicolson wrote that Fitzmaurice's statements 'may have raised hopes which cannot be realized and which had better been left unsaid'. If the Ottomans cited Fitzmaurice's conversations in the future, it would be best to change the subject. Grey agreed, because 'several things were said which we could not endorse or authorize and we should therefore say nothing'.[65]

Immediately after the Ottoman defeat in the first Balkan War, Fitzmaurice gloated over Ottoman losses in a letter to William Tyrrell, private secretary to Grey. On the embassy notepaper inscription of 'British Embassy Constantinople' he had struck through 'Constantinople' and written in 'Tzarigrad', the Bulgarian name for the city. He gloried over what he believed to be the imminent Ottoman loss of Istanbul, and blamed the loss on the CUP. The British, he stated, should back the Balkan Allies, 'undoubtedly the right horse'.[66]

Feeling, with much justification, that Fitzmaurice stood in the way of their interests, the Ottoman Government had for some time asked the British to remove Fitzmaurice from the Istanbul embassy, but with little effect. Fitzmaurice suffered a nervous breakdown and finally was sent home in February 1914.

The Foreign Office finally realised it had reason to question Lowther's judgement. Once the Turks had been defeated in the first Balkan War, Lowther predicted the imminent collapse of the Empire. 'The army is in a state of complete collapse.' Lowther expected that the Bulgarians would soon take Istanbul; it was 'just a matter of time'. As usual, he blamed the Empire's troubles on the CUP, even though they had not been in power during the losses of the first war. Lowther hoped and believed that the Bulgarians would take Istanbul, where he believed they would act absolutely correctly and restore order. He wrote that his only worry was that the Turks would massacre Christians in Istanbul and Anatolia in reprisal before the Bulgarians arrived. (Nicholson replied that, unlike Lowther, he hoped the Bulgarians would not take the city. Unlike Lowther, he expected bloodshed in Istanbul only after the Bulgarians took the city.)[67]

Lowther wrote to London with suggestions for the disposition of Edirne and the Aegean Islands, along with his usual negative statements on the Ottoman Government and a totally false statement that the Turkish fleet had been given orders to attack the Greeks. Nicolson commented that Lowther's letter was 'incomprehensible', 'very wrong' and 'misleading'. Nicolson wrote: 'At the present moment our Embassy at Constantinople should be specially careful as to what they say and abstain from giving any advice without first consulting with London.' It was as close as the Foreign Office could come to outright condemnation.[68]

Foreign Secretary Grey decided in April 1913 to remove Lowther from Istanbul. Louis du Pan Mallet was appointed ambassador on 17 June. Until Mallet could arrive, the embassy was in charge of Charles Murray Marling as Chargé d'Affaires from 2 July to 24 October 1913.[69]

Marling was an improvement on Lowther in one respect – he did not blame all evils on Jews and Freemasons. In dealing with the Ottomans, however, he was as bad as Lowther. Like Lowther before him, he hated (not too strong a word) the government of the Committee of Union and Progress. Also like Lowther, he favoured Kâmil Paşa. ('He is the only living Turk with statesmanlike qualities.') When upon taking power Kâmil rounded up CUP members, Marling applauded. ('They have to purify the Administration of Committee agents.') When Kâmil's government did not do well, Marling blamed the secret machinations of the CUP. He deprecated the chances of the CUP ever taking power, however, because he knew the army was against them, an assertion soon proven wrong.[70]

Marling oversaw the British embassy during the second Balkan War, a pivotal time for British diplomacy. He was in charge in Istanbul when the British planned to deny Eastern Thrace and the Aegean Islands to the Ottomans. During the negotiations, Marling felt no need to deal with Turkish officials respectfully and diplomatically. He threatened the Grand Vezir that Turkey would suffer greatly for its reoccupation of Thrace. He declared that all Europe was against the Turks, and soon the Powers would force them to relinquish their gains.[71]

Marling had no understanding of the Turks' desire to retake historically and demographically Turkish lands. He told London that the only reasons for the Turkish advance on Edirne was craven politics:

The existing Committee Government's sole interest in retaking Adrianople, &c., is to enhance the Committee's prestige and strengthen its hold of power, and they will stop only when they are convinced that further advance will injure their position. The Committee's record of the past five years shows that to achieve this end they are ready to risk wrecking what remains of the Empire, nor would they hesitate to embroil Europe in a general war.[72]

Marling was so set against the Turks in 1913 that he even dared to tell Grey how to conduct, or not conduct, negotiations with the Turks. He recommended that the British immediately suspend any talks with İbrahim Hakkı Paşa, who was representing the Ottomans in London, because no negotiations would succeed 'with such people'. All that would work against them would be 'forcible measures' and the loss of territory. He said, unsurprisingly, that the Russian ambassador agreed with him. Marling favoured the Russian suggestion of an occupation of the Enez–Midye Line by the Powers or at least by some of them, but he was frustrated by Austrian absolute refusal. Marling's actions and opinions earned a rebuke from Grey. Alwyn Parker of the Foreign Office was scathing in his criticism of Marling: he stated that Marling 'has lost all sense of proportion' in his proposals. Marling, Parker felt, did not know what was actually transpiring with the Turkish Government or with ongoing negotiations. 'I think the embassy at Constantinople are altogether out of touch with the Turkish Government.'[73]

## Boycott and Greek Emigration

In 1914, as Turkish refugees swarmed into Eastern Thrace and Western Anatolia, popular sentiment rose against the Ottoman Greeks, who were accused of supporting and financing the Hellenic Greeks against the Turks. The sentiment coalesced into a successful boycott of all things Greek. Turks refused to shop in Greek stores. Turkish grocers would not allow Greeks to buy food. There were attacks on Greeks and some murders in rural areas, which had the desired effect of forcing Greeks to flee. Ambassador Mallet noted that the weapon used against the Greeks was intimidation, seldom backed up by physical violence, but nevertheless effective. Large numbers of Ottoman Greeks feared for their lives and livelihoods. Greeks on the Aegean coast and in Western Thrace fled to the islands and to other new Greek territories.[74]

In Thrace, violence against the Greeks was often led by refugees who had been driven from the Balkans or who had suffered from invasions of Thrace by the Balkan Allies. Unlike corresponding conduct in Anatolia, the actions in Thrace were personal. The British head of an investigation commission in Edirne Province, Lieutenant-Colonel V. A. Nye, forwarded an accurate analysis after a tour of the province:

> Before starting, the reports from Greek newspapers had already prepared me to find that the Greeks were suffering ill-treatment at the hands of the Turkish authorities.
>
> I am bound to say that I saw nothing of it. In all the villages where the population was mixed the Greeks were living side by side with their Turkish neighbours apparently free from molestation.
>
> Every Turkish village in the vilayet and the Turkish quarters of all mixed villages are in ruins.
>
> The need of firewood for an army fighting a winter campaign must have been responsible for a large part of the destruction, but by far the greater part of the damage was done by the local Greeks after the withdrawal of the Turks towards Constantinople.
>
> The Turks having returned to their ruined villages, it is not to be expected that friendly feeling can exist between two races in villages where, on the one hand the present owners of the country are practically without shelter, and on the other hand the conquered race are living in houses untouched.
>
> In many cases the Turkish villager knows the name of his Greek neighbour who actually looted and set fire to his home.
>
> If in such a case he prefers to buy his bread from the Turkish instead of the Greek baker the boycott can hardly be attributed to orders from the Government. It is impossible also that isolated acts of aggression or reprisal should not occur. His business gone, and betrayed by his brother Christian, the Greek, either from shame or fear, decides to leave his village.

Nye stated that the local population was suffering from typhus, an infestation of locusts and raids by bands from across the Bulgarian border. A problem, he believed, might come from the mass of Turkish refugees in the province. 'They are at present being fed by the Government, but when the time comes that free bread is no longer forthcoming there is no doubt that they will live on their Christian neighbours.' Nye noted that Ottoman officials had in no way hindered his investigation: 'I journeyed wherever I wished and could have interviewed whomsoever I liked. Officers and local Governors made no attempt to hide anything from me . . .'[75]

While evidence that the boycott was centrally directed has never appeared, and the Ottomans always denied it, there is no question but that local members of the CUP directed the boycott. Refugees and local Turks both acted as 'enforcers', ensuring that Turks did not deal with Greeks. They attacked Greeks, creating an atmosphere of fear. The Ottoman Press kept up popular animosity toward the Greeks. It cited the suffering of Turks in the Greek-occupied regions, in which the Greek Government had allowed the seizure of Turkish farms and shops and had generally persecuted the Turks, as justification for the boycott of the Greeks. Even the newspapers that did not so much call for a boycott offered reasons to dislike Greeks, and surely did not oppose a boycott.[76]

British consuls made detailed lists of actions taken against local Greeks, many minor, but also including destruction of Greek property, theft, physical attacks and some murders. The accounts were often contradictory: the British consul in Salonica, James Morgan, stated that refugees arriving there showed 'no signs of ill-usage', and were 'in general well clad and well nourished', most of them 'bringing their household belongings with them', which showed that they had not been hurriedly forced out. On the other hand, some embassy officials reported fantastic pictures – 45,000 Greek refugees from regions that held less than 40,000 Greeks; 95 per cent of the Greeks had emigrated, etc. The British officials that made the claims did not offer sources for their reports, which undoubtedly came from Greek informants. One main source was the Greek ambassador in London. Ambassador Mallet considered that the reports were highly exaggerated. Nevertheless, the reports did show real attacks on, and intimidation of, Ottoman Greeks.[77]

In fact, no one ever counted the number of Greek refugees. Contemporary estimates varied widely, from 70,000 to 130,000.

Ambassador Mallet strongly protested the boycott and the emigration of Greeks, but showed an understanding of its causes:

> I have been uneasy about the anti-Greek movement and have been doing all I can to convince the Turks of their folly. They are, however, not alone or even principally to blame as refugees are still pouring in from Servia and Greece and have to be put somewhere, that somewhere – generally, unfortunately, is a Greek village – but I believe that this will be stopped.

Mallet said that Talat had given strong orders that Greek emigration should cease.[78]

German Ambassador Hans Freiherr von Wangenheim also counselled the Ottoman Government that anti-Greek activity must stop. He believed, however, that ending them completely was difficult, because Turks saw the sad state of the refugees from the Balkans and wanted revenge: 'The Turkish people are more excited every day by the stories of unspeakable agony from the muhajirs (refugees) returning from New Greece.' Wangenheim recommended strong measures against those who had oppressed Greeks. He believed '[t]he Porte would now proceed with extreme severity against the guilty, especially against offending officials'.[79]

While it never admitted concerted government or CUP-directed actions against Greeks, the Ottoman Government admitted 'excesses' by the local Turkish population in revenge for Greek actions in the war. Courts martial were instituted and arrests made. Talat Paşa was particularly active in calming the situation, touring the affected districts and punishing many of the guilty. Some Turks who had attacked Greeks were condemned to death, others given prison sentences of five to ten years, but few of the locals who sparked the events could have been punished. The government action was effective; the boycott and Greek emigration effectively ceased, although few of the Greek refugees returned.[80]

**Murder, Pillage and Expulsion of Muslims**

Reading British Central Government documents illustrates the nearly complete lack of British Government interest in the Muslim populations of the conquered lands. The settlement in the Treaty of Berlin had at least given lip service to the Muslims of lands lost to Bulgaria, Greece, Serbia and Montenegro, even though nothing was done subsequently to help them. The Treaty of London of 1913 did not even mention their existence.

The British seem to have thought that the only Ottoman concern for the conquered territories was emotional, particularly the status of the Muslim Holy Places and great mosques in Edirne, which had been the second Ottoman capital. Some sort of Bulgarian guarantee to respect the mosques, they believed, should be enough to placate the Ottomans. In fact, the main Ottoman concern was for the people of Ottoman Europe. Immediately before the start of the first Balkan

War, of all the European provinces of the Empire, only Yanya (Janina, Ioannina) did not have a Muslim majority; it was 55 per cent Greek Orthodox.

Ultimately, the Ottoman Refugee Commission (Muhacirin Komisyonu) recorded 414,000 refugees living in what remained to the Empire. The largest group of these were settled in Ottoman Europe and Southeastern Anatolia. They were the survivors. At the end of the Balkan Wars, 632,000 (27 per cent) of the Muslims of Ottoman Europe had died.[81]

The British did not lack information on attacks on Muslims in the Balkan Wars. The reports not only came from the Ottoman Government, although the Ottomans did forward accounts of massacres and forced migration. British consuls and journalists sent in extensive accounts of the theft of Muslim property and the massacre of Muslims. These were detailed and often firsthand accounts. Contrary to what Foreign Secretary Grey was to tell parliament, the consuls had often themselves seen what they reported.

The British reports, far too many to cite here, contained comprehensive and circumstantial evidence of atrocities against Muslims. Most, but by no means all, were committed by irregular bands (*komitajis*) and local Serbian, Montenegrin, Greek and Bulgarian populations. The bands were effectively doing the work of the invading Balkan Allies, ridding the conquered lands of a restive Muslim population. (Consul Greig in Monastir described the bands as 'officially organized'.) Even in the cases when regular soldiers did not take part in the massacres, they did nothing to stop them. The result was the death or expulsion as refugees of 45 per cent of the Muslims of Ottoman Europe.[82]

Examples from the consular reports:

> (Consul Morgan in Cavalla) It may be said without exaggeration that there is hardly a Turkish village in the districts of Cavalla and Drama which has not suffered at the hands of the Bulgarian Comitadjis and of the local Christian population. In many, scores of males have been massacred; in others, rape and pillage have taken place.
>
> In the Cavalla region, apart from the murder of Cavalla Turks by comitadjis, already reported, the massacre of some 200 Turks is announced from Pravishta, and of an equal number at Sarishaban. In the Drama District, Chatalja, Doxat and Kirlikova have been the scene of murders of Turks. Most of these murders took place shortly after the Bulgarian occupation, but some have been of more recent occurrence[83]

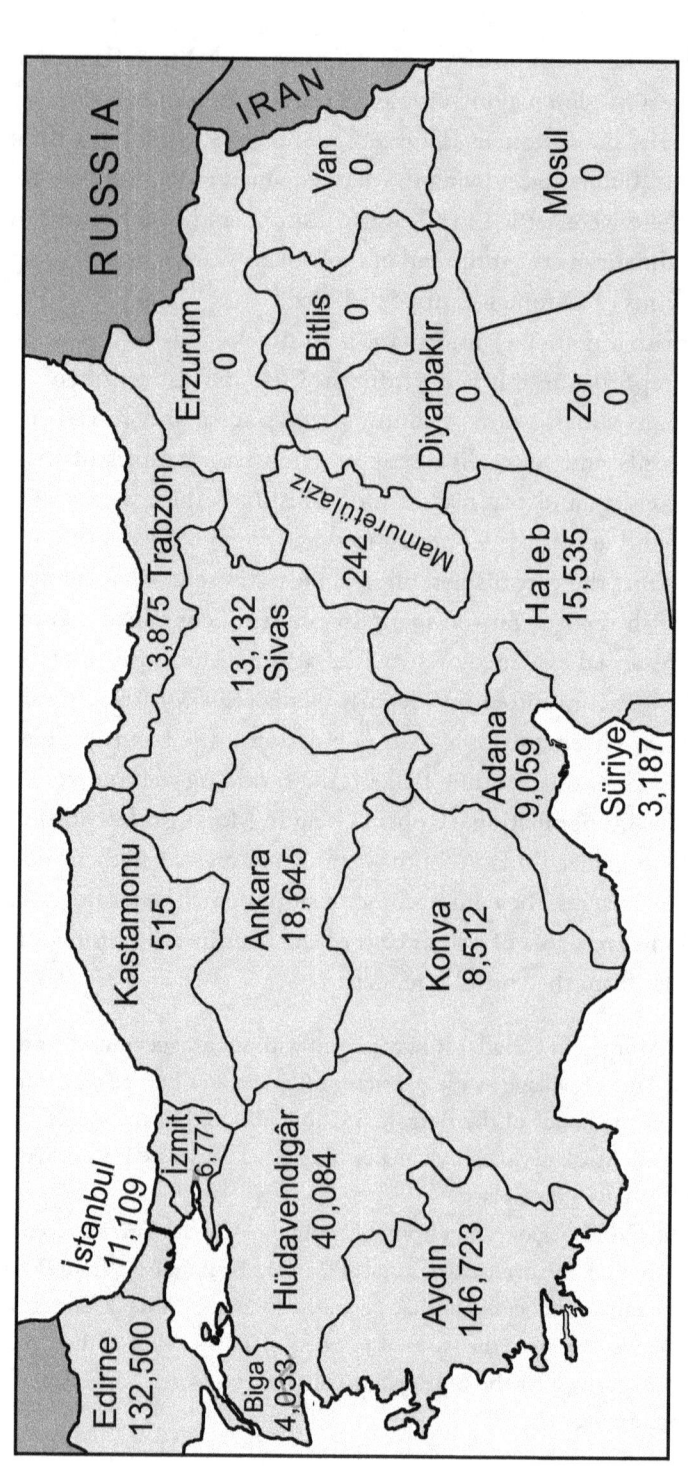

Map 7.4  Muslim refugees from the Balkan Wars

> Throughout the districts of Kilkish, Doiran, and Ghevgheli nearly all the leading Mussulmans have been put to death in one form or another, their property pillaged or destroyed and their farms and dwelling-houses burned. Their women also have been subjected to indignity and often worse.[84]
>
> All the Turks in that place (Strumnitsa) between the ages of 20 and 50, were arrested in daily batches and brought before the Commission, which examined them separately and then decided their fate by votation (that is, by vote). If six out of the seven members of the Court declared him to have been a good man, the 'suspect' was released, after being relieved of everything of value that he might happen to have upon him. If not, he was conducted to prison. After one or two days confinement, the prisoners were first stripped to their shirts, then driven at the point of the bayonet to the slaughter-houses on the outskirts of the town, and finally shot or bayonetted to death. Amongst the victims were a number of soldiers who had laid down their arms, and refugees from Radovishta and Osmanie, who had fled before the advancing foe. Many of these had previously enjoyed an excellent reputation . . . Many of the victims were atrociously mutilated by their executioners, before or after death.[85]

Scores of similar reports were forwarded to the British embassy in Istanbul and to London. The consular reports were specific. For example: in Rajanova, 'scarcely a male Muslim has been left alive'. 'All of the males of the village of Kurkut, along with many of the women and children, were collected in the mosque and in barns and were burned to death.' In Demir Hisar, sixty-four Turks were gathered together and burned to death in a coffee house. Serbian komitajis flogged the Muslim villagers of Drenova to death. '(Serres) in the space of about two hours, between 150 and 200 Turks were slaughtered and nearly every Mussulman house or shop was pillaged.'[86]

The British Government could not truthfully state that it had not received reliable information on Muslim suffering in the Balkans. The consuls who reported atrocities against Muslims included: Morgan from Cavalla, Lamb from Salonica and Vallona, Greig from Monastir, Young from Cavalla and Philippopolis, Samson from Edirne, O'Reilly from Sofia, as well as Harris from the Dardanelles. The consular reports were damning indictments of the Balkan Allies. Even Ambassador Lowther, no friend of the Turks, acknowledged the Christian massacres of Muslims, which he called 'a big thing'. Foreign Secretary Grey and the cabinet did not want them to be known.[87]

Both houses of parliament engaged in spirited debates on Muslim suffering in the Balkan Wars and the Muslim refugee problem. The debates were marked by two common factors – a general lack of real information and a great amount of misinformation; misinformation so excessive that much of it was nonsense. The fault lay with the British Government, and in particular with His Majesty's Secretary of State for Foreign Affairs, Sir Edward Grey.

Had the reports of British consuls in the Balkans been given to parliament and the public, they would have shown extensive massacres of Muslims. The foreign secretary obviously did not want such reports to be seen. Grey was asked by the MP Lieut-Colonel Walter Guinness in the Commons if the government would publish the consular documents on 'massacres and outrages in the Balkan war'. Grey responded that he would not do so, although, '[s]uch reports as I receive that seem to be well founded have been brought to the notice of the Governments that now control the territories in which outrages are said to have occurred.' Guinness then asked:

> May I ask whether it has not been the practice of the right hon. Gentleman in recent years to publish many Consular reports dealing with atrocities by Christians and Mahomedans and the like in Macedonia, and must not his refusal to publish such returns at the present juncture, dealing, as it is believed, chiefly with Christian atrocities, only lend additional colour to the present disquieting rumours (of atrocities on Muslims)?[88]

Grey refused to publish the reports. Instead, he questioned their accuracy, stating, completely falsely, that they were only hearsay and the consuls had actually seen nothing themselves. He repeatedly stated that the only action he had taken on reports of murders and pillage of Muslims was to relate them 'unofficially' to the Balkan governments. The only action Grey was willing to take on reports of atrocities against Muslims was to send the reports to those responsible for the atrocities. Even then, he stated he would only forward the few he considered 'well-founded'. His Majesty's Government, which had been willing to publish spurious and much redacted reports on Macedonia, was unwilling to publish anything on Muslim suffering in the Balkan Wars.[89]

Grey might have found comfort in at least some of the reports he received from Istanbul. In July of 1913, as the evidence of murders and forced exile of Muslims by the Balkan Allies mounted, Chargé Marling ignored the reports of the British consuls. He wrote to London that Turkish reports of atrocities by Bulgarians were fakes ('willful misrepresentations') invented by the Ottomans to enlist European sympathy. He said there was no evidence of atrocities. Less than one month later, overwhelmed by the evidence, he was forced to admit there might be some truth to the reports of barbarism. However, he wrote that, if the Bulgarians had committed any atrocities, they should be understood, because 'they were avenging centuries of "Turkish misrule and oppression"'.[90]

On 19 February 1913, Lord Lamington reported to the House of Lords on atrocities against the Muslims of the Balkans:

> [I]n numerous districts not a living soul has been left. All have been wiped off the face of the earth, occasionally women and children being spared to destitution and starvation, but mostly massacred with the rest. In some places men have been butchered like cattle.

He asked for publication of the consular reports on the war, which the foreign secretary had so far refused to provide. Viscount Morley, Lord President of the Council, responded for the government, questioning in insulting terms the statement of Lord Lamington ('His standard of proof is lower than I have ever come in contact with in my whole life.' 'Illustrations of opinion and report which struck me, if he will pardon me for saying so, as really nothing short of worthless.') Lamington responded, in effect: 'Then prove it by showing us the consular reports.' The government refused to do so. Morley did say, however, that actions against Muslims were all perpetrated by bands of irregulars who were being punished (something which never happened). 'The Bulgarian Prime Minister has stated that no outrages have been committed by the Bulgarian regular troops.' The Bulgarian prime minister's assertion was an outright lie.[91]

Lord Lamington rose once again in the House of Lords on 16 July 1913 to ask the government what it would do to secure the rights of Muslims to return to the homes from which they had been forced to flee. He spoke of 150,000 or 200,000 Muslim refugees (a large undercount) in Istanbul and Anatolia, and of terrible atrocities that had been visited on the Balkan Muslims. Their homes had been burned and their property seized. Lord Newton added that, while the Christians were aided by European consuls and missionaries, few were aiding the Muslims. The Balkan Allies would never help them. Was it not the moral duty of the Powers to do so? Again speaking for the government, Viscount Morley responded that there was no precedent for the British Government helping people in such situations (a true statement), and they would not do it now. He said the Balkan States were preserving the property of the Muslims and would return it to them after the war. The British had 'made representations' to the Balkan Allies about the state of the Muslims. 'I can assure the two noble Lords that this painful matter is, as I have already said, receiving the attentive consideration of the Foreign Office.' Whether he was simply naïve or was lying remains up for debate.[92]

The British Government wanted no public sympathy for the Turks. Worse, from the standpoint of a politician, was the fact that Britain had done nothing, not even forcibly protesting the murderous actions of the Balkan Allies. Rather, Britain had laboured to make sure the Allied invasion of the Ottoman Empire was successful.

## 'The Sympathy of Great Britain'

Harkening back to the spirit of the Congress of Berlin, and even the Congress of Vienna, the British often described a Congress of Europe – a diplomatic and political unity in which the Great Powers would insure peace in Europe. No such concert ever actually existed. It is true that Foreign Secretary Grey always worked to have unanimous decisions of the Powers to support British proposals on the Balkan problem, but the only real binding force behind agreements among the Powers was fear of a European war, not any unity of purpose. Grey worked successfully to keep the Triple Entente and the Triple Alliance from each other's throats in Albania. His commitment to Greece and Bulgaria, however, went far beyond the needs of peace among the Powers. It was another step in the longstanding British dedication to the dismemberment of the Ottoman Empire.

Whatever the political and diplomatic actions, nothing showed Britain's real attitude toward the Ottomans Muslims so much as Grey's refusal to even consider Muslim mortality in the Balkan Wars and Muslim expulsion from the Balkans. Lack of concern for Muslim lives had been the British position since 1878. It was to continue after World War I.

In 1897, when the Ottomans had won a war, they had lost more than they gained. In 1912, when the Ottomans lost, they were to lose everything. Moreover, the British upheld the 'Salisbury Principle' that no land that had been taken by Christians could ever again be ruled by Muslims; the Ottomans were not to be allowed to keep even Eastern Thrace, which they had regained after a brief loss, or islands needed for strategic defence. Muslims retaking land that had been lost to Christians offended the British, who demanded that the Ottomans abandon their gains. In Istanbul, British Ambassador Mallet told the Ottoman Government that the Turks should be happy to relinquish both Edirne and the Aegean Islands, because this 'would gain them the sympathy of Europe and especially of Great Britain'.[93]

The Ottomans knew what the sympathy of Great Britain was worth. They declined the British advice.

## Notes

1. 'Full Text of Convention Between the United Kingdom and Russia Relating to Persia, Afghanistan, and Thibet (sic), Signed at St. Petersburgh, August 31, 1907', in BDOW 4, pp. 618–20. Firuz Kazemzadeh, *Russia and Britain in Persia 1864–1914: A Study in Imperialism*, New Haven: Yale University Press, 1968, pp. 448–509.
2. Two months before the convention was signed, Grey told the Iranians the straight-out lie that Russia and Britain were not dividing Iran into spheres of influence, which they had already agreed to do. The Russians told them that Russia would not intervene in Iran unless the interests of Russian subjects were attacked. (Grey to Sir C. Spring-Rice, Foreign Office, 21 June 1907, in BDOW 4, pp. 474–5.) The terms of the convention that applied to Iran were first presented to the Iranian Government on 24 September 1907, nearly a month after it was signed. (Spring-Rice to Sir Edward Grey, Tehran, 25 September 1907, in BDOW 4, p. 599.)

    On the Russo-Japanese War, see: Kees van Dijk, 'The Russo-Japanese War', in *Pacific Strife: The Great Powers and their Political and Economic Rivalries in Asia and the Western Pacific 1870–1914*, Amsterdam: Amsterdam University Press, 2015, pp. 417–38, and John Albert White, *Diplomacy of the Russo-Japanese War*, Princeton: Princeton University Press, 1964.

    Harry N. Howard, *The Partition of Turkey: A Diplomatic History 1913–1923*, Norman, Oklahoma: University of Oklahoma Press, 1931, contains much information drawn from European printed sources. It is, however, of limited value

for this study, because its early publication date meant that few of the important British documents were available. The important BDOW volume nine and subsequent volumes had not been printed in 1931, and most of the British archival record was still closed. Even though volumes one to six of BDOW were available in 1931, he only cited BDOW twice.
3. Edward C. Thaden, *Russia and the Balkan Alliance of 1912*, University Park, Pennsylvania: Pennsylvania State University Press, 1965, pp. 9–25.
4. FO 800/357/3, Nicolson to Lowther, 11 June 1912. FO 800/355/2, Nicolson to Lowther, Foreign Office, 29 April 1912. FO 800/354/1, Bax-Ironside to Nicolson, Sofia, 24 March 1912. Serge (sic) Sazonov described Russia's fostering of the Bulgarian–Serbian alliance in *Fateful Years, 1909–1916*, London: Cape, 1928, pp. 52–5. While accurate on this point, Sazonov's self-serving book in general has to be approached with caution. For details on the dealings among the Russia and Balkan Allies before the first war, see: Thaden, pp. 58–108. Andrew Rossos, *Russia and the Balkans: Inter-Balkan Rivalries and Russian Foreign Policy: 1908–1914*, Toronto: University of Toronto Press, 1981, pp. 8–69, and the history in Bax-Ironside to Grey, Sofia, 6 January 1913, in BDOW 9/2, pp. 360–8, Fs. 468. On the diplomatic situation before the Balkan Wars, see Gül Tokay, 'The Origins of the Balkan Wars: A Reinterpretation', in M. Hakan Yavuz and Isa Blumi, eds, *War and Nationalism: The Balkan Wars, 1912–1913, and their Sociopolitical Implications*, Salt Lake City: University of Utah Press, 2013, pp. 176–96. The Greece alliance was in theory only defensive, but proved to be anything but.
5. Throughout his correspondence on the Balkan situation, Arthur Nicolson was sincerely worried that there would be a European war – Austria against Russia – drawing in the other Powers. The problem was especially to erupt over Serbia, Albania and the Adriatic. See the many examples in FO 360/2, 361/1 and 361/2. Arthur Nicolson had fairly wide experience in the Ottoman Empire, having served in the Istanbul embassy, where he developed a dislike for Abdülhamid II. He travelled extensively in Anatolia and Coastal Syria. Harold Nicolson's supposed biography of his father (*Sir Arthur Nicolson, Bart, First Lord Carnock: A Study in the Old Diplomacy*, London: Constable, 1930) is actually an incomplete and biased history of diplomatic events. It offers little light on Arthur Nicolson's opinions and actions on Ottoman problems. The book also has demonstrable errors, such as that the Ottomans did not ask Britain for mediation in the Italian Wars (p. 391).

    Arthur Nicolson's own letters, cited extensively here, are a much better guide.
6. 'Firman Providing an Organic Law, etc. for the Island of Crete, 1868', in Thomas Erskine Holland, *The European Concert in the Eastern Question*, Oxford: Clarendon

Press, 1885, pp, 77–83. Nicolson believed the Ottomans were sincere in planning reforms, perhaps Macedonian autonomy, and said Britain's pressure should be to restrain the Balkan Allies. (FO 800/359/2. Nicolson to Hardinge, 29 September 1912.)

On European diplomacy and the Balkan Wars, see Bridge and Bullen, pp. 316–28.

7. FO 424/234, Grey to Cartwright, Foreign Office, 9 September 1912; 'Draft Agreement', enclosure in Bertie to Grey, Paris, 22 September and 7 October 1912; Grey to Bertie, Foreign Office, 25 September and 12 October 1912; Bax-Ironside to Grey, Sophia, 12 October 1912. FO 800/354/1. Bax-Ironside to Nicolson, Sofia, 26 February 1912. FO 800/1/1912, Barclay to Nicolson, 21 September 1912. Cartwright to Grey, Vienna, 14 October 1912, in BDOW 9/2, pp. 20–1. Note that the documents listed here for one recipient (for example, 'Grey to Cartwright') were sometimes copied to many British ambassadors in Europe and only one is cited. Rossos, *Russia and the Balkans*, pp. 64–79. Thaden, pp. 109–16.

8. The military actions in the Balkan Wars are very well described in comprehensive detail in Edward J. Erickson, *Defeat in Detail: The Ottoman Army in the Balkans. 1912–1913*, Westport, CT: Praeger, 2003. See also the general history of the Balkan Wars in Richard C. Hall, *The Balkan Wars 1912–13: Prelude to the First World War*, London: Routledge, 2000, and, especially, Turkey, Genel Kurmay Başkanlığı, *Balkan Harbi Tarihi*, 7 vols, Istanbul and Ankara: Genel Kurmay Basımevi, 1938–65. The Carnegie Report (Carnegie Endowment, *Report of the International Commission to Inquire into the Causes and Conduct of the Balkan Wars*, Washington: The Endowment, 1914) contains interesting material, but is deeply flawed by its pro-Bulgarian, anti-Turkish and anti-Greek biases.

9. FO 800/358/2, Nicolson to Grey, relating conversations with Russian Foreign Minister Sazonov, 1 October 1912. Sazonov was particularly concerned that Austria not interfere, which might lead to war with Russia.

10. FO 424/234, Grey to Bertie, Foreign Office, 28 October 1912; Grey to Goschen, Foreign Office, 5 November 1912; Grey to Bertie, Foreign Office, 6 November 1912; Grey to Goschen, Foreign Office, 6 November 1912. Grey to Bax-Ironside, Foreign Office, 8 November 1912, in BDOW 9/2, p. 119. FO 800/359/2, Nicolson to Lowther, Foreign Office, 13 November 1912. The Ottomans had made a previous offer to Britain to take the initiative in bringing peace. (Lowther to Grey, Constantinople, 21 October 1912 in DBOW 9/2, pp. 40–1.)

11. Grey to Buchanan, Foreign Office, 1 November 1912 in DBOW 9/2, pp. 74–5. Grey to Rodd, Foreign Office, 1 November 1912, in BDOW 9/2, pp. 72–3.

    The Russian position changed significantly over the course of the Balkan Wars. At first, Russia's concern was the fate of Istanbul, and they even planned to send ships and troops to defeat a Bulgarian occupation. They were initially against Bulgarian occupation of Edirne, then supported it. (Ronald Bobroff, 'Behind the Balkan Wars: Russian Policy toward Bulgaria and the Turkish Straits, 1912–13', *Russian Review*, vol. 59, no. 1 (January 2000), pp. 76–95.)

12. The pamphlets were collected in Balkan Committee, *The Question of the Balkans, Past, Present, and Future*, London: The Balkan Committee, 1912. In fact, in Britain there was little agitation of the sort seen previously, perhaps because events had happened too quickly or because the goals of anti-Turkish groups had been met, at least during the first war. The best analysis of the British press and the Balkan Wars is Pamela J. Dorn Sezgin, 'Between Cross and Crescent: British Diplomacy and Press Opinion toward the Ottoman Empire in Resolving the Balkan Wars, 1912–1913', in Yavuz and Blumi, pp. 423–73. See also: Sevtap Demirci, *British Public Opinion towards the Ottoman Empire during the Two Crises: Bosnia-Herzegovina (1908–1909), the Balkan Wars (1912–1913)*, Istanbul: Isis, 2006, pp. 39–56. Dackombe, pp. 123–32. Georgia Kouta, 'The London Greek Diaspora and National Politics: The Anglo-Hellenic League and the Idea of Greece, 1913–1919', unpublished PhD dissertation, King's College London, 2015.

13. 'The Balkan Committee', *The Times*, 3 January 1913, p. 5. 'Balkan Committee and the Terms of Peace', *The Times*, 27 March 1913, p. 5. Another committee, the Aegean Islands Committee, had a limited effect.

14. 'The War in the Balkans', House of Lords Debate, 8 October 1912, *Hansard*, vol. 12, cc. 815–7. 'Balkan Settlement (British Interests)', House of Commons Debate, 11 December 1912, *Hansard*, vol. 45, cc. 449–52. 'War in Balkans', House of Commons Debate, 5 December 1912, *Hansard*, vol. 44, cc. 2477–8, "War in Balkans', House of Commons Debate, 15 July 1913, *Hansard*, vol. 55, c. 1036. 'War in Balkans', House of Commons Debate, 24 July 1913, *Hansard*, vol. 55, cc. 2189–90.

15. 'British Ministers and the War', *The Times*, 21 October 1912, p. 5. Charles Mastermann said he had been misquoted, but that he had not written to *The Times* for a retraction or to establish what his actual views were. Other MPs were not convinced by his denials. ('War in Balkans', House of Commons Debate, 23 October 1912, *Hansard*, vol. 42, cc. 2180–2.) 'Mr. Churchill on the War', *The Times*, 31 October 1912, p. 5. 'The Powers and the War', *The Times*, 11 November 1912, p. 9. *The Times* called it 'The Prime Minister's admirable speech'.

16. For some reason the meetings were called the Reunion of the Ambassadors in documents.
17. Justin McCarthy, 'The Population of Ottoman Europe Before and After the Fall of the Empire', in *Proceedings of the Third Congress on the Social and Economic History of Turkey*, Istanbul: Isis, 1990, pp. 281–7.
18. Grey to Cartwright, Foreign Office, 4 and 7 January 1913, in BDOW 9/2, pp. 354–5 and 372–3. The French proposed slightly different wording than Grey's; the effect was the same.
19. Grey to Cartwright, Foreign Office, 10 January 1913, in BDOW 9/2, pp. 390–1. The démarche was presented to the Ottomans on 16 January 1913, delayed by a few days.
20. FO 424/241, Cartwright to Grey, Vienna, 11 January 1913; Goschen to Grey, Berlin, 12 and 13 January 1913; Grey to Goschen, Foreign Office, 15 January 1913; Grey to Buchanan, Foreign Office, 17 January 1913. FO 424/241, Grey to Lowther, Foreign Office, 4 January 1913.
21. Grey to Cartwright, Foreign Office, 14 January 1913, in BDOW 9/2, pp. 405–6.
22. FO 424/241, Lowther to Grey, Constantinople, 22 and 23 January 1913. FO 424/242, Memorandum communicated by Tewfik Pasha, London, 26 February 1913; Lowther to Grey, Constantinople, 26 February 1913; Bax-Ironside to Grey, Sophia, 27 February 1913. On the CUP coup, see Ahmad, *Young Turks*, pp. 116–20.
23. Grey to Cartwright, Foreign Office, 9 January 1913 in DBOW 9/2, pp. 379–80. Grey to Bax-Ironside, Foreign Office, 9 January 1913, in BDOW 9/2, p. 381. Grey to Goschen, Foreign Office, 14 January 1913, in BDOW 9/2, p. 404. Cambon to Poincaré, London, 12 January 1913, in DD 5, no. 210.
24. See, among others, the many documents in FO 421/286, FO 800/372/1 and FO 800/372/2. FO 800/373/2, Nicolson to Mallet, Foreign Office, 27 April 1914. The Russians at first had intimated that they would not be averse to Ottoman retention of Chios and Mytilini, because they were so close to the mainland, but soon changed their minds. (FO 421/286, Grey to Bertie, Foreign Office, 24 November 1913.)
25. Grey to Cartwright, Foreign Office, 4 January 1913, in BDOW 9/2, pp. 354–5. Lowther to Grey, Constantinople, 1 February 1913, in BDOW 9/2, pp. 467–70. Cambon to Poincaré, London, 4 January 1913, in DD 5, no. 167. Poincaré objected to the threats to the Ottomans as 'unnecessary and imprudent'. The French were especially concerned that no financial commitment be made to the Ottomans by the Powers as inducement. (Poincaré to Cambon, Paris, 7 January 1913, and Cambon to Poincaré, London, 7 January 1913, in DD 5, nos. 187 and 188.) By

January 10, however, Cambon had submitted a draft note to the Ottoman Government, approved by the others, that included the threats and the wholly deceptive financial inducements. The note was delivered to the Ottomans on 17 January. (Cambon to Poincaré, London, 10 January 1913, and Bompard to Poincaré Pera, 17 January 1913, in DD 5, nos. 204 and 230.)

26. Enclosure in Grey to Lowther, Foreign Office, 15 February 1913, in BDOW 9/2, p. 502. Grey to Cartwright, Foreign Office, 1 February 1915, in BDOW 9/2, pp. 471–2.
27. Grey to Cartwright, Foreign Office, 1 February 1915, in BDOW 9/2, pp. 471–2.
28. FO 371/1789, Grey to Goschen, Foreign Office, 20 February 1913; 'Pro-memoria Communicated by Tewfik Pasha', 24 February 1913; Grey to Lowther, Foreign Office, 4 March 1913. FO 371/1796, Grey to Lowther, Foreign Office, 28 February 1913.
29. FO 371/1813, British Delegates on Financial Commission to Grey, Paris, 1 July 1913, which includes detailed accounts. Montenegro planned to submit more later. On the Ottoman budget: Stanford J. Shaw, 'Ottoman Expenditures and Budgets in the Late Nineteenth and Early Twentieth Centuries', *International Journal of Middle East Studies*, vol. 9, no. 3 (October 1978), pp. 373–8.
30. FO 371/1796, Bax-Ironside to Grey, Sophia, 14 March 1913. On the Allies' delays, see the extensive documentation in FO 424/243 and FO 371/1796.
31. FO 424/243, Grey to Lowther, Foreign Office, 15 March 1913. FO 800/94, in the Nicolson papers: no date and place information on the document, presumably London, May 1913. FO 424/244, Note communicated by Sublime Porte, enclosure in Lowther to Grey, Constantinople, 3 April 1913. See also FO 800/366/2, Nicolson to Lowther, Foreign Office, 30 April 1913.

    The French had suggested that if the Balkan Allies refused to accept a peace conference, the Powers tell them that they will offer no economic aid to them. They might instead threaten to give economic aid to Turkey in their fight. (FO 424/243, Bertie to Grey, Paris, 12 March 1913.)
32. FO 424/243, Grey to Goschen, Foreign Office, 17 March 1913. FO 424/244, Grey to Bertie, Foreign Office, 1 April 1913; FO 424/244, Grey to Baz-Ironside, Foreign Office, 8 April 1913. FO 424/244, Memorandum Communicated by Count Benckendorff, London, 7 April 1913. See also FO 371/1795, Grey to Bertie, Foreign Office, 1 April 1913; Buchanan to Grey, St Petersburgh, 11 April 1913. On British and bondholders' losses if an indemnity was paid, see also FO 371/1795, 'Memorandum by Sir. A. Block', enclosure in Lowther to Grey, Constantinople, 18 June 1913, and FO 371/1812, Mallet to Treasury, Foreign Office, 23 May 1913. There is much on indemnities in FO 371/1795.

33. Elliot to Grey, Athens, 21 April 1913, in BDOW 9/2, pp. 705–6. Ambassadors in the other Allies' capitals were presented with identic telegrams. The Powers had told the Allies that the Enez–Midye Line would be demanded. (Lowther to Grey, Constantinople, 31 March 1913, in BDOW 9/2, p. 624.) They notified the Allies that the questions of Albania and the islands would be decided solely by the Powers. (Grey to Elliot, Foreign Office, 23 April 1913, in BDOW 9/2, p. 710.) The Balkan Allies demands for indemnities were rejected. (FO 424/244, Paget to Grey, Belgrade, 5 April 1913.)
34. FO 424/245, Conférence de Saint-James, Protocole No. 11, Séance du 17 (30) mai 1913, Annexe. There was much debate over the terms of the draft treaty, but the British suggestions carried with minor alterations. See the many documents in FO 424/245.
35. See Erickson, *Defeat in Detail*, pp. 317–30. In March of 1913 Nicolson and the British ambassadors in the Balkans all agreed that the Balkan Allies would soon fight over the spoils. There is much on this in FO 800/364/2.

    Tevfik Paşa, the Ottoman ambassador at London, had predicted that as soon as Ottoman Europe was divided among the Allies they would be at each other's throats. (FO 424/235, Grey to Lowther, Foreign Office, 12 November 1912.)
36. 'War in the Balkans: Statement by Sir Edward Grey', House of Commons, 12 August 1914, *Hansard*, vol. 56, cc. 2281–352. In the same debate, Noel Buxton spoke in defence of the Bulgarians and of his sorrow at what they had lost. He was against the Ottomans retaining Edirne. He blamed the recent wars on the Turks. Prime Minister Asquith echoed Grey's statements that the Turks should not retake Eastern Thrace. ('Mr. Asquith on the War', *The Times*, 22 July 1913, p. 8. See also, no title, *Spectator*, 15 November 1913, p. 17.) Regarding British pressure on the Turks, see Joseph Heller, *British Policy Towards the Ottoman Empire, 1908–1914*, London: Cass, 1983, pp. 72–82, although I believe Heller has misinterpreted Grey's policy toward the Turks.
37. There are many documents on forcing the Ottomans not to advance in FO 424/247. See, for instance, Grey to Bertie, Foreign Office, 15 July 1913. The Powers had agreed to accept an advance from Çatalca to the Enez–Midye Line. (FO 424/247, Grey to Bertie, Foreign Office, 8 July 1913, and other documents in FO 424/247.) On the threat of Russian intervention, see FO 424/247, Grey to Marling, Foreign Office, 16 July 1913. For a time Grey seems to have sincerely believed that Russia would intervene. (FO 424/247, Grey to Granville, Foreign Office, 25 July 1913.)

    FO 424/247, Grey to Marling, Foreign Office, 26 July 1913. FO 424/248, Grey to Buchanan, Foreign Office, 14 August 1913. Hakki told Grey that the retaking of Edirne was so popular that if withdrawal from Edirne was ordered, it would be the government that would have to evacuate Istanbul. FO 371/1837, Minutes by Mr Parker, 25 July 1913. Parker was repeating Grey's ideas. Parker himself soon felt the Turks should stay in Edirne, as seen below. FO 371/1764, Grey to Rodd, Foreign Office, 9 January 1913. See also FO 371/1764, Grey to Rodd, Foreign Office, 13 January 1913. The Germans wanted a formal guarantee of the integrity of Asia Minor, but Grey was not willing to give it, putting the question off until the war was over. (Grey to Goschen, Foreign Office, 24 January 1913, in BDOW 9/2, p. 444.)

38. Zimmermann to Lichnowsky, Berlin, 17 August 1913, in GP 36/1, pp. 21–2.
39. Delcassé to Pichon, St Petersburg, 22 June 1913, in DD 7, no. 441.
40. Bertie to Grey, Paris, 2 November 1912, in BDOW 9/2, p. 79. Buchanan to Grey, St Petersburgh, 4 November 1912, in BDOW 9/2, pp. 92–3. FO 424/247, Telegrams from M. Sazonof to Count Benckendorff, communicated to Foreign Office, 22 and 23 July 1913. 424/247, Bertie to Grey, Paris, 26 July 1913. FO 371/1837, Grey to Cartwright, Foreign Office, 24 July 1913. FO 800/368, Buchanon to Nicolson, St Petersburg, 23 July 1913. See also FO 371/1838, 'Note Communicated by M. de Fleuriay', London, 20 August 1913. FO 424/248, Marling to Grey, Constantinople, 18 August 1913. Buchanan to Grey, St Petersburgh, 18, 21 and 23 July 1913, in BDOW 9/2, pp. 920–1, 923–4 and 931–2. Buchanan to Grey, St Petersburgh, 19 August 1913, in BDOW 9/2, pp. 989–91. FO 424/248, Buchanan to Grey, St Petersburgh, 8 August 1913. Bompard to Poincarè, Pera, 23 December 1912, in DD 5, no. 111. 'Note de l'Ambassade de Russie', Paris, 24 July 1913, in DD 7, no. 460. Pourtales to Bethmann-Hollweg, St Petersburg, 4 August 1913, in GP 36/1, pp. 14–17. Zimmerman to Tschirschky, Berlin, 11 August 1913, in GP 36/1, pp. 17–18. Kaiser Wilhelm stated that both Austria and Russia 'had made so many mistakes'. He rejected Grey's suggestion of military intervention, and felt that Germany should do nothing and wait on events. (Kaiser Wilhelm II to Foreign Office, Homburg, 16 August 1913, in GP 36/1, pp. 27–30.)

For the Russians, one possibility might be an attack on Eastern Anatolia, but they felt it would be too much trouble and little gain to them. They feared that Austria might feel free to take action against Serbia as a pretext if Russia acted alone. They believed the Ottomans would be brought to heel by notice that they would not be given the 4 per cent customs increase they desired or any financial assistance. (See FO 424/248, Buchanan to Grey, St Petersburgh, 9 August 1913; Memorandum communicated by M. Fleuriau, London, 13 August 1913; Grey to Buchanan, Foreign Office, 14 August 1913.) See also Cambon to Pichon,

London, 12 August 1913, in DD 8, no. 19. On Russian reasons for standing down, see Kurat, pp. 186–93.
41. FO 424/248, Grey to Buchanan, Foreign Office, 16 August 1913. Pourtales to Bethmann-Hollweg, St Petersburg, 21 August 1913, in GP 36/1, pp. 42–3. The Germans did not think the proposed financial pressure would work. (FO 371/1838, Goschen to Grey, Berlin, 19 August 1913.) The Germans were completely against any military or naval demonstration.
42. FO 424/248, Grey to Granville, Foreign Office, 5 August 1913. FO 424/241, Grey to Bertie, Foreign Office, 15 January 1913. FO 424/236, 'Memorandum respecting British Trade with the Balkans', Board of Trade, 11 December 1912. Grey was willing to consider an increase of Ottoman customs duties to 15 per cent, however, in exchange for a better arrangement for the British on duties in the Shatt al-Arab. Nothing came of it. (FO 424/245, 'Foreign Office Board of Trade', Foreign Office, 9 May 1913.)
43. 'War in Balkans', House of Commons Debate, 31 July 1913, *Hansard*, vol. 56, cc. 700–2.
44. FO 424/248, Goschen to Grey, Berlin, 15 August 1913. FO 371/1838, Marling to Grey, Constantinople, 8 August 1913. Granville to Grey, Berlin, 16 July 1913, in BDOW 9/2, p. 914. FO 800/180A, Bertie to Grey, Paris, 23 July 1913; Bertie Memorandum, Martigny-les-Bains, 27 July 1913.
45. FO 371/1837, Marling to Grey, Constantinople, 11 August 1913.
46. FO 371/1837, Hakki to Grey, London, 2 August 1913. For similar complaints made to the French, see Bompard to Poincarè, Pera, 30 December 1912, in DD 5, no. 147.
47. FO 371/1837, minutes in Hakki to Grey, London, 2 August 1913, and Marling to Grey, Constantinople, 15 August 1913. FO 800/369, Nicolson to O'Beirne, Foreign Office, 22 September 1913.
48. FO 800/180A, Bertie Memorandum, London, 23 July 1913.
49. Marling to Grey, Constantinople, 30 September 1913, in BDOW 9/2, p. 1002. Dedeağaç remained in Bulgarian hands. A small region of Northeastern Thrace was ceded to the Bulgarians when the Ottomans entered World War I.
50. FO 371/1764, Grey to Elliot, Foreign Office, 2 January 1913. FO 424/245, Grey to Elliot, Foreign Office, 26 May 1913; Grey to Elliot, Foreign Office, 26 May 1913. When the King of Greece visited London Grey assured him that Chios and Mytilini would go to Greece. (FO 371/1841, 27 September 1913.)

The award of the Aegean Islands to Greece was bound up in extensive negotiations and conflict among the Powers, Greece, Serbia and Montenegro. See: R. J. Crampton, *The Hollow Détente: Anglo-German Relations in the Balkans,*

*1911–1914*, London: George Prior, 1979, pp. 112–66, and 'The Decline of the Concert of Europe in the Balkans, 1913–1914', *The Slavonic and East European Review*, vol. 52, no. 128 (July 1974), pp. 393–419. William Peter Kaldis, 'Background for Conflict: Greece, Turkey, and the Aegean Islands, 1912–1914', *The Journal of Modern History*, vol. 51, no. 2 (June 1979), pp. D1119–D1146.

51. FO 371/1764, Grey to Rodd, Foreign Office, 9 January 1913. FO 424/246, Grey to Lowther, Foreign Office, 5 June 1913. FO 800/365, Nicolson to Hardinge, Foreign Office, 17 April 1913. FO 371/1764, Rodd to Grey, Rome, 14 January 1913. Cambon to Poincaré, London, 15 January 1913, in DD 5, no. 217. The Ottomans felt Crete, Cyprus and Samos had 'turbulent populations' and were willing for them to go to Greece, not the other islands. FO 371/1764, Lowther to Grey, Constantinople, 11 January 1913.
52. FO 800/362/1913, Nicolson to Lowther, Foreign Office, 8 January 1913.
53. FO 800/362, Nicolson to Lowther, Foreign Office, 8 January 1913, and FO 800/365, Nicolson to Hardinge, Foreign Office, 17 April 1913. Grey to Cartwright, Foreign Office, 7 January 1913, in DBOW 9/2, pp. 372–3. Grey to Elliot, Foreign Office, 9 January 1913, in BDOW 9/2, p. 382. FO 424/249, Grey to Dering, Foreign Office, 29 October 1913. Cambon to Pichon, London, 5 and 6 October 1913, in DD 8, nos. 265 and 274. There is extensive documentation of the deliberations over the Southern Albania question in BDOW 9/2, especially pp. 691–851. The Greek ambassador told Grey that he had heard rumours that the Powers might take the islands away from Greece. Grey told him the Powers had not lately considered the question. However, as Greece was in occupation, it was better for Greece not to raise the question. (FO 421/286, Grey to Elliot, Foreign Office, 25 November 1913.)

    I have not considered here the intense diplomatic problems over Montenegrin and Serbian access to the Adriatic, because it is beyond the scope of this study. See the extensive documentation in DD 6 and 7 and BDOW 9/2.
54. FO 800/365, Nicolson to Hardinge, Foreign Office, 17 April 1913. FO 371/1795, Grey to Cartwright, Foreign Office, 19 March 1913. Rodd to Grey, Rome, 15 and 23 April 1913, in BDOW 9/2, pp. 691–2 and 712–13.
55. FO 371/1891, Grey to Bertie, Foreign Office, 10 June 1913. Nicolson stated that the Albania–Islands exchange had been first suggested in a brief form by the French, then put into concrete form by Grey. (Cambon to Pichon, London, 14 August 1913, in DD 8, no. 321. See also: FO 371/1764, Rodd to Grey, Rome, 27 July 1913. FO 800/94, Paraphrase of Telegram to Buchanan and Bertie, Foreign Office, 14 July 1913.)

56. FO 371/1764, Grey to Dering, Foreign Office, 29 October 1913. FO 421/286, Grey to Bertie and other ambassadors, Foreign Office, 12 December 1913.
57. FO 421/286, Rodd to Grey, Rome, 13 December 1913; Grey to Bertie, Foreign Office, 16 December 1913. Flotow to Bethmann-Hollweg, Rome, 18 December 1913, in GP 36/2, pp. 435–7. Cambon to Pichon, London, 11 December 1913, in DD 8, no. 613. Flotow to Foreign Office, Rome, 2 and 4 January 1914, in GP 36/2, pp. 457 and 468. Jagow to Lichnowsky, Berlin, 7 January 1914, in GR 36/2, pp. 466–7. Lichnowsky to Foreign Office, London, 17 January 1914, in GP 36/2, p. 470.
58. FO 371/286, Mallet to Grey, Constantinople, 23 December 1913. See also the more diplomatic note of the Ottoman ambassador in London, FO 421/286, Tewfik to Grey, London, 30 December 1913, and Mutius to Foreign Office, Constantinople, in GP 36/2, p. 451. Mallet listed the Ottoman economic loss if the Ottomans lost the islands, but told Grey that security issues were the main Ottoman concern. (FO 424/251, Mallet to Grey, Constantinople, 7 January 1914.)
59. Lichnowsky to Foreign Office, London, 30 January 1914, in GP 36/2, p. 488. Jagow to Flotow, Berlin, 28 January 1914, in GP 36/2, p. 483. Jagow to Lichnowsky, Berlin, 3 February 1914, in GP 36/2, pp. 491–2. Mallet to Grey, Constantinople, 2 February 1913, in BDOW 10/1, p. 215. Grey to Mallet, Foreign Office, 3 February 1914, in BDOW 10/1, p. 216. Grey to Bertie, Foreign Office, 7 February 1914, in BDOW 10/1, p. 221.

Even when the British dropped the plan of coercion, British ambassadors were sending a confused message to other Powers. In Berlin, they stated that Grey had never wanted coercion. In Vienna they advocated coercion. (Jagow to Wangenheim, Berlin, 11 February 1914, and Tschirsky to Bethmann-Hollweg, Vienna, 11 February 1914, in GP 36/2, pp. 500–1. Lichnowsky to Bethmann-Hollweg, London, 11 February 1914, in GP 36/2, p. 507.)

60. The Germans, afraid that Austria would go to war over Albania, accepted the award of the Aegean Islands to the Greeks only to avoid problems in Southern Albania. Germany asserted that 'the retention of Aegean islands by Greece (is) conditional upon her carrying out the evacuation of Southern Albania and not causing trouble there'. FO 421/289, Grey to Gorschen, Foreign Office, 7 January 1914.)
61. FO 421/289, Grey to Bertie, Foreign Office, 4 February 1914; Grey to Bertie, Foreign Office, 9 February 1914; Buchanan to Grey, St Petersburgh, 10 February 1914; Grey to Buchanan, Foreign Office, 10 February 1914.

The Austrians saw no need to combine the Aegean Islands and Albanian issues together. On the other hand, the German ambassador in Vienna, Heinrich von

Tschirschky, felt that the Austrians would support Greek retention of the islands in the hope that it would draw Greece to the Triple Alliance side and improve Austrian trade relations in Salonica. Tschirschky to Bethmann-Hollweg, Vienna, 18 and 23 December 1913, in GP 36/2, pp. 437 and 439–40.

62. FO 421/289, Grey to Bertie, Foreign Office, 10 February 1914. Greece was notified of the decision.

63. Lowther to Grey, Constantinople, 25 August 1908, in Kuneralp and Tokay, pp. 21–3. FO 800/353/2, Nicolson to Cartwright, Foreign Office, February 19, 1912. German Foreign Minister (state secretary of the Foreign Office) Gottlieb von Jagow summarised the situation and explained Germany's acceptance of the British proposal. His main reason was avoidance of war. Jagow to Tschirschky, Berlin, 28 December 1913, in GP 36/2, pp. 444–6.

64. FO 800/364/2, Lowther to Nicolson, Pera, 13 March 1913.

65. FO 800/80, Lowther to Grey, Pera, 2 and 7 November 1912. 'Memorandum by Mr. Fitzmaurice', enclosure in FO 424/ 235, Lowther to Grey, Constantinople, 26 November 1912, and minutes by Nicolson and Grey, in BDOW 9/2, p. 213.

66. FO 800/80, Fitzmaurice to Tyrrell, Constantinople, 5 November 1912. The 'right horse' was a reference to a misunderstood quote from Salisbury. Fitzmaurice himself stated that England had backed the wrong horse in 1853 and 1878. (FO 800/80, Fitzmaurice to Tyrrell, Constantinople, 18 December 1912.)

67. FO 800/353, Lowther to Nicolson, Pera, 14 November 1912. FO 800/365, Lowther to Nicolson, Pera, 10 April 1913. Lowther to Nicolson, Pera, 7 November 1912, in Kuneralp and Tokay, pp. 417–19. FO 800/364/2, Lowther to Nicolson, Pera, 14 November 1912. FO 424/244, Lowther to Grey, Constantinople, 5 April 1913. FO 800/365, Lowther to Nicolson, Pera, 10 April 1913. Nicolson to Lowther, Foreign Office, 13 November 1912, in Kuneralp and Tokay, pp. 419–20.

68. Lowther to Grey, Constantinople, 17 January 1913, and minutes in BDOW 9/2, pp. 420–1. H. C. Norman of the Foreign Office added that he doubted the truth of what Lowther had alleged. Lowther's reputation with the Foreign Office cannot have been helped by his questions on the efficacy of Grey's policies. (See Lowther to Nicolson, Pera, 1 and 9 January 1913, in Kuneralp and Tokay, pp. 433–4 and 437–8.)

69. Letter from the king to the sultan notifying him of Lowther's removal. (FO 195/2453, Crowe for Grey to Lowther, Foreign Office, 18 June 1913.) Marling had previously served as Chargé during Lowther's absences from 12 November 1910 to 21 January 1911, from 15 June to 26 July 1911 and from 6 July to 1 October 1912.

70. FO 800/358/2, Marling to Nicolson, Therapia, 4 July, 31 July, 7 August, 3 September and 28 September 1912.
71. FO 424/247, Marling to Grey, Constantinople, 28 July 1913.
72. FO 424/248, Marling to Grey, 16 August 1913. Marling doubted that any financial inducements would work with 'such people', but thought they could be tried. He preferred the Powers to threaten to deny Imbros and Tenedos to them.
73. FO 371/1837, Marling to Grey, Constantinople, 15 and 18 August 1913; Grey to Marling, Foreign Office, 18 August 1913. See also, FO 424/247, Marling to Grey, Constantinople, 18 July 1913. FO 371/ 1837, Parker minutes of 16 August 1912.

    The borders of Ottoman Thrace were finally settled, and the Ottomans retained Eastern Thrace and Edirne. Marling reported on the Ottoman–Bulgarian Treaty, which called for demobilisation on both sides, and said the Turks would not do it. The Turks, he contended wrongly, planned to take Western Thrace, and perhaps move on to Salonica, which had been taken by the Greeks. (Marling to Grey, Constantinople, 2 October 1913, BDOW 9/2, pp. 1002–4.)

    Marling's reports on atrocities were completely unreliable. He reported Muslim actions against Christians – seldom with verifiable sources and never in context of the suffering of the Turkish refugees – based on the reports of the Armenian and Greek Patriarchs, and ignored the reports of all but one of his consuls, J. W. Streater, the unsalaried vice-consul at Rodosto (Tekirdağ), who himself accepted similar assertions. (FO 371/1834, Marling to Grey, Constantinople, 12 August 1913. See also: FO 371/1834, Streater to Marling, Rodosto, 22 July 1913. FO 424/247, Marling to Grey, 25 and 27 July 1913.) It should be noted that there was indeed some massacre of Christians at Rodosto. (FO 424/248, 'Statement by Consuls of Six Great Powers at Rodosto, July 28, 1913', enclosure in Marling to Grey, Constantinople, 30 July 1913.) Grey was against sending an international commission to investigate troubles at Rodosto, because a commission would have also had to investigate all the other atrocity reports. (FO 424/248, Grey to Marling, 19 August 1913.)
74. FO 371/1997, Mallet to Grey, Constantinople, 5 July 1914.
75. FO 424/252, Nye to Mallet, Constantinople, 12 May 1914, in Mallet to Grey, Constantinople, 14 May 1914. Consul Samson in Edirne estimated 30,000 Greeks had left Eastern Thrace and more than 60,000 Muslims had come in, not counting original Muslim inhabitants, who fled, then mainly returned. (FO 371/2133, (Major) Samson to Mallet, Adrianople, 7 July 1914.)
76. Enclosures in FO 371/2126, Mallet to Grey, Constantinople, 10 March 1914. Feroz Ahmad, *Young Turks and the Ottoman Nationalities: Armenians, Greeks,*

*Albanians, Jews, and Arabs, 1908–1918*, Salt Lake City: University of Utah Press, 2014, pp. 48–55. Aksakal, 'Defending the Nation', pp. 36–8. See also the documents in FO 371/1997.

77. FO 195/2458, Heathcote-Smith to Beaumont, 27 July 1914. FO 195/2458, Mathews to Beaumont, Constantinople, 21 July 1914. FO 421/290, Mallet to Grey, Constantinople, 12 June 1914. FO 424/252, Mallet to Grey, Constantinople, 6 May 1914. See the lists of offences against Greeks in FO 195/1997 and 2458 and FO 421/290. Numerous notices from the Greek ambassador are in FO 371/1997.
78. FO 424/252, Mallet to Grey, Constantinople, 30 April 1914. FO 800/374/2, Mallet to Nicolson, Pera, 1 June 1914. FO 371/1997, Mallet to Grey, Constantinople, 5 July 1914.
79. Wangenheim to the Federal Foreign Office, Therapia, 2, 8 and 13 June 1914, in GP 36/2, pp. 802–7.
80. FO 371/1834, Tewfik to Mallet, London, 6 August 1913; Grey to Marling, Foreign Office, 7 August 1913. FO 371/1839, Tewfik to Grey, London, 19 August 1913. FO 317/1997, Barnham to Mallet, Smyrna, 16 June 1914. At least one British consul contended that the fact the government could stop the boycott meant that they had organised it all along. (FO 195/2458, Heathcote-Smith to Beaumont, 8 July 1914.)
81. On Muslim mortality: Justin McCarthy, *Death and Exile: The Ethnic Cleansing of Ottoman Muslims 1821–1922*, Princeton: Darwin, 1995, pp. 161–4. On refugees: McCarthy, *Death and Exile*, pp. 156–62. The refugee figures were recorded in Alexandre Antoniades (*Le Développement Economique de la Thrace*, Athens: Typos, 1922, p. 217), Stephen P. Ladas (*The Exchange of Minorities: Bulgaria, Greece, and Turkey*, New York: Macmillan, 1932, p. 16) and Arnold J. Toynbee (*The Western Question in Greece and Turkey*, London: Constable, 1922, p. 138); all gave the same figures and listed the same source – the Ottoman Ministry of Refugees. Most of the Muslim refugees fled during the Balkan Wars. Bulgaria and the Ottoman Empire signed a convention (October 1913) for the exchange of Thracian Bulgarians and Bulgarian Turks, after which more Turkish refugees entered the Ottoman Empire.
82. FO 371/1762, Greig to Crackanthorpe, Monastir, 29 October 1913. A further 17 per cent came to Turkey between 1921 and 1926. The figures for mortality include deaths in Thrace to 1922, which cannot be statistically separated from the deaths in the Balkan Wars. In addition, the mortality of the Albanians, which was horrific, has not been included, because there is no statistical data. The reports are given and often quoted verbatim in McCarthy, *Death and Exile*, pp. 135–77. Most of the contents of this section have been taken from these pages of *Death and Exile*. See also, Salt, *Last Ottoman Wars*, pp. 152–68.

83. FO 195/2438, Morgan to Lowther, Cavalla, 28 December 1912.
84. FO 195/2438, Lamb to Lowther, Salonica, 3 December 1912.
85. FO 195/2438, Lamb to Lowther, Salonica, 11 December 1912.
86. FO 195/2438, Lamb to Lowther, Salonica, 3 December 1912. FO 195/2438, FO 195/2438, Lamb to Lowther, Salonica, 13 December 1912. FO 371–1762, Greig to Crackanthorpe, Monastir, 19 November 1913. FO 195/2438, no. 6866, Lamb to Lowther, Salonica, 13 December 1912. See also the descriptions in FO 371/2110. For a good short description, see Clark, *Sleepwalkers*, pp. 43–6.
87. FO 800/361/2, Lowther to Nicolson, Constantinople, 4 December 1912.
88. 'War in Balkans', House of Commons Debate, 21 January 1913, *Hansard*, vol. 47, cc. 188–9. See also 'War in Balkans', House of Commons Debate, 28 January 1913, *Hansard*, vol. 47, cc. 1150–4.
89. See the above and 'War in Balkans', House of Commons Debate, 28 January 1913, *Hansard*, vol. 47, cc. 1150–4. 'War in Balkans', House of Commons Debate, 13 February 1913, *Hansard*, vol. 48, cc. 1156–9. 'War in Balkans', House of Commons Debate, 10 April 1913, *Hansard*, vol. 51, cc. 1327–8, and 'War in Balkans (Alleged Atrocities)', House of Commons Debate, 16 January 1913, *Hansard*, vol. 46, cc. 2226–7. There were a number of similar debates in 1913, in all of which the government refused to release consular reports. It should be said that Grey was never one to share much with parliament.
90. FO 371/1834, Marling to Grey, Constantinople, 26 July 1913. FO 424/248, Marling to Grey, Constantinople, 16 August 1913.
91. 'Alleged Atrocities by the Allied Forces', House of Lords Debate, 19 February 1913, *Hansard*, vol. 13, cc. 1429–39. It should be noted, in fairness, that Grey also refused to publish any papers on the boycott of Greeks in Anatolia and the emigration of Greeks to the islands and Western Thrace. He said he could not do so because if he did he would have to also publish reports on atrocities committed on Balkan Muslims, which he would not do. ('Asia Minor', House of Commons Debate, 21 July 1914, *Hansard*, vol. 65, cc. 231–2.)
92. 'Mahomedan Refugees', House of Lords Debate, 16 July 1913, *Hansard*, vol. 14, cc. 1071–7. Morley was a member of the Asquith Cabinet.
93. Mallet to Grey, Constantinople, 29 December 1913, in BDOW 10/1, pp. 168–71. On Ottoman feelings during and after the Balkan Wars, see Ebru Boyar, *Ottomans, Turks, and the Balkans: Empire Lost, Relations Altered*, London and New York: Tauris Academic Studies, 2007.

# 8

# THE INSPECTORATES

The Balkan Wars had cost the Ottomans more than the loss of territory that had been theirs for centuries. Ottoman loss had convinced both the Europeans and domestic rebels to strike against the Empire when it was at its weakest. With much of their land lost and their army and treasury in disarray, the Ottomans had no choice but to bow to the British and Russian plans for Eastern Anatolia. Any promises that the European Powers would protect the integrity of the Ottoman Empire had long been forgotten. In the Treaty of London (30 May 1913), the Ottoman border in Europe had been placed near Istanbul. When the Ottomans retook Edirne and Eastern Thrace, the British and Russians did all they could to force them to relinquish it. The British had decided that the Aegean Islands, including those close to the Ottoman shore, would be given to Greece. No rational observer could have thought that the Eastern Anatolian 'reforms' were not another step in the dismemberment of the Empire.[1]

## Eastern Anatolia in 1913

Before the Balkan Wars, security in Eastern Anatolia had actually greatly improved. Raids and fighting among Kurdish tribes had markedly decreased. Behind the improvements in civil order were administrative reforms and especially an increased military presence in the East. Local regions were brought under the control of provincial governors. Mounted patrols improved safety in cities. New government commissions studied and adjudicated land disputes between Kurds and Armenians and between Armenians and other Armenians. The gendarmerie was slowly reformed and put under new officers. The army pursued Kurdish raiders and even managed to collect some taxes from the tribes. (An evidence of the success of the reforms was the bitter complaints from Kurdish chiefs.) The driving force behind the improvements was the need of the government to exert control, both out of good intentions to provide security and from the desire for peaceful collection of taxes. The European Powers also could take some credit for the progress – the Ottoman Government knew that troubles in Eastern Anatolia could lead to the loss of the Eastern provinces.[2]

Table 8.1   Population of the 'Six Vilâyets' by religion

|  | Muslim | | Armenian | | Other[a] | | Total |
|---|---|---|---|---|---|---|---|
| Sivas | 1,196,300 | 81% | 182,912 | 12% | 93,626 | 6% | 1,472,838 |
| Bitlis | 408,703 | 67% | 191,156 | 31% | 11,532 | 2% | 611,391 |
| Mamuretülaziz | 564,164 | 83% | 111,043 | 16% | 5,034 | 1% | 680,241 |
| Diyarbakır | 598,985 | 79% | 89,131 | 12% | 66,335 | 9% | 754,451 |
| Van | 313,322 | 61% | 130,500 | 26% | 65,975 | 13% | 509,797 |
| Erzurum | 804,388 | 83% | 163,218 | 17% | 6,590 | 1% | 974,196 |
| Total | 3,885,862 | 78% | 867,960 | 17% | 249,092 | 5% | 5,002,914 |

Some rounding errors.

[a] Primarily Assyrian and Chaldean Christians.

Source: McCarthy, *Muslims and Minorities*, p. 112.

Having failed in their 1890s rebellions, the Hunchak Party had been rent by internal dissension. Leadership of the Armenian revolution passed to the Dashnak Party (Dashnaktsutyun). The Dashnaks followed a policy of slow development of power in the Ottoman East. By no means did the Dashnaks abandon a violent revolutionary policy, but their attacks were directed to different ends than those of the Hunchaks. The most effective Dashnak technique was the organisation of cadres of dedicated fighters – *fedayi* ('those who sacrifice themselves') – trained and dedicated professional revolutionaries. These were the backbone of an organisation that enlisted Ottoman Armenians, willing or not, under revolutionary discipline. Assassination of Armenians who opposed them drove out opposition in the Armenian community. By 1908, Dashnak bands had undertaken more than seventy raids on Ottoman officials and soldiers and, in particular, on Kurds who were viewed as oppressing Armenians. In the process, they developed an image as the defenders of the Armenians.[3]

Beginning in 1908, the Dashnaks settled on a dual policy of arming and organising Armenians in the East, systematically preparing for revolution and taking part in the Ottoman political process. The Dashnaks became the leaders of Armenian nationalism in the Ottoman Empire, facilitated by the Committee of Union and Progress. A faction of the CUP had allied itself with the Dashnaks when both were revolutionaries exiled in Europe. After the 1908 revolution the CUP continued the alliance, aligning itself politically and electorally with the Dashnak organisation, which it allowed to become a legal political party. The Dashnaks became the main Armenian party in the Ottoman Parliament. However, they never abandoned their intention of creating an independent Armenia. The CUP eventually became disillusioned with Dashnak separatist aims, but meanwhile the Dashnaks had become the political image for the Ottoman Armenians. This was particularly true in Europe. When the British spoke of the 'wishes of the Armenians', it was in reality the wishes of the Dashnak Party.[4]

Some Kurdish insurgents, much less politically astute that the Armenian rebels, also planned uprisings, to be described below. They were uniformly unsuccessful, but the disruption they caused affected the European image of an anarchic Eastern Anatolia.

For the Ottoman Government, problems in Eastern Anatolia multiplied with the coming of the Balkan Wars. Both Armenian and Kurdish rebels foresaw the end of the Ottoman Empire. Both planned for a new situation in Eastern Anatolia. Although both were already armed, they increased their weapons and their plans. It would not be an exaggeration to say they hated each other. The British consul in Van, Captain Molyneux-Seel, believed the soldiers would do all they could to protect the Armenians, but they might not be able to control the Kurds.[5]

## British Domestic Pressure

The Anglo-Armenian Association had ceased to be an effective political force by the end of the Armenian troubles of the 1890s. Political and popular pressure for the Armenians was taken up in 1912 by the British Armenia Committee, an offshoot of the Balkan Committee, with many of the same members. The committee proposed a project of reforms which was essentially the same as the one proposed by the Anglo-Armenian Association nearly twenty years before:

- A European high commissioner who was to control the six 'Armenian Provinces': Van, Bitlis, Diyarbakır, Erzurum, Sivas and Mamuretülaziz (the 'Six Vilâyets').
- A Committee of Supervision and Control, representing the European Powers.
- An elected assembly, half Armenian and half Muslim, and all government functionaries to be similarly divided among the two.
- Locally recruited gendarmerie and police, again half Armenian and half Muslim.
- The judiciary and finance to be in the hands of 'European officers'.

Armenians, the committee stated, ultimately should be given the rule in Eastern Anatolia because they were the largest group, an assertion which they justified with wholly invented statistics that included only one-third of the Muslim population.[6]

The one major publication of the committee was a 1913 catalogue of evils visited on the Armenians by the Turks, as evidenced by chapter headings: 'Imprisonment', 'Torture', 'Murder and Wholesale Massacres', 'Outrages on Women', etc. The Turks had supposedly 'plundered and destroyed' 2,472 villages, burned 255,000 shops and killed 250,000 Armenians. Descriptions of Armenian suffering were graphic. The committee made great attempts to portray Armenians sympathetically. Armenians were described as 'well-built and powerful. Their women are often beautiful, with regular features, a majestic gait, large black eyes under long and thick eyelashes, and have a healthy look about them which suggests good motherhood.' They were 'serious, sober, frugal, and hospitable', with 'quick intelligence' and 'sturdiness of character'.

The book appealed to British Protestant sensibilities. It even went so far as to say that early Armenians were Protestants and had been persecuted by Jesuits.[7]

Whereas the Anglo-Armenian Association and the Balkan Committee had great effect on the public and politicians, the British Armenia Committee was a lesser force. There were no great public meetings. The committee managed to meet once with Grey to present a memorial. A small number of one-paragraph notices of committee meetings appeared in the provincial press. In 1913, the press was much more concerned with events of the second Balkan War than with the Armenian Question.[8]

By the latter part of 1913 the British public and parliament had lost their previous fervour over the Armenian issue. Previously, Lansdowne and Grey had asserted that their policies were guided by British public opinion in Eastern Anatolia in the 1890s, in Crete and in Macedonia. Lord Curzon was to make the same claim after World War I. That was to be a less important factor in Armenian issues in 1913. Although he did occasionally refer to public opinion, Foreign Secretary Grey could not accurately say that it drove his policies. Compared to past campaigns, the press devoted few articles to the issue, and newspaper opinion was mixed. Nor could it be said that parliament was especially concerned with the Armenian situation. The issue was brought up in a few debates on more general topics by MPs who were in the British Armenia Committee, but the government commented very little on the subject. In 1913 and until World War I was declared, the main Middle Eastern concerns of parliament were the affairs of Persia and the Baghdad Railway. Both topics occupied much more of parliament's time than the few debates that included Armenian reforms.[9]

In 1913 the British were occupied with the second Balkan War, the status of Albania, the Ottoman reoccupation of Western Thrace, the Aegean Islands, the Baghdad Railway and the division of power in Iran. The British Government would probably have been content to leave the Armenian issue alone but for Russian plans to detach Eastern Anatolia from the Ottoman Empire. Grey undoubtedly did feel some domestic pressure on the Armenian Question, most of it coming from his own Liberal Party and the Liberal press. In general, he could rely on the British public and the press to support actions taken against the Turks. However, diplomatic concerns, especially the Russian Alliance, and his own opinions and judgements drove his actions more than any consideration of public opinion. He stated that changes in Eastern Anatolia should be in the hands of the Russians: 'I entirely agree that it is desirable to proceed with a scheme of reforms, and I shall be delighted if the Russian Minister for Foreign Affairs will take the initiative, especially as regards Armenian vilayets.' Despite this, Grey felt that Britain had to do something itself, probably the dispatch of British officers to train gendarmes, because of what he said was the influence of Armenophiles in the public and parliament. He feared that 'people here who took considerable interest in in Armenians' would put him in an indefensible position if there were disorders and Britain had done nothing.[10]

While public opinion surely had an effect on British policy, longstanding personal beliefs of Grey and others in the Liberal government may have been as important. Grey, after all, had been an early member of the Anglo-Armenian Association who had excoriated the Ottomans in his public speeches. The prime minister with whom Grey served, Herbert Asquith, had similarly attacked the Ottomans. Grey had done all he could to remove Ottoman control over Macedonia. The policies the British followed for Eastern Anatolia were a continuity with the long-held strategies of the British politicians.

## Political Changes, but a Continuing Policy on the Armenians

The political situation between Britain and Russia had changed greatly since the Russians had blocked British plans for coercion of the Ottomans over the Armenian issue in the 1890s. Primary was the Anglo-Russian détente after 1907. Britain had become increasingly willing to cooperate with the Russians out of fear of increasing German power. Russia, defeated by the Japanese in the Far East, had begun to concentrate its ambitions in Iran and Eastern Anatolia. The perceived weakness of the Ottoman Empire after the Balkan Wars had seemed to signal the break-up of the Empire. The time had come to bring to fruition the plans for Eastern Anatolia that had been frustrated in the 1890s.

It was the British, however, not the Russians themselves, who suggested that the Russians approach the other Powers to begin investigating reforms in Anatolia. Grey said the basis of the project should be the unsuccessful British plans of 1894–5.[11]

In anticipation of European pressure, on 17 June 1913 the Ottoman Government proposed to the British a set of reforms for the Eastern provinces: a new provincial law would define the duties and powers of officials. These would be applied first to two 'sectors' of provinces: 1. Van, Bitlis, Mamuretülaziz and Diyarbakır; and 2. Erzurum, Sivas and Trabzon. The reforms would be applied gradually to the rest of the Empire. Each sector would be assigned a gendarmerie inspector, a justice inspector and an inspector of agriculture, forests and public works, all under an inspector-general, to whom they would report. The inspectors-general, in turn, would report to an inspector-general in the Department of the Interior. Britain was requested to nominate a commander for each of the seven gendarmerie corps, as well as the inspectors. However, ultimate authority remained with the minister of the interior. British Foreign Office officials at first received the Ottoman proposal well, but with the stipulation that Britain must confer with the Russians before accepting anything. Grey told the Ottoman ambassador, Tevfik Paşa, that Russia and others would have to be consulted. Tevfik accepted this, as long as none of the inspectors and officials appointed were Russian. The Ottomans were soon disappointed. Upon considering Russian objections, Grey refused the Ottoman request. He offered only 'to see if a few officers can be found to undertake the duty of organizing gendarmerie in the vilayets inhabited by Armenians'. The Russians were vehemently against Britain providing even a few gendarmerie officers. Foreign Minister Sazonov stated that no other Power but Russia could take the lead on reforms. The Ottomans would have to accept Russian gendarmerie officers, although they might accept some other nationalities along with the Russians, but no Germans. If the Ottomans did not accept Russian officers and other Russian plans for reform and there were troubles in Eastern Anatolia, Russia would intervene.[12]

In an open threat, the Russians told Grey that the British had to choose between cooperation with them or Russia taking matters into their own hands.

> It is up to him to choose between co-operation with us, based on a community of interests, or to see the Russians free from any commitment and applied to the safeguarding of its interests to the extent appropriate to the circumstances.

Grey chose the Russians. He abandoned any plan to aid the Ottomans, even with a few gendarmerie officers. He decided that he was willing to let the

Russians draw up a plan of reforms that would be presented to the Ottomans. These would then be discussed and emended by the Powers' ambassadors at Istanbul. Grey suggested the 1895 proposals as a guideline, but was willing to let Russia decide. He stated that he now wanted all matters in the Asiatic provinces of Turkey to be decided by a conference of the Powers, which would impose their wishes.[13]

The 1895 proposals that Grey suggested as the basis of reforms would have given the Powers extensive control over Eastern Anatolia: the Powers would 'supervise' the selection of provincial governors. A high commissioner and a Commission of Control, made up of three Muslim and three Christian members, supervised by the Powers, would have authority over the governors and implementation of reforms. Special officers would represent the interests of Armenians. Half the judges would be Christian, half Muslim. Special courts would try Kurdish 'brigands'. The Kurdish Hamidiye cavalry would be disarmed except in case of war. (Salisbury had felt these proposals were far too lenient on the Ottomans.) In fact, the new plan to be forced on the Ottomans went far beyond the 1895 proposals.[14]

Grey had decided the policy that Britain was henceforth to follow, with only minor variations, was to advance Russian plans for the Ottoman Empire.

## The Russians

Asking Russia to draw up a plan for reforms in Eastern Anatolia was like asking a fox to draw up a plan for the protection of chickens. The Russian position was completely duplicitous.

The stated purpose of Russian schemes for Eastern Anatolia, according to Russian Foreign Minister Sazonov, was fear of an Armenian uprising that might extend to the Russian Caucasus. He stated the only thing that had kept the Ottoman Armenians from revolt during the Balkan War was

> the constantly renewed promises to the Armenians that Russia watches over their interests and that, when the time comes, it will take up the question of reforms, by associating the Allied Powers (that is, Britain and France) and (the Armenians') friends.

Sazonov asserted that true Armenian autonomy was impossible, however, because the Armenians were 'everywhere in a minority'.[15]

The Russian plan was classic – first fomenting and supporting disorder, then being 'forced reluctantly' to step in.

The Russians had long vacillated in their relations with Armenian revolutionaries. On the one hand, they justifiably feared all revolutionary sentiment; on the other, they approved of disruption in the Ottoman East that could work to their advantage. At times the Russians interdicted Armenian rebel arms shipments to the Ottoman East from Russian Caucasian possessions; at other times they facilitated them. At first, Tsar Nicholas II was fearful of all political and nationalist revolutionary movements, including those among the Armenians. In 1885 he closed Armenian schools, which he correctly viewed as hotbeds of Armenian nationalism. Armenian revolutionary and civic organisations were banned. In 1903, when he ordered the seizure of Armenian church properties; the result was dramatic. The governor in the Caucasus, Prince Grigory Golitsyn, was wounded in an assassination attempt by Armenians. Assassinations of other officials were more successful. Demonstrations took place in the main cities, often becoming riots. Civil disruption continued while Russia lost the Russo-Japanese War of 1904–5 and barely survived the revolution of 1905. During the revolution the Russian Caucasus descended into near anarchy. Inter-communal warfare broke out between Azerbaijani Turks and Armenians. The Tsar retreated. Armenian church property was restored; Armenian schools reopened. Armenian revolutionary organisations were allowed, and flourished in public. The official policy became to allow, and even encourage, the revolutionaries, so long as they directed their attacks against the Ottoman Empire.[16]

While the Russians were protesting that their only desire was to secure a peaceful Eastern Anatolia under Ottoman reign, they were organising revolts and disruption. The Russians in the East used their power and influence to stymy Ottoman attempts at reform. For example, when the governor of Van Province convened a meeting to select members of the new provincial general council, the twenty-seven Armenian electors refused to participate and left the meeting. British Consul Molyneux-Seel stated that their objective was to make clear that the Armenians would participate in no reforms that did not include European control. In advancing this, the coordination of the various Armenian groups had been arranged through the exertions of the Russian consul. 'In the future every political step to be taken will as in the present instance be first submitted for his (the Russian consul's) approval.' Armenian rebel groups, which had sometimes been at odds with each other, coordinated their plans and activities under the auspices of the Russian Caucasus Administration in Tiflis.[17]

The Russian army invaded Western Iran in 1909, and the region passed effectively under their control. Both Armenian and Kurdish rebels benefitted from the Russian invasion. Russian occupation afforded rebels safe bases to organise without fear of Ottoman opposition. The Russians in Western Iran supported the rebels. They would not allow Ottoman troops to pursue Kurdish or Armenian rebels into Iran. Fearing war with Russia, the Ottomans could do nothing against the rebels. All this was well known to the British, reported by their consuls in the Ottoman Empire and Iran.[18]

Kurdish rebels against the Ottomans were supported and given weapons by the Russians. They paid stipends to the Kurdish rebel chiefs Şeyh Taha of Şemdinan and İsmail Simko. Simko and another Kurdish rebel, Abdürrezzak Bedirhan, were even given Russian Imperial decorations for services to the Russian cause. The Russians brought together the leaders of Kurdish rebel tribes in an attempt to forge a rebel alliance. The alliance foundered because of rivalries among the rebel chiefs, but the Russians had done what they could to cause disruption in Eastern Anatolia.

The Kurdish rebels did cause disruption, obviously the Russian intention: İsmail Simko's followers raided settlements and fought a major battle with Ottoman troops. Under the patronage of Russian consuls in Iran, Abdürrezzak organised a revolt in Southeastern Anatolia in April 1913. After attacks in the region, Abdürrezzak's revolt was put down by Ottoman troops in May of 1914. He and his followers escaped to Russian-controlled Iran. When the Russians invaded the region in World War I, Abdürrezzak was rewarded by being made governor of Bitlis Province. His uncle was named governor of Russian-occupied Erzurum. Another rebel leader, Abdüsselam Barzani, lost a battle with Ottoman troops in 1913 and fled to Russian-controlled Iran. Other rebels terrorised the region and fought against the Ottoman army in Bitlis and elsewhere. When defeated, they also fled to Russian protection. The rebels who attacked Bitlis were nearly successful in taking the city. The battle lost, the leaders fled to the protection of the Russian consulate.[19]

The Kurdish rebel tribes were no friends to the Armenian rebels. Their main reason for revolt, like that of the Armenians, was the expectation that the Russians would soon take Eastern Anatolia. They feared that the Russians would favour the Armenians if the Kurds did not themselves go over to the Russian side. The main points in Kurdish rebel proclamations were opposition to Armenian power and the creation of autonomous Kurdish control under the Tsar. The land they claimed was the same land claimed by the Armenians.[20]

The Russians did not take a side in any Armenian–Kurdish conflict. Their purpose was to cause disruption that would lead to the demise of Ottoman rule in the East.

Throughout the negotiations on Armenian reforms, German Ambassador Wangenheim correctly interpreted Russian proposals as the first step to creating an autonomous Armenia under Russian influence, then Russian control of Eastern Anatolia. He felt that England, France and Russia had determined to impose their will on a defenceless Ottoman Empire. Their machinations would ultimately lead to the destruction of the Ottoman Empire and the division of its lands among the Powers. Wangenheim's analysis was not altruistic or pro-Ottoman. Destruction of the Ottoman Empire would be disastrous for the German Empire. Germany needed a strong Ottoman Empire under German influence:[21]

> Nobody will be able to say that the Armenians are doing particularly well in the Turkish empire. On the other hand, hardly anyone will be able to prove that the other residents of Turkey and especially the Turks themselves are better off than the Armenians, or that the situation of the Armenians is worse today than at any earlier point in Turkish history. There is no doubt that the current Turkish government is fully convinced of the need to do something for the Armenians and is willing to meet the Armenian wishes as far as is possible without breaking the link between the different parts of the empire. The Armenians in Turkey are still relatively better off today than the Jews, Poles and Finns in Russia. Even so, propaganda using the most radical means today is giving the impression all over the world that the suffering of the Armenians has increased day by day and has now reached a climax that necessitates the intervention of Europe. Armenian delegates travel to European capitals in a wailing state, and a bureau has been set up here, in which the complaints of Armenians from all Turkish provinces converge, before being cleverly edited in thousands of bulletins around the world.

Wangenheim believed the Armenian demands, as presented by Russia, went far beyond what the Ottomans could accept without endangering the existence of their Empire:

> The power that is increasing the Armenian claims is Russia. With the help of Catholicos (of Echmiadzin, head of the Armenian Church), the local Armenian patriarch and countless agents in all Armenian areas and with the expenditure of significant funds, Russia has been fueling the dissatisfaction of the Armenians for years. It prevents roads and railroads from being built in Eastern Anatolia, without which the Turkish government is unable to create peace between Kurds and Armenians. In addition to the Armenians, it also supports the Kurds with money and weapons so that they can continue their predatory life at the expense of the Armenians. The local Armenian Central Committee also receives money and advice from the Russian embassy. The Armenian movement is the means by which Russia maintains Asian Turkey in a constant state of excitement and in a state which, at the moment, allows Russia, as an interested border state, to claim the right to intervene.

Wangenheim wanted Germany to resist the Russian plans. His mistake was that he hoped Britain would join in the opposition. He felt that it was in Britain's own interest to reject dismemberment of the Ottoman Empire, despite Britain's alliance with Russia. That was not to be.[22]

## The Plan of Reforms

June 1913 was a propitious time to force the Ottomans to conform to the wishes of Russia and Britain. They had lost all their European territory, and their forces could barely defend Istanbul.

The Russians suggested that a plan of reform be drawn up by the ambassadors of Russia, Britain and France in Istanbul, as had been the case in 1895. The Germans objected. All plans, they stated, would have to be the work of all the Powers. Grey told them that the three ambassadors were already discussing the matter, but others could present alternatives. The Ottomans persevered in their own reform plan, but the British categorically rejected it. The German and Austrian Governments then suggested that the Ottomans take part in the deliberations. The Russians strongly objected. They wanted no interference from the Ottomans: '(The) only logical course is for Ambassadors to elaborate a scheme of reforms, which would then be presented to Turkey with authority of all the Powers.' It seems the Germans and Austrians, like the Ottomans, were expected to accept any project without complaint.[23]

On 17 June, Ambassador Lowther forwarded to London a project of reforms. Although in theory the project was the work of the Russian, British and French embassies, it was in fact a Russian and British plan. It cannot have been incidental that the proposal was in essence the same one drawn up previously by the British Armenia Committee, although the British described it as 'the Russian proposal'. It was presented to the ambassadors of the Powers on 30 June.

- The Russian proposal envisaged one province made up of the previous Six Vilayets. One governor-general would rule over the province, appointed for a five-year term. He could be a Christian Ottoman subject, although a European was preferred. The Powers would have to assent to the person named. The governor-general would name all the administrators and judges and have control of the police and gendarmerie. All military forces would be at his disposal when he called on them. The Ottoman Government would have no control.
- An administrative council would advise the governor-general. It would consist of the heads of administrative departments (the governor-general's appointments), European technical advisors, the heads of religious communities, and six councilors, three Muslims and three Christians, named by the Provincial Assembly. That Assembly would have an equal number of Muslim and Christian members. It could be dissolved by the governor-general, who must also approve of any legislation.
- The courts would be controlled by appointees of the governor-general, as would the security forces. The police and gendarmerie would be half Muslim and half Christian. Recruits would do their military service in peacetime within the province. The Hamidiye cavalry would be disbanded.
- All officials of the administration and the judges would be Muslim and Christian in equal number
- A commission appointed by the governor would decide on Armenian land claims.
- No Muslim refugees would be installed in the province.[24]

The demographic problem with the proposal was the same as seen in all previous British and Russian proposals – Muslims made up three-fourths of the population, but only had one-half of the votes and one-half the administrative appointments. What was proposed was in fact a country excised from the Ottoman Empire. The governor-general was to function as an all-powerful king. Of all the prerogatives of a separate state, the only serious one lacking was control of the currency.

Since the Ottomans had no part in creating the proposal, the Germans and Austrians suggested that a new Ottoman plan of reform be requested and presented to the ambassadors. Even Grey agreed that this was fair, although he intimated that it need not be given serious consideration. The ambassadors, he stated, should only consider the Turkish proposal if it proved useful. The Russians were opposed to any consideration of Ottoman wishes. They insisted on 'the most rapid and complete pacification possible'. Waiting to consider an Ottoman proposal would, Sazonov stated, leave a bad impression among the Armenians. Grey then suggested that the ambassadors receive any Ottoman proposals, then quickly reject any that did not agree with the 1895 proposals. Russia found this acceptable. (In fact, the Russian proposals under consideration already went beyond the 1895 proposals, which they themselves disagreed with.)[25]

Ambassador Wangenheim accurately pointed out problems with the Russian proposal. It created one very large province. In a region with poor communications, this would make it ungovernable. Moreover, if bettering the state of the Armenians were the intention, why were areas of large Armenian population in the provinces of Adana, Aleppo and parts of Ankara Province excluded? This demonstrated that improving the lot of the Armenians was not the real Russian intention. The Ottoman plan of reform, on the other hand, applied to all provinces. It would be better for the lives of the Armenians and the rest of the population, and would not threaten Ottoman sovereignty. Wangenheim suggested that the Ottoman proposal should be strengthened by a Monitoring Commission, half appointed by the Ottoman Government and half by the Powers, to oversee reforms, as well as assigning Christian assistants in the provinces. The German State Secretary of the Foreign Office (Foreign Minister), Gottlieb von Jagow, noted his government's agreement with Wangenheim's assessment. He notified the

Russian Government of that, and stated to them that he doubted that the Russian project was appropriate.[26]

On 30 June the ambassadors in Istanbul, who could come to no agreement themselves, decided to refer consideration of the proposals to a committee made up of Gerald Fitzmaurice for Britain, André Mandelstam for Russia and Dr Schoenberg for Germany. There was never a question of the British member of the committee accepting anything but the 'Russian Proposals', which he had lent a hand in creating. Fitzmaurice was even more fanatically anti-Ottoman than his superior, Lowther. He favoured the Russian proposal throughout. He was capable of astonishing beliefs about the Turks: Fitzmaurice declared that the Six Vilâyets were actually one natural region that the Ottomans had divided into smaller provinces in order to more easily eliminate the Armenians, and that the Committee of Union and Progress had revolted against Abdülhamid mainly to forestall reforms. In 1913, he believed, the Arabs had already eliminated direct Ottoman rule. He felt the Turks were unable to govern themselves, so how could they rule 'subject races'. The Turks had oppressed their subjects because they feared that, freed from constraint, 'the subject races will progress and become his superiors'. Fitzmaurice's analysis of the Russian proposal: detaching Eastern Anatolia would actually be good for the Ottomans, saving them money. He wanted the fifty-fifty rule, stating incredibly that it would remove religious tensions. He contended that nomadic Kurds should not be allowed to vote, in order to convince them to become settled agriculturalists. Despite all consular reports to the contrary, he asserted that the Armenians would never gravitate to the Russians, but would oppose them.[27]

The Ottoman plan of reforms, submitted to the Powers on 1 July, first noted all the reforms that they had already enacted: under a new provincial law, the judiciary had been expanded and reformed. Existing and new property laws had been enforced. Gendarmerie inspectors under French Colonel Charles-Louis-Albert Baumann had been sent to each province to investigate what was needed for public security, as had new gendarmes. The Ottomans reiterated their plan to have foreign advisers and inspectors assigned to government ministries, as well as other foreign officials. Very importantly, the Ottoman plan was to apply to the entire Empire, not just the Six Vilayets.

- Inspectors-general would be assigned to each of six sectors of the Empire. They would oversee the application of all laws and, after consulting with the provincial governors, would suggest to the government new regulations. These new regulations would especially be intended to pacify the tribes. The inspectors would always work in tandem with the governors.
- An inspector-general would oversee all officials and dismiss or transfer officials found inadequate. However, those administrators reporting directly to the governors or the Central Administration would be reported to the government for action.
- Administrative, judicial, gendarmerie, public works and agricultural inspectors would be assigned to each sector. They would be bound to execute the orders of the inspector-general.
- Financial Inspectors would report directly to the Ministry of Finance, not the inspector-general.
- In cases of malfeasance by judges, the inspector-general would refer the case to the Ministry of Justice.
- 'The organization and reorganization of the police and the gendarmerie would be carried out in each inspection area, under the direction and with the knowledge of the Inspector-General.' However, the inspector-general would have to consult with the governors on suggested structural changes in the police and gendarmerie. Decisions would be made by the Central Government.
- The inspector-general would study taxation and property laws and make suggestions for changes, always in consultation with the governors. He would examine each province's budget.[28]

It is easy to see that the Ottoman proposal would not be acceptable to the Russians and the British. The real powers of the inspectors-general were extremely limited. The Ottoman proposal took the term 'inspector' seriously; the primary duty of the inspectors was to investigate and suggest changes. Their ability to make real changes was circumscribed by the need for Central Government approval. They could suggest reforms, but had few means to enforce them. The only coercive force allowed them was in the sentence: 'Gendarmes or soldiers will also be put at their disposal.' The constantly repeated phrase 'in consultation with the governors' would have been particularly bothersome to the British and Russians, because it implied the continuance of the regular Ottoman system of governance. But the greatest point of opposition was that the Ottoman proposal made no allowance for European control.

The planned creation of a committee to plan reforms did nothing to moderate the opposition among the ambassadors; it only shifted the arguments. The Germans still opposed the British and Russians. It was left to the ambassadors and their foreign offices to decide.

The Germans and Austrians wanted the Ottoman proposal to be a basis of consideration of reforms. They planned to answer the issue of European control by putting the Ottoman proposals into effect, but overseen by a Commission of Control, the members of which would be named half by the Ottomans and half by the Powers. They wanted the Ottoman proposal to be given a chance before the Russian proposal was considered. The Germans felt that the Russian plan would inevitably lead to partition and the disintegration of the Ottoman Empire. Grey at first seemed to agree with the Germans that the Russian proposal went too far:

> The German Government have pointed out the objections to them, and in some important respects they go too far and would lead to partition. They seek to create a very large and unwieldy province under a Christian governor-general with almost independent powers, and, even if accepted unanimously by the Powers, of which there is now no chance, they would, I fear, excite determined opposition on the part of the Ottoman Government and drive them to extremities.

He stated that he wanted all possibilities for reform to be considered by the ambassadors at Istanbul. This was the opposite of what the British agents were advocating at the commission meetings in Istanbul, where Fitzmaurice completely supported the Russian plan for a single province.[29]

When Lowther was relieved from his post in Istanbul, negotiations on Eastern Anatolia were left in the hands of Chargé d'Affaires Charles Marling (2 July to 24 October). Marling agreed with Fitzmaurice. He completely supported the Russian proposal. He was especially concerned to comply with the wishes of Armenians, who, he stated, all wanted European control. Marling felt the Germans were wrong in thinking the Six Vilayets would gravitate to

Russian control: '[P]ersons well acquainted with Armenian disorder believe that a prosperous Armenia is not likely to gravitate towards Russia.'[30]

At the committee and ambassadorial meetings, the Austrians and Germans continued to bring up difficulties with the Russian plan. The Austrians supported the idea of proportionality based on population numbers, rather than half-Muslims, half-Christians in governing bodies. The Russians refused to budge on their basic points: there must be no consideration of the Ottoman proposal. The governor-general must be a Christian, and the Powers must be in control. The Russians did note the objections, including those of the British, to one large province, however, and accepted that it might be split in two.[31]

The Ottomans still opposed what was to the Russians and British the essential part of the reform proposals – close European control. They did not want European inspectors-general only Ottoman subjects, in the posts. They proposed a looser system of European supervision in which European advisors (*conseiller étranger*) would be attached to each inspector-general. The advisors would report the findings of their investigations and make suggestions for reforms. If the advisors disagreed with the inspectors-general, the government Council of Ministers would make the decisions. The Ottomans did not acknowledge any plan that included absolute European control. The Russian proposal, they believed, would in effect create a separate state that would fall under Russian control, which was what the Russians intended. The British ambassador who had replaced Lowther, Louis Mallet, followed Grey's instructions. He told the Grand Vezir, Said Halim, that the Ottoman Government was entirely wrong about Russian intentions. Mallet said that the Ottoman proposal was unacceptable, because the Armenians would never accept anything but European control. Unable to convince Said, Mallet told Grey that he would leave everything to the Russian ambassador.[32]

Through July of 1913 the Germans and Russians remained at odds in Istanbul. Russian Foreign Minister Sazonov complained that Wangenheim's 'Russophobia' was delaying a solution to the reforms question. Wangenheim protested that this was untrue, even though Russian Ambassador Mikhail Nikolayevich Giers hated him, but that he opposed the Russian proposal because it was impossible. Then the German position began to change. Foreign Minister Jagow had begun a policy of attempted friendship with Britain, hoping to keep the British neutral in any coming conflict. He told

Wangenheim that he was confident the Germans could work with the British. He said he believed Foreign Secretary Grey's repeated statement that he wished only 'to maintain Asian Turkey in its current state, a goal that Sir E. Gray has repeatedly and determinedly described as the basis of English politics'. Russia, Jagow thought, currently did not want to question the integrity of the Ottoman state, but that could change if 'chauvinistic currents in Russia gain the upper hand'. If that happened, the Germans would have to count on the British to have a moderating effect on the Russians. Berlin had decided the Germans would have to cooperate with the British. That was the only way to 'moderate' the Russians.[33]

Wangenheim continued to state his opposition to any dismemberment of the Ottoman Empire. He wanted reforms, but not the Russian programme. Surely affected by Jagow's policy, however, he wrote to Berlin that he trusted Grey's intentions not to divide the Ottoman Empire, 'despite the attitude of the local British Embassy'. His reasons for this were practical: 'Russia will hardly take the step without England, and if England wants Turkey to perish, we cannot save it alone.'[34]

The embassies of the Triple Alliance (Germany, Austria–Hungary and Italy) attempted to find what Wangenheim described as a middle ground between the Russian and Ottoman plans. They proposed European control of reform actions, including organisation of the gendarmerie under European officers. The Hamidiye would be dissolved. All three languages – Turkish, Kurdish and Armenian – would be equal in law and administration. Representation in assemblies and administration would be proportionate to population. The Triple Alliance suggestion was weak on specifics (for example, 'an early solution to the agricultural question'). In particular, the manner of European control was not specified. It contained some aspects of which the Russians would approve, especially some form of European control. Others, such as proportional representation, most definitely went against Russian plans. The Russians rejected these proposals. They insisted that the individual Ottoman provinces and provincial administrations be eliminated, leaving only inspectors named by the powers in charge. The only Russian concession was that there might be two inspectorates, not one, but they wanted the region to be divided into East and West inspectorates, the former obviously under Russian control. Wangenheim personally opposed this, and believed that the Ottomans would never accept it. Despite his personal opposition to the plan, however, he followed orders from Berlin and recommended to the Grand Vezir that the only choice for the Ottomans was to put the Triple Alliance plan into effect immediately.[35]

Left with no champions, the Ottomans nevertheless rejected the Triple Alliance proposal. They knew they would be forced to accept something, but intended to use their cooperation as a bargaining chip to save their economy. The Grand Vezir stated that he could not agree to reforms unless the Powers agreed to a 4 per cent increase in customs duties. This was in the hands of Britain, which had steadfastly refused the increase. The British still refused to accept it. Other than the customs increase, Grey was willing to consent to the proposals offered by the Russians. He notified the Germans that he was not very concerned with the form of the reforms, so long as European control was assured.[36]

Instructed by his Foreign Office, Wangenheim was forced to concede much of his own opinion. He began serious negotiations with Russian Ambassador Giers. The Russians accepted two inspectorates, to be divided North–South not East–West, with governors-general to be named by the Ottoman Government. However, the Powers would name two 'advisors', who would have to agree with each governor-general's actions. Disagreements between the two would be adjudicated by the government 'after agreement with the embassies'. The embassies would have to agree with all instructions given to the governors-general. The Germans conceded that inspectorate assemblies would be half-Muslim and half-Christian, as would be administrative offices. The Russians, without notifying the Germans, then proceeded to present the Ottomans with a complicated plan that went much farther than the one to which the Germans had agreed.[37]

The Ottoman Government attempted to forestall the stringent plan by planning instead to appoint British officers in government ministries and as commanders and inspectors of the gendarmerie. The British refused. The Ottomans presented a revision of the German–Russian proposal that partially increased Ottoman control. Grey told the Ottomans he would not consider any proposals from them; the Ottomans must not put into effect any reform plans of their own. Grey stated: 'The impression in Europe, and especially in England, where people were deeply interested in the Question, would be deplorable, if after all of that had happened the assistance of Europe was refused.' Because the Ottoman Government deeply distrusted the Russians, it was left to the Germans to convince the Ottomans to accept the most recent proposal. Wangenheim told them that Ottoman refusal would be taken as an excuse by Russia to take military action against them. The Ottomans capitulated, only expressing a hope that they might later make small changes to the project.[38]

The Inspectorates Question apparently settled, Wangenheim left on vacation, leaving the embassy to his Chargé d'Affaires, Gerhard von Mutius. But when all seemed to be resolved among the Powers, the Russians demanded new Ottoman concessions on the military and the administration. The Russian Chargé d'Affaires was apologetic, but said his orders had come from St Petersburgh. The Ottomans were furious.

The new Russian demands seem to have been largely driven by events external to Eastern Anatolia: they had lost face over their failure to drive the Turks from Edirne. The Germans were increasingly influential in Istanbul, particularly in the military. This was unacceptable to the Russian hard-liners in St Petersburg. As politics and diplomacy sometimes are, the Russian reaction was irrational, and their opposition to the agreed-upon German–Russian plan made little sense. They had achieved most of what they intended in Eastern Anatolia. Extended negotiations followed in which the Germans managed to modify the Russian demands. The British advised the Russians to accept the new plan. Ultimately the Russians realised that they should not throw away their successes because of pique. They abandoned most of their new demands and accepted a final plan on 8 February 1914.[39]

The new Russian demands gave the Germans the chance to portray themselves as the friends of the Ottomans. They had stood against the Russian demands and forced changes that benefitted the Ottomans. The fact that the Germans had largely abandoned Ottoman interests in agreeing to so much of the initial Russian proposals could not have been lost on the Ottoman Government. But who else could be their friends, albeit friends who acted for their own political and military convenience?[40]

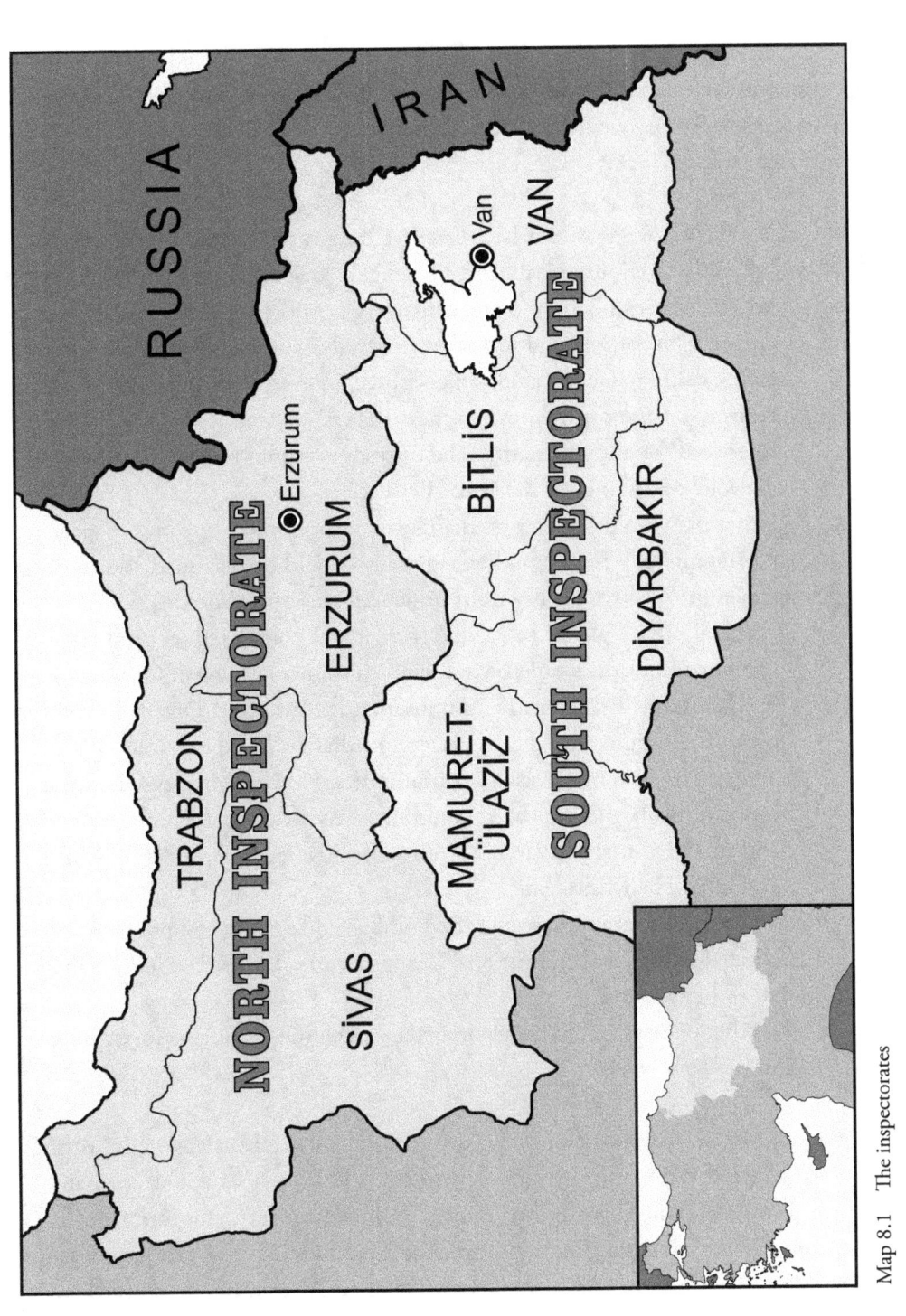

Map 8.1 The inspectorates

The inspectorates plan to which the Ottomans were forced to agree was little different from the original Russian plan. The major exception was that two inspectorates would be created, rather than the one envisaged by the Russians.

- Two inspectorates would be created: 1. Erzurum, Trabzon and Sivas. 2. Van, Bitlis, Mamuretülaziz and Diyarbakır. Inspectors-general (a deceptive term, because they were actually governors-general) would have control of the administration of justice, police and gendarmerie in their sectors, could name all senior officials except governors and could call out the army to support them when they wished. All land disputes would be 'supervised' by the inspectors. The inspectors would be chosen with 'the benevolent assistance of the Great Powers'.
- Conscripts would serve with their own inspectorate 'in times of peace and tranquility'. The Hamidiye regiments would be disarmed and transformed into reserve cavalry units under regular army orders.
- A general census would be held. Before it was completed, general councils and committees would be one-half Muslim and one-half Christian in Van, Bitlis and Erzurum. In Mamuretülaziz, Sivas and Diyarbakır proportional elections would take place immediately, based on electoral rolls and lists provided by Christian communities. However, if they found this process difficult, the inspectors could themselves decide the proportion of Muslim and Christian delegates. Administrative boards would all be half Muslim and half Christian.
- As posts came vacant, new members of the gendarmerie and police would be half Muslim, half Christian. The inspectors, however, could change that if they wished.
- All other matters would be negotiated between the Ottoman Government and the Powers.

Some of the provisions were less stringent than the Russians and British wanted: the Ottoman provinces remained. The inspectors could not name or dismiss provincial governors, only appeal to the Central Government for their dismissal. As long as the Ottomans were fighting in a protracted war in Yemen, conscripts from the inspectorates could continue to serve there, not only in their home provinces. The chaos that would ensue if all the gendarmes were changed to the 50–50 principle was avoided. The principle of proportionality in legislative bodies was at least theoretically accepted, although administrative bodies were still to be half Muslim and half Christian. Those few matters excepted, the inspectorates were still to be excisions from the Ottoman state.[41]

The British were extremely pleased with the result. The plan for the dismemberment of the Ottoman Empire in Eastern Anatolia, first suggested by Lord Salisbury, had at last come to fruition. Ambassador Mallet wrote: 'The Armenian question is solved at last, thank goodness.' Arthur Nicolson, the head of the Foreign Service, noted: 'I am glad that the Russians concluded the Armenian Reform project so successfully and I really do think that they deserve great credit for it.'[42]

**The Inspectors**

The inspectors were chosen in Europe. Selecting candidates proved to be difficult. All the Europeans agreed that neither of the inspectors should come from a Great Power. The Armenians did not want a Swiss or a Belgian. The Russians did not want a Swede. That left only Danish, Dutch or Norwegian possibilities. Ottoman diplomats were not part of the selection process, but Russian and Armenian representatives were consulted. Boghos Nubar, the representative of the Armenian Patriarch of Echmiadzin, was particularly prominent in the selection process. Louis C. Westenenk, an officer of the Dutch East India Colony, was chosen as inspector for the Northern Inspectorate (capital, Erzurum). A Norwegian major (made Lt Colonel upon his appointment), Nicholas Hoff, was appointed inspector for the Southern Inspectorate (capital, Van). Upon their selection, Westenenk and Hoff met with the Russian ambassador to the Netherlands, with Dashnak agents Hakob Zavrieb and Garo Pastermajian and with representatives of the Armenian Patriarch of Constantinople. They regaled the candidates with accounts of Armenian suffering. Neither candidate was especially concerned with the wishes of the Ottomans.[43]

The two inspectors, chosen by default politically, would not seem to have been particularly outstanding choices. Westenenk had at least been an administrator, an Assistant Resident in a province in Dutch Western Sumatra, but

Hoff had only been an army major. When he met the inspectors, Mallet was impressed with Westenenk, but worried that Hoff spoke only a few words of French. Hoff would need a Norwegian interpreter even for diplomatic communication. Neither inspector spoke Turkish, Armenian or Kurdish. The inspectors were given detailed instructions on how to carry out their duties. Oddly enough, the instructions provided for interpreters for Armenian and Kurdish, but not for Turkish.[44]

Hoff arrived in Van on 17 August 1914, where he was received coldly by Ottoman officials, but rapturously by Armenians. Ten days later, as World War I threatened, Hoff was recalled by the Ottoman Government. Westenenk never left Istanbul. All the plans for an autonomous Eastern Anatolia had been ended by war.

The inspectorates were the fulfillment of the plan first put forward by Salisbury a decade previously. Throughout the reform deliberations, the Ottoman Government had attempted to enlist the British in support of the Ottoman plans of reform. They had offered the British a large measure of control in their proposal to have British officials oversee bureaus of state and the gendarmerie. This was obviously intended to strike a balance against Russian intentions. Many Ottoman reformers also felt a kinship with what they saw as British ideals of government and economy. They naively hoped the British would apply these principles to the Ottoman Empire. The British repeatedly turned them down. Appeals to past British promises, doctrines of national sovereignty and the demographic preponderance of Muslims in Eastern Anatolia were ignored. Grey had made a point of telling them that they had no choice but to accept the dictates of Russia.

## Notes

1. On the inspectorates, see: McCarthy et al., *Van*, pp. 146–9 and 166–9. Joseph Heller, *British Policy towards the Ottoman Empire* (London: Cass, 1983), pp. 107–11. FO 371/2137, Beaumont to Grey, Constantinople, 4 December 1914. Nevzat Uyanık, 'Delegitimizing the Ottoman Imperial Order at the Threshold of New Diplomacy (The Interplay of Anglo-American Policies on the Ottoman Armenians, 1914–1923)', unpublished PhD dissertation, Princeton University, 2012, pp. 19–22. Zekeriya Türkmen, *Vilayât-ı Şarkiye (Dogu Anadolu Vilayetleri) Islahat Mufettişliği. 1913–1914*, Ankara: Türk Tarih Kurumu, 2006, and 'Birinci Dünya Savaşı Öncesinde İttihat ve Terakki Hükümetinin Doğu Anadolu Islahat

Projesi ve Uygulamaları', *Yedinci Askerî Tarih Semineri Bildirileri*, vol. 2, Ankara: Genelkurmay Basımevi, 2001. Although I disagree with many of his interpretations, see W. J. van der Dussen, 'The Question of Armenian Reforms in 1913–1914', *The Armenian Review*, vol. 39, no. 1 (Spring 1986), pp. 11–28. The embassy's 'Annual Report, 1913' is reliable only as an indication of British opinion. (FO 424/250. See pp. 24–8.)

2. On improvements made by the Ottoman Government, see, for example, McCarthy et al., *Van*, pp. 78–145. FO 195/2450, Monahan to Marling, Erzeroum, 23 and 29 September 1913; Monahan to Marling, Erzeroum, 23 September 1913; Molyneux-Seel to Lowther, Van, 9 July 1913; Monahan to Lowther, Erzeroum, 13 October 1913. FO 881/10164, Molyneux-Seel to Lowther, Van, 10 July 1912; FO 881/10339, Molyneux-Seel to Lowther, Van, 22 January 1913.

3. My colleagues and I have described the Armenian and Kurdish rebels of the pre-war period in detail in McCarthy et al., *Van*, pp. 54–175. See also Justin McCarthy, *Turks and Armenians: Nationalism and Conflict in the Ottoman Empire*, Madison, WI: Turco-Tatar Press, 2015, pp. 51–110. Hagop Manjikian, ed., *Houshamatyan of the Armenian Revolutionary Federation: Album-Atlas*, vol. 1, Los Angeles: Western United States Central Committee of the Armenian Revolutionary Federation, 2006, a long list and descriptions of Dashnak raids. There is no space here to consider the British consular reports, which are studied elsewhere, particularly in McCarthy et al., *Van*. See, for example, the various reports in FO 195/2375, 2284, 2450, 2456, 2458 and 2475, and FO 881/9542, 10164, 10339 and 10376.

4. The political developments, aims and actions of the Dashnaks have been considered in many studies, although only a few examples relevant to this period can be listed here: Hratch Dasnabedian, *History of the Armenian Revolution Federation, Dashnaktsutiun*, translated by Bryan Fleming and Vaha Habeshian, Milan: GEMME Edizione, 1989. Dikran Mesrob Kaligian, 'The Armenian Revolutionary Federation under Ottoman Constitutional Rule, 1908–1914', unpublished PhD dissertation, Boston College, 2003. M. Şükrü Hanioğlu, *Preparation for a Revolution: The Young Turks, 1902–1908*, Oxford: Oxford University Press, 2001. McCarthy et al., *Van*, pp. 130–43.

5. FO 195/2450, Molyneux-Seel to Lowther, Van, 4 April 1913 and many other references in FO 195/2450.

6. British Armenia Committee, *Armenia: Its People, Sufferings & Demands*, London: British Armenia Committee, 1913, pp. 29 and 32. In a letter to *The Times*, Aneurin Williams spoke for the committee in demanding that proposed reforms leave nothing in Eastern Anatolia under Ottoman control. ('Turkish Reforms and European

Control', *The Times*, 12 July 1913, p. 7.) See also the Commons speeches of members of the British Armenia Committee: the speech of Annan Bryce ('Albania and Montenegro', House of Commons Debate, 8 May 1913, *Hansard*, vol. 52, cc. 2298–329) in which he calls for implementation of the project that was to become the Russian proposal (see below); and the speeches of Noel Buxton, Arthur Ponsonby and T. P. O'Connor ('Civil Services and Revenue Departments Estimates, 1913–14', House of Commons Debate, 29 May 1913, *Hansard*, vol. 53, cc. 345–459.) Charitable organisations, such as the Friends of Armenia and the Armenian General Benevolent Union had little effect on British policies.

7. *Armenia: Its People, Sufferings & Demands*, pp. 4, 8–9 and 14–24.
8. 'Reforms in Armenia', *The Times*, 15 August 1913, p. 5.
9. Grey told parliament on 29 May 1913 that Britain was interested in 'the establishment of justice and sound finance' in the Asiatic Ottoman Empire, but that reform was a matter for the Powers, and he would offer no other information. ('Civil Services and Revenue Departments Estimates, 1913–14', House of Commons Debate, 29 May 1913, *Hansard*, vol. 53, cc. 345–459.) This was at a time when the reform proposals were being formulated, with British input, in Istanbul.
10. FO 424/238, Grey to O'Beirne, Foreign Office, 28 May 1913. See also, other indications of Grey's cooperation with the Russians: FO 424/238, Grey to Lowther, Foreign Office, 10 May 1913, and enclosure, Grey to Tewfiq Pasha, 10 May 1913; FO 424/238, Grey to Bertie, Foreign Office, 21 May 1913; FO 424/238, Grey to O'Beirne, Foreign Office, 23 May 1913. Judging by the diplomatic correspondence, Grey was primarily interested in the Baghdad Railway and the Shatt al-Arab, not Eastern Anatolia. FO 424/238, Grey to Bertie, Foreign Office, 28 May 1913. See also, FO 424/239, Grey to Buchanan, Foreign Office, 1 July 1913. On the political machinations of the inspectorates, see Joseph Heller, 'Britain and the Armenian Question, 1912–1914: A Study in Realpolitik', *Middle Eastern Studies*, vol. 16, no. 1 (January 1980), pp. 3–26. While his study is valuable for its depiction of European diplomacy, it suffers from its unquestioning acceptance of British official attitudes toward the situation in Eastern Anatolia, primarily caused by a lack of consideration of the consular record. Also, Heller's article was published in 1980, before most of the modern studies of the area were published.
11. Cambon to Pichon, London, 5 June 1913, in DD 7, no. 32. The Russians either acted quickly in drawing up a proposal or had one waiting. (Boppe to Pichon, Pera, 9 June 1913, in DD 7, no. 55.)

12. FO 424/238, Grey to O'Beirne, Foreign Office, 23 May 1913; Tewfik Pasha to Grey, London, 23 May 1913; Grey to Tewfik Pasha, Foreign Ministry, 24 May 1913; 'Communication from Tewfik Pasha', London, 24 April 1913. Grey to Lowther, Foreign Office, 6, 15 and 19 May 1913; and the minutes by Arthur Nicolson, Louis Mallet and Grey, in BDOW 10/1, pp. 427–33. FO 800/367, O'Beirne to Nicolson, St Petersburg, 29 May 1913. Arthur Nicolson wrote that he could see no problem with Britain sending six or seven officers: 'I cannot myself see how Sazonoff can take exception to this course.' He was wrong; Sazonov did. (FO 800/366/2, Nicolson to Lowther, Foreign Office, 30 April 1913 and 27 May 1913.) The Germans had already stated in April that they had no objections to English gendarmerie officers and advisors. (Jagow to Wangenheim, Foreign Office, 23 April 1913, in GP 38, p. 32.)

13. FO 424/238, Sazonof to Count Benckendorff (Communicated by Russian ambassador to Sir A. Nicolson, 27 May), St Petersburgh, 12 (25) May 1913; O'Beirne to Grey, St Petersburgh, 27 May 1913; Grey to O'Beirne, Foreign Office, 28 May and 9 June 1913.

14. See Chapter 2, pp. xx.

15. FO 424/238, Sazonof to Benckendorff, Saint-Petersbourg, 12 (25) May 1913 (Communicated by Russian ambassador to Sir A. Nicolson, 27 May). Kurat (pp. 206–24) gave a valuable description of the Russian plans and manoeuvring at the time of the Inspectorates Question, but not much consideration of British actions or the actual deliberations on the plans. Kurat (p. 212) believed that Russia's primary purpose in supporting the separation of Eastern Anatolia was to give it access to the Mediterranean, perhaps to build a naval base at İskenderun. I doubt if this could have been more than a long-range, and perhaps fanciful, explanation.

16. FO 424/205, Stevens to Lansdowne, Batum, numerous dispatches in September and October 1903; FO 424/205, Scott to Lansdowne, St Petersburg, 17 September 1903; FO 424/186, Stevens to Salisbury, Batoum, 23 January 1896; the entries in FO 881/8202, Scott to Lansdowne, St Petersburgh and Batum, 15, 17, 18, 19, 23, 24, 25 and 26 September and 1 and 29 October 1903; ARF History, p. 70. There had been earlier seizures. For a general picture, see Anahide Ter Minassian, *Nationalism and Socialism in the Armenian Revolutionary Movement*, trans. A. M. Berrett, Cambridge, MA: Zoryan, 1984, pp. 7, 31, 32; Ronald Grigor Suny, 'Eastern Armenia Under Tsarist Rule', in Richard G. Hovannisian, ed., *The Armenian People from Ancient to Modern Times*, vol. II, New York: St. Martin's, 1997, pp. 131–5. Hratch Dasnabedian, *History of the*

*Armenian Revolution Federation, Dashnaktsutiun*, translated by Bryan Fleming and Vahan Habeshian, Milan: GEMME Edizione, 1989, pp. 69–71.

17. FO 195/2450, Molyneaux-Seel to Lowther, Van, 11 June 1913. FO 371/2449, Molyneux-Seel to Lowther, Van, 8 May 1913.
18. See, for example, FO 371/1263, Molyneux-Seel to Lowther, Van, 31 October 1911; FO 371/2449, Molyneux-Seel to Lowther, Van, 8 May 1913. FO 195/2450, Molyneux-Seel to Lowther, Van, 24 March 1913; and the other references in this chapter.
19. On the Russians and the Kurds, see the details in McCarthy et al., *Van*, pp. 152–62. See also FO 195/2450, Molyneux-Seele to Lowther, Van, 24 May 1913. FO 195/2458, Smith to Mallet, Van, 14 February 1914; Smith to Mallet, Van, 29 May 1914. FO 371/2130, Mallet to Grey, Therapia, 2 July 1914. Michael A. Reynolds, 'The Ottoman-Russian Struggle for Eastern Anatolia and the Caucasus, 1908–1918: Identity, Ideology and the Geopolitics of World Order', unpublished PhD dissertation, Princeton University, 2003, pp. 91–138, and *Shattering Empires: The Clash and Collapse of the Ottoman and Russian Empires, 1908–1918*, Cambridge: Cambridge University Press, 2011, pp. 46–81. David McDowall, *A Modern History of the Kurds*, London: I. B. Tauris, 2000, pp. 53–9 and 112.
20. The Germans realised that the Russians were in fact fomenting trouble in Eastern Anatolia. Ambassador Wangenheim even felt that the Russians were supporting Kurdish rebels in the expectation that they would massacre Armenians, which would bring Russian intervention. He asserted that Russia was always planning to obtain 'fat morsels', as exemplified by their actions in Iran. (Wangenheim to Bethmann-Hollweg, Pera, 12 April and 20 May 1913, in GP 38, pp. 22–6 and 38.)
21. Wangenheim to Jagow, Constantinople, 7 June 1913, in GP 38, pp. 71–3.
22. Wangenheim to Jagow, Constantinople, 10 June 1913, in GP 38, pp. 73–6. On German hopes for British agreement, see also Lichnowsky to Jagow, London, 26 June 1913, in GP 38, pp. 84–5. The Germans believed the Russians intended to use the Eastern Anatolian problem to bring pressure on the Ottomans over Eastern Thrace. (Pourtales to Chancellor Bethmann Hollweg, St Petersburg, 24 July 1913, in GP 38, p. 112.) This surely was not a sufficient reason for Russian plans for Eastern Anatolia.
23. FO 424/238, Grey to O'Beirne, Foreign Office, 4 June 1913. The French had also desired that all the Powers take part, and that it was premature to draw up a plan. They nevertheless took part. (FO 424/238, Grey to Bertie, Foreign Office,

29 May 1913.) FO 424/238, Grey to Lowther, 6 June 1913; O'Beirne to Grey, St Petersburgh, 11 June 1913.

The French Government suggested in June 1913 that the Ottoman Government immediately appoint an 'Imperial High Commissioner with most extended powers to maintain order and be responsible for security of the country'. Grey agreed, if the other Powers also did, but said: 'Program of reforms to be applied in Armenia would remain quite distinct from his (the High Commissioner's) mission.' The Russians agreed to let the ambassadors consider it, but felt it was a bad idea that could not work. Nothing came of it. (FO 195/2450, Grey Telegram to Istanbul (no recipient listed), 19 June 1913. FO 424/238, Grey to Nicolson, Foreign Office, 20 June 1913; Buchanan to Grey, St Petersburgh, 21 June 1913.)

24. FO 424/238, enclosure in Lowther to Grey, Constantinople, 17 June 1913. Although the proposal was basically that of the Russian dragoman, André Mandelstam, it was finally decided upon by Mandelstam, Fitzmaurice and the Second Secretary of the French Embassy, René de St Quentin. The Armenian National Assembly was consulted, but their input is unknown. Eyre Crowe, the second in command official in the Foreign Office, wrote that the British had considerable input in the document. (September 23, Crowe minute to Marling to Grey, Constantinople, 27 August 1913, in BDOW 10/1, p. 516.) Wangenheim said the Russian proposal was not formally submitted by the committee to the ambassadors' meeting until 30 June 1913. (Wangenheim to Foreign Office, Therapia, 30 June 1913, in GP 38, pp. 86–7.)

The French, who had very little to do with the project, supported the British and Russian proposals. French Foreign Minister Gaston Domergue accepted the equal division of power between Muslims and Armenians. This, he felt, was proper because, while the Armenians were a minority, they were more prosperous:

> En effet, par son activité commerciale et son instruction, l'élément arménien représente le principal facteur de la prospérité du pays et l'emporte de beaucoup sur l'élément musulman. Il est juste que cette situation entre en balance et serve de compensation à l'infériorité numérique des Arméniens.

(Doumergue to Boppe, Paris, 17 January 1914, in DD 9, no. 96.)

25. FO 424/238, Grey to Buchanan, Foreign Office, 13 and 16 June 1913; Circular Notes from Sazonof, communicated by Count Benckendorff, London, 14 and 16 June 1913; Buchanan to Grey, St Petersburgh, 17 June 1913; Benckendorff to Sazonof (communicated to the Foreign Office, 3 June 1913). Wangenheim to Foreign Office, Therapia, 30 June and 3 July 1913, in GP 38, pp. 86–9.

FO 424/239, Grey to Granville, Foreign Office, 7 July 1913. Ambassador Lowther, as ill-informed as usual, wrote that he had not heard of an Ottoman proposal. (FO 424/238, Lowther to Grey, Constantinople, 18 June 1913.)

26. Wangenheim to Bethmann Hollweg (German Chancellor), Therapia, 3 July 1913, in GP 38, pp. 89–95. Jagow to Pourtales, Foreign Office, 14 July 1913, in GP 38, pp. 104–5.

27. Lowther to Grey, Constantinople, 30 June 1913, in BDOW 10/2, p. 468. Fitzmaurice summarised his opinions on the previous meetings of the committee in 'Memorandum by Mr. Fitzmaurice', 10 August 1913, enclosure in Marling to Grey, Constantinople, 27 August 1913. Arthur Nicolson and Eyre Crowe, the senior officials in the Foreign Office, both wrote that Fitzmaurice 'should be warmly thanked for his thoughtful and effective presentation of a very complicated problem'. (Minute to this document, 23 September 1913, in BDOW 10/1, p. 516.)

28. The text of the very detailed Ottoman reform proposal is in FO 424/239, Said Halim to Marling, 1 July 1913, enclosure in Marling to Grey, Constantinople, 3 July 1913.

29. Boppe to Pichon, Constantinople, 3 July 1913, in DD 7, no. 270. FO 424/239, Granville to Grey, Berlin, 9 July 1913; Cartwright to Grey, Vienna, 15 July 1913; Grey to Buchanan, Foreign Office, 9 July 1913. At the first meeting of the ambassadors, as instructed, the British and Russian representatives considered only the Russian proposal, but broke up when the German and Russian disagreed. They awaited further instructions from the respective governments. (FO 424/239, Marling to Grey, 4 July 1913.) The Italian Government, which was little interested, wanted an Ottoman high commissioner and was against any break-up of the Ottoman Empire. (FO 424/239, Rodd to Grey, Rome, 13 July 1913.) Wangenheim to Foreign Office, Constantinople, 7 July 1913, in GP 38, pp. 98–9.

30. FO 424/239, Marling to Grey, Constantinople, 14 July 1913.

31. Wangenheim to Foreign Office, Constantinople, 13 July 1913, in GP 38, pp. 103–4. FO 424/239, Buchanan to Grey, St Petersburgh, 13 July 1913. Cambon to Pichon, London, 12 July 1913, in DD 7, no. 349. The Ottomans still proposed to have six sectors, compromising the entire Empire. (See the above and FO 424/239, Marling to Grey, 15 July 1913.)

32. FO 424/240, enclosure and comments in Mallet to Grey, Constantinople, 12 November 1913. FO 424/240, Mallet to Grey, Constantinople, 12 November 1913.

33. Wangenheim to Jagow, Constantinople, 22 July 1913, and enclosure from Jagow, in GP 38, pp. 104–7.
34. Wangenheim to Jagow, Constantinople, 31 July 1913, in GP 38, pp. 119–21.
35. Wangenheim to Bethmann Hollweg, Therapia, 4 and 30 August 1913, in GP 38, pp. 124–7 and 136–7. Jagow to Wangenheim, Foreign Office, 1 September 1913, in GP 38, pp. 137–8. Wangenheim to the Foreign Office, 8 September 1913, in GP 38, pp. 138–40. See also Pichon to ambassadors in European capitals, Paris, 1 August 1913, in DD 7, no. 515.
36. Wangenheim to the Foreign Office, 14 October 1913, in GP 38, pp. 150–1. Kühlmann to Bethmann Hollweg, London, 8 December 1913, in GP 38, pp. 169–70.
37. Marling to Grey, Constantinople, 26 September 1913, in BDOW 10/1, p. 517. Zimmermann to Wangenheim, Foreign Office, 24 October 1913, in GP 38, pp. 154–5. Wangenheim to the Foreign Office, 7 November 1913, in GP 38, pp. 158–9. Wangenheim to Bethmann Hollweg, Pera, 26 November 1913. See also, Grey to O'Beirne, Foreign Office, 27 October 1913, in BDOW 10/2, pp. 520–1. Minute by Eyre Crowe, 1 November 1913, in BDOW 10/2, p. 522. Grey to Mallet, Foreign Office, 3 November 1913, in BDOW 10/2, p. 523.
38. FO 424/240, Mallet to Grey, Constantinople, 1 December 1913. Wangenheim to the Foreign Office, 20 and 25 December 1913, in GP 38, pp. 170–1. Mutius to Foreign Office, 29 December 1913, in GP 38, pp. 171–2. Goschen to Grey, Berlin, 10 November 1913, in BDOW 10/2, p. 526. Grey to Goschen, Foreign Office, 4 November 1913, and Grey to Mallet, Foreign Office, 8 November 1913, in BDOW 10/2, pp. 523 and 525. FO 195/2450, Grey to Mallet, FO 371/1833, Foreign Office, 3 November 1914. Grey to Mallet, Foreign Office, 8 November 1913, Mallet to Grey, Constantinople, 18 November 1913, in BDOW 10/2, pp. 529–30. FO 371/1833, Mallet to Grey, Constantinople, 5 November 1913; Grey to Mallet, Foreign Office, 8 November 1913. On the final stage of negotiations see BDOW 10/2, pp. 521–48.
39. Pourtales to Foreign Office, St Petersburg, 11 January 1914, in GP 38, p. 175. Mutius to Foreign Office, Constantinople, 16 and 20 January and 2 February 1914, in GP 38, pp. 176–9. Doulcet to Doumergue, St Petersburg, 7 February 1914, in DD 9, no. 240.
40. Mutius to Foreign Office, Constantinople, 5, 6 and 10 January and 2 and 9 February 1914, in GP 38, pp. 172–4 and 179–81.
41. FO 424/251, 'Note to be Addressed to Representatives of Great Powers', enclosure in Mallet to Grey, Constantinople, 9 February 1914.

42. FO 800/372/2, Mallet to Nicolson, Constantinople, 10 February 1914; Nicolson to Mallet, Foreign Office, 16 February 1914. See also FO 424/251, Mallet to Grey, Constantinople, 9 February 1913.
43. FO 371/2116, Mallet to Grey, Constantinople, 1 February 1914. McCarthy et al., *Van*, pp. 166–9. On the machinations of the selection of the inspectors-general and Westenenk's distinctly anti-Turkish attitude, see L. C. Westenenk, 'Diary Concerning the Armenian Mission', *The Armenian Review*, vol. 39, no. 1 (Spring 1986), pp. 29–89.
44. FO 371/2116, Mallet to Grey, Constantinople, 27 May 1914; 'Instructions relatives aux attributions et à la compétence des Inspecteurs Généraux', enclosure in Mallet to Grey, Pera, 17 June 1914.

# 9

## WORLD WAR

When World War I broke out in Europe, the British might have been expected to do all they could to attract the Ottoman Empire to their side. Having the Ottomans as allies would have been of great advantage to the British: the oil fields of Iran and the Suez Canal would have been protected without British effort or cost. The Bosporus and Dardanelles Straits would have been open to supply Russia. Failing an alliance, the British could hope for an Ottoman neutrality that would free British and Russian troops for battles in Europe. The questions for the British was what could they offer the Ottomans in return for alliance or neutrality and, for the Ottomans, whether British promises could be trusted.[1]

The answer to the question of what the British would offer the Ottomans was simple – nothing. The British were stymied by their past actions, the true intentions of British politicians and popular feeling in Britain. One thing that could easily have been promised to the Ottomans was possession of the Aegean Islands, at least those closest to the mainland of Anatolia, but Greece was sacrosanct to the British. The British would never relinquish their own possessions and protectorates in Arabia, and surely not Egypt. Western Iran and the Caucasus were held by their Russian allies. Most of Macedonia was part of Serbia and Greece; British and Russian sympathy for the Serbs and Greeks would not allow any part of their new conquests to be taken away from them.

There were some carrots that the British might offer: first among these was money. The Ottomans were in a perpetual financial bind. Indeed, it was the provision of German gold that finally committed the Ottomans to the war. The long-sought increase in Ottoman customs duty, which Britain had singlehandedly opposed, might have been granted. Foreign Secretary Grey refused. The British could have accepted the abolition of the Capitulations. Grey again refused. He offered only vague assurances that abrogation might be considered in the future.

## Ambassador Mallet

The Foreign Office replaced Ambassador Lowther and Chargé Marling with a much more able man, Louis du Pan Mallet. Mallet had extensive experience in the Foreign Office and its deliberations on the Middle East, although his only Middle Eastern posting had been two years in Cairo. He had served as Private Secretary to Grey from 1905 to 1907, then Assistant Under-Secretary of State for Near and Middle Eastern Affairs from 1907 to 1913. He proved to be an able representative of Great Britain, but one with an impossible task.

Mallet understood the difficulties of the Ottoman Government. Unlike Lowther, his relations with the Ottoman Government were amicable. (Cemal Paşa: 'We had most active and amicable relations with Sir Louis Mallet, who was a particularly fine man, thoroughly honest, and very kind.') He repeatedly counselled the Foreign Office to adopt a more sympathetic stance toward the Ottomans. He communicated well with the Ottoman leaders, and wrote that they generally wished to reform the Empire. A bit of sympathy from the British Government, he felt, would have great effect. The Ottomans should at least be consulted on matters that affected them, not only ordered to comply with British wishes. But as World War I approached, the Foreign Office had no wish to follow his advice. And the Ottomans had learned that the promises of the British were unreliable, even when transmitted by a competent ambassador.[2]

## The War in Europe Begins

Once the European war began, what Grey offered the Ottomans were threats: he offered no benefits if they joined the side of Britain, but threatened 'the gravest consequences' if they took the side of Germany. He described this as 'good advice from Turkey's oldest friend'.

> You (Chargé d'Affaires in Istanbul Beaumont) should earnestly impress upon Grand Vizier that Turkish interest would best be served by maintaining a strict neutrality. If Turkey were to be drawn into the war as an ally of Germany and Austria the gravest consequences would follow. You must, however, be careful to give to your communication the character of good advice from Turkey's oldest friend and avoid anything to give rise to an impression that we are threatening.[3]

How Beaumont could have portrayed this 'good advice' as anything but a threat was unmentioned. Grey was actually more temperate than Beaumont himself, who had suggested that the Ottomans formally be told that they would lose Eastern Anatolia if they joined the Central Powers.[4]

The use of the phrase 'make Turkey feel' in Grey's statement on British policy is instructive:

> The proper course was to make Turkey feel that, should she remain neutral, and should Germany and Austria be defeated, we would take care that the integrity of Turkish possessions as they now were would be preserved in any terms of peace affecting the Near East; but that, on the other hand, if Turkey sided with Germany and Austria, and they were defeated, of course we could not answer for what might be taken from Turkey in Asia.[5]

Of course, the 'Turkish possessions as they now were' had been much reduced. The Balkans, Crete and the Aegean Islands were gone. The British had accepted, and often even directed, the Ottoman loss. Just a few months before, the British had backed a plan to remove Eastern Anatolia from Ottoman control. The British had supported the Russians throughout the inspectorates deliberations. They could only be expected to support their Russian allies during and after the war. And the Russians had long planned to seize Istanbul and the Straits. If they won the war, they would take them, no matter any British promises. British promises had been broken often enough in the past. The British had not kept their promises to defend Ottoman territorial rights made in the Treaty of Paris, the Treaty of London, the Treaty of Berlin and the Cyprus Convention. It is true that each time Britain had broken its treaty commitments, the British had been influenced by the demands of European politics, but that was exactly the situation in 1914, and would have been the situation after the war.

Others noticed how minimal was Grey's promise on Ottoman borders, which only extended to deliberations in a future peace conference. The French suggested that the guarantee of the integrity of the Ottoman Empire be extended to the period after the war. Grey refused to consider any change in his token statement on Ottoman borders. The Russians, for their part, even refused to join the British and French in any guarantee of Ottoman border integrity. That alone made any guarantees even more meaningless.[6]

Other European Powers had cooperated with the British in coercing the Ottomans at various times, different allies in different cases, but the one consistency across all was that the British had attempted to divide and diminish the Ottoman Empire. Given their history, why would any Ottoman politician have been willing to remain neutral, and thus cooperate with the British and Russians? In their inspectorates plans, both had shown their willingness to detach much territory from the Empire, and likely to preside over the Empire's demise. If the Russians won the war, they would surely claim Eastern Anatolia, the Straits and probably Istanbul itself. The British had shown they could not be relied upon to keep to their promises on Ottoman territorial integrity. The only rational course open to the Ottomans was to do all they could to cause Russia to lose the war.

**Ottoman Attempts at Détente with Britain and France**

Geopolitical considerations were not the only factors facing the Ottoman Government. There were indeed reasons to remain neutral. After all, the Russians might lose the war despite Ottoman neutrality. One reason to avoid conflict was surely the trauma of the Balkan Wars. Soldiers and war material had been lost. Refugees packed the cities. State finances were a disaster. Would the Turkish people be willing to fight yet another war? Although not necessarily against war with the Russians, some cabinet ministers felt it better to wait until military reforms had taken effect and the army and navy were ready. And there was another reason to avoid joining the Germans – what might be called political psychology. To those had who revolted against their own autocracy, applied a constitution and looked for the eventual application of democratic values, the British and French had always seemed to be models, no matter that the British and French were democrats at home and autocrats in their colonies. Many simply did not like the Germans or the German system. Some feared that allying with the Germans would simply be choosing a new master.[7]

The disastrous effects of their past isolation had convinced Ottoman officials that the Empire needed allies. Nevertheless, the politically aware part of the Ottoman populace and members of the Ottoman Government were far from committed to opposing the British and allying with the Germans. Voices in the Ottoman Parliament and Government called for neutrality or perhaps even alliance with the British and French. Those in the Ottoman Government and political circles who wanted to avoid dependence on the Germans did all they could to ally themselves with the British and French, or at least to gain more friendly British and French policies toward the Ottomans.[8]

Ahmed Cemal Paşa, a leader of the CUP Government, was particularly active in cultivating a better relationship with the French and British. Cemal approached Ambassador Mallet and stressed that he was a partisan of Britain and France. He reminded Mallet that the Ottomans had gone far to satisfy British desires: they had agreed to British petroleum concessions in Iraq and to new shipping routes on the Tigris and Euphrates. Concessions had been given to British companies to extend the Smyrna to Aydın Railway and to build new harbours at Trabzon and Samsun. The Ottomans had settled the crisis that erupted over the construction of the Baghdad Railway by granting British and French wishes over those of Germany, in the process allowing economic spheres of interest in Iraq for the British and in Syria for the French. They had shown their friendship and respect for the British by trying to obtain British inspectors for government bureaus and for the Eastern Anatolian provinces. A British admiral had been named to reorganise the Ottoman fleet. But, Cemal stated, Britain had to show the Ottomans something in return to indicate British friendship. In reply, Mallet told Cemal quite openly that Britain would always think first of her alliance with France and Russia, not Ottoman interests. Cemal responded that Britain could at least do something. 'He pleaded strongly and earnestly with me to ask His Majesty's Government to consider whether it would not be possible to take rather a less negative line with Turkey than they had done in the past two years.' Though Mallet was personally sympathetic, Cemal pleaded in vain.[9]

In June 1914, Cemal went to Paris and made overtures for an alliance with France and Britain, but was rebuffed. The French were interested, but would not act without their allies, and Britain and Russia would never agree.[10]

Ottoman Minister of War Enver Paşa communicated to the Russians a plan for good relations and perhaps even an alliance between Russia and the Ottomans, probably to buy time until Ottoman forces were ready for war. His plan envisaged a grand alliance that would include the Balkan countries. He made various promises – to reduce troops on the Russian border and make an accommodation with Russian desires for the Straits, for example. While Cemal may have been at least somewhat sincere in his appeals to Britain and France, Enver surely was not. Talat also stated a desire for an Ottoman–Russian alliance in a visit to the Tsar in Livadia in May 1914. The Russians, and probably Talat, did not consider an alliance a real possibility.[11]

The Ottoman attempts to conciliate Britain demonstrate the naivete of new rulers unschooled in European *real politique*. Cemal Paşa and others were probably sincere in trying to draw Britain and France into a more cooperative relationship with the Ottoman Empire. They may only, as some have believed, have been disguising their real intentions. The latter seems doubtful, given Ottoman attempts at an alliance with Britain from 1911 on. Nevertheless, détente with Britain was impossible. The Russian alliance was the foundation of British plans to oppose Germany. The Russians, as always coveting the Straits, would not accept the Ottoman as allies, and the British public would probably not have stood for an alliance with the Ottomans. Moreover, the British, like most of the world, believed the Ottoman Empire was doomed.

## The Aegean Islands

One British attitude, among others, festered in the Ottoman mind – the Aegean Islands. The Ottomans never abandoned their determination to remove the threat posed by the Greek occupation of the islands close to the Anatolian coast. They announced that they would never accept that, and were not unwilling to resort to war with Greece to regain them. The Ottomans clearly understood that the British had been instrumental in delivering the Aegean Islands to Greece. When the Grand Vezir spoke of the Powers' plan for the islands, he called it 'la proposition anglaise'. Ambassador Mallet noted: 'I fear that the impression will remain for some time that we have taken a harsh line with them (the Ottomans) and sacrificed their interests with a view to propitiating Greece.' That was, of course, exactly what had happened.[12]

> (Ambassador Mallet) He (Grand Vezir Said Halım) could not understand Britain's animosity toward the Ottomans: 'His Government had honestly tried to settle all outstanding questions with His Majesty's Government, with whom they wished to be on good terms and whose friendship they valued. They hoped that this disposition on their part would have met with appreciation and encouragement, but their advances had hitherto been met with coldness, their requests for assistance refused, and now proposals had been initiated by His Majesty's Government which gave an impression of actual unfriendliness.'[13]

The main British concern in 1914 was to prevent the Ottomans from seizing any of the territory they had lost in the Balkan Wars – the same policy Britain had attempted to implement in Eastern Thrace. Britain had failed to stop the Ottoman reconquest of Eastern Thrace, but was worried that the Ottomans might try to recapture the Aegean Islands, or even go to war with Greece. Britain was much concerned that this might lead to the closing of the Straits, which it found most unacceptable. The Ottoman Government had steadfastly refused to accept any Greek possession of the islands. The Grand Vezir told Ambassador Mallet: 'Turkey could not accept their decisions unless the Powers sent their fleets to Turkish waters to impose their wishes by force.'[14]

Greece was to remain in possession of the islands, even though formal annexation was not fixed until after World War I. Ottoman representatives continued to complain to the British of the Greek occupation. They were met with British assurances that their needs would be considered and that final decisions on the islands had not been made, which was untrue. Grey even told them that the British had no interest in the islands question, and the British would only agree with the settlement decided by the other Powers – another completely untrue statement, because the British had proposed and fostered the award to Greece.[15]

## Capitulations

Externally, the lack of Ottoman power was obvious – they had just lost most of Ottoman Europe to states that had once been Ottoman possessions. Internally, the Powers planned to force them to relinquish control over even more territory – Eastern Anatolia. But perhaps nothing contributed to an accurate understanding that the Ottoman Empire was not an independent country like the Capitulations.

What were called the Capitulations were a set of privileges, some going back to the sixteenth century, granted by the Ottoman sultan to European states and eventually even to minor states. Once awarded to 'most favoured nations' as a diplomatic tool, the privileges had expanded through European military and financial power until they included many of the symbols of state sovereignty: Europeans and Americans operated their own post offices, for example. Europeans were tried in their own courts, immune from Ottoman justice. The Ottomans were not allowed to set their own customs duties or the taxes paid by Europeans within the Empire. The capitulatory privileges were extended not only to foreign nationals but to Ottoman subjects (*beratlı*) who were put under the protection of the Europeans.[16]

At the end of the nineteenth century the Ottomans had tried to alter the Capitulations and had failed. The advent of war in Europe and the failure of the Powers to give any satisfaction to their needs encouraged the Ottomans to act unilaterally. On 9 September 1914, the Ottoman Government notified the European ambassadors that it would abolish the Capitulations. The ambassadors, including those of Germany and Austria, but not Italy or the United States, protested that they could not recognise unilateral abolition. However, all but the British soon indicated that they were willing to compromise.[17]

In October of 1913, the Kaiser had sent General Otto Liman von Sanders to head a German military mission to the Ottoman Empire. Liman brought with him forty German officers entrusted with reorganisation of Ottoman army units. At first, Liman was named Commander of the First Army in the capital, but protests and extended negotiations among the Powers forced the Ottomans to change his appointment to that of Inspector-General of the Ottoman Empire, a position without line command. Nevertheless, the only Europeans with influence in the Ottoman army remained the Germans.

Once the war began, the Entente Powers believed, not without justification, that the German officers would become the nucleus of a joint Ottoman–German command.[18]

For Foreign Secretary Grey, the abolition of the Capitulations might have opened the possibility of weaning the Ottoman from their military attachment to the Germans, but Grey insisted there would be no concessions on the Capitulations unless German military and civilian advisors left the Ottoman Empire first. After that, he promised, changes in the Capitulations would be considered, but he made no commitments – the sort of vague assurance that had proved futile before. Ambassador Mallet thought Grey's position was a mistake. Mallet wanted compromise to be discussed with the Ottoman Government, because an outright refusal to consider Ottoman wishes would only strengthen the pro-Germans in the cabinet. The French proposed moderate concessions. The Ottomans agreed to reconsider their unilateral action if the British would accept equal taxation for foreigners and Ottoman subjects and allowed customs duties to be raised to 15 per cent (from 11 per cent). They also asked the British to aid them in negotiations with French bankers. The French and Russians were willing to agree to the increase of customs duties to 15 per cent. Ambassador Mallet also wanted to do so. ('There will be so many means of putting pressure on the Turks after the war that I do not much fear the concession.') But the British refused to consider even the moderate concessions on the Capitulations offered by the French.[19]

The Ottomans finally declared their full independence over all fiscal and customs matters. They unilaterally set the 15 per cent customs dues. Grey refused to accept their declaration and said the Ottomans would ultimately pay for their fiscal temerity: '[A]nd that when the moment arrives (that is, after the war) the Powers will ask the Porte to render account for them.'[20]

The Russians were much more conciliatory than the British: if the Ottomans would not mobilise their army and remained neutral, the Russians proposed, they would be given all of Germany's concessions in the Empire, including the Baghdad Railway. The island of Lemnos would be taken from Greece and given to the Ottomans. The Capitulations would be modified. The British and French opposed the proposal, primarily because changes in the Capitulations would damage them commercially, and the Russians withdrew their suggestions. On 4 September 1914, the Entente Allies agreed to act together in any negotiations with the Ottoman Empire, in effect to follow the British lead.[21]

## Ships

In the summer of 1914, the Ottoman Cabinet remained divided on joining the war, but those who wanted to join the Germans proved to be more politically adept than those who opposed it. Enver Paşa, Minister of War and a Germanophile, began secretly negotiating with the Germans in July 1914. On 2 August, Enver and Grand Vezir Said Halim, without notifying the rest of the cabinet, signed a treaty with Germany. Ottoman mobilisation began immediately, although the Ottoman Government assured the British that mobilisation was only a precaution intended to protect Ottoman territory from attack. The Grand Vezir, who had just signed the pact with Germany, declared that the Ottoman Empire would remain strictly neutral.[22]

Even as Enver and colleagues bargained with the Germans, Ottoman entry in the war was not assured. Those who advocated neutrality still had the upper hand in the Ottoman Cabinet, and the treaty with the Germans had not been known by all but rather only by a few, much less ratified. Neutrality might still have triumphed. It was British actions that changed everything.

The Ottoman Government had contracted with British yards to construct two battleships, the Reşadiye and the Sultan Osman. The Ottoman need for the ships was emotional as well as military. They were to mark a resurgence as a power able to defend itself after the Greek dominance of the sea in the Balkan Wars. Much of their £3.7 million cost had been collected in a great public campaign. Ottoman sailors went to Britain to take charge of the ships, but on 3 August Winston Churchill, the First Lord of the Admiralty, refused to release the already paid for ships to the Ottomans. The seizure was illegal, but the British Cabinet approved it. The ships became part of the British fleet.

It can be argued that Churchill's actions were pragmatically justified – the ships might have been used against British allies if the Ottomans joined the Germans. They might, and probably would, have spearheaded an attack on the Greeks in the Aegean Islands. Politically and diplomatically, however, the seizures were a disaster. The reaction in the Ottoman Empire was enormous. Public opinion turned completely against the British. Newspapers in the main cities and the provinces decried British perfidy. Street demonstrations denounced the British. Even politicians sympathetic to the British and French joined in the condemnation.[23]

Events provided the Ottomans with ships to replace those seized by the British. The German battle cruiser Goeben and light cruiser Breslau, fleeing the British Mediterranean fleet, came to the mouth of the Dardanelles on 10 August. After diplomatic manoeuvring between the Ottomans and Germans, they traversed the Dardanelles, arriving at Istanbul. The British demanded that the ships either be interned or sent out to fight, according to the rules of war. The Germans and Ottomans answered with a 'sale' of the two ships to the Ottoman navy. German sailors donned fezzes and the German commander, Rear Admiral Wilhelm Souchon, was named 'Commander of the Ottoman Fleet'.[24]

Receiving the news, Churchill, without consulting the cabinet, ordered a British blockade of the Dardanelles. The British refused to accept the 'sale'. Ambassador Mallet carried out his instructions from London: he notified the Ottoman Government that if the ships left the Dardanelles, they would be treated as German ships and attacked. He told the Grand Vezir the Ottoman Empire was now a 'German Protectorate'. He said Britain would have 'a free hand' unless the German sailors left. Grey stated the British would not remove the British fleet from the approach to the Dardanelles, but told the Ottomans that 'Turkey would have nothing to fear from British ships'.[25]

Churchill wrote a personal note to Enver Paşa, the Minister of War, in which he threatened the Ottomans, stating that:

> The overwhelming superiority at sea possessed by the navies of England, France, Russia, and Japan over those of Austria and Germany renders it easy for the four allies to transport troops in almost unlimited numbers from any quarter of the globe, and if they were forced into a quarrel with Turkey, their blow could be delivered at the heart.[26]

On 27 September, an Ottoman destroyer attempted to exit the Dardanelles. It was turned back by the British fleet. The strait was immediately closed by the Ottomans, who announced the Dardanelles would not be reopened until the British fleet left. The British refused to do so until all the German officers and men had left Ottoman waters.[27]

## War

By October 1914, the British and the Ottomans were in fact in an undeclared war. The British had interdicted the Ottoman navy at the mouth of the Dardanelles, which, by the rules of war, it could only do once war had been declared. The Ottomans had closed and mined the Dardanelles; again, this was something that treaties only allowed when the Ottomans were at war. Both sides prepared for actual war. In September, ships carrying coal that was needed for the Ottoman fleet were stopped by British ships at the Dardanelles, and the British convinced the United States not to allow any coal for the Ottomans to leave America. The Ottomans built up their forces in Syria, obviously preparing for a possible attack on the Suez Canal. In the Gulf region, the British negotiated support from the Sheikhs of Kuwait and Muhammarah (Iran, today Khorramshahr) in September. They resisted Ottoman demands that British ships leave the Shatt-al Arab. Indian troops landed at Bahrein on 22 October, preparing for an attack into Southern Iraq. The Russians were arming and financing Armenian revolutionaries in Eastern Anatolia to act in support of an anticipated Russian invasion. Russian military build-up on the Ottoman borders in Northeast Anatolia and in Iran, which had accelerated in 1910, proceeded, in preparation for invasion of the Ottoman East. Fighting broke out in September and October on the Persian border between Kurds and the Russians. Britain and Russia believed the invading Kurds were supported by Ottoman troops.[28]

On 29 October 1914, Admiral Souchon's navy attacked Russian ships in the Black Sea and shelled Russian ports. Russia began to attack in Northeastern Anatolia, and the British navy shelled Çanakkale on the Dardanelles and Aqaba on the Gulf of Aqaba. The Ottoman Empire declared war on Russia, Britain and France on 10 November.[29]

## Notes

1. On the immediate pre-war period and the Ottoman entry into the war, see: F. A. K. Yasamee, 'Ottoman Empire', in Keith Wilson, ed., *Decisions for War 1914*, New York: St. Martin's, 1995, pp. 229–68. Akşin, *Jön Türkler*, pp. 268–76. Roger Dean Adelson, 'The Formation of British Policy towards the Middle East, 1914–1918', unpublished PhD dissertation, Washington University, 1972, pp. 25–72. Feroz Ahmad, 'The Dilemmas of Young Turk Policy, 1914–1918', and

Altay Cengizer, 'The Policies of the Entente Powers toward the Ottoman Empire', in M. Hakan Yavuz and Feroz Ahmad, *War and Collapse: World War I and the Ottoman State*, Salt Lake City: University of Utah Press, 2016, pp. 66–83 and 84–112. Ulrich Trumpener, 'Turkey's Entry into World War I: An Assessment of Responsibilities', *The Journal of Modern History*, vol. 34, no. 4 (December 1962), pp. 369–80, and *Germany and the Ottoman Empire 1914–1918*, Princeton: Princeton University Press, 1968, pp. 15–61. Mustafa Aksakal, *The Ottoman Road to War in 1914*, Cambridge: Cambridge University Press, 2008. Joseph Heller, 'Sir Louis Mallet and the Ottoman Empire: The Road to War', *Middle Eastern Studies*, vol. 12, no. 1 (January 1976), pp. 3–44. Sean McMeekin, *The Berlin-Baghdad Express: The Ottoman Empire and Germany's Bid for World Power*, Cambridge, MA: Harvard University Press, 2010, pp. 7–122.

I have deliberately excluded consideration of the European development of the antagonism between the Triple Alliance and the Triple Entente. While it was indeed a background to British actions in the Ottoman Empire, it has been considered in too many studies to be needed here.

2. Mallett's actions were forced by the need, as an ambassador, to advance the decisions of his superiors in London, but he also did not always understand the Ottoman Government.
3. Grey to Beaumont, Foreign Office, 4 August 1914, in BDOW 11, p. 313. Britain declared war on Germany the same day.
4. Beaumont to Grey, Constantinople, 3 August 1914, in BDOW 11, pp. 311–12.
5. Grey to Bertie, Foreign Office, 15 August 1914, in Viscount Grey of Fallodon, *Twenty-Five Years 1892–1916*, vol. 2, London: Hodder and Stoughton, 1926, p. 167. Grey's self-serving and duplicitous account of this period (pp. 164–71) is otherwise useless as an historical source. See also Grey to Mallet, Foreign Office, 22 August 1914, Ibid., pp. 167–8. Grey made vague promises that the Capitulations, which the Ottomans had already abrogated, might be reconsidered, but made no promises. On 1 October 1914, the British notified the Ottoman Government that they could not accept the abolition of the Capitulations. (FO 438/3, enclosure in no. 572, Constantinople, 1 October 1914.)
6. FO 438/3, Mallet to Grey, Constantinople, 14 September 1914. FO 438/3, Grey to Mallet, Foreign Office, 15, 16 September 1914.
7. Some Ottoman officials understood that British promises could not be trusted:

> (Ambassador Mallet speaking to the Minister of Interior, Talat) I said that so long as a single German officer, naval or military, remained here I should consider Turkey as a German protectorate. I said that I had been informed that

Turkish Government attached no importance to written declaration which I and my French and Russian colleagues had made them respecting their integrity. I was greatly surprised at this attitude, but personally somewhat relieved, as to guarantee integrity and independence of Turkey was like guaranteeing life of man who was determined to commit suicide.

(FO 438/3, Mallet to Grey, Constantinople, 6 September 1914.)

8. See Feroz Ahmad, 'Great Britain's Relations with the Young Turks 1908–1914', *Middle Eastern Studies*, vol. 2, no. 4 (July 1966), pp. 302–29.

9. Mallet to Grey, Constantinople, 29 December 1913, in BDOW 10/1, pp. 168–71. Djemal Pasha, *Memories of a Turkish Statesman, 1913–1919*, New York: Doran, 1922, pp. 99–100. Cemal had been named military governor of Istanbul on 23 January 1913, immediately after the coup that brought the CUP back to power, a tremendously important position, then minister of public works, then navy minister.

The Baghdad Railway agreements are too detailed and too well-covered elsewhere to discuss here. See: BDOW 10/2, pp. 1–420. GP 37/2 and some documents in GP 38. Murat Özyüksel, *The Berlin-Baghdad Railway and the Ottoman Empire: Industrialization, Imperial Germany and the Middle East*, London: I. B. Tauris, 2016, especially pp. 177–203. Stuart A. Cohen, *British Policy in Mesopotamia 1903–1914*, Reading: Ithaca Press, 1976, pp. 244–357. McMeekin, pp. 32–82. William I. Shorrock, 'The Origin of the French Mandate in Syria and Lebanon: The Railroad Question, 1901–1914', *International Journal of Middle East Studies*, vol. 1, no. 2 (April 1970), pp. 133–53. Rashid I. Khalidi, 'The Economic Partition of the Arab Provinces of the Ottoman Empire before the First World War', *Review*, vol. 11, no. 2 (Spring 1988), pp. 251–64. Clark, *Sleepwalkers*, pp. 335–9. See also V. Necla Geyikdağı, 'French Direct Investments in the Ottoman Empire Before World War I', *Enterprise & Society*, vol. 12, no. 3 (September 2011), pp. 525–61. L. Bruce Fulton, 'France and the End of the Ottoman Empire', in Kent, *Great Powers*, pp. 141–72. Edward Mead Earle, *Turkey, the Great Powers, and the Bagdad Railway: A Study in Imperialism*, New York: Macmillan, 1924, suffers from its early date, in which many of the more important diplomatic documents were unavailable.

10. Djemal, *Memories*, pp. 103–7. Serge Sazonov, the Russian Minister of Foreign Affairs in 1914, wrote that Talat Paşa, the Ottoman Interior Minister, suggested an Ottoman–Russian alliance to him. (*Fateful Years, 1909–1916*, London: Cape, 1928.) I think it doubtful, if it was actually made, that this could have been a serious suggestion. I have found no indication of anything but diplomatic promises of friendship at their meetings. See Buchanan to Grey, St Petersburgh, 17 May 1914, in BDOW 10/1, p. 328, Yasamee, 'Ottoman Empire', pp. 235 and 247.

11. Kurat, pp. 230–8. Aksakal, pp. 127–30. Reynolds, 'Ottoman-Russian Struggle', pp. 76–9. Some Russians seem to have taken Enver's proposal seriously or at least considered it as a delaying tactic for them.
12. FO 424/251, Mallet to Grey, Constantinople, 3, 6, 7 and 13 January 1914. Mallet to Grey, 10 February 1914, in BDOW 10/1, pp. 228–9. Mallet wanted some sort of face-saving arrangement to be made over the islands.

    On 14 February 1914, the Six Powers presented their decision on the islands to the Ottoman Government. All the islands except Imbros and Tenedos were to be given to the Greeks. They cited the 1913 Treaty of London as their authority to make the judgement. The Ottoman Government refused to accept the decision. (FO 424/251, enclosures in Mallet to Grey, 16 February 1914.)
13. FO 424/251, Mallet to Grey, 3 February 1914. The Grand Vezir also believed that the British had proposed a naval demonstration at Istanbul in 1914, which was not true. See also FO 371/2117, Mallet to Grey, Constantinople, 29 December 1913, for Cemal Paşa's refusal to give up the islands.
14. FO 421/289, Grey to Bertie, Foreign Office, 1 January 1914; Mallet to Grey, Constantinople, 13 January 1914. FO 421/290, Grey to Mallet, Foreign Office, 16 June 1914.
15. FO 195/2455, Grey to Mallet, Foreign Office, 1 and 26 January, 2 and 16 February, 28 March, 23 April 1914. Mallet told the Grand Vezir that Grey had only 'acted as the mouthpiece of the Powers'. (FO 421/289, Mallet to Grey, Constantinople, 11 February 1914.)
16. For a detailed history of the Capitulations, especially in 1914–23, see Mehmet Emin Elmacı, *İttihat Terraki ve Kapitülasyonlar*, Istanbul: Homer Kitabevi, 2005.
17. FO 438/3, Mallet to Grey, Constantinople, 10 September 1914. On the Capitulations, see Feroz Ahmad, 'Ottoman Perceptions of the Capitulations 1800–1914', *Journal of Islamic Studies*, vol. 11, no. 1 (2000), pp. 1–20.
18. The appointment of Liman von Sanders was not the first time Prussian/German officers had advised the Ottoman army. German officers had guided the Ottoman army since the time of Helmuth von Moltke in 1835. Colmar Freiherr von der Goltz had significantly organised and improved the Ottoman army in his service to the Ottomans from 1883 to 1895, ultimately being named an Ottoman field-marshal (müşir). His reforms greatly contributed to the Ottoman success in the 1897 War with Greece.

    After much consideration, I have not included only this brief description of the so-called Liman von Sanders Affair. For the Ottomans, an upshot of the affair was an important indication that they were not masters in their own country. Matters such as who would advise or run their military were decided by diplomacy among the Powers, not by them. On this topic, see: BDOW 10/1, pp. 338–423. GP 38, pp. 191–318. Ulrich Trumpener, 'Liman von Sanders and the German-Ottoman Alliance', *Journal of Contemporary History*, vol. 1, no. 4 (October 1966), pp. 179–92. Robert J. Kerner, 'The Mission of Liman von Sanders', four parts, *The Slavonic Review*, vol. 6, no. 16 (June 1927), pp. 12–27, vol. 6, no. 18 (March 1928), and vol. 7, no. 19 (June 1928), pp. 90–112, 543–60. Liman von Sanders, *Five Years in Turkey*, Annapolis: United States Naval Institute, 1928, pp. 1–36. On the corresponding British naval interest in the Ottoman Empire, see Chris B. Rooney, 'The International Significance of British Naval Missions to the Ottoman Empire, 1908–14', *Middle Eastern Studies*, vol. 34, no. 1 (January 1998), pp. 1–29.

19. FO 438/3, Mallet to Grey, Constantinople, 17 and 20 September 1914; Grey to Mallet, Foreign Office, 18 September 1914; Buchanan to Grey, Petrograd, 21 September 1914. FO 438/3, Grey to Mallet, Foreign Office, 9 September 1914. The Russians initially felt that acceptance of the Ottoman terms would be interpreted as a sign of weakness, but did not want the issue to cause a breakdown in relations. Mallet noted the Russian attitude toward the abolition of the Capitulations: 'My Russian colleague is strongly of opinion that this should not lead to a rupture, which he is most anxious to avoid.' (FO 438/3, Mallet to Grey, Constantinople, 8 September 1914.) The Russians soon proposed more moderate terms of their own. (FO 438/3, Mallet to Grey, Constantinople, 23 September 1914.)

    On 23 September, the Ottoman Government announced the abolition of the foreign post offices. Mallet rejected this, but proposed a compromise in which British officials would be assigned to the Ottoman post offices. The Russians and French agreed to close their post offices on 30 September. Mallet wished also to do so while negotiating compromise. The Ottomans agreed to consider Mallet's plan. The British post offices were closed on 30 September. (FO 438/3, Mallet to Grey, Constantinople, 22, 23, 24 and 26 September 1914.)

20. FO 438/3, Grey to Mallet, Foreign Office, 24 and 26 September 1914.
21. Adelson, pp. 52–3.
22. Tewfik Pasha to Grey, London, 4 August 1914, and Beaumont to Grey, Constantinople, 3 August 1914, in BDOW 11, pp. 316–17. Beaumont clearly had no idea what was transpiring around him. See, for example, Beaumont to Grey, Constantinople, 31 July and 3 August 1914, in BDOW 11, pp. 238 and 310. The Germans had only somewhat earlier rejected Ottoman proposals for an alliance. When Enver Paşa suggested an alliance with Germany, Foreign Minister Jagow told him it was not possible. (Jagow to Kaiser Wilhelm II, Berlin, 23 July 1914, in GP 36/2, pp. 843–6.) See Sean McMeekin, *The Ottoman Endgame: War, Revolution, and the Making of the Modern Middle East, 1908–1923*, New York: Penguin, 2016, pp. 83–91.

23. Trumpener (*Germany and the Ottoman Empire*, p. 24) believed the Ottomans were going to give the ships to the Germans. This seems unlikely, because they were sorely needed at home.
24. Ottoman 'purchase' of the ships was theoretically a 'special provision' and not in violation of the Hague Convention, but surely violated its spirit:

> In the absence of special provisions to the contrary in the legislation of a neutral Power, belligerent war-ships are not permitted to remain in the ports, roadsteads, or territorial waters of the said Power for more than twenty-four hours, except in the cases covered by the present Convention.

(Laws of War, Article 12: 'Rights and Duties of Neutral Powers in Naval War (Hague XIII), October 18, 1907', Yale Law School, Avalon Project, https://avalon.law.yale.edu/20th_century/hague13.asp.) Aksakal, pp. 110–18.
25. FO 438/3, Mallet to Grey, Constantinople, 1, 3 and 5 September 1914. FO 438/3, Grey to Mallet, Foreign Office, 4 September 1914.
26. FO 800/80, Churchill to Beaumont (for Enver), London, 15 August 1914.
27. FO 371/2142, Mallet to Grey, Constantinople, 27 September 1914. FO 438/3, Grey to Mallet, Foreign Office, 30 September 1914.
28. FO 371/2140, Mallet to Grey, Constantinople, 4 October 1914. FO 371/2143, 'From Viceroy, 4th September 1914'. FO 371/2139, Grey to Cheetham, 31 October 1914. McCarthy et al., *Van*, pp. 168–78. Adelson, pp. 67–8. FO 371/2143, Mallet to Grey, Constantinople, 7 October 1914. Mustafa Tanrıverdi, 'Russian Military Mobilization in the Caucasus before World War I', in Yavuz and Ahmad, pp. 569–87. W. E. D. Allen and Paul Muratoff, *Caucasian Battlefields*, Cambridge: Cambridge University Press, 1953, pp. 221–43. On the coal situation, see the extensive documents in FO 371/2143. On the British incursion in the Gulf, see S. A. Cohen, 'The Genesis of the British Campaign in Mesopotamia, 1914', *Middle Eastern Studies*, vol. 12, no. 2 (May 1976), pp. 119–32.
29. The pretext for the Ottoman attack was that the Russians were laying mines at the mouth of the Bosporus, an invention. (Aksakal, pp. 182–6.) Rules on the Straits had been set in the London Straits Convention of July 1841, and reaffirmed in the Congress of Paris in 1856. Mallet felt that the Grand Vezir, Said Halim and others were against a war, but events were beyond their control. (FO 371/2145, Mallet to Grey, Constantinople, 31 October 1914.) Said Halim, who had signed the treaty with Germany, seems to have been conflicted. See McMeekin, *The Ottoman Endgame*, pp. 95–133.

# Part II

# THE FINAL CONFRONTATION

The Ottomans lost World War I. The victorious British began the final dismemberment of the Ottoman Empire.

Wartime British public statements on the fate of the Ottoman Empire had been conciliatory. The British did not pretend that they did not covet the Ottoman Arab provinces, but they did promise continuing independence for the Ottoman provinces with majority Turkish populations. In 1917, Bonar Law, British Foreign Secretary, told the House of Commons: 'We are not fighting for additional territory.' Prime Minister Lloyd George, in his 'war aims' speech of 5 January 1918, denounced the secret wartime agreements dividing the Ottoman Empire and denied all imperialist aims: 'Nor are we fighting to destroy Austria-Hungary or to deprive Turkey of its capital, or of the rich and renowned lands of Asia Minor and Thrace, which are predominantly Turkish in race.' None of this was true.[1]

The actual British intent was to divide the Ottoman Empire among Britain and her allies. On 3 January 1916, Marks Sykes for Britain and François Georges-Picot for France signed the famous Sykes–Picot Agreement dividing the Ottoman Empire. The agreement, later ratified by the French and

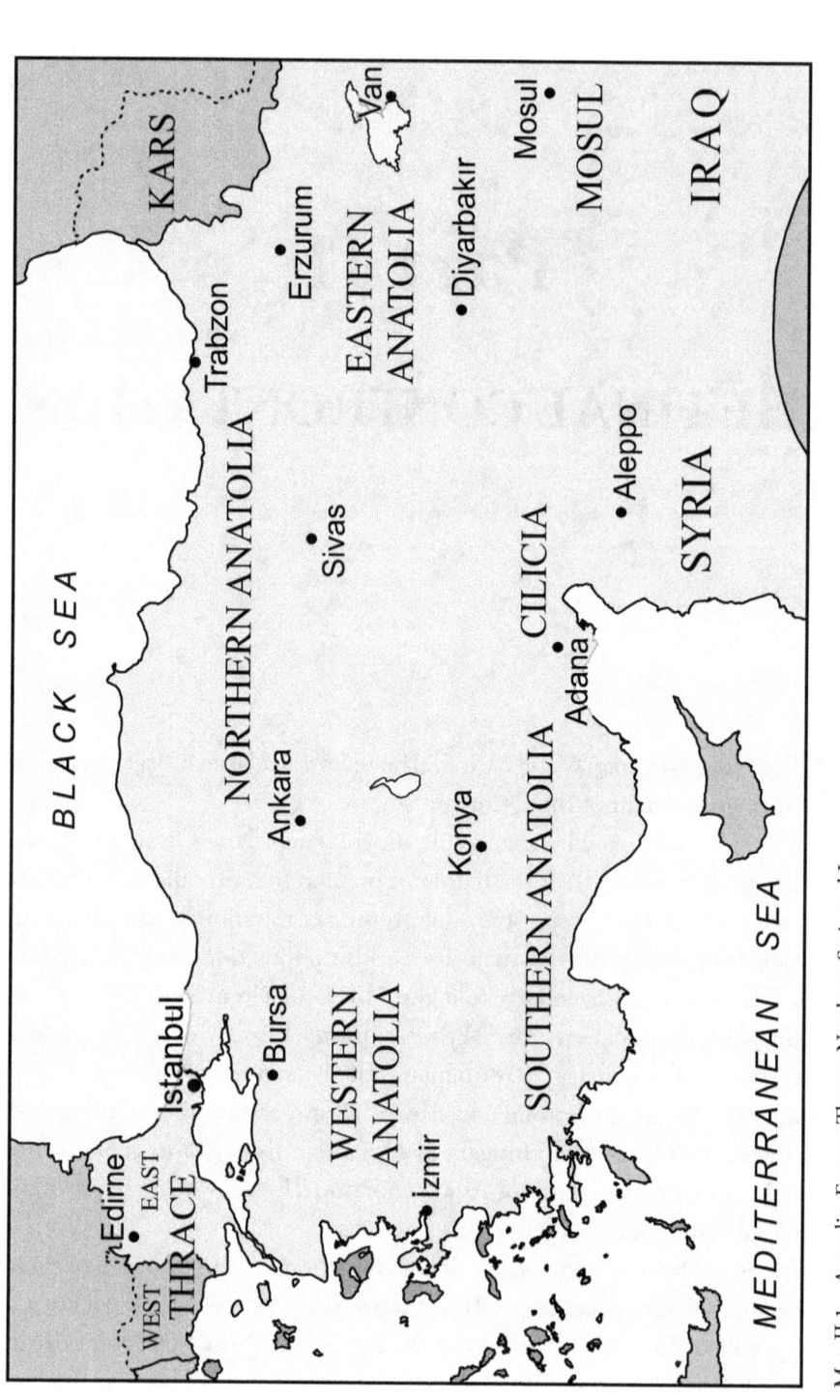

Map II.1  Anatolia, Eastern Thrace, Northern Syria and Iraq

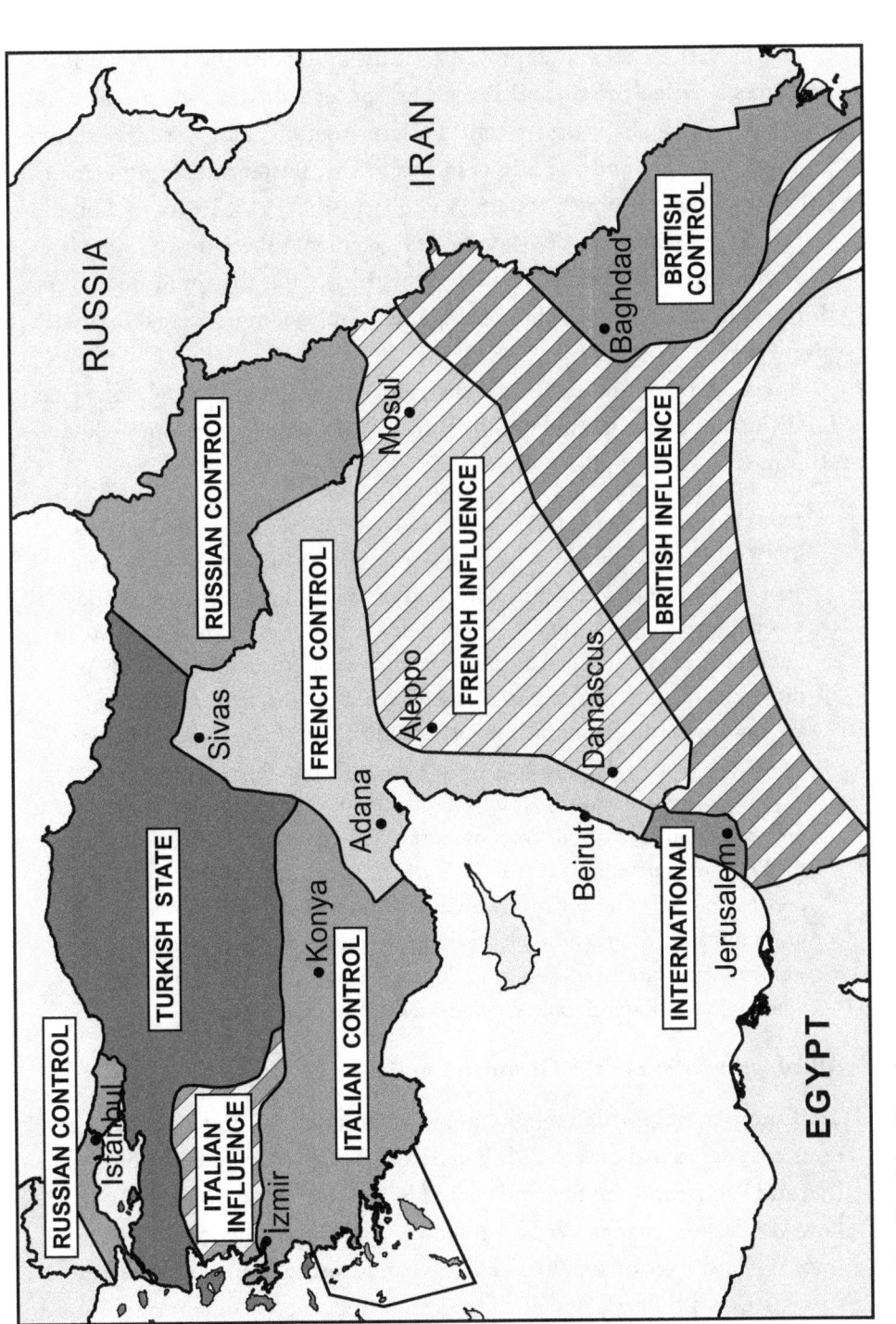

Map II.2 The Sykes–Picot Agreement

British Governments and approved by Russia, divided the Ottoman Arab provinces between Britain and France, except for Palestine, which was to be international. Russia was to receive Eastern Anatolia, and Russia had been promised Istanbul and the Straits in the 1915 Constantinople Agreement. Italy was promised Southwestern Anatolia in the 1915 Treaty of London and the 1917 Saint-Jean-de-Maurienne Agreement. These treaties were later to be broken, mainly at the pleasure of the British, but they indicate that the British had no intention of honouring their public commitments to Turkish sovereignty.

Speaking to the other British delegates at the Paris Peace Conference, Lord Curzon, then a member of the British War Cabinet, gave a more honest assessment of British post-war aims:

> Lord Curzon said that he had no desire whatever to deal gently with the Turks. The Turks had voluntarily sided with Germany; they had treated our prisoners with unexampled barbarity; they had massacred hundreds of thousands of their own subjects. They therefore deserved any fate which was inflicted upon them. He thought that they should be deprived of all their outlying provinces, that is to say Arabia, Mesopotamia, Palestine, Syria and Armenia. He was further in favour of their being turned out of Constantinople. The Turks were not an absolute majority of the population there. So long as they were there they continually intrigued throughout the Balkans and among all their neighbours. Above all unless we turned the Turks out of Constantinople the East would never believe that the Turks had been defeated in the war. The presence of the Turk in Constantinople was an outward and visible sign of his dominance. Constantinople, the ancient capital of the Eastern Empire, was a military outpost of Turkey in Europe. He was therefore strongly of the opinion that Constantinople should be taken from the Turks.[2]

## Allied Occupation of the Ottoman Empire

The Ottoman Empire had fought more successfully in World War I than any of its adversaries had expected. It had defeated the British in Gallipoli and in Iraq and had recaptured the lands seized from it by Russia in 1878. By 1918, however, lack of manpower and resources had forced the loss of Syria and Iraq. When the Ottoman allies Germany and Austria–Hungary were near to surrender, and Bulgaria had already surrendered, the Ottomans were forced to sue for peace.

The armistice signed at Mudros on 30 October 1918 allowed for only limited Allied occupation of Ottoman territory:

> Article VII. The Allies to have the right to occupy any strategic points in the event of any situation arising which threatens the security of the Allies.
> 
> Article X. Allied occupation of the Taurus tunnel system.
> 
> Article XV. Allied Control Officers to be placed on all railways, including such portions of the Transcaucasian Railways as are now under Turkish control, which must be placed at the free and complete disposal of the Allied authorities, due consideration being given to the needs of the population. This clause to include Allied occupation of Batoum. Turkey will raise no objection to the occupation of Baku by the Allies.
> 
> Article XVIII. Surrender of all ports occupied in Tripolitania and Cyrenaica, including Misurata, to the nearest Allied garrison.
> 
> Article XXIV. In case of disorder in the six Armenian vilayets, the Allies reserve to themselves the right to occupy any part of them.[3]

The armistice terms were to be ignored by the Allies almost immediately after the armistice was signed. Cilicia, Istanbul and Western Anatolia were all occupied by Allied militaries, even though the Allies were never under threat until well after their occupations. Disorders indeed continued in Eastern Anatolia, with Armenian attacks on the Muslim populations of Erzurum Province and subsequent inter-communal warfare, but the Allies never attempted to occupy there.

From the beginning, the intention of the British was to ensure that the Turks could not oppose the division of their Empire. The vehicle was clauses in the armistice agreement abolishing the Turkish military:

> Article V. Immediate demobilization of the Turkish army, except for such troops as are required for the surveillance of the frontiers and for the maintenance of internal order.
> 
> Article XX. The compliance with such orders as may be conveyed for the disposal of the equipment, arms, and ammunition, including transport, of that portion of the Turkish Army which is demobilized under Clause V.

In effect, the armistice provisions, which were soon broken, applied only to Anatolia, Istanbul and Thrace. The British were already in control of the Arab provinces.

## Military Occupation of the Ottoman Capital

On 31 October 1918, the day after the armistice was signed, the British Cabinet was already deciding that Istanbul should be occupied by the Allies. On 13 November 1918, two weeks after the Mudros Armistice was signed, the British fleet arrived at Istanbul. The first French troops had arrived one day earlier, and the Italians arrived on 7 February 1919. The Allies set up a military administration, dividing military control of the city among them.

The invasion of the Ottoman capital was in violation of the terms of the Mudros Armistice, as was recognised by the British armistice negotiator, Admiral Somerset Gough-Calthorpe:

> Admiral Calthorpe, who conducted the negotiations, in transmitting home the terms of the Armistice, made the following observations on clause 7 (of the Mudros Armistice): 'It will be observed that there is nothing in this clause, or elsewhere in the Armistice, which permits Constantinople to be occupied unless the security of the Allies is threatened.'[4]

Calthorpe was legally, and perhaps morally, correct, but his views were ignored. It was an early indication that the British were not to be bound by their commitments. Despite his misgivings, Admiral Calthorpe was a military man who followed orders. He was placed in charge of the British invasion of Istanbul and named Britain's first high commissioner for the Ottoman Empire.

The first task of the British was to remove potential opposition. London ordered High Commissioner Calthorpe to have arrested a large number of persons suspected of actual and potential threat:

> You should therefore instruct Turkish Government to take immediate steps to hand over to you or nearest Allied Commander such Turkish Officers or officials as you or the Commanders concerned consider should be surrendered for the following reasons:

1. Failure to comply with Armistice terms,
2. Impeding execution of Armistice terms,
3. Insolence to British Commanders and officers,
4. Ill-treatment of prisoners,
5. Outrages to Armenians or other subject races both in Turkey and Transcaucasia,
6. Participation in looting, destruction of property, etc.
7. Any other broaches of the laws and customs of war.[5]

The British intended the disintegration of the Ottoman Empire. Their first steps were taking control of the Ottoman Government and arresting potential political opponents. The British considered that Ottoman courts were 'too dilatory' and were acquitting too many of those arrested, so the government was ordered not to try the prisoners, but to hand them over to the Allies. The Ottoman Ministry of Foreign Affairs complained that the arrests were a breach of international law and that prisoners would not be able to properly defend themselves in Allied courts. The protest was ignored. The government had no choice but to make the arrests. The British deported the prisoners to Malta.[6]

The arrests and deportations were very much a British affair. Their French allies objected on the grounds that the deportees had not the opportunity for a fair trial. The French had not been consulted when the arrests were made.[7]

Counts of those deported to Malta differed in various documents. Despite the assertion that the arrests were to be for outrages, looting and destruction, ill-treatment of prisoners and such, the captures and detentions were obviously done primarily for political reasons. The British listed seventy-two Ottoman prisoners at Malta in July of 1920, along with the reasons they were being held: of the seventy-two prisoners recorded, twenty-one were accused of 'having troubled public security'; all but a few of these were present or past politicians or governors. Seven others were acknowledged as having been interned solely because they were politicians, with no mention of any trouble caused. No justification was given for interning thirty-nine others.[8]

Nothing in the armistice provisions justified the Allied occupation of Istanbul, much less the arbitrary arrest of Ottoman officials. Perhaps the most instructive of the British attitude as conquerors was one cause for arrests, which was '[i]nsolence to British Commanders and officers'. The British would only be satisfied with complete subservience.

## Notes

1. 'War Policy', *Hansard*, House of Commons Debate, 20 February 1917, cc. 1232. *Statement by the Right Honourable David Lloyd George, January Fifth, Nineteen Hundred and Eighteen, Authorized Version as Published by the British Government*, New York: George H. Doran Company, 1918. Ray Stannard Baker, *Woodrow Wilson and World Settlement*, New York: Doubleday, 1923, vol. 1, pp. 40–1.

    Volume Five of Stanford J. Shaw, *From Empire to Republic: The Turkish War of Liberation 1918–1923, a Documentary Study*, Ankara: Türk Tarih Kurumu, 2000, is an invaluable compendium of material for the period of the War of Independence.

It contains an extensive bibliography, lists of officials and biographical and subject dictionaries. Nothing else can compare to it in completeness.

I have not considered many of the British pre-armistice plans for the Ottoman Empire, because they were so contradictory and so few of them came to fruition. (For these, see the extensive analyses in John Fisher, *Curzon and British Imperialism in the Middle East, 1916–19*, London: Frank Cass, 1999, pp. 1–41.) What is considered here, as seen below, are some of the plans for Istanbul, Eastern Anatolia and İzmir, which are pertinent. On the pre-armistice plans, see Erik Goldstein, 'British Peace Aims and the Eastern Question: The Political Intelligence Department and the Eastern Committee, 1918', *Middle Eastern Studies*, vol. 23, no. 4 (October 1987), pp. 419–36, and 'Great Britain and Greater Greece 1917–1920', *The Historical Journal*, vol. 32, no. 2 (June 1989), pp. 339–56. The Political Intelligence Department of the Foreign Office summarised possible British plans for the Ottoman Empire in 'Memorandum Respecting the Settlement of Turkey and the Arabian Peninsula'. (ADM 116/3239, Foreign Office, 21 November 1918.)

2. CAB 23/44B/9, Minutes of a Meeting, Paris, 19 May 1919. At the same meeting, however, Curzon said he believed the Greeks should be turned out of İzmir, which was consistent with his views.
3. On the making of the armistice, see Gwynne Dyer, 'The Turkish Armistice of 1918: 1: The Turkish Decision for a Separate Peace, Autumn 1918', *Middle Eastern Studies*, vol. 8, no. 2 (May 1972), pp. 143–78, and 'The Turkish Armistice of 1918: 2: A Lost Opportunity: The Armistice Negotiations of Moudros', *Middle Eastern Studies*, vol. 8, no. 3 (October 1972), pp. 313–48. McMeekin, *The Ottoman Endgame*, pp. 393–411. The Allies pre-armistice conditions are in CAB 28/5. 'Conditions of an Armistice with Turkey', 8 October 1918, in War Cabinet, January 1919, I. C. 82.
4. FO 406/43, Foreign Office to Law Officers of the Crown, Foreign Office, 10 December 1919.
5. CAB 23/24/43, Minutes of a Meeting of the War Cabinet, 31 October 1918. Cabinet memoranda have been cited here in two ways, depending on the British National Archives system and the way in which I have seen them: some are listed by the CAB reference number (for example, CAB 24/95/37). Others are listed by their numbers in the separate National Archives collection of cabinet memoranda (https://www.nationalarchives.gov.uk/cabinetpapers/cabinet-gov/cab24-interwar-memoranda.htm#Reports%201919-1922). The latter are indicated by their Cabinet Paper identifier (for example, CAB/24/133 C. P. 3751).

For the military details of the occupation, see CAB 44/39, 'The Occupation of Constantinople, 1918–1923', pp. 6–11.

6. FO 608/109, Telegram to Calthorpe, Foreign Office, 5 February 1919. Calthorpe to Curzon, Constantinople, 30 May 1919. FO 608/109, Sublime Porte, Ministère des Affaires Etrangères, Note Verbale, 1 May 1919. Includes list of those 'arrested by Ottoman authorities'. For an Ottoman complaint that British interference in the Ottoman judicial processes was contravening international law, see Admiral Webb on 19 February 1919 in CAB 24/145/49, Eastern Report, 27 February 1919. However, Prime Minister Ferid Paşa told the British that he would arrest anyone they wished. (CAB 24/145/51, Eastern Report, 13 March 1919.) When it appeared that the courts would not convict all the accused, Ferid asked the British to deport them to Malta without trial. (CAB 24/145/61, Eastern Report, 22 May 1919. Note that the Eastern Reports do not list the recipients, which may have been the Foreign Office or the War Office.)

   On life in Istanbul and Turkish opposition to the occupiers during the occupation, see Nur Bilge Criss, *Istanbul Under Allied Occupation, 1918–1923*, Leiden: Brill, 1999.

7. FO 608/109, de Fleuriau (French ambassador in London) to Graham, 4 June 1919. The British responded that the deportees were dangerous members of the CUP who would cause trouble and might be acquitted or escape. They apologised for not consulting the French, but said the matter was urgent and needed to be acted on quickly. (FO 608/109, Foreign Office to Cambon (French ambassador in London), Foreign Office, 20 June 1919.)

8. CAB 24/109/52, Secretary of State for War (Churchill), 'Position of Turkish Political Prisoners Interned at Malta', War Office, 19 July 1920. Various lists of the prisoners deported or those who it was believed should be deported are in FO 608/109 and FO 371/5089 and 5090. There is extensive documentation on the Malta prisoners in FO 371/6499–505, especially on the prisoner exchange that freed the Malta prisoners.

# 10

## THE PARIS PEACE CONFERENCE

My Dear Prime Minister,

    I desire most sincerely to express to you, and through you, to the British Government my deep gratitude, as well as that of my country, for all you have done to enable us to obtain the fulfilment of our national unity. I feel however, that I am quite unable to give adequate expression to my feelings, for indeed, all that Greece has now realised of her legitimate claims, is due in major part, my dear Prime Minister, to your powerful and effective support, and no words of mine can efficiently express my country's deep sense of thankfulness to you.

    Greek Prime Minister Venizelos to Lloyd George, 26 April 1920.[1]

The Paris Peace Conference convened on 18 January 1919. Although delegates from twenty-seven nations attended the conference, decisions were actually made by the 'Council of Four', the so-called 'Big Four' – Britain, France, Italy and the United States – and to a much lesser extent by Japan. Although the Peace Conference ended with the signing of the treaties with Germany (Treaty of Versailles, 28 June 1919) and Austria (Treaty of Saint-Germain-en-Laye, 10 September 1919), the four Powers, again only occasionally joined by Japan, continued to exert power as an Allied Supreme Council. After the German treaty was signed, the governing body of the Peace Conference became the Council of the Heads of Delegations of the Five Powers (Britain, France, Italy, the United States and Japan), called the Supreme Council. Japan was mainly excluded from, and had no real interest in, deliberations on the Middle East or the Balkans, leaving the other four to make decisions. America largely withdrew from Supreme Council considerations after the signing of the German and Austrian treaties, and as it had never been at war with the Ottoman Empire, power was in the hands of the remaining three. The Supreme Council deliberated on, and imposed, further treaties on other enemy nations and dealt with problems arising out of the original treaties. It was the Supreme Council that made the main Allied decisions on the Ottoman Empire.[2]

Among the great European peace conferences, the Paris Congress was unique. The previous conferences of Vienna, Paris and Berlin had all included both the victors and the vanquished. It was recognised that even the defeated could aid in deliberations. Although territories were lost and reparations set in those conferences, there was no intention to destroy or economically cripple defeated foes. The 1919 Paris Congress of the wartime Allies was quite different. The intent of the victors was to impose settlements without input from the conquered. Instead, the congress specifically excluded Germany, Austria–Hungary, Bulgaria and the Ottoman Empire from its deliberative meetings. Settlements were to be imposed, not agreed upon.

The Paris Congress was the culmination of a century in which European Powers had steadily reduced the territory and power of the Ottoman Empire. It was also a triumph of imperialism. The Ottoman Empire, long accepted as a European Power, even if a second-class one, was to be treated as the European imperialists had treated South Asia and Africa. What was desired by the Europeans was to be accepted. What they allowed local peoples was to be granted, as if a gift, by the masters.

The Allies assumed that the Turks would accept whatever was ordered for them. President Wilson summarised the view of the Allies:

> All we owe the Turkish population is the right to live and the guarantee of a good administration. I don't know the Turks directly. But all witnesses agree in representing them as a docile people, against whom no reproach can be made so long as they are not granted the fatal gift of command. It is often repeated that the Turk is a gentleman; he will obey without difficulty the power which serves him as a guide.[3]

On 14 May 1919, Prime Minister David Lloyd George presented his Allies with a British plan for the Ottoman Empire, in resolutions that had been prepared by Harold Nicolson (who made no secret of his dislike of the Turks):

- Subject to acceptance by the U. S. Senate, America would take up mandates over Armenia and Constantinople and the Straits.
- Turkish sovereignty over Constantinople, Thrace and the Straits region would cease.
- Greece would receive 'complete sovereignty' over İzmir, Ayvalı and the region that connected the two districts, 'which (in 1919) embraces a predominantly Greek population'.
- The Dodecanese would go to Greece, also in complete sovereignty (even though Italy, a British ally, occupied the Dodecanese).
- The Turkish state would be to the east of the above and the west of Armenia.
- The Turkish Government had not shown it was able to protect the interests of its population, nor could it develop its natural resources. Therefore, mandates were needed over the Turkish state: Greece over the region near its İzmir borders, Italy in the South, France in the rest.
- The Ottoman Public Debt Commission would be retained, under the control of the four Powers.

Lloyd George intended that nations other than Britain, France and the United States not be allowed to change the decisions of the Powers. Italy and other nations should not be allowed to oppose Britain's plan. Lloyd George's resolutions were to take effect 'without further reference to the Council (of the Paris Conference)'. President Woodrow Wilson of the United States and President Georges Clemenceau of France accepted Britain's resolutions as a proposal to be presented to the Italian delegation, without allowing for any Italian disagreement.

It is difficult to know what Lloyd George meant by 'mandates', perhaps part of the mandate system being considered by the Peace Conference. (Mandates, theoretically under the control of the new League of Nations, were actually to be instruments of European control in regions taken from the defeated Central Powers.) He probably had no definite plan other than to insure European hegemony. Lloyd George was either ignorant of the areas proposed for the mandates or duplicitous. In the discussion of the resolutions, it was suggested that perhaps a new Turkish state should be put under two mandates – North and South. Wilson asked if Northern Anatolia were not 'more purely Turkish'. Lloyd George astonishingly assured Wilson that 'this was not the case outside the coastal districts'. Lloyd George's statement on population was so ridiculous that perhaps he meant the opposite. No one at the congress referred to his mistake. In fact, Turks were a majority in both the coasts and the interior. The provinces of Northern Anatolia – Trabzon and Kastamonu – were actually 87 per cent Muslim before the war.[4]

Five days after his first proposal, Lloyd George had somewhat changed his mind. He had decided that he did not want the Turkish state to be divided into separate North and South mandates after all. He had decided that İzmir, Armenia and a Constantinople mandate should be detached from Turkish rule, but the rest of Anatolia, theoretically still Turkish, would be under a single mandate. He wanted the same Power that had the Constantinople mandate, preferably the United States, to have the mandate for Anatolia. Italy should have no mandate in Anatolia, although Greece would have İzmir, and Eastern Anatolia would be given to the Armenians. Britain would have the mandates for Mesopotamia (Iraq, whose borders were undefined at the conference) and Palestine. The French would take Syria.[5]

## Lloyd George and Curzon

Until the very end of the British incursion in the Ottoman Empire, Lloyd George was an advocate for the Greeks.

The Chief of the Imperial General Staff, General Henry Hughes Wilson, commented:

> Lloyd George is persuaded that the Greeks are the coming Power in the Mediterranean both on land and at sea, and wants to befriend them. The whole of Lloyd George's foreign policy is chaotic, and based on totally fallacious values of men and affairs.[6]
>
> A talk early with Lloyd George, who is as much convinced as ever that the Greeks are splendid soldiers and that the Turks are perfectly useless. It is a most dangerous obsession.[7]

The reasons for Lloyd George's affection for the Greeks and hatred for the Turks can be debated. Harold Nicolson, himself a philhellene, felt Lloyd

George's reasons to be a devotion to those he felt were oppressed, confidence in Greek Prime Minister Eleftherios Venizelos, and that '[i]t was based to no small extent upon a crusading emotion, upon a strange survival of feeling regarding the crescent and the cross'. More practically, Nicolson believed Lloyd George was also motivated by the desire to have a pro-British country that would advance British interests on both sides of the Aegean and close to the Straits. Traditional Liberal disaffection for the Turks may have played a part; it surely brought him support from fellow Liberals.[8]

There has been much debate over the relative place of Lloyd George and Foreign Secretary Curzon in British foreign policy. Curzon accurately felt that the prime minister had usurped matters that should have been the province of the foreign secretary. Lowe and Dockrill have described the dominance of Lloyd George at the Paris Conference: '(Foreign Secretaries) Balfour and Curzon had little control over events and, though they attended some of the more important conferences, might just as well not have been there for all the influence they had.'[9]

After three years of subordination to Lloyd George's actions, Curzon finally wrote to the prime minister with his complaints:

> There has grown up a system under which there are in reality two Foreign Offices: the one for which I am for a time being responsible, and the other at Number 10—with the essential difference between them that, whereas I report not only to you but to all my colleagues everything I say or do, every telegram I receive or send. Every communication of importance that reaches me, it is often only by accident that I hear what is being done by the other Foreign Office.[10]

The letter was never sent to Lloyd George. Curzon was still considering it when Lloyd George was driven from office.

Curzon was the more practical, working calmly to see his prejudices and his plans succeed. He could become angry at the actions of France and Italy, but he swallowed his feelings and continued to try to obtain the cooperation of allies whom he considered duplicitous. When allowed to do so by Lloyd George, Curzon was an expert at taking charge at conferences through meticulous planning.

Lloyd George was surely the more bombastic and mercurial. His abilities to reign over parliament and the cabinet and cow his allies into submission at conferences have never been properly explained, but were very real. He usually got what he wanted, even when his allies had serious objections to his plans. Often, he did not even feel the need to explain his actions to the cabinet. When it came to the public and parliament, the prime minister routinely lied, but what else could he do when forced to defend the indefensible? His policies in the Ottoman Empire were never practical or in the best interest of Britain. His plans failed repeatedly. Only duplicity could justify them to parliament.[11]

As far as the Turks were concerned, the differences between the aims of Curzon and Lloyd George were in most cases minimal. Initially, both pursued the same goals – dividing the Ottoman Empire, ejecting the Turks from İzmir, Istanbul, Europe and Eastern Anatolia, supporting Greek expansion in Europe and Anatolia, neutering the Turks militarily and controlling Turkish finances and economy. Curzon might loathe his subsidiary position, but he publicly supported common policy with the prime minister until Lloyd George's policies began to verge on madness in 1922. Most considerations of the plans of Lloyd George and Curzon in the Ottoman Empire offer details of events. But the most important point was that those plans failed, and failed disastrously.

## Supporting the Greeks

The British were to support Greek aspirations throughout diplomatic conferences and the Greek war with the Turks. It has been advanced that the reason for British support of the Greeks was basically geopolitical. Britain needed a supportive regional power that it could depend on to advance Britain's interests in the Eastern Mediterranean and the Aegean. This is at least partially true; if Britain needed a subordinate in the region, there was no choice other than Greece. The Turks, who had just fought a war against Britain, would not fit that role. The British seldom considered the long-term implications of supporting Greece. Could Greece always be trusted to follow the British lead? The only serious consideration of this led to the conclusion that Athens was within the range of naval gunfire – Greece easily could be threatened if it did not comply with British wishes.[12]

A somewhat more convincing reason for British support of the Greeks, especially when that support became increasingly irrational, was emotional.

Perhaps affected by their own wartime propaganda, leaders such as Lloyd George and Curzon described the Turks as an evil force that could never be allowed to rule again. They described the Ottomans joining the Germans in the war as perfidious, given the friendship that Britain had always shown the Ottomans. The previous chapters demonstrated that this was self-deception, but it was believed. Throughout the events of the Turkish Independence War a theme emerged – the Turks had to be punished for fighting against the British, and the Greeks were to be the agent of British revenge. Wartime propaganda had also greatly affected the British public and domestic pressure groups, long convinced of Turkish malevolence. The campaign against the Turks was facilitated by a general anti-Turkish belief that had been inculcated in the British public since the days of the Greek Independence War of the 1820s. Politicians had no choice but to be against the Turks.[13]

The abilities of Prime Minister Venizelos in advocating for Greece cannot be discounted. His eloquence at the Peace Conference gained much for Greece, and he excelled at making the leaders of Europe and America his allies; Lloyd George was his particular friend. Venizelos came to the Paris Conference armed with positions and statistics. It made no difference that they were demonstrably false, because the Allies were more than willing to accept whatever he presented. He was greatly aided by the fact that the Allies refused to allow the Turks, Bulgarians or Albanians any opportunity to present their own cases. Again and again, Lloyd George, Curzon, Wilson and initially the French accepted Venizelos's assertions over the facts presented by their own representatives and researchers. Population statistics and descriptions of tranquility in İzmir were presented by British high commissioners and military men. They were disregarded. Had he been willing to follow the advice of his own advisors, Lloyd George would never have sent the Greeks into İzmir, but facts did not stand in the way of his intentions.[14]

Lloyd George firmly believed in the abilities of the Greeks. He saw them as a vibrant and intelligent people. He said their soldiers were superb fighting men who would easily defeat any foe. They would soon be the dominant force in the Balkans and Western Anatolia. How could such an assumption of military might and prowess be accepted? The Ottomans had easily defeated the Greeks in 1897. Serbia and Bulgaria had beaten the Ottomans in the Balkan Wars, Greece picking up her share of the spoils. Greece had fought very little when it finally entered World War I. Yet Lloyd George was convinced that the Greek army would always triumph. He was certain, moreover, that the Greeks would always be friends to the British. Prime Minister Venizelos had indeed been an ally to the British. The Greek people were not so committed, as they showed when they returned to power King Constantine, no friend to Britain, and ejected Venizelos (see Chapter 17). Yet even when his friend Venizelos was disowned, Lloyd George remained committed to the Greek cause.[15]

Without a probably fruitless examination of the imperial mindset, it is difficult to evaluate final factors behind British actions in the Ottoman Empire after the world war. Surely one factor should be the belief, seen so many times, that the British knew best what was needed by those they considered to be lesser peoples. It was the duty of those peoples to follow British advice, in particular the advice to dismember the Ottoman Empire. The British had chosen the Greeks, but the ungrateful Turks refused to conform.

Once the British had committed themselves to the Greeks, they could not bring themselves to admit they could have been wrong, even when their policies obviously had become disasters.

## The Invasion of İzmir

The British Cabinet had contemplated a Greek occupation of Western Anatolia long before the end of World War I. It had considered as early as 30 June 1915 that İzmir should go to the Greeks if Greece joined the Allies in the war. There was disagreement, however. At first, some members of the cabinet were against any occupations in Anatolia. Foreign Secretary (1916–19) Balfour stated that he felt that any occupation of Turkish towns in Anatolia should be avoided. But Prime Minister Venizelos of Greece had begun to lobby the British Government to give İzmir (Smyrna) to the Greeks before the war ended. As was so often to be the case, Venizelos's political ability and personal charm were to convince Lloyd George and the cabinet to accept Greek claims.[16]

The British offered their fellow Peace Conference delegates three justifications for the Greek invasion of İzmir: the Greeks were in jeopardy, Greeks were a majority in İzmir and Italian occupation had to be forestalled.

## Protecting Greeks from Massacre by Turks

The Greek Government conducted an active propaganda campaign with the Allied representatives at the Peace Conference. They alleged that the Turks were planning an active campaign of massacre of Christians. The only way to avoid this was by Allied military intervention.[17]

On 2 May 1919, Lloyd George announced to his fellow Peace Conference delegates, solely on the strength of a telegram from the Central Committee of Unredeemed Hellenes in Athens, that Turks in İzmir were 'continuing their policy of oppression and massacre'. He said he had shared the message with Venizelos, who agreed with the Central Committee's message. Venizelos had added that the Italians, who also wanted İzmir, were undoubtedly stirring up the Turks, and that the Greeks in the town were in danger from the Turks.[18]

Greek sources had been protesting since the end of the war that Greeks in İzmir were in danger, and that the Turks were planning massacres. Upon investigation, British authorities in Istanbul found there was nothing to the claims. In fact, the situation in İzmir had improved, as Acting High Commissioner Rear-Admiral Richard Webb noted:

> Up to the time of the Smyrna landing the situation was not only generally satisfactory but was, moreover, steadily improving, and armed conflicts between Christians and Moslems did not commence until the decision was taken by the Peace Conference to send Greek troops to Smyrna; the authority of the Central Government was, in fact, fairly well established.[19]

The British Government, however, was intent on exploiting supposed disturbances to justify Greek occupation of Western Anatolia. They would not even allow Ottoman action to try to secure the peace. When on 3 April 1919, the War Office in London suggested that a Turkish division with British officers be sent to the Aydın Province (capital İzmir) to keep the peace, the cabinet rejected the idea. 'If a Turkish division be sent to Vilayet of Aydın we should be creating difficulties for ourselves should conference pronounce in favor of union of this province with Greece.'[20]

## The Supposed Greek Majority

What might have stood in the way of the British plans for İzmir was Wilson's 'Fourteen Points'. These had promised that '[t]he Turkish portion of the present Ottoman Empire should be assured a secure sovereignty'. The question was whether İzmir was Turkish. The British had decided even before World War I ended that they would not allow the Fourteen Points to interfere with British interests. However, Wilson was active at Paris when the İzmir issue was decided, and his views had to be considered. Moreover, the British did not want to appear to be forcing a large population to accept foreign rule (unless the foreign rule was theirs). The solution was a set of counterfeit population statistics.[21]

In December 1918, the Foreign Office had recommended the boundaries of Greek acquisitions in Anatolia. It suggested an area in which, it stated, the majority of the population was Greek. A majority Turkish region would be attached 'for strategical and commercial reasons'. Greek and Turkish populations were expected to migrate to and from their respective regions, bolstering the Greek population in the area assigned to Greece. All was based on statistics provided by the Greek Government, because '[t]here is no Turkish census'. This was false. As the British well knew (see below), there was an Ottoman census and Ottoman statistics. However, choosing the falsified Greek statistics over real population records provided the British with justification for the award of İzmir, and later Eastern Thrace, to the Greeks.[22]

Greek Prime Minister Venizelos presented statistics on Greek population at meetings of Allied representatives at the Peace Conference on 3 and 4 February 1919. He listed for Eastern Thrace ('excluding Constantinople'): 267,000 Greeks, 213,000 Turks and 35,000 Bulgarians. The Bulgarians and many of the Muslims, he stated, would join with the Greeks, and it was unthinkable that any part of Europe should be returned to the Turks. For Anatolia, Venizelos stated that in the areas claimed by Greece (undefined exactly, but including İzmir) there were 1,132,000 Greeks and 943,000 Muslims, most of them Turks. He added that 100,000 Jews, Armenians and other Christians should be added to the Greek number, 'thus raising the total to 1,250,000 non-Mussulmans, as compared to 943,000 Mussulmans'. In İzmir City, he stated, there were 220,000 Greeks and 95,000 Turks.[23]

The statistics which Venizelos presented to the Peace Conference were avowedly based on population statistics collected by the Greek Patriarchate of Constantinople. When asked by President Wilson if the figures had been obtained from the Greek Patriarchate, Venizelos replied that the figures had

THE PARIS PEACE CONFERENCE | 363

Map 10.1   Foreign Office recommended boundaries

been supplied by the Greek Ecclesiastical Authorities, but he falsely stated that they had been originally derived from official Turkish statistics. (The Greek statistics were printed in various Greek Government-sponsored publications. For convenience, all are described here as 'Greek Patriarchate Statistics'.) All were fabrications created for the Greek Government to show Greek demographic dominance in large sections of Anatolia, as indicated in the map taken from the publication of the statistics (Map 10.2).[24]

The Greek statistics were obvious forgeries. There is no place here to give a detailed demographic analysis of the Greek statistics; it appears elsewhere. Briefly, the authors of the Greek statistics took data from available Ottoman statistics and especially from the books of Vital Cuinet, which were decades out of date, and added numbers to the Greek column. Sloppy work makes it easy to identify the statistics as forgeries. The creators of the Patriarchate Statistics left the numbers for all but the Greeks as they were in Cuinet's 1894 work. Table 10.1 gives an example of the process for İzmir Kaza.[25]

Table 10.1  İzmir Kaza (district): Population in Cuinet and the 'Patriarchate Statistics'[26]

|  | Muslim | Greek | Armenian | Jewish | Foreign | Bulgarian | Total |
|---|---|---|---|---|---|---|---|
| Cuinet (1894) | 96,250 | 57,000 | 7,628 | 16,450 | 51,872 | 415 | 229,615 |
| 'Patriarchate' (1912) | 96,250 | 243,879 | 7,628 | 16,450 | 51,872 | 415 | 416,494 |

These were actually statistics that had been paid for by the Greek Government. Dimitri Kitsikis has found the archival record of the Greek Government's orders for their creation and dissemination.[27]

Although there were in fact detailed Ottoman statistics on population that were not considered by Lloyd George, he and most members of the British Cabinet accepted Venizelos's figures without question. They repeatedly referred to them as fact, despite the fact that British military and Foreign Office analysts, including those on the spot in Istanbul, denied the Greek statistics' validity. Even the Political Intelligence Division of the Foreign Office, upon which the British supposedly depended for accurate information, described the Greek Patriarchate Statistics as 'very doubtful'. They were, however, positive about the Turkish statistics: 'These figures (Turkish Official Statistics for 1914) appear to be, on the

# THE PARIS PEACE CONFERENCE | 365

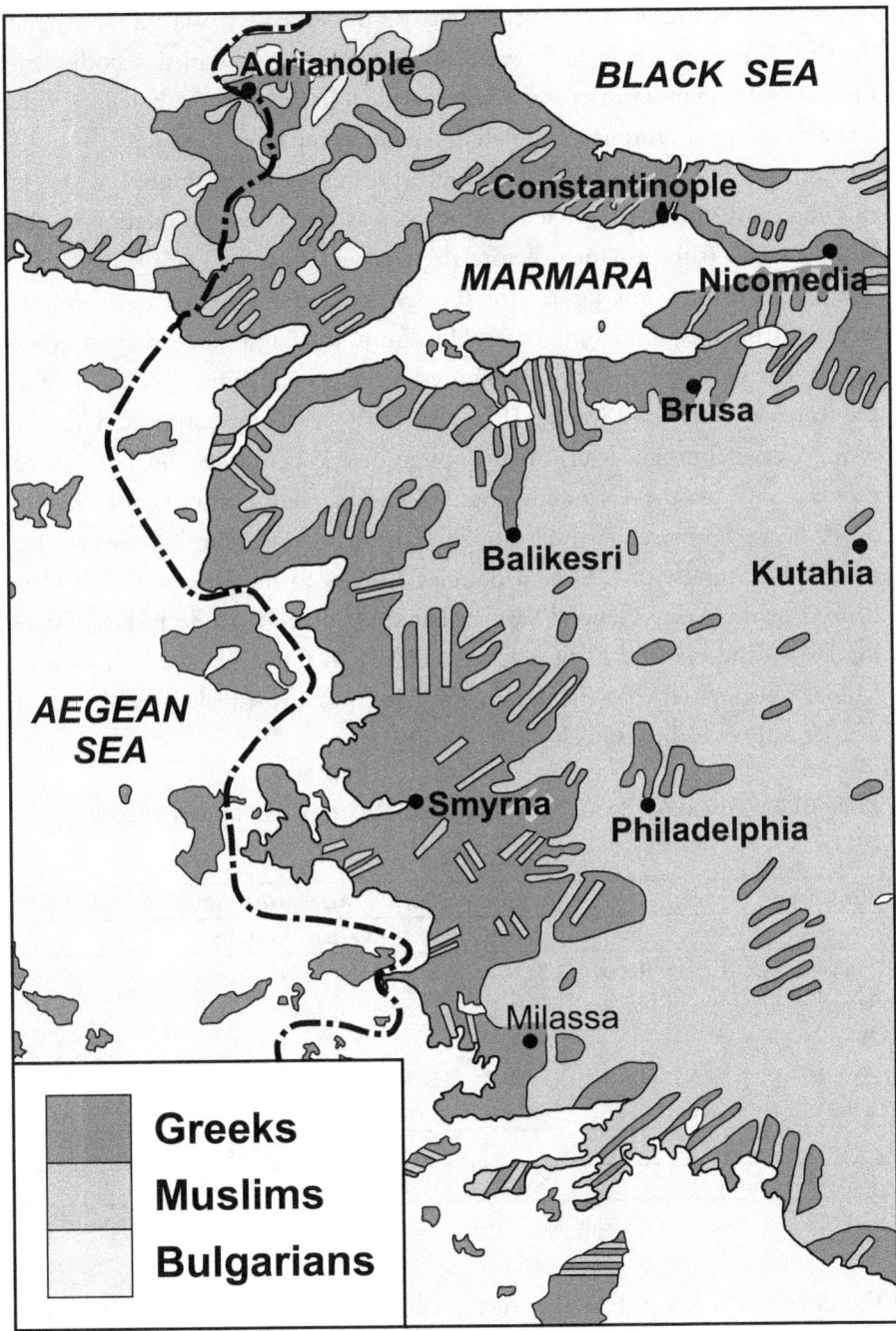

Map 10.2 'Greek Patriarchate Statistics'

whole, the best and most complete of any yet published for Asia Minor.' When the British army and navy had need of accurate population statistics, both identified the Ottoman statistics as the best available. In the past, the Foreign Office had also accepted Ottoman population records as the most accurate.[28]

Admiral de Robeck, the British high commissioner in Istanbul, wrote to the Foreign Office with what he believed was the actual population of the İzmir Sancak (sub-province) before the war, in 1914: 217,477 Greeks and 415,882 Muslims. His figures for the sancak corresponded almost exactly to the Ottoman statistics for 1914. His figures for İzmir Kaza (district) were exactly the same as the Ottoman figures: 100,356 Muslims, 73,636 Greeks. De Robeck wrote on 9 March 1920 that both the İzmir district and Thrace were 'overwhelmingly Muslim in population'. When asked by London to provide data on the Ottoman population, the high commissioner before de Robeck, Somerset Arthur Gough-Calthorpe, had simply forwarded a complete summary of Ottoman population data to the Foreign Office. The Bureau of the Army General Staff in Istanbul agreed with de Robeck's data for 1914. The General Officer Commanding in Chief in Istanbul, George Milne, telegraphed that the Aydın Province was two-thirds Turkish, İzmir district only one-third Greek.[29]

Table 10.2   Population by religion in Western Anatolia and Eastern Thrace, 1911–12[30]

| Province | Muslim | Greek | Armenian | Bulgarian | Other |
|---|---|---|---|---|---|
| Western Anatolia | | | | | |
| Hüdavendigâr (Capital Bursa) | 83% | 11% | 5% | | 1% |
| İzmit | 70% | 12% | 18% | | 0% |
| Biga | 90% | 5% | 2% | | 3% |
| Aydın (Capital İzmir) | 79% | 18% | 1% | | 2% |
| İzmir district of Aydın | 48% | 35% | 5% | | 12% |
| Eastern Thrace | | | | | |
| Edirne | 53% | 28% | 2% | 12% | 5% |

Note: These figures are for Ottoman subjects. They do not include foreign citizens.

The doyen of the British commercial establishment in İzmir, H. C. Whittall, wrote that İzmir City was one-third Greeks, two-thirds Turks, Jews, Armenians and Europeans, and 'further inland the Turks form a very great majority'. His view was endorsed both by the British Chamber of Commerce of İzmir and British High Commissioner Calthorpe. ('I most unhesitatingly and unreservedly endorse all Mr. Whitall's observations.')[31]

Albert Howe Lybyer, attached to the American mission to the Peace Conference, carefully analysed the Greek statistics, discovered the way in which they had been falsified, and remarked: 'The frank truth is that these maps and figures overestimate the proportion of Greeks in Thrace, Constantinople, and the Smyrna district in the year 1912 to a considerable extent.' Lybyer, a professor at Harvard and the University of Illinois, was one of the few American advisors to the Peace Conference with actual knowledge of the Ottoman Empire; he had taught for six years at Robert College in Istanbul.[32]

The important point is that Lloyd George and the others who presented the British case at the Peace Conference justified their position with counterfeit population statistics. The population of the İzmir region was overwhelmingly Turkish.

**Thrace**

The Allies at the Peace Conference deliberated on the possession of Western Thrace (West of the Maritsa River) and Eastern Thrace (East of the Maritsa) in 1919 (Map 10.3). At first, the American delegation wished to leave Western Thrace to the Bulgarians, who had held it since 1913. The British, French and Japanese delegations disagreed. President Wilson also wanted to give Northeastern Thrace to Bulgaria. He wrongly believed that its population was mainly Bulgarian. Curzon politely rejected this, and Wilson again changed his mind. Debate ensued on how much to give to the Greeks, how much to the Bulgarians. The delegates considered placing Eastern Thrace in an International Zone, centred on Istanbul. Finally, it was decided that all of Western Thrace and most of Eastern Thrace would be given to the Greeks, with nothing for Bulgaria. There was no agreement on the limits of an International Zone; that would be decided later. No matter the preponderance of the Turkish population, none of Thrace was to be left to the Turks, because it had been agreed that they would be expelled from Europe. A small region near Istanbul was to be left to theoretical Ottoman sovereignty, but under Allied Control, as part of the Neutral Zone.[33]

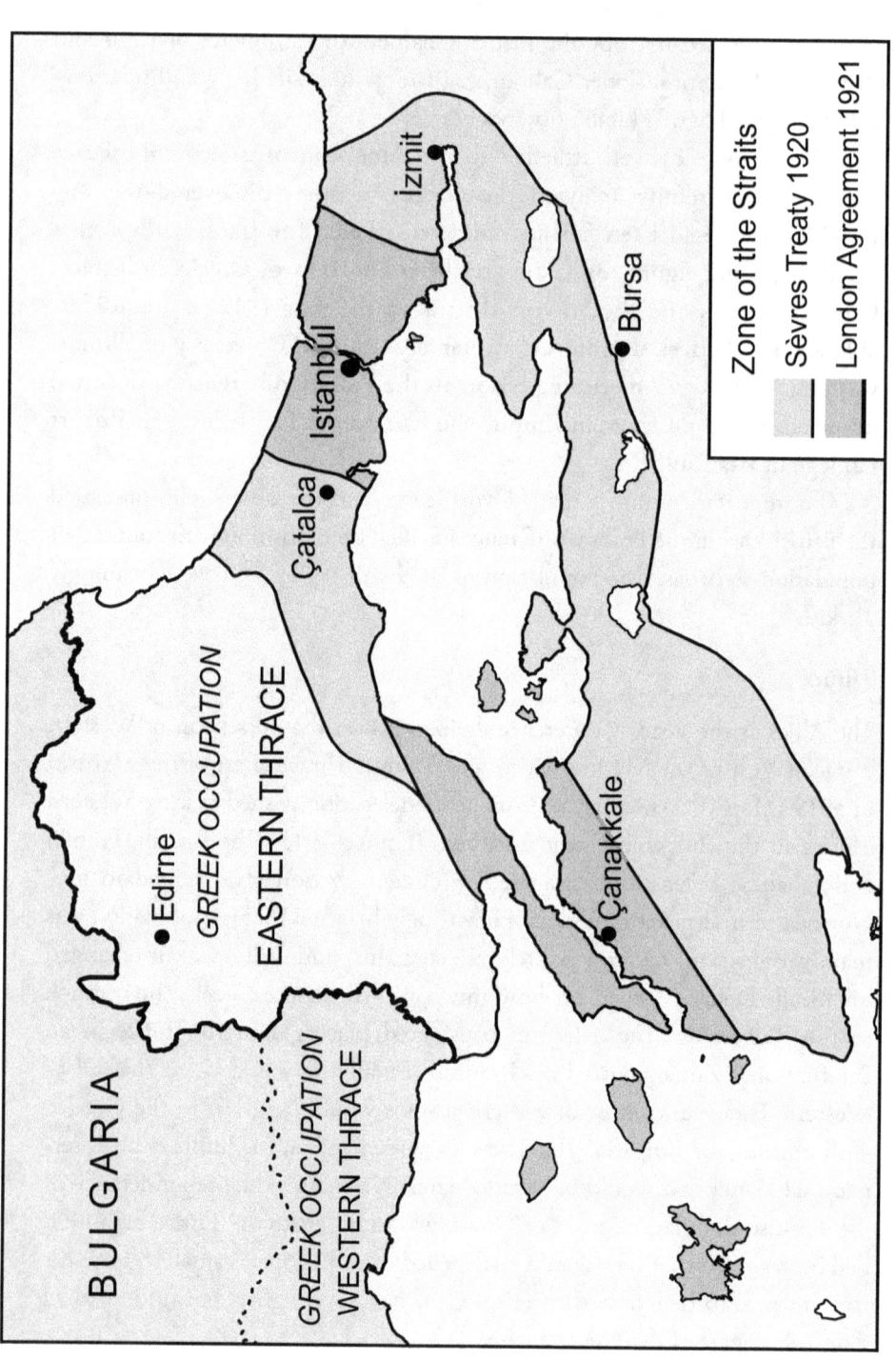

Map 10.3 Eastern Thrace and the Straits Zone

Although the Peace Conference delegates had resolved that the Turks should not be entitled to any territory in Thrace, there was still a moral problem in submitting so great a Turkish population to foreign rule. All accepted that Western Thrace would go to Greece. As they had for Western Anatolia, the British cited Greek statistics to show that Greeks were predominant in Eastern Thrace.

As seen above, Prime Minister Venizelos presented fanciful statistics on the population of Thrace (267,000 Greeks, 213,000 Turks and 35,000 Bulgarians), analogous to those he advanced on the population of Western Anatolia. British officials at the Peace Conference accepted Greek falsified statistics instead of the data from their own representatives. Before World War I, British diplomatic representatives in Eastern Thrace (the Edirne Province) had accepted Ottoman population statistics as essentially accurate: 53 per cent Muslim, 28 per cent Greek, 12 per cent Bulgarian (Table 4.1). These were the figures for 1912, before the demographic changes brought about by the Balkan Wars: from 1912 to 1920, 132,500 Turkish refugees had come to the Edirne Province, whereas approximately 100,000 Greeks and Bulgarians had left.[34]

At the end of the war, British Intelligence had provided estimates that the population of Eastern Thrace had been more than half Turkish before the Balkan Wars, and became considerably more Turkish after those wars. In 1920, the General Staff stated: '75 per cent of the population of Eastern Thrace are Moslems.' Moreover, Army Intelligence reported: 'Since the Adrianople Vilayet has been under the control of the Nationalists, it is reported that there have been no disturbances of any kind.'[35]

Lloyd George was unconcerned with the statements on population from his own officials. He only accepted Venizelos's figures. His sole interest was to maximise the area of Greek occupation in Thrace. In the plan he presented to the Supreme Council, even the Gallipoli Peninsula would be given to Greece, although with an Allied garrison to protect the Dardanelles. He hoped that Thrace would be ceded to Greece up to the Çatalca Line, with all necessary guarantees as to demilitarisation and the garrisoning of strategic points by Allied troops. Lloyd George's plan was largely to be put into effect in the Treaty of Sèvres. Greek troops, assisted by the French, had taken Bulgarian Western Thrace in November 1918. The Greeks occupied Eastern Thrace, with British military assistance, in July of 1920.[36]

## The Committee on Greek Territorial Claims

The Powers at the Paris Conference were too occupied with Germany and Austria for some time to give much consideration to the Ottoman Empire. Ottoman questions were sent to committees. On 4 February 1919, after Venizelos's testimony, the Peace Conference remanded consideration of Venizelos's proposal to a committee on territory to be given to Greece:

> That the questions raised in the statement by M. Venizelos on the Greek territorial interests in the Peace Settlement shall be referred for examination in the first instance to an expert committee composed of two representatives each of the United States of America, The British Empire, France and Italy. It shall be the duty of this Committee to reduce the questions for decision within the narrowest possible limits and make recommendations for a just settlement. The Committee is authorised to consult representatives of the peoples concerned.[37]

Although the committee was supposedly to be made up of experts, the British named diplomats with no Middle East or Balkan experience – Robert Borden, late prime minister of Canada, and Eyre Crowe, a high Foreign Office official and expert on Germany. The Americans named experts in their own fields, William L. Westermann, a professor of ancient history at the University of Wisconsin, and Clive Day, a professor of economic history at Yale, but neither had studied the contemporary Balkans or Middle East. France was represented by Jules Cambon, a diplomat who had served as ambassador in Spain, Germany and the United States. The only one with first-hand experience of the Ottoman Empire was the Italian delegate, Foreign Secretary Giacomo de Martino, who had served in Istanbul for two years as a junior diplomat from 1895 to 1897. He had also negotiated with the Ottomans in 1911.[38]

The committee members debated issues at length, but they were actually mouthpieces for the positions of their respective governments. Lloyd George was later to say that the Powers had acted as they did in Thrace and Anatolia because of the deliberations and report of the Greek Territorial Committee. He conveniently neglected to note the committee's disagreements or the fact that the British delegates were anything but neutral analysts.

According to its charge, the committee was authorised to consult 'representatives of the peoples concerned'. This charge was interpreted in a restricted manner: on a settlement in Thrace and Western Anatolia, the committee heard only from Greeks – Prime Minister Venizelos and Ottoman Greeks. No Turks

# THE PARIS PEACE CONFERENCE | 371

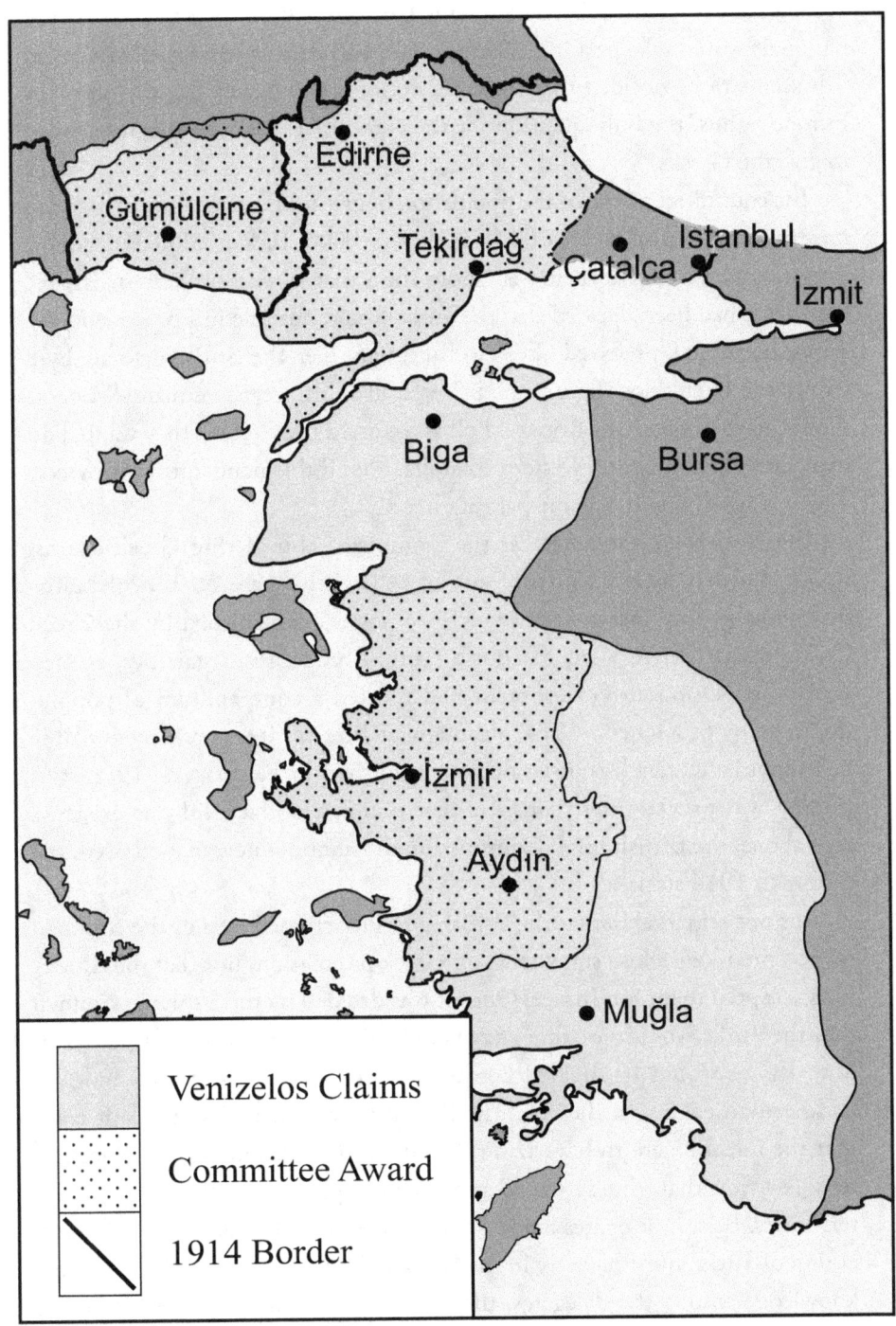

Map 10.4  Greek Territorial Committee award to Greece

or Bulgarians were heard. The Supreme Council had decided that no enemy nationals would take part in deliberations or be heard as witnesses. Moreover, '[i]t seems to be decided that there are no longer to be any Turkish states in Europe'. Thus, the only question for the committee was how much territory to give the Greeks.[39]

The committee accepted the population figures for Eastern Thrace that were presented by Venizelos: 237,000 Greeks, 193,000 Turks, 7,000 Bulgarians. Venizelos admitted that there were more Turks than Greeks in Western Thrace, but that it had been decided that the Turks would not rule in Europe, and the Turks, he alleged, preferred Greek to Bulgarian rule. The British delegate Eyre Crowe cited Venizelos's figures and believed all of Thrace, Eastern and Western, should go to Greece. The British wholly supported the Greeks. They wanted no mandates over Thrace or Western Anatolia, even if the mandatory was Greece. The territories should become part of Greece.[40]

The British representative at the committee considering Greek claims, Robert Borden, asserted in February of 1919: 'There are no Turkish statistics, and the only information which we possess is furnished by the Greek Government.' There were, of course, Turkish population statistics, as seen above. The Ottoman Government had printed a compendium of population data by province in 1914; although in Turkish, it was readily available in Istanbul. A French translation was published in February 1919, just as Borden was proclaiming that Ottoman population data did not exist. As seen above, the British High Commission in Istanbul knew of, and used, the Ottoman 1914 statistics.[41]

It is not remarkable that the British and French members of the committee accepted Venizelos's statements on Greek population, nor that the Americans accepted them for Thrace. Once it was decided by the Supreme Council that the Turks would not rule anywhere in Europe, it was only a matter of how Thrace would be divided between Greece and Bulgaria, and Bulgaria had been an enemy in the war. The British Government had made it plain that the Greeks were to have İzmir. What was remarkable was the committee's assertion that Greece would protect the rights of Muslims in her new territories. British delegates made no reference to the Greek history of persecution of Turks, most recently in the Balkan Wars. Given the lack of regional knowledge among the delegates, they perhaps did not know the history, or perhaps they did not care.[42]

By no means were all the delegates in agreement on the disposition of Ottoman lands. The French questioned the award of the region to the Greeks without Allied oversight, because Greeks would massacre Turks without it. They suggested an Allied oversight commission. On the other hand, the French stated, where Turks were in command 'order reigned' and there were no massacres. The British asserted, without offering evidence, that massacres had been carried out by Turks. There should be no Allied oversight, because it 'would weaken Greek authority in the eyes of the Turks'. Venizelos appeared before the committee and rejected the idea of Allied oversight. The commission did nothing on the oversight plan.[43]

The disagreements among the committee members reflected the positions of the members' governments. The British wanted İzmir and adjacent areas to be made a part of Greece, preferably without oversight (Map 10.1). They based their decision on Greek statistics. Even though their plan for Allied oversight had been abandoned, the French finally concurred with the British. The Americans, however, opposed separating the İzmir region from Turkish Anatolia. They did not accept the Greek statistics, stating that the region to be given to Greece was two-thirds Turkish. They proposed that the area be placed under a mandate of a Power. The British responded 'on the undesirability of placing a compact and civilized country such as that of the Hellenic colonies on the western seaboard of Asia Minor under such tutelage'. The Italians disagreed completely with the other delegations. They wanted Greece to have only a small part of Western Thrace and none of Eastern Thrace or Anatolia.[44]

In its final report on 6 March 1919, the British and French delegates asserted that the İzmir region should become part of Greece. The Americans felt it should remain part of Anatolian Turkey. The Italians protested that the region allocated to Greece had been promised to them in previous agreements. On Thrace, the Americans joined the British and French in accepting Venizelos's assertions on population and on what Venizelos said were the wishes of the people of Western and Eastern Thrace, awarding all of Thrace to Greece. The three asserted that the Greeks would guarantee the rights of the Muslims of Thrace. The Italians again disagreed on everything. In short, there was much disagreement, especially on İzmir. No committee recommendation was made, only individual recommendations. Nevertheless, both the Greeks and the British were later falsely to claim that the British position had been passed by the committee. Lloyd George told parliament that the Greeks had only been allowed to take İzmir because the committee had recommended it.[45]

## Forestalling the Italians

Like many of the deliberations of the Peace Conference, the psychology and prejudices of Britain and France were the deciding factors in how they treated Italy. In demanding what it felt it had been promised in Anatolia (Map II.2), Italy refused to come hat in hand to Britain and France. Italy planned to act exactly as Britain and France were acting, carving out a part of the Ottoman Empire for itself.

Under the terms of the 1915 Treaty of London, which brought Italy into the war, Italy would take sovereignty over the Dodecanese Islands, which she had occupied in 1912. If the Ottoman Empire was totally or partially partitioned, Italy would take Antalya (Adalia) and be allowed to occupy 'the Mediterranean region bordering on the Province of Adalia', the exact boundaries to be determined. Those boundaries were set in the 1917 Agreement of Saint Jean de Maurienne: France was to receive the Adana Province and Italy the region to its west (the southern part of the Aydın Province), including the city of İzmir. Although the British accepted these terms at the time, no formal treaty was signed. Russia, which had been expected to be part of the treaty, did not sign, due to the Russian Revolution. (The initial agreement had included the words, 'subject to Russia's consent'.) The British and French nevertheless had accepted that the agreement would be binding on them unless the Provisional Russian Government disavowed it. As there is no evidence of the agreement ever being presented to the Russians and thus it was not disavowed, it would seem that it was in force. The British, however, used the lack of Russian acceptance to declare the agreement void, and the British disavowed the agreement.[46]

The Italians naturally, and correctly, saw this as the political chicanery it was.

> Baron Sonnino (Italian Foreign Minister Sydney Sonnino) referred with a certain degree of bitterness to the difference of attitude which he had found to prevail on the part of the Allies, now that the assistance and support of Italy were no longer wanted, from that which he had encountered when Italian cooperation was eagerly desired.

Sonnino was told that all the previous agreements were being reconsidered. He remarked that this seemed to only apply to Italy, but not to British and French agreements. Foreign Secretary Balfour declared that Sonnino was in error, that the arrangements in the Sykes–Picot Agreement between France and Britain were not being put in place. He may have been theoretically correct, because the Sykes–Picot borders were indeed to be altered. The fact, however, was that Britain and France were to take Syria, Palestine and Iraq, as they had promised each other, only to divide them differently. Unlike them, the Italians were not to receive what they felt they had been promised.[47]

Britain and France had no intention of standing by the promises they had made in order to bring Italy into the war. In addition to regions in the Ottoman Empire, the Italians were not to receive extensive land on the Dalmatian coast, a protectorate over Albania and a share of the conquered German territories in Africa – all of which they had been promised. The Italians very correctly noted British duplicity.[48]

Woodrow Wilson proved to be an especially vehement opponent to the Italians. The portion of the Adriatic coast that had been promised to them, especially the port city of Fiume, was of particular importance to the Italians. Wilson contended that those lands were majority Slavic in population, and should be awarded to the new 'Kingdom of the Serbs, Croats, and Slovenes (later Yugoslavia)'. Wilson's application of his principle of self-determination made no distinction among the various Slavic peoples of the kingdom, nor was he bothered by its Serbian domination, but he knew the people were not Italian. Italian opposition made him an enemy.[49]

Part of the British attitude toward the Italians may be ascribed to negative feelings toward the Italian people and government. The Italians were felt to have 'extreme socialist' views. On the other hand, Britain had a longstanding affection for Greece. The main opposition to Italy from the British and French, however, was founded on economic, political and military power in the Mediterranean and Adriatic. Both Britain and France saw Italy as a competitor.[50]

The question of the Dodecanese, which Italy had held in its 1912 treaty with the Ottomans, was important to Italy. The Italians wished at all costs to retain them, but the British, supported by the French, were opposed. The British viewed the Dodecanese as something they could promise to the Greeks.[51]

The Italians, who seem to have been aware of British wartime plans to give İzmir to the Greeks, were already complaining about that policy at the end of the war. They stated that İzmir had been part of their sphere of influence in the Treaty of St Jean de Maurienne. Foreign Secretary Balfour told the Italian Charge d'Affaires in London that the St Jean de Maurienne Treaty was no longer valid. He admitted that Italy had been promised concessions under the Treaty of London, but said there were no special arrangements for İzmir. Balfour later told the Italian ambassador that no arrangements had yet been made on İzmir. The British ambassador in Rome was instructed to notify the Italians that they should not send any troops to Anatolia.

> You should point out again that such action on the part of the Italians will certainly provoke similar steps by the Greeks, and that His Majesty's Government in such an event would find it impossible to oppose the Greek claims to follow the Italian example.

The Italians, however, insisted on upholding at least some of their claims. Over the protests of Britain and France, Italy landed troops at Antalya. Britain announced that Italy had also sent a battleship, two cruisers and a destroyer to İzmir (there actually were never more than two ships), perhaps as a prelude to invasion.[52]

For the British and French, it became imperative that Italian plans for İzmir were thwarted.

## The Conversion of Woodrow Wilson to the Greek Cause

The Fourteen Points of Woodrow Wilson (8 January 1918) as they applied to the Ottoman Empire:

> I. Open covenants of peace, openly arrived at, after which there shall be no private international understandings of any kind but diplomacy shall proceed always frankly and in the public view.
>
> III. The removal, so far as possible, of all economic barriers and the establishment of an equality of trade conditions among all the nations consenting to the peace and associating themselves for its maintenance.
>
> V. A free, open-minded, and absolutely impartial adjustment of all colonial claims, based upon a strict observance of the principle that in

determining all such questions of sovereignty the interests of the populations concerned must have equal weight with the equitable government whose title is to be determined.

XII. The Turkish portion of the present Ottoman Empire should be assured a secure sovereignty, but the other nationalities which are now under Turkish rule should be assured an undoubted security of life and an absolutely unmolested opportunity of autonomous development, and the Dardanelles should be permanently opened as a free passage to the ships and commerce of all nations under international guarantees.

Wilson had added:

The settlement of every question, whether of territory, of sovereignty, of economic arrangement, or of political relationship, upon the basis of the free acceptance of that settlement by the people immediately concerned, and not upon the basis of the material interest or advantage of any other nation or people which may desire a different settlement for the sake of its own exterior influence or mastery.[53]

It was a very different standard that Wilson applied to European Christians than he did to the non-Christian peoples of the Ottoman Empire. Wilson's statements on the rights of peoples sounded idealistic: 'He (Wilson) believes it to be the central principle fought for in the War that no Government or group of Governments has the right to dispose of the territory or to determine the political allegiance of any free people.' As far as the Turks were concerned, it was all pious nonsense. In fact, Wilson never gave much consideration to applying his points to non-Europeans or non-Christians. But Wilson could apply the Fourteen Points to those Europeans whom he did not like. He objected mightily to the award of Slavic lands on the Adriatic to the Italians. He had no problem with Muslim lands being taken by the French, British, Greeks and Armenians, but when considering Italian claims in Anatolia he stated: 'He (Wilson) was bound to adhere to his principle that no peoples should be handed over to another rule without their consent.' Despite his promise of 'secure sovereignty', he proved unwilling to apply his avowed principles to the Turks. His only justification for awarding Turkish majority lands to others was that the lands were not really Turkish. He ignored the evidence presented by his own advisors and instead took the fabricated statistics provided by Venizelos and Armenian officials as justification for detaching regions that were overwhelmingly Turkish from Turkish rule. It is doubtful if Wilson realised any contradictions in his attitudes; he was capable of astounding self-deception.[54]

For the British, self-determination was a troublesome principle. Obviously, there was an inherent contradiction in a colonial power advocating a self-determination for Greeks and Armenians that it did not allow within its own colonies. When the colonial secretary, Lord Robert Cecil, brought the problem to the attention of the cabinet: 'It was suggested that this difficulty would be surmounted by confining the principle of self-determination to the territories actually affected by belligerent operations.'[55]

The British had never intended to apply the Fourteen Points to the Ottoman Empire. Before the armistice with the Ottomans was signed, Lloyd George had declared to the cabinet that Britain had no intention to apply the Fourteen Points to the Ottomans. After the armistice, the Foreign Office reiterated this position. Just after the Peace Conference commenced (18 January 1919), the British stated their intention not to adhere to most of the Fourteen Points as they applied to the Ottoman Empire: the British declared they would not be bound by the call for 'open agreements' in the Middle East or Thrace; pre-war agreements took precedent (although the British were to violate these also).

The Turks were by no means to be assured 'secure sovereignty'. The Allies were to decide in which regions non-Turkish minorities had not been allowed security of life and autonomous development (whatever that meant), and thus could be separated from the Ottoman Empire. In effect, this meant that the British were to detach from Turkish rule any land they wished; specific regions to which this applied were named as Armenia, Thrace and İzmir. 'Smyrna and its hinterlands' should be separated from Turkish Anatolia, and the Peace Conference should consider making them part of Greece. An Armenian state should be created in most of Eastern Anatolia, but under a European or American mandate. All the regions remaining to the Turks would come under control of a European mandate, decided by the Powers. An independent State of the Straits, including Istanbul, would be under European control, whatever the wishes of the populace. All regions detached from the Ottoman Empire would pay their share of the Ottoman debt, a vital point to the British and French.[56]

The United States at first rejected the award of İzmir to the Greeks. The American stance in the Greek Territorial Committee was instead in favour of a European mandate over the region. The American experts and diplomats disagreed with the Greek statistics that were the basis of the Greek claims. The region, they felt, was predominantly Turkish. From an economic point of view, they stated, İzmir could not be separated from the rest of Anatolia. It was the entrepot for import and export for all Western Anatolia. The American delegates to the committee were against the Greek occupation of İzmir.[57]

Woodrow Wilson, mercurial as ever, changed the American policy. He had been won over to accepting Greek claims in Western Anatolia, as well as in Thrace, by what he called 'the eloquence of Venizelos'. Against the advice of his experts and the American delegates to the Greek Territorial Commission, he became convinced that the majority of the population of the region claimed by Greece was Greek. Until he abandoned the conference and its issues, Wilson became an ardent advocate for the Greeks, insisting that they should be given the İzmir region 'in full sovereignty', united with mainland Greece and it should be given the rest of the region that Greece coveted as a mandate.[58]

## The Greeks in İzmir

The deciding Peace Conference resolution to allow the Greeks to take İzmir was on a motion by Lloyd George. President Wilson supported the motion enthusiastically. He asked that the occupation begin immediately. Lloyd George agreed. Clemenceau of France had some misgivings, but also agreed. The decision was taken in secret. Italy was not at the meeting, having temporarily boycotted the Peace Conference, and Lloyd George was anxious that the Italians would not hear of the occupation until it was a fact. He feared that the Italians, who believed that İzmir had been promised to them, might make the first move by taking İzmir themselves. He suggested the plan to Wilson and Clemenceau at a private meeting attended by Venizelos. An essential part of the plan was that both Italy and the Ottomans should not be told of it in advance. Arrangements for the occupation were completed on 11 May. Only on 12 May were the Italians notified that the Greeks would take İzmir.[59]

It was decided that one Greek division be sent to İzmir, with another to follow. The Allies would facilitate the process with their navies. Allied forces would take the forts outside the city, later turning them over to the Greeks. The Ottoman Government would only be notified of the occupation twelve hours in advance. The action was justified 'in view of reported disorders in the neighbourhood of Smyrna'. The Italians were informed of the decision as a *fait accompli*. They reluctantly agreed to cooperate with the invasion. The only Italian request was that Allied soldiers remain in İzmir, as well as Greek; the other delegates refused.[60]

In fact, the danger to the Greeks of İzmir was a complete fabrication, promulgated by Venizelos, seconded by the British. The Inter-Allied Commission of Inquiry on the Greek Occupation of Smyrna (see Chapter 11) found no such danger: 'Since the Armistice, the safety of the Christians in the Vilayet (province) of Aidin had not been threatened.' The Ottoman governor, Nureddin Paşa, had treated all ethnic groups with impartiality. Fears of massacre of Christians had never been justified. The Allied Commission wrote: 'The internal situation in the Vilayet did not call for the landing of Allied troops at Smyrna.'[61]

In May 1919, warships from Britain, France, Italy, the United States and Greece steamed into the İzmir harbour. Allied soldiers occupied coastal defences. The Greeks landed in İzmir on 15 May 1919 and swiftly took command of the İzmir Sancak, the territory that had been awarded them by the Peace Conference.

The Greek claims to large sections of Western Anatolia advanced after their occupation of İzmir. Venizelos at first claimed that he was only acting for the Supreme Council, but soon began to put forth plans to unite the Anatolian Greeks to Greece: any Greek in the Ottoman Empire could decide he wanted to be a Greek citizen. All Greeks who had gone from the Ottoman Empire to Greece were to be recognised as Greek citizens, even if they returned to Anatolia. Greek courts in the occupied territory were to have complete authority.[62]

## Opposition

Two months before the Greek invasion of İzmir, the British General Officer in Command in Istanbul, George Milne, strongly recommended against any Greek occupation. He noted that Turks were three-fourths of the population in Aydın Province. A week before the invasion, General Wilson, Chief of the

General Staff, warned Lloyd George against the invasion; he noted that the prime minister would not listen.[63]

One month before the invasion, British General Staff Intelligence reported that Greek rule in İzmir could only be successful if the Allies themselves first took control of İzmir, perhaps slowly giving more power to the Greeks. The report brought up an important point neglected in all the Allied considerations – Muslim refugees. İzmir and the Aydın Province were full of Muslim refugees from the Balkan Wars. It was not enough to consider the Greek refugees. 'The Muslim refugees in the region must be treated well, not just the Greek refugees.' (There were, in fact, 132,500 Muslim refugees from the Balkans in Eastern Thrace and 146,000 in the Aydın Province.) The General Staff report was one of the very few references to the Muslim refugees ever made by the British. It was ignored.[64]

The American high commissioner in Istanbul, Lewis Heck, reported on 4 January 1919 that American institutions (presumably missionary) at İzmir had not been molested by the Turks and were continuing their activities. The American ambassador at Athens wrote that he had received many petitions asking İzmir and elsewhere be given to Greece, but he felt that the region should remain under the Turks.[65]

The Political Officer of the Naval Command at Constantinople, H. C. Luke, wrote in a detailed report that a real threat to British interests could only be avoided if 'no predominantly Ottoman districts are to be placed under Greek rule'.[66]

Acting High Commissioner Webb in Istanbul:

> I am convinced that the present unsatisfactory situation in Anatolia, which tends to grow worse as time goes on, is the direct result of the presence of Greek troops in the Aidin vilayet, and the regrettable excesses, of which there is unfortunately no doubt, they have on several occasions been guilty ... The fact must not be lost sight of that every Turk, of no matter what party or political sympathies, is sincere in looking upon the Greek and Italian occupation as a violation of right and justice.

The only solution, he felt, was for the Greeks and Italians to leave. High Commissioner de Robeck believed that there would be no peace as long as the Greeks and Italians occupied Anatolia.[67]

Persistent advice from British observers in the Ottoman Empire was that the Allies would not be able to enforce harsh terms on the Turks unless the Allies were to devote significant troops to enforce the terms. In particular, the award of İzmir and Eastern Thrace to the Greeks would demand Allied military force.[68]

Even Lord Curzon, not yet foreign secretary himself, wrote to Foreign Secretary Balfour to complain that dire troubles awaited the British because of the decision to send them to İzmir. Curzon later said that he had opposed the Greek occupation: 'I myself thought that this was the greatest mistake that had been made at Paris, and that it was the starting point of the troubles which had since ensued.'[69]

High Commissioner Calthorpe believed that, had the Greeks not invaded İzmir, the Turks would have accepted even the worst from the Allies. After the invasion, the Turks realised they could only depend on their own efforts, not on the Western Powers. After İzmir, Turks who had received British officers well, now regarded them 'with sullen suspicion'. He expected outbreaks throughout Anatolia, as indeed became the case.[70]

None of the opposition to Greek retention of İzmir affected the plans of the British Government in London. On 14 February 1920, when French President Alexandre Millerand stated that the Greeks in İzmir had caused great problems and had to go, Lloyd George gave his colleagues a long speech: the population of İzmir was Greek. The Greeks had gone there 'not as a temporary occupation but for permanent occupation'. Venizelos was his personal friend and a staunch ally who should not be opposed. İzmir would be a 'bridgehead' for the Allies, because the Greeks shared the Allies' interests.

> He hoped earnestly, therefore, that the Entente would not dream of turning out of Smyrna that statesman (Venizelos) who had risked everything to help them in order to put in his place the worst ruler that had ever cursed any land.[71]

## The Greek Advance

The Greek army appeared to be more than a match for any force that stood against them. The fighting ability of the Greek army was largely the product of British training and supply at the end of World War I. In 1917–18, the British, with some help from the French, had supplied the Greeks with 240 trucks, forty six-inch howitzers, nine batteries of 120mm guns, supplies for the cannon, 500 mules, field hospitals, clothing and boot leather for an army, food for soldiers, etc. The supplies were intended for the wartime fight against Bulgaria, but were to become the backbone of the Greek army in Anatolia.[72]

In May and June of 1919, Greek forces advanced beyond their İzmir enclave into the rest of Aydın Province, a direct violation of the decisions of the Peace Conference. At first, Venizelos stated that he had not ordered the further incursion into Aydın – it had been a communications problem. He then recanted and admitted he had sent in the troops, but only into territories where disorders had occurred. Even though the Greek strikes into Aydın had not been sanctioned, he asserted, the Greeks needed further extension of their conquest for defence against Turkish attacks. At first, the Supreme Council accepted Venizelos's assertions that he had not personally authorised the advance, which he later recanted. They did not even question his assertion that local Turks had asked for Greek occupation. The Greeks were allowed to move into new regions on the understanding that any further advances would have to be approved by the Senior Naval Officer of the Allied Fleets at İzmir.[73]

The Ottoman Government complained to the British High Commission that the Greeks were expanding their region of control. The British responded that any problems were over; the Greeks would be restrained: '[T]he limits of tile Greek occupation had now been defined, and steps had been taken to ensure observance by the Greeks of these limits.' This was untrue. The Greeks soon advanced even further, into regions that were definitely beyond what had been agreed. The Senior Naval Officer was not consulted. By the end of July, the Greeks had occupied a large territory. Local Turks and some Ottoman army units resisted. Bands of Greek and Turkish irregulars battled each other in the villages.[74]

British representatives in Istanbul denied Venizelos's contention that the Greek advance had been needed to protect Christians. Acting High Commissioner Webb denied Venizelos's account of the Greek advance in Aydın, stating that the Greek advance was unjustifiable and contrary to Greek promises, and that Venizelos had not stated events or Turkish casualties accurately. The Greek advance, Webb stated, was not caused by the need for defence, as Venizelos had declared, but rather an 'apparent determination to seize as much territory as possible'.[75]

The question was how the Powers would deal with the Greek violation of both the Supreme Council's mandate and Venizelos's promises. As they were so often to do, the British at the Peace Conference cast themselves as defenders of the Greeks. After it had become clear in the Smyrna Report (see the next chapter) that the Greeks had massacred Muslim inhabitants in the area they had conquered and had not shown that they could rule equitably, the French and Italians suggested that the Allies should more closely control them. Clemenceau felt that the Greeks could not maintain themselves in Asia Minor by their own efforts. Turks, he believed, would never accept Greek rule 'unless obliged by force'. De Martino of Italy agreed. Speaking for the British, however, Eyre Crowe, heading the British delegation at the meeting, believed that the Greeks should be left in place and, indeed, given more power: 'Rather than create an organ of supervision it would be better to give the Greeks greater liberty of action and at the same time a larger and more definite share of responsibility.'[76]

Crowe was to continue his defence of the Greeks in a subsequent meeting of the conference delegates. He was particularly concerned that the Greeks be allowed to remain in the territory they had conquered beyond the initial award to them, although they had done so without sanction, and perhaps to expand their occupation. He felt confident that the Greeks could hold their position against any opposition. His opinion met with disagreement from Clemenceau and the American representative, F. R. Polk. Clemenceau felt that the Greeks should leave Aydın. Polk said he could not accept a further Greek advance: 'He thought that this would be tantamount to authorizing the Greeks to advance and conquer additional territory.' Crowe asserted that, if the Greek forces were not there, the Turks would massacre the local Greeks. A compromise was accepted. Greek excesses and violations of Supreme Council orders were noted, but, despite misgivings, the French and others accepted that the Greeks would be left in place in Aydın, because the Allies had no troops to take their place. The Greeks should not advance beyond the Aydın Province, and the Greek occupation in Anatolia was 'of a temporary nature'. A letter to that effect was sent to Venizelos. Crowe objected to even this compromise, stating that 'perhaps the draft letter pointed out too clearly to Venizelos that he was wrong'. Prime Minister Venizelos objected to the statement that Greek occupation was temporary. He expected the Greeks to remain.[77]

Once again, British High Commissioner de Robeck protested. He predicted both guerilla and regular warfare if the Greeks took Aydın Province. He said that all Turks, even those friendly to Britain, could not reconcile the Greek occupation with Britain's avowed principle of the rights of nationalities.[78]

**Notes**

1. David Lloyd George, *The Truth about the Peace Treaties*, vol. 2, London: Gollancz, 1938, p. 864.
2. The council was sometimes referred to as the 'Supreme Council of the League of Nations', but in fact was completely independent. See Article 4 of the League Covenant.
3. 'Conversation between President Wilson and MM. Clemenceau and Lloyd George', 13 May 1919, in Paul Mantoux, *The Deliberations of the Council of Four (March 24–June 28, 1919): Notes of the Official Interpreter*, Arthur S. Link, translator and editor, vol. 2, Princeton: Princeton University Press, 1992, p. 57.
4. Meeting of Wilson, Lloyd George and Clemenceau, Paris, 14 May 1919, *Papers Relating*, vol. 5, pp. 614–18. 'Conversation between President Wilson and MM. Clemenceau and Lloyd George', in Mantoux, pp. 39–40. Justin McCarthy, *Muslims and Minorities: The Population of Ottoman Anatolia and the End of the Empire*, New York: New York University Press, 1983, pp. 109–12.

    Largely because Lloyd George so often advanced his own ideas, the British wartime plans for the Ottoman Empire were often not the ones seen at the Peace Conference. See Erik Goldstein, *Winning the Peace: British Diplomatic Strategy, Peace Planning, and the Paris Peace Conference, 1916–1920*, Oxford: Oxford University Press, 1991, pp. 151–79. The popular work by David Fromkin (*A Peace to End All Peace: The Fall of the Modern Middle East and the Creation of the Modern Middle East*, New York: Holt, 1898) covers much more geographic ground than this study, and is not needed here.
5. Meetings of Wilson, Lloyd George and Clemenceau, Paris, 19 and 21 May 1919, *Papers Relating*, vol. 5, pp. 707–8, 711 and 756–67. Lloyd George also stated that Britain would have a mandate in Mesopotamia and Palestine and France in Syria.
6. 15 June 1920. C. E. Callwell, *Field-Marshal Sir Henry Wilson*, vol. 2, London: Cassell, 1927, p. 243. The book is drawn from Wilson's diary. Quotes here are from that diary. Wilson was appointed CIGS on 19 February 1918. He left his position on 18 February 1922. He was elected to the House of Commons on 21 February, but was assassinated by members of the Irish Republican Army on 22 June 1922.

7. 20 June 1920. Callwell, p. 245.
8. Harold Nicolson, *Curzon: The Last Phase, 1919–1925*, London: Constable, 1934, pp. 95–6. For a general view of Venizelos' diplomatic actions and policies, see Michael Llewellyn-Smith, 'Venizelos Diplomacy. 1910–23: From Balkan Alliance to Greek-Turkish Settlement', in Paschalis M. Kitromilides, *Eleftherios Venizelos: The Trials of Statesmanship*, Edinburgh: Edinburgh University Press, 2006, pp. 134–92.
9. Lowe and Dockrill, pp. 335–8. Earl of Ronaldshay, *The Life of Lord Curzon*, vol. 3, London: Ernest Benn, 1928, pp. 259–61, 314–20. Studies of the relationships of Lloyd George and Curzon and between the prime minister, his personal advisors and the cabinet are voluminous. The best summary is probably Kenneth O. Morgan, 'Lloyd George's Premiership: A Study in 'Prime Ministerial Government', *The Historical Journal*, vol. 13, no. 1 (March 1970), pp. 130–57. See also F. S. Northedge, *The Troubled Giant: Britain among the Great Powers 1916–1939*, New York: Praeger, 1967, pp. 157–9.

    There is disagreement on the relative place of Curzon and Lloyd George in policy and government actions. On the one hand is the nuanced consideration of A. E. Montgomery, which shows Curzon's subordination. ('Lloyd George and the Greek Question', in A. J. P. Taylor, ed., *Lloyd George: Twelve Essays*, New York: Atheneum, 1971, pp. 257–84.) O. H. Bennet disagreed:

    > Some critics have inferred from the Prime Minister's links to Venizelos that Lloyd George was conducting foreign policy behind Curzon's back. Through intermediaries he may have held secret briefing sessions for Venizelos on a personal level, but there was no question of secret negotiations on behalf of the two sovereign countries.

    (*British Foreign Policy during the Curzon Period, 1919–24*, London: St. Martin's, 1995, p. 94.) I believe the facts show Bennet to have been completely wrong.
10. 5 October 1922, Ronaldshay, p. 316.
11. Northedge (p. 92) commented on one of the reasons for Lloyd George's success in maintaining power over issues:

    > The 1918 Parliament was certainly one of the most insular and ignorant in British history. Yet this very fact enabled the British delegation at the Paris Peace Conference to negotiate to the accompaniment of strident clamour from home on a few sensational issues but with substantial interference on hardly any of the main problems.

12. CAB 23/35/38, Notes of a Conversation between the Prime Minister of Great Britain and the Prime Minister of Italy, Paris, 8 August 1921.

13. On the wartime British propaganda campaign against the Turks, see Chapter 11. McCarthy, *The Turk in America*, pp. 208–48.
14. In his book on the Paris Conference, Lloyd George indicated that he believed everything Venizelos told him then, and still believed it in 1938. (David Lloyd George, *The Truth about the Peace Treaties*, vol. 2, London: Gollancz, 1938, especially pp. 1228–50.)
15. Frank Owen, *Tempestuous Journey: Lloyd George His Life and The Times*, New York: McGraw-Hill, 1955, p. 631. Lord Beaverbrook, *The Decline and Fall of Lloyd George*, New York: Duell, Sloan and Pearce, 1963, p. 152.
16. FO 800/202, Balfour to C. I. G. S., London, 17 October 1918; FO 406/40, Balfour to Granville, Foreign Office, 14 October 1918. CAB 63/33, 'Extracts from the Report of an Interdepartmental Committee on British Desiderata in Turkey-in-Asia', London, 30 June 1915. On the details of Venizelos' successful seduction of the Allies at the Paris Conference, see Nicholas X. Rizopoulos, 'Greece at the Paris Peace Conference, 1919', Unpublished PhD dissertation, Yale University, 1963.
17. 'Greek Legation to the Department of State', Washington, 6 December 1918, *Papers Relating*, vol. 2, pp. 276–7. 'Conversation between President Wilson and MM. Clemenceau, Balfour, and Veniselos', in Mantoux, pp. 36–42. Admiral Webb in Istanbul reported that 'brigandage' was on the rise in the İzmir district, but blamed it on all parties – Greeks, Turks and Armenians. CAB 24/145/56, Eastern Report, 16 April 1919.
18. Meeting of Wilson, Lloyd George, and Clemenceau, Paris, 2 May 1919, *Papers Relating*, vol. 5, p. 412. Lloyd George wanted a statement sent to the press that Allied ships were being sent to İzmir because of massacres of Greeks; Clemenceau convinced the others not to do that.
19. FO 406/41, Webb to Curzon, Constantinople, 7 September 1919. See also FO 371/3429, Calthorpe Telegram, Constantinople, 18 December 1918. Note: 'Telegram' in notes indicates that no recipient is named in the source. It is presumably the Foreign Office.
20. FO 371/4166, Telegram to Paris Delegation, Foreign Office, 3 April 1919; Delegation (Balfour) to Foreign Office, Paris, 11 April 1919.
21. CAB 23/8/18, War Cabinet Meeting of 5 November 1918; FO 371/4354, Eerie Crowe, 'Turkey in Europe', Foreign Office, 21 December 1918.
22. FO 925/41129 and FO 371/4354, Foreign Office, 'The Future Turkish State', 14 December 1918. Committee for the Study of Territorial Questions Relating to Greece, Procé verbal no. 5, Meeting of 21 February 1919.
23. CAB 28/6, Meetings at the Quai d'Orsay, 3 and 4 February 1919; *Papers Relating*, vol. 3, Washington: GPO, 1943, pp. 856–72. Present were Wilson, Lloyd George,

Clemenceau, Orlando, Makino, Veniselos and numerous others. CAB 29/69, Meeting of the Heads of Delegations of the Five Great Powers, Paris, 16 July 1919. At the Peace Conference Venizelos also claimed that 300,000 Greeks had fled from Anatolia, a figure contradicted by all other sources (Chapter 7). ('Conversation between President Wilson, MM. Clemenceau, Lloyd George, and Venizelos, and Baron Sonnino', 19 May 1919, Mantoux, p. 116.)

24. George Soteriadis, *An Ethnological Map Illustrating Hellenism in the Balkan Peninsula and Asia Minor*, London: E. Stanford, 1918; Leon Maccas, *L'hellénisme de l'Asie Mineure*, Paris: Berger-Levrault, 1919; FO 608/37, E. Venizelos, *Greece Before the Peace Conference*, Appendix no. 2. Venizelos presented the book to the Peace Conference on 30 December 1918. The work was later published in the United States as Eleutherios Venizelos, *Greece before the Peace Congress of 1919; A Memorandum Dealing with the Rights of Greece, submitted by Eleutherios Venizelos*, a revised translation from the French original, New York: American-Hellenic society by Oxford University Press, American branch, 1919.

25. Vital Cuinet, *La Turquie d'Asie*, 4 vols, Paris: Leroux, 1892–4. Justin McCarthy, 'Greek Statistics on Ottoman Greek Population', in *Population History of the Middle East and the Balkans*, Istanbul: Isis, 2002, pp. 234–42 (original in *Turkish Studies*, vol. 1, no. 2).

26. Cuinet, vol. 3, p. 439.

27. Dimitri Kitsikis, *Propagande at Pressions en Politique Internationale*, Paris: Presses Universitaires de France, 1963. See especially pp. 25–36 and 81–182. Kitisikis' excellent work displays in great detail the workings of Greek and others' propaganda in favour of Greek plans and desires.

The British Foreign office officials, Philip Kerr and Eric Graham Forbes Adam, produced their own statistics, which supposedly were to bolster the case that the British were following the 'principle of nationalities' in awarding so much to the Greeks. The Forbes Adam statistics were awful, including faked Ottoman data, impossible estimates, etc. They seem to have been so bad that they were never used publicly by the British. (FO 608/272, P. H. Kerr to Robert Vansittart, 10 Downing Street, 5 May 1920, and Vansittart to Kerr, presumably Foreign Office, 10 May 1919.)

28. FO 371/4239, Foreign Office, Geographical Section (attached P. I. D.), 'Memorandum upon the Population of the Sanjak and City of Smyrna', 22 November 1919. McCarthy, *Death and Exile*, p. 308. FO 424/183, Cumberbatch to Currie, 30 May 1895.

29. De Robeck estimated 196,501 Greeks and 454,685 Muslims for 1917, but admitted he had little real information on this. (FO 371/4239, Foreign Office Telegram

to de Robeck, 11 November 1919. CAB 21/203, de Robeck to Curzon, Constantinople, 19 November 1919.) See also, FO 800/157, de Robeck to Curzon, Constantinople, 18 November 1919. The Foreign Office sent the statistics back to de Robeck to have them confirmed. He replied that they were accurate. CAB 24/101/68, de Robeck to Curzon, Constantinople, 9 March 1920. It will be noted that the analyses of the British Intelligence division and diplomats were recorded after the decision was taken to occupy İzmir. Only after strong complaints did the Foreign Office record them. However, the real Ottoman statistics had long been used by British diplomats in the Ottoman Empire. FO 371/4229, Calthorpe to Curzon, 24 May 1919. WO 138/933, GHQ General Staff Intelligence, Constantinople, 2 December 1919. An estimate for 1919 was added, showing a loss among Turks in Edirne Province, but still indicating an overwhelming numerical superiority of Turks over Greeks in Eastern Thrace, Western Anatolia and Istanbul, particularly in the regions occupied by the Greeks. FO 608/103, G. O. C. in C. to D. M. I., Constantinople, 6 March 1919.

30. Justin McCarthy, *Muslims and Minorities*, New York: New York University Press, 1983, p. 112, and 'The Population of Ottoman Europe', *Population History of the Middle East and the Balkans*, Istanbul: Isis, 2002, p. 120.

31. FO 286/702, Calthorpe to Balfour, with enclosures from the Chamber of Commerce and Whittall.

32. United States National Archives (hereafter US) 8618.014/2, A. H. Lybyer, 'Remarks on the Maps and Statistics of M. Venizelos', 6 January 1919. Lybyer was one of the most rational analysts of the Allied actions in the Ottoman Empire. See Albert Howe Lybyer, 'Turkey under the Armistice', *The Journal of International Relations*, vol. 12, no. 4 (April 1922), pp. 447–73. David Magie, professor of classics at Princeton, prepared the population estimates for the American 'Inquiry' – the group created to advise the Americans in peace deliberations. He did not understand that the Greek statistics were forgeries and used them in his estimates. Nevertheless, he stated that they were gross exaggerations. He wrote that the Greeks outnumbered the Turks in İzmir Sancak by four per cent, but that Turks were two-thirds of the population of the entire Aydın Province. (US M1107/1046, Inquiry Document 1005.)

33. Notes of a Meeting of the Heads of Delegations of the Five Great Powers, Paris, 12 August 1919, *Documents on British Foreign Policy 1919–1939*, first series, hereafter DBFP, London: H. Majesty's Stationery Office, vol. 1, pp. 399–402. For further deliberations, see: Notes of a Meeting of the Heads of Delegations of the Five Great Powers, Paris, 2 September 1919, DBFP 1, pp. 597–8. (The editors and publication years of the volumes in *Documents on British Foreign*

*Policy* changed.) CAB 24/104/91, 'Correspondence between President Wilson and the Supreme Council', 26 March and 26 April 1920. Helmreich, *From Paris to Sèvres*, pp. 153–8.

34. For the Muslim refugees in Edirne Province, see Justin McCarthy, 'Muslim Refugees in Turkey; the Balkan Wars, World War I and the Turkish War of Independence', in Justin McCarthy, *Population History*, p. 46. These figures, collected by the Ottoman Ministry of the Interior, are supported by Greek sources: Alexandre Antoniades, *Le Développement économique de la Thrace: le passé, le présent, l'avenir*, 2e édition, Athènes: Typos, 1922, p. 217, and Stephen Ladas, *The Exchange of Minorities: Bulgaria, Greece, and Turkey*, New York: Macmillan, 1932, p. 16. Ladas estimated 115,000 Greek out-migrants, but he routinely overestimated Greek numbers. See also Tevfik Bıyıklıoğlu, *Trakya'da Milli Mücadele*, vol. 1, Ankara: Türk Tarih Kurumu, 1987, pp. 159–63.

35. FO 406/41, Curzon to Granville, Foreign Office, 21 October 1919. FO 371/5044, General Staff, 'The Situation in Turkey, 15th March, 1920', War Office, 15 March 1920. FO 371/4352, War Trade Intelligence Department to Ronald Foxburgh (PID), 22 November 1918. General Staff Memorandum on the Situation in Turkey, War Office, 15 March 1920, and DBFP 13, pp. 26–38. FO 371/4160, 'Weekly Report No. 36', G. H. Q. General Staff Intelligence, Constantinople, 16 October 1919.

There are numerous British examples of a pre-war Turkish preponderance in Thrace. See, for example, FO 371/2133, Major Louis Samson (consul at Edirne) to Mallet, Adrianople, 31 March 1914.

Western Thrace is not considered in this study. For an informative description of the region under French and Greek administration, see FO 317/3527, Major A. C. M. Neate to Director of Military Intelligence, War Office, Sofia, 26 March 1920. Neate showed the result of the French census taken in Gűműlcine district: 39,601 Turks, 14,796 Bulgarians, 4,773 Greeks, 2,341 Pomaks and 3,442 Others. These can be compared to Venizelos' statistics.

36. CAB 29/86, British Secretary's Notes of a Meeting of the Supreme Council, San Remo, 21 April 1920, 4 p. m.

Eastern Thrace was often seen as a bargaining chip by those who did not want the Greeks to remain in İzmir. Just after the armistice, Eyre Crowe, while admitting that the population of Eastern Thrace was predominately Turkish, wanted the region to go to Greece, because that would keep the Greeks from demanding İzmir, of which he disapproved. (FO 371/4354, Eyre Crowe, 'Turkey in Europe', Foreign Office, 21 December 1918.)

37. Secretary's Notes of a Conversation held in M. Pichon's Room at the Quai d'Orsay, Paris, on Tuesday, 4 February 1919, *Documents Relating*, vol. 3, p. 875. The committee was created on a motion by Lloyd George. Three Commissions were set up by the Supreme Council on 17 February 1920: Smyrna Commission, Armenian Commission and Turkish Finance Sub-Commission. (CAB 24/98, C. P. 663, 'Supreme Council', 17 February 1920.)

38. The committee was sometimes called a Commission or a Committee of Greek and Albanian Affairs and other, similar names. For a complete set of minutes and memoranda of the committee, see US 181/217 – 181.21702/38. Many of the meetings of the committee are also in FO 608/272 and FO 371/4224. See also Paul C. Helmreich, *From Paris to Sèvres*, Columbus: Ohio State University Press, 1974, pp. 83–93.

    At later meetings of the committee, the British and American delegates deputised others to represent them: for the United States, William Hepburn Butler, lawyer and archeologist who had served in the US embassy in London during the war; for the British, Eric Graham Forbes Adam, a clerk in the Foreign Office in 1913, Third Secretary at the Peace Conference and member of the British Middle Eastern advisory team at the Paris Peace Conference and later conferences. Forbes Adam was First Secretary in the British delegation to the Lausanne Conference of 1922–3. Harold Nicholson for the British, well known for his dislike of Turks, and one M. Krajefsky for the French drew the outline of the committee's report.

39. US 181.21701/4. PV no. 4, Meeting of 20 February 1919.

40. US 181.21701/7, Committee for the Study of Territorial Questions Relating to Greece, Procé verbal no. 7, Meeting of 26 February 1919. Venizelos excluded the sancak of Çatalca and the Gallipoli Peninsula from his figures. US 181.21701/4. PV no. 4, Meeting of 20 February 1919. See also US 181.21701/11. PV no. 11, Meeting of 6 March 1919.

41. US 181.21701/5. PV no. 5, Meeting of 21 February 1919. Borden was speaking in response to the United States delegate, Westermann, who had said that the Greeks greatly underestimated the number of Turks in the population. On the availability of actual Ottoman population statistics, see US 185.517, 'Tableau Comparatif des Populations de quelques Vilayets de l'Empire Ottoman', in *Mémoire remis aux Haut-Commissionnaires Américain, Britannique, Français et Italien*, Constantinople, 1919, and various other sources. The inclusion in the American diplomatic record indicates that it was known.

42. In the Greek expansion from the 1820s to 1912, more than 500,000 Muslims, most of them Turks, had fled Greek conquests. Justin McCarthy, *Death and Exile:*

*The Ethnic Cleansing of Ottoman Muslims, 1821–1922*, Princeton: Darwin, 1995, pp. 10–13 and Chapter 5.

43. US 181.21701/14. PV no. 14, Meeting of 18 November 1919. PV no. 15, 19 November 1919. The United States representative (Buckler) said the United States would take no part in a commission. He preferred to let the Greeks deal with any problems.
44. US 181.21702/1, 'Report of the Committee on Greek Territorial Claims', Paris, 6 March 1919. The Italians based their claims primarily on wartime agreements.
45. 'Smyrna (Greek Landing)', House of Commons Debate, 17 July 1922, *Hansard*, vol. 156, c. 1998–2000, US 181.21702/1, Report of Committee on Greek Territorial Claims, 6 March 1919. The Italians complained of the Greek misrepresentation of the committee findings at the Peace Conference. (Notes of a Meeting of the Heads of Delegations of the Five Great Powers, 18 November 1919, DBFP, vol. 2, p. 349.)
46. For a lengthy consideration and the conclusion advanced here, see Paul C. Helmreich, 'Italy and the Anglo-French Repudiation of the 1917 St. Jean de Maurienne Agreement', *Journal of Modern History*, vol. 48, 1976, pp. 99–139. See also Christopher Howard, 'Historical Revision. No. XCVI: The Treaty of London, 1915', *History*, New Series, vol. 25, no. 100 (March 1941), pp. 347–55. For the deliberations that led to the St Jean de Maurienne Agreement, see C. J. Lowe and M. L. Dockrill, *The Mirage of Power: British Foreign Policy 1914–22*, vol. 2, London: Routledge and Kegan Paul, 1952, pp. 223–7.
47. FO 406/40, Rodd to Balfour, Rome, 10 December 1918. See also FO 371/4354, Balfour to Imperiali, Foreign Office, 25 November 1918. FO 406/40, Balfour to Rodd, London, 11 and 27 December 1918. Notes of a Meeting, Paris, 19 May 1919, *Papers Relating*, vol. 5, pp. 707–11 and 716–21. *Papers Relating* volume 5 has many examples of conflict over claims by Italy. The arguments were mainly between Lloyd George and Wilson on the one side and Orlando and Sonnino of Italy on the other.
48. FO 406/40, Balfour to Rodd, Foreign Office, 31 October 1918; Rodd to Balfour, Rome, 10 December 1918; and Balfour to Rodd, Foreign Office, 11 December 1918. FO 406/41, Rodd to Balfour, Rome, 28 December 1918.
49. The details of the quarrels over Italian claims in the Adriatic are beyond the scope of this study. They are documented from the British perspective in DBFP 4, pp. 1–240, and from the Italian perspective in Notes of a Meeting of the Delegates of the Five Great Powers, Paris, 10 January 1920, DBFP 2, pp. 789–92.
50. On the negative feelings toward Italians, see Meeting of Wilson, Lloyd George and Clemenceau, Paris, 5 May 1919, *Papers Relating*, vol. 5, pp. 463–9. FO 406/42, Stevens to Curzon, Batoum, 14 May 1919.

51. CAB 29/81, Notes of a Conversation, London, 11 December 1919.
52. Foreign Office to H. M. Ambassador at Rome, 13 December 1918, quoted in *Papers Relating*, vol. 2, pp. 277–8. FO 406/40. Balfour to Rodd, London, 14 and 16 October, 7 November, 11 December 1918.

    On the Italian ships at İzmir, see: Meeting of Wilson, Lloyd George and Clemenceau, Paris, 2 May 1919, *Papers Relating*, vol. 5, pp. 407–14. The numbers of Italian ships were routinely exaggerated, up to claims of seven battleships. There actually were never more than two. The Italians had previously notified the British that they planned to occupy Antalya and that Clemenceau had agreed to it. Britain notified them that they were opposed. FO 371/3386, Foreign Office to Rodd (Rome), 28 December 1918. See also 'Italian Memorandum Concerning Landings in Asia Minor', Notes of a Meeting, Paris, on Monday, 19 May 1919, at 4 p. m., *Papers Relating*, vol. 5, p. 726.
53. President Wilson's 4 July 1918 Speech at Mount Vernon.
54. Notes of a Meeting, Paris, 19 May 1919, 11.30 a. m., *Papers Relating*, vol. 5, p. 710. CAB 24/98 C. P. 662, 'The Adriatic, Message from President Wilson to Mr. Lloyd George and M. Millerand', 14 February 1920. CAB 24/99, C. P. 722, 'The Adriatic', 25 February 1920. See the summary of Wilson's religious and racialist prejudices in Karine V. Walther, *Sacred Interests: The United States and the Islamic World, 1821–1921*, Chapel Hill: University of North Carolina Press, 2015, pp. 271–3.

    Consideration of Woodrow Wilson's confused and contradictory views on the Ottoman Empire and the Balkans is beyond the scope of this book. See the extensive coverage of it in Laurence Evans, *United States Policy and the Partition of Turkey, 1914–1924*, Baltimore: Johns Hopkins Press, 1965.
55. The formula neglected to consider that belligerent operations had taken place in North, West and East Africa –areas of Allied countries' colonies.
56. CAB 23/5/5, War Cabinet Meeting of 3 January 1918. In November of 1918, the cabinet decided that Britain would not be bound by the Fourteen Points. (CAB 23/8/18, War Cabinet Meeting of 5 November 1918.) CAB 23/14/35, War Cabinet Meeting of 3 October 1918. FO 371/4354, Eyre Crowe, 'Turkey in Europe', Foreign Office, 21 December 1918. US 185.513/14, British Delegation, 'Statement by the British Government for the Peace Conference concerning the Settlement of the Middle East', Paris, 7 February 1919.
57. 'Dr. Clive Day and Mr. W. L. Westermann to the Secretary General of the Commission to Negotiate Peace (Grew)', *Papers Relating*, vol. 11, pp. 91, 524–5. US 181.21701/5. PV no. 5, Meeting of 21 February 1919. Fs. 130+. Helmreich, *From Paris to Sèvres*, pp. 86–93. Evans, pp. 126–8 and 173.

58. Ray Stannard Baker, *Woodrow Wilson and World Settlement*, vol. 2, New York: Doubleday, 1923, pp. 191–2. There are numerous records of Wilson's plans in the record of the Peace Conference. See, for example, Meeting of Wilson, Lloyd George and Clemenceau, Paris, 13 May 1919, *Papers Relating*, vol. 5, pp. 585–6. Lloyd George said he agreed with Wilson. Maurice Hankey, the British Conference Secretary, said that he had been to the region of Smyrna to be awarded to the Greeks, and it was poor. Wilson responded that the Greeks had great ability and 'would rise to the occasion'. Meeting of Wilson, Lloyd George and Clemenceau, Paris, 13 May 1919, *Papers Relating*, vol. 5, pp. 581–6. Wilson's conference deputy and biographer, Ray Stannard Baker, felt that Wilson joined in the 'conspiracy' to deny İzmir to the Italians and give it to the Greeks, 'because he saw no other way, at the moment, of checkmating the lawless efforts of the Italians to anticipate or force the decisions of the Peace Conference'. Baker, 1923, pp. 192 and 194.

59. Notes of a Meeting (Wilson, Lloyd George and Clemenceau), Paris, on Tuesday, 6 May 1919, at 11 a. m., *Papers Relating*, vol. 5, p. 484. Baker, v. 2, pp. 192 and 194. Churchill later wrote:

> I cannot understand to this day how the eminent statesmen in Paris, Wilson, Lloyd George, Clemenceau and Venizelos, whose wisdom, prudence, and address had raised them under the severest tests so much above their fellows, could have been betrayed into so rash and fatal a step.

(Winston S. Churchill, *The World Crisis: The Aftermath*, London: Thornton Butterworth, 1929, p. 369.)

British Intelligence in Istanbul reported on 3 July 1920 that the Ottoman Government realised that the French and Italians did not willingly join Great Britain in demanding cession of Ottoman territory to Greece. (WO 158/933, General Staff Intelligence, 'Notes on the Political Situation in Turkey', 3 July 1920.)

60. Meetings of Wilson, Lloyd George, Clemenceau and Venizelos, Paris, 7 and 10 May 1919, *Papers Relating*, vol. 5, pp. 501–5 and 553–88; Notes of a Meeting Held at President Wilson's House in the Place des Etats-Unis, Paris, on Monday, 12 May, p. 577. The ships provided were:

> British: One light cruiser, two destroyers, two sloops; One light cruiser, one leader (sic), four destroyers ordered to Aegean. French: One battleship, one cruiser; one battleship due to arrive on May 18th. Greek: One battleship, one cruiser, one destroyer. Italian: One battleship, six small vessels.

61. 'Report of the Inter-Allied Commission of Inquiry on the Greek Occupation of Smyrna and Adjacent Territories', Constantinople, 4 October 1919, *Papers Relating*, vol. 9, p. 47.
62. CAB 29/29, Notes from Venizelos to the Supreme Council: 'The Question of Nationality', 'Maintenance of the Prerogatives of the Patriarchate and of the Greeks in Turkey'. 'The Capitulations in Turkey', no place given, presumably Paris, 26 February 1920.
63. FO 371/4210. G. O. C. in C. to Director of Military Intelligence, Constantinople, 6 March 1919. Callwell, p. 190. See also FO 406/41, Milne to War Office, Constantinople, 20 October and 7 May 1919.
64. FO 371/4157, General Staff Intelligence Report (Lieut-Colonel Ian M. Smith, Area Control Officer) enclosure in Calthorpe to Foreign Office, Constantinople, 19 April 1919. See also FO 371/4165, Memorandum on Smyrna by Lieut-Colonel Ian M. Smith, Area Control Officer, Smyrna, enclosure in Calthorpe to Balfour, Constantinople, 4 March 1919. Admiral Calthorpe praised Smith's report: '(The report) states the position in that district as clearly and impartially as it can be stated.' (McCarthy, *Death and Exile*, p. 161.) The Muslim refugee figures include a small number who came after World War I.

    On Greek plans for Greek settlement, see Serdar Sarışır, 'Yunanlıların Batı Anadolu'da Nüfus Çoğunluğunu Sağlama Gayretleri ve Yunan Hükümeti'nin Bir Genelgesi', *Ankara Üniversitesi Türk İnkılâp Tarihi Enstitüsü Atatürk Yolu Dergisi*, vol. 37–8 (Mayıs-Kasım, 2006), pp. 127–39.
65. Doppers to Secretary of State, Athens, 4 December 1918; Heck to Sharp, Pera, 4 January 1919, *Papers Relating*, vol. 2, pp. 275 and 283.
66. FO 46/43, Luke to Webb, Constantinople, 25 December 1919.
67. FO 406/41, Webb (Rear Admiral Richard, Acting High Commissioner) to Curzon, Constantinople, 17 August 1919. See also, FO 406/41, Webb to Curzon, Constantinople, 7 September 1919. (Webb wrote of 'reasonable claims of the Turks that they should not be subjected to the rule of an alien and hostile race like the Greeks'.) FO 608/113, de Robeck Telegram, Constantinople, 17 September 1919.
68. See, for example, FO 406/43, Webb (Acting High Commissioner) to Curzon, 18 January 1920; FO 406/43, de Robeck to Curzon, Constantinople, 2 March 1920, the report of the (unnamed) control officer, Smyrna, in FO 608/103, Smyrna, 20 April 1919.
69. FO 406/41, Curzon to Kennard, Foreign Office, 22 October 1919. Ronaldshay, pp. 266–8.
70. FO 608/112, Calthorpe Telegram, Constantinople, 27 July 1919.

71. CAB 28/92, British Secretary's Notes of Allied Conference at London, 14 February 1920, 4 p. m.
72. CAB 25/28, Supreme War Council, British Section, Versailles, 19 September 1918; 'Supply of the Greek Army', Supreme War Council, British Section, Versailles, 15 June 1918; Supreme War Council, British Section, Versailles, 3 July 1918. There is much more in CAB 25/28 on supplies to the Greek army. It had originally planned for the British to supply equipment and clothing for 300,000 men, but this was later decided to be too high a number, and less was provided.
73. FO 608/91. Delegation Hellenique au Congrès de la Paix to the Secretary General of the Peace Conference of Peace, Paris, 26 August 1919. FO 286/714, Balfour to Webb, 10 July 1919. Note that the Peace Conference actions were actually the decisions of the Council of Four. Meeting of Wilson, Lloyd George, Clemenceau and Sonnino, Paris, 19 May 1919, *Papers Relating*, vol. 5, pp. 721–3.
74. FO 406/41, Memorandum by Ryan in Calthorpe to Curzon, Constantinople, 22 and 27 June 1919.
75. FO 608/91, Webb Telegram, Constantinople, 24 August 1919. Commodore Maurice Swynfen Fitzmaurice, in charge of the British naval detachment at İzmir, received the explanation of the Greek governor, Aristeidis Stergiadis, for the advance into Aydın, which Fitzmaurice wrote 'is so obviously incorrect in many essential points that it scarcely needs comment'. (FO 371/4222, Fitzmaurice to Commander in Chief, Mediterranean, 16 September 1919.)
76. 'Notes of a Meeting of the Heads of Delegations of the Five Great Powers', 8 November 1919, *Papers Relating*, vol. 9, pp. 36–7. See the elaborate defences of the Greek advance by Forbes Adam and Philip Herr in FO 371/4222.
77. 'Notes of a Meeting of the Heads of Delegations of the Five Great Powers', 10, 11 and 12 November 1919 and 12 November 1919, *Papers Relating*, vol. 9, pp. 78–84, 95 and 121–3. FO 371/4223, Crowe to Curzon, Paris, 26 November 1919 and enclosures. Crowe to Curzon, Paris, 26 November 1919, DBFP 4, pp. 104–5.
78. FO 800/157, de Robeck to Curzon, Constantinople, 18 November 1919.

# 11

## THE SMYRNA COMMISSION

Greek attacks on Turks in the İzmir region began on the first day of their invasion. The British could not say that they did not completely understand what occurred in İzmir. The British High Commission in Istanbul reported on the Greek atrocities on 17 May, two days after the Greek invasion. Arthur Balfour, foreign secretary, wrote to Lord Curzon, who was soon to replace him in that office:

> I transmit to your Lordship copies of various reports received either direct or through the American Delegation of the atrocities perpetrated by the Greek troops in Smyrna. The reports are detailed, circumstantial, and trustworthy, and there can unfortunately be no doubt of the disgraceful conduct of the Greek troops or the lack of control of the Greek authorities.[1]

The reports forwarded by Balfour, which included accounts by American naval officers and the Swedish consul, corroborated the reports of High Commissioner Somerset Arthur Gough-Calthorpe in Istanbul and James Morgan, his deputy in İzmir. They described ill-treatment, theft, pillage and the murders of Turkish soldiers, officials and civilians. Greek civilians and Greek soldiers took part. The descriptions by British and American officers on the scene were horrific – bayonets and torture were the weapon of choice in murdering Turks. An example:

(The statement of the Commanding Officer of the U.S.S. Arizona) Old men, unarmed, and other unoffending civilian Turks were knocked down by the Greeks, killed by stabbing with knives or bayonets, and then afterwards, having their valuables and clothing stripped off their bodies, were thrown into the sea. In one instance, the man was again shot after being thrown into the sea, this by Greek soldiers. Many of the prisoners, including high military officers, as they were marched along with hands up were permitted to be beaten by the rabble who followed. Specific instances are cited by these same eyewitnesses where Turkish soldiers and officers were bayoneted from behind by their Greek guards, while the rabble rifled their pockets and then threw their bodies into the sea. Many of the worst instances of inhuman treatment of the Turks were while they were under arrest and on the open sea front at noonday.[2]

If anything, the situation was worse in the villages surrounding the city, many of which were sacked and destroyed. Villagers fled the Greeks *en masse*. One British officer noted: 'The Greeks in the country round Smyrna have looted the arms-depots, have sacked Turkish villages, and hunted down Muslims.'[3] The reports by the Europeans and Americans are more damning than anything in the subsequent commission report, because they give great detail of the massacre of Ottoman troops and Turkish civilians.

The Supreme Council had received information of Greek attacks on Turks immediately after the Greek invasion, but at first took no action. Then, on 15 July 1919, the Şeyhülislam, head of the Islamic religious establishment in the Ottoman Empire, lodged a formal complaint on Greek excesses in İzmir with the Peace Conference.[4]

At a meeting of the Heads of Delegations of the Five Great Powers, French Prime Minister Clemenceau, Chairman of the Supreme Council, proposed the creation of a commission to investigate Greek atrocities in İzmir. While admitting the truth of the allegations, the British representative, Foreign Secretary Balfour, did what he could to forestall the naming of a commission. He said that they could not send commissions to investigate every atrocity in the world, and that they should concentrate on avoiding future troubles, rather than studying the past. Clemenceau, seconded by the Italian Tittoni, forcibly disagreed. The Italians and French felt that '[i]t was very important to make the Turks feel that the Allies did not propose to have them massacred'. Balfour finally accepted, perhaps because Clemenceau said he would send a commission on his own if the British did not cooperate.[5]

On 22 July, the Supreme Council agreed to the creation of an Allied Commission of Investigation. The commission was sent with instructions to fully investigate Greek actions in İzmir:

> The enquiry of the Committee should take as its subject matter the acts which had taken place during and after the occupation of İzmir, Aidin, Aivali and the adjacent regions by the Greek troops. These acts had been reported in the form of a complaint by the Sheikh-ul-Islam. The enquiry was to be extended to all events relative to the above from the date of occupation to the present moment. The Committee was to determine the responsibilities and to submit its report to the Supreme Council of the Allied and Associated Powers, together with such conclusions as it might consider relevant as soon as possible.[6]

Venizelos wrote to Clemenceau requesting that a Greek officer be appointed as a member of the commission. He wrote that the Greeks, unlike the Turks, were 'a friendly Allied state', whose army would be demoralised if Greece were not represented on the commission. Continuing their support for the Greek invasion, the British also attempted to place a Greek representative on the commission. Foreign Secretary Balfour did all he could to arrange it, but Clemenceau and Tittoni of Italy disagreed. Their opinion carried the day. A Greek representative would be consulted by the commission, but would not be a member. A Turkish representative would participate on the same footing as the Greek representative.[7]

The members of the commission were Admiral Mark Bristol for the United States of America, General Georges-Hippolyte Bunoust for France, General Robert Hare for Great Britain and General Alfredo Dallolio for Italy. Greek and Turkish representatives were named to consult with the commission, but not as members. The commission met for the first time in İzmir on 23 August, and held meetings there and in cities in the İzmir region until 26 September 1919. Further meetings were held in Istanbul until 15 October. In all, 175 witnesses were heard in forty-six meetings.[8]

Once the commission had taken up its investigation, Venizelos complained that the commission had not allowed the Greek representative, Col Mazarakis, to see its minutes. The Supreme Council at first decided that the Greek representative should be given all minutes, including the testimony and names of witnesses. The commission stated, however, that witnesses had been promised secrecy 'for the purpose of obtaining reliable information and avoiding reprisals'. The commission had felt, with complete justification, that they would never have been able to receive accurate testimony if witnesses knew that they would suffer from Greek or Turkish reprisals. The Supreme Council accepted the commission's rationale for secrecy. It reversed its decision and held that that neither the Greeks nor the Turks were to be given the testimony.[9]

The report of the commission was presented to the Supreme Council on 7 October 1919, and to the British Cabinet. As might be expected from such an intensive investigation, the commission's report was detailed. Its conclusions, paraphrased:

- Before the Greek invasion, İzmir was peaceful, and its inhabitants were treated with impartiality by the Ottoman Government. 'Fears of massacres of Christians were not justified.'
- The internal security situation did not justify either Allied military intervention or Greek invasion. The situation became troubled only after the Greek invasion.
- Although isolated shots were fired when the Greeks landed, shooters unknown, the Turkish authorities did not organise any resistance.
- 2,500 prisoners taken by the Greek army and civilians were treated brutally, some killed.
- Some Turks resisted; mortality statistics from the first day indicated two Greek soldiers and forty Greek civilians dead, six Greek soldiers and sixty Greek civilians were wounded. A total of 300 to 400 Turks were killed or wounded. Greek forces did nothing to restore order or restrain the Greek mob.
- As soon as word reached them of the Greek landing, Greek villagers in the villages near İzmir pillaged Turkish homes, stole Turkish livestock and killed Turks.
- The Greek troops advanced beyond the İzmir Sancak without authority. Pillage and 'excesses' followed. Turks 'in great numbers' fled and became refugees.
- The commission documented in great detail the results of the Greek invasion in Aydın Province and other areas. These included pillage and murder by both Greeks and Turkish bands opposing the Greeks. The worst were

major massacres by Greek troops in Aydın and elsewhere. In some cases, the commission felt that massacres were the fault of ill-disciplined troops, not the Greek High Command, which did not control the soldiers or civilians.
- In no way could the commission be accused of partiality. It documented attacks by both Greeks, civilians and soldiers, and by Turkish bands. It blamed both sides, and felt that '[t]he accusation (of attacks on Turks) brought by the Sheik-ul-Islam is not therefore entirely justified'.

The commission wrote an Establishment of Responsibilities, summarised below:

- The information that Christians were threatened in İzmir was false. Responsibility falls on those who forwarded this information. (The commission did not draw the obvious conclusion that responsibility also lay with those at the Peace Conference who used this false information to justify the invasion.)
- 'Their (the Greeks) occupation, far from presenting itself as the carrying out of a civilizing mission, at once took the form of a conquest and crusade.'
- Responsibility for the events of 15 and 16 May (the first days of the invasion) fell on the Greek High Command. The only claim against the Turkish authorities was that they were responsible for allowing prisoners to escape from jails.
- 'In the person of the High Civil Authority, which represents it at Smyrna, the Greek Government is responsible for the grave disorders which stained with blood the interior zone of the country during the advance of the Greek troops . . .'
- 'The Greek superior authorities are responsible because of the fact that they permitted the circulation in the country of armed civilians. In some of their military or police operations, they even tolerated the employment of these armed civilians at the same time as that of regular troops.'
- 'The hatred which has existed for centuries between the Turks and the Greeks has incontestably increased the frequency of barbarous acts. In all justice, the Greeks should not alone be held responsible.'
- 'On the other hand, the Greeks are alone responsible for the massacre at Menemen.'

- 'Even though the present situation is better, order has not yet been re-established in the Vilayet of Aidin. Practically all commercial transactions with the interior of Anatolia have ceased. This situation is incontestably the result of the occupation and the state of war existing between the Turkish irregulars and the Greek troops, even though the latter now are not further extending their zone of occupation. The heads of the Turkish national movement, who have cooperated with the former bandit chiefs, have not always had sufficient authority over their forces to prevent them from sometimes carrying out raids. Therefore, a part of the responsibility falls upon them insofar as present conditions in the country are concerned. Behind their responsibility lies that of the Turkish Government, which, up to the present time, has had no authority whatsoever over the leaders of the Nationalist Movement.' (Once again, the commission was impartial.)

The commission concluded that '[i]t (the Greek occupation) is incompatible in its present form with the return of order and of peace for which the populations, threatened with famine, have great need'. Unless the Peace Conference was prepared to accept Greek annexation of the region, Allied troops, not Greeks, should be in charge. However, annexation by the Greeks 'would be contrary to the principle proclaiming the respect for nationalities, because in the occupied regions, outside of the cities of Smyrna and Aivali, the predominance of the Turkish element over the Greek is incontestable'.

> It is the duty of the Commission to observe the fact that the Turkish national sentiment, which has already manifested its resistance, will never accept this annexation. It will submit only to force, that is to say, before a military expedition which Greece alone could not carry out with any chance of success.

Allied forces, therefore, should replace the Greeks. Turkish civil administration and the Turkish gendarmerie, under Allied officers, should be restored.[10]

The presentation of the Smyrna Report brought forth a fire storm at the Peace Conference. The commission had indicted the Greek occupiers and, by extension, those who sent them to İzmir. The Smyrna Commission Report was politically dangerous, and not only politically dangerous for the Greeks. It encountered fierce resistance from Greek and British delegates.

The Peace Conference took up consideration of the Smyrna Commission Report on 8 November 1919. Clemenceau and de Martino of Italy accepted the commission's accusations against the Greeks. They stated that the Greeks had behaved very badly, and the Turks would now never accept Greek rule unless compelled to do so by force. Clemenceau was indignant that the Greeks had gone beyond their assigned İzmir boundaries without Supreme Council approval. He doubted if the Greeks should or could long continue to occupy Southwest Anatolia.

> M. CLEMENCEAU asked if M. Venizelos did not intend to discuss the facts brought out in the report.
> 
> M. VENIZELOS said that he did not want to discuss conclusions based on testimony which had not been brought to the knowledge of the Greek representative.
> 
> M. CLEMENCEAU observed that it was a serious matter to make such a reply. The Council had expected from M. Venizelos precise answers on questions of fact. As head of the Government he must know if the alleged facts had really happened. He was astonished that M. Venizelos did not wish to discuss them.[11]

Unable to satisfactorily question the substance of the commission report, the British took up what might be called procedural objections. Eyre Crowe, speaking for the British delegation, avoided the question of whether or not the Greek occupation was justified. Instead, he attacked the commission. Crowe declared that the Supreme Council had never intended that the commission should consider whether the Greek occupation of İzmir had been justified, nor should it have commented on whether the Greeks should continue to occupy the region. The commission members, in other words, had no right to question the decisions of the Supreme Council. He added that the council was justified in allowing the Greeks to advance beyond the İzmir Sancak, with forces sufficiently strong to hold the area and guarantee the peace in the region it had taken. Although the commission's observations on the first days of the occupation were substantially correct, he felt, their procedure was flawed because the Greeks were not allowed to see the testimony. He felt that a letter notifying Venizelos of the accepted facts should be sent. He seemed to feel this was sufficient response to the commission's findings. No more needed to be done.

Crowe told his colleagues that no Allied troops could be found to take the place of the Greeks. Instead, the Greeks should be given even more latitude to govern as they saw fit. In effect, the Greeks should be rewarded, not condemned.

Venizelos took the same tack as Crowe when he addressed the meeting. Venizelos stated, although without evidence, that the commission's judgements had been wrong. Moreover, by refusing to allow the Greek representative to participate or see the original evidence, the judgement of the commission was untrustworthy. As he had previously, Venizelos complained that the Greeks were not being treated as allies. Venizelos protested to the council that placing a Turkish representative as consultant to the Smyrna Commission, on the same footing as the Greek representative, was 'offensive to an Allied people'. Greece, he said, was 'entitled to satisfaction, because it had always been loyal to the council (forgetting that the Greeks had advanced in Anatolia against the Council's directives.)'.

General Bunoust, who had sat on the Smyrna Commission, defended the need for secrecy before the council. 'It had unanimously decided that the depositions would lack sincerity if the Greek representatives had to be informed of them. The Turks would not have opened their mouths in the presence of a Greek officer.' His protests were ignored.[12]

Venizelos demanded that the commission's report be quashed, and a new commission be instituted, one in which a Greek delegate would hear all the testimony. '(Venizelos) declared that he would resent any statement being made in the British Parliament based on the findings of the Commission'. At the time, the Supreme Council had agreed with the commission's rationale for excluding the Greek and Turkish representatives. Nevertheless, Venizelos's complaints provided Lloyd George and his colleagues at the Peace Conference the opportunity to suppress the report of the Smyrna Commission.[13]

After Venizelos's testimony, the Supreme Council adjourned. It resumed its discussion of the Smyrna Report on 10 November. Eyre Crowe took up the Greek defence. He reiterated that the commission had gone too far in advising the end to the Greek occupation. He accepted Venizelos's claim that only a small number of Turks had been killed, even though all the evidence of Britain's own diplomats and soldiers had reported otherwise. 'He felt that the Greeks had done their best and that on the whole they had succeeded rather well.' The other delegates, while not persuaded by Crowe, admitted that they could not or would not carry out the commission's recommendation that the Allies take over from the Greeks. The French, in fact, were withdrawing the limited forces they had stationed in the Menderes (Meander) Valley. Primarily for this practical reason, the council decided to tell Venizelos that they accepted his argument that the Greek representative should have received all the testimony. (There was also the problem that the commission's report cast a bad light on the Supreme Council itself, which had sent the Greeks to İzmir.) It was decided not to publish the commission report.[14]

Despite the obvious logic of the commission's position, the Supreme Council made use of Venizelos's opposition to rid itself of a difficult situation. Political pragmatism won out. The British had been opposed to the commission's make-up and findings throughout the deliberations, and they had won in the end. The French were in a difficult position: largely to forestall the Italians, they had agreed to the Greek occupation. At that time, no one had wanted Turkish rule in İzmir. The French could not or would not provide troops for an Allied occupation. The Italians were not allowed any say. Better, it was felt, to avoid the problem by burying the Smyrna Commission Report.

## Ignoring Parliament and the Diplomats

The British officials in the Ottoman Empire accepted the commission report as accurate. Their representative in İzmir, James Morgan, believed the report showed that the Greeks should be evacuated:

> I would invite the particular attention of your Lordship to this report, in that it emphasises once again the desirability of the early withdrawal from Asia Minor of both the Greek and Italian troops (as set out in my telegram No. 1831 of the 17th September and in my despatch No. 1785 of the 1st October). Their presence in these regions cannot possibly be claimed to be conducive to law and order, but has shown itself to be the exact opposite.[15]

Admiral de Robeck believed the commission's report should be published.

> The Smyrna occupation has damaged our reputation for honesty of purpose very considerably in Turkish circles potentially friendly to us. Rightly or

wrongly, they attribute the decision to send Greek troops to Aidin principally to British influence; and they cannot reconcile that decision with our avowed principles as regards the rights of nationalities. The acceptance and publication of the atrocities commission's report by the Allies would go some way to rehabilitate our reputation, and I trust that this may not be found impossible.[16]

It was not to be. Despite numerous requests in parliament, the British Government steadfastly refused to publish the Smyrna Report, and has never done so. The report was only officially published by the Americans, and then not until 1946.[17]

## Suppressing the Report

On 23 February 1920, the government told parliament that it would consider publishing the report. Two days later, the government said it could not publish the report without the consent of its allies. One week later, on 2 March, when asked for the report, Andrew Bonar Law (Leader of the House of Commons, responsible for government policies in the House) stated: '[I]n the view of the Allies the publication of that report would make the position of the Allies more difficult'. It would therefore not be presented to parliament. Prime Minister Lloyd George weighed into the question on 15 March, stating that the Allies had decided to withhold the report, a decision with which he agreed. 'There is plenty of unrest in that part of the world, and we are very anxious about the position, but we do not want to pander to anything which is likely to increase it.' (The use of 'pander' is instructive.) The prime minister was asked which of the Allies had objected to the publication. He admitted that refusal to circulate the report had been at the instigation of Greece, due to the fact that Greeks had not been allowed to question the commission's witnesses. Aubrey Herbert, MP, asked: 'Are the statements in the report so bad that it is impossible to publish them?' Lloyd George did not respond. Sir J. D. Rees asked: 'Is the right hon. Gentleman aware that there is an impression that atrocities are visited with condemnation only when Christians are the victims, and as that is so, does it not point to the desirability of something being published?' Lloyd George said only that this was unfortunate. Further parliamentary requests for the report were also refused.[18]

## Notes

1. CAB 24/145/61, Eastern Report, 22 May 1919. FO 371/4218, Balfour to Curzon, Paris, 18 June 1919. High Commissioner Calthorpe's Record of the Smyrna invasion contains material on the murders of Turks, etc., but was more diffident. (ADM 137/1768, A. Calthorpe, Vice Admiral, British Commander-in-Chief, 'Report on the Greek Occupation of Smyrna', 18 May 1919.)
2. FO 371/4218, Mallet (for Balfour) to Curzon, Paris, 1919, enclosure no. 9, 'Commanding Officer USS Arizona to Senior Naval Officer, Constantinople', Smyrna, 18 May 1919.
3. FO 37/4218, 'Cable from A. C. O. Smyrna, 18th May 1919', enclosure in Calthorpe to Curzon, Constantinople, 24 May 1919. FO 371/4218 contains a great many detailed descriptions of the Greek actions. More are described and cited in McCarthy, *Death and Exile*, pp. 262–78 and 309–12, and FO 608/91 and 104.
4. Meeting of Wilson, Lloyd George, Clemenceau and Orlando, Paris, 19 May 1919, *Papers Relating*, vol. 5, pp. 733–4. The Şeyhülislam's telegram to Peace Conference: Notes of a Meeting of the Heads of Delegations of the Five Great Powers, Paris, 18 July 1919, *Papers Relating*, vol. 7, pp. 200–1.
5. Notes of a Meeting of the Heads of Delegations of the Five Great Powers, Paris, 18 July 1919, *Papers Relating*, vol. 7, pp. 191–2 and 18 July 1919, p. 207.
6. Notes of a Meeting of the Heads of Delegations of the Five Great Powers, Paris, 25 July 1919, *Papers Relating*, vol. 7, pp. 264–5. See also Peter M. Buzanski, 'The Interallied Investigation of the Greek Invasion of Smyrna, 1919', *The Historian*, vol. 25, no. 3 (May 1963), pp. 325–43.
7. Notes of a Meeting of the Heads of Delegations of the Five Great Powers, Paris, 21 July 1919, *Papers Relating*, vol. 7, pp. 238–9, 249–50; and 14 August 1919, pp. 687–8, 693; 20 August 1919, p. 730.
8. See the directives to the commission in CAB 24/145/72, Eastern Report, 7 August vol. 7,1919. See also, CAB 24/145/75, Eastern Report, 28 August 1919.
9. Notes of a Meeting of the Heads of Delegations of the Five Great Powers, Paris, 30 September 1919, *Papers Relating*, vol. 8, pp. 463–4, 476–9; 16 October 1919, pp. 675–6, 681–2. See also FO 608/86, Telegram to de Robeck, Foreign Office, 11 November 1919; FO 608/86, Foreign Office, Curzon to Crowe, 3 November 1919, and telegram to de Robeck, Foreign Office, 12 November 1919. FO 608/86 contains numerous complaints that the Greek representative was not allowed to sit at all commission meetings or see the names of the sources. The list of those interviewed and their testimony, as well as records of the commission meetings, is in US 181.8301. It shows that the commission interviewed

widely from all affected groups – including local Greeks, Turks and Europeans, as well as Greek and Turkish officials and Greek and Allied soldiers.

10. 'Rapport de La Commission Interalliée d'Enquête sur l'Occupation Grècque de Smyrne et des Territoires Adjacents', in FO 406/41, enclosure in de Robeck to Curzon, 18 October 1919, and FO 608/86, 10 November 1919.

11. Notes of a Meeting of the Heads of Delegations of the Five Great Powers, Paris, 8 November 1919, *Papers Relating*, vol. 9, pp. 36–41, CAB 21/174, 'Proceedings of the Council this Morning', 8 November 1919 and FO 406/41, Crowe to Curzon, Paris, 10 November 1919. Crowe did not at that time mention publication of the report. Other testimony revealed that while İzmir City was quiet, this was not true in other areas of the Greek occupation. After Clemenceau's admonishment, Venizelos did indeed provide a justification for Greek actions, blaming Turks. General Bunoust, who had been a member of the commission, refuted the testimony.

12. 'Notes of a Meeting of the Heads of Delegations of the Five Great Powers', Paris, 8 November 1919, *Papers Relating*, vol. 9, pp. 35–44. See also, 'Notes of a Meeting of the Heads of Delegations of the Five Great Powers', *Papers Relating*, vol. 8, pp. 476–9.

13. FO 406/41, Memorandum communicated by M. Venizelos, 23 October 1919, and FO 406/41, enclosure in Curzon to Crowe, Foreign Office, 3 November 1919.

14. Notes of a Meeting of the Heads of Delegations of the Five Great Powers, Paris, 10 November 1919, *Papers Relating*, vol. 9, pp. 78–84. CAB 21/174, Foreign Office to Harrington, 12 November 1919.

15. FO 406/41, de Robeck to Curzon, 20 October 1919. The French and British high commissioners had already suggested in August that the only solution was 'the retirement of both Greek and Italian troops from Asia Minor'. (FO 608/91, Calthorpe Telegram to Foreign Office, Constantinople, 17 August 1919.) See also the similar suggestions of Richard Webb, Acting High Commissioner, in FO 608/91, Webb to Curzon, 17 August 1919.

16. FO 800/157, de Robeck to Curzon, Constantinople, 18 November 1919. See also, CAB 24/101/68, de Robeck to Curzon, Constantinople, 9 March 1920.

17. The first official publication was an English translation: 'Report of the Inter-Allied Commission of Inquiry on the Greek Occupation of Smyrna and Adjacent Territories', *Papers Relating*, vol. 9, Appendix A to HD-87, pp. 44–78, published in 1946. The report was known, however, to diplomats and some others. See the request by the Ottoman Government that, in the light of the Smyrna

Commission Report, the Greek occupation should end. Turkish Minster of Foreign Affairs to the British High Commissioner, 20 December 1919, enclosure in de Robeck to Curzon, Constantinople, 29 December 1919, DBFP 4, pp. 979–80.

18. Bonar Law speaking for the government, House of Commons Debate, 23 February 1920, *Hansard*, vol. 125, cc. 1290–1, House of Commons Debate, 25 February 1920, *Hansard*, vol. 125, c. 1723W, and House of Commons Debate, 2 March 1920, *Hansard*, vol. 126, cc. 246–7. Speakers in the debate stated that they had received news of the report and wanted authentic copies to compare with what they had received. (House of Commons Debate, 15 March 1920, *Hansard*, vol. 126, cc. 1805–7. When asked if massacres had indeed taken place in İzmir, Lloyd George did not respond. 'Smyrna (Massacres)', House of Commons Debate, 15 March 1920, *Hansard*, vol. 126, cc. 1805–7, and 'Official Commission (Report)', House of Commons Debate, 22 March 1920, *Hansard*, vol. 127, cc. 27–9. See also House of Commons Debates in *Hansard*: 1 March 1920, vol. 126, c. 57W, 24 March 1920, vol. 127, cc. 400–1, 5 July 1920, vol. 131, cc. 1001–2, 24 May 1922, vol. 154, cc. 1205–6, and 25 May 1922, vol. 154, cc. 1395–8.

# 12

## BRITAIN, FRANCE AND ITALY

The conflict among the British, the French and the Italians over the spoils in the Ottoman Empire cannot be justified in any terms other than the archaic traditions of imperialism and warfare – 'to the victor belong the spoils'. In terms of what was best for the peoples of the region, none of the European claims could be justified. Neglecting political morality, however, in terms of the 'Allied solidarity' they always called for, the British were constantly duplicitous, demanding support from their Allies without consideration for the Allies' needs and wishes. In terms of honour and trust, the British refused to accept treaties and promises to the French in Iraq and to the Italians in Anatolia and the Balkans. They then complained at every step of disloyal allies.[1]

The French often did not agree with British plans for the Ottoman Empire. As the Turkish War of Independence wore on, the French increasingly began to doubt if the Allied plans were proving successful. They argued in Allied conferences for the lessening of strictures on the Turks. Yet until the final year of the crisis, the French capitulated to Lloyd George and Curzon. Though the French might argue against the British in meetings and conferences, the treaties and accords mainly reflected the British positions. Why were the French so compliant? The reasons were practical: the French hoped for British solidarity on many proposals for the European peace treaties – German reparations, attitude toward the Russian Revolution, the settlement of Eastern Europe and Polish–German–Russian conflicts, as well as British commitment to future French security in Europe. They looked for French economic and political benefit in Europe, and they proved to be willing to compromise in the Ottoman Empire to obtain British support for French European goals. It was practical concerns, not ideological agreement, that forced the French to cooperate with the British.

Friction between France and Britain began as soon as the world war ended. The French resented that the Mudros Armistice had been negotiated solely by the British. They thereafter strived to assert French dominance in the Ottoman Empire, but they were stymied by their need for British support for French plans for Europe and the *de facto* British occupation of the Middle East. In 1919, there was little perceivable benefit for the French in opposing the British over a settlement in Anatolia and Thrace. The Turks seemed to be completely beaten; taking their side would have yielded no benefits. Moreover, there was real advantage in supporting the British. The British controlled the oil of Iraq that the French needed. The French wanted Syria, where the British army was in control. As the treaty with the Ottoman Empire was being negotiated, the primary concern of the French was financial control. French interests held 60 per cent of the pre-war Ottoman debt, and wanted it repaid. At first, they suggested that the Ottoman Empire remain largely intact in Anatolia, Thrace and Istanbul, but with its finances under strict control by the Ottoman Debt Administration (Düyun-u Umumiye), which France mainly controlled by virtue of its holdings. The British, fearing French financial domination, were unwilling to accept that. They did, however, agree to a Financial Commission that would exercise near absolute control over the Ottoman economy and finances. The French were assured that the Ottoman debt would be paid, and they hoped for economic dominance in Turkey. In exchange, they were willing to agree to many British plans for the Sèvres Treaty. In particular, although they initially opposed it, they accepted the Greek presence in İzmir.[2]

The major agreement between the French and British was opposition to Italian goals. Italy was seen as a rival in the Eastern Mediterranean that had to be kept in check. Neither France nor Britain wished to observe the treaties signed with the Italians, and there was nothing Italy could do about it. The Italian voice was heard in the various conferences, but seldom listened to unless it supported one or both of its Allies. Once they were denied what they had been promised in Anatolia, the Italians were generally not a factor in later Allied decisions. Their interests became economic. In a meeting in August 1923, the Italian Prime Minister Giovanni Giolitti told Lloyd George 'that Italian interests were commercial and economic, and not territorial'. They would not send more troops beyond the small numbers they had in Istanbul. In the end, Britain and France were not to allow the Italians to keep even the commercial gains later promised to them. The Italians were to be denied almost everything they desired.[3]

## Mosul, Syria and Palestine

The need for oil drove British plans to claim the Mosul Province. Prior to the war, the Turkish Petroleum Company (TPC) had been granted an Ottoman concession to explore for oil in the region. The largest stockholder (47.5 per cent) in the company in 1920 was the Anglo-Persian Oil Company, of which the British Government had a controlling stake. The Anglo-Saxon Company, 40 per cent owned by British interests, held 22.5 per cent. Strong interests were therefore behind British control of Mosul. Oil had not yet been pumped in the province, but all indications were that it existed in great amounts. Mosul had not been conquered by British forces before the war ended, but the British had nevertheless advanced to Mosul and taken the city a week after the war's end, in direct violation of the armistice with the Ottomans, one of many British violations of the armistice.[4]

Possession of Iraq was also a part of the calculus of British imperialism, with its emphasis on India. Air connections were needed to replace the much slower connections by land and sea, and Iraq was needed as a base for planes, which in those days travelled only 250–400 miles between stops. While Mosul did not figure in the main air routes to India, holding Mosul was considered essential to defending Baghdad, which did.[5]

For the British, possession of Mosul made sense, primarily because of its oil, but French desire for Syria was based on hope for some sort of economic benefit. Although their trade with Syria was diminishing immediately before the war, French interests still held the majority of foreign capital there. The French hoped, with little justification, that owning Syria would aid them in economic domination of the Eastern Mediterranean. There was also emotion involved, because France had long felt a connection with Syria, especially

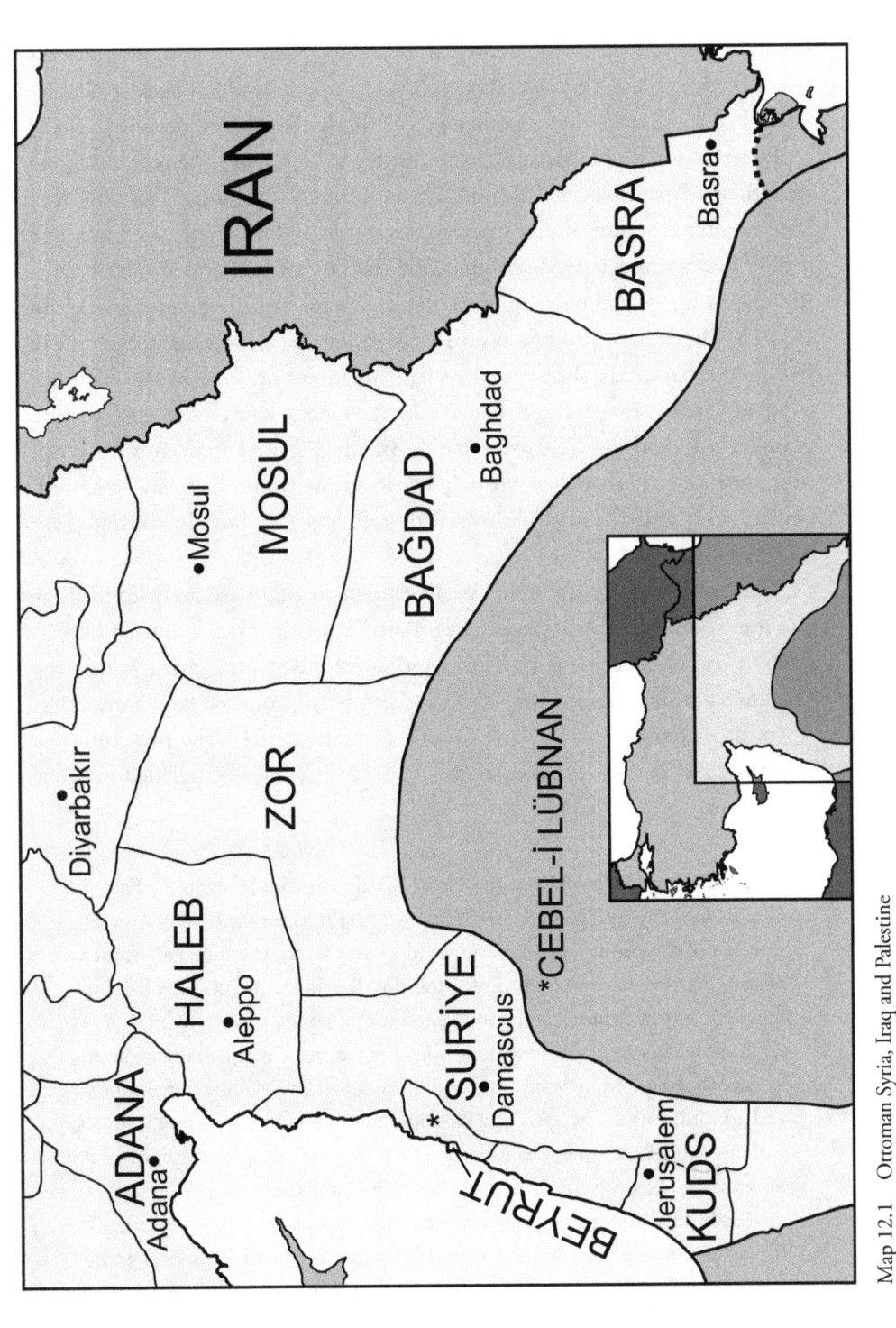

Map 12.1 Ottoman Syria, Iraq and Palestine

Lebanon. French missionary and cultural enterprises were long established there. French calculation was also typical of imperialism: land was available, and it had to be taken before others, particularly the British, took it.[6]

Palestine was the Holy Land. Even in those who had little religious concern themselves, holding Palestine was a matter of prestige. Palestine had little to offer economically; it was a backwater in all but a religious sense, but it did have a strategic value in guarding the Suez Canal and British Egypt. Attacks on Egypt had passed through Palestine for millennia, and as recently as 1915. The British also had promised it to Jews as a 'national home' in the Balfour Declaration (although they had no intention of creating an independent Jewish state). The Sykes–Picot Agreement had envisaged Palestine as under international control, but the British did not intend to give it up. All indications are that they wrongly felt Palestine would be easily governed. Unlike Syria and Mosul, rule over Palestine was not heavily contested by Britain's allies.

The main sticking point in Anglo-French relations in the Middle East was the Sykes–Picot Agreement, negotiated between France and Britain in 1916. It had divided the Arab World and most of Anatolia, giving large areas to French administration. Italy had later also been promised large territories.

In the Anglo-French Declaration of 7 November 1918, the two countries had promised that governance of the Arab lands would be decided by their populations:

> The object aimed at by France and Great Britain in prosecuting in the East the War let loose by the ambition of Germany is the complete and definite emancipation of the peoples so long oppressed by the Turks and the establishment of national governments and administrations deriving their authority from the initiative and free choice of the indigenous populations.
>
> In order to carry out these intentions France and Great Britain are at one in encouraging and assisting the establishment of indigenous Governments and administrations in Syria and Mesopotamia, now liberated by the Allies, and in the territories the liberation of which they are engaged in securing and recognising these as soon as they are actually established.
>
> Far from wishing to impose on the populations of these regions any particular institutions they are only concerned to ensure by their support and by adequate assistance the regular working of Governments and administrations

freely chosen by the populations themselves. To secure impartial and equal justice for all, to facilitate the economic development of the country by inspiring and encouraging local initiative, to favour the diffusion of education, to put an end to dissensions that have too long been taken advantage of by Turkish policy, such is the policy which the two Allied Governments uphold in the liberated territories.[7]

If there was ever an intention to keep to this declaration, it soon faded as France and Britain struggled over the spoils of war in the Arab provinces of the Ottoman Empire. British armies had conquered those territories in the war, and the British had no wish to keep to the terms of the agreement. Lloyd George told the cabinet in October 1918 that the Sykes–Picot boundaries were unacceptable. Britain, he said, had not fought the Turks for the benefit of France and Italy. The French formally complained in February 1919 that the British were not allowing them to act in Mosul, which had been awarded to them in the Sykes–Picot Agreement. Moreover, the French contended that the British in Mosul and Syria were treating the French with disrespect, notifying them that the French would not be allowed to claim either region.[8]

The British had conquered and were occupying Syria and Cilicia, the region north of Syria (Maps 12.1 and 17.1). The French had landed troops at Beirut on 8 October 1918 and were allowed to domestically administer 'Coastal Syria' (mainly Lebanon), but no more of Syria, and the British army militarily controlled Syria and Cilicia. The major cities of Damascus and Aleppo were under British control. This put the French in a difficult position. They had been promised much of Syria, Cilicia and Northern Iraq in the Sykes–Picot Agreement, but the British were in occupation. The British refused to accept the Sykes–Picot boundaries, declaring that post-war situations had made them invalid. The French complained bitterly and accused the British of bad faith, to no avail. The question for the French was what the British would allow them.[9]

At the Peace Conference, the French brought up the Sykes–Picot Agreement as the basis of dividing the Arab provinces of the Ottoman Empire. Lloyd George declared that the wartime agreement had been superseded by the solely British conquest of the Arab region and by an agreement of 9 November 1918, in which native governments were promised to the Arabs. French Foreign Minister Stephen Pichon demanded that Syria be treated as a whole and put under French mandate. Lloyd George countered that the British had promised much of Syria to an Arab state (the Hussein–McMahon Agreements of 1915–16). To give Damascus, Homs, Hama and Aleppo to the French, he contended, would mean breaking faith with the Arabs. President Wilson stated that the only question should be the wishes of the population. Neither France nor Britain wished that, and Wilson himself showed very little concern for the fate of the Arabs. Britain had no wish to apply any principle of self-determination to the areas she claimed, Iraq and Palestine, but declared the principle should be applied to French claims.[10]

On 15 May 1919, the British compromised and proposed that France take a mandate for Syria, Britain for Palestine and Iraq. This was acceptable to the French, who had given up on retaining Mosul, despite the Sykes–Picot Agreement. The problem lay with what was to be considered Syria. British leaders in Paris engaged in debate with the French over Syria, with a great deal of argument and claims of bad faith on both sides. The French made a good case that Britain had promised them Syria, and that included what today are Syria and Lebanon, as well as Cilicia. Lloyd George brought up what Britain had done for France in the war, and noted France had done nothing then in the Middle East. None of that applied to the case at hand, but it did infuriate Clemenceau, who countered that the French had done much more against the Germans.[11]

On 15 September 1919, Lloyd George announced that the British army would leave Cilicia immediately. The French army would occupy both Cilicia and Coastal Syria. The British would also leave the rest of Syria, beginning on 1 November, but they would hand over the cities of Damascus, Homs, Hama and Aleppo to the Arabs under Emir Feisal. (Feisal's supporters already controlled Damascus and much of the rest of non-coastal Syria.) Clemenceau of France agreed that the British should leave, but would not accept any turnover to Feisal. The French, he said, should occupy all of both Syria and Cilicia. The debate over Syria was one of the most vociferous arguments between Britain and France, seconded only by debates over French security and German reparations.[12]

French occupation of all of Syria and Lebanon was only decided on 25 April 1920, at the San Remo Conference. French General Gourad was named high commissioner in Syria on 9 October 1921. The French fought and defeated Feisal's forces and took over their mandate. It seems obvious that the British protestations of Arabs' rights were a bargaining chip with the French, not any sincere concern with self-determination. The British acquiescence with the French mandate was primarily based on the fact that the British did not have sufficient troops to control Syria. Lack of adequate military force was the same problem they were to have in Anatolia and Thrace, but in the case of Syria they could turn their troubles over to the French.

The San Remo Conference also saw the Mosul Question settled. Mosul was to be part of the British mandate in Iraq. In exchange, France was guaranteed a 25 per cent share of the Iraqi oil.[13]

Once the dispositions of Syria and Mosul had been decided, the British completely forgot their insistence on self-determination for the Arabs. The British treated the Arabs of the Ottoman Empire with even less respect than they showed the Turks. Once they had divided the Arab World with the French, they gave no further thought to the rights of self-determination in which they theoretically believed. Sykes–Picot promises they had made to the French were half-kept. Promises made to Zionists in Palestine were somewhat kept, although the British had no plan to turn Palestine over to them. Promises made to Arabs to draw them into the war against the Ottomans (the Hussein–McMahon Agreements) were broken, reminiscent of promises to the Italians to draw them into the war. Lloyd George had told Emir Feisal, who thought he had been promised rule in Syria, that the British considered agreements made with the Arabs of equal weight with agreements made with the French, but the claims of the Arabs in Syria soon proved to have no weight at all. Feisal protested the agreements to give Syria to France as a mandate. Curzon told him that the British had only promised 'an independent Arab state'. This, he said, was what was created – an 'independent' state under a French mandate. No one was fooled by the term 'mandate'. In internal documents, the British described the French occupation as a 'protectorate', the same term they had used for British rule in Aden, Egypt and Cyprus.[14]

The questions of occupation of Syria and Cilicia were settled at the San Remo Conference, but they had ramifications well beyond the status of the Arab provinces. The French had needed the goodwill of the British. Although it was never stated publicly as a *quid pro quo* arrangement, French acquiescence in British plans for the Ottoman Empire had been undoubtedly affected by the Syrian question. Once their possession of Syria was settled, the French, defeated in Cilicia by the Turkish Nationalists, were to sign a treaty with the Nationalists independently, ignoring the wishes of the British, and freeing Nationalist troops to fight the British protégés, the Greeks.

## Control in Thrace, Anatolia and Istanbul

Britain and France vied for supremacy in Istanbul. The conflict usually took the form of British action, followed by futile French protest. Argument included matters such as control of government ministries and buildings, seizing German and Ottoman banks, arrest and punishment of Ottoman officials and even authority over public sanitation. Perhaps most important of these was command of the Allied forces in the Ottoman Empire. France had led the defeat of Bulgaria and had an army, led by General Louis Franchet d'Espèrey, near Istanbul. According to previous Allied agreement, d'Espèrey was to be commander of Allied forces in the Ottoman Empire, but the French had agreed that an inter-Allied force at Istanbul would be led by British General George Milne. The British navy was also in command of the waters around the capital. The French demanded that Milne accept the overall authority of d'Espèrey. The British had no wish to accept that. They were the ones who had defeated the Ottomans and they planned to be in charge. The British War Council asked Foreign Secretary Curzon to arrange the abolishing of the French command, stating d'Espèrey 'has left no stone unturned in attempting to oust the British from the Turkish capital'.[15]

Lloyd George made it plain to the French delegates at the Peace Conference that the British would not accept French authority in Istanbul. If d'Espèrey gave orders to Milne, the British general was under orders not to obey. Moreover, Lloyd George said that d'Espèrey 'had constantly lacked tact in his command', and had been unable to cooperate properly with General Milne or Admiral de Robeck. Given Lloyd George's attitude, the French offered to replace d'Espèrey with General Adolphe Guillaumat, who had always had excellent relations with British military authorities, retaining French command. Of course, that was not what the British wanted.[16]

D'Espèrey was frozen out of command by the British, who acted independently of his authority. Even though d'Espèrey was theoretically in command, British Generals Wilson, Milne and Allenby acted on their own. Officers assigned to control over military disarmament in Anatolia and Syria were all British, and took their orders from their British superiors. The French responded by pulling part of their force from Istanbul, further cementing British control, but forcing the British to withdraw their troops from Batum to defend Istanbul, abandoning Trans-Caucasia. When Istanbul was occupied, General Milne appointed British officers to head the commissions that were to control major Ottoman Government ministries – to much protest from the French and Italians. Although the French eventually were allowed sops, such as control of some ministries, the British were firmly in charge in Istanbul. It was ultimately decided that the French would be in charge in Thrace and the British in Anatolia. On 19 June 1921, the French finally accepted what was already the reality and agreed that all Allied forces in Istanbul and Anatolia would be under the command of British Lieutenant-General Charles Harington.[17]

The British had won the inter-Allied battle for supremacy in Istanbul, but French ill-feeling was to continue and ultimately damage British plans for the Turks.

### The Effects of European Disputes

The French need for British support in Europe explains much of the France's (at least initially) grudging agreement with British plans for the Ottoman Empire. Events in Europe had great effect on the initial French acquiescence with British plans for the Ottoman Empire. They needed British support in Europe. For France, security against Germany and economic needs were much more essential than their interests in the Middle East or the Balkans. The Ottoman Empire, though important to the French, was of secondary concern.

Large regions of France had been devastated in the war. The French planned that reparations from Germany would pay for reconstruction. Massive transfer from Germany would also weaken Germany for decades, increasing French security. The French expected British aid in setting the amount of reparations, which were initially fixed at an astronomical amount, 11.3 billion pounds. The British demanded lower figures, much against French wishes, and the reparations were greatly reduced to 6.6 billion pounds, with Germany partly paying in coal, timber and other supplies. The Germans could not pay even the reduced amount.

The French objected vociferously when the Germans repeatedly missed payments. The British refused to agree to take action by supporting the occupation of Western Germany until the payments were made. (The French were to occupy the Ruhr in 1923 to enforce German payments.)[18]

The British Cabinet had little sympathy for the French plans for reparations from Germany:

> The suggestion was made that the difficulties of the French Government were largely attributable to the fact that France had not adopted a proper financial policy. She was still maintaining a very expensive army, fleet, and air service, and was engaging in costly adventures in the Near East. So long as she refused to economise, it would be mistaken policy for Great Britain to deal tenderly with her on the reparation question.[19]

No mention was made in the cabinet that, given British economic problems (see Chapter 20), the same could be said of Britain. In general, and with many variations of politicians' opinions, the British took the position that Germany could not be forced too hard to pay reparations – to do so would destroy her economy and lead to reparations never being paid. The French position was simple: France badly needed the money; the Versailles reparations commitments had to be upheld. Despite the fact that the Germans could never pay the sums demanded by the French, and the fact that the British stand was more reasonable, the French felt betrayed by the British.[20]

Security from possible future attacks by the Germans was understandably a primary goal for the French. The French wanted significant changes in the German border and in German control over the economy of Western Germany. An impasse among the Allies was partly settled with agreement on the separation of the Saar region from Germany and the demilitarisation of the Rhineland in the Treaty of Versailles (28 June 1919). However, the creation of that *cordon sanitaire* between France and Germany in the Rhineland did not satisfy France's desire for guarantees against future conflicts with Germany. At the Paris Conference, France had originally proposed that Allied troops be permanently stationed along a defensive border on the Rhine, but had abandoned the proposal in the face of British and American opposition. In its place, the United States and Great Britain separately had agreed to pacts in which they would come to French aid if Germany attacked France. The pact with America was dissolved when the US Senate rejected Versailles Peace Treaty. Lloyd George used American non-ratification to ignore the British commitment.

The French still felt they badly needed British agreement to a British–French alliance that would stand against Germany in future conflicts. In December 1921, the French proposed a defensive alliance with Britain. Their proposal was for a grand alliance that would unite their military forces and act if Germany violated any of the Peace Treaty, not only war against France, but against any violations of the military, naval and air clauses of the Versailles Treaty. The two governments would jointly regulate the size of their militaries, and the general staffs would act together. 'The two Governments should agree to act together on any question of a nature to engender the general peace.'[21]

The British Cabinet considered that the alliance proferred by France was unacceptable. It proposed that Britain would oppose 'unprovoked aggression' by Germany against France, but could not accept the remainder of the French plan. It would not increase British forces against that eventuality, as France wished, nor would it unite forces or have joint military planning. As for joint action against any other violations of the treaty, the cabinet did not even consider it.[22]

There was much debate over possible terms of a defensive alliance. The British postponed any final decision. Curzon considered delaying agreement on an Anglo-French treaty as a tool that could bring the French into line. 'We may find in it (the Pact) a powerful lever for securing a favourable settlement of the other issues.' Throughout the negotiations with France over a pact, Curzon delayed because of the leverage it afforded Britain: 'I think it would be unwise on our part to abandon the very powerful form of pressure which its (the pact's) non-conclusion enables us to exercise.'[23]

The British viewed negotiations over an alliance as a way to obtain French agreement with British plans for the Middle East and elsewhere. Philippe Berthelot of France made it plain to the British ambassador in Paris, Charles Hardinge, that the French expected a *quid pro quo* for support in the Ottoman Empire:

> He said that if we would support the French more on the Rhine, France would help us a great deal more in the East, recognising that the Rhine is the frontier of France and that the East is our frontier.[24]

For the French, an ever-diminishing hope that the British would cooperate with French needs continued into 1922, but the British had no desire to accede to French wishes. Ultimately, that fact was not lost on the French. Even if they gave the British the support they demanded, would the British ever agree to guaranteeing French defence? By June of 1922, France, its position rejected by the British, had abandoned its proposal for a new alliance. To the French, this was an indication that the British would not firmly support their safety. What reason, then, to support the British in the Near East? French disillusion with Britain increased through 1922, just as the British were demanding French solidarity against the Nationalist Turks.[25]

## Notes

1. I have not considered most British plans and actions for the Arab Middle East, except insofar as they affected Anatolia and Thrace. This includes negotiations over Syria and Cilicia. For the British in the Arab lands, see John Fisher, *Curzon and British Imperialism in the Middle East, 1916–19*, London: Frank Cass, 1999.
2. Minutes of the First, Second and Third Meetings of an Anglo-French Meeting, London, 22 December 1919, DBFP 4, pp. 938–69. British Secretary's Notes of an Allied Conference, London, 16 February 1920, DBFP 7, pp. 68–71. See also A. E. Montgomery, 'The Making of the Treaty of Sèvres of 10 August 1920', *The Historical Journal*, vol. 15, no. 4 (December 1972), pp. 775–87, and see also Robert Adair Burnett, 'Georges Clemenceau in the Paris Peace Conference 1919', unpublished PhD dissertation, University Of North Carolina at Chapel Hill, 1968. The bickering between Britain and France had begun even before the Ottoman armistice was signed. See CAB 28/5, 'Notes of a Conversation in M. Pichon's Room', 30 October 1918.

    The Ottomans understood the situation. British Intelligence in Istanbul reported on 3 July 1920 that the Ottoman Government realised that the French and Italians did not willingly join Great Britain in demanding cession of Ottoman territory to Greece. (WO 158/933, General Staff Intelligence, 'Notes on the Political Situation in Turkey', 3 July 1920.)
3. Notes of a Conversation (Lloyd George and Giolitti), Lucerne, 22 August 1920, DBFP 8, pp. 770–2. 'Conversation between President Wilson and MM. Clemenceau and Lloyd George', in Mantoux, pp. 564–75.
4. Stephen Longrigg, *Oil in the Middle East*, London: Oxford University Press, 1954, p. 44. These percentages were set at the San Remo Treaty. The French received 25 per cent and Calouste Gulbenkian 5 per cent. See also Daniel Yergin, *The Prize: The Epic Quest for Oil, Money, and Power*, New York: Simon and Shuster, 1991,

pp. 176–7, 184–96. Marian Kent, *Oil and Empire: British Policy and Mesopotamian Oil, 1900–1920*, New York, 1976, pp. 137–54, and *Moguls and Mandarins: Oil, Imperialism and the Middle East in British Foreign Policy 1900–1940*, London: Frank Cass, 1993, pp. 126–46.
5. There were various routes. One of them: Port Said-Baghdad-Basra-Bushire-Bandar Abbas-Chahbahar-Karachi. One route, proposed in 1923, did pass through Mosul, but came through Turkey, and was therefore impractical. ('Air Mail of the World', *Aeronautical Digest*, vol. 3, no. 4 (October 1923), pp. 272–3.)
6. See Stephen Longrigg, *Syria and Lebanon under French Mandate*, London: Oxford University Press, 1958, pp. 18–19 and 41–3, and Jukka Nevakivi, *Britain, France, and the Arab Middle East*, London: Athlone Press, 1969, pp. 4–10 and bibliography.
7. Great Britain, Parliament, 'Report of a Committee Set Up to Consider Certain Correspondence Between Sir Henry McMahon (His Majesty's High Commissioner in Egypt) and The Sharif of Mecca in 1915 and 1916', London: HMSO, 1939, Cmd. 5974, Annex I, pp. 42–3.
8. CAB 23/14/35, War Cabinet Meeting of 3 October 1918. WO 32/5602, 'Translation of Note Received by the Earl of Derby from the French Minister of Foreign Affairs, Paris, 6 February 1919'. Because they are mainly tangential to this study, the political conflicts and resolution on Syria are only considered cursorily here. For a very detailed study, see Nevakivi.
9. CAB 1/28/16, Curzon to Cambon and enclosure of 6 February from Pichon, Foreign Office, 19 March 1919. The British had already disavowed the previous treaties before the war ended. (FO 371/4354, Cecil to Pichon, Paris, 8 October 1918. FO 371/4354, Balfour to Cambon, Foreign Office, 25 October 1918.)

    Early negotiations between Britain and France and in-fighting in the British Government over Syria are described in detail in John Fisher, 'Syria and Mesopotamia in British Middle Eastern Policy in 1919', *Middle Eastern Studies*, vol. 34, no. 2 (April 1998), pp. 129–70. See also the still valuable descriptions in Longrigg, *Syria and Lebanon*, pp. 69–108, and A. L. Tibawi, *A Modern History of Syria*, London: Macmillan, 1969, pp. 209–331.
10. Notes of a Meeting, 21 May 1919, *Papers Relating*, vol. 5, pp. 756–66. See: David Watson, *Georges Clemenceau*, London: Eyre-Methuen, 1974, pp. 366–72; Northedge, pp. 126–33.
11. Notes of a Conference, 20 March 1919, *Papers Relating*, vol. 5, pp. 1–14. Notes of a Meeting (Wilson, Lloyd George, Clemenceau), Paris, 21 May 1919, and 'Memorandum Submitted to the Council by Mr. Lloyd George: Scheme for Settlement in the Ottoman Empire', *Papers Relating*, vol. 5, pp. 754–66. Notes of a Meeting, 22 May 1919, *Papers Relating*, vol. 5, pp. 807–12.

12. Notes of a Meeting, 21 May 1919, *Papers Relating*, vol. 5, pp. 756–66. Notes of a Meeting of the Heads of Delegations of the Five Great Powers, Paris, 15 September 1919, DBFP 1, pp. 685–93.
13. France was guaranteed 25 per cent of the oil produced by the British or, if a private company extracted the oil, a 25 per cent share in each company. (See 'The Anglo-French San Remo Oil Agreement, April 24–25, 1920', in H. W. V. Temperley, ed., *A History of the Peace Conference of Paris*, vol. VI, London: Hodder and Stoughton, 1924, pp. 183, 602–5.) Edward Peter Fitzgerald makes a strong case that France did not lose much in giving up Mosul in 1918. ('France's Middle Eastern Ambitions, the Sykes-Picot Negotiations, and the Oil Fields of Mosul, 1915–1918', *The Journal of Modern History*, vol. 66, no. 4 (December 1994), pp. 697–725.
14. Notes of a Meeting, London, 19 September 1919, enclosure in Hankey to Crowe, War Cabinet, 19 September 1919. BDFP 4, pp. 395–404. Feisal to Lloyd George, London, 2 October 1919, and Curzon to Feisal, Foreign Office, 9 October 1919. BDFP 4, pp. 443–9. Derby to Curzon, Paris, 20 December 1919. BDFP 4, pp. 592–5 (includes the French declaration on their rule in Syria).
15. WO 32/9552, War Council to Foreign Office, London, 21 November 1919. See also Briton Cooper Busch, *Mudros to Lausanne: Britain's Frontier in West Asia, 1918–1923*, Albany: State University of New York Press, 1976, pp. 63–6.
16. Berthelot to Millerand, Paris, 10 March 1920, in DD 1920, T 1, no. 229. Millerand to Cambon, Paris, 11 March 1920, in DD 1920, T 1, no. 233.
17. WO 106/1571, *Execution of the Armistice with Turkey: 30$^{th}$ October – 30 November, 1918*, General Staff, War Office, 1918, p. 10. On 22 November, Wilson was told to only obey orders from Milne, not d'Espèrey. (p. 17.) FO 371/3416, Enclosures in War Office to Foreign Office, 26 November 1918. The conflict between the British and French at Istanbul is considered in some detail in Alan Everard Montgomery, 'Allied Policies in Turkey from the Armistice of Mudros, 30th October, 1918, to the Treaty of Lausanne, 24th July, 1923', unpublished PhD dissertation, University of London, 1969, pp. 18–23, 34, 39 and 95–8. General Milne was under the command of General Allenby, who was in command of the Allied forces in Asia. Curzon to Hardinge, Foreign Office, 2 April 1921, DBFP 17, pp. 107–9. Hardinge to Crowe, Paris, 19 July 1921, DBFP 15, p. 598. CAB 23/26/6, Cabinet Meeting of 21 June 1921. The War Office had recommended 'complete equality' of French and British forces: British up to the Çatalca Lines, including Istanbul and Anatolia, French in the rest of Ottoman Europe. (CAB 24/100/892, 'Military Command at Constantinople', War Office, 18 March 1920.)

The abandonment of Trans-Caucasia was politically difficult for the British, implying as it did the abandonment of the Armenians. Lloyd George dithered over the question for months, even though his military advisors told him that there were insufficient troops for both Batum and Istanbul. See the descriptions by General Henry Wilson in Callwell, especially pp. 234–6 and 243. The War Office and General Staff had for some time believed that the British position in Trans-Caucasia was untenable, because they did not have adequate forces. See John D. Rose, 'Batum as Domino, 1919–1920: The Defence of India in Transcaucasia', *The International History Review*, vol. 2, no. 2 (April 1980), pp. 266–87.

French diplomatic documents contain a great number of complaints on the British takeover of control of the military and of Istanbul. See DD 1920, T 1, especially Millerand to Cambon, Paris, 17 March 1920, Paleologue to Cambon, 27 March 1920, Millerand to Cambon, Paris, 5 April 1920, in DD 1920, T 1, nos. 258, 294 and 338.

For a summary of French complaints of British actions see 'French Observations respecting Franco-British Relations in Constantinople and Syria', enclosure in FO 406/41, Director of Military Operations to Under-Secretary of State for Foreign Affairs, War Office, 21 March 1919. See also FO 406/41, Derby to Curzon, Paris, 14 February 1919; FO 406/43, War Office to Milne, 3 February 1920, F 52; and FO 406/43, de Robeck to Curzon, Constantinople, 24, 26 and 28 March 1920. There is an extensive record of the British attitude toward d'Espèrey's claims of predominance and command in WO 32/5606.

18. The French sent the British a note that they would invade the Ruhr. The British Cabinet was opposed, but could not stop it. (CAB 23/30/7, Conclusions of a Cabinet Meeting, 23 May 1922.)
19. Cab 23/27/20, Conclusions of a Meeting of the Cabinet, 16 December 1921.
20. This is necessarily a gross simplification of the problem. For a detailed consideration of the conflict over reparations and alliance, see: Jacques Bariéty, 'Le Projet de Pacte Franco-Britannique, 1920–1922', *Guerres mondiales et conflits contemporains*, no. 193 (September 1999), Paris: Editions Belin, pp. 83–99. Anne Orde, *Great Britain and International Security 1920–1926*, London: Royal Historical Society, 1978, pp. 6–36. Paul M. Kennedy, *The Realities Behind Diplomacy: Background Influences on British External Policy 1865–1980*, London: Allen & Unwin, 1981, pp. 264–7. Marc Trachtenberg, *Reparation in World Politics: France and European Economic Diplomacy. 1916–1923*, New York: Columbia University Press, 1980, especially pp. 233–6 and 253–5. W. M. Jordan, *Great Britain, France, and the German Problem, 1918–1939: A Study of Anglo-French Relations in the Making and*

*Maintenance of the Versailles Settlement, 1918–1939*, London: Frank Cass, 1943. (It should be noted, however, that the Near and Middle East do not much appear in the Jordan book, which treats British–French conflict as a purely European concern.)

21. CAB 24/132/21, 'Statement of the Views of the French Government on Anglo-French Relations', Cannes, 8 January 1922. Both the Saar and Rhineland were eventually returned to German control by a Saar plebiscite in 1935 and Hitler's military occupation of the Rhineland in 1936.
22. CAB 23/29/1, Conclusions of a Cabinet Meeting, 10 January 1922. On 24 May 1921, the cabinet had considered a defensive pact with France, but decided 'the situation was not ripe for action'. It was stated that parliament, the public and the Dominions would be suspicious of any written undertaking. It was also stated that the French would never act on their own and invade the Ruhr, which shows a certain misunderstanding of the French. (CAB 23/25/24, Conclusions of a Cabinet Meeting, 24 May 1921.)
23. CAB 24/132 C. P. 3664, Curzon, 'French Draft of Proposed Anglo-French Treaty', 28 January 1922. CAB 24/132 C. P. 3691, French ambassador, 'Memorandum Concerning the Amendments to Be Made in the British Draft Treaty between France and Great Britain', 1 February 1922. CAB/24/133 C. P. 3751, Curzon, 'The Anglo-French Agreement', 17 February 1922.
24. Hardinge to Curzon, 17 December 1920, quoted in Lowe and Dockrill, p. 367. Charles Hardinge was the British ambassador to France from November 1920 to December 1922.
25. For more detail on the deliberations for reparations and French security, see: Northedge, pp. 93–6, 161–2, 178–97 and 223–31. Montgomery, 'Allied Policies in Turkey', pp. 193–9. Bariéty, 'Le Projet de Pacte'.

# 13

## CREATING RESISTANCE – MUSTAFA KEMAL

In 1918, before the end of the war, Prime Minister Lloyd George had stated publicly that Britain was not fighting to deprive the Turks of Asia Minor or Thrace, with Constantinople continuing as the Ottoman capital. Armenia, Syria and Arabia would be detached from Ottoman rule, but Anatolia, Thrace and Constantinople would remain Ottoman. Lloyd George said there was general agreement on this among the British Government and officials such as Asquith and Grey. Later it was stated that this proclamation was only 'intended to weaken the will of the enemy, and to induce them to make a separate peace, rather than a summary of our war aims'.[1]

The private sentiments of the British Cabinet members, including Lloyd George, had been quite different to the prime minister's public statement that the Ottomans would retain their capital. Before the war ended, Foreign Secretary Balfour stated that he wanted the Turks out of Istanbul; he was 'against leaving any power for evil to the Turks'. During the war, Lord Curzon, then a member of Lloyd George's War Cabinet, later foreign secretary, made plain his desire to see the Turks evicted from Istanbul. Accompanied by descriptions of the Ottoman Empire as having 'been a source of distraction, intrigue, and corruption in European politics' and 'one of (the earth's) most pestilent roots of evil', he set forth his plan for the Ottoman capital: the sultan would retire to either Bursa or Konya, accompanied by most of the Turks resident in Istanbul. An international commission would rule the city, its immediate hinterlands and the Straits. Thrace would be divided between the Greeks and the Bulgarians. Hagia Sophia would once again become a Greek Orthodox church.²

After World War I, in 1919, Curzon had not changed his mind: 'Constantinople in his (the Turk's) hands has been, and if left there will remain, a plague-spot of the Eastern world.' Lloyd George added his agreement that the Turks should leave Istanbul. A cabinet interdepartmental committee recommended that there be no Ottoman sovereignty in Istanbul or the Straits, and that both were to be ruled by an international commission.³

On 19 May 1919, Foreign Secretary Balfour told the British delegation to the Peace Conference that he was in favour of turning the Turks completely out of Istanbul, leaving the Greeks in İzmir and placing the Turks in Anatolia under international control. He recognised that Edwin Montagu, Secretary of State for India, and others felt that the Muslim World would be incensed by ejecting the sultan/caliph from the city, but Balfour said that Constantinople was not really important to Islam, a statement that showed colossal ignorance:

> No great Mohammedan teacher has, so far as I know, ever lived there; no religious work has ever been published there or for the matter of that, anywhere else, in the Turkish language; it is adorned by no great monument of Mohammedan architecture . . .

Balfour perhaps did not know that Islamic religious works were written in Arabic, by Turks and all other Muslims, with many written and published in Istanbul, but had he not known of the great mosques of Istanbul?⁴

Lloyd George, asserting falsely that the majority of Istanbul's population was Greek, wanted the Turks out of the city. If the sultan remained, even without power, 'Constantinople would become a source of infection and war.'⁵

Prime Minister Venizelos notified the British of his views on Istanbul: 'At all costs the Turk must be removed, both as a symbol of his defeat and because his continued presence in Constantinople would be a challenge and danger in years to come.' He felt that the only solution was 'an international administration, with a High Commissioner under the League of Nations'. He called the presence of the Turks in the city 'a running sore'. Curzon told him that many in India, as well as the Secretary of State for India, felt that the Indian Muslims would consider this to be 'an intolerable insult to Islam, and would be followed by disturbances and rebellions in all parts of the Eastern

World. They had even said that it would shake our position in India. Such views could not be altogether ignored.' Venizelos said that many, including Lord Hardinge and Curzon himself, did not share those opinions. There would be no troubles in India. Venizelos would, however, accept a nominal presence of the sultan in Constantinople, 'a simulacrum of power and prestige, so long as it was unaccompanied by authority'. Curzon felt that, because an international authority would never work, Venizelos was actually planning that the city would eventually be held by the Greeks.[6]

The Allies disagreed on the fate of Istanbul. Clemenceau wanted to leave the Turks there under some system of international control. ('It would be easier to govern through the Sultan as an intermediary, and for this reason it would be better to leave him at Constantinople.') Lloyd George was vehemently opposed. Left in Istanbul, the sultan's government could close the Bosporus, and the Allies could not afford to pay for the troops to be stationed there to keep the Turks in check. Moreover, if the Turks kept Istanbul, they would not believe that they had been beaten. Curzon reversed his stand of two months before and accepted international control. Lloyd George, however, was willing to consider the idea, proposed by Venizelos, of leaving the sultan in 'a sort of Vatican' in Istanbul, but with no power. The impression was of confusion between the Allies and confusion in the mind of Lloyd George.[7]

The Secretary of State for India, Edwin Montagu, was the strongest voice in the cabinet in favour of keeping the Turks in Istanbul. Supported by letters and testimony of Indian Muslims, he asserted that Muslim sentiment in India would be deeply affected by the expulsion of the sultan–caliph from his capital. He brought Indian Muslims to London to ask for lenient treatment of the Turks. The rest of the cabinet mainly turned a deaf ear to Montagu's pleadings. He was considered a gadfly who always seemed to oppose what the majority of the cabinet thought best.[8]

The final cabinet decision to retain the sultan in Istanbul was based on military concerns and fear that evicting the sultan–caliph from a seat of Islam would spark unrest among Indian Muslims. The navy and army chiefs declared that the British would be able to bring pressure on the sultan and his government if they were under the navy's guns. In Istanbul, the government would be easy to control. If the Ottoman Government were in Anatolia, however, information from it would be limited. The Turks could organise resistance more easily. The border between the proposed international state and the Turkish State would have to be guarded. A much larger garrison would be necessary to defend Istanbul; the Chief of the Imperial General Staff, Henry Wilson, estimated 30,000 men. Curzon objected and Lloyd George did not approve, but the cabinet passed a motion that the Ottomans would remain in Istanbul. The Treaty of Sèvres was to conform with the British decision.[9]

## Istanbul and 'the Horrors in Cilicia'

Although the cabinet had already decided to retain some form of Turkish sovereignty over the capital, Curzon and Lloyd George did not give up their plan to evict the sultan from Istanbul. On 14 February 1920, two months after he had signalled in the Supreme Council his acceptance of the decision to retain the sultan in Istanbul, Lloyd George again tried to convince his Allies to evict the sultan and his government. France and Italy disagreed, pointing out that the city was 60 per cent Turkish. Lloyd George said no, Turks were a minority in the city and the region surrounding the city was Greek (Venizelos statistics, both false). However, his real reasons for eviction were emotional:

> He himself thought that the objections to turning the Turks out of Constantinople were theoretical. The Turk had been in Europe for hundreds of years, and was always a curse, an oppressor and a source of trouble. He had never become a European, he had never assimilated European civilisation, and he had been a perpetual cause of war.[10]

At a meeting of the four Powers on 28 February 1920, Lloyd George made another plea, prompted by inaccurate and one-sided reports of massacres of Armenians in Cilicia. He suggested that the Turks be evicted from Istanbul unless they controlled the situation in Cilicia, even though he knew from all British reports that the sultan's government had no control over Turkish battles against the French and Armenians in Cilicia. It was purely an attempt to achieve his aim of evicting the Turks.[11]

Lloyd George, as was his custom, gave the other Allied representatives a lengthy speech excoriating the Turks for what Armenian sources had claimed were mass murders in Cilicia. He falsely and incredibly claimed 'that Mustafa Kemal, who was responsible, presumably, for the recent horrors in Cilicia, was a high official of the Government of Istanbul and had recently been appointed

Governor of Erzerum'. Both assertions were completely untrue. He asked that, if the information he had received was *approximately* (emphasis added) true, the Allies should take over the Istanbul Government and imprison the prime minister, the minister of war and other ministers. He blamed the situation on French military failings in Cilicia, with which French General Henri Mathias Berthelot hotly disagreed. The French nevertheless stated that they 'generally favoured' Lloyd George's plan on what was to be done in Istanbul. Prime Minister Francesco Nitti of Italy was against precipitous action, as was Churchill, who felt it would be useless. Nevertheless, the Supreme Council approved a letter to the Allied commissioners in Istanbul, drafted by Curzon, that incorporated Lloyd George's threats. Nothing came of it, or could come of it, as the high commissioners understood.[12]

Foreign Secretary Curzon publicly reiterated Lloyd George's assertions. He told the House of Lords that the Turkish Nationalists did the bidding of the Istanbul Government, and that Mustafa Kemal was a high official of the Ottoman Government (once again, 'the Governor of Erzeroum'), although he thought it might be Mustafa Kemal who was giving orders to the government. Nothing, he believed, could be done in Anatolia unless the Istanbul Government was forced to take action.

> In dealing with these circumstances (hostility to the Allies) we have always had in view that the head and forefront of offending lies at Constantinople. And it is only by effective measures can be taken measures can be taken to prevent the kind of thing we have been describing this afternoon.

The kind of thing Curzon had described was not only actions in Cilicia ('the old Turkish penchant for massacre'), but humiliation of the Allies. The wishes of the Allies, he stated, were being flouted elsewhere, even in the streets of Istanbul: 'Turkish officers in the streets have shown an insolence of behaviour which can only have been the result of orders issued by their superiors.' Curzon regretted 'the revival of a national spirit among the Turks'. Its effects had to be stopped. The government in Istanbul had become nationalist and intended to make the imposition of a peace treaty impossible. Curzon firmly believed that the government must be changed, and offending ministers removed. Plans to that effect had been made. They were secret; parliament would be told after they were put in place.[13]

The British were to call upon the 'horrors in Cilicia' as justification for a number of actions against the Istanbul Government, even though all observers in Istanbul, British and otherwise asserted that the Central Government had no control over events in Cilicia or indeed in almost all of Anatolia. The belief in extensive massacres of Armenians in Cilicia were primarily founded on reports on battles in Maraş sent by Armenian and missionary organisations in Britain. These reports, according to the French, greatly exaggerated Armenian mortality. As they continued, the reports began to inflate Armenian deaths – first 5,000, then 20,000. They labelled all Armenian deaths as massacres. In reality, a war was being fought in Cilicia, with local Turks, aided by Turkish Nationalist forces, opposing French and Armenian soldiers. Neither the reports nor the British statements admitted that thousands of Turks had also died. By no means were Armenians the only ones who suffered in Cilicia. For example, Armenians slaughtered all the Muslim inhabitants in the city of Haçın, and the French had bombarded the Turkish quarter of Maraş with cannon, killing inhabitants. French and Armenian soldiers had set fire to more than twenty Turkish villages in the region. In the end, all of Maraş had burned down. There was total war in Maraş, with Armenians and Turks each suffering at least 5,000 deaths. There was great mortality, but it was mortality on both sides. Only by ignoring Turkish deaths, as he always did, could Lloyd George use the horrors in Cilicia to advance his aims.[14]

The British had no representatives in Cilicia. The closest were in Konya, Sivas or Beirut. Commissioner de Robeck lamented that he thus had no reliable information from Cilicia.

Lloyd George twice stated in parliament that he had no real information on massacres in Cilicia, but he declared nevertheless that the Turks had been guilty, without ever admitting the existence of the Turkish dead.[15]

The Allied high commissioners questioned the description of events in Cilicia as massacres, and held that any threats to the Turks on the basis of unconfirmed reports on Cilicia were wrong and would be ineffective. The Ottoman Government proposed an international commission to investigate the troubles in Cilicia. It requested Switzerland, Denmark, Spain, Sweden and the Netherlands to send representatives to investigate. The Allies refused to allow it, and instructed their representatives in European countries to direct them to decline Ottoman requests. It seems the last thing the British wanted was an independent investigation of their claims.[16]

## British Control of the Ottoman Government

The government of the Committee of Union and Progress (CUP) that had ruled the Ottoman Empire resigned on 8 October 1918. The three leaders of the ruling triumvirate, İsmail Enver, Mehmed Talat and Ahmed Cemal, fled the country on 2 November. On 13 November 1918, the Allies began the military occupation of Istanbul, occupying strategic points in the city.

Nothing indicated the British attitude toward Turkish independence as much as the subsequent British treatment of the Ottoman Parliament and Government. For the British, the Ottoman Government existed for only two purposes – to pacify Anatolia and Thrace and to ratify a peace treaty. Both aims failed.

The Ottoman Parliament that had been elected in 1914 was still dominated by ex-CUP members. The new sultan, Mehmed VI Vahdettin, who succeeded to the throne on 3 July 1918, was an enemy of the CUP and of democratic government in general. He was willing to cooperate with the British in most things, as long as his personal position was not threatened. He prorogued parliament on 21 December 1918, naming another enemy of democratic rule, Damat Mehmed Adil Ferid Paşa, as Grand Vezir. Ferid resolved that the only way to remain in office himself and to gain what little benefit the British would allow for the Empire was to cooperate with the British in all things. He began a programme of 'kangaroo courts' that prosecuted ex-CUP members for alleged crimes and did his best to cement control over an increasingly restive Turkish populace.[17]

Ferid Paşa was to find little benefit in cooperating with the British. He feebly protested the invasion of İzmir, but could do nothing. Unable to deal politically with armed Turkish opposition in Anatolia, he planned to attempt it militarily. He proposed to send a force of 2,000 men to Eskişehir to oppose the Nationalists. The British refused to allow this, fearing that the force would be too small and would probably go over to the Nationalists. Viewed as a failure by all, Ferid resigned on 1 October.[18]

Any Ottoman Government was necessarily in an impossible position. The government could not both represent the country and bow to the Allies. Many of the bureaucrats and ex-soldiers who took control after the demise of the Committee of Union and Progress bridled at the imposition of Allied control over the Empire, and especially the occupation of Istanbul. Many covertly supported the Nationalist Movement that was forming in Anatolia.

In opposition were the politicians such as Ferid who had opposed the CUP. None were allowed real power by the British.

## Mustafa Kemal

The Allied occupation of Istanbul led to the great turning point for the Turks. Mustafa Kemal Paşa, the hero of the Gallipoli campaign, a general who had, uniquely, defeated the Russians (at Bitlis in 1916), and a tactician who had led the salvation of the Ottoman army in Syria, came to Istanbul. He arrived just after the Allies had occupied the city. Mustafa Kemal made no secret of his feelings on events, so it is remarkable that the pro-British government of Damat Ferid sent him out as Inspector in charge of the Ottoman Ninth Army on the Black Sea, charged with demobilisation and the collection of arms. It has never been clear why this seemingly irrational appointment was made. Some have argued that the War Ministry hoodwinked the government. It has even been thought that the sultan was secretly in favour of resistance, though this is doubtful. Perhaps Ferid thought that he was freeing himself of a potential troublemaker who would be less of a nuisance in the provinces than in Istanbul. Whatever the cause, Mustafa Kemal arrived in Samsun just after the Greeks had landed in İzmir. He planned revolt.[19]

Turks had begun resistance to the Greek, French and Armenian occupations immediately after the invasion of İzmir. Villagers, Ottoman army units and irregulars had fought the occupiers. The opposition was disunified, however, and seldom met with more than limited local success. Now it was to become united and cohesive.[20]

Mustafa Kemal sent letters to his fellow generals in June of 1919 calling for opposition to the Ferid Paşa government. He then announced that he was taking leadership of a national movement to defend the rights of the Turks. The British in Istanbul, who had not objected initially to Mustafa Kemal's appointment, now realised he was a danger. On 6 June 1919, High Commissioner Calthorpe requested that the Ottoman minister of war remove General Mustafa Kemal Paşa from his command. Nothing was done, and High Commissioner Calthorpe reiterated the request/order on 17 June and again on 2 July. Obviously, the Ottoman Government had little desire to comply, but were forced to act. On 10 July, the Ottoman foreign minister notified the British that they had stripped Mustafa Kemal of his command as inspector-general. The foreign minister went on, however, to state that the troubles in Anatolia were the result of the Greek invasion of İzmir and extension of the territory under control of the Armenian Republic. Massacres of Muslims had occurred in both. The strictures placed on the Ottoman Government by the Allies, he said, had made it impossible to restore order. The Muslim population, exasperated by these events, had begun to resist the orders of the Allies. If the Allies wanted peace, they would have to remove those occupying Ottoman lands. Both Calthorpe's demands and the Ottoman minister's comments were forwarded to the British at the Peace Conference, where the latter were ignored.[21]

It was too late to stop the revolt. Mustafa Kemal resigned his commission in the Ottoman army. Meetings to organise the rebellion followed. In Amasya on 19 June 1919, Ottoman generals passed motions calling for an end to the demobilisation of the army and ceasing the delivery of Ottoman arms to the Allies. Nationalist congresses were held to elicit support beyond the military: Erzurum (23 July – 7 August 1919) and Sivas (4–11 September 1919). The Sivas Congress established the structure for the revolt, tying together previously disparate groups under the umbrella of the League for the Defense of Rights of Anatolia and Rumelia, led by Mustafa Kemal.

General Milne, in command of Allied troops in Anatolia, properly evaluated the situation:

> In Turkey in Asia civil war now exists. It is immaterial whether Government signs peace treaty or not. They are powerless to enforce it. It is my duty to warn you that the published details of the Peace Treaty have consolidated public opinion in Turkey, and that the inhabitants will take full measures to resist Greek aggression and to prevent the present ministry who are regarded in the light of traitors from securing their position by force of arms.[22]

## Ottoman Accommodation with the Nationalists

Damat Ferid had been forced to resign, the victim of the Greek invasion of İzmir, which his attempts to mollify the British had done nothing to prevent. The new government under Ali Riza Paşa, who succeeded Ferid as Grand Vezir, was generally sympathetic to the aims of the Nationalists. The significant post of war minister went to Mersinli Cemal Paşa, one of the generals who had decided to oppose the Allies. Another potential supporter of the movement, Hulusi Salih Paşa, became navy minister. Three weeks after it took office, the Ottoman Government of Ali Rıza came to terms with the

Nationalists, signing the Amasya Protocol (*Amasya Görüşmeleri*) with the Nationalists on 22 October 1919. The Protocol stipulated that no part of the Ottoman dominions should be under foreign control or mandate. The League for the Defense of Rights of Anatolia and Rumelia was recognised by the Ottoman Government as a legitimate organisation. Elections for a new parliament would be held.[23]

British High Commissioner Calthorpe expected the worst – incensed by the Greek invasion, the Turks would vote against the programme of the Allies and in favour of the Nationalists. He would have liked to stop the elections, but felt constrained by 'Wilsonian principles and the Turkish constitution'. 'Moreover', he added presciently, 'should meeting of Parliament be prevented here, there is nothing to prevent it assembling somewhere in the interior, indeed as you are aware Mustapha Kemal is already summoning a congress at Erzeroum'.[24]

High Commissioner de Robeck, who replaced Calthorpe in 1920, felt that the election was 'fixed' in favour of the CUP and the Nationalists. Christian minorities and the Liberal Entente had boycotted the election. The new parliament, he felt, 'will therefore simply constitute an assembly of Committee of Union and Progress and Nationalist partisans and delegates'. In fact, the Liberals had little support in the country and the minorities were too few to influence the outcome significantly. The results unquestionably reflected the will of the populace.[25]

Elections were held from October to November 1919. A new parliament that supported the cause of national independence was seated on 12 January 1920. One week later, on 28 January, the parliament aligned itself with the goals of Mustafa Kemal and the Nationalists by signing the National Pact. The Pact formalised declarations on Turkish independence previously promulgated by the Nationalists at the congresses in Erzurum and Sivas and made them Ottoman law. It was to remain the goal of the Nationalists throughout the coming conflicts in Anatolia and Thrace.

National Pact (Misâk-ı Millî), 28 January 1920

- Referendums will be held in the Arab majority provinces that were occupied at the time of the Mudros Armistice (30 October 1918). Other provinces will be joined in the Turkish homeland.

- Referendums will be held in Kars, Ardahan and Batum so that they can join the Turkish Motherland.
- The status of Western Thrace will be decided by referendum.
- The Marmara region and Istanbul will be free of (foreign) dangers. Freedom of the Straits will be guaranteed by concerned (unspecified) countries.
- Minority rights will be guaranteed as long as rights of Muslims in neighbouring countries are also guaranteed.
- There will be no restrictions (Capitulations) on political, judicial, economic and administrative freedom, although payment of past debts is not opposed.

The National Pact was democratic. This was anathema to the British. It opposed every one of their plans for the Ottoman Empire.

Hulusi Salih Paşa (Kezrak) was named Grand Vezir on 8 March 1920. Salih had signed the Amasya Protocol for the Ottoman Government and was known to be sympathetic to the Nationalist cause. The new Minister of War, Fevzi (Çakmak), was a strong supporter of the Nationalists. The political situation had evolved out of British control.

**Full Occupation of Istanbul**

Lloyd George asked his allies for a meeting in London on the question of Istanbul. He demanded complete occupation of the city, taking over the civil administration of the city, suppression of parliament and arresting officials. The French delegate, Jules Cambon, disagreed. He pointed out that the Allies already controlled Istanbul militarily. It would be sufficient to threaten the parliament with dissolution. Italian Foreign Minister Vittorio Scialoja agreed with Cambon. He felt that the radical British suggestions could not be carried out with the forces available.

Despite the disagreement of others, Lloyd George was obviously in command of the meeting. He said that any decision made would affect Greece, 'since Greece had more troops in occupation of the old Turkish Empire than any other of the Powers'. He therefore had invited Venizelos to attend the meeting. Venizelos thought that civil administration in the city should be left with the Turks, but the police should be taken over by the Allies. As for the Ottoman Parliament, he felt the threat would be sufficient for the time being, but that 'a certain number' of Nationalist leaders should be arrested. He said that two-thirds of Mustafa Kemal's force was in Aydin (completely untrue). The Istanbul Government should be ordered to disband these troops. If this had not been done in one week, 'the Allies should make it clear that the Greek Army would undertake to do this work'. Churchill disagreed with Venizelos's assessment of Turkish forces in Aydin, which were a small number of the Nationalist's total force. He said that the only way forward was to deal forcibly with Mustafa Kemal, not the powerless Istanbul Government.

Lloyd George won over the French to the occupation of Istanbul by threatening that, if France did not agree to the occupation, Britain would do it alone, and the French had no desire for the British to have complete control of the Ottoman capital. Lloyd George described the takeover as a 'precautionary measure' intended to force the Ottoman Government to obey the Allies and, especially, to disavow Mustafa Kemal. Moreover, the Turks must be shown that they had no choice but to accept whatever the Allies offered them in a peace treaty. ('He thought it would be better that the Turk should know before he came to Paris (to sign the treaty) that he would there find himself face to face with Powers that meant to enforce their will on him.') Lloyd George favoured the complete takeover of the city, but, faced with opposition to his plans from the French and Italians, he accepted that only the Post and Telegraphs Administration and the War Office be fully occupied, the police already being effectively under control. With misgivings, the French agreed with the British plan. The French did insist, however, that the notice of occupation suggested by Lloyd George be changed not to exclude the threat that the Ottoman Empire would be dissolved if the Turks did not cooperate.[26]

The Italians were unhappy with it all. The Italian high commissioner in Istanbul was ultimately to refuse to associate himself in any way with preparations for the occupation of Constantinople. He believed that the occupation would bring about the very situation the Allies were in theory trying to forestall – opposition to the peace and threats to Christians. He hoped for a lenient peace to avoid disaster, even though his colleagues told him this would never happen.[27]

By their occupation of Constantinople, the British created the situation that they most feared. They needed a pliant government in Istanbul to carry out their plans and to give an appearance of legality. It was essential that the Istanbul Government continue to command the loyalty of the Turks. But under Allied guns, the Ottoman Government obviously could not be the independent voice of the Turks. The Turks could see that orders from the sultan's government were actually orders from the British. They would not obey those orders.

The Allies decided on the full occupation of Istanbul on 5 March 1920. Orders were sent to military and diplomatic officers to arrange this. Although the high commissioners had jointly notified their superiors that they did not favour the Allied takeover, they followed orders. On 15 March 1920, the Allied commissioners in Istanbul met to carry out those orders. They decided on the form of the occupation: the city would be put under Allied military occupation on 16 March. The war and navy ministries would be occupied, and all military communications censored by the Allies. The police and the post, telephone and telegraph administration would be controlled. All security matters would be in Allied hands. The Ottoman Government was notified the next day. Almost humorously, the sultan's government was told that if it did not control Mustafa Kemal and the Nationalists, the terms of the coming peace treaty would be more rigorous and the concessions to be offered to the Ottomans would be withdrawn. (It is difficult to see how the conditions of the treaty could be more rigorous than they were to be.)[28]

An Allied proclamation to the people styled the occupation as temporary, but stated that might change if there were disturbances or massacres, without indicating where these might take place. The proclamation stated that the occupation of Istanbul was forced on the Allies by actions of the Nationalists (certaines personalités representant les idéas des chefs fugitifs du Comité Union et Progrés). The people, like the government, were told that actions against the Allies would lead to a harsher treaty. Martial law was declared. A proclamation by General Wilson, Commander of the Army of the Black Sea, leading the Allied troops in Istanbul, ordered that anyone possessing firearms or knives more than 8 cm long would be brought before a court-martial and condemned to death or perhaps a less severe penalty. Some members of the Ottoman Parliament were seized and placed under arrest. The declaration admitted that the Allied action was precipitated by actions beyond the control of the Istanbul Government, but that somehow these actions forced the occupation of Istanbul.[29] It is impossible to comprehend the logic of this.

## The End of Ottoman Democracy

One of the first acts of the Allied occupiers was the arrest of thirteen government officials and military officers, including the ex-Minister of War, Cemal Paşa, and ex-Chief of the General Staff, Cevad Paşa. Both had previously been forced from their posts by the British; now they were sent to Malta to join those who had already been imprisoned there. The decision for the arrests was made by the British; even the Italians, who opposed the arrests and the occupation, felt they had no choice but to cooperate in the name of 'Allied solidarity'. The Ottoman Parliament reacted by ceasing its meetings.[30]

The British had always viewed the Salih Paşa government as too sympathetic to the Turkish Nationalist cause. He had been the Ottoman minister who signed the Amasya Protocol. They attempted to force Salih to formally disavow the Nationalists and declare them to be enemies of the Ottoman state. Political conflict ensued.

On 16 March 1920, the high commissioners demanded that the Ottoman Government declare their disavowal of Mustafa Kemal. The Ottoman Government did nothing. On 26 March, the high commissioners repeated their demand, stating that this was a formal decision of the Supreme Council which must be carried out: 'They therefore believe it their duty to invite the Imperial Government to comply with this request without further delay, by publicly and unequivocally disavowing Moustapha Kemal Pasha and the other leaders of the movement in question.'[31]

As demanded, the Ottomans provided a disavowal of the Nationalists, stating that Mustafa Kemal had no official character and the government disapproved of 'excessive acts'. However, the Ottoman communique declared that the Nationalists had acted in response to 'the tragic events in the vilayet of Smyrna, events which were moreover noted by the investigation carried out by the Allied Powers', and 'these organizations have arisen as a result of the need for the defense of legitimate rights and the safeguarding of life and honor'.[32]

The British were incensed. They responded that, rather than disavowing Mustafa Kemal, the Ottoman communique 'would be interpreted by the population rather as an approval rather than a disavowal of Moustapha Kemal and leaders who, with him, fomented the so-called nationalist movement'. The Allies provided a substitute text, a complete disavowal and condemnation of the Nationalists. The Allied text did not mention the İzmir atrocities. It told the populace not to cooperate with Mustafa Kemal.

The British thought little of Grand Vezir Salih. Acting High Commissioner Webb (de Robeck was on leave) wrote: 'He is a man of no strength of character or ability, and he had the misfortune to take office at a moment when compromise was no longer possible.' The British were willing to tolerate Salih only because there were no better choices; Acting High Commissioner Webb wrote that no Grand Vezir could succeed, because of 'the impossibility of holding out to any Government, however disposed to work with the Allies, the prospect of a peace tolerable in the eyes of even moderate Turks'.[33]

Salih Paşa proved to have greater strength of character than the British thought. He wrote that he was 'well aware of the futility of resistance to the decisions of the Powers and the very serious consequences that such a resistance might have for Turkey', but he refused to publish the Allied declaration. Acting High Commissioner Webb wrote that a pro-British Ottoman Government would never command the loyalty of the Turks, but the 'disavowal incident' meant that the government had to be replaced. The Allies, Webb felt, had no choice but to depend on Ferid Paşa, although Ferid had little chance of success, because he had no real support in the provinces. The only thing that might save his authority was a lenient peace treaty; Webb said the only alternate to this was armed force. He believed that the experience of the Greek landing in İzmir had shown that this force had to be the Allies, not the Greeks.[34]

On 1 April the Ottoman Ministry of Foreign Affairs notified the British that the cabinet would resign rather than accept the British order. Damat Ferid Paşa once again became Grand Vezir on 5 April. The sultan's decree of his appointment conformed completely to the British wishes, declaring the Nationalists as rebels who endangered the country and would be punished. It called for cordial relations with the Allies.[35]

Ferid lost little time in telling the British they had his support. On 8 April he told High Commissioner de Robeck that 'he had come into power on a platform of subjugating such adherents of the national movement as would not submit to the will of the Central Government'. He planned to appoint a 'gendarmerie of a special kind', led by men such as the Circassian bandit Ahmet Anzavur, who had rebelled against the Nationalists in Northeast Anatolia. If the British approved, he would provide Anzavur with arms and ammunition to fight Mustafa Kemal. Ferid also requested permission to enrol and equip 15,000 regulars and 35,000 gendarmes to reclaim territory from the Nationalists. He said that 'such a force could suppress the rebel movement within three weeks'. The British War Office refused Ferid's request, correctly doubting if Ferid's plan was feasible, and assuming that Turkish troops might actually go over to the Nationalists. Ferid's impossible plan to organise Kurdish tribes to fight the Nationalists was also rejected.[36]

Ferid stated that he would provide the British with a list of those whom they should arrest. He suggested that the British should dissolve parliament (which had already itself decided not to meet, in any case).[37]

On 10 April, Ferid's government published a proclamation categorically condemning Mustafa Kemal and all who followed him of treason and high crimes. Punishment was promised to all who did not submit to the government within ten days. Newly appointed Şeyhülislam Dürrizade Abdullah issued a fetva labelling the Nationalists as infidels who must be opposed and killed. Mustafa Kemal and five other Nationalist leaders were condemned to death *in absentia* by an Istanbul tribunal.[38]

Parliament was officially dissolved by order of the sultan, as demanded by the British, on 11 April.

No more pliant official than Ferid could have been hoped for. His communications with the British smell of sycophancy. (For example, he told de Robeck that he wanted future sultans to be educated 'on sound British lines'.) Politically, the British backed him completely – a mistake for both the British and the Turks. The British in Istanbul did not like Ferid, but they needed a pliable Ottoman Government that would accept a harsh peace treaty. Elected Turkish representatives had proven they would not do so. De Robeck wrote:

> Turkey, he (Ferid) said, was confronted with treaty of utmost severity, only alternative to signing must be total ruin. This was realized by reasonable people like himself, but unfortunately country was full of irresponsible madmen, who took line that treaty was death sentence, and that Turks should not put rope around their own necks.

The only chance for the Turks, Ferid said, was British assistance in enforcing the treaty. Ferid's assistants signed the Sèvres Treaty (see Chapter 14) on 10 August 1920, but he could not produce the sultan's signature on the treaty, which was never ratified. The reward for Ferid's services – the Allies forced him from office in October 1920.[39]

The British had intended to hurt Mustafa Kemal's Nationalist Movement. Instead, their actions had the opposite effect. There had been two sources of political power – the Ottoman Parliament and the new organisation of

Mustafa Kemal. Now there was only one. The British arrested some members of the dissolved Istanbul Parliament, but most escaped to Ankara. There, on 23 April 1920, they and other supporters of the rebellion created a new parliament, the Grand National Assembly, declaring it to be the only real government of the Turks. From that point, the Istanbul Government had no power over the Turks.

When the French withdrew part of their force from Constantinople early in 1920, the British asserted that all military control of Istanbul would henceforth be in their hands, despite official French objections. De Robeck stated that the British were in charge of Istanbul and Anatolia; he only needed to notify the other high commissioners of British decisions. Although their concurrence was not necessary, he expected they would follow the British lead. In reality, the British had long been in charge.[40]

**Notes**

1. CAB 63/32, Prime Minister's Speech to the Delegates of the Trade Unions, 5 January 1918, excerpted by Hankey, London, 9 March 1922. Lloyd George never disavowed this speech, however. When in 1920 it was decided to leave some form of Turkish sovereignty in Istanbul, he told parliament that he stood by his earlier pledge ('Turks and Constantinople', House of Commons Debate, 26 February 1920, *Hansard*, vol. 125, cc. 1949–2060).
2. CAB 28/5, Notes of an Allied Conversation held in the Cabinet Room, 10 Downing Street, Tuesday, 3 December 1918. CAB 27/39, The Future of Constantinople: Memorandum by Lord Curzon, 2 January 1918. Curzon's assertions were accompanied by patently false statistics, which he may have believed: Turks were only forty per cent of Istanbul's population; Greeks were a majority in Eastern Thrace. At the time, Curzon was leader of the House of Lords and president of the council. See also, FO 371/4215, Balfour to Webb, 8 April 1919. See also: A. L. Macfie, 'The British Decision Regarding the Future of Constantinople, November 1918–January 1920', *The Historical Journal*, vol. 18, no. 2 (June 1975), pp. 391–400. Erik Goldstein, 'Great Britain and Greater Greece 1917–1920', *The Historical Journal*, vol. 32, no. 2 (June 1989), pp. 339–56.
3. CAB 24/95/95, Curzon, 'The Future of Constantinople', 4 January 1920. See also CAB 24/96/7, Curzon, 'The Peace with Turkey', 7 January 1920. FO 608/109, Harding of Penshurst, 'The Future of Constantinople and the Straits', 30 January 1919. A written note states: 'Circulated to British Delegates'. See also, CAB 28/5, Notes of an Allied Conversation, 3 December 1918.

4. CAB 63/26, The Future of Constantinople: Note by Sir Maurice Hankey, London, 6 January 1920. Hankey quoted Balfour's statements from the British records. Foreign Secretary Balfour had earlier decided that the Turks would be evicted from Istanbul. (FO 371/4215, Balfour to Webb, Paris, 8 April 1919.) See also CAB 23/44B/9, Minutes of a Meeting (sic), Paris, 19 May 1919.
5. CAB 23/44B/35, Cabinet Conference, 10 December 1919. CAB 23/35/4, Cabinet Meeting of 10 December 1919. Lloyd George seemed to change his mind on Constantinople more than once during the same meeting. Note: 'Cabinet Conference' is not a meeting of the full cabinet. 'Cabinet Meeting' is the full cabinet.
6. FO 421/297, Curzon to Granville, Foreign Office, 21 October 1919.
7. CAB 29/81, Notes of a Conversation (Lloyd George, Curzon, Clemenceau, Cambon), London, 11 December 1919, and a more complete document, Notes of a Conversation, London, 11 December 1919. DBFP 2, pp. 727–32.
8. CAB 23/44B/35, Cabinet Conference, 10 December 1919. CAB 21/184, Agha Khan to Montague, Nice, 1 August 1920. CAB 23/35/32, Meeting with Indian Muslim representations, 12 March 1921, and CAB 23/35/33, Meeting with Indian Muslim representations, 24 March 1921. CAB 24/95 C. P. 326, Edwin Montagu, 'The Turkish Peace', 18 December 1919. Curzon's rejoinder to Montagu: CAB 24/96 C. P., 'The Future of Constantinople', 4 January 1920.
9. Cab 23/20/1, Conclusions of a Cabinet Meeting, 6 January 1920.
10. CAB 89/82, British Secretary's Notes of Allied Conference at London, 14 February 1920, 10.30 a. m. Lloyd George grudgingly admitted that Britain might be forced to accept the assertions of its allies, but only if the sultan's government had no real power and a Financial Commission was in control of Turkey.

    When it had been decided to retain some form of Turkish sovereignty in Istanbul, Lloyd George was forced to change his position on the Istanbul population. In the face of difficult parliamentary questioning, he responded: 'As a matter of fact, the most recent figures show that the population of Constantinople is overwhelmingly Turkish.' ('Turks and Constantinople', *Hansard*, vol. 125, cc. 1949–2060, HC Debate, 26 February 1920. See also the speech by Bonar Law in the same session in which he stated that the Turks were a majority in Istanbul.
11. Among others, General Milne had told the Supreme Council in October 1919 that the Istanbul Government had no control over the Nationalist forces. (Notes of a Meeting of the Heads of Delegations of the Five Great Powers, 7 October 1919. DBFP 1, pp. 879–80.
12. CAB 29/83, British Secretary's Notes of Allied Conferences at London, 28 February 1920, 1.15 p. m. and 4 p. m. The British claimed the Turks had 'massacred'

20,000, which the French said was a 'wild exaggeration' of the deaths. No one considered Turkish deaths in the fighting. Churchill (war secretary) was only present at the second meeting. The source of Lloyd George and Curzon's statements on Armenian massacres may be a telegram from the Armenian Patriarchate in Istanbul. It claimed that 3,000 Armenians who fled Maraş were massacred, as were 16,000 of the 20,000 who remained in the city. Of course, no Muslim deaths were mentioned. (CAB 24/99 C. P. 752, Bishop Narayom to Nubar Pasha, Constantinople, 25 February 1920.)

13. 'House of Lords, Thursday, March 11: Armenian Massacres' and 'Lord Curzon and the Turkish Problem', *The Times*, 12 March 1920, pp. 10 and 17.
14. Robert Farrer Zeidner wrote the best description of the events in Cilicia in his PhD dissertation, 'The Tricolor over the Taurus: The French in Cilicia and Vicinity, 1918–1922', University of Utah, 1991, and a subsequent book of the same title (Ankara: Atatürk Supreme Council for Culture, Language and History, 2005). His detailed descriptions allow for no acceptance of purely Armenian mortality. See also Shaw, *From Empire to Republic*, vol. 2, pp. 890–918, and vol. 3, part 2, pp. 1386–401. For the British view, see FO 406/43, de Robeck to Curzon, 11 February 1920. See also the extensive record of the reports of massacres in FO 371/5041, FO 371/5044 and 5045, too numerous to cite individually.
15. 'Armenia (Alleged Massacres)', House of Commons Debate, 26 February 1920, *Hansard*, vol. 125, cc. 2060–2. 'Massacres in Cilicia', House of Commons Debate, 15 March 1920, *Hansard*, vol. 126, cc. 1810–1. FO 371/5044, de Robeck to Curzon, Constantinople, 13 March 1920.
16. De Robeck to Curzon, Constantinople, 7 March 1920. DBFP 13, pp. 14–16. FO 406/43, de Robeck to Curzon, Constantinople, 18 March 1920. FO 608/246, Kilmarnock (ambassador to Denmark) Telegram, Copenhagen, 27 February 1919. FO 608/247, Webb Telegram, Constantinople, 25 February 1919.
17. The term *damat* indicated a son-in-law of a sultan. Ferid had married a daughter of Sultan Abdülmecid I. The extent to which the 1914 parliament, elected under single-party CUP control, was truly democratic can be questioned. It was surely more so than either the sultan or Ferid Paşa's government.
18. De Robeck to Curzon, Constantinople, 30 September and 10 October 1919. DBFP 4, pp. 785–6 and 802–10.
19. On Mustafa Kemal's time in Istanbul before leaving East, see Andrew Mango, *Atatürk; The Biography of the Founder of Modern Turkey*, Woodstock: Overlook Press, 1999, pp. 187–224, and Gotthard Jäschke, 'Mustafa Kemal und England in Neuer Sicht', *Die Welt des Islams*, New Series, vol. 16, no. 1/4 (1975), pp. 166–228. Both accounts continue through the Lausanne Treaty.

20. Kâzim Özalp, *Milli Mücadele 1919–1922*, Ankara: Türk Tarih Kurumu, 1985, pp. 9–31; Selâhattin Tansel, *Mondros'tan Mudanya'ya Kadar*, Ankara: Başbakanlık Basımevi, 1973–4: vol. 1, contains numerous descriptions of early opposition. See pp. 72–8, 148–54 and 214–34, 240–6, 267–89. And 294–9. Shaw, *From Empire to Republic*, vol. 2, pp. 613–737, especially pp. 639–79 on armed resistance.
21. FO 608/113, Calthorpe to the (Ottoman) Minister of Foreign Affairs, Constantinople, 17 June 1919. FO 608/112, High Commissioner to Minister of Foreign Affairs, 2 July 1919; Milne to High Commissioner, Constantinople, 30 June 1919. FO 608/112, Le Ministre ad Intérim des Affaires Etrangères to Calthorpe, Sublime Porte, Ministère des Affaires Étrangères, 10 July 1919. On Mustafa Kemal's organisation of resistance, see, for example: Shaw, *From Empire to Republic*, vol. 2, pp. 661–731; Mango, pp. 224–43 and 253–73; Tansel, vol. 2, pp. 1–96. The literature on this subject is very broad, especially in Turkish.
22. FO 371/5048, GOC Constantinople to War Office, 29 May 1920.
23. The Protocol called for the new parliament to sit in Anatolia, but the Ottoman Government, citing the Constitution, which stated that parliament meet in Istanbul, refused to accept this. Parliament was to meet in Istanbul. See Dursun Gök, *Mersinli Cemal Paşa İkinci Ordu Müfettişliği ve Harbiye Nazırlığı*, Istanbul: Gençlik Kitabevi, 2015.
24. FO 608/112, Calthorpe Telegram, Constantinople, 27 July 1919.
25. FO 371/4160, de Robeck to Curzon, Constantinople, 12 November 1919., 'Elections and the Electoral Process in the Ottoman Empire, 1876–1919', *International Journal of Middle East Studies*, vol. 27, no. 3 (August 1995), pp. 265–86.
26. British Secretary's Notes of an Allied Conference, 5 March 1920, DBFP 7, pp. 411–23. Busch, pp. 203–5.
27. CAB 29/84, British Secretary's Notes of Allied Conferences at London, 10 March 1920, 12 noon. The British had actually ordered their forces 'to take steps for the military occupation of Istanbul' on 6 March. (FO 406/43, Curzon to de Robeck, Foreign Office, 6 March 1920.) See also, FO 406/43, de Robeck to Curzon, Constantinople, 8 March 1920, on preparations for the occupation.
28. British Secretary's Notes of an Allied Conference, 5 March 1920. DBFP 7, pp. 411–23. De Robeck to Curzon, Constantinople, 7 March 1920. DBFP 13, pp. 14–16. Shaw, *From Empire to Republic*, vol. 2, pp. 808–32.
29. FO 371/5045, enclosures in de Robeck to Curzon, Constantinople, 18 March 1920 and FO 371/5044, de Robeck to Curzon, Constantinople, 21 March 1920. General H. F. M. should not be confused with General H. H. Wilson, Chief of the General Staff.

30. FO 406/43, de Robeck to Curzon, Constantinople, 17 and 21 January 1920; 20 March 1920. When the French and British commissioners wrote a note demanding that the Porte remove Cemal and Cevad, because they were cooperating with the Nationalists, 'Italian High Commissioner displayed almost insuperable reluctance to agree to note.' He was finally forced to agree, but would not deliver it personally.

   The parliament acted in reaction to the occupation and especially to the arrests of its members, some of whom were actually seized on the floor of parliament. See the proposal of Riza Nur, enclosure in FO 371/5045, de Robeck to Curzon, Constantinople, 25 March 1920.

31. FO 371/5046, de Robeck to Curzon, Constantinople, 28 March 1920. Calthorpe wrote that the British had demanded that Mustafa Kemal be removed, and on 8 June the minister of war ordered it, but nothing had been done. He demanded action. (FO 406/41, Calthorpe to Turkish Minister of Foreign Affairs, Constantinople, 2 July 1919.)

   One has to have a certain amount of pity for Commissioner de Robeck. He understood full well that the Istanbul Government had no control over the Nationalists. Nevertheless, both as a military man and as a diplomatic representative of his country, he followed orders.

32. The collective notes of the high commissioners and the Ottoman proposals are enclosed in FO 371/5046, de Robeck to Curzon, Constantinople, 3 April 1920. There were two drafts of the Ottoman statement, both unacceptable to the British. See also FO 371/5045, de Robeck to Curzon, Constantinople, 30 March 1920.

33. FO 371/5047, Acting High Commissioner Webb to Curzon, 22 April 1920. FO 406/43, de Robeck to Curzon, Constantinople, 30 March 1920.

34. FO 371/5047, Acting High Commissioner Webb to Curzon, 22 April 1920.

35. FO 371/5045, de Robeck to Curzon, Constantinople, 3 April 1920; FO 371/5045, de Robeck to Curzon, Constantinople, 5 April 1920; FO 371/5047, de Robeck to Curzon, Constantinople, 9 April 1920. It should be noted that not all accept the evaluations of Ali Riza and Salih Paşas that I have given here. They condemn both for cooperating with the Allies at all, and particularly for arresting officials at the command of the British.

36. FO 371/5048: de Robeck Telegram, Constantinople, 20 May 1920; Milne Telegram to War Office, Constantinople, 25 May 1920; FO 371/5048, de Robeck to Curzon, Constantinople, 27 May 1920; FO 371/5049, Secretary, War Office, to Under-Secretary of State, War Office, 7 June 1920. Ferid also had a plan to

organise Kurds in Southeastern Anatolia to attack the Turks from behind. De Robeck thought the plan doubtful. Ferid had told the British that the Kurds would oppose the Turks because the Nationalists were trying to turn the Kurds into Bolsheviks. (FO 371/5068, de Robeck Telegram, Constantinople, 17 April 1920, and FO 371/5069, de Robeck Telegram, Constantinople, 28 July 1920.) The French approved the request for the 15,000 men if the Allied commanders were sure they would not go over to the Nationalists. (Millerand to de France, Paris, 17 August 1920, in DD 1920, T 2, no. 361.)

See also FO 406/44, de Robeck to Curzon, Constantinople, 23 September 1920. Ferid later asked for even more men. (FO 406/44, de Robeck to Curzon, Constantinople, September 24, 1920.) Later reports discussed the matter, but nothing came of it. The Commander of the Army of the Black Sea, H. F. M. Wilson, was against the idea. (Enclosure in FO 406/44, de Robeck to Curzon, Constantinople, 9 October 1920.) In the end, Ferid was basically told he could expect nothing until the treaty was ratified.

37. FO 371/5047, de Robeck to Curzon, Constantinople, 8 April 1920. Interim Commissioner Webb decided to arm the rebels, despite the fact the War Office was against any plan to arm and utilise the irregulars. (FO 371/5046, War Office to GHQ Constantinople, 16 April 1920.) Webb had faith that anti-Nationalist forces might defeat Mustafa Kemal if they were supported. (FO 406/41, de Robeck to Curzon, 2 December 1919, forwarding Webb's analysis of the situation). Anzavur was defeated by the Nationalists at Kırmastı on 16 April 1920 before any supplies could reach him. (FO 371/5046, Webb to Curzon, Constantinople, 20 April 1920.) Tansel, vol. 1, pp. 157–63 and vol. 2, pp. 22–36, 66, 102–16. Shaw, *From Empire to Republic*, vol. 2, pp. 646–7, 737–41 and 849–51.

38. Texts of the government proclamation and the fetva: FO 371/5047, enclosures in de Robeck to Curzon, Constantinople, 17 April 1920. De Robeck was hopeful that the declarations of the government and the Şeyhülislam would greatly diminish the support given to the Nationalists in Anatolia. He was mistaken. (FO 371/5046, de Robeck to Curzon, 15 April 1920.)

39. FO 800/157, de Robeck Telegram, Constantinople, 10 June 1920. FO 406/44, de Robeck to Curzon, Constantinople, 16 July 1920. See FO 371/5056, de Robeck to Curzon, Constantinople, 14 October 1920; DE Robeck to Curzon, 22 October 1920. The French especially wanted Ferid's dismissal. (FO 406/33, Note by French Minister of Foreign Affairs in Derby to Curzon, Paris, 13 October 1920; de Robeck to Curzon, Constantinople, 13, 14 and 19 October 1920.) Damat Ferid resigned on 15 October 1920.

Before he left to sign the treaty, Grand Vezir Ferid complained to High Commissioner de Robeck of the injustice of the treaty, begging piteously and futilely for help from the English. (FO 371/5049, de Robeck to Curzon, Constantinople, 10 June 1920.)

40. FO 406/43, War Office to General Milne, London, 3 February 1920; FO 371/5046, De Robeck to Curzon, Constantinople, 11 April 1920. On politics in Istanbul and other matters up to 1920 and a not overly prejudiced analysis, see FO 371/6469, 'Turkey: Annual Report, 1920', in Rumbold to Curzon, 27 April 1921.

The British limited deployment of forces in Trans-Caucasia are not within the scope of this study, but see Bülent Gökay, 'Turkish Settlement and the Caucasus, 1918–20', *Middle Eastern Studies*, vol. 32, no. 2 (April 1996), pp. 45–76.

# 14

## THE TREATY OF SÈVRES

The future of Turkey is in the hands of the Allied Governments, who have devoted long and patient effort to the construction of an equitable Treaty of Peace, and who may be trusted to act with justice to all parties and interests concerned.

King George V, responding to Sultan Mehmed VI's plea for fair terms in the peace treaty[1]

When the peace terms are published there is no friend of the Turks, should there be any left, who will not realize that he has been terribly punished for his follies, his blunders, his crimes, and his iniquities. Stripped of more than half his Empire, his country under the Allied guns, deprived of his army, his navy, his prestige – the punishment will be terrible enough to satisfy the bitterest foe of the Turkish Empire.

Lloyd George in Parliament, 26 February 1920[2]

The Allies decided on the treaty that was to be imposed on the Ottomans at the Conference of San Remo (19–26 April 1920). The treaty was very much a British creation, with a small input from the French. The Italians had little input into its provisions. American influence on the treaty, as will be seen below, was deliberately prevented. The basic form of the treaty was set in a bilateral meeting between the British and the French on 22 and 23 December 1919. Neither the Italians nor the Americans were invited. During the

Supreme Council deliberations Britain and France continued to meet outside the conference sessions to decide what would become treaty provisions.[3]

There was an elaborate procedure for the creation of the treaty, with committees and debates at many bureaucratic levels, but the treaty's main provisions were decided on 22 December 1919 when Philippe Berthelot, Chief Secretary for Political and Commercial Affairs at the French Foreign Office, and Lord Curzon, British Secretary of State for Foreign Affairs, met in London to set the terms of the upcoming treaty with the Ottoman Empire.

Curzon and Berthelot decided that Istanbul was to be lost to the Ottomans, although the sultan might be allowed some sort of fictitious sovereignty. It was to become the capital of an International State of the Straits, completely under Allied control. A new Turkish State would be founded in Anatolia, and would remain under the sovereignty of the Ottoman sultan. Bursa and Konya were suggested as possible capitals. Allied Commissions would control finances, judicial Capitulations and railways. The state would have no army, only a gendarmerie under Allied control. Italy would be expected to evacuate Southern Anatolia, encouraged by economic concessions, while France remained in Cilicia. An Armenian state would include both Trans-Caucasian Armenia and Eastern Anatolia. The French estimated 20,000 Allied troops would be needed to support it (a very minimal estimate); the British felt only 5–10,000. It would be expensive, but it was assumed the funds would be provided by America, which was not consulted on its proposed donation.

Suggestions were made of a separate status for İzmir, in theory under Ottoman sovereignty, in which the Allies elevated Greeks to hold all the key administrative positions; 'This would reduce Turkish sovereignty to an agreeable fiction.' Southwestern Anatolia would not formally become part of the Greek Kingdom, but it was hoped that the awarding of Eastern and Western Thrace would be enough to compensate the Greeks for the loss of theoretical sovereignty in İzmir.

The French and British agreed on most points for the new treaty, such as disbanding the Turkish army, but, where there were disagreements, the issues were generally decided in favour of the British position. The new Armenia was to be created according to the British plan, despite French misgivings as to its feasibility. French plans for the governance of the planned Zone of the Straits differed from those of the British, but the British plan was accepted.[4]

Both France and Britain agreed to creation of a new State of Constantinople. The British plan for the borders of the demilitarised zone on the Dardanelles and the Bosporus was accepted by the French, as was the government of the new State of Constantinople 'in principle', a formal plan for governance to be worked out later between the British and the French. The French wanted the state property and property of the sultan to be taken by the new government of the Straits. The British contended, however, that it should be used to pay reparations to the Allies. The British position was adopted. Curzon's suggestions for financial control over the new Turkish State were accepted. The French also accepted the British plans for the League of Nations. The French consented to Curzon's plan for a Kurdish state without any objection.

The British wrote that they 'note with satisfaction the degree to which the French Government are prepared to meet the views of His Majesty's Government'.[5]

The final treaty would not always be what Berthelot and Curzon envisioned. Lloyd George, not Curzon, was the final arbiter of the treaty's terms, and the ultimate decisions were his. In particular, the treaty allowed the sultan to remain in Istanbul and the Greeks were, in essence, awarded İzmir, two things Curzon was very much against.[6]

## The Treaty of Sèvres: Ottoman Land to be Appropriated

In the final version of the treaty, the sultan was to be allowed to remain in Istanbul, which was to be the capital of the new Turkish State. However, the Allied Powers retained the right to change that if they wished.

A 'Commission of the Straits' was to control the Bosporus and the Dardanelles, as well as an area three miles from each strait. The commission was to be governed by the United States, Britain, France, Italy, Japan and Russia, with two votes each. Greece, Romania, Bulgaria and Turkey (that is, the Ottoman Empire) would have one vote each.[7] In order to ensure its control, the commission would have its own police force and bureaucracy. It could sequester any property it saw fit.

A 'scheme of local autonomy' for Kurdistan would be drafted by the British, Italians and French. Kurdistan would be small – south of Armenia and north of Iraq and Syria. If the people of the new state could demonstrate their desire for independence to the Council of the League of Nations, Turkey would have to agree to this. The Allies would then agree to Mosul being included in Kurdistan.

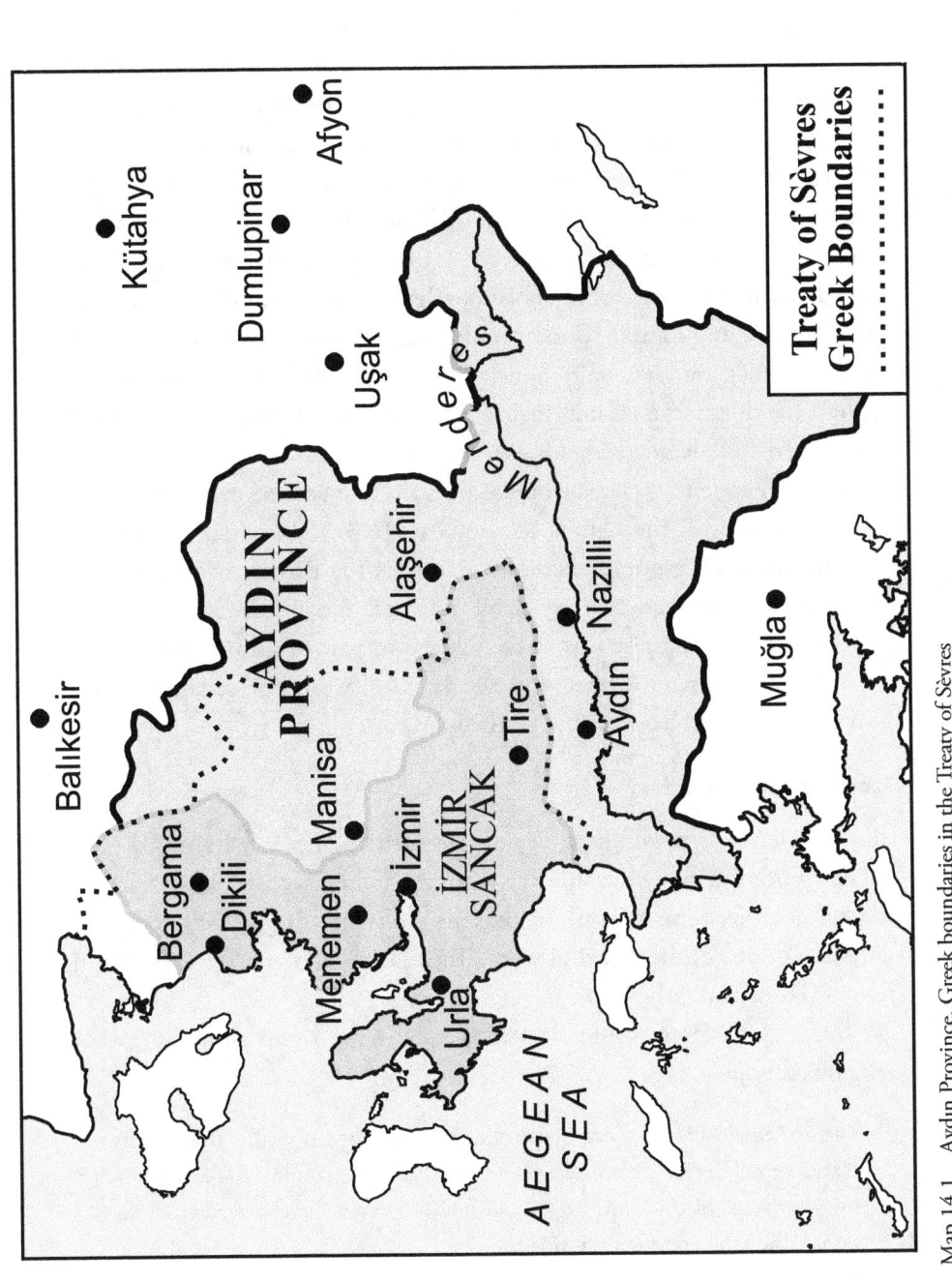

Map 14.1 Aydın Province. Greek boundaries in the Treaty of Sèvres

(A great hypocrisy, because the British had no intention of relinquishing Mosul's oil fields.)

The territory awarded to Greece conformed to the wishes of Prime Minister Venizelos. In fact, as sections of the prospective treaty were considered and revised, they were sent to Venizelos for his comments and approval. İzmir was to be ceded to Greek control, although theoretically under Turkish 'sovereignty'. Greek army presence was unrestricted. A local parliament would represent 'all sections of the population'. After five years, the local parliament could request from the Council of the League of Nations that the region be united with Greece. Both Western and Eastern Thrace would become Greek possessions, up to the borders of Bulgaria, the Straits Zone and Istanbul (the Enos–Midye line). The Eastern Mediterranean islands, including Imbros and Tenedos, became Greek. However, the Dodecanese islands were to remain Italian.[8]

An independent Armenia would be created, the borders to be defined later by the president of the United States (Map 16.3). Syria, Iraq and Palestine were to become League of Nations mandates for Britain and France. The Ottomans were to renounce any claim to Egypt, Sudan and Cyprus.[9]

The Ottoman Empire was to be reduced to part of Central and Western Anatolia. The sultan's sovereignty over Istanbul would be retained, but his government would have no real control there.

## Laws and the Judiciary

The judicial system would be decided by Britain, France, Italy and Japan. Allied military tribunals would try whomever they accused of 'violation of the laws and customs of war' or 'persons guilty of criminal acts against the nationals of one of the Allied Powers'. Those accused of massacres during the war would be similarly tried.

The Turkish State would recognise equally the rights of all 'racial' and religious groups.

> The Principal Allied Powers, in consultation with the Council of the League of Nations, will decide what measures are necessary to guarantee the execution of the provisions of this Part. The Turkish Government hereby accepts all decisions which may be taken on this subject.

In effect, the Allies could try anyone they wanted, for whatever crimes they alleged. The Turks would have no say in their own laws.

## Property

The Turkish Government would restore all property of those 'of non-Turkish race' lost after 1 January 1914. There was no mention of lost Muslim property in the territories lost to the Ottoman Empire in the Balkan Wars, World War I or post-war. Arbitral commissions made up of one Turkish Government representative, one representative of the affected community and one chairman appointed by the League of Nations would make decisions when conflicts arose. The commissions would seize all properties of those having taken an active part in massacres or deportations or having provoked them, as decided by the commission. If the owners could not be identified, the property would devolve to the community of the owner (that is, Greek or Armenian), with no right of appeal for Muslim property holders.

Turkey must return all property of Allied nationals seized in the war, but the Allies retained all seized Turkish property, including any property they still wished to take after the war. The Turkish Government would recompense its citizens for these seizures. (No consideration was given as to how the funds for this would be found.)[10]

No Turkish national was allowed to bring a legal claim against anyone acting for an Allied government after 1914. No Turkish pecuniary claims against any Allied power, from any date before the treaty took place (that is, all past history), were allowed.

## Military

A Military Inter-Allied Commission of Control and Organization would control all military matters, including organisation of gendarmerie, destruction of military material, etc. Turkey would pay for all the commission's work.[11]

The treaty in effect denied the Turks any military power. There would be no independent Turkish military or naval air forces. Turkish armed forces would number only 50,000, of which 35,000 would be gendarmes. Allied officers would train the gendarmerie officers and the police. The Inter-Allied Commission would decide the placement of gendarmes and the composition of the gendarmerie by religious group. Conscription was forbidden. The Turkish navy was allowed ships only for police and fishery duties (seven sloops and six torpedo boats). Manufacture and importation of arms would be strictly controlled by the Inter-Allied Commission. Arms, ships and airplanes either must be delivered to the Allies or destroyed, depending on Allied decisions.[12]

There would be no army; the Ottomans would be completely at the mercy of other states. Without defensive capability, it was doubtful if even the rump state left to the Turks would long remain in their hands.

## Financial

Turkey would pay reparations to the Allies, but the treaty recognised that the resources of Turkey were not sufficient at the time to pay all that was demanded. Therefore, a Financial Commission made up of France, Britain and Italy was created, with Turkey in a purely consultative capacity. The Financial Commission would have absolute control over the state budget, the financial bureaucracy and tax collection. It might demand any information and records it desired. The state might not take any loans without permission of the commission. Payments from state revenues would be made in this order: salaries and expenses of the Financial Commission, expenses of the Allied forces of occupation, indemnities (reparations) to be paid to the Allies. Only what remained would be left for operating the state.

Payment of the Ottoman Public Debt would generally continue as before the war, with all Ottoman rights abrogated in favour of the Financial Commission. The commission could apply new sources of revenue to the Public Debt.

The Capitulations remained in force, and were extended to all the wartime Allied states, even those that did not have capitulatory rights previously. Customs duties would be returned to their old rates (as of 1907). Duties could only be changed by the Financial Commission, which would authorise all prohibitions on import or export.

All previous Turkish treaties with Germany, Austria, Bulgaria and Hungary were abrogated. The Allied nations would decide which treaties with Turkey would remain in force. The treaty sections on the Financial Commission and the Ottoman Public Debt, including commission power over the Ottoman budget and government loans, were exactly as in the British plan. The order of first payments from state revenues (salaries of the commission, Allied expenses, reparations and only then state needs) were as in the initial British plan. In both the plan and the treaty, the commission was the ultimate authority.

## Wilson Wades In

The Americans had taken part in preliminary committees and early Allied decisions on the Ottoman Empire, but had disassociated themselves with the creation of the Sèvres Treaty. On 26 March 1920, as the treaty terms were being finalised, the American Secretary of State sent a dispatch to the British. It notified them of President Wilson's desires for the Turkish Peace Treaty. Wilson notified the Europeans that, although the United States had not been at war with the Ottomans, he felt a duty 'to press for a solution which will be at once lasting and just'. The communication made it clear that the United States wanted to be a party to decisions concerning the Ottoman Empire, but also stated that America would not send a plenipotentiary to the meetings discussing the Ottoman Empire. The Allies were expected to notify the United States of their deliberations, awaiting American input.

The American points:

- Turkish power should be expelled forever from Europe, including from Constantinople. Greece should receive most of Western and Eastern Thrace. The Turks of Europe, Wilson felt, would be pleased to see Turkish government end; he had been assured of that by Prime Minister Venizelos.
- The northern part of Eastern Thrace should be given to Bulgaria. The population there, Wilson (wrongly) believed, was mainly Bulgarian.
- Istanbul and the Straits should be ruled by an international commission. Soviet Russia, however, had legitimate concerns there. These should be considered, in expectation that Russia would eventually have a government 'recognised by the civilised world'.
- Armenia's 'legitimate claims' should be recognised, including access to the sea. Trabzon and Lazistan should be Armenian. The Turks of the Pontus region would prefer to be part of Armenia, rather than Turkey. He based this assessment on statements of Venizelos.
- Wilson accepted that the Great Powers would decide what happened to the Arab provinces.
- Washington took no position on the disposition of Smyrna, because it did not have enough information to make a decision.
- The economic clauses of the proposed treaty had 'grave possibilities', and needed reconsideration.
- 'Whatever arrangements or territorial changes may be made in the former Ottoman Empire, the Washington Government understand that such arrangements or changes will in no way place the citizens or corporations of the United States of America or of any other country in a position less

favorable than corporations or citizens of any Power which is a party to the Turkish Treaty.'

Wilson's views caused great consternation among the Europeans. Berthelot of France said it was pointless to waste time consulting the Americans. 'It was out of the question that they should wait for the sanction of the United States.' Lloyd George agreed, and Curzon went further, asserting that the United States would not especially benefit from the treaty, as Wilson expected: 'They would not in fact benefit from those (treaty) terms, and their nationals would not enjoy the same privileges and advantages as our own nationals.' The United States would not benefit from revisions of the Capitulations, nor would it receive any compensation for property lost by American nationals. Those who had fought the Ottomans, Curzon stated, would gain from new concessions. Others, including the Americans, would not. No one disagreed with Curzon.

There was a general feeling that Wilson was naïve and should not be listened to. The Supreme Council asked Curzon to draft a reply to Wilson. It stated, quite politely, that nothing would be delayed awaiting American participation. The treaty would conform to Wilson's ideals, except that there could not be equality in the way all peoples were treated. On Constantinople and Eastern Thrace, Wilson's views would not be followed. Greece would get all of Eastern Thrace, Bulgaria nothing. Russia would not be included in the treaty. Armenia might get much less than Wilson wanted. The Allies would take concessions only for themselves. The council decided not to send the note to the Americans until the treaty conditions had been finalised.[13]

## Tripartite Agreement

In addition to the Treaty of Sèvres, which at least in theory represented all the Allied countries, Britain, France and Italy agreed to another treaty to divide among themselves the spoils in the Ottoman Empire, the Tripartite Agreement (10 August 1920). After a dubious declaration that the three wished only 'to help Turkey develop her resources', the agreement decided on 'spheres of influence' in what were theoretically Ottoman properties. The areas of special interest for each were carefully delineated (see Map 14.2). The intent was to cease inter-Allied competition for economic and financial control of Ottoman territory.

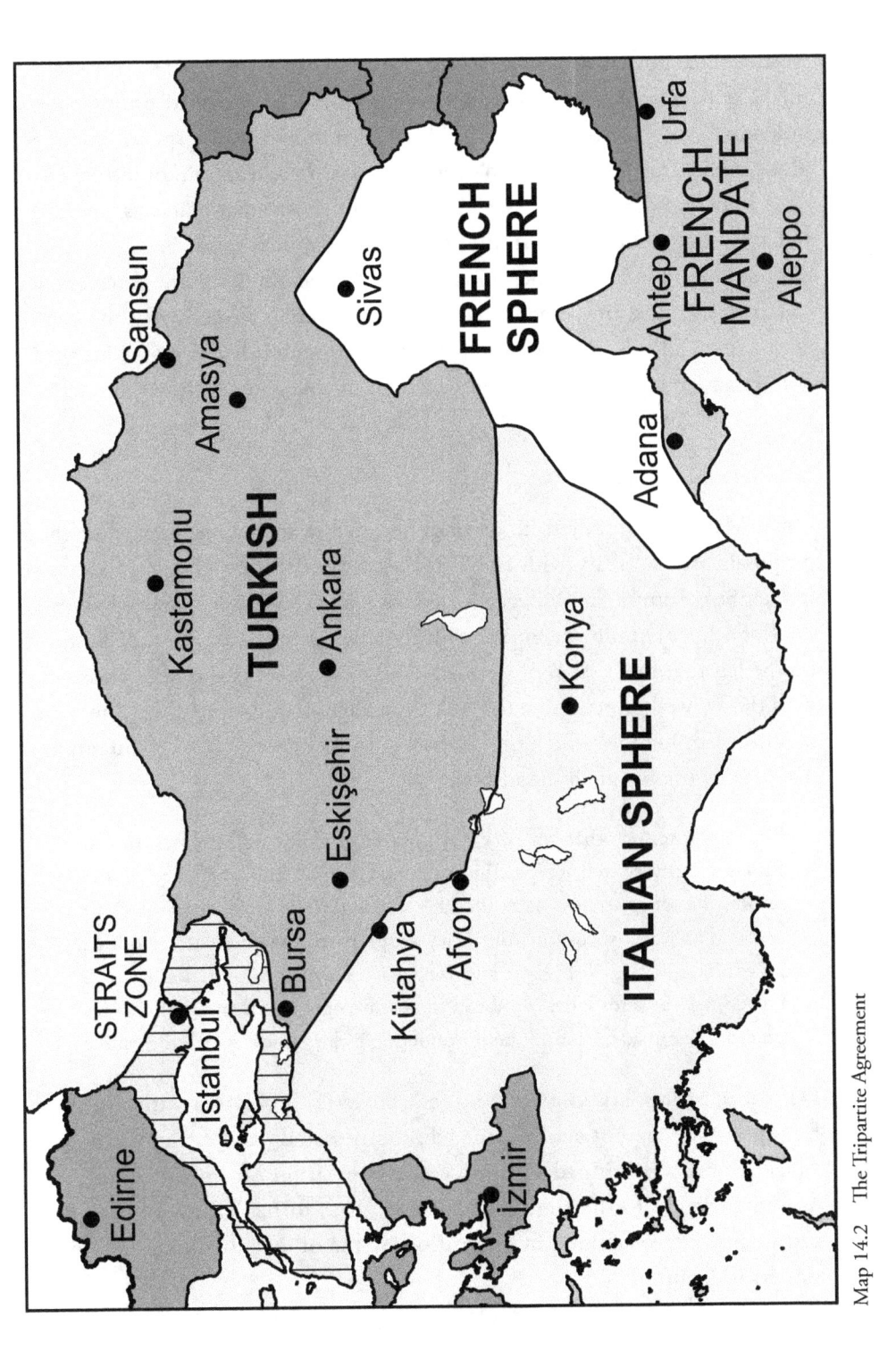

Map 14.2  The Tripartite Agreement

The three powers agreed to accept the areas of 'special interest' for each. In these areas, 'assistance' and concessions would be provided only by the individual Ally. The other two agreed not to impinge on the special interest of the other. They each agreed to support the claims and actions of the others.

A joint company was envisaged to control the Ottoman railways, and the Italians were granted ownership of the Ereğli coal mines, but the agreement did not go into other specifics on what each Ally might have. The agreement, however, signalled the intent to control the Ottoman economy for the benefit of Italy, France and Britain. From the beginning it became obvious that Britain and France did not mean to adhere to the agreement, to the detriment of Italian interests.[14]

## Doubts and Concerns

On 9 March 1920, when he was notified before their final passage of the proposals for the treaty with the Ottomans, the British high commissioner in İstanbul, Admiral de Robeck, voiced what he called his 'grave misgivings': De Robeck was in full agreement with the internationalisation of the Straits, but he felt that the cession of so much land to the Greeks was not consistent with the avowed principles of the Allies – 'a flagrant violation of the principle of self-determination' which the Turks would never accept, and could not be instituted without much bloodshed.

> The terms are such that no Turk, Committee of Union and Progress or pro-Entente, can very well accept. The Supreme Council, thus, are prepared for a resumption of general warfare; they are prepared to do violence to their own declared and cherished principles; they are prepared to perpetuate bloodshed indefinitely in the Near East; and for what? To maintain M, Venizelos in power in Greece for what cannot in the nature of things be more than a few years at the outside. I cannot help wondering if the game is worth the candle.

De Robeck summarised by stating that his letter 'is written with a strong feeling that we are not acting quite with fairness and justification'.[15]

De Robeck continued to oppose the imposition of drastic conditions on the Turks up to the time that the treaty was formally presented to the Ottomans. He was joined in opposition by the other Allied high commissioners in Istanbul.[16]

The assessment of the British General Staff echoed de Robeck's misgivings. Instructed to advise the cabinet on the situation in Anatolia and Thrace, the General Staff reported on the availability of troops in the Middle East, England and Ireland, and the rest of the British Empire. They concluded that there were none available to reinforce the proposed British commitment in the Ottoman Empire. The analysis conflicted with all that the British Government wished to be true. Its main points:

- Peace terms should be tolerable to the Turks. The present drastic terms must be reconsidered.
- 'The (peace treaty) terms, to be tolerable to the Turks, should recognize Turkish sovereignty over İzmir and Eastern Thrace, including Adrianople, and suzerainty over a substantial portion of the Eastern provinces of Asia Minor.'
- The military effort required to enforce a drastic peace would be so great that the Allied governments cannot provide it.
- The plan to deliver arms to the Armenians will depend on an Allied military expedition, which cannot occur. The Armenians cannot even defend themselves in the Trans-Caucasus, much less hold Eastern Anatolia. The only hope for the Armenian state in Anatolia is to accept 'Turkish suzerainty (undefined)'.
- 'There will be no satisfactory settlement of the Turkish question and consequently no reduction in British responsibilities until Greek ambitions are curbed.'
- The present proposals would cause the British to lose prestige, with no benefits, and probably result in the massacre of Christians.
- 'It may be that the Supreme Council prefer to include all these terms on the chance of Turkey observing them and with no intention of enforcing them if she doesn't. In this case the military opinion on such a policy is probably not desired.

  It must, however, be pointed out that the conditions of the Treaty contain little promise of bringing peace to a country which is sorely in need of peace; nor do they, from a military point of view, bring anything but anxiety and responsibility to all entrusted with the defense of the British Empire which are linked either by territorial or religious affinities to what was once the Turkish Empire.'[17]

The War Office hoped it was not too late to change the terms of the Turkish treaty. The Imperial General Staff advised that only a lenient peace with Turkey could be successful. They hoped that

> [i]t may not be too late to reconsider the terms which it is proposed to impose upon Turkey, unless his majesty's Government are prepared to face a further call for troops. There are now no reinforcements available, and indeed our military resources are strained to a dangerous extent in meeting our existing commitments.

The War Office agreed with French Marshall Ferdinand Foch on the large number of troops necessary to enforce a harsh peace, 405,000 men. Utilising the Greeks for that purpose would aid only Greek ambitions and not improve the general situation.

The plan for creation of an Armenian state in Eastern Anatolia, the General Staff felt, was unworkable. Even if Armenian forces were armed in time, which was doubtful, the Armenians could not defend themselves. The Allies could not help them.

> In short, the General Staff fail to see how the State of Armenia, if it is to include any part of the former Turkish vilayets, can be established without the goodwill of Turkey, which can hardly be obtained if the present proposals are pursued.

The Turks should retain sovereignty over İzmir and Eastern Thrace. There could be no satisfactory solution to the crisis in Anatolia 'unless Greek ambitions are curbed'.[18]

The General Staff and Admiral de Robeck were no friends to the Turks. Their objections were practical. They saw the Sèvres Treaty as unworkable, and predicted that it would end in disaster. However, such assessments of those with practical knowledge of the situation in Anatolia and Thrace seem to have had no effect on the British Government and the Supreme Council. The constant analysis of the British high commissioners and the military was that the Allies had two choices: an 'easy peace' which would be easily enforced, or a 'drastic peace' which could only be enforced by hundreds of thousands of Allied troops. Realistically, these British representatives felt, the troops would have to come from Britain.

Admiral de Robeck, the British high commissioner, wanted the Straits internationalised, close financial control over Turkey and the loss of all 'non-Ottoman' (that is, non-Turkish) provinces. He felt, however, that taking Eastern Thrace and İzmir was more than a mistake. The Muslims would never willingly accept Greek rule, 'especially after the sample of Greek methods which they have had since the Greek occupation of Smyrna'. The British military leader in the Ottoman Empire, General Harington, feared that the Supreme Council's decisions could only be enforced by reckless military action; 'Allied officers and men out here will hardly appreciate being called upon to sacrifice themselves in order to join Greeks in killing Turks.'[19]

The British Cabinet had no use for the opinions of its representatives in Turkey or its General Staff. Curzon wrote to Acting High Commissioner Webb:

> The best advice that can be given to the Turkish Government is that now the peace terms are settled they should swallow their medicine as quickly as possible and then set to work to put in order such Empire as is left to them, in which task they may look for British guidance and support.[20]

## The Outlook as Seen by the Turks

It is naturally impossible to say what would have happened if the Turks had been offered a lenient peace. Perhaps they would have accepted continued Capitulations, foreign control of government finances and other strictures. The Turkish population of Anatolia and Thrace could not be expected to have understood most of the clauses of the Treaty of Sèvres. But while the financial, economic and judicial aspects of the treaty might not have been understood by everyone, every Turk and Kurd in Anatolia and Thrace could recognize that their land was about to be taken from them and given to their enemies. İzmir, Aydın, İzmit, Cilicia and Istanbul had already been taken when the Sèvres Treaty was published. The treaty cemented these losses and also gave away Thrace and much of Eastern Anatolia. The Turks could understand what would be their fate. In the Balkan Wars, the land that had been lost was majority Muslim, and any Turk could see the effects on the Turks when that land was lost. The refugees from the Balkan Wars were all around them. Everyone was aware of what befell the Turks when their lands were taken – they were killed or expelled and lost everything. Furthermore, the Greeks in İzmir had continued the policies of the Balkan Wars. An entire nation – peasants, merchants, workers – joined soldiers in opposition to the plans of the Allies.

The Allied high commissioners wrote in a joint letter to their governments that the Sèvres Treaty had been the final straw in turning the Turks against the Allies:

> The High Commissioners note that action of Nationalist forces was set in motion, just as they had foreseen, immediately that peace conditions became known, and that nature of these conditions had made nearly all Turks Nationalists.[21]

Would the Turks have accepted a peace treaty, perhaps with some futile resistance, if it had left them with their land? British officials in Turkey felt that they would have done so. That can never be known. It is obvious, however, that by taking away such a substantial proportion of the Turkish land, the British created their own disaster.

## Enforcing the Treaty

The dangers that had been envisaged by British military and diplomatic representatives rapidly came to pass after the punitive treaty was presented to the Ottoman Government. An Ottoman delegation signed the treaty on 10 August 1920, but it was to become obvious that those who did so represented only a small number of Istanbul officials. It was never to be ratified by the Ottoman Government or the sultan. It was also obvious that the Turks would never accept the treaty unless forced.[22]

How, then, was the Sèvres Treaty to be enforced? For Lloyd George, the answer was the Greeks. Lloyd George advocated, and it was decided that Venizelos and Greek military advisors should be present when the Supreme Council considered military matters in Turkey. Lloyd George said Greece should provide the main force (100,000 men) that would enforce the treaty.[23]

The Supreme Council requested from Venizelos a military assessment of Greek assistance in 'coercing' Turks to accept the peace treaty. Venizelos appointed the military attaché to the Greek Legation at Paris to provide an assessment. The Greek report stated that: 'She (Greece) alone would be able to impose the treaty on Turkey'. Only small Allied detachments would be necessary. Thrace would be easily occupied by the Greeks. ('As a preliminary to Allied action in Asia Minor, military occupation of the whole of Thrace would offer incontestable practical advantages, and possibly also moral advantages, the Turk being, above all, a fatalist by nature.') In Anatolia, it would be necessary for Greek forces to be allowed to operate freely, attacking the forces of the Turkish Nationalists as Greece saw fit. The Turks would be easily defeated by superior Greek forces, whose morale was excellent. After defeating Turkish forces in the İzmir region, the Greeks would advance to Bursa, Afyon and the rest of Western Anatolia, joining with Allied forces on the İzmit Peninsula. By the end of the campaign, all Western Anatolia and 'a considerable part of Asia Minor' would be occupied. In order to speed up the conquest, the Allies could provide troops and military assistance. All would be aided by the low morale and lack of equipment among the Turks. (This was eventually to be the Greek action plan, even though not with full Supreme Council approval.)[24]

The Greek delegation requested Allied assistance in disarming the Turkish population and banishing and taking hostages of 'a few prominent persons'.

The Allied Military Commission at the Peace Conference reported that, in all, the Allies would need thirty infantry divisions (approximately 450,000 men), of which nineteen were at present in the theatre, including nine Greek divisions and four British divisions in Mesopotamia. The French and British forces were described as 'incomplete'. Trabzon and Batum would have to be held as bases for supply of the four divisions that would be sent to aid the Armenians. There were simply not enough troops. 'In the present circumstances, neither France, Great Britain, nor Italy can be asked to provide these reinforcements.' The desires of the Peace Conference would have to be curtailed. No force could be sent to aid Armenia. None would be available to force the Turkish Nationalists to demobilise. The Military Commission preferred to lessen Greek involvement, substituting Allied forces in Thrace and not allowing Greek advance beyond the İzmir region. The Allies proved unwilling to consider the military report. Instead, they listened to Prime Minister Venizelos.[25]

Soon after the Greeks occupied İzmir and its surroundings, going beyond the territory originally awarded by the Peace Conference, Venizelos had set his eye on more land. He coveted the region he had first requested from the conference (Map 10.4). But there were difficulties. There had been a reaction from the Allies to the unsanctioned Greek incursion into Aydın Province. Venizelos had promised that Greek forces would henceforth not go beyond their assigned boundaries without permission from the Allies' military representative in Southwest Anatolia, General George Milne. Venizelos and the Greek command tried to convince Milne that their army had to advance to counter a Turkish threat. The Turks, they alleged, were creating a large force to attack İzmir, and the Greeks should advance to counter it. British military representatives felt that the threat was greatly exaggerated in order to pave the way for an advance into new territories. Milne believed that his own Intelligence did not support the Greek claims of a pending Turkish attack. The Army Council in London stated that, if the Greeks felt threatened, they should return to Greece. Ordered to do so by London, Milne told the Greeks that they could defend against a large Turkish attack, but must return to their original lines. His plan defeated, Venizelos promised that the Greeks would not advance without Milne's permission.[26]

On 5 October 1920, Venizelos telegraphed Lloyd George, reiterating the plans for Greek military actions in Anatolia: Greek forces would drive the Nationalists out of Ankara and the Pontus (Northern Anatolia), but they would need financial assistance from Britain. Lloyd George told the cabinet that the Greeks would be able to reach Ankara. Doubts were expressed in the cabinet regarding the proposal. It was agreed to reserve a decision until the Chief of the General Staff reported on the feasibility of the plan to the prime minister.[27]

The resulting evaluation by the General Staff was not what Lloyd George wanted to hear. The General Staff wrote: 'From the moment of the arrival of the Military Section of the British Peace Delegation in Paris early in 1919 the General Staff opposed the furtherance of Greek territorial claims at the expense of Turkey.' They had believed that all Eastern Thrace and Western and Central Anatolia should remain Turkish, 'but were presented with a fait accompli by the occupation of Smyrna by Greece in May 1919, which was executed in spite of their repeated protests'. Unless ordered by the cabinet, the General Staff stated, no British troops should ever form part of an Allied force in Asia Minor. Prior to the San Remo Conference, where the Treaty of

Sèvres was finalised, they once again protested that Turkish administration should not be removed from Eastern Thrace and Western Anatolia, unless the Allies were willing to make available greatly increased military forces. Under orders, the General Staff did what it could to cooperate with the Greeks, but noted: 'This situation now exists and the General Staff views future developments with the greatest anxiety.'[28]

This was not the only time the General Staff gave a judgement against using the Greeks to enforce the treaty. In January 1921, it wrote: 'It is unsafe to rely on the Greek Army to cover the Allied position in Turkey. HMG (His Majesty's Government) should either A. Send reinforcements to Constantinople; B. Withdraw the existing British troops, or C. Re-adjust the Allied policy.' Since no troops were permanently available for option A, what was needed was a 'drastic revision' of the treaty over İzmir, Kars and possibly Thrace. The General Staff wanted 'gracious concessions' to the Turks, 'recreating Turkey as a buffer state between the Entente Powers and Russia, and removing some of the principal underlying causes of unrest throughout the British dominions in Egypt, Mesopotamia and India'.[29]

High Commissioner de Robeck in Istanbul warned against any Greek advance further into Anatolia, which would alienate both Turks and the rest of the Muslim World: 'A renewed Greek advance will perpetuate disorder and rebellion.' Curzon responded that he would discuss the matter with Venizelos and inform de Robeck of the outcome.[30]

As on so many questions, the judgements of his military and diplomatic advisors did not sway Lloyd George. He resolved to make the Greeks the agents that would impose the Treaty of Sèvres on the Turks.

## Notes

1. FO 371/5048, Curzon to de Robeck, Foreign Office, 5 June 1920.
2. 'House of Commons: Thursday, February 26', *The Times*, 27 February 1920, p. 8.
3. There is extremely extensive documentation on the deliberations that led to the treaty. See DBFP 7 (740 pages of argument and agreement).
4. The French and British disagreed on the extent of the new Armenian state. The French wanted to exclude Erzurum Province, the British to include it.
5. CAB 28/9, Anglo-French Conference on the Turkish Settlement, London, 22–3 December 1919, and meeting minutes in DBFP 4, pp. 938–70. For the French

plans for the treaty, see CAB 1/29, Vansittart to Curzon, Paris, 12 January 1920. For the British plans for the treaty, see the following: FO 371/4239, Robert Vansittart, S. Armitage Smith, E. G. Forbes Adam, 'British Peace Delegations Draft Proposals for the Financial Conditions of Peace with Turkey', Foreign Office, 29 December 1919; E. G. Forbes Adam and Robert Vansittart, 'Memorandum on Turkish Settlement by Political Section of British Peace Delegation', Foreign Office, 18 December 1919.

6. Curzon laid out his own plans and complained of what others had done in a long memorandum of 22 April 1919. (FO 371/4180, Curzon, 'Note Respecting the Middle Eastern Question', 22 April 1919.) Much of what he discussed did not conform to later events and British policies. For a general consideration of the treaty, see Helmreich, *From Paris to Sèvres*, pp. 242–337.
7. The United States would only take part if it agreed, which it had not yet done. The chairman of the commission, who had a casting (a second) vote, would be selected from the members with two votes for a two-year term.
8. FO 371/4239, Adams (British Delegation) to Phipps, Paris, 19 January 1920.
9. Another hypocrisy:

> Certain communities formerly belonging to the Turkish Empire have reached a stage of development where their existence as independent nations can be provisionally recognized subject to the rendering of administrative advice and assistance by a Mandatory until such time as they are able to stand alone. The wishes of these communities must be a principal consideration in the selection of the Mandatory.

(League of Nations Covenant, Article 22.)
10. This also applies to intellectual and artistic property, as well as industrial property.
11. There were also naval and aeronautical commissions of control.
12. The actual terms did not specifically indicate absolute Allied control of the military: 'Officers or officials supplied by the various Allied or neutral Powers shall collaborate, under the direction of the Turkish Government, in the organization the command and the training (of the gendarmerie and police).'

    The British General Staff disagreed with the abolition of a Turkish army. They felt there should be a Turkish army, officered by Turks, for defence. (CAB 21/184, 'General Staff on the Reason for the Retention of a Regular Army by Turkey', 14 January 1920.)
13. CAB 29/31, British Secretary's Notes of Meetings of the Supreme Council, San Remo, 19 April 1920.

14. Great Britain, Parliament, *Tripartite Agreement between the British Empire, France and Italy respecting Anatolia, Signed at Sèvres August 10, 1920*, London: HMSO, 1920, Cmd. 963.
15. CAB 24/101/68, enclosure in Curzon memorandum to the cabinet, Foreign Office, 26 March 1920. Even Curzon expected the Turks might make trouble over the harsh treaty stipulations, although this did not stop him from supporting the treaty. (CAB 25/107, 'A Note of Warning about the Middle East, by Lord Curzon', in Wilson (CIGS) to PM, 4 April 1919.)
16. See, for example, FO 371/5043, de Robeck to Curzon, Constantinople, 7 March 1920 and 10 March 1920. FO 371/5043 contains other calls for a more lenient peace and plans for one. There are also dire warnings of disaster if a harsh peace was passed.
17. WO 106/64, General Staff, War Office, 'The Situation in Turkey, 15$^{th}$ March, 1920', 15 March 1920. The General Staff had hoped for lenient terms, predicting trouble if harsh terms were exacted. (CAB 21/154, General Staff, 'Military Policy in Asia Minor', presented to the cabinet by the Secretary of State for War (Churchill), 9 October 1919.)
18. CAB 24/103/14 and FO 371/5046, 'General Staff Memorandum on the Turkish Peace Treaty', War Office, 1 April 1920.
19. CAB 24/101, de Robeck to Curzon, Constantinople, 9 March 1920.
20. Curzon to Webb, Foreign Office, 5 May 1920, BDFP 13, p. 68.
21. FO 371/5050, de Robeck to Curzon, 17 June 1920. The high commissioners stated that either the treaty terms would have to be relaxed or would have to be implemented by force, with additional forces dispatched immediately. The Ottoman Government might sign the treaty, they said, but there was a question of whom that government actually represented.
22. It is often falsely stated that Damat Ferid signed the treaty, but the official treaty document listed as Ottoman signatories only Hadi Paşa, Riza Tevfik and Reşad Halis.
23. CAB 29/31, British Secretary's Notes of Meetings of the Supreme Council, San Remo, 20 April 1920. See also CAB 29/32, 'Protection of Minorities in Turkey', Paris, 11 April 1920.
24. CAB 24/103/35, Colonel Ractivan (representing the Greek Government), 'Supplementary Note on the Execution of the Treaty of Peace with Turkey' and 'Note Regarding the Peace with Turkey', Paris, 19 and 27 March 1920.
25. CAB 29/31 and CAB 24/103/35, Paris Allied Military Committee (Foch) to Lloyd George, President of the Peace Conference, and enclosures, Paris, 30 March 1920.

26. FO 371/5132, Army Council to Under-Secretary of State, War Office, 14 February 1920, and enclosure: G. O. C., Constantinople (Milne); Fitzmaurice to Commander in Chief, Mediterranean Station, Smyrna, 22 January 1920. G. O. C. in C., Constantinople to War Office, 29 February 1920. FO 371/5132, War Office to Milne, 3 March 1920. FO 371/5132, Venizelos to Curzon, London, 25 February 1920. Even Curzon felt at the time that the Greeks should not be allowed to advance, although he left the decision to Milne. (FO 371/5132, Foreign Office to Secretary of the Army Council, 24 February 1920.) Prime Minister Venizelos had offered on 8 March to attack Mustafa Kemal's forces in cooperation with the British. (FO 371/5132, Kerr Interview of Venizelos, London, 9 March 1920.)
27. CAB 23/22/16, Cabinet Meeting of 12 October 1920; FO 800/157, Venizelos telegram to Lloyd George, Athens, 5 October 1920. A similar but less extensive plan had been presented by Greece earlier. (CAB 24/103/35, 'Note regarding the Treaty of Peace with Turkey: Collaboration of Greece', enclosure in Letter from Marshal Foch to Lloyd George, Paris, 30 March 1920.)
28. WO 32/5772, General Staff, 'Aide Memoire: General Staff Protests against Greek Territorial Claims in Turkey', War Office, 22 November 1920. The General Staff questioned Venizelos' statistics, noting, for example, that the majority of the population of the Adrianople vilayet was Turkish. Admiral Webb had earlier warned of the trouble that would ensue if the Greeks were used to enforce the treaty. (FO 406/43, Webb to Curzon, Constantinople, 23 April 1920.)
29. CAB 29/33, General Staff, 'The Military Situation in Russia, Caucasia, Turkey and Greece, Brought Up to Date (19th January, 1921)', War Office, 19 January 1921.
30. FO 371/5053, de Robeck to Curzon, 29 July 1920; FO 371/5053, Curzon to de Robeck, Foreign Office, 30 July 1920.

# 15

# AT WAR WITH THE TURKS

The invasion of İzmir and the Allied occupation of Istanbul were catalysts that drove the Turks to resistance. Immediately after the armistice, Turks had done little to oppose the Allies. Allied 'control officers' moved through Northern and Western Anatolia gathering weapons and asserting Allied authority. Allied 'relief officers' seized houses that had been occupied by Turkish refugees from the Balkans and gave them to Greek refugees returning to Anatolia. Allied officers in many, although not all, regions remarked on the cooperation shown them by local officials. With the İzmir occupation, all that changed. The mass of the Turks saw that the Allies, the sponsors of the Greeks, were the enemy. Those who still wished to cooperate with the Allies found it impossible, even dangerous, to defy the populace.

The Turkish Nationalist forces under Mustafa Kemal organised their forces politically and militarily. Mustafa Kemal managed to bring together, under the aegis of the Ankara Grand National Assembly, a disparate group of Ottoman politicians who had fled Istanbul, army officers, local armed bands who had opposed the Greeks and Armenians, and religious leaders.

The Ottoman army in Syria, though defeated, had retired intact, led by Mustafa Kemal Paşa. The army in the Northeast had retreated to the 1914 borders, also intact. Both had suffered desertions, but many of the deserters returned to the Nationalist colours. The Nationalists began military organisation and trained new recruits. What had begun as a political movement now was an army.[1]

The Nationalist army was not ill-equipped. Under the terms of the Mudros Armistice, the Allies were to collect the weapons of demobilised Ottoman army units. They had begun to do so in Western Anatolia and Thrace, but had not yet been able to seize the military supplies in other parts of Anatolia when the İzmir invasion halted Turkish cooperation. And the sequestered weapons in regions of Allied control began to disappear, sent secretly to the Nationalists by sympathisers in the Istanbul Government and army. When the Nationalists raided an arms dump at Gallipoli, 80,000 rifles were taken.

The Turkish Nationalists and the Soviet Russians shared a common desire to act against British imperialism. The Soviets also hoped that revolutionary Turkey would at least be friendly to Communism. Any hope of turning the Turks into Communists was unlikely, but the Soviets were satisfied with the actions undertaken to defeat English power at their doorstep. The Soviets and the Nationalists signed a Turkish–Soviet Treaty of Friendship on 16 March 1921. The Soviets sent military supplies to the Nationalists, at first smuggled across the Black Sea, then, when the Caucasus border was secured, also by land. Finances remained a problem for the Nationalists, cut off from many traditional forms of taxation and customs duties. The Soviets did much to alleviate the problem by delivering 10 million gold rubles to the Nationalists by 1922.[2]

## The Failures of British Intelligence

Obviously, the British could have had little information on Ottoman Anatolia or Thrace when the Allies began their occupation in 1918–19. Remarkably, the voluminous documentation of the British High Commission in Istanbul and the cabinet shows few references to the pre-war Foreign Office records. It is likely that no one took on the task of sifting through thousands of pages of documents. Had they done so, the British officials would have found many detailed descriptions of the environment they had decided to rule – yearly reports of trade, life, local government, ethnic relations, etc. – but they seem not to have been concerned enough to search the archives.

The British had some good, but limited sources of Intelligence. The best of these were intercepts of telegraph traffic. British spies read the diplomatic and other telegrams of not only the Nationalists, but their own Allies. These intercepts were often cited in British diplomatic documents. The British also had spies, never all identified, in Nationalist circles. The spies' reports were sometimes accurate, sometimes not. They related, for example, the refusal of the Nationalist leaders to cooperate with the sultan, whom they despised, and gave accurate summaries of the debates in the Ankara Assembly. They also, however, invented political events in Ankara that had not occurred. For example, the spies reported that Nationalist morale had been broken and Mustafa Kemal only wanted to negotiate with the Istanbul Government. Separating the accurate from the many false reports would have been difficult.[3]

For their main military and civilian Intelligence, the British relied on military officers, usually junior officers, sent to the provinces. Some few were dedicated Intelligence officers. Some were 'control officers' whose main duty was supervising demobilisation of the Ottoman army and seizing of military stores, as prescribed by the armistice terms. Other British officials were not specified by the armistice terms, but were sent to the provinces by the British without armistice authority. These were 'relief officers' (sometimes called 'repatriation officers'), operating under the aegis of the Armenian–Greek Section of the British High Commission in Istanbul, a committee which included British, Greek and Armenian members. Their duty was to oversee the return of Christians who had left or been deported, and to order the return of Christian property. They sent in reports on what they believed were local political and military conditions, based on what they heard from local Christians and greatly affected by their own preconceptions. (Only a few examples can be given here, but they are representative of what was to be found in the reports.)

The information that was the basis of the reports of the relief officers was seldom given. When it was, it was questionable. For example, in a report on the state of the town of Vezirköprü:

> The following information concerning Vizir Keupru and the conditions there is collated from that obtained from three sources: one, from two Syrian Catholics (one previously Dragoman (translator) at the Italian Consulate at Damascus) who were interned there; two, from five Greeks who left Vizir Keupru on March 24 last; and three, from three Armenians who returned to that town.[4]

The relief officer reporting this, Leonard Henry Hurst, had been an 'assistant' in the Istanbul embassy before the war.

A report from an Intelligence officer in Adana demonstrated the type of sources that formed the bases of Intelligence reports. The report was 'obtained from a reliable agent (Armenian)'. According to the reliable agent, Indian soldiers were deserting the British army and joining the Nationalists. Enver Paşa had organised troops in Azerbaijan, which, it was expected, would soon come to Anatolia to join the Nationalists. A secret pro-British society had been founded, with members given cards which would identify them to the British. Turks had been sent to India to organise rebellion there. 'Many hundreds' of Bolsheviks had joined Mustafa Kemal's forces, including Russian officers. No reflection seems to have been given to the question of how an Armenian in Adana could have known such ridiculous things.[5]

The British officers' opinion of the Turkish populace was none too good. General Staff Intelligence in Istanbul reported that the Turk was a 'slow mover with no initiative'. He did not realise that he had been defeated, and was worried that the Christians were plotting against him. He feared the Christians, 'whom he knows can outwit him'. One British relief officer described the members of the Nationalist forces as 'the riff-raff of the country'. The inclination to think the worst of the Turks coloured the Intelligence reports and made dubious sources believable. For example:

> A Jew mentioned during the course of conversation that he heard some Moslems state that in case of trouble they proposed bringing out the 'Green Flag of the Prophet.' This according to my knowledge of the Turk means 'massacre of the Christians.'[6]

British Army Intelligence in Istanbul forwarded a 'Report on the Situation in Anatolia (from a trustworthy Turkish source)' on 23 February 1920, in which it stated that Mustafa Kemal was controlled by the CUP, who in turn were controlled by Talat and Cemal Paşas from Zurich. (Neither was, in fact, located in Zurich.) However, the report stated, so many officers of the regular army did not support the Nationalists that firm Ottoman ministers could easily defeat all the Nationalist plans. The source should not have inspired confidence: it stated that Mustafa Kemal was from Polatlı, a Kurdish area in Central Anatolia, and so the Kurds liked him. Mustafa Kemal was actually from Salonica, so it is doubtful if the Polatlı residents would have claimed him as a neighbour.[7]

The British high commissioners often doubted the reports they were receiving from the interior, but they themselves might rely on questionable Intelligence. Admiral Webb sent to the War Office a description of fighting near Bursa, based on what he called 'impartial sources, neither Turkish nor Greek'. The source (there was only one) was actually a newspaper article. Admiral Calthorpe complained to the Ottoman authorities of the unsatisfactory situation in Kayseri. He told the Ottoman Minister of Foreign Affairs he had received the information from 'very reliable sources'. In fact, as he noted in a letter to Lord Curzon, his source was one Armenian gentleman.[8]

Some of the Intelligence reports can only have derived from arrogance, or perhaps wishful thinking. According to the officers, one thing that united the Greeks and Turks of Anatolia was that they both wanted British control. If British officers were to be believed, all the Turks of Anatolia wished for was that the British would take charge. In Ankara, 'many of the more enlightened Turks' desired it. One officer, returning from İzmit, found the Turks to be 'child-like and credulous' people who were being misled by Mustafa Kemal. Given the chance, they would welcome British control. Relief officer J. S. Perring reported from Adapazarı in June 1919 that all the Turks he met had asked for 'British protection and guidance'. The Turks told him that 'a national vote would be unanimously in favor of Great Britain'. Even Greeks who had been refugees from Anatolia supposedly preferred British control, rather than Greek.[9]

None of the officers seems to have considered that the Turks with whom they spoke might have been telling their conquerors what they wanted to hear.

*Lack of Support for the Nationalists*

Anyone relying on the officers' 1919 reports would have thought that the Nationalists would be no problem for the British or the Greeks. It would not be an exaggeration to say that in 1919, the Intelligence on the Turkish National Movement was usually wrong. The will of the Turks to oppose the Allies and to resist the Greeks, Armenians and French occupiers in Anatolia was discounted. The increasing authority of Mustafa Kemal was denied. Coupled with the British disdain for the defeated Turks, the Intelligence received by the British led them to vastly overestimate their own power in Anatolia and underestimate the power of the Turkish Nationalists.

It is understandable that the British Government underestimated the power and influence of the Nationalist Movement, given the Intelligence reports they received. One example: on 20 October 1919, British Military Intelligence in Istanbul circularised the control officers on the situation in Anatolia. They reported:

> The Nationalist Movement has probably reached the zenith of its popularity, and it is generally thought that – unless the Movement receives some new impetus – it will lose its present influence. This would account for the fact that recently, in most quarters, the nationalists have been carrying on a strong Pan-Islamic propaganda, with a view not only to gaining further influence, but also to retaining what support they already possess.
>
> The progress of the Movement is really fictitious, inasmuch as at the present tine there is no national unison in support of its ideas. The Movement has progressed only in the sense that it has gained isolated support from the efforts of certain military and civil officials in the chief centres of Anatolia and Eastern Thrace.[10]

Further reports continued to assert that the Nationalists had no real support from the peasantry, that they only enrolled with the Nationalists when forced or occasionally influenced by religious propaganda. Turks in the interior were indifferent to the fate of Smyrna. It was the officer class, not the people, who supported the Nationalists. The Turkish people would never make sacrifices for the Nationalist cause.[11]

Reports presented a bleak picture for the Nationalists: Mustafa Kemal reportedly had few followers, and his movement would soon fizzle out. The reason for this was inertia; the Turks were tired of war and would not listen to Mustafa Kemal's call to fight. The Nationalists 'had failed to touch the mass of the people, who sat docile, praying for peace and security'. The Nationalist Movement 'did not meet with much favor among the Turks'. 'Opinions from all quarters agree that the people are not willing to make any great sacrifices for the Nationalist cause.' Army Intelligence in Istanbul summarised the information they had received:

In carrying out preparations for armed resistance against the terms of peace, the Nationalist leaders, who attempt to control affairs in Anatolia and in Thrace, have little expectation that actual resistance on a wide scale will be found either possible or necessary.[12]

It is no wonder, with Intelligence as this, that the British underestimated the Turkish dedication to the Nationalist cause.

*Enver Paşa and the Committee of Union and Progress*

The British were obsessed with Enver Paşa, the former Ottoman War Minister. Even though Enver had fled the Ottoman Empire and had virtually nothing to do with the Turkish Nationalist Movement, they long remained fixed on the idea that he was in control of it, or at least that he would soon return to Anatolia to take charge of the movement. At first, the British were confused about control of the Ottoman Government. In November 1918, the British first reported that Enver, Talat and Cemal were in Istanbul, organising resistance to the Allies, then that they had escaped, then that the three had returned to the city, once again organising resistance. Later, when they realised that Enver, Talat and Cemal had in fact left Istanbul and not returned, the British decided that the three had left behind an organisation of resistance that they still controlled. The Committee of Union and Progress (CUP), a remnant of the Ottoman wartime government, was believed either to be in control of the Nationalist Movement or to be about to seize control.[13]

In February 1919, the Intelligence Department of the Naval Staff provided the government with brief summaries of politics and events of countries of the world. Their information on the Ottoman Empire seems to have been based wholly on hearsay from unnamed sources. For example, the Intelligence summaries firmly stated again and again that the Committee of Union and Progress were in charge in the Ottoman Empire, even after the armistice and the departure of Enver, Cemal and Talat. The Ottoman Cabinet was reportedly controlled by puppets of the CUP. Talat Paşa was in control behind the scenes. All sorts of CUP conspiracies were taking place in Istanbul and throughout the Empire.[14]

Enver Paşa remained a dominant factor in many reports in 1919: when Mustafa Kemal convened his Erzurum Conference, it was reported that Enver was actually calling the shots from Nahçıvan. He would soon (October 1919) arrive to take charge. Enver would be leading an army, either from Azerbaijan or Iran, either to assist or to take over the Nationalist Movement. British Intelligence was never sure whether Enver Paşa was cooperating with Mustafa Kemal or was an enemy of Kemal who planned to seize control of the Nationalist forces. Enver was either in constant communication with Mustafa Kemal, supporting Kemal's movement or was planning to usurp Kemal's position. Or perhaps, as the Foreign Office's Eastern Department reported, the old CUP leaders would join the Nationalist government and 'Mustapha Kemal and Enver, despite personal differences, would bury the hatchet.'[15]

British Intelligence felt that the CUP was cooperating with another perceived menace – Bolshevism. Dismayed by the success of the Bolsheviks in Russia, many British officials in Istanbul began to see the Turkish Nationalists as allies in an international Communist conspiracy. In February 1920, G. H. Q. in Constantinople forwarded a report to London from 'a trustworthy Turkish agent in high position'. Among reports on ammunition available, troop strength, etc., he reported that Nationalist officers planned to join the Bolsheviks if the peace terms were harsh. In February 1920, another 'secret source' reported that the Nationalist leaders in Ankara had decided to embrace Bolshevism. A proclamation asking all Muslims to adopt Bolshevism was to be promulgated. Even more moderate assessments stated that Bolshevik influence over the Nationalists was growing ever stronger.[16]

A 'Political Report, Asia Minor, from our Representative (in Istanbul)' from the Intelligence and research branch of the Foreign Office, the Political Intelligence Division, was read by the British Government. The source was 'a well-educated and intelligent Turkish gentleman'. According to the report, once they had lost the war, the Committee of Union and Progress had decided to spread Bolshevism as the vehicle for their return to power. Aided by the Soviets, the CUP Communists were taking over the Grand National Assembly. Mustafa Kemal would not be able to resist them. The Bolshevik/CUP supporters planned to depose the sultan/caliph and replace him in the caliphate with the Emir of Afghanistan, who would do their bidding. The report was forwarded to British officials in India and the Middle East. According to initials and comments on the cover sheet, it was read by top officials of the Foreign Office – Curzon, Eyre Crowe (Permanent Under-Secretary of State) and William George Tyrrell (Assistant Under-Secretary).[17]

The reports were uniformly wrong. Enver had no army and no authority in the Nationalist Movement. Although Enver surely wanted a place in the Nationalist organisation, Mustafa Kemal made sure he did not have one. He was never a part of the Nationalist revolution in Anatolia and Thrace. Although a minority of members of the Grand National Assembly may have supported Enver and the dominance of the old CUP, on 12 March 1921 the Assembly as a whole passed a law prohibiting Enver from entering Anatolia. CUP members undoubtedly provided considerable backing for the Nationalist Movement, especially on the local level. Mustafa Kemal and the Nationalists depended on the old CUP organisation, but broke completely with its old leaders. Those CUP leaders (not Talat, Enver or Cemal) who did attempt to take power in the movement were effectively suppressed by Mustafa Kemal. 'Bolshevism' never took over the Turkish struggle.[18]

*Intelligence on Eastern Anatolia and Cilicia*

The British had few British sources of Intelligence on Eastern Anatolia. What they believed was usually drawn from Armenian and missionary sources and from the dubious reports of sources in Istanbul that knew as little as did the British. General Milne, the British military commander in 1919, for example, wrote to London that the Turks were on the defensive against the Armenians; Turks could not take the offensive. The sources believed that Kâzim Karabekir, commander of the eastern Turkish forces, was willing to concede territory to the Armenians. All Karabekir wanted, a 'secret source' reported, was to avoid trouble with the Armenians. This proved not to be the case. Karabekir was in fact organising his forces to resist the Armenians and reclaim lost Ottoman territory.[19]

There were a small number of accurate reports from the East. The best of these were not what the British Government wanted to hear, and were thus ignored. A good example are the reports of Lt. Col. Alfred Rawlinson from Northeastern Anatolia. Rawlinson reported the oppression of the Muslim population by the Armenian Republic army and armed Armenian civilians and bands. He listed numerous murders of Turks and Kurds and destruction of Muslim villages: 'Armenian troops are not under control. Looting and worse crimes are general.' The Armenians were opposed by Kurdish tribes, in effect controlling the mountains, while Armenians controlled the plains. Rawlinson described it as a state of war, and blamed it on the Armenians. He sent a note to the Armenian commander to that effect. Armenians opposed his presence and even attacked him and the British soldiers who protected him.[20]

Rawlinson ceased to send in reports when he was detained by the Nationalists in March 1920. After that, no British officials witnessed events in the region themselves. By 1920 the amount of Intelligence from the East, never good, had significantly decreased. What little that was sent by 'agents' was described by the British as complex and inconsistent. Agent reports alleged amalgamation of the forces of Azerbaijan and the Turkish Nationalists and agreement among the Soviets, Georgia and Armenia to divide up Azerbaijan territories. The reports came from outside Eastern Anatolia, usually Tiflis (Tbilisi) in Georgia, and were uniformly untrue.[21]

In the face of a hopeless situation in Northeastern Anatolia, one in which they were powerless to intervene, the British might have found some comfort in reports from Istanbul that the Turkish Nationalist forces in the East were opposed to Mustafa Kemal. Kazim Karabekir, the Nationalist leader in the East, reportedly was at odds with Kemal because Karabekir favoured the Bolsheviks. An Intelligence report from Istanbul on 29 July 1920 stated 'on the authority of the Greek High Commissioner' that Karabekir was moving 12,000 troops west to fight Kemal. Karabekir was actually remaining in the East, preparing to begin his attack on the Armenians on 28 September.[22]

As in Eastern Anatolia, the British had few real Intelligence resources in Cilicia. Once the French occupied Cilicia, the British were dependent on reports from their allies, the French. Reports on Cilicia from actual British officials originated at some distance, from Beirut. The French Government naturally spoke of French success against the Turks. They provided little real information, especially when they were being defeated by the Nationalists. British army headquarters in Istanbul complained: 'French have given me no information as to real military position at Marash which they are shrouding in a veil of secrecy.' But when the French finally admitted they were in trouble in Cilicia, they were not believed. General Gourad reported to the British, quite accurately, that Nationalist forces were concentrating against them in Cilicia. The French reports were discounted by the British as only attempts to gain British support.[23]

Good Intelligence scarce, the British were forced to rely on missionary reports, secondary sources from Paris (French parliamentary committees, newspaper accounts, etc.) and on reports sent to the British by local Greeks and Armenians, as well as from Greek and Armenian political groups in London and America. These were particularly influential in forming British opinion for areas, such as Cilicia and Eastern Anatolia, in which the British had few of their own sources.

The result of the lack of Intelligence on Cilicia, and on the French intentions there, was that the British were surprised and dismayed when the French came to terms with the Turks (see Chapter 17).

*Changes in 1920*

In 1920, many of the sources of British Intelligence disappeared. As the Turkish Nationalists organised, Turks no longer followed Allied orders to demobilise army units or turn in their weapons. Anatolia was no longer a safe place for control officers. After the Greek invasion of İzmir and the Allied occupation of Istanbul, the Turks refused to cooperate with relief officers. The relief officers reported that the İzmir invasion meant that their mission to restore property to Greeks had become impossible. Unless the agents were in regions controlled by the Allies or the Greeks, Intelligence from control and relief officers ceased. In addition, the Nationalists rounded up many of the Turks who, friends to the British or loyal to the Istanbul Government, had been sources of information. Feeling the need to concentrate their limited forces in the Istanbul region, the British withdrew the forces that had occupied Batum and Samsun, curtailing information from the Black Sea region. Information, bad as it had been, became scarce.[24]

As the flow of what had been bad information ceased, some in the British power structure began to reevaluate the Turkish Nationalists. By March 1920, the General Staff in London had developed a very different picture of the Nationalists, admitting they were in effective control of Anatolia. The Nationalists had demonstrably become stronger and were firmly under Mustafa Kemal's command. The General Staff believed that, if the Nationalists were to be defeated, it would take large, fully equipped armies, not 'control officers'. It was becoming evident to anyone not blinded by prejudice that the tales of Turkish weakness, lethargy and lack of commitment to the national cause were false. Unfortunately for the British, Lloyd George and other ministers were full of prejudice that discounted Turkish abilities. A conflict between the General Staff assessments and the prime minister's beliefs developed. It was to continue until the end of the British intervention in the Ottoman Empire.[25]

In 1919, the Intelligence appraisals of the Turkish Nationalists were the reports that were seen by Curzon, Lloyd George, the Foreign Office and the British delegation at the Peace Conference. In the early days of Mustafa Kemal's revolt, the British consistently downplayed the strength of the national movement. Coupled with unjustified belief in the declarations of Venizelos, British Intelligence played its part in the great British misunderstanding of Turkish Nationalist power and capabilities. British Intelligence had failed badly. Nevertheless, the Intelligence reports had great effect, and not only in 1919; Lloyd George was to continue to rely on and promulgate the false image of Turkish power generated in 1919 until his final defeat in 1922.

**Too Few Troops**

The fate of Turkey was decided militarily. If British plans were to succeed, Mustafa Kemal's army had to be defeated. It took some time before the British Government appreciated this. From the Mudros Armistice until the Treaty of Sèvres, British political leaders had what can only be described as blind faith that the Turks would simply surrender to Allied plans. No military force need be applied. The Turks would realise that they had been beaten and would accept whatever fate the Allies intended for them. As the Turks organised to resist the British plans and the Nationalist army grew ever stronger, that proved not to be true.

Throughout the duration of their conflict with the Turks, the British were unable or unwilling to provide the military force that their military advisors felt was necessary. Driven by financial considerations and the political difficulties of retaining a large force after the end of the war, the British had greatly reduced their army. By the end of 1919, the 3.8 million-strong force at the end of World War I had been decreased to less than 900,000. The numbers were to fall to just over 230,000 by 1922. Demobilisation radically reduced the British military position in the Ottoman Empire. In 1919, the

22nd and 26th Divisions at Salonica were demobilised, and the 27th Division was withdrawn from the Caucasus and demobilised. The French 122nd Division was also withdrawn. A further reduction in the British Army of the Black Sea was affected on 29 September 1920, just as local military commanders were pleading for more men.[26]

Any attempts at using Ottoman Government troops against the Nationalists was a failure. When sent to oppose the Nationalists in the İzmit region, Ottoman troops refused to fight and often deserted to the Nationalists. After that, the British refused to allow the Ottomans to even organise army units. The War Council in London realised that any soldiers, weapons or ammunition allowed to Ottoman troops would quickly be passed over to the Nationalists. 'The greatest optimism cannot suggest that Turkish forces of any description can be relied on to participate in the enforcement of these (treaty) terms.'[27]

The General Staff noted in April 1919 that British troops were insufficient to enforce a peace treaty, and that all troops should be taken from outlying areas and concentrated in areas 'vital to the British Empire'. The General Staff noted that plans being suggested by the Allies included, among others, creation of a Greater Armenia and Greek occupation in Western Anatolia and Thrace. These plans would demand significant Allied forces. The General Staff recommended that '[o]nly such terms will be seriously considered by His Majesty's Government, in the first place, as may be reasonably compatible with the resources which exist or which it may be intended to provide for their execution'. Churchill, then Secretary of State for War, told the cabinet in August of 1919 that he wanted all British troops to be withdrawn from Turkey (not including Iraq). His reason was the great cost of keeping the troops there.[28]

In 1920 the Allied high commissioners each wrote to their governments questioning whether the Allies had enough troops to control Istanbul, much less to enforce the peace treaty. Significant navy and army reinforcements were needed. The only good alternative, they felt, was to lessen the strictures of the Sèvres Treaty.[29]

The problem of the military situation became obvious in February 1920, when the British military felt it necessary to leave their forward positions in Anatolia and concentrate on Istanbul. Admiral Richard Webb, the Acting

British High Commissioner, sent many reports to London declaring that the British plans would never succeed in Anatolia and Thrace, nor would they be able to enforce a 'drastic peace', unless they were willing to send sufficient numbers of troops. Using the Greek army for that purpose, he believed, would lead to disaster and much bloodshed.[30]

As seen above, the British General Staff's detailed analysis of the availability of troops in the Middle East, England and Ireland, and the rest of the British Empire concluded that there were none available to reinforce the British commitment in the Ottoman Empire: General Milne, in command of Allied forces in October 1920, wrote that the forces at his disposal were only sufficient to control Istanbul, not further into the country. If peace terms were harsh (as they would be), he would need a much greater force. When the plans for the Turkish peace were proposed, the three Allied high commissioners in Istanbul wrote to the Supreme Council at the Peace Conference that the plans suggested for Turkey were 'neither opportune nor effective'. The Allies would be able to impose their will on Turkey, they stated, only if significant armed forces were sent. In its response to the commissioners' note, the Supreme Council did not mention the problems noted by the commissioners, nor did they mention financial support or reinforcements. They seem to have assumed there would be no problems, despite the judgement of those actually in Istanbul.[31]

In one way, Curzon had shown himself in 1919 to be somewhat prescient:

> Lord Curzon said that on the assumption that something like the present proposals for peace terms with Turkey were accepted by the other Allies, he hoped that the military difficulties of imposing them on Turkey would not be ignored. It would be disastrous to dictate a peace which the Allies had not the military strength to enforce.[32]

## Expert Advice Ignored

The British and their Allies could not say that the advice of their military advisors had misled them. In April 1920, when the Allies considered what was needed to enforce the Turkish Treaty, Marshall Foch reported to the Supreme Council that his advisors had calculated that twenty-seven divisions (405,000 men) were necessary. Venizelos reported that Greece had ten divisions on a war footing and four on a peace footing that could easily be brought to a war footing. Foch believed that this was adequate to defend the İzmir enclave, but not nearly enough to extend into interior Anatolia and enforce the treaty provisions. Extensive use of Greek forces, it was stated, would incense Turkish feelings and greatly increase the difficulties of the plan. 'In the present circumstances, neither France, Great Britain, nor Italy can be asked to provide these reinforcements.' The best that could be hoped for would be holding what was already occupied. In addition, no troops could be sent to Armenia.

The British General Staff were in complete agreement with Marshal Foch's analysis of the situation. They agreed that many divisions would be needed and that depending solely on the Greeks was a questionable policy. In any case, they insisted that Greek forces must be under Allied commanders. The Allies would never provide twenty-seven divisions, but Lloyd George and Curzon, ever optimistic, thought that a much smaller force could seize ports and strategic points: 'Turkey should be strangled at her Capital and at her ports on the sea-coast.' (This strategy had been first suggested by Venizelos in October of 1918.) Armenia could defend herself without Allied soldiers. The United States, Lloyd George hopefully believed, would provide 10,000 men.[33]

The British Government proved to be more willing to believe the military assessments of Greeks and Armenians than those of their own military men. Avetis Aharonian, representing the Armenian Republic at the Peace Conference, stated that Turkish soldiers were 'greatly inferior', badly equipped, badly trained, etc. Armenians could easily hold their territory, including a large section of Eastern Anatolia, against them if they were provided with ammunition and equipment. No Allied soldiers were needed. The other Armenian representative, Boghos Nubar, agreed, saying that there were more Armenian than Turkish soldiers. Commenting on the Armenian assertions, Marshall Foch, president of the Inter-Allied Military Committee, painted a much bleaker picture. He and the other Allied military advisors completely disagreed with the Armenians; they believed the Armenians could not hold out against the Turks. (It turned out the military advisors were correct.)[34]

The British answer to Allied military weakness in Western Anatolia was to depend on the Greeks to enforce the terms of the Sèvres Treaty, a decision taken despite the misgivings of the military and the high commissioners, who felt that the solution was to lessen the strictures of the treaty, not to employ the Greek army.

Despite earlier misgivings, High Commissioner de Robeck at first thought that using the Greeks had turned out better than he had expected. His sentiments, on 22 October 1920, were probably coloured by Greek reports that all was going well. Less than one month later, he had altered his opinion. He believed that by November of 1920 the situation had become so bad that the British faced disaster. The Armenians had been defeated and the Soviet victory in Russia insured that the Caucasus was lost. The Nationalists would not be disposed to accept the Treaty of Sèvres, even with amendments. The Allied forces had been so weakened by reductions that they could do nothing in Anatolia and perhaps could not even control the local situation in the Istanbul region. They would have to rely on the Greeks, but Greek forces would be insufficient unless strengthened by significant Allied reinforcements. Otherwise, the Ottoman Government would never ratify the treaty. The Foreign Office responded that de Robeck should threaten even worse treatment for Turks than in the treaty if they delayed in ratifying. They said nothing about his request for increased forces.[35]

By 1921, when Turkish forces had proved to be more of a threat to Allied plans than the British Cabinet had anticipated, the military experts were again pessimistic. Generals Henri Gourad and Colonel Alphonse Georges, giving the Allied High Command opinion, stated that the Turks were sufficiently armed, including artillery, to resist the Greeks. 'He (Georges) could not say that a successful operation against Angora was impossible, but he did say that such an operation with the existing Greek resources was one of a hazardous character.' Greek representatives at the council meeting, on the other hand, asserted that the Turkish Nationalists would be easily defeated. They would soon take the Nationalist capital at Ankara. Lloyd George disagreed with the Allied experts. He said that his own experts were not capable of making an accurate assessment, but the Greeks were.[36]

Analyses by the British General Staff did not hesitate to place the blame for the situation on the politicians. Despite the signing of the Sèvres Treaty, the General Staff had not changed its views on the Turkish settlement. Indeed, the analysis they delivered to the cabinet on 16 February 1921, as the British were trying to salvage what they could of their quagmire in Anatolia, can only be described as 'I told you so':

> The General Staff have always been strongly opposed to the invasion of Anatolia by Greece and have considered this to be the greatest source of irritation to the Turks, who regard it, not without reason, as a dishonourable breech of the Armistice.

They had always said that 'there will be no satisfactory settlement of the Turkish question until Greek ambitions are curbed'. That judgement had not changed. Contrary to the plans of Curzon and the Foreign Office, the General Staff believed that the Turks should have a regular army under Turkish officers and control of their own state. The General Staff also believed the Wilson Award to Armenia was far too big (see Chapter 16). They doubted if the pre-war boundaries in Eastern Anatolia (that is, Kars and Ardahan) should be included in an Armenian state.[37]

The General Staff believed the only possible policy was 'to make gracious concessions to the Turks'. The British did not have sufficient force available to do anything else.[38]

Lloyd George doubted his military advisors at every turn. To him, the British generals wrongly minimised the fighting prowess of the Greeks and Armenians, and the generals, both British and French, had grossly overestimated Allied military needs. He had faith in the Greeks and Armenians and in his own wisdom. That faith was to him a more reliable guide than the evaluations of his generals.

**Attacking the Turkish Nationalists**

It was not only the desire to enforce the Sèvres Treaty that led the British to support Greek plans. They also feared that Istanbul could be taken by the Turks. At British Cabinet meetings on 17 and 18 June 1920, military advisors told them that Istanbul could not be held with the British force available if the Nationalist army attacked, and the French and Italians would not offer much help. The solution, the cabinet decided, was to support the Greeks in attacks to destroy Mustafa Kemal's forces. 'To retire from Constantinople before a bandit Mustapha Kemal would deal a shattering blow to our prestige in the East, and this could not possibly be contemplated.' Extension of Greek forces into Anatolia was authorised.[39]

British armed conflict with the Turks did not end with the Mudros Armistice. By summer of 1920, the British were once again at war with the Turks,

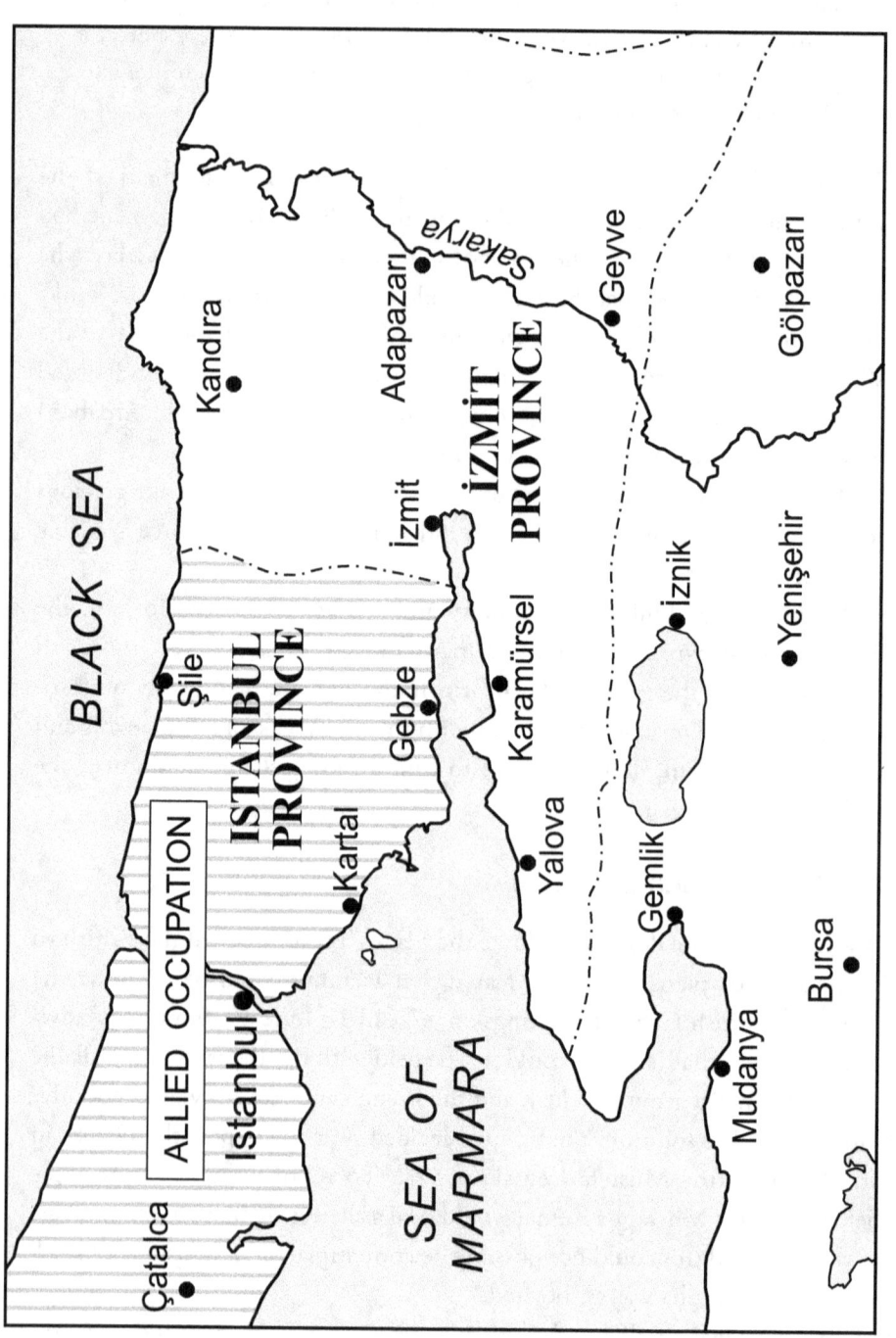

Map 15.1 The İzmit–Yalova region

this time against Mustafa Kemal's Turkish Nationalists. The British and, to a much lesser extent their French and Italian allies, had two goals – to enforce the terms of the Sèvres Treaty and to protect occupied Istanbul. The British in Istanbul feared that the Turks might advance to take the city. High Commissioner Admiral de Robeck wrote in the summer of 1920 that a largely increased army would be necessary to control even just Istanbul and the Straits.[40]

Nationalist forces had occupied Yalova and Karamursel, near İzmit, in May of 1920. In June, Nationalist infantry and artillery advanced into the İzmit Peninsula. Ottoman Government troops, whom the Allies had counted on to defend the road to Istanbul, proved to be totally inadequate. On 14 June 1920, the Ottoman troops in the İzmit Peninsula began to retreat toward Istanbul. They were attacked by Nationalist forces and driven to the British lines, which the British soldiers at first did not allow them to cross. They were finally allowed to retreat to İzmit City, where the British disarmed them and put them on ships to Istanbul.[41]

The Nationalist Turks began attacks and artillery bombardments on British positions near İzmit. Turkish units were manoeuvring to cut off the British from Istanbul. The Turks reportedly had greatly superior forces. Local British authorities and the War Office agreed that much larger forces were needed if the Turks were to be confronted. Because no reinforcements were to be sent, the War Office recommended British abandonment of the region.[42]

On 18 June 1920, the cabinet considered the situation in the İzmit Peninsula. General Milne had notified them that one new British division was needed to defend the peninsula. The General Staff agreed. However, Prime Minister Venizelos was in London at the time. He assured the cabinet that Greece could bring troops from İzmir and Western Thrace to defeat the Nationalists. The Chief of the General Staff felt this to be unwise. General Milne, commanding British troops in the region, had concurred. His views and those of the General Staff were ignored. The cabinet decided to accept Greek help, and Lloyd George explained the decision to the French at a meeting at Lympne (the Second Conference of Hythe, in Kent). The French were notified of the British decision, of which they had no part, but to which the French agreed. (It should be noted that Lloyd George explained British decisions to the Allies, not that the Allies affected the decision.)[43]

The Allies authorised the Greeks to send troops to the İzmit and Marmara regions. The Greeks were to be assisted by British naval forces. Seven dreadnought battleships, six destroyers, an aircraft carrier, a minesweeper and a number of smaller vessels were devoted to the task. All were British ships; Britain's allies, even though they had ships in the area, contributed nothing. Aiding the Greeks was a purely British enterprise. In the İzmit region that was being contested with Turkish forces, the British landed marines on 14 June. The battleships Ramillies and Revenge fired at Nationalist targets. Turkish troops were observed to be entering a drapery factory in İzmit; the British ships bombarded and destroyed the factory, with at least 100 estimated casualties. Other areas were similarly bombarded. Houses around the factory and near the shore were hit and burned down. Further naval artillery fire struck suspected Nationalist outposts. The Nationalists attacked İzmit in force over the week of 14 to 21 June, but they were frustrated by naval gunfire.[44]

On 22 June 1920, British landing parties destroyed seventy-six Turkish field guns at the Derince artillery depot, seven miles west of İzmit. Joint British and Greek forces undertook a reconnoitre of the region. On 24 June, the navy fired on enemy encampments near Karamürsel. Landing parties then raided Karamürsel, occupied the town and arrested officials. They sent out repeated landing parties and aerial reconnaissance, but the Nationalist troops had left. The British attacked Mudanya on 5 July with overwhelming force (two dreadnought battleships, two destroyers, an aircraft carrier, two lighters and a tug), landing parties of 834 officers and men. The Turks could only respond with sporadic fire from rifles and one machine gun. They nevertheless managed to repel British landing parties on the beach near Mudanya and, for a time, at the town itself. In the end, however, resistance was stilled by heavy fire from naval guns. Houses in the city were destroyed by the bombardments. Outside Mudanya, ships were 'bombarding the hillsides wherever any sign of movement was seen'. Turkish villages in which it was suspected Nationalist troops were billeted were destroyed. The Turks were forced to retreat, and Mudanya and Karamürsel were turned over to the Greeks on 10 July. Gemlik was taken (6 July) more easily than Mudanya; fire from two battleships had quelled Turkish resistance. The town was turned over to a Greek army battalion that marched in on 16 July.[45]

Admiral de Robeck (Commander of the Mediterranean Fleet, as well as high commissioner), despite his opposition to the plan to utilise the Greek army, was a military man who followed orders. He also personally feared that the Turkish Nationalist build-up of forces threatened the British position in Istanbul. He told the Admiralty that he felt that the attitude of Turks in the Marmara coastal towns was becoming 'more hostile'. He therefore acted 'by undertaking raids on these towns with a view to ensuring respect to the British flag and British officers'. (It should be noted that the British Intelligence reports included with de Robeck's report to the Admiralty indicated that the only Turkish offence in the region was drunkenness among some Turkish troops, who harassed, but did not harm, some Greeks.) He intended to go on and further shell at İzmit, but changed his mind when the Greek bishop came aboard and asked him not to do so, because Greeks and Greek property would suffer.[46]

> (De Robeck's) Instructions to Officers and Men Landing.
> Out of ten persons you will see, nine will probably be Greek and one Turk, in other words the great majority of the inhabitants are friends, a small portion only are hostile.
> The first object of the expedition is to arrest certain Civil and Military Authorities who have shown disrespect to our Service and openly defied Great Britain.
> Admiral de Robeck, 24 June 1920[47]

Judging by his other, more accurate comments on population, seen above, it is impossible to believe that de Robeck actually believed that 90 per cent of the population was Greek.

Admiral de Robeck and General Milne agreed with the Greek commander that the Greeks should advance to Bursa. De Robeck telegraphed the governor of Bursa, warning him if the Turks offered opposition: 'I shall not hesitate to bombard the town of Brussa with the heavy guns of the fleet, nor shall I hesitate to attack with aircraft.' The Greeks took Bursa on 8 July.[48]

The British in Istanbul reported: 'We are now in open hostilities with the Nationalists.' The British naval commander wrote: 'It is my intention to help them (the Greeks) wherever and however I can.' The Admiralty agreed. However, asked in parliament if the British were helping the Greeks, Lloyd

George lied and stated they were not doing so. Speaking for the government, Bonar Law told parliament that 'His Majesty's Government are only engaged in resisting attacks'.[49]

The British remained in charge of the İzmit region until the end of September, when they gave over control to a Greek army division, although nominally under the command of the British Commander-in-Chief. (The Greek army remained until June of 1921, when they left to join the general fight with the Nationalists. İzmit and the nearby Marmara region were then occupied by the Nationalists, up to the border of the Neutral Zone.)[50]

British assistance having allowed them to take Northwest Anatolia, the Greeks turned their attention to Eastern Thrace, which was under the effective control of Turkish Nationalists, except for strategic areas occupied by the French. The Greek Commander-in-Chief asked the British forces for assistance. De Robeck disapproved of the move: 'This proposal of Mr. Venizelos is, I think, most rash and ill advised. Thrace is at present perfectly quiet and Nationalists there are giving no trouble.' British Intelligence had reported that '[s]ince the Adrianople Vilayet has been under the control of the Nationalists, it is reported that there have been no disturbances of any kind'. De Robeck was overruled from London. British forces were ordered to 'render all aid possible' to the Greek invasion. A Greek force of 12,000 men and 6,000 animals was landed at Rodosto (Tekirdağ) and elsewhere, supported by three British battleships and four destroyers. British ships bombarded the shores wherever Turks showed signs of resistance to the conquest. The French continued only to occupy strategic positions, not interfering with the Greek conquest.[51]

The Greek army appreciated the British assistance:

> The Army under my orders and myself express our heartiest thanks for the previous aid and co-operation afforded with so much readiness and enthusiasm by the British Navy during the landing operations at Panderma. The Greeks will never forget this new mark of sympathy given by the sons of our great British Ally and our gratitude for her will remain eternally engraved in our hearts.
>
> (Signed) PARASKEVOLPOULOS (Greek Commander-in-Chief)[52]

The fact that it was only the British who supported the Greeks militarily was significant. Neither the French nor the Italians provided any military support.

By the summer of 1920, the British alone were carrying out the war against the Turks alongside the Greeks.[53]

On 23 June 1920, the Greeks began to extend their attack in Western Anatolia. Turkish cities fell to them rapidly: by 2 July they had taken Salihli, Alaşehir, Kula, Balıkesir, Edremit, Bandırma and Biga. They were not stopped until their loss to the Nationalist army at the First and Second Battles of İnönü on 9 January and 26 March 1921. It was a temporary setback; a major Greek offensive was to begin. On 2 August 1920, Venizelos had announced that the Greek army was about to 'enforce the orders given at (the Conference at) Spa' and advance to Afyon and Eskişehir. He said nothing would be done without the 'consentement et la co-opération du Gouvernment anglais'.[54]

It must be said that the British in Istanbul admitted that '[w]e possess no trustworthy information on the situation in Anatolia and Angora'. De Robeck recognised that the Allies would never send forces sufficient enough to enforce the peace terms. The Greeks might do it, but they 'would doubtless insist on excessive recompense'. His only suggestion was that the Ottoman Government be asked to send a commission to Anatolia to explain British terms to the Nationalists and convince them to comply. Curzon approved the plan. This was an indication of how little they understood the situation.[55]

**Turkish Refugees**

When Greek forces, aided by the British, advanced beyond the İzmir region, villages, towns and refugee camps in Western Anatolia and the Istanbul region were already full of refugees from the initial Greek invasion. Many of those refugees had first been forced from their homes in Europe in the Balkan Wars, then disposed a second time by the Greeks. Now they were forced to flee once again, along with Turks from the new Greek conquests. The number of Turkish refugees was immense, 1.2 million from Anatolia and 30,000 from Eastern Thrace. One-third of the Turkish refugees died of starvation and disease.[56]

General Harington visited some of the Turkish refugee camps in the Istanbul area:

> I have paid a visit to many of the Turkish refugee camps. Of the 65,000 refugees about 23,000 are in real distress. On my last visit I saw 7,000 composed of old men, almost beyond work, women and children. Their condition is

deplorable. One bowl of soup every second day and a bit of bread on alternate days is all that I saw are getting. Excellent work is being done by British Relief Committee, under Sir Adam Block, and they are deserving of every support. They are working up to one bowl every day. Their clothing is mere rags. Their state is worse than that of the Russians.[57]

There were also Greek and Armenian refugees who had fled from Nationalist-held territories; the Greek Government estimated 7,500 in İzmir, Bursa and İzmit.[58]

The British made no public acknowledgment of the Turkish refugees. Unlike Greek and Armenian refugees, they were never mentioned in notices to parliament or to the press.[59]

## Yalova, Gemlik, İzmit

The Greek occupation of the Eastern Marmara region had terrible consequences for its Turkish inhabitants. Ottoman representatives in London protested Greek attacks on Turkish civilians in the İzmit/Yalova area. Based on British accounts they had received, High Commissioner Rumbold and General Harington reported on 10 April 1921 that it was probable that Greek outrages had been committed at Yalova and elsewhere. Rumbold proposed that a commission of enquiry be sent. The Foreign Office agreed on 16 April. London thought that the reports had been exaggerated, which may be why the British agreed.[60]

Two commissions set out on 12 May, one to Yalova/Gemlik; one to the İzmit Peninsula.[61]

As its investigation continued, Colonel Farmar, the British head of the commission, sent reports by telegram to British headquarters in Istanbul. These demonstrated attacks by Greek regular soldiers, as well as by Greek bands of irregulars, often assisted by soldiers; 'ill-treatment', 'incendiarism', 'serious misbehaviour' and 'crimes' were all reported.

> General Franks (of the commission), in making an appeal yesterday for full liberty of action for Red Crescent to succour and remove Moslem population of Gemlek area, telegraphed that this Commission is convinced that Power in occupation (Greece) is proceeding upon system of destruction of Moslem element, Greek troops and brigands appearing to act on programme in complete accord.[62]

Farmar presented a preliminary report on 18 May 1921. In the report the commission provided evidence of attacks on Turkish civilians by Greek bands and soldiers:

> To report in general terms:—Credible evidence has been produced as to crimes committed by both Greek officers and soldiers during the last year, and more especially lately, when the troops have been on the march. This is set out in the attached schedule; a few examples in *précis* only.
>
> During the occupation by regular Greek troops there has been either entire or partial interruption of civilian police jurisdiction.
>
> Civilian control has not been replaced by any capable military organisation. Full advantage has been taken of this by all bad characters, probably including deserters from the Greek army.
>
> The commission is of opinion that the Greek military authorities did not take adequate steps to safeguard the civilian inhabitants from the depredations and acts of violence of outlaws, nor did they make adequate provision for the maintenance of discipline amongst their regular troops.
>
> Turkish officials appear to have done their best to carry out their duties, but have been much handicapped, and charges preferred by them against the Greek soldiers do not appear to have been investigated.
>
> There appear to be no complaints by Greek civilians of any trouble caused to them by Moslems during the last few months. The commission recommend that full advantage should be taken at once of existing Turkish machinery for the maintenance of order and that this should be expanded and made more powerful. European officers to be made available to give their assistance as far as this may be practicable.
>
> There is evidence that adjacent villages of different creeds exist side by side in the same districts without trouble when the Greeks are in a minority and the administration Turkish.
>
> It is certain that many people have been prevented from settling on the land owing to the disturbed conditions. Some Greeks have already left and others will try to get away if the Kemalist troops come forward, as there is often only a shadowy distinction between brigand bands and groups calling themselves Nationalist soldiers. The Greek civilians are in dread of being made to suffer in their turn and the Moslems are in very genuine fear of the return of the Greek troops.
>
> The countryside is sparsely populated and many villages are in a state of decay.

> The members of the commission are of opinion that the displaced population will speedily return when they are assured of protection, and emphasise their opinion that the forces of law and order should be made under Moslem administration.

The evidence attached to the commission précis was a list of a small number of the crimes against Turks that it had discovered during the course of its investigation; full evidence was sent in great detail in a separate volume of interviews. The commission noted that Greek soldiers and civilians had pillaged and burned Turkish villages, stealing all the villagers' flocks and murdering those Turks that could not escape. Lists were provided of destroyed Turkish houses and entire villages. Turkish women were raped all across the region, with some women taken away and raped multiple times. Extortion was common; often the only way Turks could survive was to pay the Greek soldiers, and the Turks were often murdered after they had paid. The commission noted widespread murders committed by Greek regular troops, stating: 'Everywhere the Greek soldiers behaved savagely.'[63]

Member of Parliament Aubrey Herbert asked in June of 1921 if the Yalova Report would be presented to parliament. Speaking for the government, Austen Chamberlain responded: 'His Majesty's Government are not convinced of the advisability of publishing this Report at present, but will consult the Governments who, with them, were represented on the Commission.'[64]

Three weeks later, after the reports of the Yalova Commission had been thoroughly edited, the evidence altered by omission and unsubstantiated claims of Turkish attacks on Greeks added, Lloyd George announced to parliament that he would release a commission report. He even quoted the first paragraph of the new 'report':

> There is no doubt that there have been a large number of atrocities in the Ismid Peninsula, and it appears that those on the part of the Turks have been more considerable and ferocious than those on the part of the Greeks.[65]

By the time the 'Report of the Ismid Commission of Enquiry' was published by the British, it had undergone a transformation:

> Credible evidence has been produced as to crimes committed during the last twelve months by both Greeks and Turks. There is no doubt that there have

been a large number of atrocities in the Ismid peninsula, and it appears that those on the part of the Turks have been more considerable and ferocious than those on the part of the Greeks.

The titles of the brief descriptions provided in the report are instructive in themselves: 'Excesses of Which the Greeks are *Accused*'; 'Excesses *Committed* by the Turks' (emphases added). Although Greek atrocities were considered, the report did not include most of the voluminous evidence against the Greeks gathered by the commission's own members – Allied military men. The evidence against the Turks, on the other hand, was taken from accusations provided by 'the Greek Authorities'. The Greek assertions were for the prior year, when the Allies and Greeks had been fighting the Nationalists in the region, and obviously could not be verified. The commission had originally asked that the region be put under Muslim administration; the new report asked for Allied administration.[66]

What was presented to parliament in no way represented what had actually been found by the commission.

The disaster in the İzmit region culminated with the Greek withdrawal from the İzmit region (27–8 June 1921). When asked in parliament about the Greek evacuation of the İzmit Peninsula, the government response was duplicitous:

> (Cecil Harmsworth, Undersecretary of State for Foreign Affairs) The situation in the Ismid Peninsula is obscure, but according to information received this morning the town of Ismid was evacuated by the Greek forces on the evening of 27th June. It is further reported that the town is in flames and that great panic prevails in the district. Numbers of Armenians and neutral Turks are fleeing towards Constantinople. Having regard to the general confusion, there appears to be considerable danger of massacres, and Mr. Rattigan, in concurrence with the Allied high commissioners, is taking all possible steps to prevent such outrages by one side or the other.[67]

In fact, the situation in İzmit was anything but obscure. British agents had for some time reported massacres of Turks and the flight of Turkish refugees in the region. War Office and Foreign Office officials in Istanbul reported that Greek soldiers and local Greeks and Armenians had conducted large-scale massacres of Turks before they left the city. According to British reports,

Greeks in İzmit had been notified by the Greek forces that they had two-and-a-half hours to evacuate the city. The Greeks then burned down İzmit and killed the Turkish populace. General Harington wrote of fierce massacres by Greeks at İzmit. Harmsworth had obviously seen the reports, because he knew the city was in flames, but he did not mention who had burned it, that most of those who fled were Turks or that the Greeks and Armenians had killed Turkish inhabitants.[68]

The massacres extended beyond İzmit as the Greeks retreated. British navy and army authorities reported that the Greek army was destroying everything in its path:

> Greeks behaved atrociously before leaving. Kemalist troops are well disciplined and have restored order in town. Greek troops are retiring westward along Southern coast of Gulf of Ismid burning and bombarding villages as they retire.[69]
>
> No evidence of any massacre of Christians (when Turkish Nationalist troops occupied İzmit). Officials of American hospital and French priests speak highly of Kemalist discipline and demeaner. Atrocities of appalling nature, including murder, torture, and mutilation, were verified by exhumation. Statements that these were committed by Christian, Armenian and Circassian brigands assisted by drunken and undisciplined Greek troops, whilst was in Greek military occupation, are supported by American evidence.[70]

This evidence was never presented to parliament or the public.[71]

## Notes

1. Edward J. Erickson, *Ordered to Die: A History of the Ottoman Army in the First World War*, Westport, CT: Greenwood, 2001, pp. 199–203. W. E. D. Allen and Paul Muratoff, *Caucasian Battlefields*, Cambridge: Cambridge University Press, 1953, p. 497. Turkey, Genelkurmay Başkanlığı, *Türk İstiklâl Harbi I, Mondros Mütarekesi ve Tatbikatı*, Ankara: Genelkurmay, 1999, pp. 71–7. Turkey, Genelkurmay Başkanlığı, *Türk İstiklâl Harbi II/2, Batı Cephesi*, Ankara: Genelkurmay, 1999, pp. 31–4.
2. Busch, pp. 201–2. Bülent Gökay, *A Clash of Empires: Turkey between Russian Bolshevism and British Imperialism, 1918–1923*, London and New York: I. B. Tauris, 1997, pp. 63–123. Although dated 16 March, the treaty was actually

signed some days later. There is disagreement on exactly how much finance was delivered, but Gökay believed 10 million was approximately correct (Gökay, pp. 110–11). Riza Nur reported to Kâzim Karabekir that 10 million was sent to Istanbul with 'a Communist named Hilmi' (Kâzım Karabekir, *İstiklâl Harbimiz*, Istanbul: Türkiye Yayınevi, 1960, p. 964). On the delivery of weapons by the Russians, see Karabekir, pp. 604–5, 799–800, 822 and 971. See also Tansel 4, pp. 65–6 and 140–3.

3. Robin Denniston, 'Diplomatic Intercepts in Peace and War: Chanak 1922', *Diplomacy and Statecraft*, vol. 11, no. 1 (March 2000), pp. 241–56. FO 406/49, Rumbold to Curzon, Constantinople, 7 March 1922. FO 371/5166, 'Weekly Summary of Intelligence Reports Issued by M. I. 1. C., Constantinople Branch, for the Week Ending 29th July, 1920'. Note: this 'weekly summary' is different than the weekly summaries issued in London. See Salâhi R. Sonyel, *Kurtuluş Savaşı Günlerinde İngiliz İstihbarat Servisi'nin Türkiye'deki Eylemleri*, Ankara: Türk Tarih Kurumu, 1995, which goes into great detail, A. L. Macfie, 'British Intelligence and the Turkish National Movement, 1919–22', *Middle Eastern Studies*, vol. 37, no. 1 (January 2001), pp. 1–16, and 'British Views of the Turkish National Movement in Anatolia, 1919–22', *Middle Eastern Studies*, vol. 38, no. 3 (July 2002), pp. 27–46. Macfie detailed many of the Intelligence reports, and some of his conclusions have been used here. His descriptions of the workings of Intelligence gathering are valuable. However, he often simply paraphrased the reports and seldom considered how wrong many of the reports were. For a general view on British Intelligence, see C. Andrew and J. Noakes, *Intelligence and International Relations, 1900–1945*, Exeter: Exeter University Press, 1987. Most of the actual Intelligence reports – that is, those from Intelligence professionals, not control or relief officers – have been destroyed or kept secret to this day. They are sometimes listed in the National Archives indexes, but do not exist in the files. Those few that exist do not inspire confidence. It can be assumed that they were used to compile the often laughable naval and foreign office weekly reports. For examples of existing reports, see FO 406/45 and FO 371/3404.

4. FO 608/113, 'Political – Greek and Armenian', Captain L. H. Hurst (relief officer at Samsun) to British High Commission, Samsoun, 4 April 1919.

5. FO 371/4159, 'Special Report No. 24 of the Intelligence Officer, Adana', 24 September 1919. The French had occupied Adana in December 1918, so the sources of such an Intelligence officer were not military.

6. WO 158/933, General Staff Intelligence, 'Notes on the Situation in Anatolia', Constantinople, 3 March 1919. FO 371/4157, General Staff Intelligence, 'Notes

on the Situation in Anatolia', Constantinople, 16 March 1919. FO 371/4161, Hadkinson to High Commissioner, Constantinople, 12 November 1919. FO 608/113, control officer in Uzun Keupru (no name given) to British High Commission, Uzun Keupru, 22 May 1919.

7. FO 106/1505. General Staff Intelligence, Army of the Black Sea, 23 February 1920. The secret source gave detailed but doubtful information of Turkish armaments.
8. ADM 137/1772, 'Extract from "Orient News" – 22 Jan. 1921', enclosure in Mediterranean Letter of 7 February 1921 (Webb). FO 608/113, Calthorpe to Curzon, Constantinople, 12 July 1919.
9. FO 371/4158, Perring to Calthorpe, Constantinople, 8 June 1919. FO 371/4159, Perring to Calthorpe, Samsoun, 17 and 23 August 1919. FO 371/4159, Webb to Curzon, Constantinople, 11 September 1919. FO 371/5042, W. Gordon Campbell, 'Memorandum on the Situation in Asia Minor', London, 17 February 1920. FO 608/113, Hole to Webb, Smyrna, 7 May 1919.
10. FO 371/5041, 'The Nationalist Movement in Turkey: Summary of Reports Received from Various Central Officers in the Interior, in Reply to a Questionnaire Issued by G. S. "I"', General Staff Intelligence, Constantinople, 6 January 1920. The report stated that Christians had been unharmed by the Nationalists.
11. FO 371/5041, General Staff Intelligence, Army of the Black Sea, Constantinople, 28 October 1919. The report included lists of those whom the authors identified as supporters or opponents of the Nationalists. One relief officer reported that, rather than support other Turks, the Turks in Thrace planned to overthrow the sultan's government and declare an independent state. (FO 371/4142, A. J. Wilson to Armenian–Greek Section, British High Commission, Constantinople, Kirk Kilisse, 16 July 1919.)
12. FO 371/4158, Perring to Webb, Samsun, 29 July 1919. Perring based his analysis on an unnamed source. FO 406/41, Perring to de Robeck, Samsoun, 11 November 1919. FO 371/4160, 'Notes on the Nationalist Movement in the Samsun Area', enclosure in de Robeck to Curzon, Constantinople, 28 October 1919. FO 406/41, enclosure in de Robeck to Curzon, Constantinople, 23 November 1919; FO 406/41, Hadkinson to de Robeck, Constantinople, 12 November 1919. FO 371/5041, General Staff Intelligence, Army of the Black Sea, 'The Nationalist Movement in Turkey: Summary of Reports Received from the Various Control Officers, October 28, 1919', Constantinople, 1 June 1920. FO 371/5166, General Staff Intelligence, Constantinople, Weekly Report No. 58, 3 March 1920.

13. WO 106/1571, 'Execution of the Armistice with Turkey: 30th October – 30 November, 1918', General Staff, War Office, 1918.
14. ADM 137/3846, Naval Staff, Intelligence Department, 'The International Situation and General Intelligence', 14 November 1918, 9 December 1918, 2 January 1919, 9 January 1919, 24 January 1919.
15. There are many reports alleging this. See, for example: FO 371/4161, 'Weekly Summary of Intelligence Reports Issued by the Constantinople Branch', 22 November 1919. 'Record by Sir E. Crowe of a Conversation with the French Charge d'Affaires', Foreign Office, 7 January 1921, DBFP viii, no. 6, p. 5. (Crowe at the time was Permanent Under-Secretary for Foreign Affairs.) FO 371/6517, Eastern Department, 'Turkey', 5 May 1921. FO 371/4158, Heathcote-Smith to Calthorpe, Constantinople, 24 July 1919. He based his report on a journey from Istanbul to Trabzon from 3 to 24 July 1919. FO 371/4160, Perring to de Robeck, Samsoun, 1 October 1919 and Webb (for de Robeck), Constantinople, 18 October 1919. See also FO 371/5041, G. H. Q. Istanbul to War Office, 17 February 1920. The War Office based a question on Enver Paşa on a 'very confused French report'. (FO 371/5041, War Office to G. H. Q. Istanbul, 9 February 1920.) The French report falsely placed Enver at Sivas.
16. FO 371/5042, G. H. Q. Constantinople to War Office, 18 February 1920. FO 371/5166, General Staff Intelligence, Constantinople, Weekly Report No. 58, 3 March 1920. FO 371/5166, 'Weekly Summary of Intelligence Reports Issued by M. I. 1. C., Constantinople Branch, for the Week Ending 29th July, 1920'. Note: This is different than the London weekly summaries. See Macfie, 'British Views', pp. 34–41.
17. FO 371/5178, 'Political Report: Asia Minor, Constantinople, August 9, 1920', in W. J. Childs, PID, to Terrell, 20 September 1920. The document cover indicates that the report was sent by the SIS.

The Ottoman Government of Damat Ferid was not above spreading the Bolshevik scare in appealing for support from the British. The minister of the interior sent a telegram claiming that the army commanders in Konya, Kütahya and Karası had revolted in favour of Bolshevism, and were collecting money to aid the Bolshevik cause. Nationalist organisers in Eskişehir were arrested 'on the ground of spreading CUP and Bolshevist propaganda'.

18. On the CUP and the Turkish Revolution and Independence War, see Erik Jan Zürcher, *The Unionist Factor*, Leiden: Brill, 1984, especially pp. 127–32. On Enver's actual movements, see Şuhnaz Yılmaz, 'An Ottoman Warrior Abroad: Enver Paşa as an Expatriate', *Middle Eastern Studies*, vol. 35, no. 4 (October

1999), pp. 40–69. See Gwynne Dyer, 'The Origins of the "Nationalist" Group of Officers in Turkey 1908–18', *Journal of Contemporary History*, vol. 8, no. 4 (October 1973), pp. 121–64. On the realities of the Nationalists relations with the Bolsheviks and Communism, see Shaw, *From Empire to Republic*, vol. 3, part 1, pp. 1092–106 and vol. 3, part 2, pp. 1542–9.

The myth of Bolshevik intervention did not completely die. In May 1921, British army representatives in Istanbul fully expected that the Greeks would defeat the Nationalists. They expected, however, that the Russian Bolsheviks would intervene on the side of the Turks, both sending troops overland and landing at Trabzon. Mustafa Kemal was reportedly resisting this, but others wanted Bolshevik assistance and the return of Enver Paşa. (FO 371/6525, General Officer Commanding, Constantinople, 4 August 1921, 5 August 1921.)

19. CAB 24/93/60, Milne to the Secretary of the War Office, Constantinople, 20 October 1919. FO 406/41, Milne to War Office, Constantinople, 20 October 1919. See also FO 371/4159, GHQ Constantinople to War Office, 12 September 1919. FO 371/4160, 'Weekly Report No. 39', G. H. Q. General Staff Intelligence, Constantinople, 23 October 1919.
20. FO 371/4159, Rawlinson, 'Camp on Allah Akbar Mt. (Between Sarikamish & Oltu), July 22', enclosure in de Robeck to Curzon, Constantinople, 25 September 1919. See also Rawlinson's memoir, A. Rawlinson, *Adventures in the Near East 1918–1922*, London: Melrose, 1924.
21. See, for example, FO 371/4938, Luke Telegram, Tiflis, 18 May 1920. FO 371/4940, Luke Telegram, Tiflis, 15 June 1920.
22. FO 371/5170, General Staff Intelligence, Constantinople, Weekly Report No. 79, 28 July 1920. (Note that this report admitted that the British had no information on the 'Army of the East', but nevertheless offered its assessment.) FO 371/5166, 'Weekly Summary of Intelligence Reports Issued by M. I. 1. C., Constantinople Branch, for the week ending 29th July, 1920'. Note: This is different than the London weekly summaries. FO 608/113, Calthorpe to Curzon, Constantinople, 2 July 1919; Webb to Curzon, Constantinople, 24 August 1919.
23. FO 371/5041, G. H. Q. Istanbul to War Office, 17 February 1920. FO 371/5041, Army Council to the Under-Secretary of State, Foreign Office, War Office, 12 February 1920. The British had at least one Intelligence officer, whose absurd information is described above.
24. FO 608/113, Webb to Curzon, Constantinople, 21 August 1919. FO 371/4160, Perring to de Robeck, Samsoun, 1 October 1919.
25. FO 371/5044, General Staff, 'The Situation in Turkey, 15th March, 1920', War Office, 15 March 1920.

26. CAB 44/39, Brigadier-General Sir James Edmonds, 'The Occupation of Constantinople 1918–1923', War Cabinet Secretariat, 27 September 1944.

    According to General Milne, at the end of 1919, the British Army of the Black Sea had 9,834 men, of which 7,398 were in Anatolia and Istanbul: in the Batum area 1,874, at Salonica 562, in the Istanbul area 4,469, along the railway from İzmit to Afyon 2,272, at the Dardanelles 657. The figures did not include two brigades of artillery. The forces at Batum and Afyon and along the rail line were later withdrawn, mainly to the Istanbul region. The French had six battalions at Istanbul and in Thrace under British command and a division under French command. The Italians had 6–7,000 men in South and Southwest Anatolia. The Greeks had 75,000 at İzmir.

    Milne stated that the Ottoman army had 'an authorized armistice establishment of 57,000'. It seems doubtful, however, that these were all actually Ottoman troops, many having already gone over to the Nationalists.

    FO 406/43, de Robeck to Curzon, Constantinople, 23 December 1919.

27. FO 371/5048, Vice Admiral Commanding First Battle Squadron to Commander in Chief, Mediterranean, 7 May 1920; FO 371/5048, Webb to Curzon, Constantinople, 13 May 1920; FO 371/5049, GOC Constantinople to War Office, 14 June 1920. Webb had asserted as early as summer 1919 that any Ottoman troops sent to 'suppress disorder' would join the Nationalists. (FO 406/41, Webb (Rear Admiral Richard, Acting High Commissioner) to Curzon, Constantinople, 17 August 1919.)

    On demobilisation, see Stephen Richards Graubard, 'Military Demobilization in Great Britain Following the First World War', *The Journal of Modern History*, vol. 19, no. 4 (December 1947), pp. 297–311.

    The British refused numerous requests by the Ferid Paşa government to equip troops and send them to fight the Nationalists. See, for example, FO 371/5049, de Robeck to Curzon, Constantinople, 13 July 1920; FO 371/5049, Curzon to de Robeck, Foreign Office, 16 June 1920.

28. FO 371/4215, General Staff, Paris, 'The Situation in South Eastern Europe and Turkey in Asia', Paris, 5 April 1919. A cover letter from General Wilson, Chief of the Imperial General Staff, to the prime minister stated: 'I would welcome a decision which definitely proclaimed that we would not interfere, in a military sense, in the chaos and welter which is coming in Central Europe, the Balkans, and Turkey.' (CAB 24/93/60, Milne to the Secretary of the War Office, Constantinople, 20 October 1919.) Even Lord Curzon, who definitely did believe in interfering militarily in the Balkans and Turkey, believed it could not be done without more military force. He nevertheless went ahead with intervention without force.

(CAB 24/77/38, 'A Note of Warning about the Middle East. By Lord Curzon', 25 March 1919.) CAB 24/95 C. P. 342, General Staff, 'The Military Aspect of the Turkish Peace Settlement', 24 December 1919. CAB 23/11/29, War Cabinet Meeting of 14 August 1919.

29. FO 406/43, de Robeck to Curzon, Constantinople, 17 June 1920. See also FO 371/5050, de Robeck to Curzon, 17 June 1920.
30. FO 371/4159, War Office to GOC Constantinople, 10 February 1919. FO 371/5041, G. H. Q. Constantinople to War Office, 12 February 1920. FO 406/43, Webb to Curzon, Constantinople, 22 and 23 April 1920; FO 371/4162, Webb to Curzon, Constantinople, 18 January 1920.
31. WO 106/64, General Staff, War Office, 'The Situation in Turkey, March 15, 1920'. FO 406/41, Milne to War Office, Constantinople, 20 October 1919. FO 406/43, de Robeck to Curzon, Constantinople, 7 March 1920; FO 406/43, Curzon to de Robeck, Foreign Office, 10 March 1920. See also FO 406/43, de Robeck to Curzon, Constantinople, 13 February 1920, FO 371/5042, de Robeck to Curzon, Constantinople, 29 February 1920.
32. CAB 28/9, Anglo-French Conference on the Turkish Settlement, London, 22–3 December 1919.
33. CAB 24/103/35, Allied Military Committee, 'Note Regarding the Treaty of Peace with Turkey', enclosure in letter from Marshal Foch to Lloyd George, Paris, 30 March 1920. CAB 29/86, British Secretary's Notes of a Meeting of the Supreme Council, San Remo, 20 April 1920. (Foch estimated a division as made up of 15,000 men.) CAB 24/103/27, 'General Staff Comments on the Report from Marshal Foch on the Military Measures Required to Put into Execution the Treaty of Peace with Turkey', 7 April 1920. Berthelot said that the United States would never provide soldiers. Venizelos plan: FO 406/40, Balfour to Granville, Foreign Office, 14 October 1918.

> As regards Thrace War Office consider that Greek troops should not be utilized in first instance, and that at least four Allied Divisions (ca, 60,000 men) would be necessary. They point out that only 5,000 French troops are now available. In conclusion, they draw attention to Marshal Foch's report on measures to enforce peace.

(FO 371/5046, Foreign Office to British Delegation, San Remo), 17 April 1920.
34. CAB 29/86, British Secretary's Notes of Meetings of the Supreme Council, San Remo, 23 April 1920, 11 a. m. and 22 April 1920, 4 p. m.
35. FO 371/5057, de Robeck to Curzon, Constantinople, 22 October and 30 November 1920. WO 32/5771, de Robeck Telegram, Constantinople, 10 November 1920.

FO 371/5057, de Robeck to Curzon, Constantinople, 11 November 1920. FO 372/5057, Foreign Office to de Robeck, 17 November 1920.
36. CAB 29/91, British Secretary's Notes of an Allied Conference, London, 21 February 1921, 4.30 p. m. Lloyd George: 'No-one believed that Mustafa Kemal would be able to drive the Greeks out of Asia Minor.' (CAB 29/86, British Secretary's Notes of a Meeting of the Supreme Council, San Remo, 21 April 1920, 4 p. m.)
37. CAB 24/119/100, 'The Treaty of Sèvres: General Staff Views on Modification of Terms', 16 February 1921.
38. CAB 24/120/8, War Office, 'The Military Situation in Russia, Caucasia, Turkey and Greece', 19 February 1921.
39. CAB 23/22/15, Conclusion of a Conference of Ministers, London, 17 and 18 June 1920.
40. FO 406/43, de Robeck to Curzon, Constantinople, 15 and 16 June 1920.
41. FO 371/5050, G. H. Q. Constantinople to War Office, 17 June 1920.
42. FO 406/43, Webb to Curzon, 13 May 1920. De Robeck Telegram to Curzon, 10 June 1920, BDFP 13, pp. 83–4. FO 371/5049, GOC Constantinople to War Office, 14 and 15 June 1920; FO 371/5049, Secretary, War Office, to Under-Secretary of State, War Office, 14 June 1920; FO 371/5050, C in C Mediterranean to Admiralty, 15 June 1920; FO 371/5050, GOC Constantinople to War Office, 17 June 1920. British forces withdrew to Tuzla, near Istanbul.
43. CAB 23/37/42, Conference of Ministers, 18 June 1920. FO 371/5048, GOC Constantinople to War Office, 29 May 1920. FO 371/5049, de Robeck to Curzon, Constantinople, 8 June 1920. The cabinet had previously decided in general to support the Greeks in Anatolia and Eastern Thrace. (CAB 37/41, Conference of Ministers, 17 June 1920.) Notes of a Conversation, Lympne, 20 June 1920, DBFP 8, 1920, pp. 307–9.
44. British Secretary's Draft Notes of a Conference, Boulogne, 21 June 1920, DBFP 8, pp. 347–9. FO 371/5054, Sydney R. Fremantle, Vice Admiral, to Commander-in-Chief, Mediterranean, 25 June 1920, enclosure in Admiralty to Under-Secretary of State, Admiralty, 10 August 1920.
45. FO 371/5055, Reports from Vice Admiral Sydney R. Fremantle and other officers to the Commander-in-Chief, Mediterranean, enclosures in Admiralty to Under-Secretary of State, Admiralty, 21 August 1920. FO 371/5050, War Office to Milne, 18 June 1920; Admiralty to C in C Mediterranean Afloat, 18 June 1920; CIGS War Office to Milne, 20 June 1920; FO 371/5051, C in C Mediterranean to War Office, 26 June 1920. FO 371/5054, Admiralty to Under-Secretary of State, London, 4 August 1920. There are extensive military reports of British

naval actions in ADM 137/1768 and 1769. On the use of joint forces, see FO 371/5055, Commanding Officer Ajax, 'Letter of Proceeding', 19 August 1920.

46. FO 371/5054, de Robeck to Secretary of the Admiralty, Iron Duke at Beicos and attachments, 4 July 1920. British officers who had visited Pandırma the previous May had found no unsettled conditions and no animosity toward the British. They were surprised at how well they were received. (FO 371/5054, Major Warder, 'Report on Information Obtained at Panderma', 5 May 1920, enclosure in Admiralty to Under-Secretary of State, Admiralty, 6 August 1920.) Greek bands, however, had been attacking Turkish villages in the region since 1919. (WO 32/5733, Hadkinson to Curzon, Constantinople, 6 October 1919.)

47. ADM 137/1768, Med. No. 6667, 24 June 1920.

48. ADM 137/1768, the British Admiral to Vali and Military Governor of Brussa, 25 June 1920; FO 371/5052, de Robeck to Curzon, Constantinople, 5 July 1920; FO 371/5053, C in C Mediterranean to Admiralty, 10 and 11 July 1920. See also the Istanbul meeting in which the British decided to aid the Greek conquest of Bursa. (FO 406/44, de Robeck to Curzon, Constantinople, 5 July 1920.)

49. FO 371/5051, de Robeck telegram, Constantinople, 23 June 1920; FO 371/5051, C in C Mediterranean telegram, 30 June 1920; FO 371/5051, Admiralty to Commander-in-Chief Mediterranean Afloat, 30 June 1920; FO 371/5051, Parliamentary Question from Lieutenant Kenworthy, 28 June 1920. FO 371/5052, Parliamentary Questions by Dr Douglas Murray and Mr Malone, also in 'Greek Operations', *Hansard*, HC Debate, 5 July 1920, vol. 121, cc. 1001–2.

50. FO 371/5056, War Office to Under-Secretary of State for Foreign Affairs, War Office, 1 October 1920. CAB 23/24/16, Cabinet Meeting, 22 March 1921.

51. FO 371/4160, General Staff Intelligence, Constantinople, Weekly Report No. 38, 16 October 1919. FO 371/5052, de Robeck telegram, Constantinople, 8 July 1920; FO 371/5053, Director of Naval Intelligence describing Admiralty orders to C in C Mediterranean, 13 July 1920; FO 371/5053, telephone message from Admiralty to Foreign Office, 20 July 1920, ADM 137/1768 and enclosures, de Robeck Telegram, 8 July 1920. See also FO 371/5053, C in C Mediterranean to Admiralty, 21 July 1920; CAB 24/109/68, Admiralty Weekly Intelligence Summary, 17 July 1920. See the detailed reports of British actions in Thrace in FO 371/5055, Admiralty to Foreign Office, London, 6 September 1920, and many other reports of British aid to the Greeks in FO 371/5055. Grand Vezir Damat Ferid had ordered Turkish forces not to resist, but Turks resisted where possible. (FO 371/5252, de Robeck to Curzon, Constantinople, 29 July 1920.) On the

Greek occupation and Turkish resistance, see Tevfik Bıyıklıoğlu, *Trakya'da Milli Mücadele*, vol. 1, Ankara: Türk Tarih Kurumu, 1987, pp. 314–407.

The cabinet decided to support the Sèvres's award of all of Thrace to the Greeks. (CAB 23/37/18, Cabinet Conference on 5 January 1920.)

52. FO 371/5055, Milne to de Robeck, Constantinople, 7 July 1920.
53. De Robeck notified Curzon that an attack on the Turks needed military support from the French and Italians. Curzon wrote that he agreed. It rested there, with no French or Italian troops provided. (FO 371/5049, de Robeck to Curzon, Constantinople, 10 June 1920, and Curzon to de Robeck, Foreign Office, 21 June 1920.)
54. FO 371/5054, Venizelos to Gen. Wilson, Paris, 2 August 1920. Venizelos also had promised this on numerous earlier occasions. See, for example, FO 371/5132, Telegram to de Robeck, Foreign Office, 3 March 1920. Venizelos was mistaken in stating that the orders for the Greek advance had been given at Spa. They were actually given at the Boulogne Conference, earlier than the Spa Conference. Lloyd George, however, did exalt at Spa on the Greek success. (British Secretary's Notes of an Inter-Allied Conference, Spa, 7 July 1920, DBFP 8, pp. 443–9.) At that meeting, Venizelos stated with the approbation of his allies:

> The only way to bring Mustafa Kemal to heel was to defeat him everywhere. A military defeat was the one thing that would bring him to his senses. He himself (Venizelos) was born in Turkey and knew Turkey well, and he was perfectly certain that the only right way to deal with the Turks was by conquest.

55. FO 371/5054, de Robeck to Curzon, Constantinople, 30 July 1920; FO 371/5054, Curzon to de Robeck, Foreign Office, 4 August 1920.
56. McCarthy, *Death and Exile*, pp. 300–5, gives details of the refugee numbers, drawn from British diplomatic and Ottoman sources.
57. FO 371/7931, Harington to War Office, Constantinople, 31 January 1922.
58. Bureau de la presse du Ministère des Affaires Etrangeres (sic), *La Grèce en Asie-Mineure*, Athens, 1921, pp. 27–9. Another estimate in the same source gave 16,000 Christian refugees in İzmit and Bursa. In 1920, Ambassador Rumbold estimated the city of İzmit and its surroundings held 12,000 Greek, 6,000 Armenian and 10,000 Turkish refugees. (FO 371/5214, Rumbold to Curzon, Constantinople, 19 November 1920.)
59. Turkish refugees were not specifically mentioned, but, asked by the MP Aubrey Herbert if an inquiry would be made into 'the sufferings of the Moslem population under the régime introduced by the Greeks in the territories occupied by

them in Asia Minor', Lloyd George said only that he was considering sending someone to investigate 'allegations by both parties'. ('Greece and Turkey', House of Commons Debate, 21 April 1921, *Hansard*, vol. 140, cc. 2057–8.)

60. FO 371/6510, Reshid Pasha Memorandum, London, 18 April 1921. FO 371/6508, Rumbold Telegram, Constantinople, 10 April 1921; Foreign Office to Rumbold, 16 April 1921. FO 371/6511, War Office to Under-Secretary of State, 29 April 1921.

61. The commission members: Lieut.-Colonel H. M. Farmar, President, Lieut.-Colonel S. Vitelli, Lieut.-Colonel De Witkowski and Major O. H. Van Millingen. There was some question regarding if the British would send only their own officers on the investigation, but the others finally joined. (Rumbold Telegrams, Constantinople, 23 April and 7 May 1921, in DBFP 17, pp. 152–3 and 173. FO 371/6511, Rumbold Telegrams, Constantinople, 6 and 7 May 1921.) See also: Shaw, *From Empire to Republic*, vol. 3, part 1, pp. 1261–89. Mehmet Kaya, 'Yalova-Gemlik Bölgeleri ve İzmit Yarımadası'nda Yunan Mezalimine Dair İtilaf Devletleri Araştırma Komisyonu Raporları (12–22 Mayıs 1921)', *Ankara Üniversitesi Türk İnkılâp Tarihi Enstitüsü Atatürk Yolu Dergisi*, no. 51 (Spring 2013), pp. 563–78 The mission was accompanied during part of its investigation by delegates of the Red Cross. Their report supported in every particular the commission's report of ill-treatment and the murders of Turks, as well as the burning of Turkish villages. The Red Cross facilitated the evacuation of thousands of Turks from the stricken region. (Maurice Gehri, délégué du Comité international de la Croix-Rouge, 'Mission d'enquête en Anatolie (12–22 mai 1921)', *Revue Internationale de la Croix-Rouge*, vol. 3, no. 31 (July 1921), pp. 721–35. Arnold J. Toynbee observed many of the attacks on the Turks, as well as Greek efforts to hide them. (*The Western Question in Greece and Turkey*, London: Constable, 1922, pp. 259–319.) Toynbee only had the official report to supplement his own observations, but what he reported from his own observations was damning. Before his book was published, Toynbee had described much of what he observed in the *Manchester Guardian*. His articles sparked questions in parliament, which were not answered by the government. (See, for example, 'Near East', House of Commons Debate, 30 May 1922, *Hansard*, vol. 154, cc. 2027–54.)

62. FO 371/6513, Rumbold Telegram, Constantinople, 21 May 1921. For other examples, see: ADM 137/2502, Farmar Telegram to High Commissioner, 16 May 1921; Farmar Telegram to High Commissioner, 17 May 1921. FO 371/6513, GHQ Constantinople to War Office, 17 May 1921.

63. FO 406/46, Enclosure in Rumbold to Curzon, Constantinople, 20 May 1921. See the hundreds of pages of testimony in ADM 137/2502 and the more limited reports in Gehri.
64. 'Greek Atrocities, Yalova (Commission's Report)', House of Commons Debate, 9 June 1921, *Hansard*, vol. 142, c. 2095W. See also 'Greece and Turkey', House of Commons Debate, 16 June 1921, *Hansard*, vol. 143, cc. 593–6, and the excerpts of parliamentary questions and responses in FO 371/6518.
65. 'Greece and Turkey', House of Commons Debate, 30 June 1921, *Hansard*, vol. 143, cc. 2321–3.
66. Great Britain, Parliament, Turkey No. 1 (1921), *Reports on Atrocities in the Districts of Yalova and Guemlik and in the Ismid Peninsula*, London: HMSO, 1921 (Cmd. 1478). The archival documents do not indicate how much pressure was put on the commission to produce its altered conclusions.
67. *Hansard*, HC Deb, 29 June 1921, vol. 143, cc. 2126–7, and FO 371/6520, Question in parliament, 29 June 1921.
68. FO 371/6523, Knight to Granville, Volo, 30 June 1921, among other reports. FO 371/6520, Harington to War Office, Constantinople, 28 June 1921. See also, FO 371/6520, Commander-in-Chief, Mediterranean to Admiralty, 29 June 1921, Rattigan Telegram, Constantinople, 28 June 1921; and Rattigan Telegram, Constantinople, 28 June 1921.
69. FO 371/6521, Commander-in-Chief, Mediterranean telegram, 30 June 1921. See also ADM 137/1774, C. in C. Mediterranean to Admiralty, 1 July 1921.
70. FO 371/6521, Rattigan Telegram, Constantinople, 1 July 1921. See also Rattigan Telegram, Constantinople, 5 July 1921. British military officials in Istanbul put the blame on the Armenians:

> The Greeks decided to evacuate ISMID altogether and this was done accompanied by incendiarism and a massacre of Turks by the local Armenians under the eyes of the Greek troops. The Turks occupied ISMID with a battalion on 28th June.

(WO 158/933, 'British Army in Constantinople. Summary of Events for June 1921'). Harington cited a different date for the Turkish entry into İzmit, 29 June 1921. He wrote that a commission under General Franks was sent to İzmit: 'Franks commission to investigate atrocities has landed and has been well received.' (FO 371/6520, Harington to War Office, Constantinople, 30 June 1921.)
71. Another commission, headed by Major-General G. N. Franks, was sent to investigate reports of atrocities in the Marmara region. It found evidence of robbery,

murder, torture and extortion of Turks by Greek villagers and the abduction of Turkish women. One Turkish village, Arablar, was burned down. However, the atrocities were much fewer than in Yalova–Gemlik. Greek soldiers, except for some officers who led guerilla bands, had neither killed nor protected the Turks. The commission rather lamely satisfied itself by telling the Greek authorities that the Turks 'are equally entitled to protection with the Greek inhabitants'. (FO 286/759, 'Report', Franks to Rattigan, 25 June 1921, enclosure in Rattigan to Curzon, Constantinople, 25 June 1921.)

# 16

## KURDS AND ARMENIANS

During World War I the British made various vague promises to the Armenians, never committing themselves to definite boundaries of a new Armenia. The cause of the Armenians was a convenient propaganda tool against the British enemies, the Turks. Britain also wanted the Armenians of Trans-Caucasia to do all they could to fight the Ottomans, who were taking Trans-Caucasia after the evacuation of Russian troops in the Russian Revolution. The British encouraged the Armenians, but promised little. Nevertheless, the British were willing to create an Armenian state, as long as it needed little military or financial commitment from them.[1]

Before the war ended, Lloyd George and the cabinet felt that the creation of an Armenia in Eastern Anatolia and the Caucasus would be an easy task: 'The Prime Minister said that, as far as Armenia was concerned, the argument when the decision was taken had been that if the Allies were in Constantinople they could do what they liked as regards Armenia.' He was mistaken.[2]

Ottoman troops had abandoned Trans-Caucasia and Northeastern Anatolia, approximately to the pre-war boundary, after the Mudros Armistice. A new Armenian Republic, with a capital at Erivan, had moved troops into the Kars-Ardahan region. It claimed large territories in Eastern Anatolia. By the summer of 1919, however, it had become obvious to everyone but Lloyd George that the Armenian state could not defend even its limited territory that had been part of Russia (mainly the Russian Erivan Province), let alone

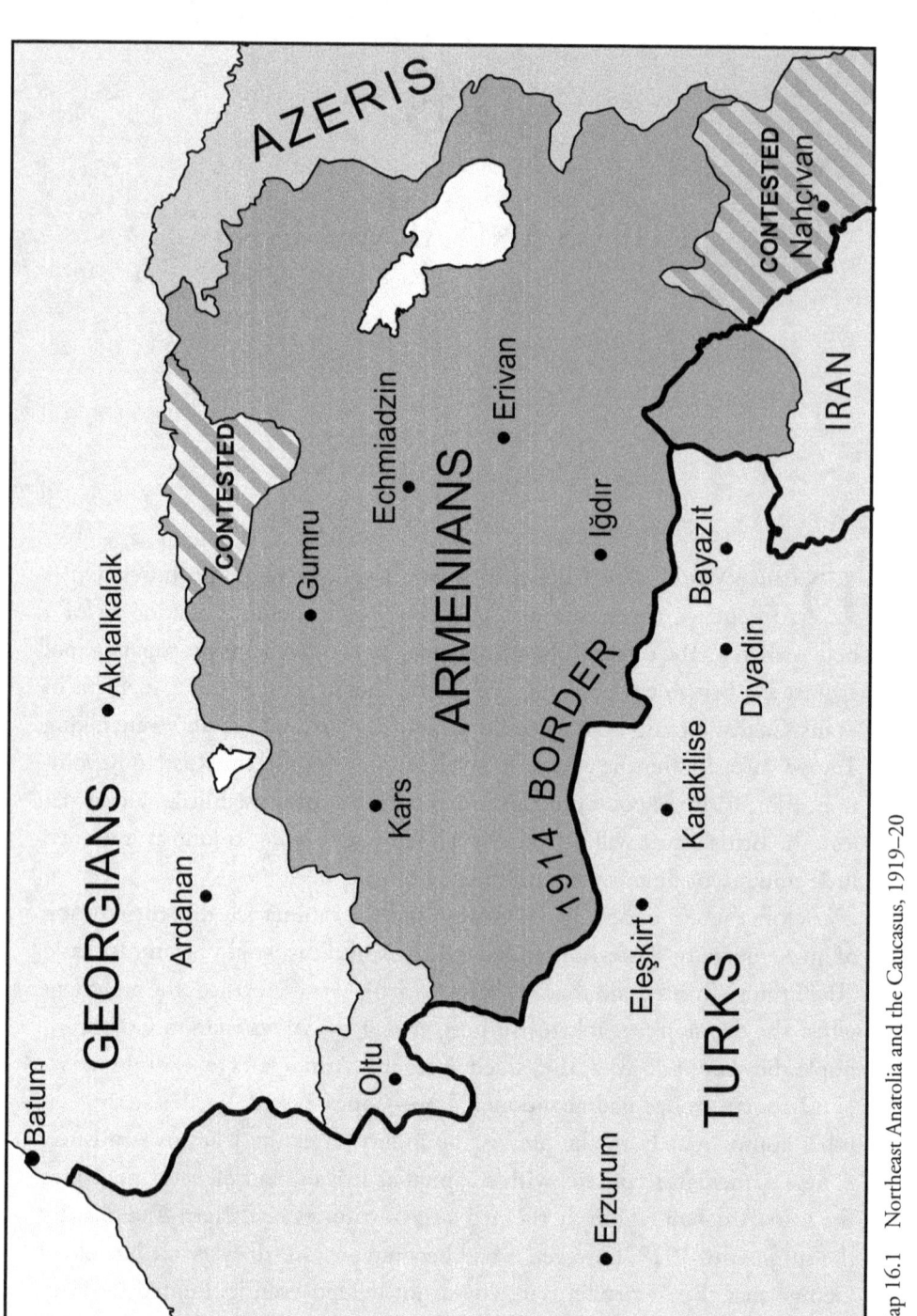

Map 16.1 Northeast Anatolia and the Caucasus, 1919–20

claim large territories in Anatolia. British military analyses stated categorically that the Armenian Republic would only survive if the Allies supported it with significant military force. Instead of that, the British withdrew even their small expeditionary force in the Trans-Caucasia, only temporarily remaining in Batum in September 1919. Clemenceau summarised the situation:

> The conclusion was that France could do nothing; Italy could do nothing; Great Britain could do nothing and, for the present, America could do nothing. It remained to be seen whether, as the result of this any Armenians would remain.

However, rather than undertake a costly (and perhaps impossible) military invasion, the Peace Conference (bureaucrats all) created a committee – the Commission for the Delimitation of the Boundaries of Armenia.[3]

The Armenian Commission was created on 17 February 1920. Its remit was to assume that Armenia would be an independent state that would include the Erivan Republic and 'portions of the adjacent Turkish vilayets'.[4]

The commission heard testimony from representatives of the Georgian and Armenian Republics. No Turks or other Muslims were heard. The commission's proposals were typical of the process by which imperialists so often created states – drawing of boundaries without consideration of the rights of the inhabitants or the 'facts on the ground'. The Ottoman provinces of Erzurum and most of the provinces of Bitlis and Van were to be given to the Armenian Republic. Autonomous states of Batum and Lazistan were to be created (Map 16.2). These states would grant free passage and port privileges to Armenians, who needed access to the Black Sea. No thought was given to the possibility that the region's peoples might not accept such a situation. The commission decided that it should be defended by creating a demilitarised zone around Armenia, and all Turkish forces were to be stationed at a distance from the borders.[5]

The commission gave no real consideration to the actual population of its proposed Armenia, although both Turks and Armenians had presented population data to the Peace Conference delegations.[6]

Significantly, the Armenian Commission offered no decision on the actual process of bringing the commission's plans to fruition. The commission assumed that the League of Nations would resolve all problems, taking

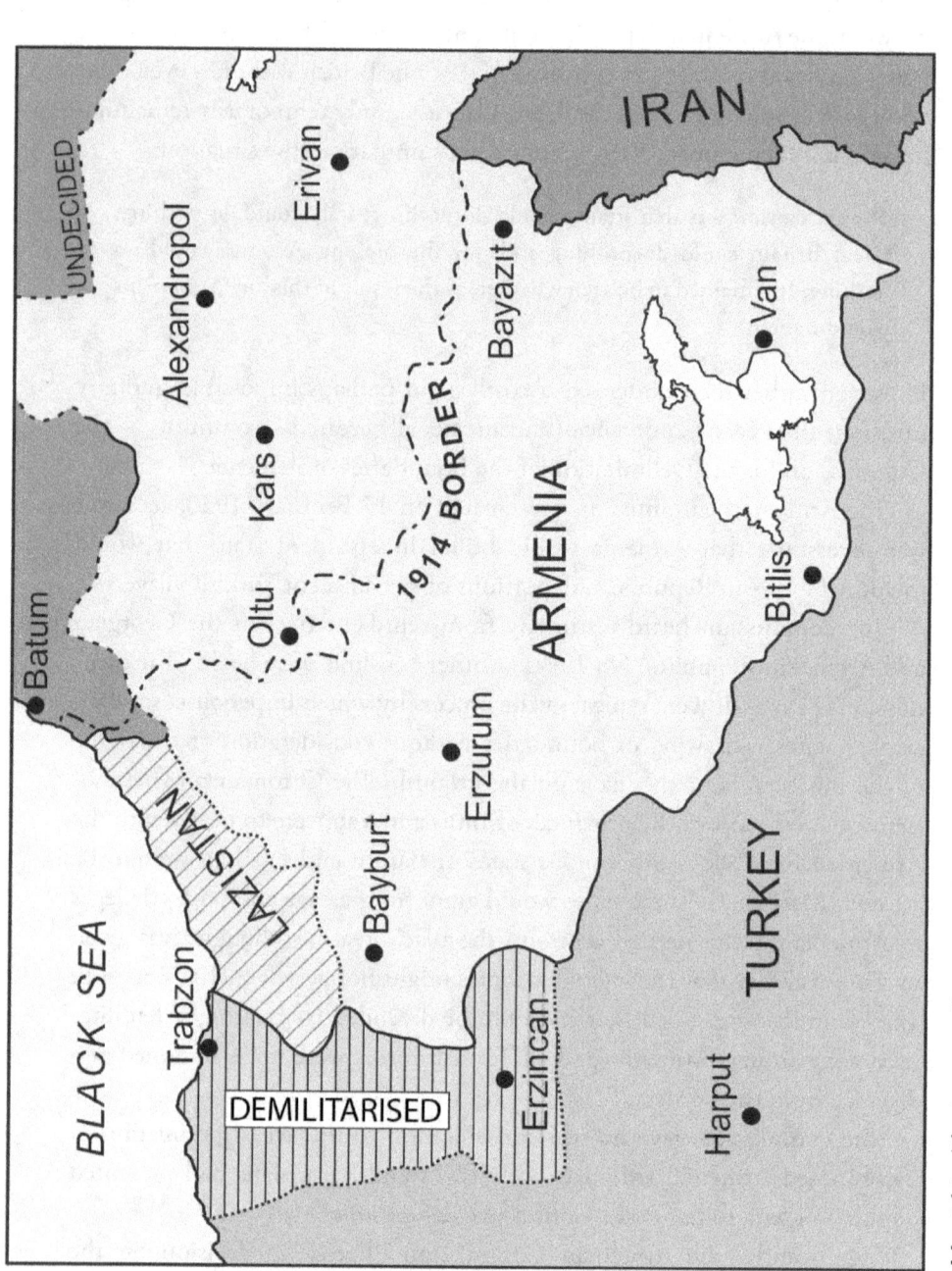

Map 16.2  The Armenian Commission proposal

Armenia under its wing. The League was formally asked 'to place the future of the Armenian State under the protection of the League of Nations'. The League's reply stated, in much political verbiage, that it could not do anything, because it had neither money nor troops. It stated that someone else would have to take a mandate for Armenia, preferably America. That, of course, was the problem; neither America nor anyone else would take on the obligation. American interest in the Armenian cause remained high, but with the American Senate's disavowal of the peace process, it had lost any leverage on the issue. In other words, the League washed its hands of the problem.[7]

The commission encouraged the Allies to assist Armenia financially and by recruiting overseas Armenians for the Armenian army; no more Allied assistance was offered. No Allied troops were to be involved. The Supreme Council decided to implement the decisions of the commission, except for the creation of autonomous Batum and Lazistan. Consideration of these was wisely deferred.[8]

At the San Remo Conference, one month after the Supreme Council had accepted the Armenian Commission's recommendations, the Allies had already begun to abandon Armenia. On 11 April 1920, before the San Remo meeting, the Supreme Council had received the League of Nations memorandum that said it could do little to help on Armenia. The League had written that a mandate for Armenia was necessary. A plea was sent to Wilson. An American mandate, however, had already seemed unlikely. Curzon suggested that Norway might take the mandate, a truly ridiculous idea. He wanted the Supreme Council to aid Armenia with equipment and officers. Both Millerand of France and Nitti of Italy said that neither France nor Italy would send money or men. Nitti said that if Erzurum were given to Armenia, the Allies would have to go to war with Mustafa Kemal to enforce the award, which was impossible. Needed forces could not be found. He believed, accurately, that Norway would never take the mandate.[9]

Lloyd George said Britain would not spend any money, but that Armenia could defend itself: 'The Armenians had an army of 30,000 or 40,000 armed men. What they required was equipment. Among them the Allies could certainly supply this.' Then he suggested the question be referred to military advisors, and its consideration postponed. Curzon spoke of 'moral responsibility' to aid the Armenians. Lloyd George suggested a loan of 10,000,000 pounds, which would be provided by America. Berthelot and Nitti agreed that America should pay. All agreed that Batum should be a free port, but no one was willing to support that militarily. Instead, they voted, '[t]hat it was highly desirable to obtain an agreement between (sic) Armenia, Georgia, and Azerbaijan regarding the port of Batum'.[10]

Allied advocacy for an Armenia in Eastern Anatolia had descended into a combination of wishes and impossibilities, all to be funded by America. Of course, America, not represented at the San Remo Conference, had not been consulted. In fact, the American Government, while full of heartfelt concern for the Armenians, would prove to be willing to contribute neither money nor men to the Armenian cause. Lord Curzon finally admitted that the British could do nothing for the Armenians; the British did not have the military force and parliament would not pay the bill.[11]

The basic problem for any British plans for Eastern Anatolia was military. The British military believed that action in the East would demand what they called 'heavy military commitments'. That would mean either moving troops, including heavy artillery, from Iraq or by sea, probably through Trabzon. In Iraq, the British barely had enough troops to control the Kurdish tribes and the potential oil fields of Mosul. The logistics of landing and transporting troops and artillery over the Eastern Anatolia mountainous terrain were a nightmare. In addition, they would face entrenched Turkish troops and possibly Soviet troops. Finally, no matter the logistic problems, the British simply did not have the troops.[12]

In September 1920, Turkish forces under Nationalist General Kâzim Karabekir attacked into the lands that had been claimed by the Armenian Republic, defeating the Armenians. In the Treaty of Alexandropol (Gümrü) of 3 December 1920, the Turks regained the Kars-Ardahan regions that the Ottomans had lost in 1878. The Armenian Republic was occupied by the Bolsheviks in 1921. Independent Armenia was gone.[13]

It had been decided in the Treaty of Sèvres that the borders of Armenia would be set by President Wilson. On 22 November 1920 Wilson delivered his map of the borders he had set. They included a large region, much more than had been envisaged by the Armenian Commission. His decision arrived just as the Turks defeated the Armenian Republic, setting the actual borders

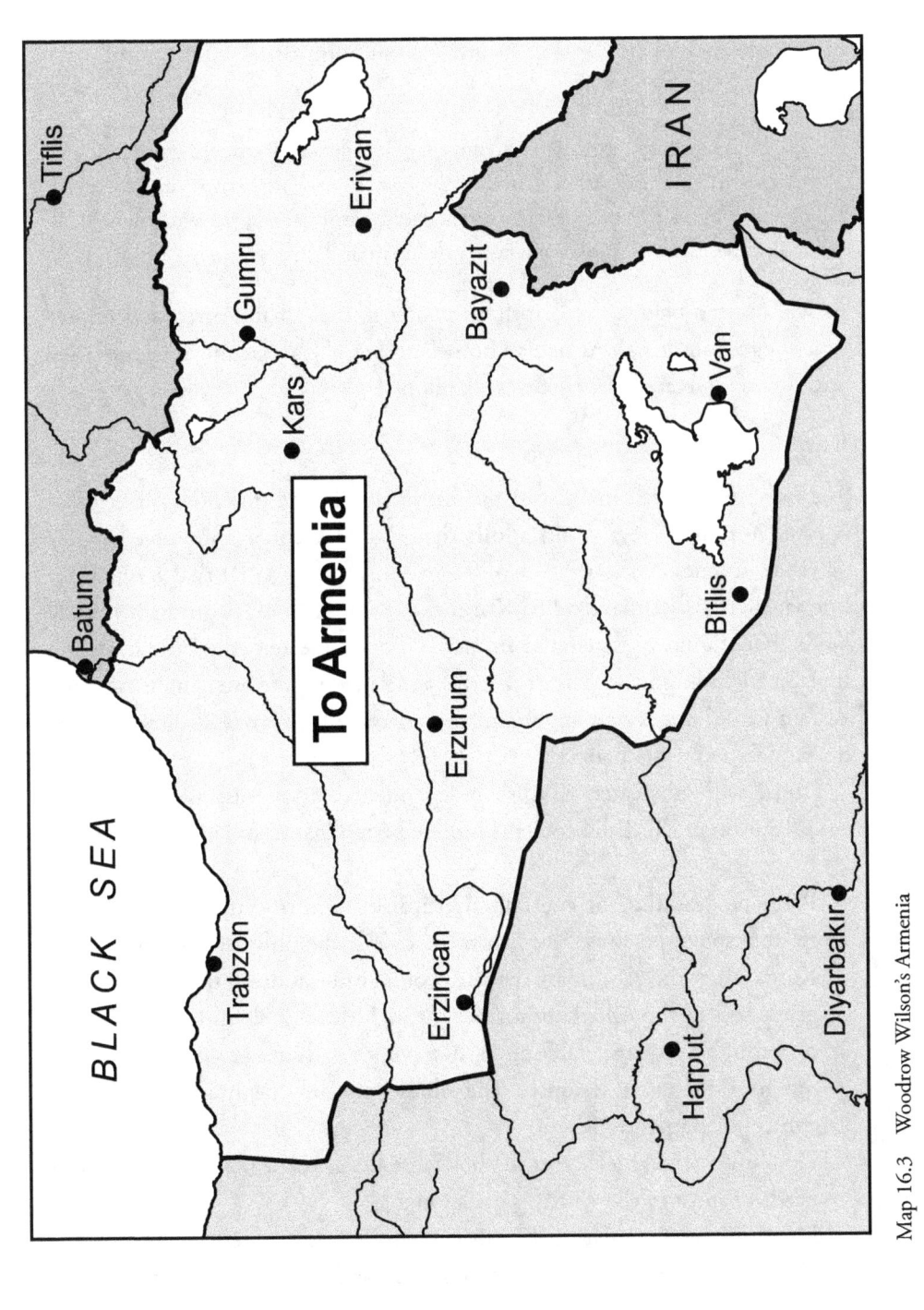

Map 16.3  Woodrow Wilson's Armenia

of Eastern Turkey. The Wilson Award was stillborn. Britain, Italy and France jointly decided:

> The boundaries of Armenia, as defined by President Wilson, are boundaries which, without close examination in the light of existing events, the Powers who belong to the League of Nations could hardly at the present moment accept the responsibility to guarantee or maintain.[14]

As will be seen below, the British were later to make halfhearted and impossible suggestions for an Armenian homeland in Cilicia, but the once promised creation of a Greater Armenia was abandoned.

## Kurds

The only real British interest in the Kurds was in the potential oil fields of Mosul, not that they would admit that. Lloyd George announced to his Allied colleagues at the Peace Conference in January 1919 that he had not known there was a place called Kurdistan, so he had left it out of his list of lands that should be separated from the Turks. He remedied the omission by later including it on his list. At the same meeting he amazingly said that Britain would not accept any mandate over the oil wells of Kurdistan, which he had learned was a place.[15]

Those who advocated Kurdish independence, or at least asked for some consideration of Kurdish problems, suffered from insurmountable difficulties:

- With no tradition of centralised Kurdish authority, the Kurds had no reliable spokespersons. Kurdish tribal chiefs, the only real authority over Kurds after the Ottoman demise, could only address their hopes and grievances to the Allied authorities through the British authorities in Iraq or through a few unreliable and self-serving Kurds in Paris or Istanbul. No one took the latter seriously. The Allies were only really concerned with control of Iraq and oil.
- How much the chiefs, even if they were listened to, represented the real needs of most of the Kurds is questionable.
- Much of the land with a Kurdish majority was claimed by Armenians. The Allies, especially the British, were, at least in theory, committed to the Armenian cause.

- While vocal advocates in Britain and France took up the causes of Armenians, Greeks and even Turks, there were no important advocates for the Kurds. Basically, few cared about the Kurds.
- Many of the Kurds in Anatolia took up the cause of the Turkish Nationalists, which further alienated the British.

Self-styled representatives of the Kurds and Kurdish societies sent numerous memoranda and desiderata to the British, whom they properly believed to be the only ones who could help their cause. These included arguments for Kurdish independence, based on population numbers and history. Wilson's Fourteen Points were cited in claims for self-determination. Appeals were made for the retention of the oil fields by a Kurdish state that would badly need revenue. Protestations for love of the British were ubiquitous. None of them were given any consideration.[16]

Mohammed Cherif Pasha (Mehmet Şerif) had been briefly an Ottoman diplomat, but had fallen out with both the governments of Abdülhamid II and the Committee of Union and Progress. After the war he rejoined the Ottoman Government, again briefly, before he abandoned it and became a spokesman for Kurdish nationalism to the Allies in Paris. Cherif sent the British a proposal for an extensive Kurdistan under British mandate. He was a self-promoter, often offering himself to the Allies as a candidate for president of Kurdistan. The British never took Cherif or his plan seriously.[17]

Cherif became anathema to other Kurdish nationalists when he signed an agreement with Armenian representatives that accepted Armenian rule in Van and Bitlis Provinces, both overwhelmingly Kurdish in population. Ultimately, the British also rejected him and the other nationalist groups that claimed leadership of the Kurdish cause. It had become obvious that he had no support in the Kurdish region. Power there was held by tribal chiefs, not nationalists based in Paris and Istanbul.[18]

A seemingly more likely claimant for British support was Shayh Seyyid Abdulkadir, scion of the powerful Şemdinan family in Southeastern Anatolia and an influential member of the Ottoman Senate (higher house of the parliament). Abdulkadir wished for autonomy of the Kurdish region under the Ottoman Empire, and thus was an enemy of the Turkish Nationalists, who were opposed to it. He asked the British to support him financially and to send him first to Southeastern Anatolia, and then to Mosul, to organise Kurdish tribes. Initially his plan was to oppose the Turkish Nationalists, but in 1921 the plan changed. He told the British that the Kurds under his leadership were to oppose fanciful Bolshevik incursions. Abdulkadir's plans played cleverly into British fears of Turkish Nationalists and Soviet Russians, but foundered on the facts in the Kurdish territories: Abdulkadir and his family had enemies, particularly the powerful Bedirhan family. There was general disunity of the Kurds – more tribal loyalties than the desire for a Kurdistan. If the British were to bring the Kurds together, of course under British guidance, they would have to work with local chiefs.[19]

In the end, the British supported none of the Kurds who approached them in Istanbul or Paris. Instead, the British supported local solutions – Kurdish chiefs who would support the British. British efforts with the chiefs were notable failures.

Plans and negotiations for a Kurdish autonomous state were in the hands of British representatives in Baghdad, a division of the government of India. The real concern of the British was not Kurdish self-determination, but rather protection of the northern borders of Iraq. They defined Kurdistan as being cut into two parts – a northern region (promised to the Russians in the Sykes–Picot Agreement and now to be given to the Armenians), and a southern region, which included southern parts of Van and Bitlis Provinces and much of the Mosul Province (not including the town of Mosul itself). In December 1918, it was proposed that Mosul be included in British Mesopotamia, and that a Kurdish confederation under British control ('British protection') be put in place in the southern region.[20]

Immediately after the end of the war, the British agent in Sulaymaniyah, Major Edward William Charles Noel, reported that there would be no problem with creating a Kurdish state under British protection. Noel arranged a meeting of Kurdish chiefs with the British Civil Commissioner in Iraq. On 4 December 1918, the Civil Commissioner, Colonel Albert Wilson (1918 to 1920), met with the Kurdish chiefs, some of whom agreed to accept British officers for all government departments, including officers for Kurdish levies. Not all the chiefs agreed, but Colonel Wilson decided that the chiefs had exercised their right of Kurdish self-determination, as promised by the

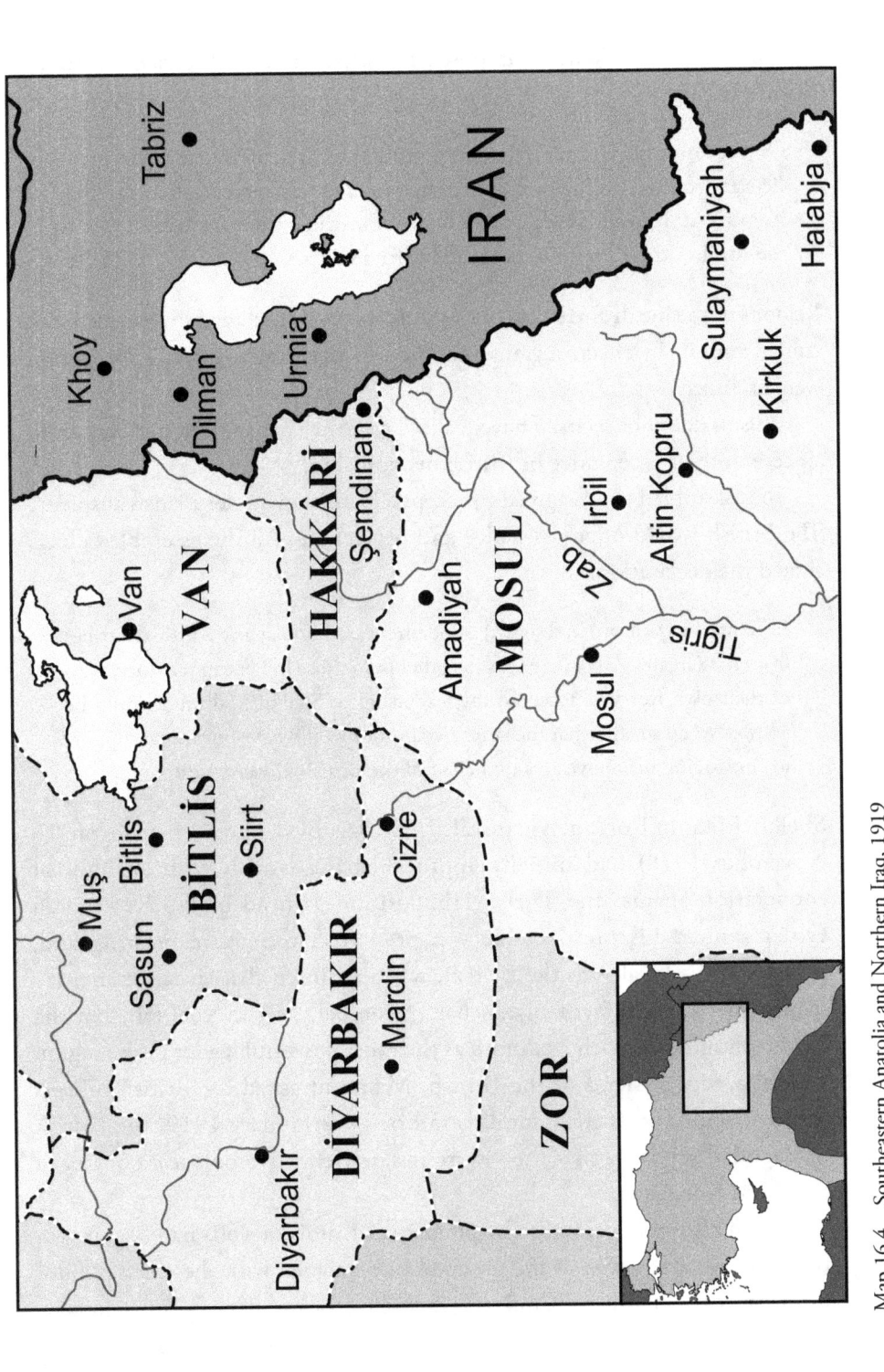

Map 16.4  Southeastern Anatolia and Northern Iraq, 1919

British. The region Wilson proposed for what the British styled as 'South Kurdistan' was:

> On the north the Greater Zab, on the south the Diala, on the east the Turco-Persian frontier, on the west an irregular line, to be fixed hereafter, running from the Zab to the Diala and so drawn to exclude from the confederation the Arbil, Altun Keupri, Kerkuk, and Kifri districts.

Regions to the north and south of this were not to be included in the Kurdistan confederation. In effect, regions promised to the Armenians and oil regions were excluded.

Wilson does not seem to have realised that the chiefs might not have been sincere in their acceptance of British overlordship.[21]

The assembled chiefs agreed to accept a Kurdistan 'under British auspices'. The British would offer 'assistance and protection'. All the assembled chiefs signed the declaration.

> In return he (Wilson) had signed a document stating that any Kurdistan tribes from the Greater Zab to the Dialah (other than those in Persian territory) who of their own free will accepted the leadership of Shaikh Mahmud would be allowed to do so, and that the latter (Mahmud) would have our moral support in controlling the above area on behalf of the British Government.

Sheikh Mahmud of Sulaymaniyah (first occupied by the British on 16 November 1918) had initially approached the British with an offer of cooperation against the Turks. His position as head of the Kadiri Sufi Order assured his prestige. He was present at the above meeting and, professing his loyalty to the British, was appointed British representative in the district of Sulaymaniyah that December. Major Noel felt that the British should side with Mahmud as the most powerful leader in the region and avowedly a friend of the British. Mahmud asked for British officers for his troops and British administrators. By 2 January 1919, the British in Baghdad reported that they 'were in fairly effective political control of Southern Kurdistan'.[22]

British assurance proved to be premature. Kurdish revolts had begun near the Persian border, even as the pact was being signed with the chiefs. Minor disturbances in 'Southern Kurdistan', including the murder of a British officer, began in April 1919. Anti-British pamphlets appeared throughout the region. British Intelligence reported that a loose confederation of chiefs had formed against British plans. By May, a full-blown revolt had broken out. When it became obvious that he would not become the leader of all Kurdistan in its entirety, Mahmud turned against the British. His forces seized Sulaymaniyah from the British, capturing British officers and troops and cutting telegraph wires. Halabja and other towns were taken. Ottoman forces sent to the area of rebellion did little to stop the revolt. Support for Mahmud was limited, however. Other Kurdish chiefs had always opposed him. Some, such as Abdulkadir of the Şemdinan, suggested that they should be the leaders of Kurdistan. (Probably mistakenly, Baghdad officials believed that Abdulkadir was actually one of the instigators of Kurdish revolt.) Others, such as Shaikh Taha, refused to accept any authority.[23]

In the end, politics and diplomacy having failed, the British used force. Troops defeated Sheikh Mahmud and other chiefs. Two infantry brigades, mountain guns, cavalry and bombing airplanes defeated the Kurds. A brigade was left in the Sulaymaniyah region to enforce British control. Outside of 'Southern Kurdistan', however, armed reaction to British occupation continued: Kurds from Iran attacked British outposts. To the north, tribes increasingly began to take the side of the Turkish Nationalists. In 1919, Kurdish tribes attacked and sometimes defeated British occupiers in Northeastern Anatolia. The Greek occupation of İzmir greatly increased Kurdish anxiety. Kurds feared that Kurdish areas in and near Mosul would be taken from them, which is exactly what happened.[24]

The greatest fear of all the Kurds, whether tribal chiefs or nationalists in Paris, was domination by the Armenians, whom they had been fighting since 1915. The British were never willing or able to assuage their fears. All the British offered to the Kurds was meaningless advice: 'Remain quiet and desist from agitation pending the decision of the (Peace) Conference, where their (Kurdish) views are known.' Curzon made it plain that no definite promises should be made to the Kurds. The Kurds, he felt, should be placated with meaningless assurances. For example, because the Kurds were worried about domination by the Armenians, they should be assured that there would not be '*unrestricted* Armenian domination' (emphasis in original). Not fools, they realised that they could not trust the British to satisfy Kurdish desires.[25]

Faced with Armenian atrocities against Muslims, the Kurds of Northeast Anatolia took the side of the Turks in opposition to the Armenians in occupation. They were particularly effective as guerillas and in mixed bands of Turkish Nationalists and Kurdish tribesmen.[26]

In the light of Kurdish unrest, the British Cabinet began to rethink its entire Kurdish policy. In opposing the Kurdish revolt, British forces had initiated what was in effect a military occupation of 'Southern Kurdistan'. Britain did not have the force or the financial ability to control the region; it was now beyond their present military control:

> Future of Kurdistan is still unsettled, but it may be taken as certain that permanent responsibilities of His Majesty's Government in these regions will in no event go beyond loose political supervision, and that anything in nature of direct British administration is out of question. In these circumstances His Majesty's Government are very reluctant to take what would in effect be first step towards effective military occupation. They have hitherto supported policy of extending British influence to South Kurdistan because they believed that inhabitants themselves welcomed it. It was on this understanding that they sanctioned your (Commissioner in Baghdad's) proposal to create fringe of autonomous Kurdish States under Kurdish Chiefs with British political advisers; see my telegram of 9th May. It would now appear that belief was misplaced, and that inhabitants, so far from welcoming British influence, are so actively hostile that strategic railways are required to keep them in check. In these circumstance's (sic) might it not be the better course to withdraw our political officers, &c, and leave Kurds to their own devices? Alternative of maintaining order by force among recalcitrant mountain tribesmen opens up prospect of military commitments, which His Majesty's Government contemplate with gravest apprehension.[27]

Only one British official evidenced actual concern for the Kurds, Major Noel, sent by British Intelligence to investigate the Kurdish situation. Noel let it be known that he intended to investigate matters that others perhaps did not want to consider, such as actual population numbers, Armenian attacks on Muslims and true Kurdish feelings toward the British. The British administration in Iraq, which searched for anything that would protect their northern border, initially supported Noel's investigations.

Major Noel's report proposed significant differences from anything being considered by the Allies: all of Eastern Anatolia (the 'Six Vilayets') should be placed under 'a single mandatory rule, backed by an army of occupation'. The mandate would be divided into three zones: a Northern Zone, where there were no Kurds (a false statement); a Central Zone, where Kurds and Armenians were mixed; a Southern Zone, exclusively Kurdish. Each zone would have its own local administration. If this were not achieved, Trabzon and Erzurum Provinces should become Armenian; Van, Bitlis, Diyarbakır and Mamuretülaziz Provinces should be a Kurdish state, 'under presumably British auspices'. Perhaps wisely, given the political realities, Noel did not include the Northern Iraq oil region, Kurdish and oil-producing, in his Kurdish state. He also recommended that the British should not oppose independence for Persian Kurds.

Unfortunately for the Kurdish cause, Noel proved to be an intemperate lover of all things Kurdish. His report on the Kurds was so overblown that it could not be taken seriously. (One British official styled Noel as 'the Apostle to the Kurds'.) Every foreign traveller had a favourable impression of the Kurds, Noel stated. The Kurd was more receptive to modern education and progress than the Arab, the Turk or the Persian. Of all the Middle Eastern peoples, the Kurds were the most capable of stable and progressive government. They all had a deep sentiment of Kurdish nationality. Turks, never Kurds, had decided to massacre Armenians. During the war, the Kurds had refused to fight for the Ottomans. Kurds hated the Turks, but would live alongside Armenians and Assyrians peaceably. And, finally, the Kurds loved the British and would be glad to accept British guidance.[28]

Coupled with so many false assertions, it is no wonder that Noel's recommendations for Kurdish independence were disregarded. The British Commission that governed Mesopotamia profoundly disagreed with his assessments on almost every point. His more accurate statements, such as that Kurds were a large majority in Southeast Anatolia and Northern Iraq or that American missionary statements on Armenians could not be trusted, were likewise ignored by the British Government and the Supreme Council. His proposal that all of Eastern Anatolia be under a single European mandatory or that the Armenians should have no more than the Erzurum and Trabzon Provinces was never even considered by the Allies.[29]

In the Sèvres Treaty, the putative autonomous Kurdistan was relegated to the small region north of Mosul Province. When the treaty was revised, the

Kurds were forgotten completely. The British claimed Mosul, and the Turks took the rest of Noel's Kurdistan.[30]

The Turkish Nationalists had never accepted the idea of an independent or autonomous Kurdistan. They viewed what the British called 'Southern Kurdistan' as an integral part of Turkish Anatolia. They also claimed Mosul Province, which the British had never planned to give up to the Kurds. The populace of the Kurdish-speaking regions was represented by elected deputies in the Grand National Assembly in Ankara. This was significantly different than the claims of so-called Kurdish spokesmen such as Cherif, who represented no one but themselves.[31]

## Notes

1. See: Artin H. Arslanian, 'British Wartime Pledges, 1917–18: The Armenian Case', *Journal of Contemporary History*, vol. 13, no. 3 (July 1978), pp. 517–30. Richard G. Hovannisian. 'The Allies and Armenia, 1915–18', *Journal of Contemporary History*, vol. 3, no. 1 (January 1968), pp. 145–68, and 'Armenia and the Caucasus in the Genesis of the Soviet-Turkish Entente', *International Journal of Middle East Studies*, vol. 4, no. 2 (April 1973), pp. 129–47. Levon Marashlian's PhD dissertation is decidedly one-sided, but does provide much detail on the Allied deliberations regarding the Armenians. ('The Armenian Question from Sèvres to Lausanne: Economics and Morality in American and British Policies, 1920–1923', unpublished PhD dissertation, University of California, Los Angeles, 1992.)

    British policymakers were confused by conflicting reports from Eastern Anatolia and Trans-Caucasia, actions of General Denikin's army in Russia, and further confusion over Armenia's military power. As an example, see the letter by Eyre Crowe, which turned out to be wrong in almost every particular. (Crowe to Kidston, Paris, 17 November 1919, DBFP 4, pp. 892–5.) Crowe at the time was British representative at the Supreme Council in Paris. He became permanent under-secretary, the head of the Foreign Office bureaucracy, in 1920. See also the mistaken optimism about Armenian success in Kidston to Crowe, Foreign Office, 28 November 1919, and Crowe to Kidston, Paris, 1 December 1919, DBFP 4, pp. 907–10 and 912–14.

2. CAB 23/14/40, War Cabinet Meeting of 26 October 1918.
3. FO 406/42, 'Notes on Present Conditions in the Caucasus', enclosure in Director of Military Intelligence to Under-Secretary of State for Foreign Affairs, War Office, 11 August 1919. See Artin Hagop Arslanian, 'The British Military Involvement in

Transcaucasia, 1917–1919', unpublished PhD dissertation, University of California, Los Angeles, 1974, pp. 204–61, and John Fisher, '"On the Glacis of India": Lord Curzon and British Policy in the Caucasus, 1919', *Diplomacy and Statecraft*, vol. 8, no. 22 (July 1997), pp. 50–82. 'Situation in Armenia', Notes of a Meeting of the Heads of Delegations of the Five Great Powers, Paris, 11 August 1919, DBFP, vol. 1, pp. 387–90.
4. CAB 24/98, C. P. 663, 'Supreme Council', 17 February 1920.
5. The commission's report was indefinite on the borders of Lazistan and Batum. The map has been drawn from the commission's own map (MPKK 1/38), which did not give definite borders for the Batum state or the northern borders of Armenia. In addition, the report seemed to give slightly larger Lazistan borders than the map. It is doubtful if the commission really knew the geography very well.
6. See the numerous examples in US 868.014 and FO 608/78. On various claims on population numbers, see especially FO 608/78, 'Les Revendications Armeniennes et les Preuves sur les Quelles Elles Se Basent (sic)'. In December 1918, War Office Intelligence estimated that Kars (Kars-Ardahan) Province had 131,000 Turks and 91,000 Armenians before World War I. FO 371/4352, Director of Military Intelligence, 'Population of Trans-Caucasia', War Office, 23 December 1918.
7. CAB 24/104/87, 'Correspondence between the Supreme Council and the Council of the League of Nations', San Remo, 12 March 1920. Balfour, head of the British delegation to the League, later said that the suggestions were impossible; the League had neither money nor arms for such undertakings. (CAB 24/100, 'Memorandum by Mr. Balfour on Suggestions Made to the Council of the League of Nations in Reference to the Peace with Turkey', no place given, 15 March 1920.) The cabinet agreed to drop all the suggestions on the League. (CAB 24/101/24, Hankey to Drummond, London, 20 March 1920.) On the Americans and the Armenians, see Mark Malkasian, 'The Disintegration of the Armenian Cause in the United States, 1918–1927', *International Journal of Middle East Studies*, vol. 16, no. 3 (August 1984), pp. 349–65.
8. CAB 29/29, 'Report and Proposals of the Commission for the Delimitation of the Boundaries of Armenia', London, 24 February 1920. Commission members: for Britain, R. Vansittart and Col. W. H. Gribbon; for France, M. Kammerer and Col. Chardigny; for Italy, M. Galli and Col. Castaldi; for Japan, Lieutenant Commander Anno. CAB 29/30. Supreme Council, Summary of decisions made on 27 February and 6 March 1920.
9. The Americans were told that the mandate would entail financial and military factors, but would not be as bad as some had assumed. (CAB 24/104/88, 'Despatch to President Wilson', 26 April 1920.)

10. CAB 29/31, British Secretary's Notes of Meetings of the Supreme Council, San Remo, 20 April 1920. See also CAB 29/32, 'Protection of Minorities in Turkey', Paris, 11 April 1920. The British did suggest an arrangement in which they would sell the Armenian Republic war materials, paid for with Armenian notes. Armenia could not pay anything, as it was soon taken over by the Soviets. (T 160/8 contains much correspondence on this.)
11. Curzon to Aneurin Williams, Foreign Office, 6 December 1921, DBFP 17, pp. 515–16, no. 475. Aneurin Williams, M. P., was Chairman of the Armenian Refugees (Lord Mayor's) Fund.
12. See FO 248/1225, GOC Constantinople to War Office, 30 January 1920. The lack of British military wherewithal is not given enough consideration in Fisher's otherwise admirable 'On the Glacis of India'.
13. Allen and Muratoff, pp. 499–500. Turkey, Genelkurmay Başkanlığı, *Birinci Dünya Harbinde Türk Harbi, Kafkas Cephesi, 3ncü Ordu Harekâtı*, vol. 2, Ankara: Genelkurmay, 1993, pp. 629–42. The Alexandropol Treaty was confirmed by the Bolsheviks in the Treaty of Moscow of 23 October 1921.
14. British Secretary's Note of a Conference, London, 3 December 1920, DBFP 8, p. 849. The conferees decided they were not bound by the Treaty of Sèvres on Armenia, since the treaty had not been ratified. Note in this document the complete lack of understanding of Soviet–Turkish Nationalist relations. Evans, pp. 262–3.
15. Secretary's Notes of a Conversation, Paris, on Thursday, 30 January 1919, *Papers Relating*, vol. 3, pp. 805–6.
16. There are a great number of these in FO 608/95, far too many to cite independently. The British in Istanbul, Paris and London had extensive, fruitless exchanges with Kurdish notables. A summary of the various British dealings with Kurdish representatives is in FO 608/95, 'Situation in Kurdistan', Inter-Departmental Conference on Middle Eastern Affairs, enclosure in Curzon to Balfour, Foreign Office, 12 September 1919. See the summary of Commissioner Rumbold in FO 371/6346, Rumbold Telegram, Constantinople, 1 January 1921. See FO 371/6346, Rumbold to Curzon, 29 December 1920. Like other British officials, Rumbold feared the Bolsheviks and hoped the Kurds might help oppose them, but he felt they were too disunited to be an asset. See also CAB 24/145/51, Eastern Report, 13 March 1919.
17. FO 248/1225, Général Cherif Pasha, Président de la Délégation Kurde a la Conférence de la Paix, enclosure in Crowe to Curzon, Paris, 12 October 1919. He made his offer to assume the presidency a number of times. See, for example, FO 608/95, Cherif to Mallet, Paris, 20 May 1919, and Mallet to Curzon, Paris,

27 May 1919. See also in FO 371/5008, the conflicts among those who said they represented the Kurds.
18. See FO 608/95, Cherif, Ohandjanian and Boghos Nubar to President of the Peace Conference, Paris, 20 November 1919.

    When Cherif claimed he had been elected as the head of the future state, Admiral Webb in Istanbul commented: 'I have no reason to suppose Sherif has been elected by any one except himself. I agree as to his utter unsuitability for position of responsibility in Kurdistan.' (FO 608/95, Webb Telegram, Constantinople, 8 September 1919.) It is unclear if Cherif claimed to be president of Kurdistan or only president of 'The Kurdish Delegation at the Peace Conference', which would also be a dubious election. (See FO 608/97, Cherif to Derby, Paris, 24 March 1919.) Secretary of State for India, Edwin Montagu, and Col. Wilson in Baghdad agreed that Cherif was unfit for the position. (FO 608/95, Wakely to Under-Secretary of State, India Office, 13 September 1919.)
19. See: Hakan Özoğlu, '"Nationalism" and Kurdish Notables in the Late Ottoman–Early Republican Era', *International Journal of Middle East Studies*, vol. 33, no. 3 (August 2001), pp. 383–409. Saad Eskander, 'Britain's Policy in Southern Kurdistan: The Formation and the Termination of the First Kurdish Government, 1918–1919', *British Journal of Middle Eastern Studies*, vol. 27, no. 2 (November 2000), pp. 139–63. There are a large number of documents in FO 371/4193 on the actions of self-appointed Kurdish representatives. I have not considered them here, because the British never took them seriously and nothing came of their efforts.
20. Baghdad had always had *de facto* control of the political situation, but the Civil Commissioner's authority over the Kurdish Question was formalised in June 1919. (FO 608/95, Secretary of State to Civil Commissioner, Baghdad, London, 5 June 1919.)
21. FO 371/3385, 'From Civil Commissioner, Baghdad', 16 November 1918. FO 371/3386, 'Kurdistan (Note by the Political Department, India Office), December 14, 1918', enclosure in Secretary of State for India to Secretary of State for Foreign Affairs, India Office, 17 December 1918. In October 1918, the Political Department had proposed including part of Iran, west of Lake Urmia, in the Kurdish district. (FO 371/3407, 'From Political. Baghdad, October 15, 1918', enclosure in Secretary of State for India to Secretary of State for Foreign Affairs, India Office, 17 October 1918.) Arnold Toynbee of the Foreign Office suggested that the region might be given to Iran. The suggestion went nowhere.
22. FO 608/95, 'Mesopotamia: British Relations with Kurdistan', Political Department India, 27 August 1919. FO 608/95, Circular Memo from Major E. W. C. Noel, Sulaimaniyah, 8 December 1918, enclosure in Office of the Civil Commissioner,

Baghdad, 30 December 1919. Noel admitted that Mahmud was not a good man, but felt he had to be accepted for purely political reasons. FO 608/95, 'Kurdistan', enclosure in Gribban of the General Staff to Military Section, British Delegation, Paris, 31 March 1919. Calthorpe believed that the Kurds sincerely wished for the British to control Kurdistan, one of many instances of wishful thinking. (Calthorpe to Curzon, Constantinople, 10 July 1919, DBFP 4, pp. 678–80.)

23. FO 608/95, Telegrams from Baghdad: 7, 9, 15 April and 25 May 1919; G. O. C., Mesopotamia, to War Office, 25 May and 12, 22 July 1919; Calthorpe Telegram, Constantinople, 13 April 1919; Webb, Constantinople, 26 April 1919. The British commander in Iraq estimated the Kurdish force at '8,000 rifles'. (FO 608/95, G. O. C., Mesopotamia, to War Office, 2 August 1919.)

24. FO 608/95, G. O. C., Mesopotamia, to War Office, 5, 22 July, 2, 12 August 1919; 'From Baghdad', 26 June 1919; Calthorpe Telegram, Constantinople, 10 July 1919. G. H. Q., Constantinople, to War Office, 25 August, 12 September 1919.

25. FO 608/95, Balfour to Curzon, Paris, 3 May 1919. Foreign Office to Under-Secretary of State, India Office, Foreign Office, 29 May 1919. See also FO 608/95, Webb to Foreign Office, Constantinople, 21 May 1919. The Armenian national representatives at the Peace Conference stated that the Kurds in Northeast Anatolia were allied with the Turks, unlike many of their statements, an accurate assessment. (CAB 28–6, Secretary's Notes of a Conversation, Paris, 26 February 1919.) The Kurds had good reason to fear the results of an Armenian conquest. See Justin McCarthy, 'American Commissions to Anatolia and the Report of Niles and Sutherland', in *Türk Tarih Kurumu Kongresi XI, Ankara: 5–9 Eylül 1990*, Ankara: Türk Tarih Kurumu, 1994, pp. 1809–53.

26. CAB 24/45/12, Intelligence Bureau, Department of Information, Weekly Report on Turkey and Other Moslem Countries, 12 March 1918.

27. FO 608/95, Secretary of State to Civil Commissioner, Baghdad, Foreign Office, 22 August 1919.

28. FO 608/95, India office, 'From Baghdad', 4 June 1919. E. W. C. Noel, 'Notes on the Kurdish Situation', enclosure in Calthorpe to Curzon, Constantinople, 23 July 1919, later printed by the Office of Civil Administration in Mesopotamia. (FO 371/5008, *Diary of Major E. Noel, C. I. E., D. S. O., on Special Duty in Kurdistan.*) Noel later modified his proposals to accept nominal Turkish sovereignty over Eastern Anatolia, but with Kurdish administrators and gendarmes in the Six Vilayets. The official language would be Kurdish. (FO 608/95, 'From Civil Commissioner, Baghdad', 22 October 1919.) See also, Hohler to Tilley,

Constantinople, 21 July 1919. Hohler also commented: 'I wish Noel wasn't such an out-and-out Kurd!' On Noel's unrealistic plans, see also, FO 248/1225, Noel Telegram to Civil Commissioner, Baghdad, Aleppo, 20 September 1919 and Malatia, 6 September 1919. A number of Noel's reports are in FO 248/1249.

29. FO 608/95, 'From Civil Commissioner, Baghdad', 27 November 1919.
30. On 9 May 1919, the British administration in Baghdad was authorised by the cabinet to treat Mosul as part of Iraq. (FO 608/95, 'British Relations with Kurdistan', Political Department, India Office, August 1919.) The French refused to accept any independent Kurdish state in Mosul under 'British protection', but this was before they grudgingly accepted British rule over Mosul. (FO 608/95, Military Intelligence Report of 27 January 1919, enclosure in Curzon to Secretary of State for Foreign Affairs, Foreign Office, 5 February 1919.)

In February 1921, Curzon was still advocating some sort of autonomous state of Kurdistan, but now believed it might be under 'Turkish supervision'. (CAB 23/38/29, Cabinet Conference on 13 February 1921.)

31. British Secretary's Notes of an Allied Conference, London, 26 February 1921, 11 a. m., DBFP, vol. 15, pp. 213–14, and CAB 29/91. On the Nationalists and the Kurds, see Andrew Mango, 'Atatürk and the Kurds', *Middle Eastern Studies*, vol. 35, no. 4 (October 1999), pp. 1–25.

# 17

## THE FALL OF VENIZELOS – NEUTRALITY

King Constantine of Greece, himself from a Germanic background and married to a sister of Kaiser Wilhelm II, was believed by the British and their Allies to be a pro-German who wished to make Greece an ally of the Central Powers. Public anti-war sentiment and the presence of Allied warships forced him to remain neutral, but the British always viewed him as an enemy.

Prime Minister Venizelos deeply wanted the Greeks to side with the Allies in World War I. On his own initiative, he invited the British and French to occupy Thessaloniki as a spearhead in their fight against the Bulgarians and Ottomans. The king prorogued parliament, forcing Venizelos from power.

In 1916, supporters of Venizelos staged a revolt, and Venizelos became the prime minister of a revolutionary government in Thessaloniki. A civil war ensued between Royalists supporting King Constantine and Venizelists. The Allies, confident that Venizelos would join their side in the war, recognised the revolutionaries as the government of Greece. They instituted a blockade of more than three months of Royalist-controlled regions of Greece to force the Royalists to resign power. The French occupied Thessaly and threatened to bombard Athens if Constantine did not abdicate. In June of 1917 he left Greece, but never formally abdicated. His second son, Alexander, became king, reigning as the puppet of Venizelos and the Allies. Venizelos became prime minister of all Greece. He brought Greece into the war on the side of the Allies.

Greece remained deeply divided. King Constantine retained much support. While Venizelos was the image of Greece for the Allies, he was not nearly as popular in war-weary Greece. Much of Greece opposed the entry into the world war and the subsequent Greek occupation in Anatolia. King Alexander died on 26 October 1920. Venizelos's Liberal Party lost the election of 1 November 1920 to the People's Party of Dimitrios Gounaris. Dimitrios Rallis became prime minister on 17 November 1920, replaced in two months by Nikolaos Kalogeropoulos, who lasted for three months. Gounaris became prime minister on 8 April 1921. A plebiscite on 22 November 1920 returned Constantine as king by an overwhelming majority, to the consternation of the Allied Powers. He retook the throne on 19 December.[1]

Gounaris's party had campaigned against the Anatolian war in the 1920 election. Once in power, however, it continued the war. King Constantine supported an escalation of the fight against the Turkish Nationalists. It would appear that, for the Allies, little had changed. The new Greek Government remained as committed against Mustafa Kemal as had been Venizelos. But among the Allies, emotion defeated clear thinking. Britain and France viewed Constantine as a pro-German who had kept Greece from their side in the war (not a completely fair assessment). Moreover, the British loved Venizelos. Throughout the peace negotiations and the Anatolian war, they had given him their support. Indeed, it is not too much to say that it was Venizelos who was the deciding factor in British positions on both Anatolia and Thrace. British affection for him and hatred for his enemies was deep. For the Allies, Venizelos's defeat had changed everything.

The French proposed complete disavowal of the Greeks as long as Constantine ruled. The British hated Constantine, calling him and his staff 'traitors' for their past pro-German sympathies. They felt, however, that they could not take military or effective political action against Constantine. Instead, Curzon told Georges Leygues, Prime Minister and Foreign Minister of France:

> There is in Greece only one man who, by the prestige he enjoys in the army, can maintain the Treaty of Sèvres, this man is Constantine; he alone can decide that the army stays in Smyrna and in Asia Minor.

Lloyd George said that the Allies must not forget that Turkey was worse than Constantine, and no action against Greece in İzmir or elsewhere should aid

Turkey. Curzon wanted no actions that would 'tear up the treaty of Sèvres', including taking İzmir from Greece. France, seconded by the Italians, wanted strong opposition to the king and his government. Despite British feelings, a somewhat milder version of the French and Italian opinion took hold. No direct action would be taken against the Greeks, but the Allies would end their direct support of the Greeks, declaring neutrality in the war between the Greeks and the Turkish Nationalists. The warring sides were forbidden from importing arms, a prohibition that mainly affected the Greeks.[2]

The French must have seen Constantine's return as a convenient reason to disavow what had become a quagmire in Anatolia and Thrace. The Italians had always opposed the Greek incursion. France suggested that the Treaty of Sèvres be modified to account for the new conditions. Lloyd George and Curzon seriously objected. Curzon announced:

> He, personally, could take no part or lot in any policy which would have the result of placing the Christian population of Smyrna and Thrace back under the Turkish heel. Such a policy undertaken by the Allies would be regarded by the world and by history, as infamous and cowardly.

As long as Constantine respected the treaty, the British contended, the treaty should stand. That meant that the Greeks should remain in Western Anatolia. Only if the Greeks abandoned the treaty would the Allies take action against them. A letter to that effect was sent to the Greek Government.[3]

British support for the Greeks did not disappear with a declaration of neutrality. The majority of the cabinet continued to hope for a Greek victory, although some voices, Churchill's in particular, openly doubted past and present British policy, which he described as a complete failure in need of change.

> It would appear, therefore, that we should initiate and pursue steady and consistently a policy of friendship with Turkey and with the Arabs, and that we should not hope for any effective assistance either from the Bolshevik Russians or the pro-German Greeks.[4]

The British publicly proclaimed their neutrality. Despite their past support for the Greeks, they began to portray themselves as neutral mediators between the Greeks and the Turks. However, in a speech in the Commons on 22 December 1920, Lloyd George indicated that the British were anything but honest brokers between the Greeks and Turks. Repeating the old refrain, he declared that both İzmir and Thrace had Christian majorities that the British could not abandon. In a previously unknown assertion, he said that the Greek majority in İzmir was even greater than was usually thought, because many of those called Muslim were actually Greek Muslims who supported Greece ('there are scores if not hundreds of thousands of Greeks that are Mussulmans'). Despite what he called the blunder of the recent election in Greece, he continued to support the Greeks. He had no doubt that the Greeks would defeat the Nationalists.

The prime minister showed little understanding of the situation in Anatolia. Giving no indication that he knew of the National Pact that set out exactly what the Nationalists wanted, he said he had no idea what Mustafa Kemal wanted. He thought that the Nationalists would be satisfied with Constantinople. Forgetting the Gallipoli campaign, where Mustafa Kemal had successfully opposed the British, he said that no one had ever heard of Mustafa Kemal before 1919. To Lloyd George, Mustafa Kemal was a 'mutinous general' who could not be trusted to comply with any peace terms he entered into. Mustafa Kemal and the Bolsheviks were 'in a state of conflict' over control of Azerbaijan. (The Soviets had taken Azerbaijan in April 1920, eight months before Lloyd George's speech.) He stated that Enver Paşa was holding the purse strings of the Nationalists. Lloyd George did make one accurate statement in his speech: 'I do not know what is happening in Greece. I do not know what is happening in Asia Minor. Who does?'[5]

High Commissioner de Robeck had relinquished his post, replaced in November 1920 by a steady Foreign Office hand, Horace Rumbold. High Commissioner Rumbold had an intelligent understanding of the situation. He wrote on 20 January 1921 that it was useless to regard Mustafa Kemal as anything but the master of Anatolia. The bulk of the Turkish population supported him. Christians under Nationalist control were being treated well. The Nationalist economy, though poor, would not collapse. The Bolsheviks assisted, but did not dominate the Nationalists. The only hope for the Allies would be to make substantial concessions to the Turks.

> All this amounts to saying that Turkish situation as a whole has become almost inextricable, it is true – inextricable if Treaty of Sèvres is still to be regarded as basis of future (sic) unless Allies are united and are prepared to fight new war on large scale.

Although he did not state it, Rumbold must have known that the Allies were neither united nor willing to fight a large war.[6]

The prime minister had defined the British attitude toward the Greeks – disappointed over their electoral decision, but supportive of the Greek army in Turkey. The British nevertheless continued to present themselves as honest brokers, as if the Turks did not know of Lloyd George's opinions. Viewed by their actual intentions, as opposed to their public declarations of neutrality, the British remained committed to the Greeks. They finally realised, however, that the situation in Anatolia had been changed by the rise of Turkish Nationalist power. They felt some alterations would have to be made to the Sèvres Treaty to appease the Turks. Their intention, as always, was to obtain as much as possible for the Greeks. The medium was to be a new conference at which the Allies would dictate new terms.

## The London Conference

The military situation in Anatolia was fluid at the beginning of 1921. The Greeks, with British assistance, had driven Nationalist forces from much of Western Anatolia, but their advance was halted on 11 July at the First Battle of İnönü. The Nationalists were increasing their forces as soldiers were transferred from the victory over the Armenians. The French had suffered heavy losses in Cilicia. They and the Italians were negotiating with the Nationalists. The Greeks were also increasing their forces, planning a final push against the Turks.

The Allies held a preliminary conference among themselves in Paris on 25–7 January 1921. French Prime Minister Aristide Briand wanted a complete disavowal of the Greeks, who had discarded Venizelos and chosen King Constantine. Although the Greeks had recently had some military success against the Nationalists, he felt that the Greek army would soon be in disarray due to the loss of purged Venizelist officers. The Allies would have to come to terms with the Nationalists. Italian Foreign Minister Carlo Sforza agreed. Both Briand and Sforza stated that the public in their countries wanted a compromise with the Nationalists and would not support any military intervention. ('The Allies had no solid ground on which to base extreme measures.')

Curzon stated that the Greeks were about to begin a major operation in Asia Minor, which the Allies could not oppose, because it was the same plan proposed earlier by Venizelos. (He did not explain why this made it acceptable. The Supreme Council had not accepted Venizelos's plan at the time.) The Treaty of Sèvres must be maintained, he said, perhaps with some modifications. Lloyd George wanted the Allies to give the Greeks the financial support they needed to defeat the Turks. He wanted no surrender to Mustafa Kemal:

> Mustapha Kemal was scheming to revert to the pre-war condition of things, and for the Allies to agree to any such proposition would mean that, as regards Turkey, the war had not been an overwhelming victory, but a disgraceful defeat.

The most the British were willing to accept was nominal Turkish sovereignty over İzmir, but actual Greek rule.

The Allies decided that the Ottoman and Greek Governments would be invited to a conference in London to modify the conditions of the Sèvres Treaty. The Nationalists were invited to join the Ottoman delegation, not to appear separately. Despite the Allied intentions, the Nationalists nevertheless sent their own delegation, to which the Ottoman delegation deferred in the subsequent meetings.[7]

Officials at the Foreign Office prepared suggestions for Curzon at the meeting. The head of the Foreign Service bureaucracy, Eyre Crowe (Permanent Under-Secretary of State for Foreign Affairs), felt that Mustafa Kemal would come to terms with the Allies because he was feeling political pressure from the Bolsheviks. Harold Nicolson and D'Arcy Osborne, influential First Secretaries in the Foreign Office, wrote memoranda for the foreign secretary. They suggested as little revision of the Treaty of Sèvres as possible, and that very few concessions be made to the Turks at the upcoming conference; no modifications should be made in most clauses of the treaty, including the Straits, Constantinople and the Arab provinces. 'Kurdistan' should be excised from the treaty – and no mention made of the Kurds. The Turks should lose Eastern Anatolia and Cilicia. Smyrna should remain under Greek control, although with purely nominal Ottoman sovereignty. The Smyrna award province would be called 'the Province of Ionia'. The Straits and Eastern Thrace should not be considered at all, left as in the Sèvres Treaty. Whatever the Turks suggested at the conference should be rejected, because it would be sure to be 'immoderate'. Nicolson and Osborne prepared a conference agenda for Curzon.[8]

For the British, the only serious question was the British attitude toward King Constantine and the new Greek Government. Some, such as Nicolson and Osborne, wanted recognition of the king and British aid for the Greeks. Crowe disagreed, advocating a postponement until events in Anatolia had died down, because there was too much anti-Constantine feeling to risk a change in the British position. Curzon agreed with Crowe, and even Lloyd George, in the face of public and cabinet opposition, did not feel able to openly support the Greeks, although he planned to do so covertly.[9]

On 13 February 1921, the cabinet considered the British position at the upcoming London Conference. Speaking for himself and Lloyd George, Foreign Secretary Curzon outlined British demands: the Sèvres Treaty must be retained, although certain features might be modified. The Greeks would retain Thrace ('the population is more Greek than Turk'), and the Straits would be under international control. İzmir, while under nominal Turkish suzerainty, would be under a Christian governor. Civil order in İzmir would be kept by a gendarmerie under control of the Powers. The proposals, he said, by no means indicated that Greek ownership of İzmir was being abandoned, only delayed. Curzon called upon the example of Eastern Rumelia, which had been first made autonomous within the Ottoman Empire, then annexed by Bulgaria. He felt that control of İzmir would eventually 'slip away' to Greece.

Not all of the cabinet agreed with Curzon. Balfour was against giving anything to the Turks. He wanted no revision to the Sèvres Treaty. Venizelos had assured him that the Greeks could defeat the Nationalists. Churchill was completely against both Curzon and Balfour. The comments of the prime minister at the cabinet meeting did not indicate an understanding of the problems Britain faced: Lloyd George said that he doubted that the Nationalists were being financed by the Bolsheviks. He suggested that Mustafa Kemal would accept Azerbaijan instead of Thrace, because it was in Azerbaijan that Mustafa Kemal 'was basing his strength'. (All the statements were untrue.) He wanted no surrender to what he called the wishes of Mustafa Kemal.[10]

Before the conference began, Lloyd George met with Nikolaos Kalogeropoulos, the Greek prime minister. Kalogeropoulos told him that the Greek army was strong. It could defend its possessions; the Greeks would never relinquish İzmir or Thrace. 'The (British) Prime Minister said that he was glad to hear this, and that he relied upon the spirit of the Greek people not to surrender legitimate rights.' He only asked that the Greeks accept some temporary expedient in İzmir, after which it would surely revert to Greece.[11]

As the conference progressed, the French showed little willingness to press their points. They could not apply much pressure on the British, who were in control of the Allied position in the Ottoman Empire. Lloyd George reminded the French of their place by suggesting the conference hear Emir Feisal, the enemy of the French in Syria, and telling the conference that all aspects of the Sèvres Treaty might be considered. The treaty, of course, included the award of Syria to the French.[12]

The London Conference met from 21 February to 12 March 1921.[13]

In light of future events, one of the most interesting testimonies came on the first day of the conference when the Greek prime minister and military staff spoke of their plans for war with the Turkish Nationalists. The testimony was choreographed by Lloyd George, who fed the Greeks questions that must have been presented to them beforehand. (For example: 'Mr. Lloyd George enquired whether any enthusiasm existed amongst the population of Greece in regard to the liberation of the Greek population in Asia Minor?' The response: 'Yes. All parties were united in that goal.') The Greeks assured the conference that they would soon attack the Turks, and defeat them in three months: 'The Kemalists were in fact not regular soldiers; they merely constituted a rabble worthy of little or no consideration.'

Prime Minister Briand of France disagreed; the French experience in Cilicia had shown that the Turks were excellent fighters. French General Gourad, a military advisor to the conference, seconded Briand. In fact, he said, 15–20,000 of the Nationalist troops were seasoned regulars. Others were also excellent soldiers. No one, he felt, could defeat them in Central Anatolia. The Greek plan could not succeed. Lloyd George questioned the judgement of his own military experts, who agreed with Gourad. In support of the Greeks, he stated that the opinions of the Allied generals had in the past been wrong and the opinion of the Greeks had been right.[14]

Lloyd George had further questions for the Greeks. It is difficult to believe that the questions and answers were not prepared in advance. For example:

> (MR. LLOYD GEORGE) would like to know in what proportion the total wealth was held by Turks and Greeks respectively.
>
> M. GOUNARAKIS regretted that he had no figures available, and he could only therefore give a very rough idea. If real property was added to industry and commerce, he thought that the percentages would work out at something like 60 per cent. to 65 per cent. Greek, and 35 per cent. Turkish.
>
> MR. LLOYD GEORGE then enquired whether good order prevailed in the Smyrna vilayet.
>
> M. GOUNARAKIS said that not only he himself, but the representatives of the Great Powers could testify that excellent order had always been maintained in the town and vilayet of Smyrna.
>
> MR. LLOYD GEORGE then enquired whether there had been any trouble from the Mussulman population.
>
> M. GOUNARAKIS . . . The Turkish population was quiescent because it had the most complete confidence in the Greek administration.
>
> MR. LLOYD GEORGE then enquired whether historically Smyrna had been Greek or Turkish territory.
>
> M. GOUNARAKIS replied that for many centuries prior to 1453 the district had been Greek. Since 1453 the Greek population had diminished owing to Turkish misrule, but the fact that Greek ideals and culture had survived, in spite of Ottoman oppression, indicated how strongly and vigorously Greek sentiment and sympathies had permeated the district.[15]

Turkish and Greek delegates were heard. The Greeks said they were confident of victory, so none of the suggested plans for Allied mediation were necessary. They insisted on the complete Sèvres Treaty. The Turks demanded full acceptance of the National Pact, including the return of both İzmir and Eastern Thrace. For the Turks, Bekir Sami presented a detailed plan which specified Turkish rule in all of Anatolia and Thrace, economic independence, protection for minorities, military independence and neutrality of the Straits. The usual conflicting statements on population were heard.[16]

After dissension and debate, the Allies decided to present a plan, drafted by Curzon, to the Greeks and Turks: hostilities would cease. The question of who should rule İzmir and Eastern Thrace would be decided by a commission named by the Allies, based on population. (Briand said the Greeks should accept this, because 'M. Kalogeropoulos had just said to him that he had absolute certainty in being able to prove his figures.') The commission would study the population question and make political recommendations. The Greeks and Turks would bind themselves to accept the commission's decision, and would agree to accept all the other provisions in the Sèvres Treaty. Neither Greeks nor Turks were satisfied, but the Turks were conciliatory. The Nationalist representative, Bekir Sami, agreed to a cessation of hostilities while the commission worked. The Turks agreed to abide by the commission's findings on İzmir and Thrace, but needed to consult Ankara on the rest of the treaty, although Bekir Sami made plain that retaining the rest of the Sèvres Treaty would not be acceptable. The Ankara Grand National Assembly voted agreement with Bekir Sami's position – a commission on İzmir and Thrace, to whose judgement they would adhere, but not the rest of the Sèvres Treaty.[17]

In fact, the British themselves were not willing to abide by the commission's findings. Lloyd George stated that only if the Nationalists agreed to the rest of the Sèvres Treaty would an international commission be considered. At the conference he told the Turks that the questions of İzmir and Eastern Thrace would be decided by the Great Powers upon receipt of the report of the investigating commission. In other words, the Turks were told to accept whatever the Allies wished, not what the commission stated:

> M. Lloyd George desired the Turkish Delegates thoroughly to realize, before proceeding further, that every question in the Sèvres Treaty must be considered as closed, with the exception of the ones relating to Thrace and Smyrna, which were to be adjudicated upon by the Great Powers.

Lloyd George told the Turks that they would also have to accept an Armenian state in Eastern Anatolia.[18]

Any Turkish acceptance of the proposed commission would appear to have been madness. Nothing in past British actions indicated that such a commission, controlled by the Allies, would be impartial. They must have known from experience of the suppressed Smyrna Commission Report that the British would not let any commission, especially an impartial commission, affect their plans. One explanation is that, when they accepted a commission in a conference meeting, they did not fully understand what Lloyd

George intended. The other more likely explanation for the Turks' acceptance was that they were sure the Greeks would reject it completely, which was true. Better to let the Greeks bear the onus of rejection.[19]

The Greeks protested everything. For the Greek Government, Prime Minister Nikolaos Kalogeropoulos complained that: 'The Greek Government was now asked to nullify a title-deed which bore the signatures of the Great Powers.' He objected that the Greek army was about to begin a victorious advance, and now it was being told to cease hostilities. Kalogeropoulos said the Greeks would only accept the proposals if they retained military control of İzmir and the entire region, including naming the governor. He said he could not accept or reject the terms offered without consultation from Athens. In the end, the Greek National Assembly unanimously rejected any alteration of the Sèvres Treaty. Instead of accepting terms that obviously favoured them, the Greeks asked for British credits to continue their fight. The Greeks went forward with their attack. Lloyd George said he did not want to give any impression that the Allies wished to prevent the Greeks from attacking.[20]

In rejecting the Allied proposals, the Greeks believed they actually had the support of the British. Curzon had presented them with very favourable terms, but they had been assured by Lloyd George that they would achieve more if they refused the London Conference terms. Lloyd George had notified them privately of his support for a refusal. The British prime minister had no difficulty in opposing his own foreign secretary.

Lloyd George was hampered by a neutralist policy that had developed in parliament and the press over Constantine's return to rule in Greece. His dealings with the Greeks were therefore private and secret, going behind the backs of the British delegation to advise the Greek delegation during the conference. Lloyd George's henchman (not too strong a description), Philip Kerr, distributed the conference's plans to the Greeks during the conference meetings, and advised them not to accept the conference proposals. Lloyd George even edited the draft text of the proposed Greek rejection, suggesting revisions to make it more palatable to public opinion. He assured the Greeks that when they attacked the Turks, 'they need fear no obstacle from them (the British)'. 'Mr. Lloyd George informed us (the Greek delegation) that Great

Britain has consecrated a warm corner in her heart for Greece and proposes to assist her to return to her pristine glory.' The Greeks realised that, no matter what Curzon and the Allies decided, British foreign policy was effectively in the hands of Lloyd George. The Greeks indicated that they were confident of his support.[21]

While they awaited the Turkish and Greek responses, the conference delegates considered the Armenian Question. Curzon was particularly vociferous in his demands that the Turks give land to an Armenia: 'He wished the Turkish delegation to understand clearly that Europe—that is, the Powers who had been victorious in the war—were solemnly pledged to create an independent State of Armenia.' Bekir Sami responded that Turkey would gladly see an independent Armenia in all the regions where Armenians were a majority (that is, no part of Anatolia). Lloyd George met with Bekir Sami and made a last effort to change the Turkish position in the light of the Greek refusal. He asked the Turks to accept modifications in their proposal. Bekir Sami politely refused.[22]

Meeting with Kalogeropoulos, Lloyd George told him that all he asked from the Greeks in return for his support was their acceptance of some sort of change in the legal status, but not the actual rule, in İzmir. He himself supported the Greek position, but he needed something to present to France and Italy, who were increasingly against the Greeks. The Greeks gave him nothing. Not even when the British prime minister asked for a Greek plan for treaty revisions that he could present to the conference did they budge from absolute refusal of any change in the Sèvres provisions. In the end, this had little effect on Lloyd George, who continued his constant support of the Greeks.[23]

Lloyd George had orchestrated the entire London Conference. He and Lord Curzon had prepared the proposals and the final decisions. They had hobbled discontent from their Allies. The assumption was that the Greeks and Turks would humbly accept the decisions of the Great Powers, but as the conference closed, it was obvious that neither Greeks nor Turks would accept British guidance. Both groups refused, the Greeks categorically, the Turks in part. Frustrated by the results of the conference, the Allies, by themselves, wrote a set of proposals that satisfied no one. The proposals for modification of the Sèvres Treaty were handed formally to the Greek and Turkish delegations on 11 March 1921, although the proposals had been known before. The main points:

- Turkey would be admitted to the League of Nations if they executed the modified Sèvres Treaty.
- Turkey would not be expelled from Constantinople 'in certain contingencies'.
- The demilitarised zone would be decreased in size. 'The Allies might also consent to the rapid evacuation of Constantinople, of the Ismid Peninsula, and to limit the Allied occupation to Gallipoli and Chanak.' (Note the 'might'.)
- Turkish membership on the Commission for Judicial Reform and the Straits Commission.
- Turkey would have a member on the Financial Commission. The Turkish member would have a vote on internal financial matters and 'a consultative voice in those affecting more specially the financial interests of the Allies'. The Allies would have the majority on all commissions.
- The Turkish Parliament could modify their budget 'prepared in agreement between the Minister of Finance and the Financial Commission', but the Financial Commission would have final approval. This was also true of concessions granted to Europeans.
- Turkish forces would be increased to '30,000 special elements and 45,000 Gendarmerie'. There would be more Turkish and fewer European officers (numbers unstated), and there might be other military allowances. A Turkish navy 'might' be allowed.
- Kurdistan aspects of the Sèvres Treaty 'might' be modified.
- 'In regard to Armenia the present stipulations might be adapted on condition of Turkey recognising the rights of Turkish Armenians to a National home on the Eastern Frontiers of Turkey in Asia, and agreeing to accept the decision of a Commission, appointed by the Council of the League of Nations, to examine on the spot the question of the territory equitably to be transferred to Armenia.'
- 'The region called the Vilayet of Smyrna would remain under Turkish sovereignty.' However, İzmir would have a Christian governor, appointed

by the League of Nations, and Greek troops would remain in the city. Outside the city, an Allied Commission would have authority, supported by 'a gendarmerie with Allied officers and recruited in proportion to the numbers and distribution of the population as reported by an Inter-Allied Commission'. This proportional arrangement would also apply to the administration.[24]

The international commission on İzmir and Thrace, the only thing the Turks had accepted, was not in the final proposal, because the Greeks had immediately rejected it.

For the Turks, the Allied proposals were in fact insignificant modifications of the Sèvres Treaty. Stripped of promises, they left the Turks with little actual control over their state. Turks would have a member on the various commissions that would govern their lives, but no actual say in decisions. Given past history of broken promises, Turks could only doubt promises, such as the evacuation of Istanbul and İzmit, a navy being allowed or other military concessions. Significantly, Eastern Thrace was not mentioned in the Allied proposals, which meant the Sèvres Treaty stipulations still applied. It would remain Greek.

The provisions in the Sèvres Treaty that were not modified were to remain in place. The financial, economic and judicial terms of Sèvres that would restrict a future Turkish State remained. They were expected to accept the rulings of Allied Commissions, whatever they might be. They would lose Thrace, Eastern Anatolia and, effectively, İzmir and its region. The area actually ruled by the Turks would be nearly the same as in the Sèvres Treaty. The Turks were expected to concede land to an Armenia after that same land had just been reconquered from occupying Armenians. Turkish 'sovereignty' over İzmir was an almost humorous concession – an Allied-appointed Christian governor, Greek troops and Allied gendarmerie officers would really rule. (As Curzon noted, the same situation had resulted in the lost Ottoman provinces of Crete and Eastern Rumelia.)[25]

The British seem to have had a low estimation of the intelligence of the Turks. They promised possibilities, completely dependent on Allied intentions to carry them out. The Turks knew what such promises were worth. As far back as the Mudros Armistice and for decades before, the British had shown that their promises were worthless. The Turks could see that the British had never abandoned their preference for the Greeks, nor their wish for Greek success. If they had accepted British 'mediation', they would have been as incompetent as the British assumed.

The Turkish refusal to accept the Allied proposals is understandable; to do so would have been to deny what they had pledged in the National Pact. Their economy and much of their land would have remained in the hands of their enemies. The Greek refusal was driven by their military plans. In July they began their great assault against the Nationalists. They expected to reach Ankara and claim much more land than the London Accords had allowed them.

**Allied Unity Disabled**

After events in İzmir, the Italians were at best half-hearted allies of the British, as the British realised. Curzon confronted the Italian Foreign Minister, Count Carlo Sforza, at the Allied Conference at Spa, Belgium (5–16 July 1920). Not mincing words, he accused the Italians of being disloyal allies. Curzon accused them of consorting with both the Bolsheviks and the Turkish Nationalists. The Italians, Curzon alleged, had assured the Nationalists that they were behind them in resisting the Sèvres Peace Treaty.[26]

In March 1921, the French and Italians altered what had been an increasingly superficial alliance. The French accepted that they had been defeated

Map 17.1   Cilicia: Treaty boundaries

in Cilicia and signed a treaty of peace with the Nationalists on 9 March, superseded by the Treaty of Ankara (20 October 1921), setting the borders between Turkey and Syria. Hostilities ended. The French gained mining concessions – a concession to operate the Baghdad Railway from Cilician ports westward – and promises of economic cooperation in the region. The Italians had begun to withdraw their troops from Southern Anatolia in July of 1920. They signed a treaty with the Nationalists on 12 March 1921. The Italians gained economic concessions in Anatolia. The clause that particularly galled the British was: 'Clause 4. Italian Government undertakes to support vis-à-vis its Allies all demands of Turkish delegation about the Peace Treaty, especially with regard to the restitution of Thrace and Smyrna to Turkey.' The Italians promised to remove their troops from Ottoman territory once a peace treaty had been signed. In May and June, Italian troops evacuated Marmaris and Antalya.[27]

The Italians and French also gave concrete support to the Nationalists, leaving behind military supplies when they evacuated. The French left enough weapons and equipment to outfit 40,000 men. Most of the 80,000 Turkish soldiers in Cilicia were able to join the fight against the Greeks.

The Italians also allowed some guns and ammunition to be imported for the Nationalists. French and Italian actions were thus a significant factor in the subsequent Nationalist victory.[28]

In the cabinet Curzon described the French agreements as 'a breach of honour and good faith and were most detrimental to British Interests'. He believed that 'France appeared to be adopting an attitude definitely hostile to British interests in the Near East'.[29]

## Renewed Mediation

The Allies considered making further offers of mediation between the belligerents, but it was recognised that the Greeks would not accept as long as they seemed to be winning. Lloyd George blamed the Turks, but complained that the Greeks should have been supported by the British. Now nothing could be done. In fact, it was the Greeks who had completely refused British mediation. They notified the British that they were relying on their great offensive against the Nationalists.[30]

By the middle of 1921 the British Cabinet was searching for a solution to their entanglement in the Near East. Meeting on 1 June as the 'Committee on the Future of Constantinople' – Lloyd George, Curzon (Foreign Affairs), Churchill (Colonies), Montagu (India), Worthington-Evans (War) and Mond (Health) – considered the British options. The committee heard dispiriting evidence from General Wilson, the Chief of the General Staff, and General Harington, who had come from Istanbul to testify. Attempts to deal diplomatically with the Nationalists and the Greeks had failed. The French and Italians, far from supporting Britain, had presented obstacles to British plans. Militarily, the situation was also dire. The Dardanelles could only be held with a significant military reinforcement. The British, it was suggested, might ask for assistance from the Greek army, but only if 'Greece would be willing to place herself in our hands'. There were questions regarding whether Greece was worthy of support: Intelligence reports described the Greek army as lacking in morale, troop discipline, strategic planning and, especially, capable officers. The committee was unwilling to commit to significant reinforcements, because it believed there was not yet a significant danger to Constantinople.

Obviously, the British Cabinet still hoped for a Greek victory, despite their despair at the triumph of the Greek King. The possibility of British armed assistance to the Greeks was suggested, or at least a threat to Mustafa Kemal that they would do so if he did not accept 'a reasonable peace'. The military representatives held that even a great military effort by Britain might not defeat the Nationalists. Perhaps the Greeks might abandon İzmir if they were guaranteed Thrace? The committee decided to hear the testimony of Venizelos, now out of office but still influential. As might have been expected, Venizelos told them that the only hope for success was active British military support for the Greek army.

In the end, the committee recommended what appeared to them to be a moderate position. Mustafa Kemal would be threatened with British support of the Greeks if he did not accept the Sèvres Treaty, with modifications. That support, however, would be limited to allowing the Greeks to purchase munitions and war materials, as well as a naval blockade of the Black Sea, not British troops.[31]

The cabinet deemed it essential that the British were to appear truly neutral if their mediation were to succeed. To that end, the cabinet resolved to strengthen neutrality by denying some of their previous support of the

Greeks. Throughout their war with the Nationalists, the Greeks had used Istanbul as a base for resupply of their navy. The Marmara had been open to their troop movements and supply. Allied voices began to question this as a violation of declared Allied neutrality. The French ambassador suggested to Curzon, in view of Greeks refusing Allied mediation, that the Greeks should be told that the continuation of the war was their fault, and that the Allies should now refuse to let them use Istanbul for revictualling, and not allow them the use of the Sea of Marmara at all. Curzon emphatically disagreed; the French suggestion was ignored. He said the Greek army was now in good shape and would be victorious – after which the Greeks would 'appeal to our good offices'. Despite Curzon's feelings, the government decided that it was still better to present an appearance of neutrality.[32]

Despite Curzon's avowed belief in the triumph of the Greeks, he was deeply worried that the Turkish Nationalists might win, which eventuality he called 'a catastrophe'. 'A Turkish success would jeopardize every Allied gain in the war and remove all prospects of peaceful reconstruction in the Middle East.' The Allies would either have to strengthen Iraq, Syria and Palestine or abandon them. Thrace and Istanbul would be lost. There would be 'disastrous consequences which might overtake all Allied interests in the East in the event of a Greek retreat'. Curzon did not quite assert that a Turkish victory would bring about the Apocalypse and the End of Days, but he surely adopted an apocalyptic tone. Curzon said that if the Greeks won, all would be well, but if it looked as if the Turks would win, something would have to be done to save the situation. Agreement between the two sides would then have to be forced by the Allies, along much the same lines as put forward in the London Conference. If the Greeks lost, they would agree. If the Turks refused, the British should support the Greeks financially, facilitate the supply of arms, ammunition and supplies to them, and create a naval blockade that would interdict arms shipments to the Nationalists. To Curzon, British neutrality was obviously a gesture forced on the cabinet by circumstances, not a real declaration of British desires.[33]

While Lloyd George had been constrained, despite his wishes, not to support the Greeks militarily, both he and his representative, Kerr, privately notified the Greeks of his support in their battle with the Turkish Nationalists. The Greeks were encouraged. Depending on Lloyd George, they had good reason to believe that the British would come over to the Greek side completely if the Greeks defeated the Turks in the great Greek push toward Ankara.

On 18–19 June 1921, the Allies convened in Paris for a further meeting on proposed mediation between the Greeks and the Turks. Neither of the belligerents were present. At the meeting Curzon proposed that the Turks be presented with a plan that was little different than that proposed in London. He suggested that if the Turks did not agree to the Allied demands, then all the 'concessions' offered to them in the London Agreements would be withdrawn, the Greeks would be given financial assistance and would be able to purchase weapons of war and the Allies might blockade Turkish Black Sea ports. As for the Greeks, they were only to be asked politely to agree: 'Lord Curzon repeated that there was no case for threatening the Greeks, but that the British Government feared that concessions to the Turks would be fruitless unless accompanied by a threat.' Foreign Minister Briand, on the other hand, felt that both sides should be threatened or neither. He thought, however, that the Allies did not have the force to really threaten either. Curzon, stressing the need for Allied unity, condemned his Allies, France and Italy, for signing separate agreements with the Turks.

The main positive offer to the Turks was abandonment of the Tripartite Agreement that had divided Anatolia in economic spheres of control. France and Britain were in favour; Italy firmly opposed.

It was decided to first approach the Greeks to seek their agreement to a new conference. Only if they agreed would the Turks be asked. The Greeks were told that if they did not agree, all would be abandoned. They did not agree. It was all abandoned.[34]

The Greeks began their final offensive to seize Ankara on 27 June. Lloyd George justified the attack. He alleged that the Greeks were forced to attack because of 'a large concentration' of Turkish troops threatening their position. He was lying. He knew there was no such large concentration. General Wilson noted that both the British and Greek authorities knew that the prime minister's statement was untrue.[35]

## Questions on Neutrality

Even the appearance of neutrality soon was further diminished by the British prime minister. On 10 August 1921, Lloyd George had convinced the other three powers at the Peace Conference to allow the Greeks to purchase weapons from arms merchants. The British immediately took steps to facilitate arms purchases from British suppliers. An ineffective blockade was put in place on the Black Sea; Soviet vessels supplying arms to Nationalists were to be seized.[36]

Allowing the Greek navy to use Istanbul as a base in their war with the Nationalists was a major breach in the British policy of neutrality. British and Allied high commissioners and military representatives in Istanbul felt that the Greek bases should be closed. The Admiralty agreed. The high commissioners in Istanbul redoubled their efforts to evict the Greeks from Istanbul after the Greek massacres of Turks in the İzmit region. The commissioners took neutrality seriously. They met and decided on a proclamation of neutrality: all areas occupied by the Allies were to be neutral, and both Greek and Turkish forces were to be excluded from them. They declared that allowing the Greeks to use Istanbul as a naval base was a violation of neutrality. They therefore requested their governments to ask the Greeks to remove all their warships from the Allied Constantinople Zone, close their naval base there and not allow Greek forces to enter the neutral zone. A proclamation to that effect was prepared. Curzon delayed the commissioners' proclamation on the false pretext that the French objected to denying the Istanbul base to the Greeks. The French, however, had authorised the proclamation, so the British were forced to admit it was they who favoured the Greeks. Lloyd George disagreed with the high commissioners.[37]

Counsel from the British representation in Istanbul was disrupted when it was sorely needed, just as the Greeks prepared and began the offensive against the Nationalists. The British had mainly received good advice from their high commissioners in Istanbul. The commissioners did not care for the Turks, and surely never considered as important the welfare of Turks or of the Ottoman Government. Their advice on major issues, such as the İzmir occupation, was seldom followed by Lloyd George or Curzon. Nevertheless, at the critical juncture in the summer of 1921, the British greatly needed accurate analyses from Istanbul. Unfortunately, High Commissioner Rumbold was on leave during the difficult time in 1921 when the British were trying to salvage what they could in their Turkish quagmire. Frank Rattigan, Rumbold's deputy, took charge (26 May – 31 July 1921) until Rumbold returned.

Rattigan was vehemently pro-Greek and questioned the policy of neutrality. Rattigan asked the British Government to reverse its policy and support the Greeks militarily. He stated that 'our military experts' (unnamed) supported British intervention on the side of the Greeks. In fact, this was untrue – the British military, both in Istanbul and in London, gave him no support. Rattigan went so far as to write to London that General Harington supported his view that neutrality should not be extended. In particular, the Greeks should not be restricted from using Istanbul as a base. Although he had been ordered to restrict the Greeks, Rattigan did not do so. Because Harington reportedly had felt it wise not to further restrict the Greeks, London agreed to relax the policy, allowing the Greeks to use Istanbul as a military base.[38]

Harington became apprised of this and protested that Rattigan had misrepresented his position. (He politely did not openly say Rattigan had lied.) He stressed that he completely disagreed with Rattigan. Restricting the Greeks was the only way the British could demonstrate their neutrality. The War Office agreed with him that neutrality should be strengthened. Moreover, Harington felt that it was a mistake not to meet with Mustafa Kemal. The Foreign Office changed its position, noting that Rattigan had misrepresented Harington's views. Obviously, Rattigan had blotted his copybook. In transmitting Harington's letter to the War Office, the Foreign Office noted rather pointedly that Rumbold would shortly return to his post, relieving Rattigan.[39]

Much debate and communications among British officials and with the French and Italians took place over the Greek bases. Rumbold repeatedly told London that he and the other commissioners felt that the Greek naval base should be closed, and the Greeks refused the use of Istanbul for all military purposes. It all came to nothing. Rumbold and Harington (but obviously not Rattigan) wanted to close the base, as did France and Italy. In the meeting of the Supreme Council of 10 August 1921, however, Lloyd George stated that neutrality had gone too far. To deny their Istanbul base to the Greeks, he said, 'would amount to taking steps against Greece since it would prevent Greece from delivering decisive blow'. France, still under pressure in Europe, was forced to agree. The Greeks were allowed to keep their base.[40]

## The Prime Minister Explains to Parliament

Lloyd George seldom felt it necessary to explain his government's actions in the Ottoman lands, much less ask for parliamentary support. On 16 August

1921, however, he felt pressured by parliamentary and public questions to offer brief explanations in parliament; his main points:

> The assignment of İzmir and Thrace, he said, was based on the recommendation of the British in the Greek Territorial Committee, which he described as 'impartial' and 'judicial'. (False. The differences among the members of that committee and its lack of unanimity went unmentioned.)
>
> Any Greek failures in Anatolia were the fault of Britain's Allies: 'What has happened since shows that Veniselos (sic) was quite justified in the view which he took that he could have disposed of that insurrection without the slightest difficulty.'
>
> The French had occupied Cilicia mainly to protect Armenians. He stated that the Italians had occupied Southern Anatolia also to protect Armenians (although in fact there were very few Armenians there).
>
> The Greeks and Turks had refused to accept British mediation. The British could not defeat the Turks militarily. 'There is only one other alternative, and that is to leave both of them to fight it out.' He was confident that the Greeks would realise the impossibility of advancing into 'the fastnesses of Asia Minor'. (An odd assertion, since the Greeks had begun their final attack into those 'fastnesses' one month earlier.)

Lloyd George said he believed that both sides would now accept mediation. The battle that decided the fate of Anatolia, the Battle of the Sakarya, began one week after the prime minister spoke.[41]

As was so often the case, the prime minister's actions belied what he told parliament. He did not support mediation; he supported Greek attack. In private transactions with the Greeks, Lloyd George told them that he and the other Allies understood that the Greeks would find it necessary to attack the Turks, but that '[i]t was imperative to Greece to make it quite clear to the Western Powers, and particularly to the people of England, that responsibility for bloodshed and strife rested with the Turks and not with the Greeks'.[42]

**Notes**

1. Venizelos' party's loss was due to the eccentricities of the Greek electoral system. Even though the party won 50 per cent of the votes, the opposition claimed 70 per cent of the seats in parliament.

2. Berthelot to de Peretti de la Rocca, London, 27 November 1920; de Peretti de la Rocca to Cambon, Paris, 28 November 1920; and Berthelot to all posts, Paris, 7 December 1920, in DD 1920, T 3, nos. 239, 245 and 279. CAB 29/90, British Secretary's Notes of a Conference between Representatives of the British and French Governments, London, 26 November 1920. The political changes in Greece have not been considered here in any detail. See DBFP 12, pp. 503–56. On the arms boycott, see the many documents in FO 371/6513.
3. CAB 29/90, British Secretary's Notes of a Conference between Representatives of the British, French and Italian Governments, London, 2 December 1920.
4. CAB 24/117/87, Secretary of State for War (Churchill), 'The Situation in the Middle East', 16 December 1920.
5. *The Parliamentary Debates*, Fifth Series, vol. 136, London: HMSO, 1920, pp. 1893–902.
6. FO 406/45, Rumbold to Curzon, Constantinople, 20 January 1921.
7. British Secretary's Notes of an Allied Conference, Paris, 25 January 1921, DBFP, vol. 15, pp. 29–39. CAB 24/119/13, 'Conclusions of the Paris Conference, Note by the Cabinet Secretary (Hankey)', 3 February 1921.
8. Record by Sir E. Crowe of a conversation with the French Charge d'Affaires, Foreign Office, 7 January 1921, DBFP 17, pp. 5–7. See also Harold Nicolson's advice to the cabinet that the British give up none of the Treaty of Sèvres, which gives a picture of at least some of the foreign advice. FO 371/6077, 'Revision of the Treaty of Sèvres: Memorandum by Mr. Nicolson', January 1921. 'Memorandum by Mr. Osborne and Mr. Nicolson on the Graeco-Turkish Conference', Foreign Office, 17 February 1921, DBFP 17, pp. 61–5. Nicolson wanted any plebiscite on Greek rule to be excluded. Osborne's full name was Francis D'Arcy Godolphin Osborne.
9. On the Foreign Office disagreements, see Eleftheria Daleziou, 'Britain and the Greek-Turkish War and Settlement of 1919–1923: The Pursuit of Security by "Proxy" in Western Asia Minor', unpublished PhD dissertation, University of Glasgow, 2002, pp. 177–9.
10. CAB 23/38/29, Cabinet Conference on 13 February 1921. An earlier cabinet meeting had shown a great deal of confusion and differences with what was decided on 13 February. (FO 371/6464, Cabinet Meeting on 20 January 1921.) On British plans for the London and Paris Conferences, see FO 371/6531, annex in 'Minutes by the Secretary of State of September 28'.
11. CAB 29/91, 'Interview between the Prime Minister and Monsieur Kalogeropoulos', 18 February 1921. Kalogeropoulos did not give an answer to Lloyd George's plan. He said he would have to consult his government. The Greek

Government in a later formal message refused the plan, and said it would fight the Turks and win, obviating any need for changes in the Treaty of Sèvres. ('Athens Note Communicated to M. Kalogeropoulos', in British Secretary's Notes of a Meeting, London, 21 February 1921, DBFP, vol. 15, pp. 131–7.) Nikolaos Kalogeropoulos (sometimes spelled Calogeropoulos) was Greek prime minister from 24 January to 26 March 1921.

Lloyd George later told Briand a version of his conversation with Kalogeropoulos. It was at great variance with the record of that conversation. He told the French that he had threatened the Greeks with action if they did not comply with Allied plans – very different than what he had said. ('Notes of a Conversation between Mr. Lloyd George and M. Briand', London, 21 February 1921, DBFP, vol. 15, pp. 127–30.)

12. CAB 29/91, British Secretary's Notes of an Allied Conference, 22 February 1921, 11 a. m. The minutes of the London Conference are in DBFP, vol. 15, pp. 137–216, 278–86, 344–7, 360–96 and 403–11.
13. Each conference sitting is described in detail in Adnan Sofuoğlu and Seyfi Yıldırım, *Arşive Vesikalarına göre 1921 Londra Konferansı*, Ankara: Atatürk Kültür, Dıl ve Tarih Yüksek Kurumu, Atatürk Araştırma Merkezi, 2018, pp. 189–372. See also Busch, pp. 236–47.
14. CAB 29/91, British Secretary's Notes of an Allied Conference, 21 February 1921. Lloyd George asked Gourad: 'How many white troops the French had on the Cilician Front?' The obvious implication was that the cause of the French loss in Cilicia was the use of African troops.
15. British Secretary's Notes of an Allied Conference, London, 24 February 1921, DBFP, vol. 15, pp. 181–8.
16. Sofuoğlu and Yıldırım, pp. 230–2, 235–7 and 253–7.
17. CAB 24/120 P. C. 2666, 'Reply of Angora Government to Allied Conference in Regard to Smyrna and Eastern Thrace'. The Turks particularly stated that they would never accept some parts of the Sèvres Treaty, particularly on Armenia and Kurdistan.
18. CAB 29/91, British Secretary's Notes of a Conference, London, 24 February 1921; British Secretary's Notes of an Allied Conference, London, 25 February 1921, two meetings, at 11.30 a. m. and 5 p. m.; British Secretary's Notes of an Allied Conference, London, 26 February 1921.
19. See FO 371/6467, Granville to Curzon, Athens, 1 March 1921.
20. CAB 29/91, British Secretary's Notes of an Allied Conference, London, 4 March 1921, 11.30 a. m. and 4.05 p. m. CAB 29/92, British Secretary's Notes of an Allied Conference, London, 10 March 1921, 5.15 p. m. and 9.30 p. m. CAB

24/120 C. P. 2699, 'Reply by the Greek Government', 10 March 1921. Lloyd George had already told his allies on 9 March that the Greeks would attack and win easily, something of which he was all in favour. (British Secretary's Notes of an Allied Conference, London, 9 March 1921, DBFP 15, pp. 344–7.)

21. FO 371/6467, M. Calogeropoulos to Ministry of Foreign Affairs, Athens, London, 19 March 1921 (a British Intelligence intercept). Michael Llewellyn Smith, *Greece in Asia Minor 1919–1922*, New York: St. Martin's, 1973, pp. 189–97. Daniel-Joseph MacArthur-Seal, 'Intelligence and Lloyd George's Secret Diplomacy in the Near East, 1920–1922', *The Historical Journal*, vol. 56, no. 3 (September 2013), p. 714. In addition to private papers, MacArthur-Seal's very valuable analysis made use of secret intercepts of Greek telegrams.

22. British Secretary's Notes of an Allied Conference, London, Meetings of 25, 26 February and 4 March 1921, and Notes of a Meeting between Lloyd George and Bekir Sami Bey, London, 4 March 1921, DBFP 15, pp. 194–285. Further discussions are included in this source, but they show no change in the stands of the Greeks or Turks. Lloyd George felt the Turks were only willing to accept a commission so that they could reopen the population question, which had already been decided against them. (FO 286/760, 'Notes of a Conversation (British and Greek) held at 10 Downing Street', 10 March 1921.)

23. Interview between the prime minister and M. Kalogeropoulos, London, 4 March 1921, DBFP, vol. 15, pp. 265–9. Lloyd George uncharacteristically practically begged the Greeks for help with his allies.

24. FO 371/6467, 'Proposed Modification of the Treaty of Sèvres as Submitted to the Greek and Turkish Delegations on March 12th, 1921', Vansittart to Howarth, 14 April 1921. (This document includes a 'mark-up' of the treaty with proposed changes.) CAB 24/120/96, 'Proposals of the Allies in regard to the Dispute between the Greeks and Turks', 10 March 1921. Sofuoğlu and Yıldırım, pp. 340–5. CAB 29/92, British Secretary's Notes of an Allied Conference, London, 25 February 1921, 11.30 a. m.; British Secretary's Notes of an Allied Conference, London, 12 March 1921.

25. FO 286/760, 'Notes of a Conversation (British and Greek) held at 10 Downing Street', 10 March 1921.

26. FO 406/44, Curzon to Buchanan (ambassador at Rome), Foreign Office, 10 July 1920. Sforza told Curzon that Italy did disagree with Britain over İzmir and Thrace, but that he was personally friendly with Britain.

27. FO 406/44, de Robeck to Curzon, Constantinople, 16 July 1920. De Robeck believed that the Italians could not be trusted to aid the British after that.

FO 406/46, 'Accord franco-turc politique, militaire, économique sur les Fontières enter la Turquie et la Syria', in Hardinge to Curzon, Paris, 2 April 1921; 'Agreement between the Italian Government and the Angora Government', in Buchanan to Curzon, Rome, 19 April 1921. FO 406/48, 'Accord signé á Angora. Le 20 Octobre 1921, entre M. Franklin-Bouillon, ancien Ministre, et Youssouf Kemal Bey, Ministre des Affaires étrangères du Gouvernement de Grande Assemblée nationale d'Angora', in Hardinge to Curzon, Paris, 30 October 1921. See also Leygues to Gouraud, Paris, 2 January 1921, in DD 1920, T 3, no. 417. Reports and Intelligence intercepts had shown the British that the French were negotiating with the Turks long before actual treaties were signed. See the many examples in FO 371/5054.

On the French and Cilicia, see: Kemal Çelik, *Milli Mücadele'de Adana ve Havalisi (1918–1922)*, Ankara: Türk Tarih Kurumu, 1999. Yücel Güçlü, 'The Struggle for Mastery in Cilicia: Turkey, France, and the Ankara Agreement of 1921', *The International History Review*, vol. 23, no. 3 (September 2001), pp. 580–603.

28. Shaw, *From Empire to Republic*, vol. 3, part 2, pp. 1437–8. Güçlü, p. 598.
29. CAB 23/27/11, Cabinet Meeting of 1 November 1921. See also Güçlü, pp. 598–601.
30. British Secretary's Notes of an Allied Conference, Paris, 10 August 1921, Documents XV, pp. 652–7. FO 371/6519, Granville Telegram, Athens, 25 June 1921.
31. CAB 27/133, Meetings of the Committee on the Future of Constantinople, 1, 2 and 9 June 1921.

    Churchill recommended a belligerent policy, sending fresh divisions and threatening both the Greeks and the Turks if they did not acquiesce to British plans. Mond, a wealthy industrialist, must have had political importance, because his office as minister of health was accorded cabinet rank, which was unusual. See also CAB 23/26/6, Cabinet Meeting of 21 June 1921.

    By no means were all British officials agreed on neutrality. Eyre Crowe stated that if the Turks took İzmir and Istanbul, then a Turkish–Bolshevik alliance would threaten India. Lord Grenville in Athens wanted complete British support for the Greeks – supplies and equipment (including airplanes), officers and especially financial assistance. ('Memorandum by Sir E. Crowe on the Hostilities between Turks and Greeks', Foreign Office, 30 May 1921, in DBFP 17, pp. 209–11. Granville to Curzon, Athens, 3 June 1921, in DBFP 17, pp. 216–17.)
32. FO 371/6521, Curzon to Hardinge, Foreign Office, 1 July 1921.
33. FO 371/6517, Curzon to Hardinge, Foreign Office, 14 June 1921.

34. Conversations in Paris between British, French and Italian Representatives, 18–19 June 1921, DBFP, vol. 15, pp. 588–98. See Curzon's description of the meeting in CAB 23/26/6, Cabinet Meeting of 21 June 1921. The Greeks refused Allied offers on 27 June 1921. (CAB 23/23/26/9, Cabinet Meeting of 27 June 1921.)
35. 22 June 1921. Callwell, pp. 281–2. Wilson tried to convince the cabinet to withdraw completely from Turkey and make friends with Mustafa Kemal. (Callwell, pp. 92–5, 312–13.)
36. FO 371/6526, 'Message for Cabinet on Meeting of Supreme Council on August 10th', Paris, 10 August 1921. FO 371/6526, Lloyd George to A. Chamberlain, Paris, 10 August 1921 in Cabinet Meeting of 11 August 1921. See also FO 371/6526, Foreign Office to Board of Trade, London, 20 August 1921. FO 371/6526, Secretary, Admiralty to Under-Secretary of State, Foreign Office, London, 18 August 1921. FO 371/6526, Foreign Office to Admiralty, Foreign Office, 18 August 1921. MacArthur-Seale, p. 719, 796–7.
37. Rumbold to Curzon, Constantinople, 9 May 1921, DBFP 17, p. 174. FO 371/6513, 'Amended Draft of Proposed Proclamation of Neutrality', 11 May 1921. See also, FO 371/6556, Meeting of the Allied High Commissioners, Constantinople, 9 May 1921. FO 371/6512, Rumbold Telegram, Constantinople, 9 May 1921; Curzon to the Secretary of the Admiralty, Foreign Office, 18 May 1921; Rumbold Telegram, Constantinople, 16 May 1921. ADM 137/1774, Hardinge Telegram (for Cabinet), Paris, 10 August 1921; Admiralty to Commander-in-Chief, Mediterranean, 12 August 1921. See also the numerous communications from British officials in ADM 137/1772 and 1774 and FO 371/6514.
38. FO 371/6516, Rattigan to Crowe, Constantinople, 1 June 1921. FO 371/6521, Rattigan (William Frank Arthur Rattigan) Telegram, Constantinople, 8 July 1921; FO 371/6521, Telegram to Rattigan, Foreign Office, 12 July 1921. The Army Council in London complained that Rattigan had done nothing to enforce the policy of neutrality. (FO 371/6523, Army Council to Under-Secretary of State, War Office, 15 July 1921.)
39. FO 371/6523, Harington Telegram, Constantinople, 21 July 1921. See also FO 371/6523, Harington Telegram, Constantinople, 13 July 1921. FO 371/6523, Telegram to Rattigan, War Office, 19 July 1921; FO 371/6523, Osborne to the Secretary to the Army Council, Foreign Office, 21 July 1921. Rattigan wrote that Harington had changed his mind, a doubtful statement, but that neutrality still should not be enforced. (Rattigan to Curzon, 22 July 1921, in DBFP 17, pp. 324–5, no. 314.) In DBFP 17, there are numerous examples of Rattigan

changing his mind on the issue, depending, I believe, on what he perceived as his superiors' wishes. Rattigan was forced to resign from the Foreign Service in 1922 after an affair in which he impregnated Princess Elizabeth of Romania.

40. Rumbold gave examples of Greeks using the base to supply their army. See, for example, Rumbold to Curzon, Constantinople, 21 April 1921, DBFP 17, pp. 148–9. Curzon, reversing his earlier opinion, stated that the base should not be used, but changed his mind again in accordance with Lloyd George's position. (Oliphant to Secretary of the Army Council, Foreign Office, 4 May 1921, DBFP 17, pp. 167–8. Curzon to Rumbold, Foreign Office, 12 August 1921, BDFP 17, p. 352. DBFP contains much on the closing of the bases, none of which had any effect on the final decision.
41. FO 371/6526, Eastern (Turkey) Confidential, 'Extract from Prime Minister's Speech of August 16, 1921: Asia Minor'.
42. Lloyd George met with Kalogeropoulos and Gounaris. (Notes of a Meeting, London, 18 March 1921, DBFP 15, pp. 447–52.)

# 18

## SAKARYA

The Greek army launched what they expected to be their final campaign against the Nationalists in June of 1921. They rapidly advanced as the Turks fell back to a position near their capital, Ankara. There they held the Greeks (Battle of the Sakarya, 23 August to 13 September 1921). The Greeks retreated, badly beaten, but the exhausted Turks were not yet able to press the attack against them. In a memorandum of 7 October 1921, Curzon wrote that the time had come for further mediation between the Greeks and Turks, because both sides were exhausted, a stalemate. He did not foresee that the Greeks could be driven from the positions to which they had fallen back after the Sakarya defeat. Curzon was willing to give very little to the Turks; his proposed terms were similar to those that had been previously on offer: only a slightly increased portion of Eastern Thrace over that allowed in the Sèvres Treaty was to be Turkish, Edirne would remain Greek, Allied 'advisors' would oversee Turkish government ministries and an autonomous İzmir would be under a Greek governor. Curzon proposed a purely Allied conference that would set terms to be given to the Greeks and Turks. The Allies would remain in charge, preparing terms for acceptance by the belligerents.[1]

For the Greeks, their failure to defeat the Turkish Nationalists changed everything. The London Accords now looked much better to them. The Greeks told the British in November 1921 that they were now willing to place Greek interests in the hands of Great Britain. They would accept British mediation

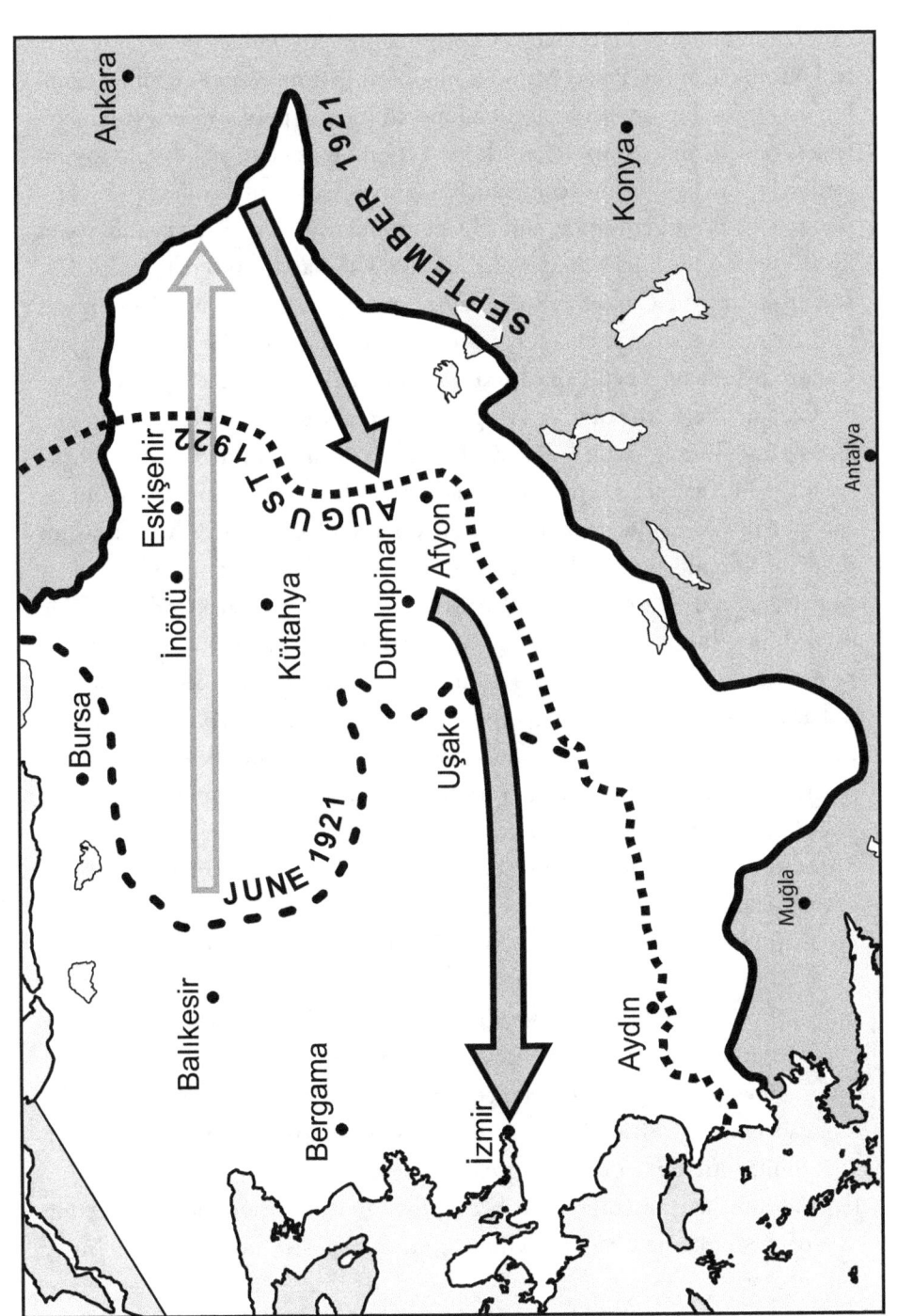

Map 18.1 The Greek army advance and retreat

over İzmir, but not Thrace. Lloyd George met secretly with a Greek delegation in London, assuring Prime Minister Gounaris that he would do all he could for the Greeks in any peace negotiations. In a more public meeting, Curzon told Gounaris that he would work for a solution as close as possible to that arrived at in the previous conference: İzmir to be an autonomous province under a Christian governor, and Thrace to be as provided for in the Sèvres Treaty, with some minor border rectification. Gounaris found that acceptable, as well he might. Curzon felt the Turks might accept, because '[t]he forces of the Angora Government were wasted and exhausted'. The British did not want to believe how badly the Turkish victory had affected their plans.[2]

Curzon offered the cabinet a lengthy memorandum, 'Intervention between Greece and Turkey', which indicated that he had little understanding of the situation in Anatolia. He admitted that he had little real information, but he thought the two sides were at stalemate. Some of his sources had told him that Greek morale was high, some that it was low. But Curzon felt both sides were exhausted. It was time for British intervention to force mediation. He also admitted, however, that both sides had refused mediation. They might be more reasonable as winter set in, and the stalemate continued. When they did accept mediation and agreed to a new conference, Curzon offered much the same terms as in the London Conference: İzmir would be under Turkish sovereignty, but with a Greek governor and a gendarmerie under Allied officers. Greece would retain Eastern Thrace, with small border modifications. There would still be international control over the Straits. The financial and economic clauses of the Sèvres Treaty would remain; Turkey would pay Allied occupation expenses and reparations. Curzon's plan for a conference:

(a.) A very early effort to ascertain what are the bases on which mediation can now take place with a reasonable prospect of success – such effort involving an urgent conference with the Greeks, upon whom we alone can exercise a friendly pressure, to be accompanied or followed by a similar attempt to resume discussion with the Turks.
(b.) As soon as the bases have been provisionally determined, a meeting of the Supreme Council to draw up the proposed revision of the Treaty of Sèvres.
(c.) A summons to Greeks and Turks to attend and receive the revised conditions.[3]

Events had not caused much change in Curzon's plans. One wonders how he could have thought that the Turks would accept what they had refused when they were threatened by the Greek army now that the Greek threat was alleviated? It is worth noting how much Curzon and his colleagues retained their mindset as imperial conquerors. The Allies, not the belligerents, would prepare a treaty. It would then be presented for acceptance. The British were to remain in charge.

As always seemed to be true, the General Staff disagreed with Curzon's assessment. They stated that the Nationalist army's morale was high, and the army was gaining strength. Greek morale, they assumed, must have declined. The Greeks had lost trust in their higher officers. If the Greeks were to save anything, they had to come to terms with the Turks, but this might not be possible: 'Mustapha Kemal is in such a strong military position, that there appears to be no reason why he should moderate his political demands, in the event of peace negotiations being re-opened.'[4]

Curzon felt that the main problem for the British was not the military prowess of the Turks, but the disloyalty of Britain's allies. In a cabinet meeting on 1 November 1921, Curzon spoke for the British amazement and feeling of betrayal at the Franco-Turkish Pact. His long speech against the French was not an example of diffident British understatement, employing language such as: 'breach of honour and good faith', 'violations', 'reprehensible', 'hostile' and 'sinister'. Curzon was furious at the French for dealing independently with the Turks. He summoned the French ambassador to signal his protest. The French, he accurately claimed, had violated the Allies' understanding not to take independent action in the Ottoman Empire. They had violated the Treaty of Sèvres and their compact with Britain and Italy in the Tripartite Agreement. Curzon might have been correct in stating that the British had been betrayed by their ally, but the British protest that they had not been consulted before the treaty was signed can only be called hypocritical, since they themselves had been acting independently for some time. In their response, the French noted this, and stated that they had no choice but to negotiate with the Nationalist victors in Cilicia. They refused to accept any British criticism as valid.[5]

The British ultimately decided that, while the French had acted reprehensibly, there was no purpose in further discussion of the matter. French acquiescence was needed to create a new conference.[6]

## Montagu is Forced to Resign

Curzon's plans for the upcoming conference were the undoing of the Secretary of State for India, Montagu, and the loss of a usually reasonable voice in the cabinet. In March 1922 he authorised the publication of a message from the Viceroy in India, setting out India's wishes for the revision of the Treaty of Sèvres, which were much at variance with the plans of Lloyd George and Curzon. Curzon contended that this publication severely embarrassed him in the negotiations for a new peace conference. Montagu had already challenged cabinet policy on Egypt and Kenya, and Lloyd George was finding him increasingly an opponent to his policies. He took the opportunity of the publication to force Montagu to resign on 9 March. Montagu was devastated and vigorously denounced Lloyd George in a speech to his constituents: 'For heaven's sake, let the British people know the facts, and don't let them go hoodwinked and blindfolded under the leadership of the Prime Minister.' He called Lloyd George a dictator and condemned the Middle East policies of both Lloyd George and Curzon. A voice that had questioned those policies was lost to the cabinet.[7]

## The Paris Conference, 22–6 March 1922

The great Greek offensive against the Turkish Nationalists had foundered. The Turks had defeated the French in Cilicia and the Armenians in the Northeast, freeing men and supplies for the fight against the Greeks. But years of setbacks had only slightly diminished British confidence that they could bend the situation to their will.

Curzon made another attempt at British mediation. He proposed to the cabinet that they offer a new plan to the Turks and Greeks. There was to be a meeting of the British, French and Italian foreign ministers in Paris to agree on terms to be presented to the warring sides. The Supreme Council would then present the terms to the Greeks and Turks. Curzon suggested a meeting in Istanbul, where it was hoped Mustafa Kemal would attend.[8]

On 21 December 1921, Curzon presented the cabinet with his plan for a new conference to settle the problem in the Near East. His new plan was only a slight variation on the old plan: İzmir would still not be under Turkish control; France and Britain would be in charge, under an undefined mandate from the League of Nations. Slightly more land in Eastern Thrace would be allowed to the Turks. The Straits would be under an international commission, but the Neutral Zone slightly reduced. The Turks would create an Armenian state in the Cilician area (which the Turks had recently reconquered).[9]

The British were to suggest supervision or outright governance in the Middle East by the League of Nations. It was not a body from which the Turks could expect much comfort. The secretary-general of the League from 1920 to 1933 was Sir Eric Drummond. He was a British diplomat who had served as Private Secretary for foreign secretaries Asquith, Grey and Balfour, and had been a member of the British delegation to the Peace Conference. The four Permanent Members of the Executive Council of the League, where actual authority lay, were Britain, France, Italy and Japan. In 1920, Greece was one of the Non-Permanent Members which also sat on the council. Arthur Balfour, whose negative feelings on the Turks are described above, was president of the Assembly of the League. It can be easily seen why the British wished to send so many decisions to the League.

The Italians were almost solely concerned with retaining financial clauses in any treaty that would benefit Italy, including the Tripartite Agreement. The British felt that they would support the British plan in most matters.[10]

Curzon felt that French Prime Minister Briand would approve of his plan, but the British soon had a setback. The British were faced with a new French administration. Raymond Poincaré became French prime minister on 15 January 1922. He had often disagreed with his predecessors, Georges Clemenceau and Aristide Briand, over cooperation with British plans. Indeed, Clemenceau and Poincaré hated each other. (Clemenceau had famously said: 'There are only two perfectly useless things in this world. One is an appendix and the other is Poincaré.') Poincaré resented British control of Allied plans. Much more than the British, he wanted rigorous enforcement of German reparations. On a personal level, the old friendship that had characterised relations between Clemenceau and Lloyd George disappeared: Lloyd George thought very little of Poincaré, who he alternately accused of unbendingly steadfast erroneous convictions and of 'tricky' duplicitousness. He thought Poincaré not very intelligent and described his actions as 'sinister'. In short, Lloyd George ascribed to Poincaré some of his own character traits.[11]

Many of the reasons that had forced French compliance with British wishes in the past were gone. The Syrian and Mosul Questions had been decided. The French correctly viewed issues of Istanbul and the Straits as matters under British control, and knew the British had frozen them out. The Turks could offer the French possible trade concessions and guarantees not to interfere in Syria. The British offered only a vague commitment to 'Allied solidarity'. And the British had shown, again and again, that to them Allied solidarity meant agreement with the British. British cooperation with France on reparations and French security in Europe was still possible, but was beginning to appear unlikely.

Curzon at first hoped that Poincaré would prove at least as amenable to British plans as his predecessor, Briand – and remain in, at least limited, agreement. That was not to be. Poincaré notified Curzon that the French would henceforth not support any coercive measures against the Turks. He was against giving any consideration to Greece. Whereas Briand usually had been content to allow Britain to set the agenda and formulate the basic proposals for conferences, France would now propose their own agenda and plans. Curzon reluctantly accepted. The French, British and Italians would meet in Paris to confer.[12]

The French proposed a completely different set of priorities for a revision of the Sèvres Treaty, agreeing to most parts of the Turkish National Pact: the Greeks were to leave both Anatolia and Eastern Thrace. Greek evacuation must be 'immediate and complete'. The Turks would hold Anatolia and most of Eastern Thrace in complete dominion. Allied Commissions would oversee both Anatolia and Eastern Thrace for a brief period, perhaps six months to a year, until the Turks took over. Istanbul would be returned to Ottoman control, with only a small Allied garrison outside the city. Allied control of the Straits would be minimal. Nothing would be done about an Armenia. The Turks should have a larger army, under their own control, and would be allowed conscription. The French only agreed with Britain on two matters – retention of a Financial Commission and some sort of Straits Commission.[13]

Before the conference began, Curzon met separately with the Ottoman Foreign Minister İzzet Paşa and the Nationalist representative Yusuf Kemal. He gave them Britain's non-negotiable demands: an immediate armistice as a precondition to everything, a system in İzmir that would protect the Greeks, a reduced army without conscription, neutralisation of the Straits and Turkish recognition of pre-war debts and of claims arising out of the war, including the costs of the army of occupation. Curzon said the British could never abandon Gallipoli, for what he called 'sentimental reasons'. He told the Turks that they were ungrateful for all the British good intentions:

> We had been victorious, but we were not anxious to be harsh in the hour of victory. (He obviously did not consider the Sèvres Treaty to have been harsh.) His Highness must, however, realise that it was out of the question for the vanquished to dictate terms like victors. The Allies were entitled to take steps to prevent a recurrence of such events and Turkey must pay the price of the error of 1914. We were, however, anxious to forget the past and to re-establish the Turkish Government and nation in a position of independence and strength, in which they could, on friendly terms with Great Britain, renew their national existence, and play a considerable part in Eastern politics. With this object we had joined with the Allies in drawing up the Treaty of Sèvres.[14]

Curzon's attitude signalled what were to become the British proposals at the upcoming conference.

The reception the British gave the Greeks was quite different than the one they offered the Turks. On 12 January 1922, Lloyd George and Curzon met at Cannes with Prime Minister Dimitrios Gounaris and Georgios Baltatzis of Greece. The British prime minister and foreign secretary told them that they would do all they could for the Greeks at the upcoming conference. They would have to leave İzmir, but would retain most of Eastern Thrace; 'Greece would be in possession of very considerable new territories.' Lloyd George assured the Greeks: 'It was quite certain that our proposals were now the utmost that could be secured for Greece.'[15]

Whether Curzon's stressing his neutrality between the Turks and the Greeks was self-deception or political manoeuvring cannot be known. When the French accused him of favouring the Greeks, he denied it. His Majesty's Government, he wrote, did not take sides. He then went on to praise the Greeks as allies and described the Turks as enemies. He wanted the fact that the Turks had been wartime enemies of the Allies to be considered when they were dealt with in 1922. When the French mentioned the atrocities of the Greeks in Anatolia, Curzon went so far as to falsely state that the Turks had been more ferocious than the Greeks and their attacks more considerable than those of the Greeks. Curzon called for unity among the Allies; it was obvious that he meant unity in supporting the British position.[16]

From 22 to 26 March 1922, the British, French and Italians met in Paris to try yet again to create peace diplomatically. It was not to be a meeting of allies, nor even friends. Curzon took charge of the meetings. He presented the proposal and framework under which the conference would deliberate. He made suggestions that his Italian and French colleagues repeatedly disparaged but still often accepted, either out of deference to the British place in the occupied Ottoman lands or sheer lack of interest. Curzon continued to quote the same counterfeit population statistics to show how much should be given to the Greeks. The Treaty of Sèvres (which had in fact never been ratified), he said, was still in effect, it only needed to be modified. The Greeks would have to evacuate Anatolia, but the Turks would pay for the evacuation. A homeland for the Armenians should be created in Cilicia. Curzon's plans thoroughly ignored the actual situation in Anatolia.[17]

Poincaré and Marshal Foch, military advisor to the conference, suggested a commission to oversee the Greek evacuation of İzmir. The commission would look after the local population and ensure that the Greeks did not engage in massacre and pillage as they retreated. Curzon was against this, declaring that the Greeks would never do such things. (He was not prescient.) Curzon was only concerned with the fate of the area's Greeks. He wanted an unspecified 'special administration' to protect the Greeks of İzmir. Poincaré did not want special favours for the Greeks. Curzon once again quoted the spurious statistics that Greeks were a majority in the İzmir region, and thus deserved special consideration.[18]

Concerning Thrace, Curzon did all he could to maximise the territory retained by the Greeks. The French had suggested a separate buffer state, under the League of Nations. This was an impossible solution; the League had no army to defend it. Curzon felt, however, that practicality was not the important question:

> There was another point to consider, namely that of Greece. We were going to ask the Greeks to withdraw their army with 80,000 bayonets from Asia Minor, and to give up all claims to Smyrna. The Greeks were our Allies; the Turks were our enemies, and had caused enormous sacrifices to all the Allies. The Greeks really deserved some consideration. Were we really to accept the dictation of Mustapha Kemal?

Curzon fell back, as always, on invented statistics showing a Greek majority in Eastern Thrace. When Poincaré doubted the statistics, Curzon said that 'his case rested upon Turkish official statistics'. He must have known this was false. The deciding factor was the testimony of military advisors, who stated that the Greeks could not be forced militarily from Thrace (at least at that time; their opinion was to change).[19]

Curzon defended the Treaty of Sèvres, and wanted to keep as many of its provisions as possible. In particular, Curzon wanted the Turks to agree not to persecute minorities. Curzon had lost none of his animosity toward the Turks. He stated that the Turks still planned massacres and had to be stopped. 'While the Greeks had been guilty of misdeeds, it was broadly speaking true that the Turks had stood for barbarity and savagery for sixty years.' Provision had to be made in agreements to stop Turkish evil deeds. Curzon would keep in force all the minorities clauses of the Sèvres Treaty. The League of Nations should appoint commissioners all over Anatolia to monitor Turkish actions. Curzon asked his colleagues, as Christians, to agree that they were charged with a particular duty to the Christian minorities.

Poincaré of France, on the other hand, spoke against the Sèvres Treaty. He said the treaty had been created by the British; no French Government would support it. If there were to be clauses in any treaty to provide Turkish guarantees on the treatment of minorities, clauses should also be inserted stating that Greece and Bulgaria should also agree to such guarantees for Muslim minorities. Poincaré was both practical and more sympathetic to the Turks:

> They (the Allies) could not to-day impose terms which it had been impossible to impose even in 1921. They must face realities. They could not resuscitate the Treaty of Sèvres. They must not give the Angora Nationalists the impression that they were to be treated as savages; they must treat them like the inhabitants of a European country.

Curzon replied, basically, that Poincaré was wrong; the Turks were not to be trusted. They could not be treated like Europeans. However, he was forced to be satisfied to include only general principles in the committee's recommendations.

Curzon did not attempt to placate his supposed allies. He criticised the French in particular: 'M. Poincaré's argument was in favor of giving way at every point to the Turks.' In fact, by no means did Poincaré oppose Curzon 'at every point'. Poincaré deferred to Curzon on those matters in which France had little interest, such as the Turkish military establishment. Unlike Curzon, Poincaré's interests were practical, not at all ideological. Poincaré was willing to agree with Curzon's suggestions only when he thought they were realistic. For example, Curzon produced a catalogue of what he called Turkish crimes against Armenians, blaming France for the exodus of Armenians from Cilicia. He wanted an autonomous region for the Armenians in Cilicia, naively planning to wrest from the Turks what they had taken from the French. Poincaré said it would never work. Argument followed, France against Britain. (Curzon told the House of Lords that the meetings with Poincaré were 'very friendly', which they surely were not.) In the end, the Allies put into their plan a Cilician homeland for the Armenians. France knew it would never work, but that it would conciliate Curzon. No one opposed Curzon on the important matter of the Turks paying for everything – the occupation, reparations, the Public Debt.[20]

Poincaré had opposed much of the British proposals, but these points were only somewhat modified in the final proposals. In order to gain French support, the British played their strongest card to bring the French to at least some agreement with the British proposals – a proposed pact guaranteeing French security from future German attack in Europe. As Lloyd George told Gounaris:

> We had made a settlement of the Eastern Question a condition of our Treaty of Guarantee to France and this settlement was the best that we could hope to have. We had done our utmost to help Greece by making the Treaty of Guarantee conditional on a settlement of the Eastern Question and there was nothing better in sight for Greece.[21]

Despite their disagreements with the British plans, security in Europe was more important to the French. While the British held them hostage over defence cooperation in Europe and reparations from Germany, the French only could bring some modifications to the proposals. Once the Paris Proposals were passed, the British rejected any plan for French security guarantee in Europe.[22]

## The Paris Proposals, 26 March 1922

- Greece and the Nationalists would agree to an armistice.
- Once a peace treaty was signed, the Allies would leave Istanbul.
- The region to be evacuated in Anatolia would be demilitarised and would be controlled by an Allied Commission and Allied military forces and police. However, '[t]he Allies cannot in any case accept responsibility for the maintenance of order during the evacuation, nor the direct control of the civil administration; in each zone, this care will fall to the Greek authorities until the evacuation, and to the Ottoman authorities when the Hellenic troops leave'.
- Christians in Turkey and Muslims in Greece would enjoy special protection, supervised by League of Nations representatives. (Curzon had opposed the inclusion of protection for Greek Muslims, but finally agreed.)
- The three powers declared that they supported a National Home for the Armenians, but left its creation to later negotiations between the League of Nations and the Turks (that is, recognition that nothing could be done).
- Greece would retain Western Thrace and approximately half of Eastern Thrace (to Babaeski and Kırk Kilisse (Kırklareli)). The Turks would have the Eastern half. (This was an impossible border. They did not even try to consider natural features.) Edirne was to be lost to the Turks. All of Eastern Thrace would be demilitarised, except for Allied forces, which would be in military control.[23]
- The Allies would maintain military and naval forces in the Gallipoli Peninsula and Rodosto (Tekirdağ).
- An Allied Commission would exercise effective control over the demilitarised zones in Anatolia and Thrace. Its expenses would be paid by the Turks.
- The Turks would be allowed a slightly larger armed force than had been permitted in previous plans: 45,000 in the gendarmerie, 40,000 in the army. Conscription was forbidden. It was recommended, but not required, that Allied officers be used 'for the organization, command and training of the army'.
- The Ottoman debt would be paid by Turkey. All military expenses of the Allies after the armistice would also be paid by the Turks. Collection would be completely in the hands of an Allied Commission. (Five million pounds sterling annually, reduced to three million for the first three years,

paid by concessions from Turkish taxes, until all was paid.) Any increase in customs duties would have to be approved by the Allies. A commission composed of Britain, France, Italy, Japan and Turkey would decide on revisions of the financial Capitulations. A similar commission would be in charge of changes in the judicial Capitulations.[24]

Like the earlier schemes for dismembering the Ottoman Empire, the Paris Proposals were typical of the calculations of imperialists. The British assumed that they could sit down in Paris, pore over maps and 'expert' opinion and devise a solution to an imperial problem, breaking for tea. The Allies would decide all. Little consideration was given to the attitudes and positions of the Turks, or even of the Greeks.[25]

The official proposals sometimes spoke of 'Turkey', sometimes of the 'Ottoman Government', but gave no formal recognition to the Nationalists. Nevertheless, the Nationalists still considered the Paris Proposals seriously, but would only commit to an armistice if the Greeks agreed to withdraw within four months. They agreed to a further Allied proposal that the population numbers in Western Anatolia and Thrace be examined by a commission, a proposal which the Greeks understandably declined. The Turkish Nationalists did not even respond to the other conditions in the proposal that would never have been acceptable to them: Turkish sovereignty would actually have been abandoned in Eastern Thrace and Western Anatolia. State finances would have been controlled by foreigners, as would much of the court system. The amounts demanded by the Allies could never have been paid. The army was restricted. These, for the Turks, were impossible suggestions. Much of the Paris Agreement was a watered-down version of the Sèvres Treaty. This was not at all what the Nationalists had fought for. It was especially unlikely that the Turks would accept the proposals just as they were preparing a final push against the Greek forces. They planned a Greek evacuation that would not depend on the Allies. Just as the Greeks had rejected Allied proposals when they believed they would triumph militarily; the Turks rejected the proposals when they were confident of military victory.[26]

The Greeks had promised to place their fate in the hands of the British, but found it impossible to accept the Allied proposals. Either because they misunderstood their perilous military position or were forced by domestic

Map 18.2   Paris proposals, British plans for Greek evacuation

politics, the Greeks categorically dismissed the Paris Agreement and Allied mediation. The Greek Government declared that it would never allow Western Asia to be returned to Turkish administration. Curzon had tried to save what he could for the Greeks. Foolishly, the Greeks did not want his help.[27]

The Allies planned to call the Greeks, the Turkish Nationalists and the Istanbul Government to a new conference. They styled it as a 'preliminary conference', because it was assumed that after debate, a final conference and peace treaty would follow. At first it was suggested that the conference be held in the Ottoman Empire, but this was viewed as impractical. Venice was chosen. The date of the conference was put off, however, as administrative differences arose among the Allies. A major problem arose over the precondition of an armistice between the combatants. Both sides insisted that the other cease fire first. The plans of the conference foundered.

## The 'Treachery' of Britain's Allies

Curzon was not willing to blame the failure of the Paris Conference on the Greeks and the Turks. His mindset, and the mindset of the British Cabinet as a whole, was always that any problems would be solved by Europeans. Therefore, failure must also be blamed on Europeans:

> The failure to give effect to that agreement was due to the consistent treachery of France. The French Government had been in constant communication with Kemal and had urged him to pay no attention to what had been agreed to at Paris.[28]

The British complained that the French and Italians had provided arms to the Nationalists. The French had undoubtedly worked in their own interests and against British interests in Anatolia, but the amount of weapons in question could not have been significant, compared to the arms available in Ottoman army ammunition dumps and those provided by the Soviets.[29]

Although they exaggerated the effect of the further French supply of weapons to the Turks, the British were correct in believing the French and Italians were aiding the Turkish war effort. That aid was primarily political.

After the Paris Conference, Curzon became more and more convinced that the French and the Italians were working with the Nationalists against the conference proposals, which they had never sincerely accepted. If true, as was probable, this was exactly the advice that Lloyd George had given the Greeks at the London Conference – ignore the conference proposals. Curzon's convictions on the power of Europeans were arrogance that often led him to erroneous analyses, but he may have been correct on French intentions and actions. That, as well as the threat to the pact in Europe, may explain why the French had been willing to agree to meet in the Paris Conference, when it was obvious that they had great differences with the British. It may also explain much of the French attitude during the conference. For example, when Curzon brought forward his plan that an armistice must be the first condition of any peace, Poincaré objected that the Nationalists would never agree to that. When Curzon insisted, however, the Frenchman rather meekly agreed. Poincaré wanted no mention of the name Smyrna, but accepted its use. Poincaré questioned everything about Curzon's suggestion for the creation of a home for the Armenians. He stated that the Turks would never accept it, but allowed it to be retained in the conference proposals. The French wanted the Turks to be allowed conscription, but Poincaré gave way to Curzon's insistence that it not be allowed. It is understandable that the supremely self-confident British believed that the Paris Proposals might work. It is unlikely that the more practical French might have believed that.[30]

The Italians correctly believed that the London and Paris Agreements were a further step in denying their place in the Middle East. The promises made to them during the war had been denied. The French and British were to receive Ottoman lands, the Italians nothing. The Tripartite Agreement, which had promised the Italians commercial concessions and a 'sphere of influence' in Anatolia, had been abandoned.

In the all-important matter of oil, the Italians rightly felt that they had been frozen out of oil concessions in the Ottoman lands. The British had compromised with the French over the oil of Mosul. The Italians received nothing. When the Italians complained of unjust treatment, Curzon said he was shocked that the Italians should complain of the British San Remo oil agreement. He told the Italians that nothing in the agreement would preclude the Italian commercial interests from exploiting oil resources and, basically, the Italians would be able to buy oil at the same prices as anyone else. The British would not interfere with existing oil concessions (for example, the British-controlled Turkish Petroleum Company), which were commercial, not governmental enterprises.

He said, duplicitously, that the British Government had no hand in British commercial oil enterprises, which were as open to the Italians as to anyone. In other words, the Italians were to be treated just like those who had never joined the Allied war effort. The Italians made their bitterness known. The British paid no attention to their complaints. The cavalier treatment of the Italians was to haunt the British when they asked for assistance in defending the Straits against the Turks and did not receive it.

Poincaré suggested a completely new plan to the British on 15 May. Ankara would be approached to arrange a meeting at İzmit to include the Allies, the Nationalists, the Istanbul Government and the Greeks. It would be a conference in which all sides would consider a preliminary peace. The British wanted none of that. For them, the only plan was complete acceptance of the Paris Accords. Poincaré expressed his regret that the British would not accept his proposal for a preliminary conference. If that meeting had been arranged, he believed, a new Allied plan would have been a success.[31]

Three months later, Curzon had decided that he did want a conference after all, but it would be a conference to solidify the Turkish acceptance of the Paris Accords. Even as the Turks were advancing on İzmir, the British were still planning a conference in Venice at which the plan of the Paris Conference would be largely passed. They were still labouring to save what they could for the Greeks. Commissioner Rumbold in Istanbul rightly described the British efforts as made 'in order to save [the] Greek army from a complete disaster'. The cabinet met on 7 September and decided that the Paris Accords would be the base of British policy. The Paris Agreements, the cabinet decided, must be accepted by the Turks. Commissioner Rumbold in Istanbul felt that the victorious Turks would never agree to the Venice conference. The Italians and French agreed that the conference described by the British would be impossible. Moreover, the French plan for a guarantee pact with the British in Europe had been abandoned. The British had lost their strongest card to force the French to accept British proposals. After debate among the Allies, Curzon's plans were dropped.[32]

The British politicians kept developing plans to save the Greek army, despite the advice from the military that the Greeks would lose and the best course for the British would be to completely abandon the Ottoman Empire. When approaching the Turks, the British were hampered by their own position and pride. Rumbold noted that in a proposal to Ankara, '[g]reatest care was taken to avoid any appearance of humiliating solicitation on the part of the Allies'. The plans were useless; as the British themselves described, the Greeks were destroying and killing all they found on their path of retreat. This made the Turkish agreement with any British plans impossible.[33]

Despite all evidence to the contrary, the British, especially Lord Curzon, believed that they could salvage at least some of their plans and give some advantage to the Greeks. The British in Istanbul were ordered to construct complicated blueprints to execute the Paris plan: in true bureaucratic fashion, an order was sent to Istanbul to create a committee to consider the details of Greek evacuation and an Allied occupation in Anatolia and Thrace – the 'Directing Committee of Allied Generals at Constantinople under the presidency of Lieutenant-General Sir Charles Harington'. With no input from the League of Nations itself, the committee considered a plan that was to be overseen by the League. Greek refugees would be concentrated in İzmir, Mudanya and Bandırma, where they would be protected by Allied troops until loaded onto ships for Greece. Italy, France and Britain would each control an area of Western Anatolia until the evacuation was complete (Map 18.2). The Turks would proclaim a general amnesty. No consideration was given to the fact that the Allied generals had declared that they had no troops for such an effort, or that the Turks might not cooperate in the midst of a war that they were winning. But most telling was one statement by the committee: 'Nothing should be done to encourage the population to look for the assistance of the Allies in facilitating their flight.'[34]

The plan drawn up by the Generals' committee was detailed and complicated. In its completed summary form, it included twenty-nine printed pages of detailed plans, maps and tables. It was distributed on 14 August 1922, twelve days before the swift defeat of the Greeks (Battle of Dumlupınar, 26 August) rendered it useless.[35]

## The Greek Plan to Take Istanbul

Beginning in June 1922, the Greeks moved 30,000 troops from their defensive lines in Anatolia. By the end of July, they had 45,000 men in Thrace. In July 1922, the Greek army began to move troops to Midye, on the border of the Thracian Neutral Zone. The Greek Government notified the British that it had decided that peace could only come if the Greeks occupied Istanbul. They requested approval from the Allies, but did not receive it. All sides believed that the Greek plan was to seize Istanbul.[36]

The Greek threat to Istanbul was taken very seriously by the British, both in Istanbul and in London. General Harington in Istanbul suggested that the Greek fleet should be interned immediately if Greek troops crossed the Neutral Zone in Thrace, and that Greek navy vessels met at sea by the British navy should be sunk. London cabled its agreement with Harington's plans. The Admiralty further suggested that Piraeus might be bombarded and Greek merchant ships interned. London advised Harington to make preparations for defence, but actions suggested by the admirals in Istanbul, such as ordering Greek ships to remain in port and out of the Straits, should not be taken yet. The Greek Government was told that any advance into the Neutral Zone or attempt to occupy Istanbul would be met by force.[37]

The Greek threat was met with rare complete agreement among the Allies. The French in Istanbul believed that the Greeks actually planned to attack, and must be stopped. High Commissioner Rumbold felt that 'the Greek menace to Constantinople is 50% bluff and 50% serious', but agreed with the French that the Greeks should be told to remove their troops from the Neutral Zone border. The Italian Government completely supported any British and French actions against the Greeks. The only question was whether the Allies had enough force to stand against the Greeks. General Harington moved most of what forces he had ('less than 2,000 British rifles and sabres and the French little more') from the İzmit Peninsula to Çatalca to oppose the Greeks. This would leave Istanbul open to attack from the Nationalists from İzmit. However, if the Greeks attacked in Thrace, he expected the French to aid the British if the Nationalists advanced from İzmit; the French provided three battalions of infantry and a regiment of cavalry. The Greeks abandoned their attack.[38]

Why did the British oppose the Greek seizure of Istanbul? It would seem that their continuing support of the Greeks might have led them to accept a Greek occupation of the capital. Both Lloyd George and Curzon had long thought that the Turks should be evicted from Istanbul. But when it came time to actually evict the Turks, the British found that British power to force their own plans on the Ottoman Empire was at stake. The Greeks would have been egregiously opposing the decisions of the Allies, which the British could not abide. It was a matter of British imperial prestige, something that had proven to be most important to them. The Greeks could not be allowed to insult the British plans. Moreover, the French and Italians were committed to opposing the Greeks. The defence of Istanbul against the Greeks was one of the very few instances in which the French and Italians were willing to commit fresh troops. The British could not be seen to be giving Istanbul to the Greeks while their allies defended it from the Greeks. In the worst case, what would the British do if their allies fought the Greeks?

Characteristically, Lloyd George weighed in on the side of the Greeks after the issue had been decided. On 4 August 1922, Lloyd George spoke before parliament and considerably complicated the British assertion that they were acting as honest brokers between the Greeks and the Turks. He excoriated the Turks and praised the Greeks. He blamed the failure of the British attempts to negotiate solely on the Turkish Nationalists. He intimated that the Greeks would have defeated the Turks if the Allied policy of neutrality had not tied their hands and refused to let them occupy Constantinople. The Turks, he said, planned a policy of extermination of Christians; the Christians had to be protected. (He did not say Britain was willing to send troops for the purpose.) His speech made clear his sympathies. The Greeks took comfort from the speech, hoping that the British might intervene militarily, but the British had neither the troops nor the desire to intervene.[39]

The Greeks complained 'that the decision of the Powers against the occupation of Constantinople by the Greeks is an obstacle to decisive action on the part of the Greeks for the conclusion of peace', but they stood down, abandoning their plans. The only chance for the Greeks to take the city had been Allied compliance, but Allied support for Greek plans had disintegrated. The plan to take Istanbul demonstrated Greek desperation and the hope that, despite declarations of neutrality, the Allies would once again support them, because the British had long wanted the Turks out of Istanbul. That sentiment, the Greeks hoped, might triumph, but the time for such hopes was over.[40]

The Greek attempt was a last throw of the dice. The removal of so many troops from the battle against the Nationalists probably was a contributing factor in the subsequent Greek defeat in Anatolia. Surely it was a colossal military blunder.[41]

Mustafa Kemal's forces had spent the time after the Sakarya victory recuperating, training and replenishing military stores. They advanced from their forward positions on 14 August 1922. By 30 August, they had decisively defeated the Greek army and begun to advance rapidly to the West and Southwest. Greek soldiers fled before them toward İzmir and other ports (Dikili, Çeşme) for evacuation to Greece. The Turks entered İzmir on 9 September and Bursa on 10 September. Cilicia and the Northeast had already been conquered. The Nationalists occupied all of Anatolia up to the Allied Neutral Zone.

## Notes

1. FO 371/6533, 'Intervention between Greece and Turkey: Memorandum by the Secretary of State for Foreign Affairs', 7 October 1921.
2. CAB 23/27/11, Cabinet Meeting, 1 November 1921. MacArthur-Seal, p. 715, CAB 24/131 C. P. 3504, Minutes of a Fifth Meeting between Lord Curzon and M. M. Gounaris, Baltazzis and Rangabe, 19 November 1921. 'Minutes of a Meeting held at the Foreign Office between the Marquess Curzon of Kedleston and Greek Representatives', in DBFP 17, 2 November 1921, pp. 460–1.
3. CAB 24/128/83, 'Memorandum by the Secretary of State for Foreign Affairs', Foreign Office, 7 October 1921. Churchill, now colonial secretary, agreed with Curzon on the exhaustion of the warring parties and the need for a conference. (CAB 24/128/27, Churchill, 'Greece and Turkey', Colonial Office, 26 September 1921.)
4. CAB 24/129 C. P. 3434, General Staff, 'The Situation in Anatolia, 1st October, 1921', in 'Memorandum by the Secretary of State for War', 21 October 1921.
5. Curzon to Hardinge, Foreign Office, 3 November 1921. Curzon followed with a letter stating the same objections. (FO 406/48, Curzon to Saint Aulaire, Foreign Office, 5 November 1921.) FO 406/48, Montille to Curzon, Embassy of France, London, 17 November 1921.
6. CAB 23/27/15, Cabinet Meeting, 22 November 1921.
7. 'Peace in the East', *The Times*, 18 March 1922, p. 9. See 'Statement by Mr. Chamberlain', *Hansard*, House of Commons Debate, 9 March 1922, vol. 151, cc. 1489–94; 'Notice of Motion', *Hansard*, House of Commons Debate, 13 March 1922, vol. 151, cc. 1757–65; 'India (Mr. Montagu's Resignation)', *Hansard*,

House of Commons Debate, 15 March 1922, vol. 151, cc. 2291–320. There were many articles on this in *The Times*. See especially 'Mr. Montagu's Reply' (13 March 1922, p. 7) on his speech against Lloyd George and Curzon, and the summary of events in 'The Montagu Dispute' (14 March 1922, p. 12).

8. CAB 24/131/72, Lord Curzon, 'Proposed Meeting at Paris for Revision of Treaty of Sèvres', 19 December 1921. See also, FO 371/6481, Draft Conclusions of a Conference of Ministers, 21 December 1921.
9. CAB 23/29/2, Cabinet Meeting, 21 December 1921. The Curzon plan was not specific about the rule in İzmir, except to suggest a system similar to that which had been applied in the Saar Basin. In that instance, Britain and France had been in control. Curzon's plan was detailed in an extensive communication sent to Italy and France. (FO 286/760, 'Memorandum of Proposals at the Conference of Allied Foreign Ministers on the Revision of the Treaty of Sèvres', 30 December 1921.) His plan demonstrated Curzon's faith in Greek assertions and population estimates. Montagu, as so often was the case, disagreed with Curzon, stating that he preferred Anatolia and Eastern Thrace go to the Turks. (CAB 24/131 C. P. 3576, E. S. M(ontagu), 'Turkish Peace', 22 December 1921. See also CAB 23/27/20, Conclusions of a Meeting of the Cabinet, 21 December 1921.)
10. FO 371/7854, enclosure in Graham (ambassador in Italy) to Curzon, Rome, 27 January 1922.
11. David Lloyd George, *The Truth about the Peace Treaties*, vol. 1, London: Gollancz, 1938, pp. 249–52, 581.
12. CAB 23/29/2, Cabinet Meeting, 18 January 1922. Curzon felt that Poincaré wanted to drag out Allied negotiations to give the Turks time to regroup to attack the Greeks.
13. CAB 24/132/65, French Embassy to Curzon, London, 27 January 1922. FO 371/7854, 'French Proposals of January 27th 1922'. French plans on numerous other parts of the treaty are included, as well as British objections to the French plan. For the detailed British objections, see FO 371/7854, 'Propositions en Vue de la Reunion des Ministers des Affaires Etrangeres', London, 26 January 1922. The French backtracked somewhat, stating that disagreements would be easily sorted out in the conference, but insisted the Greeks should be ejected from Anatolia. (FO 371/7854, Hardinge Telegram, Paris, 1 February 1922.)
14. 'Memorandum of an Interview between the Marquess Curzon of Kedleston and Izzet Pasha' and 'Memorandum of an Interview between the Marquess Curzon of Kedleston and Yussuf Kemal Bey', Foreign Office, 16 March 1922, DBFP 17,

pp. 654–7. CAB 23/29/19, Cabinet Meeting, 20 March 1922. Curzon's position was the same in an interview with İzzet Paşa, the Ottoman Foreign Minister. (CAB 24/134 C. P. 3860 and 3861, Curzon, 'Memorandum of an Interview between Lord Curzon and Izzet Pasha', 18 March 1922.)
15. FO 371/7853, 'Note of Conversation, Cannes', 12 January 1922.
16. FO 406/49, Saint-Aulaire to Curzon, French Embassy, London, 27 January 1922 – Saint-Aulaire's descriptive letter and Poincaré's propositions for the upcoming Paris meetings. FO 406/49, Curzon to Hardinge, Foreign Office, 30 January 1922, a message for Poincaré. Curzon assured the Greeks that his avowed neutrality only went so far. Before the meeting began in Paris, he told Gounaris that he hoped the Greeks would be able to hold their line in Anatolia. (FO 406/49, Curzon to Gounaris, Foreign Office, 6 March 1922.)
17. WO 32/5658, Minutes of the Third Meeting of Foreign Office Ministers at the Quai d'Orsay, at 3 p. m., 23 March 1922. The minutes of the Paris Conference are in DBFP 17, pp. 668–763, and in the documents cited below.

    The idea of an Armenian homeland in Cilicia seems to have been suggested in a letter to the League of Nations from the Conseil Mixte Armenien, signed by the Armenian Gregorian and Catholic Patriarchs and the head of the Armenian Protestant community, Constantinople, 15 October 1921 (T 161/145).
18. CAB 29/95, Minutes of a Meeting of Foreign Ministers, Paris, 22 March 1922, 1.20 p. m. Curzon wisely did not mention the Greek Patriarch statistics. Instead, he cited specious 'American statistics of 1914'. The minutes of these meetings are also in FO 406/49.
19. FO 406/49, Minutes of the Fifth Meeting of Foreign Ministers, 24 March 1922.
20. 'Near East Conference', *Hansard*, House of Lords Debate, 30 March 1922, vol. 49, cc. 985–1009. Curzon's long speech was a self-serving justification of the terms of the Paris Conference. CAB 29/95, Minutes of the Second Meeting of Foreign Ministers, Paris, 23 March 1922, 10.30 a. m. The Italians were primarily concerned with their economic position in Turkey. (FO 406/49, 'Memorandum from Italian Ministry of Foreign Affairs', in Graham to Curzon, Rome, 27 January 1922.
21. FO 371/7853, 'Note of Conversation, Cannes', 12 January 1922. On the French–British conflicts over actions in Europe, see Andrew Barros, 'Disarmament as a Weapon: Anglo-French Relations and the Problems of Enforcing German Disarmament, 1919–28', *Journal of Strategic Studies*, vol. 29, no. 2 (April 2006), pp. 301–21. Hines Hall III, 'Lloyd George, Briand and the Failure of the Anglo-French Entente', *The Journal of Modern History*, vol. 50, no. 2, On Demand Supplement (June 1978), pp. D1121–38. Anne Orde,

*Great Britain and International Security 1920–1926*, London: Royal Historical Society, 1978, pp. 6–36.
22. On the security pact, see Jacques Bariéty, 'Le Projet de Pacte Franco-Britannique, 1920–1922', *Guerres mondiales et conflits contemporains*, no. 193), Paris: Editions Belin, September 1999, pp. 83–99. Orde, pp. 6–36.
23. The map has been drawn from the agreement's provisions and from General Harington's plan for Allied control of the evacuation process (see below). On the proposal, the Greek–Turkish border in Thrace is poorly defined, so that border on the map is speculative.
24. 'Text of Resolutions, &c. of Paris Near Eastern Conference of March 1922', DBFP 17, pp. 756–63. Curzon had attempted to have his scheme for an Armenia in Cilicia included in the plan, but France's objections forced instead mild inconsequential terms. Curzon was also forced by the others to include protection of the Muslims of Greece, in order that the proposals would seem even-handed. In a break with the usual policy, Curzon explained the plans to the House of Lords in great detail. ('Near East Conference', 30 March 1922, *Hansard*, vol. 49, cc. 985–1009. The public was given a summary of the plans, involving more platitudes than substance. (House of Commons, Miscellaneous No. 3, 'Pronouncement by Three Allied Ministers for Foreign Affairs respecting the Near East Situation, Paris, March 27, 1922', London: HMSO, 1922. Cmd. 1641.) Curzon explained and justified the Paris plan in a long speech in the House of Lords. (FO 406/49, 'Near East Conference: Speech by the Secretary of State for Foreign Affairs in the House of Lords', 30 March 1922.)
25. On the Allied disagreements, see FO 371/7858 and FO 371/7859, Meetings of the Foreign Ministers, Paris, 22–6 March 1922. The British had their way in the discussions – a great amount of debate that, in the end, came to nothing when it was rejected by both the Greeks and the Turks.
26. FO 371/7860, Rumbold Telegram, Constantinople, 5 April 1922. FO 371/7861, Youssef Kemal, 5 April 1922, in A. Hamid to Rumbold, Constantinople, 5 April 1922. FO 371/7862, Rumbold Telegram, Constantinople, 23 April 1922. On the opinion of the Istanbul Government, see FO 371/7862, Rumbold to Curzon, Constantinople, 9 and 10 April 1922; FO 371/7863, Rumbold Telegram, Constantinople, 30 April 1922. For the Istanbul Government's response to the Paris Proposals which, given their position, was essentially meaningless, see FO 406/49, İzzet Pasha to Rumbold, 29 April 1922, enclosure in Rumbold to Curzon, Constantinople, 30 April 1922. High Commissioner Rumbold had predicted before the conference met that the Turks would never accept such terms. (FO 371/7853, Rumbold Telegram, Constantinople, 15 January 1922.)

27. WO 32/5658, Bentinck Telegram, Athens, 3 August 1922; Telegram to Bentinck (Athens), War Office, 12 August 1922. See also the comments on 27 July by Aristeidis Stergiadis (Sterghiades), the Greek Governor of İzmir. He was confident that the Greeks would win against the Nationalists, and there would be no Greek evacuation. (WO 32/5658, 'Interview with Sterghiades by HMR Smyrna', 2nd Bureau, GHQ Constantinople, 2 August 1922.) Greek public opinion was against the Paris Proposals, and the Greek Government felt, probably correctly, that acceptance would lead to its fall. (Lindley, Athens, to Curzon, 30 and 31 March 1922, DBFP 17, pp. 768–9.)
28. CAB 31/1, Cabinet Meeting of 7 September 1922.
29. Harington believed the Greeks were 'hobbled' by the aid that the French and Italians gave the Turks, including arms they allowed the Turks to take from Ottoman depots. FO 371/7885, Harington to War Office, Constantinople, 2 September 1922. This volume contains much on the British effort to arrange an armistice and save what they could of the Greek army. Events on the battlefield transpired too fast for this to have any effect. See also WO 106/1505, Harington, 'Appreciation of the Military Situation in the Near East, November 1920 to December 1922', Constantinople, 6 January 1923.

   On the available evidence, it is not possible to know the extent of the supply of arms to the Nationalists by the Italians and French: arms and munitions were undoubtedly left behind by both as they departed from Cilicia and Antalya. There were Greek complaints and rumours reported by the British consul in Beirut ('80,000 rifles, guns, etc.') and others ('military stores, equipment and munitions for two divisions'). (CAB 24/129/48, Eastern Department Memorandum, 26 October 1921.) Most reports were general in form, without specifics. For example, a 'very secret source', otherwise unidentified, told British Intelligence that the French had facilitated the removal of 1,000 rifles and ammunition from the 'arms dump' at Gülhane. British officials at the time had mentioned nothing. (FO 371/6530, Director of Military Intelligence to Under-Secretary of State for Foreign Affairs, War Office, 20 September 1921.) In all the reports I have seen, the British did not have evidence of these arms deliveries, although some British officials stated they had taken place, again without evidence. On Greek allegations, see the numerous examples in FO 371/6509. The French did not consider the arms question in their lengthy justification of their pact with the Nationalists. (CAB 24/131/1, Saint-Aulaire to Curzon, London, 17 November 1921.)
30. Curzon's memorandum of 22 April 1922, cited in DBFP 17, p. 792.

31. FO 406/49, Poincaré to Hardinge, Paris, 15 May 1922, enclosure in Hardinge to Curzon, 15 May 1922. FO 406/49, Foreign Office Memorandum to Poincaré, 7 June 1922, enclosure in Balfour to Hardinge, Foreign Office, 7 June 1922. Poincaré also noted that the British were too consumed with defending the Greeks. He wrote that the British were only concerned with Turkish massacres, but the Greeks were also guilty. FO 406/49, Poincaré to Hardinge, Paris, 16 June 1922, enclosure in Hardinge to Balfour, Paris, 17 June 1922.
32. FO 424/254, Rumbold to Curzon, Constantinople, 3 September 1922. FO 371/7872, T. Jones to Curzon, London, 7 September 1922. FO 371/7886, Rumbold Telegram, Constantinople, 6 September 1922; Kennard (ambassador in Italy) Telegram, Rome, 7 September 1922.
33. General Harington's assessment in CAB 23/25 /28, Cabinet Meeting of 31 May 1921. General Wilson:

> I think the chances are that the Turks will drive the Greeks back on to Smyrna, and quite likely out of Smyrna too, and that our troops in Constantinople will be in danger. Nor in such a case can I see any possibility of holding the Dardanelles. In short, I think we ought now to take the necessary steps to withdraw, and withdraw completely, both from the Bosporus and the Dardanelles. (Callwell, p. 292)

On plans, see FO 424/254, Rumbold to Curzon, 7 September 1922. There are too many documents on the various British plans to cite here, especially because the plans were all unavailing. See the dozens of communications in FO 424/254, pages 141–69. The letters of Cabinet Secretary Maurice Hankey to Lord Balfour and Hankey's summaries of cabinet meetings in CAB 63/32 and CAB 63/33, while they do not offer much real information, do indicate the feelings in the cabinet.

34. Committee meeting of 27 August 1922, enclosure in T 161/145, Rumbold to Balfour, Constantinople, 6 June 1922; WO 32/5658, Rumbold Telegram, Constantinople, 31 August 1922; WO 32/5658, 'Special Paper No. 6, Regarding the Evacuation and Demilitarization of Thrace', revised 18 July 1922. A plan, later revised, had already been begun before the Paris meeting, but the General Staff had felt that the scheme could only work with complete agreement by the Greeks and Turks and an extensive commitment of British, French and Italian forces. (WO 32/5658, War Office File: Harington, 'Scheme for Evacuation of Asia Minor by Greek Army and Appendices', 3 January 1922.) British Consul Lamb was convinced that there could not be a peaceful evacuation of Greek

troops without a strong Allied force to cover it. (FO 406/49, Lamb to Rumbold, Smyrna, 1 May 1922, enclosure in Rumbold to Curzon, Constantinople, 13 May 1922.) See also the plans in WO 158/787.

35. 'Instructions Regarding the Allied Control' was first printed on 30 May 1922, revised in June, and distributed on 14 August (WO 32/5658, War Council to Under-Secretary of State, War Office, 14 August 1922.) Among Britain's allies, there were significant arguments over the plan; the final product was almost entirely a British production. (WO 32/5658, British High Commission to Balfour, Yeni-Keuy, 13 June 1922 and other documents in WO 32/5658. Numerous descriptions are in FO 371/7870.)

36. FO 371/7868, Bentinck Telegram, Athens, 29 July 1922. ADM 137/1771, Harington to Chief of the Imperial General Staff, 17 July 1922. See Bentinck's summary of the event in FO 372/7871, Bentinck to Curzon, Athens, 11 August 1922, and FO 371/7871, War Office Intelligence, 'Greece: A Secret History of the Recent Threat to Occupy Constantinople', 29 August 1922. For extensive further documents on the Greek plan to take Istanbul, see DBFP 17, pp. 900–12. Michael M. Finefrock, 'Atatürk, Lloyd George and the Megali Idea: Cause and Consequence of the Greek Plan to Seize Constantinople from the Allies, June–August 1922', *The Journal of Modern History*, vol. 52, no. 1, On Demand Supplement (March 1980), pp. D1047–66.

37. ADM 137/1771, Harington to War Office, Constantinople, 27 July 1922; Harington to Chief of the Imperial General Staff, 17 July 1922; Admiralty to Harington, 29 July 1922; Foreign Office to Rumbold, London, 1 August 1922; Foreign Office to Bentick (ambassador at Athens), London, 1 August 1922; Rumbold Telegram, Constantinople, 2 August 1922.

38. ADM 137/1771: Harington to War Office, Constantinople, 27 July 1922; Rumbold Telegram, Constantinople, 31 July 1922; Graham (ambassador at Rome) to Foreign Office, 3 August 1922. WO 32/5743, Harington Report. WO 32/5742, Harington to War Office, Constantinople, 20 October 1923, 'British Forces in Turkey. Commander-in-Chief's Despatch. Period 1920–1923'. Harington believed that Mustafa Kemal took advantage of the Greek movement of troops to Thrace to commence his attack in Anatolia.

39. 'Near East', 4 August 1922, *Hansard*, vol. 157, cc. 1986–2008. FO 371/7887, Bentinck to Curzon, 29 August 1922. Bentinck himself felt that the British should give Istanbul to the Greeks. (DBFP 17, pp. 939–41, Bentinck to Curzon, Athens, 29 August 1922.)

The Greek Government received the British prime minister's statement enthusiastically. The Greeks hoped that the prime minister might now let them

occupy Istanbul after all; Lloyd George's verbal support did them no good. (Bentinck to Curzon, Athens, DBFP 17, 29 August 1922, p. 939, no. 181. FO 371/7869, Bentinck Telegram, Athens, 7 August 1922. FO 424/254, Rumbold to Curzon, Constantinople, 15 August 1922.) Rumbold mistakenly stated that the Lloyd George speech had been on 14 August.
40. Bentinck to Balfour, Athens, 3 August 1922, DBFP 17, p. 913, no. 719.
41. Finefrock (pp. D1059–60, D1064–5) makes a case for this, and notes from Turkish sources that Mustafa Kemal was fully aware of the weakness caused by the removal of troops to Thrace. WO 32/5743, Harington Report.

# 19

## CHANAK

The Greeks had withdrawn their remaining forces from Anatolia to mainland Greece and Thrace. All indications were that they could no more resist the Turkish army in Thrace than they had been able to do in Anatolia. The Turks swiftly withdrew their army to the border of the Neutral Zone of the Straits. The question was whether the British would attempt to stand in the way of a Turkish attack into Eastern Thrace. They resolved to hold the Straits against the Turks, both to keep their control of the waterway and to retain what they could for the Greeks in Thrace. The French and Italians, on the other hand, realised that standing against the Turks would be folly. They had no desire to do so. The British were to stand alone in defence of the Straits.

There were two potential possibilities for Nationalist attack – the İzmit Peninsula and the South side of the Dardanelles. Both were held only by small British detachments. The danger at the İzmit border was that the Turks could easily defeat a small British force and advance to Istanbul. At the Dardanelles, the Turks could easily take the Southern shore, shell the defences of Gallipoli and likely advance to attack the Greeks in Thrace. Despite Greek protestations that they could defend Thrace, all military assessments were that they would be easily defeated. The Allies had no force capable of assisting the Greeks, and the French and Italians had no desire to do so.

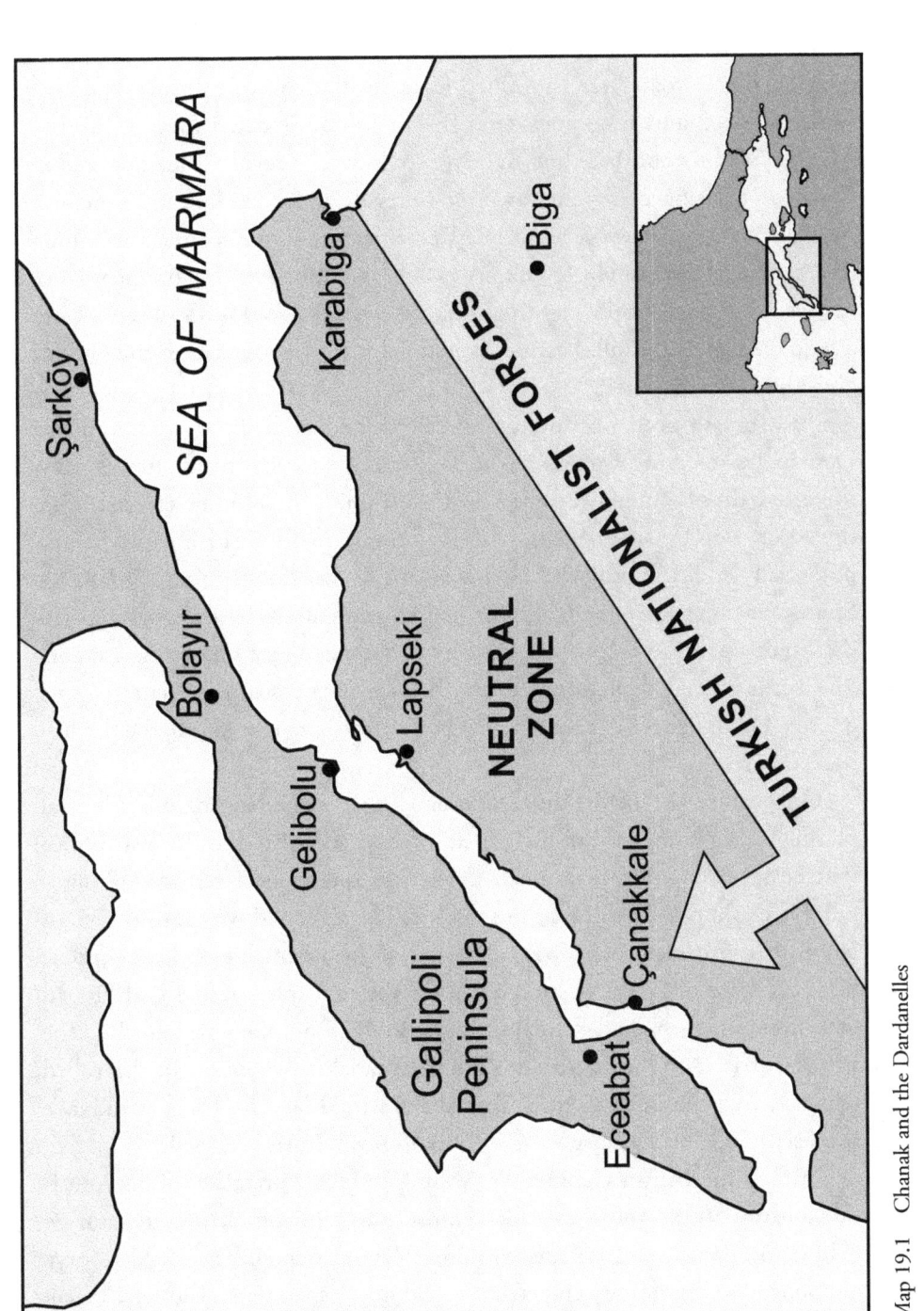

Map 19.1 Chanak and the Dardanelles

Of the two potential areas for Turkish attack, the assault would probably come at the Dardanelles. The Allied forces in the İzmit Peninsula could be easily defeated and Istanbul taken. The British anticipated that, if Turkish forces moved toward Istanbul, the city would rise in revolt. They doubted if the forces available could put down such a revolt, much less defeat the incoming Turkish army. However, Mustafa Kemal had no desire to attack Istanbul. There would have been little military benefit in taking Istanbul on the way to Thrace, and much of the city might have been destroyed in the attack, with a high civilian death toll. Istanbul would fall readily enough after the Greeks and Allies were defeated.

The Turkish need was to cross to Thrace and evict the Greeks, and the Dardanelles crossing was much more attractive to the Turks. It was only three-fourths of a mile wide at its narrowest point. It could be crossed from the Asian side by small boats, as it was traditionally. British capital ships potentially could interdict traffic between the two sides of the Dardanelles Strait. Wartime losses at Gallipoli had shown, however, that warships in the Strait could be readily targeted by mobile artillery on the Asian side. The Turks moved their troops to the British defences in the Neutral Zone on the Dardanelles. Ultimately, 50,000 Turkish troops faced the British barbed wire.[1]

On 3 June 1922, before the Greeks had been defeated in Anatolia, General Harington, in command of the Allied forces, had written to the War Office that he saw no point, and much danger, in the Allied retention of Istanbul. He could not defend it against attack. He suggested withdrawal. On 14 September he cabled to the War Office that if the other Allies did not support him, his force of 2,700 was too small for the task. He stressed that he had little hope unless he had French assistance, which he thought doubtful. The British garrison on the South side of the Dardanelles (which the British called Chanak, after the small town of Çanakkale) would fall, the Turks would take the Asiatic side of the Bosporus, and Istanbul would rise in revolt.[2]

At first, the British Cabinet was willing to take a practical military position on the Straits and the İzmit Peninsula which, they felt, could not be held if the French and Italians withdrew. On 11 September, Lloyd George announced to his military chiefs that he did not wish to defend either Chanak or the İzmit Peninsula. Only Gallipoli and Istanbul were to be retained. What was important was that the Nationalists not be allowed to cross the Straits and attack Gallipoli from the North. The cabinet did not intend to send reinforcements to hold the South side of the Dardanelles, which was considered indefensible; it would be abandoned, and British forces would transfer to Gallipoli. General Harington was given permission to leave the İzmit Peninsula, at his discretion. The navy, the cabinet believed, would be enough to keep the Nationalists from crossing the Dardanelles to Thrace. Lloyd George stated that the important point was to retain Gallipoli, in order to allow warships to pass the Straits and threaten Istanbul, although the Admiralty doubted the possibility of this.[3]

Two days after it had been decided to abandon Chanak and İzmit, the British Cabinet changed its mind and determined to defend both. The ostensible reason was the belief that the French and Italians had agreed to assist in their defence. General Harington felt that he could hold Chanak with French and Italian assistance. This was a hope, rather than a reality, because the two planned to send only a token force. Curzon, although doubtful of the cabinet decision, decided to accept retention of the two positions. The British Cabinet began to approach the situation as a clash of wills in which the British must be triumphant, even if it meant war with the Turks. Lloyd George, Winston Churchill (Secretary of State for the Colonies) and Austen Chamberlain (Lord Privy Seal) were particularly vociferous in advocating war, rather than what they viewed as dishonour.[4]

The General Staff recommended that the British abandon the İzmit Peninsula, Istanbul and Chanak. The cabinet, however, was unwilling to pay attention to assessments by the military. Lloyd George's hold on the reality of the situation was deteriorating. He suggested that the Greek defeat in Anatolia had been engineered by King Constantine for his own purposes. Despite the Greek loss, he wanted the Paris Agreements to still take effect, because he thought that nothing much had changed: 'Nothing, however, had happened which was inconsistent with the Paris arrangement. The Greeks had voluntarily (sic) evacuated Asia Minor, for, so far as he could judge, there had been practically no fighting.' The prime minister even stated that Mosul was of no account to the British, compared to Istanbul. Even Mosul's oil, so long demanded by the British throughout lengthy negotiations, could not compare, in the prime minister's mind, to the need to salvage what little the

British still controlled – Istanbul and the Straits. Wounded pride was not lacking in Lloyd George. He declared that the British could not 'run away before Mustapha Kemal'.[5]

Lloyd George's understanding of the situation was inexplicable, except perhaps by psychiatric analysis. Even though the Turks had quickly defeated the Greeks, how could anyone have believed that the battles of 1922 had not existed? And the Greek evacuation of Anatolia had been anything but voluntary. Lloyd George had never been practical, or even completely rational, in his plans for the Ottoman Empire. Now he was willing to court a Götterdämmerung, fighting overwhelming Turkish forces and perhaps destroying much of Istanbul in the fight. Yet, if Lloyd George's irrationality is understood as an aberration, how can one explain the war fever that gripped his cabinet colleagues, who presumably knew better? The cabinet agreed with the prime minister. Despite the failure of the Paris Accords, the cabinet voted to retain them as essential to any British position. They realised that a small number of British troops faced a large Turkish army. Their military advisors had described nothing but dangers. But those Curzon described as the 'fire-eaters' in the cabinet did not shirk at the prospect of a new war. Churchill, Lloyd George and others fiercely advocated retention of both the Bosporus and the Dardanelles, even if it meant war.[6]

The cabinet gave little consideration to the feelings of the British public; much of the opposition coming from their political enemy, the Labour Party. Placards appeared all over London protesting against British plans for war. Mayors called public meetings of protest. In public meetings, labour union leaders and Labour MPs spoke against the government's intentions for war with the Turks. At one of them, Ramsay MacDonald said: 'We regard him (Lloyd George) as a public danger to the peace of the world.' The General Council of the Trades Union Congress met with Prime Minister Lloyd George. They notified him in most definite terms that the working class was completely against any new war. They threatened hostility and resentment toward any politicians who drove the country to war. Lloyd George told them that the measures being taken by the cabinet were intended to avert war. He asserted that all the British wanted was 'Freedom of the Straits', and said, falsely, that the Kemalists had not guaranteed that, and wanted to be able to close the Straits. The Trades Union representatives were not convinced; they wanted no war.[7]

## Humiliation

The issue of control of the South side of the Dardanelles had become an emotional one. A rational calculation would seem to have been to abandon the conflict with the Turks. The only real desire of the British now was Freedom of the Straits, and the Turkish Nationalists had already promised neutralisation of the Straits. Surely that could have been negotiated, as it ultimately was. And if it came to war, the British did not have the troops to fight. Defending a world-wide empire was already taxing their strength. How many British casualties could the Dardanelles be worth? But the dominant fear of the British prime minister and cabinet was not military defeat or the loss of soldiers' lives; they most feared humiliation. Already in June of 1920 the cabinet had decided that 'to retire from Constantinople before a bandit like Mustapha Kemal would deal a shattering blow to our prestige in the East, and that this could not possibly be contemplated'. It was easy to advance that sentiment when the Nationalists were weak, but the fear of humiliation continued when Mustafa Kemal was strong.[8]

Mustafa Kemal's existence and success were an affront to the British. He was an image of opposition to British imperialism. One of the main complaints of the British was that the Turkish Nationalists refused to abide by the terms set by Allied conferences. Obviously, the Turks rejected the Sèvres Treaty. They also refused to abide by the terms of the Allied conferences of London and Paris. Why should they have done so? The only valid reasons to comply with the conference decisions would have been benefit for the nation or compulsion by military force. The Allies, led by the British, offered neither to the Turks. Instead, they repeatedly expected the Turks to accept Allied judgements simply because the Allies had made them. For example, after the Greek defeat, one of the main British objections was that Mustafa Kemal was not adhering to the Paris Proposals. Those proposals had been drawn up without any input from the Turks, on the continuing assumption that the European Powers knew what was best. Mustafa Kemal even had the effrontery to announce that he refused to accept even the concept of a neutral zone created solely by the Allies. Mustafa Kemal was not playing the game as the British expected it to be played. Imperial Powers were supposed to set the rules, and subject peoples to obey.[9]

Whereas Lloyd George's motivation had long been to defend the Greeks, he now defended the image of Britain in the world. 'The Prime Minister thought that the evacuation of Chanak, having regard to all that had happened, would be the greatest loss of prestige which could possibly be inflicted on the British Empire.' When General Harington suggested that the Turkish army might be allowed to pass into Thrace, the prime minister was aghast. His reason was that it would be 'most humiliating' for the British. 'The Prime Minister considered the action of the Turkish Nationalists an insult to the British Empire.' He was certain, despite all his generals having declared the overwhelming power of the Turkish force, that the Turks were cowards who would recoil before the small number of British soldiers who stood against them:

> I cannot help thinking that by a combination of naval guns, and howitzers on Gallipoli, machine-guns, bombing and firing we could make it impossible for the Turks to approach Chanak and as all one hears about them leads one to believe that they are inferior, certainly out of trenches, to European troops; they might be effected with panic and disperse. It would be a great triumph if we could defeat a heavy Turkish attack alone without any assistance from the French and demonstrate to the world that even from a military point of view we are not as helpless as our enemies of every description imagine us to be.[10]

Lloyd George was not alone in his sentiments. Other powerful members of the cabinet echoed his determination. In the past, Winston Churchill had generally been a rational voice, calling, for example, for the Greeks to leave İzmir, but he was a man who never shied away from conflict. Throughout the Dardanelles crisis, Churchill held that the reason to hold the line was the loss of prestige if the British did not fight: 'There could be no greater blow to British prestige than the hurried evacuation of Chanak in face of Turkish threats.' 'To give up Chanak would be a serious blow to the prestige of the Empire.' 'If it was now decided to clear out of Chanak, we should become the laughing-stock of the world.'[11]

## Britain Stands Alone

The British knew they needed support, so they grasped at whatever possibility they imagined might be available: at Lloyd George's suggestion, the cabinet asked the Dominions and the Romanians and Yugoslavians to send troops to come to their aid. The British force in Istanbul and the Straits, the prime minister said, would with that assistance swell to 60,000 men. But neither the Romanians nor the Yugoslavs were willing to aid the British. Even the British Dominion friends in Australia, South Africa and Canada refused. The French and Italians had already abandoned them. The British were alone.[12]

A frantic scramble to find reinforcements for the British positions at Istanbul and especially at the Dardanelles ensued. The cabinet at first decided to send a relatively small force to Harington, an understaffed division of 7,000 men, because more troops were thought to be unavailable. On 16 September, the cabinet decided that more troops might be found, and one or possibly two full divisions, previously planned to be demobilised or in training, could be sent from Britain. This, however, could not have caused much cheer to Harington. The first division would not arrive for a month after it was mobilised. The divisional artillery would not embark from Britain for fourteen to twenty-one days. It would take a further thirteen days for it to arrive from England. Only two battalions would leave from Malta and Gibraltar at once. The men of two howitzer batteries would accompany them, but their guns and horses would not arrive until the end of the month. The War Office assumed that these forces would only assist in joint operations with the French, which was not about to happen. In any case, the cabinet reversed its decision two days later, deciding to send only one brigade from England, a quarter to a half of their original intention. Then, obviously in confusion, on 18 September, an ever more bellicose cabinet found more forces to send to Harington – 1,000 marines, a squadron of 'bombing airplanes', a brigade of field artillery, two regiments of cavalry from Egypt and, if Lord Allenby in Cairo approved, two more battalions of infantry. Thirty-eight field guns were soon on route from Egypt and Gibraltar. Forty more were being prepared, expected to be ready to sail between 30 September and 7 October. The ships sailing on 30 September were expected to arrive on 13 October. Many of the combat units would not embark until 30 September. The horses needed to move the cannon could not sail before 4 October. Unloading the cannon at Gallipoli and Chanak would be a difficult task, so a ship was to be sent with a 12-ton crane.[13]

The question before the cabinet was whether reinforcements would reach Istanbul, Chanak and Gallipoli in time, and whether they would be enough to deter Mustafa Kemal from attacking. Would the Turks conveniently wait until the reinforcements arrived? The Chief of the General Staff, Field Marshal Frederick Rudolph Lambert, Earl of Cavan, reported that the Turkish Nationalists had a force of 52,000 within 50 miles of Chanak. These would quickly defeat the British. Cavan said the total Nationalist army was estimated at 300,000. Lloyd George, as usual doubting his military advisors, stated that the Turkish Nationalist army was only 72,000 in total, not 300,000. With reinforcements, he said, the British force would be enough to deter Mustafa Kemal.[14]

An interesting point was the assumption made by the cabinet, although not by the generals, that the British would be able to land reinforcements at the Dardanelles without opposition. It stretches credulity that the Turks would have held back their attack as the British landed their battalions and cannon. A 12-ton crane hoisting howitzers would have made plain to the Turks that something was afoot, and that it was time to attack before the howitzers could be put into action. It was assumed that if Mustafa Kemal agreed to an armistice meeting, he would demand that the British not employ any reinforcements. It was decided, therefore, that the Turks would be told that the British would send no more reinforcements, except those that were at sea. (Almost all their reinforcements were already at sea.) They more than somewhat underestimated Mustafa Kemal's intelligence.[15]

General Cavan repeatedly questioned the military assumptions of the cabinet. He stated that the British perimeter at Chanak was only four miles wide, not enough to house and supply the expected reinforcements. Moreover, he believed that Kemal would not hesitate to attack reinforcements. He felt that Turkish guns on the Asiatic shore would make it impossible to land troops at Chanak. They would have to land on the North side of the Gallipoli Peninsula, march across the peninsula, then be ferried across the Strait under heavy fire. 'This would be a very difficult operation and heavy losses would probably be incurred in transferring troops across the Dardanelles.' The navy, however, believed they could silence the Turkish guns with naval gunpower. One wonders if they had learned the lessons of a previous Gallipoli campaign.[16]

Throughout the cabinet debates the prime minister clashed with the military. When told that the delivery of 6-inch howitzers from Malta would be delayed because ships had to be refitted for the mobile howitzers' horses,

Lloyd George said that the guns should be dragged up the hills by men. Cavan thought this impossible, and nothing larger than 4-and-a-half inch guns could be used at Gallipoli. Lloyd George insisted that an inquiry be launched regrading transporting 6-inch guns up the hills. Again and again, Cavan told Lloyd George that the prime minister's plans would not work. Lloyd George, seconded by Churchill, persisted. Cavan said that the cabinet's plans were based on French support, which he doubted would appear. Despite all the reports to the contrary that had reached the cabinet, Lloyd George was confident of French support. Curzon, who was beginning to doubt that, differed with the prime minister; the British ambassadors in Paris and Rome had written that the French and Italians would send neither troops nor ships.[17]

In Istanbul it had become obvious that the French and Italians would not support the British against the Turks. The French and Italian high commissioners in Istanbul had originally agreed (10 September 1922) to send, as a token, small numbers of troops to Chanak and Scutari (Üsküdar, on the Asiatic side of Istanbul), one company at each place, to reinforce the British, who held those positions against the Turks, but would do no more. By 19 September, Harington had become sure that the French and Italian support upon which he depended would not be forthcoming. His Allied colleagues refused to send any more men to Chanak or İzmit unless they received orders from their governments. Instead, the French and Italians withdrew their forces from Chanak, although the French left a small force on the European side of the Dardanelles. Commissioner Rumbold believed that the French High Commission was unwilling to do anything that would be unwelcome to the Nationalists.[18]

**Curzon Appeals for Allied Solidarity**

Curzon, increasingly dismayed by the war fever he saw in the cabinet, decided to approach the French in a last attempt at Allied solidarity. French Prime Minister Poincaré met with Curzon in Paris on 20 September 1922. It became obvious in the acrimonious proceedings that the French would offer no real assistance to the British. Of the tools that had insured French compliance with British aims, only ongoing talks on German reparations still held any hope for leverage with the French. The French proved not to believe the

British would assist them on that issue; Britain, therefore, could no longer force the French to agree with them in negotiations. For the first time in all the discussions and conferences on the Ottoman Empire, the French and British were equals.[19]

Curzon began the discussion with Poincaré by asserting that the British could never allow Mustafa Kemal to decide the fate of Thrace, Istanbul or the Straits. Those were matters to be decided by the Allies, not the Turks. The British had ordered a battalion to Chanak. They had reinforced the British position in the İzmit Peninsula insofar as they were able. Curzon expressed amazement that the French, whose support he had hoped the British could have relied on, had withdrawn their battalion from Chanak. He politely asked Poincaré to explain his actions.

Poincaré responded, also politely, that he had warned the British at the March meetings (the Paris Accords) that the Turks would never accept the Allied proposals. Mustafa Kemal had told French representatives that his troops would occupy all the territory specified in the National Pact, including Istanbul and Eastern Thrace. Poincaré accepted that the Turks would cross the Straits into Thrace. The French had neither the men nor the money to oppose them, and, moreover, France had no wish to do so. As for removing troops from Chanak, the French, he said, had never agreed to send troops to enforce the Neutral Zone of the Straits.

The only solution, Poincaré felt, was to invite Mustafa Kemal to a conference, and to tell him that he would have Istanbul and 'an acceptable settlement in Thrace and Gallipoli'. The Turks would never come to a conference unless they were promised that. Curzon disagreed. He wanted any conference with the Turks to be held on the basis of the Paris Accords. He would not make any promises to the Turks before a conference. Instead, he offered that the Allies should tell the Turks that they would take the Turks' desires 'into grave and sympathetic consideration'. Poincaré replied that such a policy was 'blindness'; the Turks had already rejected the Paris Accords. Poincaré implied, although not overtly stated, that past experience had forced the Turks not to trust such unconditional assurances.

From that point the conferees became less polite. Poincaré stated that it was for the French alone to order French troops. Curzon said if the French withdrew, leaving the British to face Kemal alone, 'public opinion would hardly regard this as a just and loyal arrangement'. Poincaré said the Allies were exposed to a great peril, and he would not expose French soldiers to that peril. Curzon said that the French were destroying the *entente* in Asia. He 'deplored' the French position. Count Sforza, the Italian ambassador to France, had entered the room and joined the discussion. (Curzon had not wanted the Italians to take part in the meeting, but Poincaré brought them in.) Sforza said he shared Poincaré's views. Italy, like France, would not fight against the Turks.[20]

British and French admirals were brought in to assess the possibility of a naval defence of the Straits. British Admiral David Beatty assured that it could be done. Poincaré, seconded by Admiral Grasset, doubted that such naval action was feasible, referring to the British experience at Gallipoli.

Curzon and Poincaré traded insults until both finally began to act maturely. Curzon found himself forced to accept most of the French plan, not the plan of the British Cabinet. He and Poincaré set out to write an invitation to the Turkish Nationalists to a meeting with Allied generals at Mudanya to conclude an armistice. Curzon did not get any reference to the Paris Accords, which were obviously dead. The French had demanded that the Allies notify the Turks that they would be allowed to take Eastern Thrace. Curzon wanted no such admission, but finally agreed to include a reference to Allied support for ultimate Turkish occupation of Eastern Thrace. Curzon's one success was an agreement that upcoming armistice talks 'should be strictly confined to the single point of fixing the line in Thrace to which the Greek troops might be withdrawn'.[21]

The cabinet at first had not approved of notifying the Turks that they would surely gain Eastern Thrace, but decided to give Curzon a free hand in his talks with Poincaré. It later accepted the Poincaré–Curzon plan. The cabinet described this as an unfortunate necessity. It put the blame on French and Italian duplicity in withdrawing from Cilicia and Antalya, the refusal of the United States to accept a mandate and the deficiency of the Greek army. Nothing was the fault of the British. 'In these circumstances it would be advisable to avoid any phrase which might be construed as committing the British Government to the moral responsibility for the inevitable change of policy in regard to Eastern Thrace.' The cabinet authorised Lloyd George to tell the press that Britain had acted wisely over Chanak. All problems were the fault of others.[22]

The three Allies finally agreed on 23 September to send an invitation to the Nationalists to a conference to be held at Venice or another place. Plenipotentiaries of Great Britain, France, Italy, Japan, Romania, Yugoslavia ('l'Etat serbe-croate-slovène') and Greece would also be invited. The conference would negotiate a treaty of peace among Turkey, Greece and the Allied Powers. In the letter, the Nationalists were told that the Allies favoured Turkish rule in Eastern Thrace, up to the Maritsa, including Edirne. The Allies would 'use their influence' to have the Greeks evacuate Eastern Thrace, to a line determined by Allied generals, before the conference opened. The only necessary Allied condition was that the Turks hold back from attack at the Neutral Zone before the conference, but they also held that some agreement would have to be met on demilitarising the Straits under the aegis of the League of Nations and on the protection of minorities. The three Allies would sponsor Turkey for membership in the League of Nations. On completion of the peace conference, the Allies would withdraw their forces from Anatolia, Istanbul and Eastern Thrace.

The Allies suggested that a meeting could take place between Mustapha Kemal and Allied generals in Mudanya or İzmit to set the line behind which the Greeks would withdraw, the only subject to be discussed at the meeting. Curzon was pleased that the invitation to the Turks did not go into details. He was insistent that the upcoming armistice conference would only be on the specific topic of Greek withdrawal, not other matters. The British, he felt, would have more control over these at the ensuing peace conference.[23]

The Allied proposal was sent to Istanbul on 23 September for transmission to Mustafa Kemal; it was not sent directly to Mustafa Kemal, who expected a formal request. One assumes he distrusted a verbal note from the British. Yusuf Kemal, Nationalist representative in Istanbul, left Istanbul for Ankara with the Allied proposal on 29 September. It was expected that it would be a week before the Allied governments received his reply.[24]

The meetings in Paris had reached more reasonable conclusions than had the London or Paris Accords, but they shared one defining characteristic with the earlier conferences. All assumed that the structure of the region would be set by outsiders. Until they were forced to the table with the Turks at Lausanne, the Allies had always presented 'peace plans' that were in fact thinly disguised orders to the Turks. Turkish input was not desired. The Paris meeting between

Poincaré and Curzon had been no different: the British and French drew up a plan that was communicated to the Turks for their acceptance, although the French and Italians had unsuccessfully advocated a position that would be more acceptable to the Turks. Throughout the meetings with Poincaré and Sforza, Curzon repeatedly stated that he was anxious to ensure unity among the Allies. He may or may not have consciously understood that the unity he demanded was actually a united support of Britain's plans. His frustration was that he did not receive that support. Nevertheless, in accepting the final Allied plan the cabinet praised Curzon for what it considered his great success.[25]

The cabinet finally and grudgingly accepted General Harington's assessment that Istanbul and the Bosporus could not be held against Turkish attack. For them, the essential issue was control of the Dardanelles. Harington was even told to evacuate Istanbul and concentrate his forces on the defence of Chanak and Gallipoli, if that were necessary. The French, however, felt that all Allied forces should be withdrawn from the Asiatic shore of the Straits. They were to have nothing to do with British conflict with the Turks over Chanak.[26]

Despite the Allied invitation to an armistice conference, Harington continued to make preparations for defence of his Chanak Neutral Zone position and of İzmit and Istanbul: the navy was in place to defend the Dardanelles. Howitzers and newly arrived troops were dispatched to Gallipoli and Chanak. British wives and children left. Harington advised that all arrangements for reinforcements be retained. The Turks kept up pressure. Turkish cavalry reconnoitred within the Neutral Zone, then retired. The British threatened the Turks with airplane and naval bombardment. Harington, however, held off hostile encounters.[27]

The cabinet was in no mood to accept pacific measures. On 19 September, the Chief of the Imperial General Staff, Earl Cavan, once again spoke against defence of Chanak. He listed the troop numbers of the Turks and the British, 52,000 Turks opposed to one British battalion: 'The Kemalists could push that small force into the sea within a fortnight.' Lloyd George told him that he knew that the Nationalist force was much smaller than the general had stated. If only the British stood firm, the prime minister believed, the Nationalists would never attack. At a meeting on 27 September, Lord Cavan once again advised that the position at Chanak could not be held for long. He recommended evacuation of the Chanak position. He was met with obstinacy derived from pride.

> Mr. Chamberlain (Austin Chamberlain, Lord Privy Seal, in the chair at the meeting) observed that the proposals for withdrawal were based on purely military considerations, and he was of the opinion that we could not now withdraw from Chanak with credit to ourselves in order to avoid Kemal's irregulars (sic). He would regard such a withdrawal as an humiliation to the British Empire.

Churchill suggested various plans that could be used to hold and reinforce Chanak. The military view was unheeded.[28]

On 28 September, Harington notified the War Office that he had received a pacific telegram from Mustafa Kemal. Harington did not believe the Turks wanted war: 'I do not think Mustapha Kemal wants to attack us and I feel myself that if we go straight now we may remove all danger of attacks from our troops.' Harington believed it was possible, and legal according to the rules of war, to allow the Turkish army to cross into Eastern Thrace, avoiding the Neutral Zone and the British army. The Greeks would have to withdraw to the Maritsa, into Western Thrace. He was most concerned with saving soldiers' lives. He proposed to meet personally with Mustafa Kemal.[29]

London received Harington's cable at 10 a. m. The cabinet considered it that day, then replied that night. The substance of their reply was that Harington's suggestions were different from the plan decided recently in Paris: the Paris meeting had stated that the Turks would not be allowed to cross into Europe except by decision of a peace conference. The proposals did not allow the personal meeting Harington wanted. The Greeks could only be definitively told to retreat by act of an upcoming armistice conference. The cabinet then admonished Harington for his involvement: 'He (Harington) will no doubt express his opinions on the matter at Mudania, and final decision should not be made without reference to High Commissioners and to Allied Powers, since matter is evidently political rather than military.' The reply was sent by the Foreign Office not to Harington, but to High Commissioner Rumbold. The cabinet obviously thought Harington had to be put in his place.[30]

On 29 September, at 11.30 a. m., the cabinet finally decided on war. Six days had passed since the Allies had proposed an armistice meeting to Mustafa Kemal. The cabinet suspected that the Nationalists were using the time to prepare their attack. Lloyd George called the inactions of the Nationalists 'an insult to the British Empire'.

> The Secretary of State for the Colonies (Churchill) suggested that the time had come for General Harington to give an ultimatum to the Turkish Nationalist troops to withdraw outside the neutral zone and to employ force if they did not agree to the ultimatum.

Lloyd George, supported by Churchill and Lord Chancellor Birkenhead (Frederick Edwin Smith, Viscount Birkenhead), presented a motion to the cabinet that a telegram be sent to Harington:

> The Turkish Nationalists are obviously moving up troops and seeking to net your forces in. Cabinet are advised by the General Staff that if we allow continuance of this, the defensive position will be imperiled and that the moment to avert the disaster has arrived. It has therefore been decided by the Cabinet that the Officer Commanding the Turkish forces around Chanak is immediately to be notified that, if his forces are not withdrawn by an hour to be settled by you, at which our combined forces will be in place, all the forces at our disposal—naval, military and aerial—will open fire. In this latter event the air forces should be used so long as the Turkish forces are inside the neutral zone. The time limit should be short and it should not be overlooked that we have received warning regarding the date (of a Turkish attack)—September 30th, from our intelligence.[31]

On 29 September at 3 p. m., the same day the British ultimatum was sent to Istanbul, Commissioner Rumbold received a message from the Nationalists that the Turks agreed to meet at Mudanya. They notified the Allies that they had stopped any advance toward Chanak or Istanbul, although they did not say they would retreat from their positions inside the Neutral Zone. It was obvious that the Turks did not trust the British, but Turkish agreement to meet had been negotiated by the French representative, Franklin-Bouillon. İsmet Paşa would represent Mustafa Kemal at the meeting at Mudanya, which would begin on 3 October.[32]

By the evening of the 29th, the newspapers in London and Paris carried news of Mustafa Kemal's acceptance.

Curzon, whose low opinion of the Turks did not stop him from wanting to avoid war, asked his colleagues for an immediate cabinet meeting. It convened at 10 p. m. on the 29th. Curzon told his colleagues that he had met with the Nationalist representative in London, Nihad Reşat, at 4 p. m. Curzon had told him that Mustafa Kemal had not yet replied to the invitation to meet at Mudanya, and that on 30 September General Harington would demand the withdrawal of Turkish troops. If they did not do so, the British troops would open fire. Nihad Reşat explained that the Turkish response had been delayed while they waited for Franklin-Bouillion's report. He said he would telegraph Ankara immediately.

Curzon asked the cabinet for a 48-hour delay in the ultimatum until the British could formally receive Mustafa Kemal's response, but powerful voices in the cabinet spoke against any delay. The Lord Privy Seal and Leader of the House of Commons (Austen Chamberlain), Lord Chancellor (Viscount Birkenhead), Chancellor of the Exchequer (Robert Horne) and the Secretary of State for the Colonies (Winston Churchill) all spoke against a delay. They argued that the Turks had been given enough time. Moreover, it was too late to stop the ultimatum, which they assumed had been delivered by Harington, or to delay the military preparations for the British attack. The prime minister was not at the meeting, but Chamberlain told them that Lloyd George was also against a delay. Churchill announced that British action at Chanak would teach the Turks that the British could not be 'trampled on and ignored'. 'When Mustapha Kemal found he was up against people who would stand up to him he might change his attitude.'[33]

Poincaré, notified of the British ultimatum by the newspapers, not by the British Government, told the British that he would not be bound or responsible for any action taken by General Harington. If Britain attacked the Turks, he would withdraw all French forces from the Neutral Zone. Poincaré lamented that France and Italy had not been notified before the British took such drastic action. He felt the solidarity shown so recently among the Allies had been destroyed.[34]

The cabinet waited for a telegram from Harington, notifying them that war had begun. The telegram had been sent to Harington at 3 p. m. on the 29th. No answer had been received by 4 p. m. on the 30th. The cabinet adjourned until Harington's reply was received. News finally came in a telegram from Commissioner Rumbold: Harington had not acted on their order. The bellicose members of the cabinet were dismayed. Nothing had been received from Harington himself. It was agreed that nothing could be done until Harington's message was received.[35]

When Harington's message finally reached the cabinet, they found that he admitted not having acted on their ultimatum, although he perhaps assumed too much regarding their desire for peace:

> I was convinced that I was acting in the interests of peace, and in accordance with what I felt would be the wishes of His Majesty's Government, in withholding the warning, as I alone was in a position to judge the situation on the spot.[36]

Frustrated in their desire for war and presented with Harington's *fait accompli*, the cabinet sent orders to Harington for an upcoming meeting with the Turks at Mudanya. Harington was to demand that the Turks abandon their incursions into the Neutral Zone, because the Greeks would not evacuate Eastern Thrace until the Turks had done so. He was to leave political questions to the diplomats and only consider military matters, such as evicting the Greek army beyond the Maritsa. Administration and occupation of Eastern Thrace was to be decided later by the Allied high commissioners, not by the generals at Mudanya. Finally, Harington was advised that he need not send the ultimatum to Mustafa Kemal after all.[37]

## Mudanya

When the Allied generals met at Mudanya on 3 October 1922, they found that the Turks would not accept their proposals for Eastern Thrace. İsmet Paşa, the Turkish Nationalist representative, refused to accept anything but that Eastern Thrace be handed over completely to the Turks before any final peace treaty was signed. He demanded that all Allied officials and soldiers should leave Eastern Thrace. Moreover, Turkish forces had withdrawn from the British lines, but not completely from the British-defined Neutral Zone, and were still in position to attack the British. Harington felt that İsmet threatened hostilities unless his conditions were met. The French General Charles Antoine Charpy agreed with İsmet. The meeting recessed to consider this. Curzon decided that in view of the situation he would have to go to

Paris to confer with Poincaré. Harington was instructed by the cabinet not to return to Mudanya without further instructions.[38]

Curzon once again met with Poincaré about the Mudanya Conference. Animosity between the French and the British had not ended with agreement on the letter to be sent to the Turks. There were still disagreements that would drive them to insult:

> (Curzon) And if Mustapha Kemal attacked again what would M. Poincaré propose to do? The Paris note spoke of the respect of the neutral zones, but M. Poincaré thought Mustapha Kemal might have already attacked. If so, what course was M. Poincaré going to adopt.
>
> M. Poincaré retorted that if the Turks advanced he would do nothing. Let there be no doubt of that. He would do nothing in any circumstances. French troops would never fire a shot in the East. He had said that before. France could not fight in the East, and would not. If concessions must be made she would make them reluctantly.
>
> Lord Curzon said that this seemed to be a most humiliating position, and he could not conceive that any Great Power should adopt it.
>
> M. Poincaré replied with great heat that there was no question of humiliation. He needed no lessons from anyone and would take none.

The British described the French plan for the Mudanya Armistice Conference as simple – to restore Turkish rule in Anatolia, Istanbul and Thrace up to the 1914 borders. Curzon, on the other hand, wanted no questions on the status of the region until a final conference. Insults aside, before long a compromise was found. Curzon, bereft of the tools that had so often forced French compliance with British plans, was forced to accommodate the French position.[39]

The Allies presented their terms to İsmet Paşa on 6 October:

- Greek troops would retire west of the Maritsa – that is, out of Eastern Thrace.
- An Allied force would occupy Eastern Thrace.
- Within a month after the Greek withdrawal, the Turks would establish an administration and a gendarmerie.
- The Allied force would then occupy 'certain points on the right bank of the Maritza and the places where they are at the present moment (unspecified, but intending to include Gallipoli, İzmit and Çatalca) during the upcoming peace conference'.[40]

The British Cabinet had accepted the terms only with further stipulations: the Turks would have to remain out of the Neutral Zone. The Allied generals would set the numbers of the Turkish gendarmerie. The Allied force would only withdraw at the end of the thirty-day period, and only if they were assured that order and protection existed. The French and Italians agreed.[41]

Presented with the Allied terms, İsmet requested an adjournment until the next day. Meanwhile, the French tried to convince Harington to yield further to the Turkish demands. Harington, citing his orders from the cabinet, refused. Poincaré sent a telegram notifying the delegates that under no circumstances would France go to war with the Turks. Harington still refused. Then, to the surprise of all, İsmet returned and basically accepted the Allied terms.[42]

## The Terms of the Armistice

The representatives of the Allies and the Turkish Grand National Assembly signed an armistice treaty on 11 October 1922. It was to take effect on midnight of 14 October, but Greece did not sign until 15 October. The convention finally took place on midnight of 16 October. The provisions:

> Hostilities between the Greek and Turkish armed forces were to come to an end.
>
> Greek forces and their equipment were to leave Eastern Thrace, to the East of the Maritza River, within fifteen days.
>
> Greek civil authorities would withdraw as soon as possible. Allied Commissions and seven Allied battalions would take control. The Allied missions and troops would leave within thirty days after Greek troops had evacuated, transferring authority to Turkish administrators.
>
> The Turkish army was not to enter Eastern Thrace until a final peace treaty was signed. However, a Turkish gendarmerie force of up to 8,000 would police the region.
>
> The İzmit and Gallipoli peninsulas, Istanbul and other regions of the Neutral Zone were to remain in Allied hands until the final treaty was signed.
>
> The Allies and the Turks agreed not to erect fortifications or artillery emplacements in or near the borders of the Neutral Zone.
>
> Other provisions regarding railroads, the status of Karaağaç (near Edirne), etc.[43]

The Mudanya Agreement was a reasonable compromise, with concessions from all sides. The British Cabinet had instructed Harington not to consider what it called 'political questions', but he had to accept Turkish administration of Eastern Thrace, effectively putting it under control of the Grand National Assembly.[44]

### The Frustration of Those who had Wanted War

While the Mudanya meeting was drawing to a close, Lloyd George vented his frustration to the cabinet. All his plans for the Greeks had been thwarted. He implied that the Greeks would have won if the Allies had not stopped them from taking Istanbul. Now it was the duty of the British to stop the Turkish army from crossing into Europe and upsetting the plans that had been set in the Paris Agreements. His grasp on reality had not improved. Even his fellow cabinet members saw that the Paris Agreements were long dead. Two days after Lloyd George spoke, the cabinet accepted the Mudanya Agreement.[45]

Lloyd George then took his frustration to the public. Speaking in Manchester on 15 October, after the Mudanya Agreement had been signed, he blamed all on the treachery of the French and Italians, and on the Americans for not taking mandates. He defended past British actions as necessary to keep the Turks from massacring the people of Istanbul and Thrace ('intolerable horror', 'a horrible massacre'), defending the Freedom of the Straits and keeping war from spreading into Europe. (He did not note that he had been willing to abandon Istanbul.) If not for the British, he declared, the Turks would have spread the war to Salonica and beyond, igniting the sort of Balkan War that had led to World War I.[46]

Austen Chamberlain concurred with the prime minister's defence in a speech in Birmingham on 13 October: the fault for British defeat was in the hands of the French, Italians and Americans. The British had crusaded for the Freedom of the Straits; the British had saved Europe from a new war. 'I believe our policy has been successful. (Cheers.) If so, it will be because the Government from the first firmly but temperately impressed its will and pursued with unanimity the simple objects which it had set before itself.' Perhaps knowing that the documentary evidence to the contrary would never be seen by his audience, Chamberlain stated, one assumes with a straight face, that the Chiefs of Staff had always supported the cabinet's plans for Chanak.[47]

The Lloyd George Coalition Cabinet fell on 19 October 1922. His policies over the Chanak problem were the main cause of his defeat. The Conservatives who had dominated his cabinet rebelled and forced him from office. On 19 October 1922, Lloyd George and his fellow Liberals left the government, as did Conservatives who had supported Lloyd George's Coalition Cabinet. Their place was taken by a Conservative administration under Andrew Bonar Law as prime minister. Curzon, a Conservative who had become increasingly disenchanted with Lloyd George, remained as foreign secretary, but those who were most insistent on forcing an attack against the Turks at Chanak – Lloyd George, Churchill and Chamberlain – were no longer in power. Even those whose support was less enthusiastic – Birkenhead, Horne and Lord Lee – left the cabinet.[48]

The new cabinet wanted to see the end of the interminable troubles in Turkey, by then extending nearly four years after the Ottomans had been defeated in World War I. The cabinet gave Curzon their support to end what had become an impossible, and expensive, situation. 'We cannot alone act as the policemen of the world', Law had written in a letter to *The Times*. 'The financial and social condition of this country makes that impossible.' If the French would not cooperate (as they had shown they would not), Britain would henceforth restrict itself 'to the safeguarding of the more immediate interests of the Empire'.[49]

## Notes

1. On the number and placement of Nationalist troops, see Turkey, Genelkurmay Başkanlığı, *Türk İstiklâl Harbi II/6/4, İstiklâl Harbi'nin Son Safhası*, Ankara: Genelkurmay, 1995, pp. 81–95.
2. FO 406/49, Harington to Chief of the Imperial General Staff, Constantinople, 3 June 1922, in Worthington-Evans to Balfour, War Office, 22 June 1922. Worthington-Evans, Secretary of State for War, wrote that he generally concurred with Harington's views. FO 371/7888, Harington to War Office, Constantinople, 14 September 1922. Harington had been against retaining Istanbul since he took command (WO 32/5743, 'British Forces in Turkey. Commander-in-Chief's Despatch. Period 1920–1923', Harington to Secretary of State for War, Constantinople, 20 October 1923 (hereafter, Harington Report)). Note that Harington had already left Istanbul by 20 October 1923. Harington reported much the same material found in his report in his later book, *Tim Harington*

*Looks Back*, London: John Murray, 1940, pp. 100–59. See also A. L. Macfie, 'The Chanak Affair (September–October 1922)', *Balkan Studies*, vol. 20, no. 2 (1979) pp. 309–41.

There is a temptation to comment on David Walder's *The Chanak Affair* (London: Macmillan, 1969), which contains much analysis of which I disagree and much that I find incorrect. The main problem is that Walder cites no sources. There are no footnotes, even for the few quotes he provides. For the most basic of sources, the British National Archives, he lists only 'The Records of the Cabinet Office' and 'The Public Record Office', with no indication of what was seen in those sources. How can one evaluate his facts or use his analyses?

3. CAB 23/39/38, A Conference of the Prime Minister, the Secretary of State for War and the First Lord of the Admiralty, 11 September 1922. The War Office and Admiralty both felt that Turkish 6-inch guns could stop all naval ships except major battleships, and these would have to return to the open sea 'to refurnish'. (FO 371/7887, Notes of a Conference held at Churt, 11 September 1922.)
4. FO 371/7887, Foreign Office to Rumbold, 13 September 1922. See Busch, pp. 344–8, on Harington's initial misplaced optimism.
5. WO 106/1505, 'Rough Notes on the Turkish Situation', General Staff, War Office, 10 September 1922.
6. CAB 31/1, Cabinet Meeting of 7 September 1922. CAB 23/31/2, Cabinet Meeting of 15 September 1922. Curzon, it should be added, was not willing to give up Istanbul (CAB 23/39/50, Cabinet Conference, 27 September 1922), and no one but Lloyd George said they were willing to give up Mosul.
7. CAB 24/139 C. P. 4219, 'Situation in the Near East', 21 September 1922. I only cite here some articles in *The Times*, which did not itself join the condemnations: 'Turkey's Claims' and 'How to Stop Wars', 20 September 1922, p. 10; 'Labour Against War', 22 September 1922, p. 22; 'Stop the War', and 'Call to Prayer', 21 September 1922, p. 12; 'Peace Words and War Words', 26 September 1922, p. 12.
8. CAB 37/41, Conference of Ministers, 17 June 1920. No personal name was given in the source.
9. See CAB 23/39/54, Conference of Ministers, 29 September 1922.
10. CAB 23/39/50, Cabinet Conference, 27 September 1922. CAB 23/39/54, Minutes of a Conference of Ministers, 29 September 1922. CAB 23/39/45, Conference of Ministers, 22 September 1922. Lloyd George felt that Istanbul could be held with the aid of 20,000 Greeks in the city, 'who had offered their assistance'. (CAB 23/39/42, Conference of Ministers, 20 September 1922, 6.30 p. m.) Venizelos (asked by the new Greek Government to represent Greece

to foreign countries) said the Greeks still had strong forces and would join the British in war against the Turks. (CAB 23/36/27, Note of a Conversation between Sir Edward Grigg, Mr Vansittart of the Foreign Office and M. Venizelos, Paris, 30 September 1922.)

11. CAB 23/39/42, Conference of Ministers, 20 September 1922, 6.30 p. m. CAB 23/36/26, A Conversation (Chamberlain, Curzon, Churchill, Worthington-Evans, Lee), 27 September 1922, 3.00 p. m. Churchill even said that the British should accept help from the Greek army. On Churchill's past moderation, see CAB 24/117/87, Secretary of State for War (Churchill), 'The Situation in the Middle East', 16 December 1920, and 'Mr. Churchill to Lord Curzon. April 26, 1922', Churchill, *The Aftermath*, pp. 414–16. Throughout the past crises, Churchill had questioned Britain's support of the Greeks. Now, with the scent of blood, he changed his mind.

12. CAB 23/31/2, Cabinet Meeting of 15 September 1922. New Zealand was willing to send a small force, a show of support for the Motherland. FO 424/254, H. Dering (ambassador at Bucharest) to Curzon, Bucharest, 19 September 1922. See the telegrams to the Dominions and their responses in CAB 24/138 C. P. 3857–61 and 4200. See also the various telegrams, mainly refusals of the British requests, in CAB 24/138 and 139. On 5 September 1922, General Pellé, the French high commissioner in Istanbul, was approached to consider a Greek request for mediation for a ceasefire, which the Greeks had asked from the British alone. Pellé's response, sent to Paris: 'At this moment we French have no interest in risking compromising, by posing as mediators, the excellent position that only among our allies we have vis-à-vis the Turkish nationalists.' (Pellé to Poincaré, Constantinople, 5 September 1922, in DD 1922, T 2, no. 149.)

13. CAB 23/31/2, Cabinet Meeting of 7 September 1922. FO 371/7891. War Office to Harington, 16 September 1922. FO 371/7892, 'Conclusions Reached at a Conference of Ministers', 18 September 1922. Ships were also to be sent on 19 September and later, but were to have no effect on the outcome of the conflict. (FO 371/7890, Admiralty to Commander-in-Chief, Mediterranean, 18 September 1922; War Office to Harington, 18 September 1922. CAB 39/46, Committee of Ministers, 23 September 1922. CAB 23/39/47, Committee of Ministers, 26 September 1922.) See also CAB 23/39/39, Conference of Ministers, London, 19 September 1922, and WO 32/5743, Harington Report.

14. FO 371/7892, Draft Minutes of a Conference of Ministers, 18 September 1922. Another War Office estimate of the size of the Turkish army at the time was 140,000 soldiers and cavalry. (WO 106/6326, General Staff, 'General Staff Appreciation for a Plan of Campaign Against Turkey, in the Event of War', War

Office, 28 September 1922.) The 300,000 figure probably included irregulars and ancillary personnel. In any case, all the figures were rough estimates, although all were above Lloyd George's ridiculous figure.

15. CAB 23/39/47, Committee of Ministers, 26 September 1922. The General Staff felt that the Chanak and Gallipoli positions could be held, but only if the reinforcements were in place. (CAB 24/139 C. P. 4240, 'Appreciation by the Combined Staffs of the Position at Chanak—Constantinople', 28 September 1922.)
16. CAB 23/39/50, Minutes of a Conference of Ministers, 27 September 1922. CAB 23/39/49, Committee of Ministers, 27 September 1922.
17. CAB 23/39/40, Conference of Ministers, 18 September 1922. CAB 23/39/41, Conference of Ministers, 19 September 1922. The French press overwhelmingly objected to Britain's policy in Istanbul and the Straits. Ambassador Hardinge noted: 'If the press be a correct indication of French policy, there seems but small chance of inducing French Government to give their active support in the defence of the Dardanelles against Kemalists.' (FO 424/254, Hardinge to Curzon, Paris, 18 September 1922.)
18. FO 371/7886, Rumbold Telegram, 10 September 1922. FO 371/7888, Harington to War Office, Constantinople, 10 September 1922. FO 371/7891, Harington to War Office, Constantinople, 19 September 1922. FO 406/49, Rumbold to Balfour, Yenikeuy, 19 June 1922. FO 371/7893, Harington Telegram in Draft Minutes of a Conference of Ministers, 21 September 1922. See also, FO 424/254, Rumbold to Curzon, Constantinople, 19 and 20 September 1922; Rumbold to Hardinge and Foreign Office, Constantinople, 20 September 1922. CAB 23/39/44, Conference of Ministers, 21 September 1922.
19. The best the British could do was to withhold from the French notice of major disagreements on reparations because it would affect Near East negotiations. (CAB 24/138, C. P. 4194, 'Conference on Inter-Allied Debts and Reparations: Memorandum by the Secretary of State for Foreign Affairs', 17 September 1922.)
20. Count Carlo Sforza, *Makers of Modern Europe*, London: Elkin Mathews & Marrot, 1930, pp. 84–6. Sforza gives an insightful evaluation of Curzon's character (pp. 80–90).
21. CAB 29/97, Conference between the French President of the Council and the British Secretary of State for Foreign Affairs, Paris, 20, 22, 23 September 1922, Curzon fairly accurately summarised the first part of the talks in FO 371/7890, Telegram from Hardinge, Paris, 20 September 1922, and similar reports in FO 371/7891 and 7892. FO 424/254, Hardinge (for Curzon) to Tyrrell, Paris,

22 September 1922. Sforza was appointed ambassador to France in February 1922, but resigned from office nine months later on 31 October after Benito Mussolini had gained power.

Curzon remarked: 'I grieve to have to report to my colleagues an experience as painful as that which I have passed through this afternoon, and which I hope never to be compelled to repeat.'

22. FO 371/7893, Draft Minutes of a Conference of Ministers, 21 September 1922. CAB 23/31/3, Conclusions of a Meeting of the Cabinet, 23 September 1922.
23. CAB 29/97, Conference between the French President of the Council, the British Secretary of State for Foreign Affairs and the Italian ambassador in Paris, Saturday, 23 September. FO 371/7893, Telegram from Hardinge (for Curzon), 23 September 1922.
24. FO 424/254, Rumbold to Curzon, Constantinople, 27 September 1922. Text of the Allied note: CAB 24/139 C. P. 4238, 'Situation in the Near East: Allied Note to Turkey', 29 September 1922.
25. CAB 23/31/4, Conclusions of a Meeting of the Cabinet, 25 September 1922. One success of Curzon was actually gaining cabinet acceptance of an armistice meeting. Lloyd George was not in favour of a preliminary conference, because he feared 'the Kemalists putting forward extreme views at the Preliminary Meeting'. (CAB 23/39/41, Conference of Ministers, 19 September 1922.)
26. The cabinet ranked in terms of importance: retention of, first, Chanak and the Gallipoli Peninsula, second Istanbul and third the İzmit Peninsula. (CAB 23/31/4, Cabinet Meeting, 25 September 1922.) FO 371/7896, 'Conclusions Reached by the Cabinet in regard to the Naval and Military Situation in the Near East', 25 September 1922. CAB 23/39/50, Cabinet Conference, 28 September 1922, 4 p. m. Hardinge to Curzon, Paris, 26 September 1922, BDF P18, p. 100.
27. FO 371/7895, Harington to Dardanelles Sector Defence Force, Chanak, Constantinople, 26 September 1922 (two telegrams); G. H. Q. Constantinople to War Office, 26 September 1922. FO 371/7896, Harington to War Office, Constantinople, 27 September 1922. See the numerous descriptions of the reinforcement actions in FO 371/7895.
28. CAB 23/39/39, Conference of Ministers, London, 19 September 1922. FO 371/7896, Draft Minutes of a Committee of Ministers, 27 September 1922.
29. FO 371/7896, Harington to War Office, 28 September 1922.
30. FO 371/7896, Telegram to Rumbold, Foreign Office, 28 September 1922. Lloyd George's previous view was that no Nationalists should be allowed to cross

the Straits. 'The moment a Kemalist gets afloat he must be dealt with.' In this, he disagreed with the other cabinet members, who felt such decisions should be left to the military commanders in the area. (CAB 23/39/45, Conference of Ministers, 22 September 1922.) See also CAB 23/39/51, Cabinet Conference, 28 September 1922.

31. CAB 23/31/5 and 23/39/54, Conclusions of a Conference of Ministers, 29 September 1922. The 'Intelligence' on the date, 30 September, was weak, and described as 'various indications'. See FO 424/254, Harry Lamb to Foreign Office, 21 September 1922.

    J. G. Darwin demonstrated how the cabinet supported the actions of Lloyd George, Churchill and the other 'fire eaters'. He contended, however, that the British actions were proper and rational, given the British need to defend the Freedom of the Straits, a totally questionable assertion, especially because he gives only one reason for why the Straits were so important – defence of India. He believed that the British traditionally supported the integrity of the Ottoman Empire because it was 'a strategic outwork of British India', again, as demonstrated above, doubtful. (J. G. Darwin, 'The Chanak Crisis and the British Cabinet', *History*, vol. 65, no. 213 (1980), pp. 32–48.)

32. Franklin-Bouillon to Poincare, Smyrna, 29 September 1922, in Poincaré to ambassadors in London, Rome and Constantinople. Paris, 1 October 1922, in DD 1922, T 2, no. 217. CAB 24/139/85, Youssouf Kemal to the Allied representatives, 29 September 1922. FO 371/7897, Commander-in-Chief Mediterranean to Admiralty, 1 October 1922.

33. CAB 23/39/55, Conference of Ministers, 29 September 1922, 10 p. m. Curzon wrote to his wife late on 30 September: 'I have had to sustain the battle single-handed against all the fire eaters and war-mongers.' (Earl of Ronaldshay, *Lord Curzon*, London: Ernest Benn, vol. 3, p. 307.) On Curzon's personal opposition to the cabinet's plans, see CAB 23/39/45, Minutes of a Committee of Ministers, 22 September 1922; David Gilmour, *Curzon: Imperial Statesman*, New York: Farrar, Strauss and Giroux, 1994, pp. 543–7.

34. FO 424/254, Hardinge Telegrams, Paris, 19 and 30 September 1922.

35. CAB 23/39/56, Conference of Ministers, 30 September 1922, 4 p. m. CAB 23/31/6, Cabinet Meeting, 30 September 1922, 10.30 p. m.

36. WO 32/5743, Harington Report.

37. CAB 23/31/7, Cabinet Meeting, 1 October 1922, 10 a. m. CAB 23/31/8, Cabinet Meeting, 1 October 1922, 3 p. m. FO 371/7899, Hankey (for the Cabinet) to Curzon, London, Offices of the Cabinet, 2 October 1922.

38. One element of confusion was that the term 'neutral zone' was ill-defined. When some in the cabinet spoke of the zone from which the Turks should withdraw, they obviously referred to the large zone envisaged in earlier conferences, called the Neutral Zone of 1921. This was not the actual zone occupied by British troops. Curzon decided that the term meant 'line which had been held by British troops for past three years'. (Curzon to Rumbold, Foreign Office, 9 October 1922, DBFP 18, pp. 180–1.) For the French instructions for the Mudanya meeting, see Poincaré to Franklin-Bouillon and Pellé, DD 1922, T 2, no. 204, which stresses how much the French had done for the Nationalists.
39. CAB 29/97, 'Meeting at the Quai d'Orsay (Poincaré, Curzon, Galli)', Paris, 6 October 1922, FO 371/7899, Rumbold Telegram, Constantinople, 5 October 1922, two telegrams; Curzon to Rumbold, Foreign Office, 6 October 1922. CAB 23/31/12, Cabinet Meeting, 7 October 1922. See also the meeting descriptions in CAB 23/81/10–14. Curzon's report on the meetings with Poincaré are in CAB 23/31/12 and FO 371/7900. The French report on the meeting reflects closely the British report. ('Notes by the French Secretary Taken during a Meeting at the Quai d'Orsay', Paris, 6 October 1922, in DD, T 2, no. 232. Other French reports on the Mudanya Conference are in DD, T 2.
40. FO 424/255, Rumbold to Curzon, Constantinople, 6 October 1922. Rumbold to Curzon, Constantinople, 6 October 1922, BDFP 18, p. 146.
41. FO 371/7900, Telegram to Rumbold, Foreign Office, 7 October 1922 and Rumbold Telegram, Constantinople, 6 October 1922. Curzon and Poincaré agreed to the cabinet's stipulations. (FO 371/7900. 'Message by Telephone from Lord Curzon to Prime Minister', 7 October 1922.)
42. FO 424/255, Rumbold to Curzon, Constantinople, 17 October 1922. Harington Report. Harington felt that the French were a hindrance at Mudanya, with Franklin-Bouillon as a 'perfect curse'. (FO 424/255, Rumbold to Curzon, Constantinople, 5 October 1922.) Franklin-Bouillon was not an accredited representative at the conference, but he often spoke for the French Government view.
43. CAB 24/139/84, 'Cabinet: The Near East Situation, Terms of the Mudania Convention', Telegram from General Headquarters, Constantinople, 12 October 1922.
44. Bıyıklıoğlu, pp. 450–63.
45. CAB 23/31/9, Cabinet Meeting of 5 October 1922.
46. 'The Premier's Defence', *The Times*, 16 October 1922. See also 'Freedom of the Straits: Mr. Lloyd George's Statement', *The Times*, 25 September 1922, p. 15. Lloyd George told cabinet members some of what he planned to say in Manchester. Curzon begged him to moderate his attacks. They were exactly the wrong

thing to say when delicate negotiations were in progress. Lloyd George refused. Ronaldshay, *Lord Curzon*, vol. 3, p. 314.
47. 'Mr. Chamberlain's Appeal', *The Times*, 14 October 1922, p. 12.
48. For the story of Lloyd George's downfall by one with firsthand knowledge of the political machinations and the centrality of the Chanak Crisis, see Lord Beaverbrook, *The Decline and Fall of Lloyd George*, New York: Duell, Sloan and Pearce, 1963, pp. 149–205. For details of the cabinet's fall and the political machinations that led up to it, see Kenneth O. Morgan, *Consensus and Disunity: The Lloyd George Coalition Government 1918–1922*, Oxford: Clarendon Press, 1979, especially pp. 324–56.
49. 'We Cannot Act Alone', *The Times*, 7 October 1922, p. 11.

# 20

# LAUSANNE

The two cards the British had held before the Mudanya Armistice were possession of Istanbul and control of the Dardanelles Strait. After Mudanya, the military situation at the Straits was much as it had been, with continuing dangers for the British. A breakdown in treaty deliberations might still lead to war at Chanak, which the new British Cabinet was completely against. Nevertheless, the British position at the Dardanelles could be used by the British at the upcoming peace conference, because the Turks also did not want war. What had been another British strong point before Mudanya, occupation of Istanbul, had in practice ceased to exist.

## The Situation in Istanbul

The situation in Istanbul had turned decidedly against the British. General Harington reported

> a considerable influx of Kemalist soldiers into Constantinople, and it was evident throughout that they had been preparing organizations, both in Eastern Thrace and in Constantinople, which, in the event of a rupture, would have carried out active operations against the Allies.

He estimated that the Nationalist forces he faced were '40,000 at Chanak, 50,000 on the Ismid Peninsula, 30,000 Central Reserve, 20,000 at Constantinople, and 20,000 in Eastern Thrace'.[1]

Even before any decision at Lausanne, the Nationalists had begun to recover control of the Ottoman capital. If peace talks failed, the British could expect a well-planned revolt in Istanbul, supported by most of the populace. On 19 October 1922, immediately after the signing of the Mudanya Armistice, the representative of the Nationalist Government, Refet (Bele) Paşa, arrived in Istanbul with 100 Nationalist guardsmen. The Nationalists notified the British that the Ankara Government intended to take over the civil administration and gendarmerie of Istanbul. Refet effectively assumed control of the city administration, leaving most Ottoman officials in place, but demanding that they now answer to Ankara. He abolished the emergency courts that had been created by the Allies, set new customs fees and censored pro-Allied newspapers. Commissioner Rumbold told Refet that the Allies were still in charge, and the high commissioners complained to their governments that they had lost control. In fact, all the Allies had left to enforce their control of the city was their armed force, which they could not use without sparking an uprising, and was too small a force to resist one.[2]

The Ankara Parliament abolished the sultanate on 1 November 1922. On 4 November, Grand Vezir Tevfik Paşa asked the British high commissioner if, in light of events, the Istanbul Cabinet should resign. Commissioner Rumbold told Tevfik Paşa that he could not give him any advice, because 'His Majesty's Government did not interfere with internal affairs of other States'. It is not recorded if Tevfik or Rumbold resisted the impulse to laugh. The cabinet decided to resign the next day.[3]

## Problems at Home and in the Empire

Great Britain had social and economic problems that made it imperative to put an end to adventures in Turkey. By the end of 1919, sterling had dropped 22 per cent. The national debt had risen from seven million pounds before the war to eight billion in 1919. Service on the debt was more than ten times its pre-war level. Foreign trade had halved from 1920 to 1922. By the end of 1921, industrial production had dropped drastically. Coal mining was depressed, and the miners launched a great strike in October of 1920. The textile industry was even more depressed, with 50 per cent of the looms idle and great unemployment. Railroad workers had struck in 1919. From 1919 to 1920 unemployment had risen from 2.4 per cent to more than 10 per cent, and was to go as high as 17 per cent. Although wages improved, they did not meet price increases, because domestic prices had more than doubled. The improvements that had been promised to the British people in wartime were abandoned when the funds were needed to pay off Britain's debts. Rather than offer new benefits, the British could not pay for the old ones.[4]

The British army was spread thinly across the Empire. Since 1914 the British had faced revolts in Egypt, Iraq, Ireland and South Africa, and Gandhi had begun his resistance movement in India. The demobilisation of British forces left a professional army that strained to control a vast empire. Britain could little afford to support its military commitments in the Empire, much less support military effort in Turkey. All this had been known by Lloyd George and his coterie of warmongers. They had not allowed it to affect their bellicose plans in Turkey, but their successors could not avoid the economic realities.[5]

Public opinion, which had so often supported British action against the Ottomans, now turned against it. The losses of World War I resulted in a public rejection of further war. No matter Britons' opinions of Turks, there was no longer any appetite to lose British lives to oppose them. Moreover, British intervention against the Turks had failed at every turn. The old saying – 'Don't throw good money after bad' – applied.[6]

The British entered the Lausanne Conference with a poor bargaining position. They badly needed to put their Turkish enterprise behind them. The Turks realised that those who had badly wanted war had been ejected from power in London. When your adversary knows that you want something desperately, you are never in a good bargaining position. The only positive factor for the British was that the Turks also wanted peace, and were willing to offer limited concessions to gain it.

Poincaré made the French position plain:

> We ourselves have an interest in maintaining unity to avoid a general rupture of the Agreement (with Britain). But England has made no concessions to our ideas and our rights in matters of reparations, and has disregarded the commitments she made in the Treaty of Versailles. In Eastern affairs, therefore we must not allow our collaboration to subordinate our policy to English policy. The main considerations which must dictate our conduct are the will to maintain peace and defend French interests in Turkey.[7]

The standard in past conferences had been for the British to prepare the draft of points to be considered, giving them some control over deliberations. Now the French guaranteed to the Turks that they would in no way be forced to accept a British draft of the treaty.[8]

## The British Plan for Lausanne

The Treaty of Lausanne was the capstone of the ultimate defeat of British plans for the Turks. The details of the Lausanne Conference have been described in great detail in government publications, books and learned articles. Much of what has been written about the conference deals with the minutia of the meeting – Curzon's manoeuvres to chair the various committees, İsmet Paşa's firmness (usually exemplified by his act of turning off his hearing aid), the British use of telegram intercepts and the general bickering – in hundreds of pages of discussion and scholarly conflict. There is no need for that here. What is considered here is only the place of the conference in the development and collapse of British plans for the Turks.[9]

In October of 1922 the Foreign Office, Colonial Office and the Treasury prepared a detailed joint list of British desiderata at the upcoming conference:

- Syria would be left to the French, and Iraq and Palestine to the British, although the Colonial Office was suggesting modifications of the Sèvres borders, 'all to Iraq advantage'.
- The Straits should be open to ships of war, not just commercial ships, but, if necessary, the British will accept freedom for merchant ships alone.
- All Ottoman Government pre-war debts would be repaid, collection to be supervised, as before the war, by a Public Debt Commission, which would also collect the payments on any new Turkish loans.
- An Allied Commission would decide on judicial Capitulations, as in the Sèvres Treaty, although Turkey might be given membership on the commission, along with Britain, France, Italy and Japan. 'Judgments given by the national or consular courts of an Allied Power or new State whose territory is detached from Turkey or orders of the (Judicial) Commission' must be enforced by the governments.
- A Liquidation Commission composed of British, French and Italian representatives would enforce the collection of Turkish financial obligations to

the Allies. All costs of the commission, including salaries, would be paid by Turkey. All revenues of Turkish customs, the tithe (head tax) and the sheep tax not already taken by the Public Debt Commission would be granted to the Liquidation Commission. If those revenues were insufficient, Turkey would increase taxes or find new revenues. If Turkey defaulted on payments, the commission would take over 'full control and management' of Turkish state finances to collect the sums owed. The Liquidation Commission would be able to visit and inspect any places in Turkey. The Turkish Government would provide any documents the commission might require.
- Concessions held by Allied nationals and companies before World War I and any concessions awarded by the Liquidation Commission would be accepted by Turkey. The commission must approve any new concessions, even those awarded to Turkish nationals.
- Turkey would pay an indemnity and the expenses of the Allied occupation, but the demand for the occupation costs might be abandoned. The indemnity, suggested to be 50 million gold Turkish lira, could be paid for by an Allied loan.
- Numbers of the Turkish military would be limited, and conscription forbidden.
- Kurdistan and Armenia would not be considered.
- Because any special reference to minorities would be difficult to obtain, 'a stock European minority treaty' would suffice.[10]

The list was an impossible dream, filled with provisions that the Turks had previously rejected. The General Staff, conspicuously not a part of these plans, felt that there should be no limits on the Turkish army, which was needed to defend a state surrounded by potentially hostile neighbours. They saw an armed Turkey to be no threat to British interests.[11]

On 1 November 1922 Lord Curzon gave the new British Cabinet a summary of the history of British negotiations for peace in the Near East. He stated that the British had always insisted that peace could only come if the Allies acted in unison. The British had been betrayed, however, by the French and the Italians. The French had always been unreliable, as had the Italians, although he expected that the new Italian Government of Benito Mussolini would bring honest, and presumably more reliable, government in Italy.

The French, who had 'hitherto been in the pocket of the Turks', would now cooperate, because circumstances had changed: 'The French support of the Turks had been based on the fact that France was jealous of our position in the Moslem World.'

All Britain wanted now, Curzon told the cabinet, was an honourable peace and to convince the Turks that the British were willing to be their friends. However, despite all that had passed, Curzon still believed he would meet at Lausanne 'to revise the Treaty of Sèvres'. He listed the various countries that would take part in the conference; trouble was expected from the Soviets and the Turks. In Turkey, 'he would be faced with a victorious Turkey, utterly unscrupulous, which would raise questions of the most troublesome description'. And 'on the question of Capitulations he must expect a bitter struggle. The Turks were standing out for equality, whereas no European could live and do business in Constantinople without the Capitulations, or at least some mixed tribunal'.[12]

It cannot be said that Curzon had abandoned all his grievances, but he went to Lausanne as a more practical advocate than the Curzon of old. Curzon disliked the Turks as much as any British politician. He had always been in favour of the complete dissolution of Turkish power and the relegation of the Turkish land to a small part of Anatolia. He had wanted European control over all the important parts of the Turkish Government and economy. But Curzon was a practical man. Compared to Lloyd George, he was a paragon of moderation. The 'Freedom of the Straits' had been the main demand of the British, but he was even willing to compromise over control of the Straits. If, he said, Freedom of the Straits meant freedom for merchant ships, the Turks would make no difficulties. If, however, it meant free access for British warships to threaten Istanbul, there was no chance for success. All the other nations opposed this – not only Turkey, but France, Italy and all the Black Sea states. Freedom for warships to threaten the Turks could only be ensured by large forces permanently maintained on both sides of the Dardanelles, which the British could not do.[13]

Curzon's aim always had been to achieve the maximum British goals. At each stage of the British conflict with the Turks he had failed to get what the British wanted. But at each stage he had proved willing to lower his expectations and demands, although he had often not been supported by the rest of the cabinet. Before he left for Lausanne, Curzon notified the cabinet of the positions he would take at the upcoming conference:

Essential
- Western Thrace to remain Greek.
- The Straits to be demilitarised.
- The British and French were to remain in Iraq and Syria, with unchanged borders.
- The Capitulations would remain, but with modifications to be suggested by Britain.
- Turkey would pay indemnities, as described in the Paris Conference, the amount to be determined by the Allies.
- Allied troops would only be withdrawn from Istanbul after a new treaty was ratified.

Desirable
- Some protection of minorities.
- Turkish military to be as set in the Paris Conference of 1922: 45,00 in the gendarmerie, 40,000 in the army, no conscription.
- Financial clauses, to be set by Allied experts.
- Economic clauses, to be set by Allied experts.[14]

Before he left for Lausanne, Curzon presented the British people with a mixture of hope in the alliance and defiance of the Turks. Speaking at a Conservative meeting in London on 8 November 1922, Curzon asserted that France could be counted upon for support. ('In reality, the points which divide us from France are very small, while the interests which link us together are very large.') He also stated that the French would be satisfied with the knowledge of British–French 'mutual trust and esteem', and that no written treaty between them would be needed. He gave a totally false story of harmonious meetings with Poincaré in Paris. For his ally, Benito Mussolini, he had great praise. Mussolini would support the British. ('He is a man very young, of great character and power. Signor Mussolini has lost no time in stating his earnest desire to act in complete accord with the Allies on the Eastern question.')

Curzon described the Turkism Nationalists as 'nationalism gone wild'. The Turks, he said, had demanded that the British withdraw from Istanbul and the Straits. They had abolished the Capitulations and closed the Mixed

Courts. They had sought to levy an 'illegal and intolerable tariff' (raising the customs duties). They had abolished the Administration of the Public Debt (which was untrue). 'These pretensions cannot be tolerated. They have no conceivable justification; they are an affront to the Allies and a challenge to Europe'; an affront and challenge that would not be tolerated. 'Turkey must learn that there is a limit to the concessions which we are willing to make to her, and that we cannot purchase peace at the cost of humiliation or disgrace.'[15]

Armed with his plans, his opinions and the need to avoid humiliation, Curzon set off for Lausanne.

## The Conference

The delegates met at Lausanne, Switzerland. After preliminary meetings, the conference officially began on 21 November 1922. Others gave their opinions, agreements and disagreements, but the conference was primarily a negotiation among the British, the French and the Turks. Curzon expected the support of his supposed allies, but the French proved to be supporters of most of the Turkish positions, except those on finance. Although many of the main points of a treaty had been accepted, İsmet Paşa refused to even consider British demands on matters such as the judicial Capitulations and state finances, and the conference broke down on 4 February 1923, which Curzon characteristically blamed on the French.[16]

New Turkish proposals and Allied meetings in London came forth that seemed to indicate that progress might be made. When the delegates returned on 23 April, Curzon refused to attend, leaving the British representation to Sir Horace Rumbold, who proved to be a more able negotiator. After three months of often rancorous deliberation, a treaty was signed on 24 July 1923.[17]

## The Lausanne Treaty[18]

- Territory. The Turkish state was to include Anatolia, Istanbul and Eastern Thrace, including Edirne. The status of Mosul would be decided later. Turkey gained Imbros, Tenedos and the small Rabbit Islands. Greece retained the rest of the Aegean Islands, which she had held after the Balkan Wars. Italy retained the Dodecanese islands, Britain Cyprus and Egypt. Decisions in various previous treaties and British wartime claims were accepted.

- The Straits. Turkey guaranteed the Freedom of the Straits to all ships. The only exception would come in time of war, when Turkey could refuse the Straits to enemy vessels.[19]
- Istanbul. The Allies agreed to remove their troops and ships from Istanbul and the neighbouring regions within six weeks of the ratification of the treaty.
- Mosul. No agreement was possible on the status of Mosul. A final determination was left in the hands of the League of Nations. This was the only important Turkish setback at the conference.[20]
- Rights. The Capitulations were completely abolished. Turkey and Greece both recognised equality before the law for minorities. The Turkish Government undertook to assure full and complete protection of life and liberty to all inhabitants of Turkey without distinction of birth, nationality, language, race or religion.
- Financial. The Ottoman Public Debt would be apportioned among Turkey and the Ottoman successor states.[21]
- Reparations. Greece recognised her duty to pay reparations for damage done in Anatolia, but Turkey released Greece of the obligation. No reparations or occupation expenses were to be paid to the Allies.[22]
- Demilitarised zones. The Straits, with the exception of Istanbul, were demilitarised, as were large regions of Eastern Thrace, Western Greece and Southern Bulgaria (Map 20.1).[23]
- Population Exchange. Turkey and Greece agreed to a compulsory exchange of Muslims in Greece and Greek Orthodox in Turkey. The Greeks of Istanbul and Muslims of Western Thrace were excluded.[24]

Curzon claimed credit for what he described as British success at the Lausanne Conference, when the achievements had been largely the work of Rumbold. But the British had actually achieved little. They had gained some of Curzon's 'essential' wishes: Greece would retain Western Thrace; the Straits would be demilitarised; Syria and Iraq would remain French and British. These were things that the Turks could easily accept. They had long accepted the demilitarisation of the Straits and the loss of Western Thrace, Syria and Iraq. On Curzon's other 'essential' and 'desirable' wishes, however, the British failed: The financial and judicial Capitulations were gone. Turkey would pay no

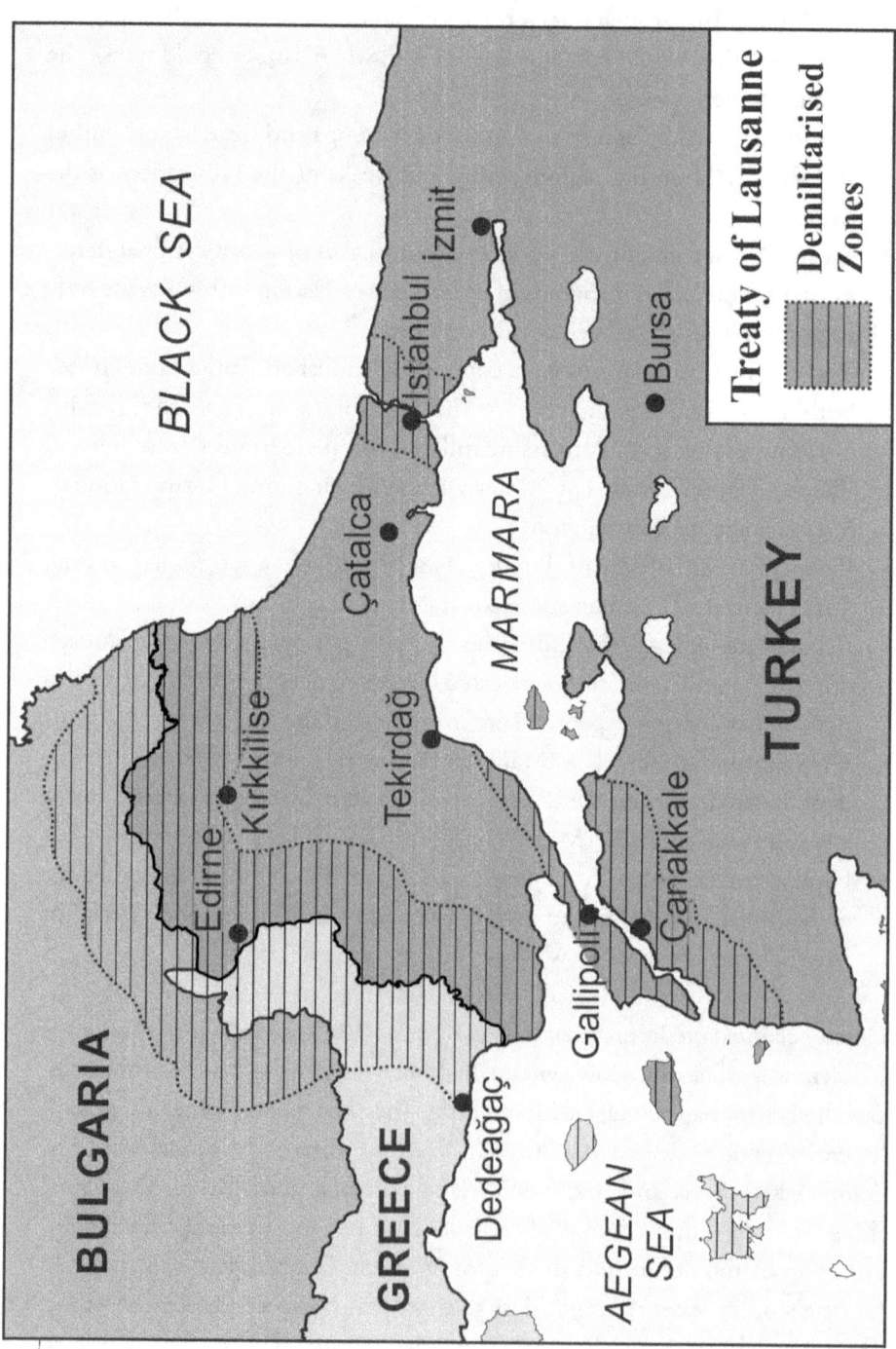

Map 20.1 Lausanne Treaty and demilitarised zones

indemnity to the Allies. The Turkish army would be at full strength, and conscription would remain. Protection of minorities would depend on Turkish goodwill, not on foreign wardens. There would be no Allied Commissions to rule over Turkish state expenditures and the national economy. Subject only to the need to pay off their share of the Ottoman debt, the Turks would control their own taxes. The Turks even retained new territory in Northeast Anatolia, regaining land that had been lost to the Russians in 1878. Politically and economically, the new Turkey was more in control of its own house than the Ottoman Empire had been for many decades.[25]

Curzon gave a long justification for the treaty to the House of Lords. It did not dwell on the disappointment of British aims, but described the treaty as a relief from a long nightmare:

> This Peace Treaty, which I conclude by recommending to your Lordships, is one which, if it does not give complete satisfaction to anybody, has given, I think, absolutely unmitigated relief to all. It is the last of the Peace Treaties. It shuts the door; we are no longer at war. We have been able to take our troops from Constantinople. We have sent a Chargé d'Affaires to Constantinople, and there is now a Turkish representative in London whom the noble and learned Lord can see at the Foreign Office whenever he likes. The sky is for the moment clear, at any rate as regards international relations between us. And here I say, not without a touch of pride, that I believe at this moment if there is a country that stands high in the regard and esteem of Turkey it is this country. I challenge contradiction on that point; and if that be so, let us, instead of diving again into the troubles and anxieties of the past, devote ourselves with as much devotion and sincerity as we can to assist our old friend Turkey and our former Ally Turkey in the difficult future that lies before her.[26]

## The Final British Defeat

The Lausanne Treaty in fact represented a great defeat of the British plans for the Turks. Rather than a triumph, the Treaty of Lausanne was the dying gasp of British imperialist aims for the Turks. Very little of what the British had hoped for when they occupied Istanbul had been achieved (Table 20.1). Instead of a humbled Turkey, much limited in area and controlled by Britain and its allies, the Turks had themselves created a new national state, free from outside control.

Table 20.1    British plans for Turkey

| | Sèvres Treaty August 1920 | London Accords March 1921 | Paris Accords March 1922 | Lausanne Treaty |
|---|---|---|---|---|
| İzmir and Western Anatolia | Greek Control Greek Army | Christian Governor Greek Garrison Allied Gendarmerie Officers | Greeks Evacuate Demilitarised | Turkish |
| Istanbul | Allied Control | 'Possible' Allied Evacuation | Allied Evacuation After Treaty | Turkish |
| Straits | Allied Control | Reduced Territory Allied Control | International Allied Military | Turkish Control Demilitarised |
| Kurdistan | Small Territory British Control | 'Turkish Sovereignty' Autonomy | Ignored | Ignored |
| Cilicia | French | French | Autonomous Armenia in Cilicia | Ignored |
| Eastern Anatolia | Independent Armenia | Independent Armenia | No Specifics (Already Held by Turks) | Ignored |
| Eastern Thrace | Greek Control Greek Army | Greek Control and Army 'Modifications' | Half Greek Half Turkish | Turkish |
| Finances | Allied Control Turks Pay: Ottoman Debt Indemnity Occupation Costs | Allied Control Turks Pay: Ottoman Debt, Indemnity Occupation Costs | Allied Control Turks Pay: Ottoman Debt Indemnity Occupation Costs | Turks Only Pay: Ottoman Debt Turks Control Own Finances |
| Judicial/ Capitulations | Allied Control | Allied Control 'Turkey Represented' | Allied-Controlled Commission to Decide | Capitulations Ended |
| Army and Gendarmes | Allied Control 15,000 in Army 35,000 Gendarmes No Conscription | Allied Control 30,000 in Army 45,000 Gendarmes No Conscription | Allied Control 30,000 in Army 45,000 Gendarmes No Conscription | No restrictions Conscription |

## Notes

1. WO 32/5743, Harington Report. Harington noted that the Nationalist troops at the Neutral Zone had kept to the terms of the Mudanya Convention.
2. Pellé to Poincaré, Constantinople, 7 November 1922, in DD 1922, T 2, no. 300. Cavan, the Chief of the General Staff, ordered Harington to evacuate by sea if necessary. (WO 106/63266, Cavan private letter to Harington, War Office, 20 November 1922. There are other planning documents in WO 106/6326, but these turned out to be unneeded.)
3. Rumbold to Curzon, Constantinople, 4 and 5 November 1922, DBFP 18, pp. 226–7 and 229–30. FO 5743, Harington Report. Curzon to Hardinge, Constantinople, 4 November 1922, BDFP 18, pp. 227–9. Rumbold stated that the Allies would only exercise 'surveillance'. (Rumbold to Curzon, Constantinople, 6 November 1922, BDFP 18, pp. 232–3. A 'state of siege' was considered,

but abandoned. The cabinet told Harington to delay taking any action. (CAB 23/32/4, Cabinet Meeting, 16 November 1922.) See the more extensive description in Criss, *Istanbul under Allied Occupation*, pp. 145–55.

4. These statistics are drawn from Albert T. Lauterbach, 'Economic Demobilization in Great Britain After the First World War', *Political Science Quarterly*, vol. 57, no. 3 (September 1942), pp. 376–93. On the perilous state of Britain's finances, see the very detailed Treasury reports in 'Report of the Committee on Expenditure (Civil Departments)', 11 October 1922, in CAB 24/139/69, and 'Report of Committee Appointed to Examine Part 1 (Defence Departments) of the Report of the Geddes Committee on National Expenditure', 4 February 1922 in CAB 24/132/91 and 92. See also: Kennedy, *Realities*, pp. 226–30, 247–51. F. W. Hirst, *The Consequences of the War to Great Britain*, London: Oxford University Press, 1934. More than four billion dollars was owed to the United States alone. The cabinet felt that there would be great difficulty in balancing the next year's budget, and that plans for assisting unemployment would be hard to realise. On the economic difficulties of the British, see CAB 23/27/20, Conclusions of a Meeting of the Cabinet, 16 December 1921. Morgan provides an accurate and detailed account of the British economic woes. (*Consensus and Disunity*, pp. 243-4, 256–62 and 280–301). The disastrous monetary policies of successive British Governments exacerbated the economic problems and unemployment. (Keith Laybourn, *Britain on the Breadline*, London: Alan Sutton, 1990, pp. 7–15.) On the problem of military manpower, see Keith Jeffery, *The British Army and the Crisis of the Empire, 1918–1922*, Manchester: Manchester University Press, 1984, pp. 11–74.

5. It was primarily the costs of putting down rebellions that were to lead the British to accept domestic home rule in Egypt and Iraq.

6. See Sevap Demirci, 'The Lausanne Conference: The Evolution of Turkish and British Diplomatic Strategies 1922–1923', unpublished dissertation, the London School of Economics and Political Science, London, 1997, pp. 48–50.

7. Poincaré to the French Delegation at Lausanne, Paris, 5 January 1923, in DD 1923, T 1, no. 5. French records of the Lausanne meetings (DD 1923, T 1) indicate that their main concerns were financial, particularly the Ottoman debt.

8. Poincaré to the French Delegation at Lausanne, Paris, 29 January 1923, in DD 1923, T 1, no. 94.

9. Very extensive British documents on the Lausanne Conference are in DBFP 18, pp. 320–1,064. Some interesting analyses of the Lausanne Conference: Demirci, 'The Lausanne Conference', which has an extensive bibliography. A. L. Macfie,

'The Straits Question: The Conference of Lausanne (November 1922 – July 1923)', *Middle Eastern Studies*, vol. 15, no. 2 (May 1979), pp. 211–38; Bilâl Şimşir, ed., *Lozan Telgrafları I, 1922–1923*, and *Lozan Telgrafları II, 1922–1923*, Ankara: Atatürk Kültür, Dil ye Tarih Yüksek Kurumu, 1990 and 1994. Öke, Mim Kemal, *İngiliz Belgelerinde Lozan Barış Konferansı (1922–1923)*, Istanbul: Boğaziçi Üniversitesi Yayınları, 1983. Salahi R. Sonyel, 'The Foreign Policy of the Turkish Nationalists 1919–1923', unpublished dissertation, University of London, London, 1971.

10. FO 371/7907, Forbes-Adam to Crowe, 'Revision of Turkish Treaty', 25 October 1922; 'Treaty of Peace with Turkey', Financial and Economic Clauses, 18 and 22 October 1922. Forbes-Adam suggested organisational procedures for the conference. These were generally followed later by Curzon at Lausanne. It was felt that other desirable provisions, such as Turkey's not being allowed submarines and turning over all its military aircraft, would probably have to be abandoned. I have omitted the suggestions on the Hijaz, Egypt, etc.

    The Forbes-Adam list did not include the Straits Question. That was reserved for a paper to be prepared by Harold Nicholson. Its conclusions are included in this list. ('Memorandum Respecting the Freedom of the Straits', FO 424/255, 15 November 1922.)

11. FO 371/7952, 'Memorandum by the General Staff on the Proposed New Treaty between the Allies and Turkey', 19 October 1922. The General Staff had believed there should be a Turkish army of 60,000 as far back as January of 1920. (CAB 21/184, 'General Staff on the Reason for the Retention of a Regular Army by Turkey', 14 January 1920.)

12. CAB 23/32/1, 'Summary of Statement made to the Cabinet by the Secretary of State for Foreign Affairs', 1 November 1922.

13. CAB 23/39/58, Conference of Ministers, 13 October 1922, before the change in government. At the same meeting, Churchill demanded that no fortifications be built in the Straits, so that the British navy could threaten Istanbul.

14. CAB 23/32/4, Cabinet Meeting of 16 November 1922 and FO 424/255, Curzon to Graham (Rome), 14 November 1922. See also the various documents on planning for the Lausanne Conference in FO 371/7952.

15. 'Lord Curzon on Near East', *The Times*, 9 November 1922, pp. 12 and 14. The speech was quoted verbatim or in part in numerous newspapers.

16. Saint-Aulaire to Poincaré, London, 6 February 1923. 'He (Eyre Crowe, because Curzon was ill) read to me from a note dictated by Lord Curzon in such a violent tone that I declared that I could not accept it.' Saint-Aulaire thought it best to wait until Curzon better controlled himself. Curzon's note contained numerous

allegations against the French, all of which were successfully refuted by Poincaré. (Poincaré to Saint-Aulaire, Paris, 8 and 12 February 1923, in DD 1923, T 1, nos. 140 and 150. See Curzon's justification for leaving the conference and comments on Turkish 'intransigence'. ('Lord Curzon on Lausanne', *The Times*, 7 February 1923, p. 9.) Curzon's ill-temper may have been driven by his illness, which would be the most charitable explanation.

17. The treaty was ratified by Turkey on 23 August 1923. The other signatories had ratified it by 16 July 1924. It officially came into force on 6 August 1924.
18. Great Britain, Parliament, *Treaty of Peace with Turkey, and Other Instruments, Signed at Lausanne*, London: HMSO, 1923, Cmd. 1929.
19. 'Convention Relating to the Regime of the Straits', 24 July 1923. The Bosporus, the Dardanelles, the Marmara Islands and the Aegean Islands of Samothrace, Lemnos, Imbros, Tenedos and the Rabbit Islands were to be demilitarised zones. There were to be no fortifications or troop emplacements in the zone, although Turkish troops could transit between Anatolia and Thrace, and the Turkish navy could use all Turkish waters. Turkey could maintain 12,000 men, an arsenal and a naval base at Istanbul. All would be overseen by an international commission composed of Turkey, Britain, France and the Balkan countries. In times of peace and when Turkey was neutral in times of war, there would be complete freedom of passage of merchant vessels and a limited number of belligerent warships. When Turkey was at war, she could prevent enemy vessels from using the Straits, but not vessels of neutrals. In 1936 the Montreux Convention returned control of the Straits to Turkey.
20. The League of Nations, where Britain was predominant and Turkey not a member, made a highly questionable decision to award Mosul to Iraq in 1925. Turkey and Britain signed a treaty to that effect in 1926. See Nevin Coşar and Sevap Demirci, 'The Mosul Question and the Turkish Republic: Before and After the Frontier Treaty, 1926', *Middle Eastern Studies*, vol. 42, no. 1 (January 2006), pp. 123–32, and Peter J. Beck, '"A Tedious and Perilous Controversy": Britain and the Settlement of the Mosul Dispute, 1918–1926', *Middle Eastern Studies*, vol. 17, no. 2 (April 1981), pp. 256–76.
21. As might be imagined, given the importance of financial matters to all, the financial clauses were voluminous. The treaty considered matters of repayment of the Ottoman debt in great detail (Articles 46–57).
22. Property seized by the Ottoman Government during World War I and by the Balkan Allies during the Balkan Wars was be returned to its owners or compensation paid. A Mixed Arbitral Tribunal would adjudicate disputes. Little of the property seized in the Balkan Wars was ever returned.

23. 'Convention Respecting the Thracian Frontier', 24 July 1923. In the Thracian demilitarised zone, Turkey would be allowed 5,000 gendarmes, police, customs officers and frontier guards. Greece and Bulgaria would be allowed 2,500 each.
24. 'Convention Concerning the Exchange of Greek and Turkish Populations', 30 January 1923. Emigrants were allowed to take all moveable property. Property left behind would be liquidated, as evaluated by a Mixed Commission. The Mixed Commission would have members from Greece, Turkey and three neutral members named by the League of Nations. It had full powers to decide all matters relating to the population exchange.
25. It was Rumbold who negotiated the final treaty, but Curzon took all the credit. Rumbold was disgusted: 'Curzon is a man who accepts the cream brought to him by someone and kicks the man who brought it.' (Rumbold to Henderson, quoted in Erik Goldstein, 'The British Official Mind and the Lausanne Conference, 1922–23', *Diplomacy and Statecraft*, vol. 14, no. 2 (June 2003), p. 203.) Harold Nicolson wrote detailed praise for Curzon at Lausanne, describing it as a triumph. ('The odds against him were tremendous.') Nicolson, pp. 281–349.
26. 'Treaty of Peace (Turkey) Bill', House of Lords Debate, 28 February 1924, *Hansard*, vol. 56, cc. 426–56.

# APPENDIX: GOVERNMENT OFFICIALS

## Ottoman Empire

| Grand Vezir | Foreign Minister |
|---|---|
| Mehmed Kâmil 1885–91 | Said Halim 1885–96 |
| Ahmed Cevat Şakir 1891–5 | Turhan 1896–9 |
| Mehmed Said 1895 | Said Halim 1899 |
| Mehmed Kâmil 1895 | Ahmed Tevfik 1899–1909 |
| Halil Rifat 1895–1901 | Mehmed Rifat 1909–11 |
| Mehmed Said 1901–3 | İbrahim Hakkı 1911 |
| Mehmed Ferid 1903–8 | Mustafa Asım Bey 1911–12 |
| Mehmed Said 1908 | Gabriel Noradunkyan 1912–13 |
| Mehmed Kâmil 1908–9 | Said Halim 1913–15 |
| Hüseyin Hilmi 1909 | Halil 1915–17 |
| Ahmet Tevfik 1909 | Ahmed Nesimi 1917–18 |
| Hüseyin Hilmi 1909–10 | Mehmed Nabi 1918 |
| İbrahim Hakkı 1910–11 | Mustafa Reşid 1918–19 |
| Mehmed Said 1911–12 | Yusuf Franko 1919 |
| Ahmed Muhtar 1912 | Mehmed Ferid 1919 |
| Mehmed Kâmil 1912–13 | Abdüllatif Safa 1919 |
| Mahmud Şevket 1913 | Mustafa Reşid 1919–20 |
| Said Halim 1913–17 | Abdüllatif Safa 1920 |

Mehmed Talat 1917–18
Ahmed İzzet 1918
Ahmed Tevfik 1918–19
Mehmed Ferid 1919
Ali Rıza 1919–20
Salih Hulusi 1920
Mehmed Ferid 1920
Ahmed Tevfik 1920–2

Mehmed Ferid 1920
Abdüllatif Safa 1920–1
Ahmed İzzet 1921–2

## Great Britain

| Prime Minister and Party | Foreign Secretary |
| --- | --- |
| Salisbury (Conservative) 1886–92 | Northcote 1886–7<br>Salisbury 1887–92 |
| Gladstone (Liberal) 1892–4 | Rosebery 1892–4 |
| Rosebery (Lib.) 1894–5 | Kimberley 1894–5 |
| Salisbury (Cons./Lib. Union) 1895–1902 | Salisbury 1895–1900<br>Lansdowne 1900–5 |
| Balfour (Cons./Lib. Union) 1902–5 | Lansdowne 1900–5 |
| Campbell–Bannerman (Lib.) 1905–8 | Grey 1905–16 |
| Asquith (Lib.) 1908–16 | Grey 1905–16 |
| Lloyd George (Lib.) 1916–22 | Balfour 1916–19<br>Curzon 1919–24 |
| Law (Cons.) 1922–3 | Curzon 1919–24 |
| Baldwin (Cons.) 1923–4 | Curzon 1919–24 |

## British Ambassadors to the Ottoman Empire

White 1886–91
Ford 1891–3
Currie 1893–8
O'Conor 1898–1908
Lowther 1908–13
Mallet 1913–14

*War*

Calthorpe 1918–19 (High Commissioner)
Rumbold 1920–4 (High Commissioner)

## France

| President | Prime Minister* | Foreign Minister |
|---|---|---|
| Poincaré 1913–20 | Briand 1915–17 | Briand 1915–17 |
|  | Ribot 1917 | Ribot 1917 |
|  | Painlevé 1917 | Barthou 1917 |
|  | Clemenceau 1917–20 | Pichon 1917–20 |
| Deschanel 1920 | Millerand 1920 | Millerand 1920 |
| Millerand 1920–4 | Leygues 1920–1 | Leygues 1920–1 |
|  | Briand 1921–2 | Briand 1921–2 |
|  | Poincaré 1922–4 | Poincaré 1922–4 |

* Officially President of the Council of Ministers

## Italy

| Prime Minister | Foreign Minister |
|---|---|
| Giolitti 1911–14 | San Giuliano 1910–14 |
| Salandra 1914–16 | Salandra 1914 |
|  | Sonnino 1914–19 |
| Boselli 1916–17 | Sonnino 1914–19 |
| Orlando 1917–19 | Sonnino 1914–19 |
| Nitti 1919–20 | Tittoni 1919 |
|  | Nitti 1919 |
|  | Scialoja 1919–20 |
| Giolitti 1920–1 | Sforza 1920–1 |
| Bonomi 1921–2 | Torretta 1921 |
| Facta 1922 | Schanzer 1922 |
| Mussolini 1922–43 | Mussolini 1922–9 |

# BIBLIOGRAPHY

Articles are cited only in the notes.
Document collections are cited on page v.

Adanır, Fikret, *Die Makedonische Frage: Ihre Entstehung und Entwicklung bis 1908*, Wiesbaden: Steiner, 1979.

Adelson, Roger, *London and the Invention of the Middle East: Money, Power, and War, 1902–1922*, New Haven: Yale University Press, 1995.

Adıyeke, Ayşe Nükher, *Osmanlı İmparatorluğu ve Girit Bunalımı (1896–1908)*, Ankara: Türk Tarih Kurumu, 2000.

Ahmad, Feroz, *Young Turks and the Ottoman Nationalities: Armenians, Greeks, Albanians, Jews, and Arabs, 1908–1918*, Salt Lake City: University of Utah Press, 2014.

——, *The Young Turks: The Committee of Union and Progress in Turkish Politics 1908–1914*, Oxford: Clarendon, 1969.

Aksakal, Mustafa, *The Ottoman Road to War in 1914*, London: Cambridge University Press, 2008.

Akşin, Sina, *Jön Türkler ve İttihat ve Terakki*, İstanbul: Remzi, 1987.

——, *Turkey from Empire to Revolutionary Republic*, New York: New York University Press, 2007.

Allen, W. E. D., and Paul Muratoff, *Caucasian Battlefields*, Cambridge: Cambridge University Press, 1953.

Anderson, M. S., *The Eastern Question 1774–1923*, London: Macmillan, 1966.

Antoniades, Alexandre, *Le Développement économique de la Thrace: le passé, le présent, l'avenir*, 2e édition, Athènes: Typos, 1922.

Bağçeci, Yahya, *İngiltere'de Ermeni propagandası (1878–1898)*, İstanbul: Yalın Yayıncılık, 2013.
Baker, Ray Stannard, *Woodrow Wilson and World Settlement*, 2 vols, New York: Doubleday, 1923.
Bayur, Hilmi Kâmil, *Sadrazam Kâmil Paşa*, Ankara: Sanat, 1954.
Bayur Yusuf Hikmet, *Türk İnkılâbı Tarihi*, third printing, 3 vols, in 10, Ankara: Türk Tarih Kurumu, 1983.
Beaverbrook, Lord, *The Decline and Fall of Lloyd George*, New York: Duell, Sloan and Pearce, 1963.
Bennett, O. H., *British Foreign Policy during the Curzon Period, 1919–24*, London: St. Martin's, 1995.
Berridge, G. R., *Gerald Fitzmaurice (1865–1939), Chief Dragoman of the British Embassy in Turkey*, Leiden: Nijhoff, 2007.
Bıyıklıoğlu, Tevfik, *Trakya'da Milli Mücadele*, 2 vols, Ankara: Türk Tarih Kurumu, 1987.
Blaisdell, Donald C., *European Financial Control in the Ottoman Empire*, New York: Columbia University Press, 1929.
Bosworth, R. J. B., *Italy, the Least of the Great Powers: Italian Foreign Policy before the First World War*, London: Cambridge University Press, 1979.
Bourne, Kenneth, *The Foreign Policy of Victorian England 1830–1902*, Oxford: Oxford University Press, 1970.
Bournoutian, George A., *A Concise History of the Armenian People: (From Ancient Times to the Present)*, Costa Mesa, CA: Mazda Publishers, 2002.
Boyar, Ebru, *Ottomans, Turks, and the Balkans: Empire Lost, Relations Altered*, London and New York: Tauris Academic Studies, 2007.
Bridge, F. R., *Great Britain and Austria-Hungary 1906–1914: A Diplomatic History*, London: Weidenfeld and Nicolson, 1972.
Bridge, F. R., and Roger Bullen, *The Great Powers and the European State System, 1814–1914*, Toronto: Pearson Longman, 2005.
Brown, Keith, *Loyal unto Death: Trust and Terror in Revolutionary Macedonia*, Bloomington: Indiana University Press, 2013.
Burman, John, *Britain's Relations with the Ottoman Empire during the Embassy of Sir Nicholas O'Connor to the Porte, 1898–1908*, Istanbul: Isis, 2010.
Busch, Briton Cooper, *Mudros to Lausanne: Britain's Frontier in West Asia, 1918–1923*, Albany: State University of New York Press, 1976.
Callwell, C. E., *Field-Marshal Sir Henry Wilson*, vol. 2, London: Cassell, 1927.
Carnegie Endowment, *Report of the International Commission to Inquire into the Causes and Conduct of the Balkan Wars*, Washington: The Endowment, 1914.

Cecil, Gwendolen, *Life of Robert, Marquis of Salisbury*, vol. 1, London: Hodder & Stoughton Limited, 1921.

Childs, Timothy W., *Italo-Turkish Diplomacy and the War over Libya*, Leiden: Brill, 1990.

Churchill, Winston S., *The World Crisis: The Aftermath*, London: Thornton Butterworth, 1929.

Clark, Christopher, *The Sleepwalkers: How Europe Went to War in 1914*, New York: Harper, 2012.

Coates, Thomas F. G., *Lord Rosebery: His Life and Speeches*, 2 vols, London: Hutchinson, 1900.

Cohen, Stuart A., *British Policy in Mesopotamia 1903–1914*, Reading: Ithaca Press, 1976.

Crampton, Richard J., *Bulgaria 1878–1918*, Boulder, CO: Eastern European Monographs, 1983.

———, *The Hollow Détente: Anglo-German Relations in the Balkans, 1911–1914*, London: George Prior, 1979.

Criss, Nur Bilge, *Istanbul Under Allied Occupation, 1918–1923*, Leiden: Brill, 1999.

Dakin, Douglas, *The Greek Struggle in Macedonia*, Thessaloniki: Institute for Balkan Studies, 1966.

———, *The Unification of Greece, 1770–1923*, New York: St. Martin's, 1972.

Dasnabedian, Hratch, *History of the Armenian Revolutionary Federation, Dashnaktsutiun, 1890–1924*, trans. Bryan Fleming and Vahe Habeshian, Milan: Oemme Edizioni, 1990.

Deliorman, Altan, *Türklere Karşı Ermeni Komitecileri*, Istanbul: Boğaziçi Üniversitesi, 1975.

Djemal Pasha, *Memories of a Turkish Statesman, 1913–1919*, New York: Doran, 1922.

Earle, Edward Mead, *Turkey, The Great Powers, and The Bagdad Railway: A Study in Imperialism*, New York: Macmillan, 1924.

Elmacı, Mehmet Emin, *İttihat Terraki ve Kapitülasyonlar*, Istanbul: Homer Kitabevi, 2005.

Erickson, Edward J., *Defeat in Detail: The Ottoman Army in the Balkans, 1912–1913*, Westport, CT: Praeger, 2003.

———, *Ordered to Die: A History of the Ottoman Army in the First World War*, Westport, CT: Greenwood, 2001.

*Ermeni Komitelerinin Amal ve Harekât-i İhtilâliyesi*, Istanbul: Matbaa-i Amire, 1332.

Evans, Laurence, *United States Policy and the Partition of Turkey, 1914–1924*, Baltimore: Johns Hopkins Press, 1965.

Findley, Carter Vaughn, *Bureaucratic Reform in the Ottoman Empire*, Princeton: Princeton University Press, 1980.
_____, *Ottoman Civil Officialdom*, Princeton: Princeton University Press, 1989.
Fisher, John, *Curzon and British Imperialism in the Middle East, 1916–19*, London: Frank Cass, 1999.
Gallant, Thomas W., *The Edinburgh History of the Greeks, 1768–1913: The Long Nineteenth Century*, Edinburgh: Edinburgh University Press, 2015.
Gilmour, David, *Curzon: Imperial Statesmen*, New York: Farrar, Straus and Giroux, 1994.
Glenny, Misha, *The Balkans: Nationalism, War and the Great Powers, 1804–1999*, New York: Viking, 1999.
Gök, Dursun, *Mersinli Cemal Paşa İkinci Ordu Müfettişliği ve Harbiye Nazırlığı*, Istanbul: Gençlik Kitabevi, 2015.
Gökay, Bülent, *A Clash of Empires: Turkey between Russian Bolshevism and British Imperialism, 1918–1923*, London and New York: I. B. Tauris, 1997.
Graves, Robert, *Storm Centres of the Near East: Personal Memories, 1879–1929*, London: Hutchinson, 1933.
Grenville, J. A. S., *Lord Salisbury and Foreign Policy*, London: Athlone Press, 1964.
Grey, Viscount Grey of Fallodon, *Twenty-Five Years: 1892–1916*, 2 vols, London: Hodder & Stoughton, 1925–6.
Hall, Richard C., *The Balkan Wars 1912–13: Prelude to the First World War*, London: Routledge, 2000.
Hanioğlu, M. Şükrü, *A Brief History of the Late Ottoman Empire*, Princeton: Princeton University Press, 2008.
_____, *Preparation for a Revolution: The Young Turks, 1902–1908*, Oxford: Oxford University Press, 2001.
_____, *The Young Turks in Opposition*, Oxford: Oxford University Press, 1995.
Harington, Tim, *Tim Harington Looks Back*, London: John Murray, 1940.
Heller, Joseph, *British Policy Towards the Ottoman Empire, 1908–1914*, London: Cass, 1983.
Helmreich, Ernst Christian, *The Diplomacy of the Balkan Wars, 1912–1913*, Cambridge, MA: Harvard University Press, 1938.
Helmreich, Paul C., *From Paris to Sèvres*, Columbus: Ohio State University Press, 1974.
Hertslet, Edward, *The Map of Europe by Treaty*, vol. II, London: Butterworths, 1875.
Hinsley, F. H., ed., *British Foreign Policy under Sir Edward Grey*, London: Cambridge University Press, 1977.

Hirst, F. W., *The Consequences of the War to Great Britain*, London: Oxford University Press, 1934.
Hocaoğlu, Mehmed, *Arşiv Vesikalarıyla Tarihte Ermeni Mezâlimi ve Ermeniler*, Ankara: Anda, 1976.
Holland, Robert, and Diana Markides, *The British and the Hellenes: Struggles for Mastery in the Eastern Mediterranean 1850–1960*, Oxford: Oxford University Press, 2006.
Holland, Thomas Erskine, *The European Concert in the Eastern Question*, Oxford: Clarendon Press, 1885.
Hovannisian, Richard G., ed., *The Armenian People from Ancient to Modern Times*, vol. II, New York: St. Martin's, 1997.
Howard, Harry N., *The Partition of Turkey: A Diplomatic History 1913–1923*, Norman, Oklahoma: University of Oklahoma Press, 1931.
Hüseyin Nâzım Paşa, *Ermeni Olayları Tarihi*, 2 vols, Ankara: Osmanlı Arşivi Daire Başkanlığı, 1994.
İnal, İbnülemin Mahmut Kemal, *Osmanlı Devrinde Son Sadrâzamlar*, 4 vols, Istanbul: Tarih ve Medeniyet, 1982 (original 1940–53).
Jeffery, Keith, *The British Army and the Crisis of the Empire, 1918–1922*, Manchester: Manchester University Press, 1984.
Jelavich, Barbara, *The Ottoman Empire, the Great Powers, and the Straits Question*, Bloomington: Indiana University Press, 1973.
Jordan, W. M., *Great Britain, France, and the German Problem, 1918–1939: A Study of Anglo-French Relations in the Making and Maintenance of the Versailles Settlement, 1918–1939*, London: Frank Cass, 1943.
Kansu, Aykut, *The Revolution of 1908 in Turkey*, Leiden: Brill, 1997.
Karabekir, Kâzım, *İstiklâl Harbimiz*, Istanbul: Türkiye Yayınevi, 1960.
Kardjilov, Peter, *The Cinematographic Activities of Charles Rider Noble and John Mackenzie in the Balkans*, Volume One, translated from the Bulgarian by Ivelina Petrova, Newcastle upon Tyne: Cambridge Scholars Publishing, 2020.
Karpat, Kemal H., *Ottoman Population, 1830–1914*, Madison, WI: University of Wisconsin Press, 1985.
Kazemzadeh, Firuz, *Russia and Britain in Persia 1864–1914: A Study in Imperialism*, New Haven: Yale University Press, 1968.
Kennedy, Paul M., *The Realities Behind Diplomacy: Background Influences on British External Policy, 1865–1980*, London: Allen & Unwin, 1981.
Kent, Marion, ed., *The Great Powers and the Ottoman Empire*, second edition, London: Cass, 1996.
Kitsikis, Dimitri, *Propagande et Pressions en Politique Internationale*, Paris: Presses Universitaires de France, 1963.

Küçük, Cevdet, *Osmanlı Diplomasisinde Ermeni Meselesinin Ortaya Çıkışı (1878–1897)*, İstanbul: İstanbul Üniversitesi, Edebiyat Fakültesi, 1984.

Kuneralp, Sinan, ed., *Ottoman Diplomatic Documents on 'The Eastern Question': Crete and Turco-Greek Relations (1869–1896)*, Istanbul: Isis, 2012.

Kuneralp, Sinan, and Gül Tokay, *The Private Correspondence of Sir Gerard Lowther, British Ambassador to Constantinople (1908–1913)*, Istanbul: Isis, 2018.

Kurat, Akdes Nimet, *Türkiye ve Rusya*, Ankara: Kültür Bakanlığı, 1990 (original 1970).

Ladas, Stephen, *The Exchange of Minorities: Bulgaria, Greece, and Turkey*, New York: Macmillan, 1932.

Lange-Akhund, Nadine, *The Macedonian Question 1893–1908. From Western Sources*, translated by Gabriel Topor, Boulder, CO: East European Monographs, 1998.

Langer, William L., *The Diplomacy of Imperialism*, 2d ed., New York: Knopf, 1951.

Laybourn, Keith, *Britain on the Breadline*, London: Alan Sutton, 1990.

Liman von Sanders, Otto Viktor Karl, *Five Years in Turkey*, Annapolis: United States Naval Institute, 1928.

Llewellyn Smith, Michael, *Greece in Asia Minor 1919–1922*, New York: St. Martin's, 1973.

Lloyd George, David, *The Truth about the Peace Treaties*, vol. 2, London: Gollancz, 1938.

Longrigg, Stephen, *Oil in the Middle East*, London: Oxford University Press, 1954.

———, *Syria and Lebanon under French Mandate*, London: Oxford University Press, 1958.

Lowe, C. J., and M. L. Dockrill, *The Mirage of Power: British Foreign Policy 1914–22*, vol. 2, London: Routledge and Kegan Paul, 1952.

Lowe, C. J., and F. Marzari, *Italian Foreign Policy 1870–1940*, London: Routledge & Kegan Paul, 1975.

Luke, Harry, *Cities and Men*, vol. 2, London: Geoffrey Bles, 1953.

Maccas, Leon, *L'hellénisme de l'Asie Mineure*, Paris: Berger-Levrault, 1919.

Mango, Andrew, *Atatürk; The Biography of the Founder of Modern Turkey*, Woodstock: Overlook Press, 1999.

Manjikian, Hagop, ed., *Houshamatyan of the Armenian Revolutionary Federation: Album-Atlas*, vol. 1, Los Angeles: Western United States Central Committee of the Armenian Revolutionary Federation, 2006.

Mantoux, Paul, *The Deliberations of the Council of Four (March 24–June 28, 1919): Notes of the Official Interpreter*, Arthur S. Link, translator and editor, 2 vols, Princeton: Princeton University Press, 1992.

Matthew, H. C. G., and Brian Harrison, *Oxford Dictionary of National Biography, in Association with the British Academy: From the Earliest Times to the Year 2000*, Oxford: Oxford University Press, 2004.

Mazıcı, Nurşen, *Belgelerle Uluslar arası Rekabette Ermeni Sorunu'nun Kökeni (1878–1918)*, İstanbul: Genel dağıtım, Der Yayınevi, 1987.

McCarthy, Justin, *Death and Exile: The Ethnic Cleansing of Ottoman Muslims, 1821–1922*, Princeton: Darwin, 1995.

———, *Muslims and Minorities: The Population of Ottoman Anatolia and the End of the Empire*, New York: New York University Press, 1983.

———, *The Ottoman Peoples and the End of Empire*, London and New York: Arnold and Oxford University Press, 2001.

———, *Population History of the Middle East and the Balkans*, Istanbul: Isis, 2002.

———, *The Turk in America: Creation of an Enduring Prejudice*, Salt Lake City: University of Utah Press, 2010.

———, *Turks and Armenians: Nationalism and Conflict in the Ottoman Empire*, Madison, WI: Turco-Tatar Press, 2015.

McCarthy, Justin, Cemalettin Taşkıran, and Ömer Turan, *Sasun*, Salt Lake City: University of Utah Press, 2014.

McCarthy, Justin, Esat Arslan, Cemalettin Taşkıran, and Ömer Turan, *The Armenian Rebellion at Van*, Salt Lake City: University of Utah Press, 2006.

McMeekin, Sean, *The Berlin-Baghdad Express: The Ottoman Empire and Germany's Bid for World Power*, Cambridge, MA: Harvard University Press, 2010.

———, *The Ottoman Endgame: War, Revolution, and the Making of the Modern Middle East, 1908–1923*, New York: Penguin, 2016.

Medlicott, W. N., *The Congress of Berlin and After: A Diplomatic History of the Near Eastern Settlement 1878–1880*, London: Cass, 1963, originally published by Methuen in 1938.

Michail, Eugene, *The British and the Balkans: Forming Images of Foreign Lands, 1900–1950*, London: Continuum, 2011.

Michelleta, Luca, and Andrea Ungari, *The Libyan War 1911–1912*, Newcastle: Cambridge Scholars, 2013.

Millman, Richard, *Britain and the Eastern Question 1875–1878*, Oxford: Clarendon Press, 1979.

Morgan, Kenneth O., *The Age of Lloyd George*, London: Allen & Unwin, 1971.

———, *Consensus and Disunity: The Lloyd George Coalition Government 1918–1922*, Oxford: Clarendon Press, 1979.

Nalbandian, Louise, *The Armenian Revolutionary Movement*, Berkeley: University of California Press, 1963.

Nevakivi, Jukka, *Britain, France, and the Arab Middle East*, London: Athlone Press, 1969.

Nicolson, Harold, *Curzon: The Last Phase, 1919–1925*, London: Constable, 1934.

──────, *Sir Arthur Nicolson, Bart, First Lord Carnock: A Study in the Old Diplomacy*, London: Constable, 1930.

Northedge, F. S., *The Troubled Giant: Britain among the Great Powers 1916–1939*, New York: Praeger, 1967.

Öke, Mim Kemal, *İngiliz Belgelerinde Lozan Barış Konferansı (1922–1923)*, İstanbul: Boğaziçi Üniversitesi Yayınları, 1983.

Orde, Anne, *Great Britain and International Security 1920–1926*, London: Royal Historical Society, 1978.

Otte, T. G., *The Foreign Office Mind: The Making of British Foreign Policy, 1865–1914*, Cambridge: Cambridge University Press, 2011.

Özoğlu, Hakan, *Kurdish Notables and the Ottoman State: Evolving Identities, Competing Loyalties, and Shifting Boundaries*, Albany: State University of New York Press, 2004.

Özyüksel, Murat, *The Berlin-Baghdad Railway and the Ottoman Empire: Industrialization, Imperial Germany and the Middle East*, London: I. B. Tauris, 2016.

Pamuk, Şevket, *The Ottoman Empire and European Capitalism, 1820–1913*, Cambridge: Cambridge University Press, 1987.

Perry, Duncan M., *The Politics of Terror: The Macedonian Liberation Movements, 1893–1903*, Durham, NC: Duke University Press, 1988.

Popovic, Alexandre, *L'Islam Balkanique: les musulmans du sud-est européen dans la période post-ottomane*, Berlin: Osteuropa-Institut an der Freien Universität Berlin, 1986.

Pribram, Alfred Franzis, and Archibald Cary Coolidge (English edition), *The Secret Treaties of Austria-Hungary*, vol. 1, Cambridge, MA: Harvard University Press, 1920.

Psomiades, Harry J., *The Eastern Question: The Last Phase*, Thessaloniki: Institute for Balkan Studies, 1968.

Reynolds, Michael A., *Shattering Empires: The Clash and Collapse of the Ottoman and Russian Empires, 1908–1918*, Cambridge: Cambridge University Press, 2011.

Robbins, Keith, *Politics, Diplomacy and War in Modern British History*, London: Hambledon Press, 1994.

──────, *Sir Edward Grey: A Biography of Lord Grey of Fallodon*, London: Cassell, 1971.

Roberts, Andrew, *Salisbury: Victorian Titan*, London: Phoenix, 2000 (paperback of 1999 book).

Rodogno, Davide, *Against Massacre: Humanitarian Interventions in the Ottoman Empire 1815–1914*, Princeton: Princeton University Press, 1912.

Ronaldshay, Earl of, *The Life of Lord Curzon*, vol. 3, London: Ernest Benn, 1928.

Rossos, Andrew, *Macedonia and the Macedonians: A History*, Stanford, CA: Hoover Institution, 2008.

_____, *Russia and the Balkans: Inter-Balkan Rivalries and Russian Foreign Policy: 1908– 1914*, Toronto: University of Toronto Press, 1981.

Salt, Jeremy, *Imperialism, Evangelism and the Ottoman Armenians 1878–1896*, London: Frank Cass, 1993.

_____ *The Last Ottoman Wars: The Human Cost, 1877–1923*, Salt Lake City: University of Utah Press, 2019.

Şaşmaz, Musa, *British Policy and the Application of Reforms for the Armenians in Eastern Anatolia 1877–1897*, Ankara: Türk Tarih Kurumu, 2000.

Sazanov, Serge, *Fateful Years, 1909–1916*, London: Cape, 1928.

Schöllgen, Gregor, *Imperialismus und Gleichgewicht: Deutschland, England und die orientalische Frage 1871–1914*, München: R. Oldenbourg Verlag, 1984.

Şenışık, Pınar, *The Transformation of Ottoman Crete: Revolts, Politics, and Ideology in the Late Nineteenth Century*, London: I. B. Tauris, 2011.

Sforza, Count Carlo, *Makers of Modern Europe*, London: Elkin Mathews & Marrot, 1930.

Shaw, Stanford J., *From Empire to Republic: The Turkish War of Liberation 1918–1923, a Documentary Study*, 5 vols in 6, Ankara: Türk Tarih Kurumu, 2000.

Shaw, Stanford J., and Ezel Kural Shaw, *History of the Ottoman Empire and Modern Turkey*, vol. 2, Cambridge: Cambridge University Press, 1977.

Şimşir, Bilâl, ed., *Lozan Telgrafları, 1922–1923*, 2 vols, Ankara: Atatürk Kültür, Dil ye Tarih Yüksek Kurumu, 1990 and 1994.

Smith, Michael Llewellyn, *Ionian Vision: Greece in Asia Minor 1919–1922*, New York: St. Martin's, 1973.

Sofuoğlu, Adnan, and Seyfi Yıldırım, *Arşive Vesikalarına göre 1921 Londra Konferansı*, Ankara: Atatürk Kültür, Dıl ve Tarih Yüksek Kurumu, Atatürk Araştırma Merkezi, 2018.

Soteriadis, George, *An Ethnological Map Illustrating Hellenism in the Balkan Peninsula and Asia Minor*, London: E. Stanford, 1918.

Sowards, Steven W., *Austria's Policy of Macedonian Reform*, Boulder, CO: East European Monographs, 1989.

Steele, David, *Lord Salisbury: A Political Biography*, London: UCL Press, 1999.

Steiner, Zara S., *Foreign Office and Foreign Policy, 1898–1914*, Cambridge: Cambridge University Press, 1969.

Tansel, Selâhattin, *Mondros'tan Mudanya'ya Kadar*, 4 vols, Ankara: Başbakanlık Basımevi, 1973–4.

Tatsios, Theodore George, *The Megali Idea and the Greek-Turkish War of 1897: The Impact of the Cretan Problem on Greek Irredentism, 1866–1897*, Boulder, CO: East European Monographs, 1984.

Taylor, A. J. P., *English History 1914–1945*, Oxford: Oxford University Press, 1965.

_____, ed., *Lloyd George: Twelve Essays*, New York: Atheneum, 1971.

_____, *The Struggle for Mastery in Europe*, Oxford: Clarendon Press, 1954.

Ter Minassian, Anahide, *Nationalism and Socialism in the Armenian Revolutionary Movement*, trans. A. M. Berrett, Cambridge, MA: Zoryan, 1984.

Thaden, Edward C., *Russia and the Balkan Alliance of 1912*, University Park, PA: Pennsylvania State University Press, 1965.

Tibawi, A. L., *A Modern History of Syria*, London: Macmillan, 1969.

Tokay, Gül Tokay, *Makedonya Sorunu: Jön Türk İhtilali'nin Kökenleri, 1903–1908*, İstanbul: AFA Yayınları, 1996.

Toynbee, Arnold J., *The Western Question in Greece and Turkey*, London: Constable, 1922.

Trachtenberg, Marc, *Reparation in World Politics: France and European Economic Diplomacy. 1916–1923*, New York: Columbia University Press, 1980.

Trumpener, Ulrich, *Germany and the Ottoman Empire 1914–1918*, Princeton: Princeton University Press, 1968.

Turkey, Başbakanlık Devlet Arşivleri Genel Müdürlüğü, Osmanlı Arşivi Daire Bşk., *Ermeni Komiteleri (1891–1895)*, Ankara: T. C. Başbakanlık Devlet Arşivleri Genel Müdürlüğü Osmanlı Arşivi Daire Başkanlığı, 2001.

Turkey, Genel Kurmay Başkanlığı, *Balkan Harbi Tarihi*, 7 vols, Istanbul and Ankara: Genel Kurmay Basımevi, 1938–65.

_____, *Birinci Dünya Harbi'nde Türk Harbi*, Ankara: Genel Kurmay, 1993 (various printings).

_____, *Türk İstiklâl Harbi*, Ankara: Genel Kurmay, 1991–9 (various printings).

Uras, Esat, *The Armenians in History and the Armenian Question*, Istanbul: Documentary Publications, 1988.

Uyar, Mesut, and Edward J. Erickson, *A Military History of the Ottomans*, Santa Barbara, CA: Praeger/ABC-CLIO, 2009.

Venizelos, Eleutherios, *Greece Before the Peace Congress of 1919; a Memorandum Dealing with the Rights of Greece, Submitted by Eleutherios Venizelos, a Revised Translation from the French Original*, New York: American–Hellenic Society by Oxford University Press, American branch, 1919.

Vovchenko, Denis, *Containing Balkan Nationalism: Imperial Russia and Ottoman Christians, 1856–1914*, Oxford: Oxford University Press, 2016.

Walther, Karine V., *Sacred Interests: The United States and the Islamic World, 1821–1921*, Chapel Hill: University of North Carolina Press, 2015.

Woodward, E. L., et al., eds, *Documents on British Foreign Policy 1919–1939*, First Series, vols 1–17, London: H. Majesty's Stationery Office, 1947–70.

Yasamee, F. A. K., *Ottoman Diplomacy: Abdülhamid II and the Great Powers, 1878–1888*, Istanbul: Isis Press, 1996.

Yavuz, Hakan, and Peter Sluglett, eds, *War and Diplomacy: The Russo-Turkish War of 1877–1878 and the Treaty of Berlin*, Salt Lake City: University of Utah Press, 2011.

Yavuz, Hakan, and Isa Blumi, eds, *War and Nationalism: The Balkan Wars, 1912–1913, and their Sociopolitical Implications*, Salt Lake City: University of Utah Press, 2013.

Yergin, Daniel, *The Prize: The Epic Quest for Oil, Money, and Power*, New York: Simon & Schuster, 1991.

Yosmaoğlu, İpek, *Blood Ties: Religion, Violence, and the Politics of Nationhood in Ottoman Macedonia, 1878–1908*, Ithaca: Cornell University Press, 2014.

Zeidner, Robert Farrer, *The Tricolor Over the Taurus: The French in Cilicia and Vicinity, 1918–1922*, Ankara: Atatürk Supreme Council for Culture, Language and History, 2005.

Zürcher, Erik Jan, *The Unionist Factor: The Role of the Committee of Union and Progress in the Turkish National Movement 1905–1926*, Leiden: Brill, 1984.

## Dissertations

Adelson, Roger Dean, 'The Formation of British Policy towards the Middle East, 1914–1918', Washington University, 1972.

Akarlı, Engin Deniz, 'The Problems of External Pressures, Power Struggles, and Budgetary Deficits in Ottoman Politics under Abdulhamid II (1876–1909): Origins and Solutions', Princeton University, 1976.

Antonoff, Anne Louise, 'Almost War: Britain, Germany, and the Bosnia Crisis, 1908–1909', Yale, 2006.

Brooks, Julian, 'Managing Macedonia: British Statecraft, Intervention, and "Proto-peacekeeping" in Ottoman Macedonia, 1902–1905', Simon Fraser University, 2014.

Burnett, Robert Adair, 'Georges Clemenceau in the Paris Peace Conference, 1919', University of North Carolina, Chapel Hill, 1968.

Dackombe, Barry Patrick, 'Single-Issue Extra-Parliamentary Groups and Liberal Internationalism, 1899–1920', Open University, 2008.

Daleziou, Eleftheria, 'Britain and the Greek-Turkish War and Settlement of 1919–1923: The Pursuit of Security by "Proxy" in Western Asia Minor', University of Glasgow, 2002.

Demirci, Sevap, 'The Lausanne Conference: The Evolution of Turkish and British Diplomatic Strategies, 1922–1923', the London School of Economics and Political Science, 1997.

Kaligian, Dikran Mesrob, 'The Armenian Revolutionary Federation under Ottoman Constitutional Rule, 1908–1914', Boston College, 2003.

Karagiannis, Alexander, 'Greece's Quest for Empire at the Paris Peace Conference, 1919–1920: The Diplomacy of Illusions', Indiana University, 1981.

Marashlian, Levon, 'The Armenian Question from Sèvres to Lausanne: Economics and Morality in American and British Policies, 1920–1923', University of California, 1992.

McTiernan, Mick, 'A Very Bad Place for a Soldier: The British Involvement in the Early Stages of the European Intervention in Crete, 1897–1898', University of London, 2014.

Mohammed, Adnan Amin, 'British Representations of the Kurds and the Armenian Question, 1878–1908', University of Leicester, 2018.

Montgomery, Alan Everard, 'Allied Policies in Turkey from the Armistice of Mudros, 30th October, 1918, to the Treaty of Lausanne, 24th July, 1923', University of London, 1969.

Odoms, H. J. R., 'British Perceptions of the Ottoman Empire, 1876–1908', Oxford, 1995.

Perkins, James Andrew, 'British Liberalism and the Balkans, c. 1875–1925', University of London, 2014.

Psilos, Christopher, 'The Young Turk Revolution and the Macedonian Question 1908–1912', University of Leeds, 2000.

Reynolds, Michael A., 'The Ottoman-Russian Struggle for Eastern Anatolia and the Caucasus, 1908–1918: Identity, Ideology and the Geopolitics of World Order', Princeton University, 2003.

Rice, Eber Harold, 'British Policy in Turkey: 1908–1914', University of Toronto, 1974.

Rizopoulos, Nicholas X., 'Greece at the Paris Peace Conference, 1919', Yale University, 1963.

Snodgrass, Nancy Therese, 'The Chanak Crisis: A Study in British Diplomacy', University of Illinois, 1971.

Sonyel, Salahi R., 'The Foreign Policy of the Turkish Nationalists, 1919–1923', University of London, 1971.

Tokay, Ahsene Gül, 'The Macedonian Question and the Origins of the Young Turk Revolution, 1903–1908', University of London, 1994.

Uyanık, Nevzat, 'Delegitimizing the Ottoman Imperial Order at the Threshold of New Diplomacy (The Interplay of Anglo-American Policies on the Ottoman Armenians, 1914–1923)', Princeton University, 2012.

Yanatma, Servet, 'The International News Agencies in the Ottoman Empire (1854–1908)', Middle East Technical University, 2015.

Zeidner, Robert Farrer, 'The Tricolor over the Taurus: The French in Cilicia and Vicinity, 1918–1922', University of Utah, 1991.

# INDEX

1877–8 Russo-Turkish War, 3, 7, 27, 31, 117, 122, 221
    mortality and refugees, 3
1897 Ottoman–Greek War, 89–92
    British pressure on the Ottomans, 91–5
    Britain's dual standards for conquest, 95
    indemnity, 91–4

Adana, 10, 125, 305, 374, 474
Albania and Albanians, 118, 123, 126, 134, 140, 143, 190, 250, 252, 260–4, 276, 296, 359, 375
Aleppo (Haleb), 305, 415, 416
Antalya, 374, 376, 547, 599
Armenians, 7, 9–31, 346–8, 494, 497, 498
    conferences (1921–3), 536, 541, 543–5, 553–6, 568, 570, 571, 575, 621
    Paris peace conference, 355, 356, 362, 364, 366, 377, 378, 427, 430, 432, 451, 452, 454, 455, 457, 458, 461, 462, 511, 513, 515, 516, 518, 519
    reforms, 46–66
    *see also* inspectorates; Paris Peace Conference; Turkish Independence War
Armenian Apostolic Church and patriarchs, 9, 18, 46, 47, 303, 315
Armenian Republic, 435, 479, 485, 511, 513, 516
Armenian revolutionaries and rebellions
    Dashnaks, 13–15, 293, 294, 315
    Hunchaks, 9–14, 21, 64, 65, 293
    mortality, 7, 9–14, 65
    Ottoman Bank, 15, 56
    Sasun, 10, 11, 13, 14, 21, 24–7, 50, 57, 64, 65
    Van, 10, 13, 14, 21, 22, 23, 24
    Zeytun, 10–14, 24, 64
Athens, 22, 75, 84, 90, 358, 532
Austria-Hungary, 1, 2, 56, 58, 60, 78, 80, 81, 84, 85, 92, 94, 95, 97–9, 222, 223, 229, 239–41, 245–7, 254, 255, 257, 259, 260–3, 267, 303–5, 308–10, 332, 354
    Aehrenthal, Alois Lexa von, 186, 194
    Bosnia annexation, 218, 220, 221
    Emperor/King Francis Joseph, 175, 180
    Goluchowski, Agenor Maria, 58, 97, 98, 174
    *see also* Macedonia

Aydın, 361, 366, 374, 380, 381, 383–5, 400, 401, 437, 438, 466
Azerbaijan, 300, 480, 516, 535, 538

Baghdad Railway, 296, 329, 333, 547
Balkan Wars, 240–2, 245, 249, 252, 253
   Aegean Islands, 257, 259–63, 327, 330, 331
   boycott and emigration of Greeks, 267–70
   British neutrality, 242–4
   British pressure on the Ottomans, 253–67
   Çatalca Line, 242, 245, 253
   mortality, 270, 271, 273–5
   refugees, 267–71, 381
banks and bankers, 60, 62, 94, 174, 177, 222, 333, 418
Batum, 419, 437, 465, 481, 513, 515, 516
Beirut, 415, 432, 480
Bitlis, 9, 10, 22, 48, 65, 293, 295, 298, 301, 314, 434, 513, 519, 520, 525
Black Sea, 174, 220, 227, 254, 336, 472, 513, 548, 550, 551
Bosnia and Bosnians, 2, 94, 175, 197, 218, 220, 221, 239, 240
Bulgaria, 121, 354, 367, 369, 372, 452, 457, 458, 625
   in San Stephano treaty, 2, 117, 118
   King Ferdinand, 218, 462
   unification, 118, 218–21
   *see also* Balkan Wars; Macedonia
Bursa, 366, 427, 451, 465, 475, 491, 494, 580

Caucasus *see* Trans-Caucasia
Circassians (Çerkes), 12, 441, 498
conferences
   Lausanne, 617–25, 627
   London (1921), 536–45, 549, 562, 575
   Mudanya, 490, 577, 599, 600, 603–8, 617, 618
   Paris (1921), 550

   Paris (1922), 564–72, 575, 593
   Saint-Germain-en-Laye, 353
   San Remo, 416, 417, 450, 515, 516, 575
   Second Conference of Hythe, 489
   *see also* Paris Peace Conference
Crete, 73, 74, 250, 252
   blockade, 80, 81, 83, 84, 85, 98
   Powers' intervention, 78, 79–85, 91, 92, 96–100
   Prince George, 79, 95, 97, 98, 100, 101
   rebellion, 73, 74–6, 79
   reforms, 76–8
Crimean War, 1, 31, 136, 139
Cyprus, 4, 454, 624

Damascus, 415, 416
Diyarbakır, 47, 48, 295, 298, 314, 525
Dönmes, 211, 213, 214, 216

Eastern Rumelia, 117, 118, 122, 218, 220, 221
Edirne (Adrianople), 118, 120, 131–3, 181, 182, 245–57, 260, 263, 266–8, 270, 292, 312, 366, 369, 461, 492, 560, 571, 600, 624
Erivan (Yerevan), 7, 511, 513
Erzincan, 23, 65
Erzurum, 9, 10, 48, 62, 65, 347, 435–7, 513, 515, 525; *see also* inspectorates
European Concert, 81, 84, 85, 93, 94, 194, 245, 249, 255, 276

France, 2, 25, 31, 61, 213, 343
   Armenians, 32, 48, 50–4, 59, 60
   Balkan Wars, 245–7, 253, 254
   Briand, Aristide, 536, 539, 541, 550, 565, 566
   Cambon, Jules, 370, 437
   Chanak and Lausanne, 598–600, 604–7, 619–24
   Clemenceau, Georges, 355, 379, 384, 398, 399, 403, 416, 429, 513, 565

Crete and 1897, 78, 80, 83, 93–5, 96, 98–100
Constans, Jean Antoine Ernest, 122, 130
Foch, Ferdinand, 462, 484, 485, 568
Franklin-Bouillion, Henry, 604
Hanotaux, Gabriel, 80
inspectorates, 303, 304
Italian War, 222, 223, 228
Macedonia, 187, 194
Millerand, Alexandre, 382, 515
Pichon, Stephen, 415
Poincaré, Raymond, 565, 566, 568–70, 575–601, 604, 606, 607, 619, 623
post-war conflicts with Britain, 410–12, 414–22, 438, 539, 547–52, 566, 569, 570, 608, 609
*see also* Paris Peace Conference: France; Turkish Independence War; World War I: preliminary disputes
Freemasons, 211–18

Georgia, 480, 513, 516
Germany, 2, 50, 53, 60, 78–81, 83–5, 92–9, 187, 194, 222, 223, 239, 240, 245–8, 252, 254, 255, 257, 259, 260, 262, 263, 297, 298, 302–6, 308–12, 375, 410, 411, 416, 418, 419–21, 532–4, 565, 570, 597
  Eulenburg, Philipp Friedrich Alexander zu, 97
  Fürst von Radolin, Hugo, 33
  Hatzfeldt, Paul von, 31
  Jagow, Gottlieb von, 305, 309, 310
  Kaiser Wilhelm II, 31, 79, 80, 85, 86, 332
  Liman von Sanders, Gen. Otto, 332
  Marschall von Bieberstein, Adolf, 84, 89, 101
  Wangenheim, Hans Freiherr von, 270, 302, 303, 305, 309–12
  *see also* Balkan Wars; Crete; Macedonia; World War I: preliminary disputes

Great Britain, ambassadors and consuls
  Beaumont, Henry, 327
  Bertie, Francis, 225, 257
  Biliotti, Alfred, 74–7, 101, 126–8, 149, 150
  Currie, Philip, 19, 20, 29, 31–3, 46–56, 59, 95
  Egerton, Edwin, 22, 75
  Fitzmaurice, Gerald, 214–17, 264, 265, 306–8
  Lamb, Harry, 190, 191, 273
  Lowther, Gerard, 211–18, 263–6, 273, 304, 306, 308
  Mallet, Louis, 248, 256, 257, 262, 267, 269, 270, 277, 309, 315, 316, 326, 329–31, 333, 335
  Marling, Charles, 266, 267, 274, 275, 308, 309
  Maunsell, Francis, 132
  Morgan, James, 269, 271, 273, 397, 405
  O'Conor, Nicholas, 132, 144, 149, 179, 185, 194, 196
  Rattigan, Frank, 497, 551, 552
Great Britain, army, 466, 474, 483
  Allenby, Edmund, 418, 595
  Cavan, Earl of, 596, 597, 601
  General Staff, 229, 356, 366, 369, 381, 430, 440, 461–3, 466, 468, 474, 481–9 548, 563, 591, 596, 601, 603, 621
  Harington, Gen. Charles, 463, 493, 494, 498, 548, 552, 577, 578, 590, 591, 594, 595, 597, 601–7, 617
  Milne, Gen. George, 366, 380, 418, 419, 435, 466, 479, 484, 489, 491
  Rawlinson, Lt Col Alfred, 479, 480
  War Office, 361, 438, 441, 462, 489, 497, 552, 590, 595
  Wilson, Col Albert, 520, 522
  Wilson, Gen. Henry F., 418, 439
  Wilson, Gen. Henry H., 356, 379, 380, 430, 548, 550

Great Britain, cabinet, 273, 346, 357, 358, 360, 361, 378, 420, 421, 427–30, 466, 486, 487, 489, 511, 534, 538, 547–9, 563, 564, 576, 590–609, 617, 621

Great Britain, Foreign Office, 18, 20, 28, 145, 173, 190, 196, 210, 213–15, 217, 240, 256, 265–7, 276, 298, 326, 357, 362, 364, 366, 378, 472, 478, 486, 487, 494, 497, 537, 552, 602, 620

  Crowe, Eyre, 370, 372, 384, 403–5, 537, 538

  Nicolson, Arthur, 197, 217, 223, 227, 230, 245, 257, 259, 315

  Nicolson, Harold, 355–7, 537

  Sykes, Mark, 343, 344, 346, 375, 414–17

Great Britain, foreign secretaries

  Curzon, Marquess, 63–5, 346, 356–9, 367, 382, 417, 418, 421, 427–31, 451, 452, 458, 463, 468, 484, 485, 493, 515, 516, 523, 533, 534, 536–8, 540, 542, 543, 545–51, 560, 562–71, 574–8, 591, 597–601, 604–6, 609, 620–5, 627

  Grey, Edward, 20, 171–3, 178, 192–7, 210, 211, 216, 220, 221, 223–7, 241, 242, 244–9, 252–67, 274, 276, 296–9, 303, 305, 308–12, 316, 326–8, 331, 333, 335

  Kimberley, Earl of, 19, 20, 27–30, 32, 47, 51, 52

  Lansdowne, Marquess of, 87, 133, 169–71, 176–9, 181, 182, 186

Great Britain, high commission, Istanbul

  control officers, 471, 473, 476, 481

  de Robeck, John, 366, 381, 385, 405, 418, 432, 436, 440–3, 460–3, 468, 486, 489, 491–3

  Gough-Calthorpe, Somerset, 348, 366, 367, 382, 397, 434–6

  intelligence, 364, 369, 381, 466, 472–82, 491, 492, 523, 524, 548, 603, 620

  İzmit-Yalova Commission, 494–7

  relief officers, 471, 473, 474, 475, 481

  Rumbold, Horace, 494, 535, 536, 551, 552, 576–8, 597, 602, 603, 605, 618, 624, 625

  Webb, Richard, 361, 381, 383, 440, 441, 463, 475, 483

Great Britain, ministers of state

  Chamberlain, Austen, 496, 591, 602, 604, 608, 609

  Churchill, Winston, 245, 334, 335, 431, 438, 483, 534, 538, 548, 591, 592, 594, 597, 602, 603, 604, 609

  Montagu, Edwin, 428, 429, 564

Great Britain, navy, 31, 52, 55, 187, 188, 220, 247, 253, 335, 336, 358, 381, 383, 418, 421, 429, 477, 490–2, 498, 578, 591, 594, 596, 599, 601; *see also* Crete

Great Britain, parliament 15, 19, 28, 53, 57, 63, 64, 86–8, 170, 181, 193, 194, 225–7, 244, 254, 255, 271, 274, 296, 297, 357, 358, 404–6, 431, 432, 491, 492, 496–8, 542, 552, 553, 579

Great Britain, political parties

  Conservative, 27, 30, 142, 144, 169, 171, 178, 225, 609, 623

  Labour, 592

  Liberal, 15, 30, 52, 87, 88, 134, 144, 171, 172, 192, 296, 297, 357, 609

Great Britain, prime ministers

  Asquith, Herbert, 87, 136, 172, 226, 244, 245, 297

  Balfour, Arthur (also foreign secretary), 144, 171, 357, 360, 375, 376, 382, 397–9, 414, 427, 428, 538

  Campbell-Bannerman, Henry, 141, 172

  Gladstone, William Ewart, 15–17, 24, 27, 29, 172

Lloyd George, David, 87, 343, 353, 355–61, 364, 367, 369, 370, 374, 378, 379, 381, 382, 406, 410, 412, 415–18, 421, 427–32, 437, 438, 450, 452, 458, 464, 466, 468, 482, 485–7, 489, 496, 511, 515, 518, 533–43, 547–53, 562, 564, 565, 567, 570, 575, 578, 579, 590–2, 594, 596, 597, 599, 601, 603, 604, 608, 609, 619

Rosebery, Earl of, 16, 27, 28, 30, 32, 52, 87

Salisbury, Marquess of, 19, 20, 29–32, 52–4, 56–60, 63, 80–8, 92–101, 118, 175, 228

Great Britain, propaganda and public opinion
  Anglo-Armenian Association, 15–21, 24, 28, 30, 87, 134, 171, 225, 295–7
  Armenians, churches and clergy, 16, 17, 19, 20, 28
  Armenians, newspapers and public opinion, 21–7
  Balkan Committee, 19, 134–41, 144, 145, 169–73, 193, 194, 225, 244, 295, 296
  Balkan Wars, 244
  Brailsford, Henry, 135, 136, 140, 145
  Bryce, James, 15, 30, 134, 135, 170
  Buxton, Noel, 134, 136, 138, 139, 170
  Crete and 1897 war, 85–9, 93
  inspectorates, 295, 296, 304, 312
  Italian War, 225, 229
  Macedonia, churches and clergy, 134, 136, 138, 141, 142, 172
  Macedonia, newspapers and public opinion, 131, 133, 143–50, 169
  post-World War I, 542, 619
  Stevenson, Francis, 15, 16, 18, 30, 87

Greece
  Deliyiannis, Theodore, 75
  Ethniki Etaireia (National Society), 75, 89, 188

Gounaris, Dimitrios, 533, 562, 567, 570

Greek High Commission, Istanbul, 480

Kalogeropoulos, Nikolaos, 533, 539, 541, 542, 543

King Alexander, 533

King Constantine, 360, 532–4, 536, 538, 542, 591

King George, 75, 79, 95, 96, 450

Megali Idea, 75, 89

Rallis, Dimitrios, 533

Venizelos, Eleftherios, 260, 262, 353, 357, 359–62, 364, 369, 370, 372, 373, 378–80, 382–4, 399, 403–5, 428–30, 437, 438, 454, 457, 460, 464–6, 468, 482, 484, 485, 489, 492, 493, 532, 533, 536–8, 548

*see also* 1897 War; Balkan Wars; Crete; Paris Peace Conference; Turkish Independence War

Hüdavendigâr *see* Bursa

India, 336, 412, 428, 429, 468, 520, 564
inspectorates, 292–316
  Armenian input, 303, 305, 308, 315
  British Armenia Committee, 295, 296, 304
  Germany and Austria, 303, 308, 309–12
  Great Britain, 297, 298, 306, 309
  inspectors-general, 299, 307, 314–16
  Russia, 299–306
Iran, 14, 15, 239, 240, 296, 297, 301, 325, 336, 412, 522, 523, 525
Iraq (Mesopotamia), 31, 329, 336, 356, 410–12, 414–17, 454, 518, 520, 549, 620, 623, 625; *see also* Mosul
Italian War, 224–8
  British neutrality, 223–7
  Dodecanese, 227, 228

Italy, 99–101, 187
  conferences (1920–3), 534, 536, 546–8, 550, 552, 553, 563–6, 568, 572, 574–9, 588, 590, 591, 595, 597, 599–601, 604, 607, 620–2
  de Martino, Giacomo, 370, 384, 403
  Dodecanese (1912–23), 248, 257, 261–4, 355, 374, 375, 454, 624
  Giolitti, Giovanni, 412
  Imperiali, Guglielmo, 223
  Mussolini, Benito, 621, 623
  Nitti, Francesco, 431, 515, 516
  Scialoja, Vittorio, 437
  Sforza, Carlo, 536, 546, 599, 601
  Sonnino, Sydney, 374, 375
  Tittoni, Tommaso, 398, 399
  see also Italian War; Ottoman Empire, Allied Occupation; Paris Peace Conference
İzmir (Smyrna) see Ottoman Empire, Allied Occupation; Paris Peace Conference
İzmit, 366, 463, 475, 483, 489–92, 494–8, 578, 588, 590, 591, 597, 598, 601, 606, 607, 617

Japan, 239, 240, 335, 353, 354, 452, 454, 565, 572, 600, 620

Kurds, 9–11, 13, 14, 21, 24–7, 47–50, 54, 57–9, 62, 65, 292–4, 299, 301–3, 306, 310, 336, 442, 452, 479, 480, 511, 516, 518–20, 522–6, 537, 544, 621
  Abdulkadir, 519, 520, 523
  Mohammed Cherif, 519, 526
  Noel, Major Edward, 520, 522, 524–6
  Shaikh Mahmud, 522

League of Nations, 355, 428, 452, 454, 455, 513–15, 518, 544, 545, 564, 565, 568, 569, 571, 577, 600, 625
  mandates, 355, 356, 372, 373, 378, 379, 384, 416, 417, 436, 454, 515, 518, 519, 525, 564, 599, 608
Libya see Italian War

Macedonia, 117–20
  Bulgarian Orthodox Exarchate, 121, 123, 128
  Bulgarian Orthodox (Exarchists), 121, 123, 124, 129, 130, 188, 189, 190
  Greek Orthodox (Patriarchists), 121, 123, 124, 129, 130, 188, 189, 190, 191
  reforms, 176–84, 186, 187, 191, 193–6
Macedonia, revolts
  destruction and mortality, 123–33, 189–91
  Edirne Revolt, 131–3
  guerilla bands (komitadjis), 122–6, 188–90
  Ilinden Revolt, 128, 129, 178
  IMRO, 121, 129
  Krushevo Revolt, 125, 129–31
  SMAC, 121, 128, 129, 146
Manastır, 123, 126, 131, 135, 143–5, 147, 148, 271, 273
Montenegro, 3, 228, 240–2, 260, 270, 271
Mosul, 412, 414–17, 452, 454, 516, 518, 520, 523, 526, 575, 591, 624, 625
Muş, 9, 10, 26, 50, 63
Mustafa Kemal (Atatürk), 430, 431, 434–6, 438–43, 471–82, 535, 537, 538, 548, 552, 564, 580, 590, 593, 596, 598, 600, 602–5

Ottoman Empire
  1908 revolution, 197, 209–11
  army, 12–14, 77, 82, 83, 90, 98–100, 123–6, 129, 130, 132, 133, 179, 182, 209, 215, 216, 224, 242, 332
  cabinet, 59, 210, 247, 253, 328, 333, 334, 441, 618

capitulations, 91, 92, 94, 221, 248, 249, 254, 326, 332–4, 437, 451, 456, 458, 463, 572, 620, 622, 623, 624, 625
counter-revolution, 215–17
customs tariffs, 61, 73, 74, 77, 185–8, 194, 221, 246–9, 252, 254, 256, 311, 316, 326, 332, 333, 455, 456, 472, 495, 572, 618, 621, 624
elections, 209, 210, 436
finances, 48, 57, 60–3, 74, 141, 185–9, 195, 221, 254, 255, 328, 358, 411, 451, 452, 456, 463, 472, 544, 572, 608, 609, 620–5
governors-general, 18, 30, 31, 51, 76, 77, 95, 100, 101, 125, 126, 145, 178, 180, 187, 195, 304, 305, 308, 309, 311, 314
Hamidiye, 24, 25, 49, 299, 304, 310, 314
navy, 62, 185, 224, 335, 336, 455, 544
parliament, 209, 210, 214, 216, 294, 433, 436, 437, 439, 440, 442, 443, 544
Public Debt Commission, 60, 187, 249, 355, 456, 570, 620, 621, 624, 625
Refugee Commission, 271
taxes, 11, 61–3, 73, 77, 91, 100, 123, 128, 177, 180, 183, 187, 189, 195, 214, 293, 307, 332, 333, 456, 572, 621, 627
Ottoman Empire, Allied occupation (1918–23)
occupation and control of Istanbul, 348, 349
Allied conflicts over authority, 409, 411, 414, 415, 418, 419
Allied neutrality, 532, 534, 536, 540, 548–52, 567, 579
British plans for the Ottoman Empire, 343, 346, 427–30, 511, 513; *see also* Paris Peace Conference,
expert advice ignored, 460–6, 468, 482–6

Ferid Paşa government, 433, 441, 442
France, 346, 349, 41, 412, 414–16, 418–22, 430–7, 459, 489, 533, 534, 536, 539, 543, 547, 550, 552, 564–6, 569, 572, 574
Italy, 348, 360, 361, 437, 430, 438, 440, 450, 451, 452, 454, 456, 458, 460, 465, 473, 485, 487, 489, 492, 513, 515, 518
Malta prisoners, 349, 440
Mudros Armistice, 347, 348, 411, 436, 472, 482, 487, 511, 545
Ottoman Government and the Nationalists, 435–7
seizing control of the government, 437–42
*see also* conferences; Great Britain, high commission, Istanbul; Mustafa Kemal; Ottoman Empire: parliament; Paris Peace Conference; Treaties: Lausanne; Turkish Independence War; Turkish National Movement; Venizelos
Ottoman grand vezirs and ministers of state
Ahmed Cemal, 217, 326, 329, 330, 433, 474, 477, 479
Ahmed İzzet, 566
Ahmed Tevfik, 618
Hulusi Salih, 435, 437, 440, 441
Hüseyin Hilmi, 125, 126, 128, 145, 170, 176, 178, 209
İsmail Enver, 217, 247, 330, 334, 335, 433, 474, 477–9, 535
Mahmud Şevket, 228, 229
Mehmed Ferid, 210, 217, 433–5, 441, 442
Mehmed Kâmil, 209, 210, 215–17, 220, 264, 266
Mehmed Said, 209, 226
Mehmed Talat, 217, 247, 270, 330, 433, 474, 477, 479
Mersinli Cemal, 435, 439
Said Halim, 309, 331, 334

Ottoman political parties
　Committee of Union and Progress, 209–17, 247, 264–6, 269, 270, 294, 306, 329, 433, 436, 460, 474, 477–9, 519
　Liberal Entente, 210, 215, 217, 436
Ottoman sultans
　Abdülaziz, 121
　Abdülhamid II, 12, 32, 33, 51, 52, 55–7, 59, 60, 63, 66, 74, 76, 82, 91, 96–8, 144, 171, 209, 210, 214, 216, 306, 519
　Mehmed VI, 433, 450

Palestine, 212, 346, 356, 375, 414, 416, 417, 454, 620
Paris Peace Conference and Supreme Council, 353–9, 369, 380, 398, 403–5, 430, 431, 484, 515
　Armenia Commission, 513, 515, 516
　Armenians, 515, 516
　France, 353, 355, 370, 374–6, 379, 456, 458, 460
　Greek invasion and occupation of Anatolia, 360, 374–85, 464, 484
　Greek Patriarchate Statistics, 362, 364, 369, 372
　Greek Territorial Committee, 370, 372–4, 379, 553
　Istanbul, 428–31, 437
　Italy, 346, 353, 355–7, 374–7, 379, 380, 384, 398, 403, 410–12
　Kurds, 518, 525
　Smyrna Commission, 380, 397–406
　Thrace, 367, 369
　see also political leaders by country; treaties: Sèvres; treaties: Versailles
petroleum, 325, 329, 411, 412, 417, 454, 516, 518, 519, 522, 525, 575, 576

population, 259, 263
　Crete, 73, 74
　Eastern Anatolia, 10, 46, 47, 50, 293, 295, 305, 519
　Istanbul, 428
　Macedonia, 117, 118, 120, 184
　Ottoman Europe, 3, 4, 7, 131, 245, 246, 256, 270, 271, 362, 366, 369, 371–3
　Western Anatolia, 359, 362, 364, 366, 367, 369, 380

Romania, 117, 170, 253, 256, 452, 594, 595, 600
Russia, 2, 7, 197, 346, 374
　Armenian reforms, 48–54, 56, 58, 60
　Balkan Wars, 239–42, 244, 245, 246, 247, 250, 253, 254, 257, 263, 267
　Benckendorff, Alexander von, 244
　Bosnia and Bulgarian Unification, 220, 221
　Crete and 1897 War, 76, 78, 80–3, 85, 89, 91, 93–101
　Giers, Mikhail Nikolayevich, 309, 311
　Kapnist, Pyotr, 182, 183
　Isvolsky, Alexander Petrovich, 197
　Lobanov-Rostovsky, Aleksey, 21, 56
　Macedonia, 117, 118, 133, 137, 141, 144, 150, 174–82, 185, 187, 190, 192, 194–6
　Mouravieff, Mikhail Nikolayevich, 98
　Sazonov, Sergei Dmitriyevich, 240, 254, 298, 299, 305, 309
　Russian Revolution and Bolsheviks, 374, 410, 511, 516
　Tsar Nicholas II, 30, 58, 91, 96, 175, 180, 300, 302
　see also inspectorates; World War I
Russo-Japanese War, 174, 300

Salonica (Selanik), 30, 31, 118, 126, 127, 132, 133, 174, 188, 196, 252

Samsun, 273, 434, 481
Serbia and Yugoslavia, 3, 61, 117, 118, 135, 228, 375, 594, 595, 600; *see also* Balkan Wars; Macedonia
Sivas, 47, 48, 293, 295, 298, 314, 435, 436
Straits (Bosporus and Dardanelles), 17, 93, 174, 220, 221, 227, 242, 247, 325, 327, 328, 330, 331, 335, 336, 346, 355, 357, 378, 428, 429, 437, 451, 452, 457, 460, 463, 537, 538, 540, 544, 562, 565, 566, , 590, 591–601, 608, 620, 622, 623, 625
Syria and Lebanon, 31, 227, 329, 336, 343, 356, 375, 411, 412, 414, 415–19, 427, 434, 452, 454, 471, 539, 547, 549, 566, 620, 623, 625
    King Feisal (Fayṣal bin al-Ḥusayn ), 416, 417, 539

Thrace *see* Balkan Wars; Edirne; Ottoman Empire, Allied Occupation; Turkish Independence War
Trabzon, 298, 314, 356, 457, 465, 525
Trans-Caucasia, 53, 299, 300, 301, 325, 348, 419, 451, 461, 483, 486, 511, 513
treaties and agreements
    Anglo-Russian Convention (1907), 239, 297
    Alexandropol (1920), 516
    Ankara (1921), 547
    Berlin (1878), 2–4, 56, 92, 94, 117, 118, 169, 218, 220, 221, 225, 226, 241, 256, 270
    Constantinople (1913), 257
    Lausanne (1923), 620, 624, 625, 627
    London (1913), 252, 257, 259, 270, 292, 327, 376
    London (1871), 2
    London (1913), 257, 259, 292

    London (1915), 374
    Ouchy (Lausanne, 1912), 228, 261
    Paris (1856), 1, 2, 3, 226, 227, 327, 354
    St Jean de Maurienne (1917), 346, 374, 376
    San Stephano (1878), 2, 28, 117, 118, 140, 141, 169, 172, 256
    Sèvres (1920), 369, 411, 430, 442, 450–8, 462–4, 467, 468, 483, 485–9, 516, 525, 526, 534–46, 548, 560, 562–9, 572, 593, 620, 622
    Tripartite Agreement (1920), 458, 459, 550, 563, 565, 575
    Versailles (1919), 353, 420, 421, 619
Triple Alliance, 229, 230, 240, 247, 254, 260, 276, 310, 311
Triple Entente, 220, 226, 239, 240, 245, 247, 254, 260, 276
Turkish Independence War
    Cilicia, 347, 415, 430, 432, 480, 481, 518, 536, 539, 546, 547
    Eastern Anatolia, 479–81
    Greek advance, 379–83, 487, 489–93, 560, 564, 577, 578
    İsmet Paşa (İnönü), 603, 605–7, 620, 624
    İzmit-Yalova Commission; Paris Peace Conference and Supreme Council: Smyrna Commission
    Karabekir, Gen. Kâzım, 479, 480, 516
    mortality, 397, 432, 498; *see also* Great Britain, high commission, Istanbul: refugees, 400, 471, 493, 494, 497
    Soviet assistance, 471, 472, 478, 480, 520, 551, 574
    Turkish advance, 489, 516, 560, 579, 580, 588, 590, 591, 601
    *see also* Mustafa Kemal
Turkish National Movement, 402, 431, 434–42, 464–6, 471–98, 516, 526, 536–41, 548, 572, 617, 618

Turkish National Movement *(cont.)*
  Amasya Protocol, 435–7
  Bekir Sami, 541
  Grand National Assembly, 443, 471, 478, 479, 526, 541, 607, 608
  National Pact, 436, 437, 535, 540, 546, 566, 598
  Refet, 618
  *see also* Mustafa Kemal

United States of America, 61, 332, 336, 353–6, 367 370, 373, 379–81, 384, 397–9, 420, 421, 451, 454, 456–8, 485, 515, 516, 608
  Bristol, Mark, 399
  Fourteen Points, 361, 362, 376, 377, 378, 519
  Heck, Lewis, 381
  Wilson, Woodrow, 354–6, 359, 361, 362, 367, 375–9, 416, 456–8, 487, 515, 516, 518, 519
Üsküdar (Albania, Shkodër), 181, 250
Üsküdar (Istanbul), 597
Üsküp (Skopje), 125, 147

Van, 10, 48, 62, 293–5, 298, 300, 513, 519, 520, 525; *see also* inspectorates
Varna, 132

World War I, 301, 336, 343, 346, 382, 383
  preliminary disputes, 327, 328, 330–5

EU representative:
Easy Access System Europe
Mustamäe tee 50, 10621 Tallinn, Estonia
Gpsr.requests@easproject.com

www.ingramcontent.com/pod-product-compliance
Lightning Source LLC
Chambersburg PA
CBHW061702300426
44115CB00014B/2526